U·X·L

ASIAN AMERICAN

ALMANAC
2ND EDITION

U·X·L
ASIAN AMERICAN
ALMANAC   2ND EDITION

**Edited by Irene Natividad
and Susan B. Gall**

Detroit • New Yor   ⁱe • London • Munich

U•X•L ASIAN AMERICAN ALMANAC, 2ND EDITION

Irene Natividad and Susan B. Gall, Editors

Project Editor
Diane Sawinski

Permissions
Margaret Chamberlain

Imaging and Multimedia
Lezlie Light, Randy Bassett

Product Design
Cindy Baldwin

Manufacturing
Rita Wimberley

Composition
Evi Seoud

ISBN 0-7876-7598-9

Library of Congress Control Number: 2003110047

Printed in the United States of America
10 9 8 7 6 5 4 3 2 1

CONTENTS

Reader's Guide ix
Photo Credits. xi
Words to Know xiii

1   Who Are the Asian Americans? 1
    Asian Indian Americans. 5
    Cambodian Americans. 9
    Chinese Americans 14
    Filipino Americans. 18
    Hmong Americans 21
    Indonesian Americans 23
    Japanese Americans 26
    Korean Americans 30
    Laotian Americans. 36
    Pacific Islanders. 39
    Pakistani Americans. 43
    Thai Americans 45
    Vietnamese Americans 47
    Suggestions for Further Reading 51

2   Significant Documents 53
    Chinese Exclusion Act, 1882. 53
    Joint Resolution Annexing the Hawaiian Islands to the United States, 1898 54
    Cable Act, 1922 56
    Immigration Act, 1924. 56
    Presidential Proclamation, 1938 57
    Executive Order 9066, 1942 58
    Public Proclamation, 1942. 59
    Public Law 503, 1942 62
    Repeal of Chinese Exclusion Acts, 1943. 62
    Immigration and Nationality Act, 1952. 62
    Immigration and Nationality Act Amendments, 1965. 63
    Refugee Relief Act, 1980. 63
    Commission On Wartime Relocation and Internment of Civilians Act, 1980 65
    Civil Liberties Act, 1988 Public Law 100-383 67
    Hate Crimes Statistics Act, 1990 68

Asian /Pacific American Heritage Month, 1991 and 1992 69
Joint Resolution on the 100th Anniversary of the Overthrow of the Hawaiian Kingdom, 1993 .71
Executive Order 13216, 2001 74
A Proclamation by the President of the United States of America on the 100th
Anniversary of Korean Immigration, 2003 77

3   Landmarks **79**
Arizona 79
Arkansas 80
California 81
Colorado 89
Florida 89
Hawaii 89
Idaho 92
Illinois 93
Massachusetts 93
New York. 93
Oregon 94
Pennsylvania 94
Utah 95
Washington 95
Washington, D.C. 96
Wyoming 97
Suggestions for Further Reading 97

4   Immigration **99**
Beginnings: 1850 to 1920 100
Between the Wars: The Triumph of Exclusionism 102
Post-World War II Liberalization 104
After the Vietnam War: Refugees from Southeast Asia 106
Anti-Immigration Trends. 108
Suggestions for Further Reading 109

5   Civil Rights **111**
The Student Movement 111
The Labor Movement 113
Anti-Asian American Violence 116
Suggestions for Further Reading 118

6   The Legal System in the United States **119**
Laws Against Asian Americans. 119
Mobilization Against Anti-Asian Laws and Judicial Decisions 123
Lawmakers and Lawyers. 125
The Criminal Justice System. 128
Suggestions for Further Reading 133

7 Population... **135**
    Population Trends 135
    Asian Americans and the Census.. 136
    1790 to 1890.. 137
    1900 to 1960.. 137
    Post-1965 Immigration and Refugee Resettlement 140
    1980 Census... 141
    1990 Census... 142
    2000 Census... 143
    Population Projections 144
    Suggestions for Further Reading 144

8 Jobs and Money **145**
    Immigration and Entrepreneurship 146
    Entrepreneurs and Ethnic Firms....................................... 148
    Consequences of Entrepreneurship 151
    Suggestions for Further Reading 153

9 Women and Families **155**
    Family Life Before World War II 156
    Family Life from World War II to 1965 159
    Family Life after 1965 160
    Marriage... 161
    Family Size 161
    Children and Child-Rearing... 161
    Women's Resource Groups 162
    Suggestions for Further Reading 162

10 Languages **163**
    Bengali.. 163
    Chinese Languages 164
    Japanese... 165
    Korean Language.. 167
    Pilipino... 168
    Urdu and Hindi... 168
    Suggestions for Further Reading 169

11 Education **171**
    Asian Americans 171
    Elementary through High School....................................... 172
    Higher Education 173
    Teaching and Teacher Education....................................... 177
    Summary 177
    Suggestion for Further Reading 178

12 Science and Engineering **179**
  Anti-Asian American Bias: Fear or Reality? 179
  Success Factors 180
  Asian American Milestones in Science 182
  College Education in Science and Engineering 183

13 Religion **187**
  Hinduism 188
  Buddhism 188
  Islam 190
  Confucianism 191
  Taoism 192
  Shintoism 192
  The Unification Church 193
  Suggestions for Further Reading 195

14 Literature **197**
  Asian American Literary History 198
  Asian American Writers of Adult Literature 199
  Children's Literature 207
  Suggestions for Further Reading 211

15 Theatre **213**
  Early Asian American Theatre 213
  New Generation of Theatres 217
  Emerging Companies 218
  Playwrights 220
  Behind the Scenes in Theatre 224
  Asian American Theatres 226
  Suggestions for Further Reading 227

16 Sports and Athletics **229**
  Sumo 230
  Japanese Athletic Leagues and Clubs 231
  Surfing 234
  Martial Arts 236
  Suggestions for Further Reading 239

17 Military **241**
  Before World War II (Pre-1939) 241
  World War II (1939–45) 243
  Korean War (1950–53) 246
  Asian/Pacific American Service Personnel 247
  Asian Pacific Military Heroes 247
  A Special Presentation 251
  Suggestions for Further Reading 256

Index 257

READER'S GUIDE

U•X•L Asian American Almanac, 2nd Edition, explores the history and culture of the major ethnic groups comprising Asian America, the fastest growing minority population in the United States. Like the first edition, this second edition of the *Almanac* is organized into 17 subject chapters, including landmarks, significant documents, literature, religion, immigration, civil rights, law, sports, employment, and the family. The volume contains more than 90 black-and-white photographs and maps and concludes with a subject index. The volume begins with a glossary of terms; words are also defined in a Words to Know box within the chapter in which they appear. Charts, graphs, sidebars, and Fact Focus boxes provide complementary and engaging information, and a list of sources is provided at the end of each chapter for the student who wishes to pursue further readings or research.

Related Reference Sources:

U•X•L Asian American Biography, 2nd Edition, profiles more than 150 Americans who trace their ancestry to Asia and the Pacific Islands. Included are prominent men and women of Asian Indian, Cambodian, Chinese, Filipino, Native Hawaiian, Hmong, Japanese, Pacific Island, Pakistani, Taiwanese, and Vietnamese descent, both living and deceased. Profilees are notable for their achievements in fields ranging from civil rights to sports, politics to academia, entertainment to science, religion to the military. Early leaders in Asian America as well as contemporary figures are included. A black-and-white photograph accompanies most entries, and a list of sources for further reading or research is provided at the end of each entry. Cross-references to other profiles in these volumes are noted in bold letters within the text. The volumes are arranged alphabetically and conclude with an index listing all individuals by field of endeavor and a subject index.

U•X•L Asian American Chronology, 2nd Edition, explores significant social, political, economic, cultural, and professional milestones in Asian American history. Arranged by year and then by month and day where applicable, the chronology spans from prehistory to modern times. Entries range from a few lines to one page in length and describe topics such as immigration, discriminatory legislation, the world wars, the formation of activist organizations, and the contributions Asian

Americans have made to all aspects of American society. The *Chronology* contains more than 100 illustrations and maps as well as charts and boxes that highlight important information. The extensively cross-referenced volume concludes with a list of sources for further reading or research and a subject index.

U•X•L Asian American Voices, 2nd Edition, presents 20 full or excerpted speeches, orations, testimony, and other notable spoken works of Asian Americans. Each entry is accompanied by an introduction and a glossary explaining some of the terms and events to which the speech refers. The volume is illustrated with 100 black-and-white photographs and drawings and features a subject index.

Comments and Suggestions

We welcome your comments on *U•X•L Asian American Almanac,* 2nd Edition, as well as your suggestions for topics to be featured in future editions. Please write: Editors, *U•X•L Asian American Almanac,* U•X•L, 27500 Drake Road, Farmington Hills, MI 48331-3535; call toll-free: 800-877-4253; fax: 248-699-8097; or send e-mail via http://www.gale.com.

Advisors

Special thanks are due to Helen Zia, Frank Wu, Kristine Minami, and Karen Narasaki, each of whom provided valuable information and insights.

PHOTO CREDITS

The photographs used in *U•X•L Asian American Almanac,* 2nd Edition, were received from the following sources:

Cover: New York City Chinese New Year, **Archive Photos.**

AP/Wide World Photos: pp. 12, 16, 29, 32, 38, 39, 48, 49, 68, 70, 77, 82, 84, 86, 92, 96, 107, 131, 150, 152, 194, 224, 250; **G. Asha:** page 7; **Courtesy of Kamla Motihar:** page 8; **Photo by Floyd Lumbard, courtesy of Lee and Barbara Lumbard and Connie Young Yu:** page 15; **Courtesy of Office of Hawaiian Affairs:** page 40; **Courtesy of Representative Eni Faleomavaega:** pp. 42 and 247; **Courtesy of Shazia Rafi:** page 44; **Photo by Hope Cahill, courtesy of Connie Young Yu:** page 80; **Photo by Randy Curtis:** page 85; **Corel Corporation:** page 90; **Library of Congress:** pp. 101 and 103; **Photo by Yoichi R. Okamoto, LBJ Library Collection:** page 105; **Courtesy of Jon Melegrito:** page 114; **Filipino American National Historical Society:** page 116; **Bill Burke/Page One Photography, Inc.:** page 117; **Courtesy of Connie Young Yu:** page 158; **Courtesy of Lynda Barry:** page 199; **Photo by Karen Dacker, courtesy of Penguin Books:** page 200; **Courtesy of Le Ly Hayslip:** page 201; **Courtesy of Ha Jin:** page 203; **Courtesy of Ruthanne Lum McCunn:** page 204; **Photo by Joan Chen, courtesy of Pantheon Books:** page 205; **Courtesy of G. P. Putnam's Sons:** page 206; **Courtesy of Jose Aruego:** page 208; **Courtesy of Allen Say:** page 209 (left); **Photo by Deborah Storms, courtesy of estate of Yoshiko Uchida:** page 209 (right); **Photo by K. Yep, courtesy of Laurence Yep:** page 210; **Courtesy of Mako:** page 214; **Photo by Corky Lee, courtesy of Frank Chin:** page 216; **Photo by Howard Hsieh, courtesy of Lodestone Theatre Ensemble:** page 219; **Courtesy of Berkeley Repertory Theatre:** page 220; **Photo by Hideo Yoshida, courtesy of Philip Kan Gotanda:** page 222; **Courtesy of David Henry Hwang:** page 223; **Photo by Marty Umans:** page 225; **Courtesy of Dale F. Yee and Connie Young Yu:** page 230; **Courtesy of Jhoon Rhee:** page 238; **U.S. Army Military History Institute:** pp. 243 and 248.

WORDS TO KNOW

A

acculturation: adjusting to or acquiring the culture of a society

activist: a person who takes action supporting or opposing a political issue

adherents: followers of a leader, an idea, a church, or political party

affirmative action: programs designed to remedy the effects of past discrimination and to end such discrimination

alien: foreign-born resident of a country

annex: to incorporate, or add, territory to an already existing state or nation

appurtenance: a secondary right, or something added on

assembly center: a temporary holding facility, such as a race track, where West Coast families of Japanese descent were taken when the U.S. military forced them to leave their homes at the start of American involvement in World War II; after a short stay at an assembly center, prisoners were moved to internment camps

assimilate: to become like or similar to; to join

asylum: shelter, protection

audit: methodical examination or review

B

bachelor society: community comprised primarily of men; usually refers to an immigrant community where only men have immigrated

backlash: a strong negative public or group reaction to a recent social or political event

bilingual: able to speak, read, and write two languages with equal skill

C

canon: accepted rules and standards

cede: to transfer property or rights to territory by treaty

Chinatown: neighborhood in a city where people of Chinese descent live and often operate businesses and restaurants

civil rights: the rights of an individual to equal treatment and equal access to the benefits of society, such as housing, free speech, employment, and education

coalition: two or more groups working together toward a common goal

D

decennial: occurring every ten years

deity: a god or goddess

demographics: statistical data, such as age or income, to describe the characteristics of a group

dialect: a regional variety of a language

discrimination: treatment or judgment of a person based on something other than merit

draft: in the military, to select for compulsory, or involuntary, service

E

emigration: to leave the country of one's birth with the intention of living somewhere else

enclave: a distinct territorial or cultural unit, such as a Chinatown

enlightenment: achievement of spiritual insight; complete understanding

entrepreneurship: organizing, starting, and running a business

evacuation: the removal of people from a zone of danger or military activity

exclusion: barring from participation in an activity or group

extended family: family unit consisting of parents and their children, as well as aunts, uncles, cousins, or grandparents

G

Great Depression: the severe downturn in the U.S. economy from 1929 to about 1939, marked by heavy unemployment

H

hate crime: illegal acts committed against a person because of the victim's characteristics, such as race, religion, or sexual orientation

Hispanic: one who traces his or her ancestry to Spain, or to Spanish-speaking countries such as Mexico and the countries of South and Central America; Hispanics may be of any race

homogeneous: similar; the same

humanitarian: promoting human welfare

I

immigration: to move to a country where one was not born for the purpose of living there

immortality: a state of eternal life without vulnerability to death

indigenous: original or native to an area

inflection: changes in the form of words that make distinctions pertaining to case, gender, number, tense, person, mood, or voice

internment: holding and confining a group of people, against their will, away from society

internment camp: remote, primitive camp where Americans of Japanese descent were held as prisoners during World War II, on the theory that they were risks to U.S. military security

interracial: combining two or more races

interrogate: ask questions in a formal and systematic way

issei: first-generation Japanese Americans; those who emigrated from Japan

M

mainstream society: the majority or dominant group in a culture, which shares certain customs, assumptions, and ways of interacting

manong: immigrant to the United States from the Philippines

meditate: to focus thoughts; to enter a state of deep contemplation

miscegenation: marriage between two races, especially between a white person and a person of another race

monarchy: government headed by a king or queen

multiethnic: reflecting two or more ethnic groups

multilingual: speaking three or more languages with fluency

N

nationals: people who receive the protection of a country and owe allegiance to that country, but are not formally citizens

naturalization: admission as a citizen

naturalize: to admit as a citizen

nisei: second-generation Japanese Americans; those whose parents emigrated from Japan

nuclear family: family unit consisting of parents and their children

O

Oriental: belonging to the countries of Asia. This term was used until the 1950s, when it was replaced by the term "Asian"; many Asian Americans consider "Oriental" an offensive term

ostracized: kept from participating in a group by agreement among the members of the group

outmarriage: marriage to a spouse outside one's own ethnic group

P

pantheon: official gods of a group of people; supreme beings

phoneme: a single, distinct speech sound; one of the smallest units of speech that distinguish one utterance from another; for example, the *g* sound or *h* sound

phonetic spelling: using the alphabet of one language to represent the sounds of another

picture bride: a woman whose marriage is arranged through the exchange of letters and photographs

playwright: the author of a work for performance on stage

postdoctoral: study after completing the requirements for a doctorate

Q

queue: a braid of hair usually worn hanging down from the back of the head

quota: numerical limit; the number of people from a particular country allowed to immigrate to another country

R

redress: act of compensating for a loss

refugee: one who leaves his or her homeland to escape a dangerous or unlivable condition

reincarnation: rebirth of a soul in a new body

repatriation: the returning of an individual to the country of his or her origin or birth

repertory: several different plays produced over the course of a season, usually by a performing group or theatre

resettlement: establishing a home in a new location

resolution: formal expression of opinion by the U.S. Congress

revelations: teachings revealed by a god or supreme being to humans

ritual: ceremony or pattern of behavior, often used in religious worship

S

sansei: third-generation Japanese Americans

scripture: sacred writings

sect: a group within a larger religious body that follows specific teachings or rules

segregation: the enforced separation of a race, ethnic group, or social class in education, housing, and other social arenas

Selective Service: U.S. government agency that oversees the military registration of men at age 18 and administers the draft

stereotype: oversimplified image based on a characteristic or trait of group members

stress: to place emphasis on; to accent

surveillance: watching someone or something closely

syllabary: a set of symbols or characters in written language, each representative of a syllable (rather than a single sound, as in the English language's alphabet)

T

tenet: a belief held to be true

theism: belief in the existence of a god or gods

theology: the study of religious faith and practice

tone: the pitch of a word, often used to express different meanings

W

war bride: a woman who meets and marries a soldier from another country serving in her country during wartime

1

Who Are the Asian Americans?

A Demographic Overview

FACT FOCUS

- *Asian Americans include 30 separate ethnic groups who trace their roots to Asia and the islands of the Pacific Ocean.*
- *The six largest Asian American ethnic groups are Asian Indian, Chinese, Filipino, Japanese, Korean, and Vietnamese.*
- *Asian Americans make up almost 4 percent of the total U.S. population.*
- *The five U.S. states with the largest Asian American populations are California, New York, Hawaii, Texas, and New Jersey.*
- *The number of Americans of Asian or Pacific Island descent grew by 63 percent between 1990 and 2000.*
- *By 2020, Asian Americans are projected to number 19.7 million, or 6 percent of the total U.S. population.*

Asian American is a term that describes over 30 ethnic groups from different parts of Asia. Asians include people from Cambodia, China, India, Indonesia, Japan, Korea, Malaysia, Pakistan, the Philippines, Singapore, Vietnam, American Samoa, Northern Mariana Islands, Micronesia, Guam, Marshall Islands, Palau, and Hawaii. This group had the highest rate of population growth of any in the United States during the 1990s. Between 1990 and 2000, the U. S. Census Bureau reported the Asian/Pacific Islander population grew from 7.3 million to 11.9 million, an increase of 63 percent, and totaled 4.2 percent of the U.S. population in 2000. By the year 2020, it is estimated that Asian/Pacific Islanders will number over 19.7 million, or 6 percent of the total projected U.S. population. In 2000, the U.S. states with the largest Asian and Pacific Island populations were California (4,155,685), New York (1,169,200), Hawaii (703,232), Texas (644,193), and New Jersey (524,356).

POPULATION PROFILE: ASIAN AND PACIFIC ISLANDER AMERICANS

Feature	API	Total, U.S.
U.S. Population of Asian and Pacific Islander (API) descent (2000)	11.9 million	281 million
—as percent of U.S. total, 2000	4.2%	100%
—percent male	49%	49%
—percent female	51%	51%
—median age	30.4	33
Income, employment, and poverty (2000)		
—households with annual income of $35,000 or more	47.8%	44.3%
—households with five or more members	16.7%	10.4%
—unemployment rate	3.9%	4.4%
—poverty rate	10.2%	11.7%

Source: U.S. Census Bureau, *Asian and Pacific Islander Population in the United States: March 2000 Current Population Survey (Update).*

Income

Income statistics for Asian and Pacific Island immigrants to the United States tend to be conflicting. While the median income of Asian and Pacific Island immigrants is higher than that of non-Hispanic whites, their poverty rate is the highest rate among all new immigrants. Both extremes in income are reflected by the fact that immigrants who are both skilled and unskilled, educated and uneducated are attracted to the United States from Asia. In some cases, family-run businesses and extended households produce higher incomes, but the number of people among whom the income is divided reduces its benefits.

Education

Asian and Pacific Islander cultures place an emphasis on education, hard work, and striving for excellence. Forty-four percent of this population continue into higher education, compared with half that rate for non-Hispanic whites. While under 18 percent of Asian and Pacific Islanders in 2001 had less than a high school education, the average income of this group was slightly higher than that of non-Hispanic whites. Although more Asian and Pacific Islanders attend college than their non-Hispanic white counterparts, educated Asian Americans also earn less. This fact has been attributed to the "glass ceiling," a barrier that seems to exist in many U.S. corporations that prevents this ethnic group from advancing within certain organizational structures.

Stereotype and Reality

One popular, seemingly positive, stereotype of Asian Americans is that of the

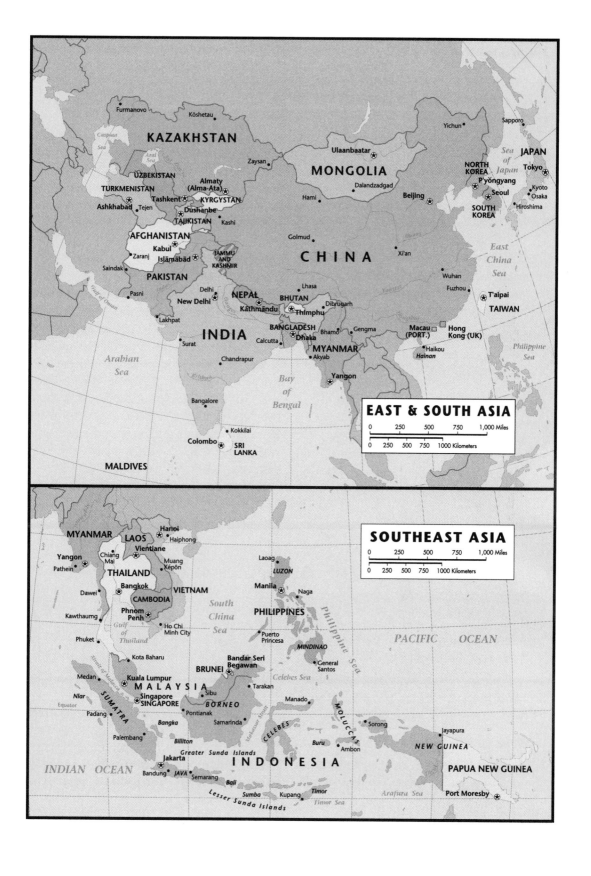

WORDS TO KNOW

acculturation: adjusting to or acquiring the culture of a society

affirmative action: programs designed to remedy the effects of past discrimination and to end such discrimination

assimilate: to become like or similar to; to join

extended family: family unit consisting of parents and their children, aunts, uncles, cousins, grandparents

Great Depression: the severe downturn in the U.S. economy from 1929 to about 1939, marked by heavy unemployment

homogeneous: similar; the same

internment camp: remote, primitive camp where Americans of Japanese descent were held as prisoners during World War II, on the theory that they were risks to U.S. military security

issei: first-generation Japanese Americans, those who emigrated from Japan; second generation Japanese Americans are called nisei, and third generation, sansei

nuclear family: family unit consisting of parents and their children

queue: a braid of hair usually worn hanging down from the back of the head

quota: numerical limit; the number of people from a particular country allowed to immigrate to another country

redress: act of compensating for a loss

stereotype: oversimplified image or model

"Whiz Kid," or academically gifted student. Another common, but clearly negative, stereotype is that of the young Asian and Pacific Islander refugee immigrant easily lured into criminal ways, lost to a culture that does not understand or easily assimilate him. Like all stereotypes, these are applied unfairly to Asian Americans, often because of the way they look.

Also promoted in the media is the image of Asian and Pacific Islanders as a "model minority," which assumes that this ethnic group is a single, homogeneous, and stable population that, on the whole, is successful in schools and the workplace. This stereotype is often used as justification for the belief that if people of color simply work hard enough, they can achieve the American dream. As a result of this stereotypical attitude, Asian and Pacific Islanders are given low priority for affirmative action programs and social service support in different areas. Thinking based on this stereotype leads to the assumption that if one minority can succeed with little or no intervention or assistance, the same should be possible for another. This leads to tension between Asian Americans and other racial and ethnic minorities. In addition, it places unreasonable expectations on all Asians to conform to the "success model." Furthermore, the "model minority" stereotype reinforces the conclusion that racism is not a factor that impedes socioeconomic success in America, because Asian and Pacific Islanders have succeeded through self-reliance and hard work.

Print, electronic, and motion picture media from the 1980s through the early twenty-first century have perpetuated negative stereotypes of Asian criminals and drug gangs. Distorted perceptions based on ethnic and racial stereotypes dehumanize groups of people, in this case Asian and Pacific Islanders, and may lead to discrimination, hate crimes, and policies directed against them.

Seeking a deeper understanding of the complex issues determining success and failure among ethnic minorities in the United States demands avoidance of stereotypical thinking and an appreciation of the true diversity of the cultures represented by this subpopulation.

Asian Indian Americans

History of Immigration and Population Statistics

Since the eighteenth century it is estimated that approximately 18 million Asian Indians, sometimes referred to as East Indians, have settled in different parts of the world outside their homeland, India. Of these, nearly one million Asian Indians have immigrated to the United States since 1850, when immigration records began. Although the first Indian immigrants were laborers, recent changes in the law have resulted in an influx of people with technological skills and high ability in the sciences, arts, education, business, and athletics.

In 2000, the U.S. Census estimated the number of Asian Indians at 1,899,599, or 0.67 percent of the total population. This represented a 141 percent increase since 1990 and was due, in large part, to provisions of immigration policy that allowed naturalized citizens to bring family members to the United States.

Education and Employment

The educational attainment of the U.S.

Asian Indian population is high: 73 percent of Asian Indians 25 years of age and older in the United States have more than a high school education. A 1984 study also found that Asian Indians had a mean high school grade point average of 3.8—the highest of all Asian Americans. Because of their academic accomplishments, Asian Indian students constitute a sizable proportion of the student population at many elite universities.

Most Asian Indian immigrants in the 1960s and 1970s were professionals and almost 50 percent of those living in the United States in 1980 held either managerial or professional positions. However, more recently, family sponsorship provisions have attracted people from a vast spectrum of economic and professional backgrounds. Occupational choices among Indian immigrants in the United States have been influenced by ethnic networks existing in certain professions, such as New York City's newsstand industry, which some claim is operated by a virtual monopoly of Asian Indians, as well as that city's jewelry trade, where Indians as an ethnic group are outnumbered only by Hasidic Jews in the Diamond District.

Asian Indian-owned businesses also experienced tremendous growth during the 1980s and 1990s. Asian Indians are more likely to be affluent than any other ethnic group in the United States. In 2000, only 7.1 percent were below the poverty level; of these, the majority were recent immigrants.

Political Participation

Political participation among Asian Indians lags behind that of other ethnic minorities in the United States. In a California voter registration study it was found that while 73

POPULATION PROFILE: ASIAN INDIAN AMERICANS

Feature	Asian Indian
U.S. Population of Asian Indian descent, 2000	1,899,599
—as percent of U.S. total, 2000	0.67%
—percent increase in population 1990–2000	132%
—as percent of Asian and Pacific Islander total, 2000	15.9%
—percent foreign-born (not born in the United States)	75%
—percent native-born (born in the United States)	25%
—households with 5 or more persons	21.6%
—households with 4 persons	27.9%
—households with 3 persons	19.8%
—households with 2 persons	18.6%
—households with 1 person	12.1%
Income, employment, and poverty	
—median income,1990	$44,696
Education	
—percent with less than 12 years of school	15.3%
—percent with at least high school degree	11.6%
—percent with at least bachelor's degree	25%

Source: U.S. Census Bureau, *Asian and Pacific Islander Population in the United States: March 2000 Current Population Survey (Update)*.

percent of the state's population was registered to vote, only 16.7 percent of its Asian Indian population was. This compared to a Japanese rate of 43 percent and a Chinese rate of 35.5 percent. Despite this lack of involvement in conventional electoral politics, Asian Indians have exercised considerable political influence through lobbying (promoting special interests by actively attempting to influence public officials) on issues such as immigration policy, antidiscrimination legislation, and opposition to military aid to Pakistan. (The nation of Pakistan was partitioned from India in 1947 as a separate country for Indian Muslims. Violence between Hindus and Muslims nonetheless continued, escalating into a series of India-Pakistan Wars. Although a cease-fire has been declared, relations between India and Pakistan remain strained.)

Ten U.S. States with Highest Population of Asian Indians, 1990	
State	**Population**
California	159,973
New York	140,985
New Jersey	79,440
Illinois	64,200
Texas	55,795
Florida	31,457
Pennsylvania	28,396
Massachusetts	28,330
Michigan	23,845
Oklahoma	20,848
Virginia	20,494

Source: Susan B. Gall and Timothy L. Gall, editors, *Statistical Record of Asian Americans*, Gale, 1993, p. 689; see www.census.gov for state data from the 2000 census of population, scheduled for release in fall 2003.

Asian Indian American professional on the job.

Affirmative Action

Affirmative action, a program designed to remedy the effects of past discrimination and to end such discrimination, has existed in the United States for the past thirty years. A debate whether or not to include Asian Americans as minorities in affirmative action programs is ongoing. The National Association of Americans of Asian Indian Descent (NAAAID) campaigned for and won the designation known as "8A–minority status" from the Small Business Administration for businesses owned by Asian Indian Americans. But some argue that the affluence and success of Asian Indian businesses should disqualify them from the category of "disadvantaged business enterprises." Others argue that discriminatory barriers in the workplace prevent Asian Americans from advancing and that historic discrimination based on race entitles them to participate in affirmative action programs.

Religion

In the late nineteenth and early twentieth centuries, Indian religious movements impacted American culture. The two most significant influences were theosophy and Hinduism. Theosophy is a mystical (involving meaning or reality that is not apparent to the senses or the intellect)

Asian Indian woman wearing a sari.

Asian Indian woman in Rajasthani dress.

philosophy that asserts that there is one God and that all nature is spiritual. The religions and philosophies of India were based in theosophy, and the nineteenth-century Theosophical Society, a religious reform movement, drew heavily from Indian doctrines. Swami Vivekananda's Vedanta Society brought Hindu teachings to the United States.

Today, in many communities throughout the country, Hindu and other religious centers are focal points for the celebration of religious festivals (Dussehra, Diwali, Janmashtami, Id-Uz-Zuha, and Muharram); secular festivals (Independence Day, Republic Day); seasonal festivals (Pongal, Onam, and Basant Panchmi); and the preservation of Indian religion, art, and culture.

Dress

The most common traditional dress for Asian Indian women is the sari (sometimes spelled saree), which consists of six yards of

POPULATION PROFILE: CAMBODIAN AMERICANS

Feature	Cambodian Americans
U.S. Population of Cambodian descent, 2000	206,052
—as percent of U.S. total, 2000	0.07%
—as percent of Asian and Pacific Islander total, 2000	1.7%
—percent foreign-born (not born in the United States)	94%
—percent native-born (born in the United States)	6%

Source: U.S. Census Bureau, *Asian and Pacific Islander Population in the United States: March 2000 Current Population Survey (Update)*.

fabric draped or pleated around the waist and hung over a long petticoat with the end gathered on one shoulder. A *choli,* or matching, tight-fitting blouse, is worn underneath.

Traditional dress varies by region in India. Immigrants to the United States who choose traditional dress will reflect the region from which they came. Women from Punjab wear a *kurta,* or long dress over baggy trousers called *salwar,* or tight trousers gathered in pleats at the ankles called *churidar.* A *dopatta,* or matching scarf, is draped over the shoulders. In Rajasthan women wear a *ghaghra* or flared skirt, a *choli,* and long scarf. Men's traditional dress is a long robe called a *sherwani,* worn over tight-fitting *churidars* (pants). Sometimes a *kurta* (long chemise or dress) is worn over pants with a vest or over a dhoti, several yards of fabric draped into trousers around the legs. In the Sikh community, a turban is worn along with a steel bangle around the wrist, a comb in uncut hair, a dagger (*kirpan*), and a pair of shorts. By the mid-1990s, Western dress by most Asian Indian men

and many Asian Indian women in both the United States and India was common.

Music

Two main styles of vocal and instrumental music exist in India—Hindustani, in the north, and Karnatak, in the south. Favorite instruments include the sitar, a gourd with a long neck, frets, and strings popular in the north, and the veena, two gourds with strings and frets similar to the sitar but popular in the south.

Cambodian Americans

History and Immigration

A southeast Asian country of ten million people bordered by Thailand, Laos, and Vietnam, Cambodia is a nation composed of 90 percent ethnic Cambodians or Khmer, 5 percent Vietnamese, 1 percent Chinese, and 4 percent other ethnic minorities. Most people live in the countryside and subsist by farming. The climate is tropical. Cambodia is 95 percent Buddhist, with a literacy rate

Cambodian Refugees Arriving in the United States, 1975 to 1990

Year	Refugees Arriving
1975	4,600
1976	1,100
1977	300
1978	1,300
1979	6,000
1980	16,000
1981	27,100
1982	20,100
1983	13,191
1984	19,849
1985	19,237
1986	10,054
1987	1,949
1988	2,900
1989	2,220
1990	2,325

Source: Susan B. Gall and Timothy L. Gall, editors, *Statistical Record of Asian Americans*, Gale, 1993, p. 451.

of 48 percent among men and 22 percent among women.

Large numbers of Cambodian immigrants began entering the United States in the 1970s and 1980s following the Vietnamese war and during the devastating regime of the Khmer Rouge. The Khmer Rouge was a Communist guerilla revolutionary group that toppled the government of Cambodia in 1975. An extremely brutal and violent group, it instituted a policy of anti-Western, anti-intellectual reform. It meant to return Cambodia to the agricultural country it was before colonial domination by Europe and America. The Khmer Rouge killed an estimated one to two million Cambodians in a population of about 7.5 million.

During the 1980s, thousands of Cambodian, Vietnamese, and Laotian refugees entered the United States each year. The U.S. government's program for Cambodian refugees ended in 1985, and the numbers of new refugees entering the country after that year decreased significantly. The 2000 census reported over 200,000 Cambodians Americans in the United States, with the largest population concentration in California. However, even these numbers were probably underestimates.

Assimilation and Acculturation

Cambodian immigrants, especially older ones, have had difficulty assimilating (blending in by becoming like) into the American culture. In 1990, only about one in five foreign-born Cambodians in the United States had become a naturalized citizen. While many younger Cambodians have adopted the American culture as their own, racism directed toward them as "foreigners" has resulted in some degree of alienation. In addition, cultural differences have brought misunderstanding. An example of this can be seen in the value Cambodians and Americans tend to place on courtesy and graciousness: Cambodians highly prize these characteristics while Americans consider them passive traits of less value.

Language

Cambodian, or Khmer, is an Austro-Asiatic language related to Vietnamese as well as to other tribal languages of Southeast Asia. It is not a tonal language like the major Asian languages. Its alphabet of 47 letters is derived from the ancient Indian alphabet and has many sounds quite different from those of English. Early Cambodian literature is based on Indian models and written in Sanskrit. The most famous classical poem, the *Reamker*, is still known by Cambodians today. The *Chbab*, a collection of aphorisms (laws) is memorized by school children as is the *Kotilok*, fables designed to teach moral lessons. Modern literature largely consists of autobiographical accounts of the horrors suffered under the Khmer Rouge from 1975 to 1979.

Music

Six types of traditional Cambodian musical ensembles exist. They consist of a variety of instruments, some unfamiliar in Western cultures, including the two- and three-stringed fiddles, monochord, lute, goblet drums, oboe, gongs, flute, zither, cymbals, dulcimer, and xylophone.

The best-known Cambodian dance is called the "masked dance." It always tells the story of the *Ramayana,* a Cambodian epic borrowed from ancient India. The art of dance in Cambodia is only now being revived after the blow dealt it when 90 percent of all trained dancers were killed during the Khmer Rouge regime.

Religion

Buddhism, the traditional religion of Cambodia, was protected by the rulers of the country prior to 1975, and the hierarchy of its monks was overseen by the government.

Ten U.S. States with Highest Population of Cambodian Descent, 1990	
State	**Cambodian Population**
California	68,190
Massachusetts	14,050
Washington	11,096
Texas	5,887
Pennsylvania	5,495
Virginia	3,889
Mississippi	3,858
Rhode Island	3,655
North Carolina	3,646
Indiana	3,026

Source: Susan B. Gall and Timothy L. Gall, editors, *Statistical Record of Asian Americans*, Gale, 1993, p. 689; see www.census.gov for state data from the 2000 census of population, scheduled for release in fall 2003.

Religion was, and is, an important part of the culture because the monks educate the children and pass on traditional religious rituals.

The essence of the Buddhist faith is the belief that all worldly things are changing and impermanent. To become attached to worldly things leads to suffering, which continues as the soul goes through a cycle of rebirths, continually attracted to worldly desires. Overcoming these desires can be accomplished through meditation and by leading a moral, disciplined life. Then the soul reaches nirvana, or the state of blissful oblivion to the cares of the world.

The cycle of death and destruction that occurred in Cambodia between 1975 and 1979 caused a spiritual crisis among some

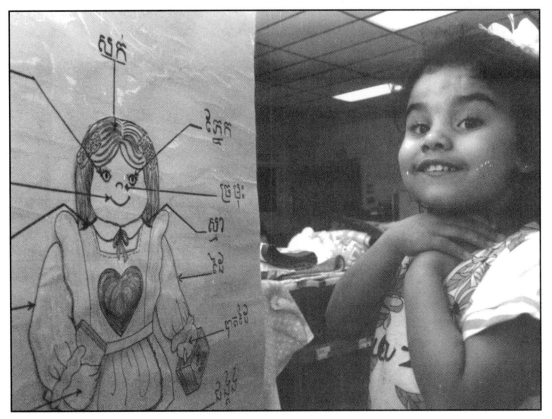

In 1991, Angelina Melendez, then age four, was a student at the Demonstration School in Lowell, Massachusetts. She studied the parts of the body from a poster written in the Cambodian language, Khmer. Established by the University of Lowell, the Demonstration School has a trilingual curriculum, teaching in English, Spanish, and Khmer.

Cambodians, who feared it was a sign that Buddhism had failed. Though some Cambodian Americans have converted to Christianity through cultural assimilation, the majority of Cambodian Americans continue to practice their traditional religion.

Family and Community

Children in Cambodian families are highly treasured, and families tend to be large—the average family has 5.03 members. In 1990, 20 percent of Cambodian households in the United States were headed by women because much of the male population was killed during the war years. In Cambodian culture the ideal woman is obedient to her husband, has practical intelligence for household business and family decision-making, and is expected to cook, wash clothes, and care for babies. Although women's advice and opinions are highly regarded in traditional society, primarily men receive education, and only men can occupy the prestigious status of the Buddhist monk.

POPULATION PROFILE: CHINESE AMERICANS

Feature	Chinese Americans
U.S. Population of Chinese descent, 2000	2,734,841
—as percent of U.S. total, 2000	0.96%
—as percent of Asian and Pacific Islander total, 2000	23%
—percent foreign-born (not born in the United States)	63%
—percent native-born (born in the United States)	37%

Source: U.S. Census Bureau, *Asian and Pacific Islander Population in the United States: March 2000 Current Population Survey (Update)*.

Because many Cambodian communities are located in urban areas of the United States, social contact with other minorities is common. Due to their dark complexions, many Cambodians experience racial prejudice which, while separating them from the white population in some areas, actually promotes assimilation with other groups, such as the Mexican population in Texas, where the two cultures intermingle freely. In Lowell, Massachusetts, Hispanics and Cambodians live together, and the community has responded by developing services to meet the needs of both ethnic groups.

Employment and Economics

Due to lack of formal education, job skills, and unfamiliarity with English, first-generation Cambodian Americans have a high rate of unemployment in the United States. Those who work find employment mostly in low-paying service and manual labor jobs. U.S. Census figures indicate that 42 percent of Cambodian families live below the poverty line, and 51 percent rely on some form of public assistance income. However, statistics also show that the longer Cambodians live in the United States, the lower their rate of unemployment becomes. Dedication to acquiring more education is reflected in the low high school dropout rate for Cambodian Americans between the ages of 16 and 19: 6 percent, compared with 10 percent for whites and 14 percent for African Americans.

Politics

Perhaps because survival and economics are priorities for Cambodian immigrants in the United States, their political concerns center primarily on the reconstruction and rebuilding of their native country.

An additional consequence of the stress experienced by those who lived through the war years in their land is the increased incidence of mental and physical health problems in those who have fled to the United States.

Chinese Population in the United States
1900 to 2000

Year	Chinese Population	Asian Population, Total	U.S. Population, Total
1900	118,746	204,462	76,212,168
1910	94,414	249,926	92,228,531
1920	85,202	332,432	106,021,568
1930	102,159	489,326	123,202,660
1940	106,334	489,984	132,165,129
1950	150,005	599,091	151,326,798
1960	237,292	877,934	179,323,175
1970	436,062	1,429,562	203,211,926
1980	812,178	3,466,421	226,545,805
1990	1,645,472	7,273,662	248,709,873
2000	2,734,841	11,898,828	281,421,906

Source: Susan B. Gall and Timothy L. Gall, editors, *Statistical Record of Asian Americans*, Gale, 1993, p. 572; and U.S. Census Bureau, *Asian and Pacific Islander Population in the United States: March 2000 Current Population Survey (Update)*.

Chinese Americans

History of Immigration and Discrimination

For centuries, the Great Wall of China symbolized the isolation of that country from Western influence. Emigration from China was forbidden by imperial decree—the rulers believed that China alone embodied civilization—and was even punishable by death. In 1757, however, the emperor opened the port of Canton for the first time to foreign trade. Then, in 1851, a peasant uprising in Kwangsi was crushed by the ruling dynasty; 30 million lives were eventually lost and internal disorder, chaos, and famine plagued southern China. These two factors caused men and women to begin to look outside China for a place to live and raise families. It was around this time that Chinese immigration to the United States began.

With the California Gold Rush of 1848 attracting thousands of Chinese to U.S. shores, immigrants arrived without money or jobs and in debt to brokers who advanced them the cost of transport to the United States. Most men arrived in the United States with plans to make money and then return to China. If they were married, their wives remained in China, looking after their in-laws, according to custom. Very few women traveled alone. Thus, early arrivals were almost all men, and their communities in America were known as "bachelor societies." Chinese men formed district associations to support each other in the search for jobs, to provide loans, and to socialize. As Chinatowns sprang up across the West Coast, Chinese American men

Children with queues around 1910.

Ten U.S. States with Highest Population of Chinese Descent, 1990

States	Chinese Population
California	704,850
New York	284,144
Hawaii	68,804
Texas	63,232
New Jersey	59,084
Massachusetts	53,792
Illinois	49,936
Washington	33,962
Maryland	30,868
Florida	30,737

Source: Susan B. Gall and Timothy L. Gall, editors, *Statistical Record of Asian Americans*, Gale, 1993, p. 689; see www.census.gov for state data from the 2000 census of population, scheduled for release in fall 2003.

outnumbered women 21 to 1 by 1880, and 28 to 1 by 1890.

During the second half of the nineteenth century, a wave of intolerance against the Chinese was set in motion. Oppressive taxes were levied on Chinese, and a California judge ruled that a Chinese person could not give evidence in court against a white man. These discriminatory forces plagued Chinese Americans, who were already tormented by hate crimes and discrimination. Chinese who refused to comply with the law and pay fines levied were jailed and punished by having their braids, or queues, cut off.

Throughout the nineteenth century, Chinese workers were a major labor force behind the development of the American West. They supplied factory labor, making cigars, shoes, clothing, and gunpowder. They labored in mines, built railroads (particularly the Central Pacific Transcontinental Railroad), levees, and dams, and farmed the land. Hatred for people of color, and fear that cheap Chinese labor would drive down white men's wages, produced a bigoted fear of the "Yellow Peril" during the 1870s. Riots and mob violence erupted in Chinatowns across the West. The issue of Chinese labor was also controversial on the East Coast and in the South, where the emancipation of slaves created a need for labor in the cotton industry.

Dragon dancers lead a parade through the streets of Chicago's Chinatown to celebrate the Lunar New Year.

In an attempt to halt Chinese immigration, President Chester Arthur signed the **Chinese Exclusion Act** in 1882, barring the immigration of laborers for ten years and strictly limiting the immigration of many professionals. In 1892, the exclusion law was extended indefinitely, reducing the Chinese population considerably. The 1890 Census reported 107,488 Chinese; in 1900, there were 118,746, and in 1910, 94,414. The **Immigration Act** of 1924 prevented Chinese wives of U.S. citizens from entering the country for the first time. In addition to the Immigration Act, between 1910 and 1940 the Angel Island Immigration Station at San Francisco Bay, a holding site where many Asian immigrants were detained, limited numbers of Chinese from entering the United States. (Texts of the two acts appear in the **Significant Documents** chapter of this volume.)

In 1943, during World War II, when China became an ally of the United States against the Japanese, Congress repealed the exclusion acts, but still limited Chinese immigration to 105 per year. By 1960, there were 237,292 Chinese in the United States, about 60 percent of whom were American born. About 50 percent of these lived in Hawaii, California, and New York. In 1962, President Lyndon B. Johnson, prompted by John F. Kennedy's vision of a fairer immigration policy, abolished the national quotas system, ending the era of discriminatory exclusion in immigration policy.

POPULATION PROFILE: FILIPINO AMERICANS

Feature	Filipino Americans
U.S. Population of Filipino descent, 2000	2,364,815
—as percent of U.S. total, 2000	0.8%
—as percent of Asian and Pacific Islander total, 2000	20%
—percent foreign-born (not born in the United States)	65%
—percent native-born (born in the United States)	35%

Source: U.S. Census Bureau, *Asian and Pacific Islander Population in the United States: March 2000 Current Population Survey (Update).*

Religion, Traditions, and Customs

While nineteenth-century Chinese immigrants usually clung to the beliefs and traditions of their ancestors, twentieth-century immigrants incorporated many new customs into their lives.

Traditional religion in China is a mixture of Buddhism, Confucianism, and Taoism. Buddhism teaches that all human life is bound in a cycle of rebirth and suffering, and that only through a life of contemplation and discipline can nirvana, or a state of blissful detachment from worldly cares, be reached. The principles of Taoism espouse a life of simplicity and harmony with nature. The teachings of Confucius (551–478 B.C.) stress self-improvement, good deeds, harmony in the home, and a respect for one's ancestors.

In Chinese religion there are no set services. Worshippers can visit a temple at any time, make an offering to the gods, and ask for their help. If prayers are answered, a gift or plaque may be offered to the temple. Chinese homes may also have altars. Christianity is also followed by some Chinese Americans, and in many Chinatowns, Christian services are held in Chinese.

Medicine

Traditional Chinese medicine is different from Western medicine. Herbs and medicinal soups are used for minor ailments, and acupuncture, an ancient Chinese medical practice using needles on special points of the body, is common treatment for a variety of illnesses.

Holidays

The 5,000-year old Chinese lunar calendar is divided into 12 cycles of planting and harvesting, each ruled by an animal deity: dragon, ram, monkey, rooster, dog, boar, rat, ox, tiger, rabbit, snake, and horse. Among traditional holidays celebrated by Chinese Americans are the Moon Festival (in the

17

**Filipino Population in the United States,
1900 to 2000**

Year	Filipino Population	Asian Population, Total	U.S. Population, Total
1900	N/A	204,462	76,212,168
1910	2,767	249,926	92,228,531
1920	26,634	332,432	106,021,568
1930	108,424	489,326	123,202,660
1940	98,535	489,984	132,165,129
1950	122,707	599,091	151,326,798
1960	176,310	877,934	179,323,175
1970	343,060	1,429,562	203,211,926
1980	781,894	3,466,421	226,545,805
1990	1,406,770	7,273,662	248,709,873
2000	2,364815	11,898,828	281,421,906

Source: U.S. Census Bureau, *Asian and Pacific Islander Population in the United States: March 2000 Current Population Survey (Update).*

fall), Ching Ming (a spring visit to ancestors' graves), and Chinese New Year.

Celebrations for longevity (old age), funerals, births, and weddings mark the life cycle. The color red is symbolic of good luck and happiness and is prominent in New Year's celebrations.

Filipino Americans

Population Statistics

Filipino Americans are persons of Filipino ancestry who are U.S. citizens by birth or naturalization, or Philippine nationals who are permanent U.S. residents. Since the Census Bureau first counted the Filipino population in the United States, the number of Filipinos has grown from 2,767 in 1910 to 2,364,841 in 2000. In that year, Filipino Americans accounted for 20 percent of all Asians in the United States, and constituted the second largest group of Asian Americans. In the decade between 1980 and 1990, Filipinos led all other Asian Americans in immigration, and that growth continued in the 1990s. The average age of the Filipino population in 1990 was 31.1 years and the male/female ratio was 86 males to 100 females.

"Pilipino" is another term sometimes used to refer to those who trace their ancestry to the Philippines. Its use is preferred by some Filipinos.

History of Immigration

Filipinos were the earliest Asians to cross the Pacific Ocean for North America with the Manila Galleon Trade, which prospered between Mexico and the Philippines from 1565 to 1815. During the eighteenth century, sailors, stowaways, and domestic workers jumped ship in New Orleans, Louisiana, settling there and migrating westward to settle in territory now occupied by the states of California, Texas, and New Mexico.

After the defeat of Spain in the Spanish-American War (a war fought in 1898 that resulted in Spain ceding the Philippine Islands to the United States), the United States annexed the Philippines, which had been a Spanish colony for over 400 years. Between 1903 and 1934, hundreds of Filipino students called *pensionados* immigrated to attend U.S. colleges with scholarships provided by the United States. Upon graduation, they were expected to return to their native country to spread the ideals of democracy; however, many remained in the United States to work. Additional waves of Filipino immigrants found jobs in industry and agriculture on the American West Coast and later sought employment in the Merchant Marine and the U.S. Navy.

When the Hawaiian Sugar Planters Association began importing Filipino laborers between 1907 and 1929, 30 percent of all plantation workers were Filipino. By 1930, Filipino residents accounted for 18 percent of the total population of the Hawaiian Islands. From 1920 to 1930, labor needs in California agriculture and the Alaskan salmon industry prompted another major exodus of Filipino workers from Hawaii to the mainland. During the Great Depression in the 1930s, when many Americans lost their jobs, discrimination toward immigrant aliens was prevalent. Laws forbidding marriage between Filipinos and white women were passed, depriving some Filipino laborers of family life and social acceptance.

Ten U.S. States with Highest Population of Filipino Descent, 1990	
States	**Filipino Population**
California	731,685
Hawaii	168,682
Illinois	64,224
New York	62,259
New Jersey	53,146
Washington	43,799
Virginia	35,067
Texas	34,350
Florida	31,945
Maryland	19,376

Source: Susan B. Gall and Timothy L. Gall, editors, *Statistical Record of Asian Americans*, Gale, 1993, p. 689; see www.census.gov for state data from the 2000 census of population, scheduled for release in fall 2003.

Between 1945 and 1965, a third wave of Filipino immigrants came to the United States. Most were descendants of veterans of the Spanish-American War or soldiers who served in the U.S. armed forces and their dependents. Then, with the passage of the **1965 Immigration Act,** the quota system was abolished. The Filipino population jumped from 176,310 in 1960 to 1,406,770 in 1990. This population included many highly skilled and technically trained men and women.

Education

The Filipino American community includes large numbers of educated people. In 1990, 82.8 percent of all Filipinos age 25 and over were high school graduates, surpassing the Asian American graduation rate of 75 percent. Both groups had equal percentages of college graduates—approximately 38 percent. Despite high levels of education, however, many Filipinos educated in the Philippines find it difficult to get U.S. jobs commensurate with their academic credentials. Professional obstacles encountered include lack of proficiency in English, lower standardized test scores, and rigorous U.S. licensing requirements.

Family

Most Filipino families are headed by couples (78 percent) and the average family had 4.0 members in 1990. The extended family (a family that includes not only parents and children, but other relatives as well, all living in one home) common in the Philippines is not the norm in the United States, although the church and extended community do often serve a strong family support function.

Languages

More than 70 dialects are spoken by Filipinos. The most common of these are Tagalog, Visayan, and Ilocano, which are spoken by 66 percent of all Filipinos in the United States. In addition to their native dialect, many Filipinos also speak English. English was introduced as the language of instruction in the U.S.-run Philippine public schools early in the twentieth century. But according to the 1990 census, only 63 percent of Filipino Americans five years old and over speak English very well.

Labor Force

Since early immigration to the United States, the Filipino American labor force has undergone change. In 1990, Filipino Americans age 16 and over had the highest civilian labor force participation rate among all U.S. citizens—both male and female at 75 percent. The 1990 census also revealed that over 55 percent of Filipino Americans hold white-collar jobs, including professional, sales, and administrative positions. Compared with other Asian Americans, however, Filipinos have a relatively low level of small business ownership. Of the remaining Filipinos in the labor force, 16.8 percent were in service occupations; 11 percent were operators, fabricators, and laborers; 7.4 percent were in precision production, craft, and repair occupations; and 1.5 percent were in farming, forestry, and fishing occupations. In the 1950s and 1960s, a shortage of medical professionals in the United States attracted thousands of Filipinos, who trained as physicians or nurses either in the Philippines or in the United States. There is also a high representation of Filipinos in government and the U.S. Navy.

Income

The median income of Filipino American families in 1990 was $46,698, which exceeded the average Asian American family income by $5,000. This is due to the presence of many highly skilled professionals in the Filipino population and also to the larger number of workers in Filipino families (30 percent have three or more workers). The 1990 per capita income of Filipinos was $13,616, a figure only slightly below the U.S. average. The poverty rate among Filipino families in 1990 was only 5

POPULATION PROFILE: HMONG AMERICANS

Feature	Hmong Americans
U.S. Population of Hmong descent, 2000	186,310
—as percent of U.S. total, 2000	0.06%
—as percent of Asian and Pacific Islander total, 2000	1.6%
—percent foreign-born (not born in the United States)	75%
—percent native-born (born in the United States)	25%

Source: U.S. Census Bureau, *Asian and Pacific Islander Population in the United States: March 2000 Current Population Survey (Update).*

percent, the second lowest rate among all Asian Americans.

Religion

The majority of Filipinos in the United States are Christian and most are Roman Catholic. During the 350 years of Spanish colonial rule of the Philippines, the rituals of the Church were the center of family life. Today, in addition to religious holidays, cultural celebrations and festivals include parades, folk dances, food and craft fairs, and music and other forms of performance. These holidays include Philippine Independence Day on June 12; Rizal Day on December 30, commemorating the martyrdom of national hero José Rizal; and Philippine-American Friendship Day on July 4.

Hmong Americans

History and Immigration

The Hmong are an ancient people whose origins date back to 2000 B.C. in China. Probably originating in Siberia and then migrating south into the mountains of China, the Hmong struggled for centuries against Chinese rule to maintain their cultural identity. However, in the eighteenth century, they were ultimately vanquished and assimilated by the Chinese. As a Chinese minority, the Hmong waged a series of wars and rebellions during the nineteenth century. Unsuccessful in these, they fled south into the territory now occupied by Laos, Vietnam, and Thailand.

Here the Hmong encountered new oppression under the French, who ruled a vast Indochinese empire. In 1920, after a revolt led by Pa Chay, who called for establishing a separate Hmong kingdom, the French created an autonomous (self-governing) Hmong district in Laos. However, competition for leadership between clans led to the permanent political separation of the Hmong in Laos. The Ly clan allied themselves with the French and later the Americans in their fight against the North

Vietnamese communists and their Laotian supporters. The Lo clan joined forces with the Lao nationalists who wanted independence from France and who later became the Pathet Lao, or the Communist forces.

When the United States became involved in the war in Southeast Asia in the 1960s, the Pathet Lao guerrillas joined with the Viet Cong in Vietnam to fight the South Vietnamese government and Americans for Vietnamese reunification. By 1969, 40,000 Hmong soldiers, led by anticommunist Vang Pao, were assisting the royal Lao government and the Americans.

After the American withdrawal from southeast Asia in 1973 and the fall of South Vietnam in 1975, the royal Lao government also collapsed. Those Hmong who were not resettled in the United States were either sent to reeducation camps in Laos or exterminated as rebels of the new government. Some also managed to escape to Thailand, where they stayed in refugee camps.

Beginning in 1975, the resettlement of Hmong in the United States began. By the early 1980s, there were approximately 50,000 Hmong living in the country and by 1990, the number had doubled.

Resettlement agencies in the United States dispersed Hmong refugees to over 53 cities in 25 different states. However, because of separate tribal identities and the desire to reunify clans, between 1981 and 1985 the Hmong undertook a secondary migration in small family groups to reform their communities on the Pacific Coast. They reunited in Fresno, Merced, Sacramento, Stockton, Chico, Modesto, and Visalia, California. The three states with the largest Hmong population are California, with 46,892; Minnesota, with 14,050; and Wisconsin, with 16,373.

Religion and Customs

The Hmong regard religion as the foundation of life. Their religion is pantheistic (believing that spirits reside in all things) and is composed of three parts: the cult of spirits, shamanism, and ancestor worship. The Hmong believe that all life is divided between the invisible world of the spirits and the visible world of human beings, objects, and nature. An intermediary between the two worlds is the shaman, a holy man who can contact the world of the spirits. The shaman is also considered a healer, who uses herbal medicines and massage to cure illnesses believed to be spiritual in nature. Many Hmong in both Laos and the United States have converted to Christianity.

Births, marriages, and funerals all feature important Hmong ceremonial customs. The Hmong believe that every child born is a reincarnated soul who joins human society three days after birth. In a ceremony, a shaman invokes the soul and bestows upon the baby a silver necklace symbolic of it.

In Laos, marriage within a clan is forbidden and only men and women with different family names may marry. This does not prevent marriage between first cousins and some blood relations. Tradition dictates that Hmong men marry between the ages of 18 and 30 and women between the ages of 14 and 18. Courtship occurs during the New Year's Festival when many young people from different villages come together for the celebration. To find a bride, a Hmong man hires a go-between who bargains with the woman's family to secure a bridal price. Occasionally in Laos, elopements and wife kidnapping when bridal price cannot be agreed upon are practices allowed under Hmong law. The custom of polygyny, or marriage with several women, is also condoned.

In Asia, the death of a family member is announced by firing three shots. Funerals are attended by mourners bearing gifts for the family. A shaman makes an offering to the departing soul of the deceased and tells it which route is safe to follow to rejoin its ancestors.

Language

Hmong is a language consisting mostly of one-syllable words, spoken with eight different tones. The language was written with Chinese characters until the 1950s when the Romanized Popular Alphabet (RPA) used by English and other western European languages was applied to the Hmong language. A consonant at a word's end is a code indicating the tone. Most other vowels and consonants not at the end of a word are pronounced the same as in English. A common greeting in Hmong, *Koj tuaj los?*, means literally "You've come?" (the "j" indicates a falling tone and "s" is a mid-low tone). *Kuv tuaj* means "I've come" (the "v" is a mid-rising tone). Blue and White Hmong, two tribal dialects, are spoken in the United States.

Myths and Legends

Folktales predating the Hmong's assimilation into Chinese culture were passed on orally from generation to generation. A comprehensive collection is the bilingual volume *Myths, Legends, and Folktales from the Hmong of Laos* (1985). Hmong stories use magic, the supernatural, spirits, animals, and people to convey moral lessons such as the value of hard work, honesty, and virtue and the unfortunate results of evil, laziness, and selfishness.

Economics and Family

High levels of economic hardship exist in the Hmong American community due to the low level of formal education among Hmong born outside of the United States, who were predominantly farmers. In 1990, two-thirds of this population (63.6 percent) lived beneath the poverty level. However, among Hmong born in the United States, 32 percent of those aged from 18 to 24 were in college in 1990, a rate only slightly lower than that of white Americans (39.5 percent).

The average Hmong family is composed of 6.38 individuals. While the extended family is the basic social unit in Asia, Hmong Americans live in nuclear families in which the husband is the decision-maker and head of the family and the wife has primary responsibility for the household and children. Parental control over children is highly respected in traditional Hmong culture.

Indonesian Americans

Overview

The Republic of Indonesia is located in Southeast Asia on the Malay Archipelago, a group of more than 13,000 islands along the equator. It occupies an area approximately the size of Mexico and spans about one-eighth of the world's circumference. The Indonesian islands consist of a Pacific Ocean set including Borneo, Celebese, and the Moluccas and an Indian Ocean set including Sumatra, Java, Bali, and the Lesser Sundas.

The fourth most populous country in the world, the Republic of Indonesia had a population of 231 million in 2002. Its people are physically, culturally, and ethnically diverse, reflecting centuries of immigration and domination by a variety of nations. The largest ethnic group is the Javanese, who comprise 45 percent of the total population. The Sudanese make up 14 percent, followed by Madurese at 7.5 percent, and coastal Malays at 7.5 percent.

The climate of Indonesia is generally tropical with heavy rainfall, but it can vary according to altitude and exposure to the ocean. A land rich in natural resources such as oil, liquefied natural gas, rubber, palm oil, and tin, Indonesia exports to the United States, Japan, Singapore, the Netherlands, and Germany.

History

Two advanced civilizations flourished on the islands of Indonesia centuries before the Renaissance in Europe. From the seventh to the fourteenth centuries, the Buddhist kingdom of Srivijaya flourished on Sumatra, reaching as far west as Java and the Malay Peninsula. By the fourteenth century, the Hindu kingdom of Majapahit in eastern Java ruled most of what is today Indonesia and the Malay Archipelago.

Between the twelfth and sixteenth centuries, Islam replaced Buddhism as the dominant religion everywhere in the archipelago except Bali, which remained predominantly Hindu. In the seventeenth century, the Dutch established themselves as rulers of most of Indonesia, which they called the Netherlands East Indies and controlled for the next three hundred years.

The Indonesian independence movement began during the first decade of the twentieth century and grew in force during the three-year Japanese occupation during World War II (1939–45). With the Japanese surrender on August 17, 1945, Sukarno, a nationalist leader of the Indonesian independence movement, established the Republic of Indonesia. After defeating attempts by the Dutch to regain colonial territories lost to Japan, Indonesia joined the United Nations in 1950.

Economic conditions deteriorated under Sukarno's leadership, and in 1965 a coup by the Indonesian army resulted in the death of hundreds of thousands of people and an outlawing of the Communist Party. General Suharto was elected president in 1968 and, in the mid-1990s, remained in power.

Immigration and Acculturation

Since the mid-1950s, when the United States and Indonesia began cooperating in the field of education, increasing numbers of Indonesians have come to the United States to pursue studies, especially in the fields of engineering and social sciences. However, a 1993 immigration bill by the Indonesian parliament barred individuals from entering or leaving the country under certain conditions and limited their time of travel in and out of the country. This effectively restricted recent immigration flow between the United States and Indonesia.

The Indonesian community in the United States is smaller than other Asian American communities and is located predominantly in Los Angeles, San Francisco, Houston, New York, and Chicago. The 2000 census reported only 63,073 Indonesians or Indonesian Americans (0.01 percent of population)

POPULATION PROFILE: JAPANESE AMERICANS

Feature	Japanese Americans
U.S. Population of Japanese descent, 2000	1,148,932
—as percent of U.S. total, 2000	0.4%
—as percent of Asian and Pacific Islander total, 2000	9.7%
—percent foreign-born (not born in the United States)	28%
—percent native-born (born in the United States)	72%

Source: U.S. Census Bureau, *Asian and Pacific Islander Population in the United States: March 2000 Current Population Survey (Update)*.

in the United States. The Indonesian American population is diverse and is composed of more than three hundred distinct ethnic groups, each with its own social classes, language, religion, and cultural background. Cultural assimilation for many Indonesian Americans depends on such factors as age, length of residency in the United States, degree of isolation or support from friends and family, and religion.

Language

The official language of Indonesia, proclaimed in 1928, was Bahasa Indonesian, a modified form of Malay. However, there are more than three hundred regional languages and dialects used in Indonesia. The majority of educated people who live in urban areas have command of at least two languages.

Family and Economics

According to the 1990 census, 78 percent of Indonesian American families are married-couple families. Intermarriage between Indonesians and non-Indonesians in the United States is more common in the 1990s than in the past. The 1990 census reported that one-third of employed Indonesian American adults are managers; one-third are professionals; and one-third are in technical, sales, and administrative-support positions. The importing and exporting business also employs many Indonesians.

Religion

Five major religions influence Indonesian culture: Islam (90 percent of the population); Protestantism (6 percent); Catholicism (3 percent); Hinduism (2 percent); and Buddhism (1 percent).

The high percentage of Muslims makes Indonesia the largest Islamic nation in the world. Introduced by traders from India in the twelfth century, Islam was founded by the prophet Muhammad, who was selected by the Islamic god, Allah, to spread his word

**Japanese Population in the United States,
1900 to 2000**

Year	Japanese Population	Asian Population, Total	U.S. Population, Total
1900	85,716	204,462	76,212,168
1910	152,745	249,926	92,228,531
1920	220,596	332,432	106,021,568
1930	278,743	489,326	123,202,660
1940	285,115	489,984	132,165,129
1950	326,379	599,091	151,326,798
1960	464,332	877,934	179,323,175
1970	591,290	1,429,562	203,211,926
1980	716,331	3,466,421	226,545,805
1990	847,562	7,273,662	248,709,873
2000	1,148,932	11,898,828	281,421,906

Source: U.S. Census Bureau, *Asian and Pacific Islander Population in the United States: March 2000 Current Population Survey (Update).*

through the Koran, Islam's holiest book.

In Java, a blend of Islam, Hinduism, and Buddhism has produced a religion known as Javanism, officially recognized in 1945. On Bali, Hinduism, the predominant religion, is observed through ritual and art and in Balinese ceremonies marking puberty, marriage, and death.

However, the most rapidly growing religions in Indonesia are Roman Catholicism and Protestantism, introduced respectively by the Portuguese in the sixteenth century and the Dutch in the seventeenth century. For a variety of reasons, membership in the Christian church remained low for several hundred years until the 1965 military coup, when Indonesians who had not practiced a religion found themselves being labeled "communist." In order to avoid political reprisals, many joined Christian churches.

Only 1 percent of Indonesians practice Buddhism, a belief system brought to Indonesia by the Chinese along with Taoism and Confucianism.

Japanese Americans

History of Immigration

For centuries, Japan's ruling dynasty forbade travel to and from the country. Fear of foreigners and the penalty of death for defying imperial policy kept the Japanese people on their home soil. From the seventeenth through the mid-nineteenth centuries, only stranded or shipwrecked fishermen rescued by ships escaped the country's total isolation.

In 1868, the importation of Japanese contract laborers by Hawaiian sugar plantations broke this isolation and, in 1869, a small group of Japanese exiles founded the short-lived Wakamatsu Tea and Silk Colony in Coloma, California, near Sacramento. Between 1880 and 1900, the number of Japanese residing in the United States grew from 148 to 85,716. This increase was due in part to the importation of Japanese women known as "picture brides," who came to the United States to marry Japanese men after a period of exchanged letters and photographs. Japanese immigrants in the early twentieth century were also needed for the Yamato Colony communities in California, Florida, and Texas. These experimental cooperative farm communities imported contract laborers from Japan. Although the first workers were unmarried young men, later settlers married and raised families, making the colonies into permanent settlements.

However, as the Japanese American population grew, so too did anti-Japanese sentiment. Fear of a "Yellow Peril" resulted in discriminatory U.S. laws, such as alien land laws prohibiting Asians from owning land. The 1924 **Immigration Act,** commonly known as the Asian Exclusion Act, prohibited alien immigration, including Japanese. They would be ineligible for citizenship until 1952, and then only a limited number of Japanese immigrants were allowed to enter the country. Despite deteriorating relations between the United States and Japan throughout the 1930s, the Japanese American population continued to grow and prosper and, in 1940, there were 285,115 people of Japanese descent in the United States, more than half of whom were U.S.-born.

World War II and Internment

On December 7, 1941, Japan attacked Pearl Harbor, Hawaii, destroying the U.S. Pacific fleet and prompting a backlash of

Ten U.S. States with Highest Population of Japanese Descent, 1990	
States	**Japanese Population**
California	312,989
Hawaii	247,486
New York	35,281
Washington	34,366
Illinois	21,831
New Jersey	17,253
Texas	14,795
Oregon	11,796
Colorado	11,402
Michigan	10,681

Source: Susan B. Gall and Timothy L. Gall, editors, *Statistical Record of Asian Americans*, Gale, 1993, p. 689; see www.census.gov for state data from the 2000 census of population, scheduled for release in fall 2003.

furious anti-Japanese sentiment. In 1942, as a response to the suspicion that the attack on Pearl Harbor was due to espionage committed by Japanese Americans, President Franklin D. Roosevelt signed **Executive Order 9066,** which dictated the removal and internment (confinement) of Japanese Americans. The assumption that U.S.-born Japanese, or nisei, would bear allegiance to Japan and engage in acts of wartime sabotage fueled pro-internment sentiments. Farming interests in California saw in Executive Order 9066 the opportunity to rid themselves of competition from Japanese American farmers who, as internees, were forced to abandon their farms as well as businesses, jobs, and homes.

HOUSE OF REPRESENTATIVES DEBATE ON THE CIVIL LIBERTIES ACT OF 1988

Among those who testified during the debate on the Civil Liberties Act of 1988 in the House of Representatives was Congressman Norman Y. Mineta of California. Mineta recounted wearing his Cub Scout uniform when he and his family were forced to leave their home and were taken to an "assembly center":

"I respectfully urge my colleagues to approve the rule for the Civil Liberties Act of 1987. Now, after 45 years, Congress has the opportunity to close the book on one of the most shameful events in our nation's history: The internment, beginning in 1942, of 120,000 loyal Americans, simply on the basis of their ethnic ancestry. There was no trial; there was no jury.

"Those interned were not foreign spies disloyal to the United States.... Among those interned were old men and women who had toiled in the fields of California. Their hard labor made barren lands productive, lands that many would lose as a result of the internment.

"Those interned were not unscrupulous agents of a foreign power: They were business people who had worked long and hard to build small businesses and to become respected members of their communities. And, those interned were not recent immigrants of uncertain loyalty; most were born in this country and were proud citizens from birth.

"I was one of those interned. I was 10 years old. If someone, anyone, could show me how by any stretch of the imagination any reasonable person could suspect me to have been a security threat, I would abandon this effort here and now.

"The fact remains that no Americans of Japanese ancestry committed any acts of treason or disloyalty, and the fact remains that the internment was not a mere inconvenience to Japanese Americans.

"Evacuated with little notice and little explanation, thousands of Americans lost their homes, their businesses, their farms. And we lost 3 years of our lives. The financial losses were enormous. But the losses of friends, education, opportunity, and standing in our communities were incalculable.

"The internment was not, as some say, 'regrettable but understandable.' It was wholly unjustified in light of what we know now and, even more distressing, unjustified in light of what anyone could have known in 1942. As a consequence, our entire Nation was and still is shamed by the internment.

"Yes, it was a time of great national stress. But moral principles and rules of law are easy to uphold in placid times. But are these same principles upheld by great nations under great difficulty and stress? Sadly, we as a nation failed such a test in 1942."

—*Congressional Record,* vol. 133, no. 141, September 17, 1987

Japanese Americans were sent first to "assembly centers" and then to remote and desolate desert area camps. Termed "relocation camps" by the government, these internment camps were surrounded by barbed wire fences and armed guards. Japanese Americans were forced to live in wooden barracks covered in tar paper. A family was crowded into a single 20 by 20-foot cubicle with a potbellied stove, a single electric light, and army cots for beds. Latrines and bath facilities were shared, ensuring a lack of privacy, and waiting in lines for every daily task became a fact of life. Internees struggled to provide makeshift schools to educate the thousands of school-aged children interned in the camps.

The U.S. government had classified all young Japanese American men as enemy aliens in 1942. In 1943, all interned Japanese Americans over the age of 17 were administered a loyalty questionnaire, causing bitter divisions in the Japanese American community. It required all Japanese Americans to swear allegiance to the United States and renounce allegiance to Japan. One thousand two hundred volunteers did so, and these young Japanese American men were recruited to serve in the 442nd Regimental Combat Team. The 442nd united with the 100th Infantry Battalion (another all-Japanese American group) and was sent to fight on the front lines in Italy and France, where it suffered enormous casualties.

By the end of World War II, these veterans returned to the United States, only to be reinterned in camps. In 1944, when the Supreme Court ruled against further detainment of loyal citizens, many Japanese Americans returned to their homes and were met with reactions from the local citizenry ranging

Takashi Tanaka, Japanese American entrepreneur, owns a bookstore in Columbus, Ohio.

from acceptance to hostility. Others relocated in other cities across the United States.

It was not until the Civil Rights Movement took hold in the 1960s that Japanese Americans publicly addressed what they viewed as a chapter of shame in their history. Because the internment was a painful experience that many issei (first-generation Japanese Americans) and nisei (second-generation Japanese immigrants) wished to forget, it had not been discussed. However, in the 1960s and 1970s, many sansei, or third-generation Japanese Americans, began to learn about their parents' and grandparents' ordeal. In 1968, the Asian American Political Alliance (AAPA) was formed. With help from the Japanese American Citizens League, AAPA succeeded in 1971 in repealing the Emergency Detention Act of 1950, thereby preventing future internment of those who might be suspected of "acts of espionage or sabotage."

Redress for Internment

At this same time, the demand for redress—compensation for those who had been interned—began to gain favor. Redress resolutions were passed in 1970, 1972, and 1974 by the Japanese American Citizens League, which worked steadily to raise the level of public consciousness about Japanese internment. A variety of commissions, councils, and committees studied the impact of the internment experience on Japanese Americans and sought to recommend appropriate remedies. On July 31, 1980, President Jimmy Carter signed a bill to create a Commission on Wartime Relocation and Internment of Civilians (CWRIC) to review the actions that resulted from Executive Order 9066, which ordered the imprisonment of Japanese Americans. During the summer of 1981, the CWRIC began its series of ten public hearings on the internment experience. Over 750 people testified during the hearings, which were held in different cities around the United States.

On June 23, 1983, the CWRIC issued its report, *Personal Justice Denied.* The report found that there had been no justifiable reason to deny the constitutional rights of the Japanese Americans who were interned. The Commission recommended that an apology be issued and that each surviving victim of the internment be granted a sum of $20,000 in redress.

Several bills supporting these redress recommendations were proposed in Congress,

Immigration to the United States from Korea by Decade, 1901 to 1990	
Decade	Number of Immigrants
1901–1910	7,697
1911–1920	1,049
1921–1930	598
1931–1940	60
1941–1950	N/A
1951–1960	6,231
1961–1970	34,526
1971–1980	271,956
1981–1990	338,824
1991–1999	148,952

Source: Susan B. Gall and Timothy L. Gall, editors, *Statistical Record of Asian Americans*, Gale, 1993, p. 411; and Table 2: Immigration by region and selected country of last residence: fiscal years 1820-2001, Immigration Information, Fiscal Year 2001 Statistics.

but each failed. Finally, the **Civil Liberties Act** of 1988 authorized compensation of $20,000 to Japanese who were eligible under certain conditions for redress. In 1989, Senator Daniel Inouye proposed the addition of an entitlement program to be instituted in 1991 to fund the redress payments. Although fully half of the victims of internment did not live to see redress achieved, it was nonetheless a monumental victory for the Japanese American community.

Korean Americans

History of Immigration

In little more than one hundred years, the Korean American community has grown

Ten U.S. States with Highest Population of Korean Descent, 1990

States	Korean Population
California	259,941
New York	95,648
Illinois	41,506
New Jersey	38,540
Texas	31,775
Maryland	30,320
Virginia	30,164
Washington	29,697
Pennsylvania	26,787
Hawaii	24,454

Source: Susan B. Gall and Timothy L. Gall, editors, *Statistical Record of Asian Americans*, Gale, 1993, p. 689; see www.census.gov for state data from the 2000 census of population, scheduled for release in fall 2003.

from a small group of political exiles and immigrant laborers in Hawaii and California to become one of the fastest-growing ethnic groups in the United States. According to the 2000 census, Americans identifying themselves as of Korean descent numbered 1,228,427.

Early Korean immigrants, with the exception of a handful of exiled political and social reform movement leaders, were male contract workers recruited by the Hawaiian sugarcane industry. The first wave of Korean immigration to the United States consisted of two thousand workers who left the Hawaiian plantations in the first decade of the twentieth century and moved to the mainland to operate small farms or retail businesses. This immi-

gration slowed between 1905 and 1924, when Japan—which then occupied Korea—allowed only Korean women to enter the United States. The Japanese government wanted to keep men from emigrating and joining the Korean independence movement based in the United States and from competing with Japanese immigrants for U.S. jobs.

The result of Japanese restrictions was an influx of Korean "picture brides"—women introduced to their prospective husbands through letters and photographs. Family life brought new stability to Korean communities in the United States.

As was the case for many immigrant groups, Korean Americans faced open discrimination during this time in the form of anti-Asian laws. Laws barred Asians from intermarrying with whites, residing in certain desirable neighborhoods, holding government jobs and teaching positions, and owning land. These difficulties, however, did not prevent Korean Americans from focusing their energies on fighting for Korean national independence from Japan. This effort, led by patriots-in-exile Park Yong-man, Suh Jae-pil (also known as Philip Jaisohn), and Syngman Rhee, finally celebrated victory when independence from Japan was declared in 1945. In 1948, with U.S. backing, Syngman Rhee was elected president of the Republic of Korea. Korea was divided into democratic South Korea—known as the Republic of Korea—and communist-controlled North Korea (Democratic Republic of North Korea).

American involvement in the Korean War in the 1950s produced a second wave of immigration, including 6,500 wives of servicemen and 6,300 war orphans adopted by

Korean American children wave the flags of the United States and South Korea in the Los Angeles neighborhood known as Koreatown during a March 2003 rally against the development of nuclear weapons in North Korea. The rally was sponsored by a coalition of Korean American churches, businesses, and community groups.

Americans. In addition, increasing numbers of Korean students came to study in the United States along with Korean doctors who sought to continue their training in U.S. hospitals.

The **Immigration and Nationality Act** of 1965 banished the quota system for immigrants, giving Asians an equal chance to immigrate for the first time. Korean families, students, and professionals finally became eligible to apply for permanent residency and U.S. citizenship. Between 1966 and 1970, Korean immigration surpassed 25,000, and it

more than quadrupled in the succeeding three-year period. Between 1981 and 1990, the number of Koreans entering the United States reached a new high of 338,824.

Community and Religion

Contrary to many Asian immigrant settlement patterns, Korean Americans are widely dispersed throughout the United States. According to the 1990 census, 44 percent of all Korean Americans live in the West, 23 percent in the Northeast, 19 percent in the South, and 14 percent in the Midwest.

Yung Kim, a Korean American businessman in Baltimore, stands between a revolving Plexiglas window and the wire-grated door to his store.

Korean communities include a complex network of churches, recreational clubs, business and professional associations, alumni organizations, and civic groups. These connections are reinforced by the Korean-language news media. As with many immigrant groups, cultural and language differences exist between the older and younger Korean Americans. Younger Korean Americans have formed their own organizations.

Churches are the foundation of the Korean community in America. Although Buddhism is the predominant religion in South Korea and most early immigrants were non-Christians, today 75 percent of Korean Americans affiliate with a Christian church and 65 percent attend church regularly. Churches are more than places of worship; they also function as surrogate extended families for Koreans in the United States, affirming Korean culture, values, and nationalism. At church, Korean Americans share information on employment, housing, immigration, naturalization, income taxes, health care, social security, and education. Churches also support causes of interest to Korean Americans. In March 2003, when North Korea appeared to be developing nuclear weapons, Korean Americans rallied in support of South Korea and the U.S. efforts to keep nuclear weapons out of the region.

Employment

Although Korean Americans can be found in all walks of life, they have the highest business ownership rate of all racial and ethnic groups in the United States. Approximately one-third of Koreans living in urban centers run small businesses, including import-export firms, neighborhood grocery stores, dry cleaners, fast-food restaurants, and clothing stores. The high degree of Korean entrepreneurship can be traced to several factors. Although college educated, many immigrants have language differences that prevent them from gaining access to white-collar jobs in the United States. This obstacle, plus the attraction of independence and profit from business ownership, leads many to this career.

During the 1970s and 1980s, Korean Americans took advantage of opportunities to buy inner-city businesses. However, caught up in the problems of crime, poverty, and an ongoing urban race/class struggle, many Korean business owners had mixed experiences. Misunderstandings between Korean American shopkeepers and their clientele—often African American or Hispanic American—have resulted in conflicts that occasionally have become violent. The riots that erupted in Los Angeles in 1992 after the police officers accused of beating African American motorist Rodney King were acquitted resulted in the looting and destruc-

Korean Business Ownership, 1977–1997		
Year	Korean-Owned Businesses	Total Asian-Owned Businesses
1977	9,000	83,000
1987	69,000	355,000
1997	137,000	913,000
2000	135,571	922,000

Source: Susan B. Gall and Timothy L. Gall, editors, *Statistical Record of Asian Americans*, Gale, 1993, p. 44; and 2000 U.S. Census of Population.

tion of more than 2,000 Korean-owned businesses and approximately $350 million loss in damages. Many of these businesses did not reopen.

Customs

Traditional Korean beliefs are based on Confucianism. Confucianism emphasizes strict obedience to elders, responsibility to one's family, and respect for hierarchies of authority—a value reflected in most Korean businesses and community organizations. The extended family is the basic social unit among Korean Americans. Family groups provide financial assistance, information, employment, and emotional support for many Korean immigrants.

A custom unique to Korean Americans is a rotating credit system called *kye,* which has existed for centuries in Korea. A *kye* is a small group of 12 to 20 individuals who meet once a month to contribute a fixed sum of money to a "pot." This money is then distrib-

Laotian Population in the United States, 1980 to 2000

Year	Laotian Population	Asian Population, Total	U.S. Population, Total
1980	47,683	3,726,440	226,545,805
1990	149,014	7,273,662	248,709,873
2000	198,203	11,898,828	281,421,906
Percent increase, 1980–1990	212.5%	95.2%	9.8%
Percent increase, 1990–2000	33%	64%	13%

Source: Susan B. Gall and Timothy L. Gall, editors, *Statistical Record of Asian Americans*, Gale, 1993, p. 569; and U.S. Census Bureau, *Asian and Pacific Islander Population in the United States: March 2000 Current Population Survey (Update)*.

uted—as a loan—to any member of the group who needs it. Reasons for requesting money from the *kye* include opening a business or paying for a wedding, funeral, or college tuition. *Kyes* can generate pools as small as one thousand dollars or as large as one million dollars. They depend on trust among members. *Kyes* are an important factor in the success of small business ownership among Korean Americans, since many new immigrants would have difficulty getting a loan from a commercial bank.

Language

There are more than 68 million Korean-speaking people in the world. In fact, Korean ranks as the fifteenth most-spoken language in the world. It is spoken in both North and South Korea, although with different accents. Hangul, the Korean alphabet dating from the fifteenth century, is phonetic (based on the sound of the spoken language) and is composed of ten vowels and fourteen consonants. Due in part to the simplicity of the language, over 95 percent of all Koreans can read and write—one of the highest literacy rates in the world. Because many Korean words have been borrowed from Chinese, South Korean (Republic of Korea) script is often an intermingling of Chinese characters and Hangul. North Korea (Democratic Republic of Korea), on the other hand, has eliminated Chinese characters from its written Korean by law.

Korean names usually consist of three syllables. The surname, or family name, comes first. The second syllable stands for the generation name; it tells a person's place in the extended family. For example, all the siblings and cousins of the same generation have the same second syllable. The third syllable is the person's first name. When the first child in a generation is born, the generation name is determined according to a twelve-year cycle on the father's side. This system makes it possible to maintain genealogies and extensive family trees. The most

Ten U.S. States with Highest Population of Laotian Descent, 1990

States	Laotian Population
California	58,058
Texas	9,332
Minnesota	6,381
Washington	6,191
Illinois	4,985
Massachusetts	3,985
Wisconsin	3,622
Iowa	3,374
Oregon	3,262
New York	3,253

Source: Susan B. Gall and Timothy L. Gall, editors, *Statistical Record of Asian Americans*, Gale, 1993, p. 689; see www.census.gov for state data from the 2000 census of population, scheduled for release in fall 2003.

common family name in Korea is Kim, which 20 to 25 percent of all families bear. Fifty percent of the population bears one of five surnames, which, besides Kim, include Lee, Park, Choi, and Chung. Other common family names are Ahn, Cho, Han, Kang, Lim, and Yoo.

Laotian Americans

Overview

Located in Southeast Asia and slightly larger than the state of Utah, Laos measures 91,400 square miles. It is bordered by Cambodia in the south, Thailand in the southwest, Burma in the west, China in the north, and Vietnam in the east. A country of 5,800,000 people, Laos is a small mountainous country with a tropical climate. Most Laotians earn a living by subsistence farming. Three main ethnic minorities comprise the population: the Mon-Khmer; the Yao; and the Hmong. The principal religion is Theravada Buddhism, heavily influenced by the cult of *phi*, or spirits, and Hinduism.

History

Laotians trace their ancestry to the T'ai, a people who migrated south from China in the sixth century. Although originally part of the Khmer Empire (Cambodia), Laos was created as an independent state in 1353 when a prince from the city of Luang Prabang declared himself king of Lan Xang, or the "Kingdom of a Million Elephants." Luang Prabang was its capital for two hundred years until the site changed to Vientiane, the present capital of Laos. The kingdom reached its height in the 1600s, but with the death of King Souligna Vongsa in 1694 it was broken into the kingdoms of Vientiane, Luang Prabang, and Champassak. By the mid-1800s, only Luang Prabang remained independent, with the north of Laos controlled by Vietnam and the southern and central parts of the country under the rule of Thailand.

By the 1880s, all of Vietnam was controlled by France, and by 1899 the French succeeded in unifying all the old Laotian territories under their rule. Despite small rebellions, widespread Laotian resistance to the French began only after World War II with the defeat of Japan in Indochina. Many Laotians opposed to French control joined together with the Viet Minh under the command of Ho Chi Minh and defeated the French at Dien Bien Phu in Vietnam in

1954. Ho Chi Minh's communist government assumed control of Vietnam north of the seventeenth parallel and invaded South Vietnam in 1959. Both Laos and the United States were drawn into the war. In 1975, communist forces overthrew the Laotian government, renaming the country the Lao People's Democratic Republic.

History of Immigration

Beginning in 1975 during the communist takeover, thousands of Laotians fled their homeland for the United States. They were aided by the Indochina Migration and Refugee Assistance Act, which allowed up to 200,000 Vietnamese and other Southeast Asians to enter the United States without going through the normal immigration process. Between 1975 and 1978, 18,600 Laotian refugees entered the United States, followed by another 105,000 from 1979 to 1981. This resettlement continued throughout the 1980s and 1990s with somewhat reduced numbers.

The 1990 census revealed that there were 150,000 Laotian Americans (excluding Hmong) living in the United States, with the majority located in California, Texas, Minnesota, and Washington. Ninety-six percent of all Laotian Americans live in urban areas and only 4 percent live in rural communities.

In 1991, Laos was the third highest source of refugees admitted to the United States, after Vietnam and the former Soviet Union. As of 1989, 94 percent of Laotians in the United States were foreign-born, the highest of any Asian ethnic group.

Laotian Americans are a young population, whose average age is 20.4 years compared to 34.1 years for other U.S. citizens. The average Laotian family consists of 5.01 members, compared to an average white family of 3.06 members and African American family of 3.48 members.

Religion and Community

The practice of Buddhism pervades all aspects of Laotian American family life. Theravada Buddhism, predominant in Laos, stresses that all worldly things are impermanent and attachment to them leads to suffering, which continues through a cycle of rebirths. This suffering can be broken only by overcoming desire through meditation and a moral, disciplined life. At this point, the soul reaches nirvana, a state of blissful detachment from worldly cares and desires. All Laotian men are expected to become monks and women may become nuns. Because of the scarcity of temples in the United States, Laotian American monks sometimes share temples with Thai American or Cambodian American monks.

Laotian communities are closely knit and personal respect for each individual is highly prized. Families often live in close proximity to one another, and Laotian children are taught to respect and care for their elders throughout their adult lives.

Language

Lao is a tonal language that has different regional dialects. Its alphabet is phonetic; each letter represents a sound. Lao writing has 27 consonant symbols that are used for 21 consonant sounds. This disparity in number is because different consonants are used to begin words of different tones. The tones of Lao words are indicated by four different tone marks written above the consonant of a syllable. The Lao alphabet also has 38 vowel symbols representing 24 vowel sounds,

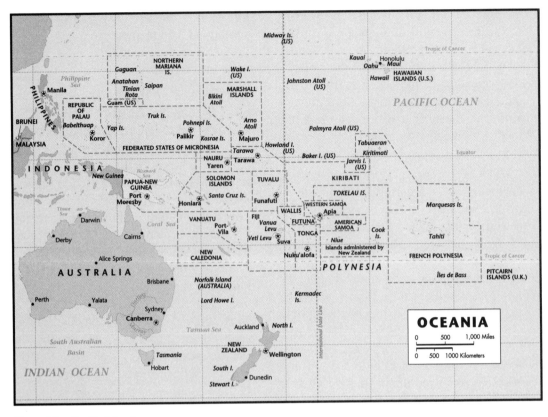

Map of the Pacific Islands.

because some sounds are written differently in the middle or at the end of a word. The letters of the Laotian alphabet are based on the Khmer alphabet, which was developed from an ancient writing system in India and is similar to the Thai writing system.

A common Laotian greeting is *Sabai dee baw,* which means "How are you?" The reply, "I'm well," is *Koy sabai dee.*

Employment

In 1990, one out of every three Laotians lived in households with income below the poverty line. The median household income for Laotian Americans that same year was only $23,019, compared to $30,056 for other Americans, and the unemployment rate among Laotian Americans was 9.3 percent.

Most of the economic hardship is due to lack of education. The work skills of most Laotians were acquired in their homeland, a predominantly agricultural society rather than a highly industrialized one. Thus, most jobs held by Laotian Americans are in manual labor. Also, lack of proficiency in speaking English has proved a hindrance to economic advancement.

Pacific Islanders

Overview

Pacific Islanders are people of the islands of Fiji, Guam, Hawaii, the Commonwealth of the Northern Mariana Islands, the Republic of Palau, American and Western Samoa, and Tonga, located in the Pacific Ocean. They are divided into three main ethnic groups: Polynesians, Micronesians, and Melanesians.

Polynesians come from the many islands within the triangle formed by Hawaii, New Zealand, and Easter Island. Micronesians are people from the small islands stretching west from Polynesia and north of the equator and New Guinea. Melanesians ("black islanders") are inhabitants of the islands south of the equator and west of Polynesia, including New Guinea.

Scholars of Pacific Island migration speculate that the first nomadic people came from the Southeast Asian peninsula when New Guinea and Australia were still linked by land. After the melting of the polar ice cap, these hunter-gatherers developed a farming culture and moved into New Guinea and onto other islands of Melanesia. Much later, other highly developed cultures from Southeast Asia and later from the Philippines migrated from Indonesia north into Micronesia and from Micronesia east into Polynesia.

Fijians

Fiji, a country of about 320 islands located in the belt of islands known as Melanesia in the southwest Pacific Ocean, covers an area slightly smaller than the state of New Jersey. Fijians, or Fiji Islanders, are descended from seamen who reached the

Madeleine Z. Bordallo was elected delegate to the U.S. Congress from Guam in 2002.

islands from mainland Asia 3,500 years ago. After discovery by the Dutch in 1643, the islands were fought over by various European powers for the next two hundred years until 1874, when Fiji was declared a crown colony of the British Empire. During the 1800s, the population was decimated by vast epidemics that killed almost half of all native Fijians. This led to the importation of Indian and Chinese plantation laborers who settled on the islands. In 1970, Fiji became an independent nation within the British Commonwealth and in 1990, it became a republic. Its estimated population in 2002 was 856,346.

Fijian society is organized around patriarchal clans (groups organized by a family

Women and girls in Hawaii learn the expressive hula. These dancers also wear the lei, a traditional necklace of flowers.

structure in which the father dominates, wives and children are legally dependent, and inheritance is based along the male lines of relationship) headed by a hereditary chief and tribes consisting of multiple hereditary clans. Men perform farming and fishing tasks, while women tend the home and children. Christianity, brought to the Fiji islands in the 1800s, became mixed with native beliefs and is today the principal religion along with Hinduism, Islam, and Chinese Confucianism. Fiji's official language is English, but Fiji is widely spoken. In 1999, the nation had a literacy rate of over 92 percent.

Guamanians

The largest of the Mariana Islands in the western Pacific Ocean, Guam is volcanic in origin, has a tropical climate, and lies in the typhoon belt of the western Pacific. In 2002, its population was 160,796, excluding U.S. military personnel.

The original inhabitants of Guam, the Chamorro, migrated from the Malay Peninsula to the Pacific around 1500 B.C. In 1521, Portuguese navigator Ferdinand Magellan landed on Guam, bringing disease, war, and Spanish rule. By 1741, only 5,000 Chamorro out of the original 100,000 remained. In

1898, Guam was ceded to the United States by Spain. Occupied briefly by the Japanese during World War II (1939–45), Guam was recaptured in 1944 by the United States. In 1950, the island became an unincorporated U.S. territory, and Guamanians were granted U.S. citizenship. The island is a multicultural society, composed of descendants of the original Chamorro (about 47 percent of the population), Filipino (the largest ethnic minority group, about 25 percent of the population), American, British, Korean, Chinese, and Japanese immigrants. English is the official language, although Chamorro is taught in the primary schools. Roman Catholicism is the predominant religion.

Native Hawaiians

Stretching for 390 miles in the Pacific Ocean 2,100 miles southwest of San Francisco, California, are the eight Hawaiian Islands. The islands—Niihau, Kauai, Oahu, Molokai, Lanai, Maui, Kahoolawe, and Hawaii—were formed by volcanic eruption 70 million years ago. The islands are mountainous with an even temperate climate and low humidity despite their tropical latitude.

Originally settled between A.D. 300 and 500 by seafaring peoples called Polynesians, the Hawaiian Islands were "discovered" by British navigator Captain James Cook in 1778. In the 1860s, the American sugar industry was established on the islands, importing Asian and European workers. These influences changed Hawaiian culture. In 1893, the Hawaiian Islands became a U.S. territory and the center for military operations in the Pacific Ocean until the Japanese attack on the naval base at Pearl Harbor in 1941. This attack resulted in the United States entering World War II (1939–45). In 1959, Hawaii became the fiftieth state in the United States.

Hawaii's population is comprised of people of European, African, Japanese, native Hawaiian, Filipino, Chinese, and Korean descent. The 2000 U.S. Census reported 282,667 Americans of Hawaiian descent. English and Pidgin English are the spoken languages. The Hawaiian language survives mainly in oral form and in phrases and names of places. The ancient Hawaiian religion, largely replaced by Christianity in the 1800s, coexists today with a variety of modern religions. Many ancient customs have survived in Hawaiian society, such as *kapu* (today known as taboo), or the prohibition of certain kinds of behavior. The ukulele (Hawaiian guitar), hula dance, muumuu (a loose-fitting dress worn by Hawaiian women), and the lei (a necklace of flowers worn around the neck) are all traditional parts of Hawaiian culture.

The principal food export crops, which constitute one-third of all exports in the islands' economy, are sugar, pineapple, Macadamia nuts, papaya, and coffee. Tourism, however, remains the major source of revenue.

Northern Mariana Islanders

The Northern Mariana Islanders are descendants of the original Micronesian inhabitants known as the Chamorro and migrants from the Caroline Islands, the Philippines, Korea, and America. The Northern Mariana Islands, a U.S. commonwealth in the western Pacific Ocean, consist of a group of sixteen volcanic islands, three of which are inhabited. The climate is tropical.

Eni Faleomavaega is the delegate to the U.S. Congress from American Samoa. Both Guam and American Samoa send representatives to Congress.

Settled by migrants from the Philippines and Indonesia, the Marianas were "discovered" by Ferdinand Magellan and ruled by Spain from 1521 until 1898, when the United States won the Spanish-American War and sold them to Germany. During World War II (1939–45), they were occupied by the Japanese until taken by the United States. In 1947, the Northern Mariana Islands became a United Nations trust territory administered by the United States. In 1986, they became a self-governing U.S. commonwealth of American citizens.

Palauans

Palau (also known as Belau) is a nation consisting of two hundred tropical islands located in the western Caroline Islands in the far western Pacific Ocean near the equator. The 19,409 Palauans (2002) are descended from Micronesians and Melanesians with influences from the immigration of Filipinos, Chinese, and Europeans.

Discovered by Spanish explorers in the sixteenth century, the Carolinian archipelago remained under Spanish dominion until it was sold to Germany after the Spanish-American War (1898). Japanese occupation of the islands began in World War I (1909–14), followed by American occupation in World War II (1939–45). In 1980, Palau became a self-governing republic.

Palauan economy is based on farming and raising livestock. Commercial fishing and tourism are also important industries. Palauan, a language related to Indonesian, is the official language and Roman Catholicism is the dominant religion. Palauan society is based on maternal clans, ten of which usually form a village with a chief as leader. In recent history, Palau has been beset by the social problems prevalent in economically underdeveloped nations.

American and Western Samoans

In 1990, the U.S. Census reported 49,345 Americans of Samoan descent living in the

United States. Samoans are Polynesians from the islands composing American and Western Samoa, located in the Pacific Ocean 2,300 miles southwest of Hawaii. Tropical islands of volcanic origin, Western Samoa is an independent nation of 1,090 square miles with a population of 159,862, and its southeast neighbor, American Samoa, is a U.S. territory of 76 square miles with a population of 51,115.

According to one historical theory, Samoa was settled by Polynesian migrants from the east Asian mainland, who expanded into the Malay Peninsula and then traveled to various islands in the Pacific during the Paleolithic era, or Old Stone Age. Samoa was ruled by a series of powerful chiefs and priests from the thirteenth through the nineteenth centuries. Although the islands were visited by Europeans in 1722, trade bases and missionary work were not established until the mid-nineteenth century. After years of rule by Germany, New Zealand, and the United Nations, Western Samoa gained independence in 1962, while American Samoa remained under U.S. control.

Samoa is a multicultural society composed of descendants of Polynesians, Europeans, Asians, and Americans. Extended families of two or three generations live together and groups of related families are bound together under a village chief (*matai*) and princess. The economy is primarily agricultural. Fishing and tourism are important industries. Western dress is customary, and Christianity is the dominant religion. English is the official language, and the Samoan population is 99 percent literate.

Tongans

The Tongan archipelago consists of 172 volcanic, subtropical islands—127 uninhabited and 45 inhabited. They are located east of Fiji in the South Pacific Ocean. Ruled by native kings since the tenth century, Tonga is today an independent nation of roughly 100,000 people where both Tongan and English are the spoken languages. The Tongan adult literacy rate is more than 98 percent. Family life is strongly influenced by Polynesian traditions and Christianity, the dominant religion. Tonga has a primarily agrarian economy with fishing, tourism, and exports of copra (dried coconut meat), coconuts, and bananas as principal industries.

Pakistani Americans

Overview

Pakistan, an Asian country of 310,402 square miles with a population of 147,663,429 in 2002, is bordered on the east by India, on the west by Afganistan and Iran, on the north by China, and on the south by the Arabian Sea. Pakistan consists of three very different geographical areas, the Himalayan mountains, the fertile plains of the Punjab, and the desert areas of Sindh and Balochistan. Although Pakistan's cultural heritage dates from the prehistoric Indus Valley civilization, its history as a nation is relatively short. Once part of India, Pakistan was created as a separate country for Indian Muslims by the Indian Independence Act of 1947.

Approximately 204,000 U.S. residents reported being of Pakistani descent in 2000. The Pakistani American population tends to be concentrated in large urban areas. Until 1947, people emigrating from what is now

Family and Community

Many Pakistani Americans aspire to the American dream of high salaries, homes in the suburbs, and academic success. To achieve this goal, Pakistani Americans depend on extended family networks. Often one member of a family will immigrate to the United States and then will bring other relatives until the entire clan is reunited. Most Pakistani families prefer to raise their children according to Islamic tradition, rather than have them assimilated into Western culture. Consequently, some send their children to study in Pakistan. Some Pakistani American communities have established mosque schools for Islamic training. Many marriages are arranged and it is considered a fortunate match if a Pakistani American marries within the Pakistani community or with a native-born Pakistani.

Although women in the Pakistani labor force work primarily in agriculture and industry, Pakistani American women enter medicine, business, and teaching. Women may come to the United States from Pakistan as brides, mothers, or sisters of immigrants; they may also come to pursue an education.

Religion and Language

Religion is a central force in Pakistani life. Islam is the state religion and the professed belief of 98 percent of the population. The remainder are Hindus, Christians, and Buddhists.

The national language of Pakistan is Urdu, which is spoken by 7 percent of the people. English is spoken primarily in business and government circles. The dominant local language, Punjabi, is spoken by 65

Pakistani American family, dressed in traditional costume, ready for a holiday dinner.

Pakistan were citizens of India. Early immigration to the United States by Asian Indians was restricted by law until the **Immigration and Nationality Act** of 1965, which abolished the quota system and admitted large numbers of skilled professionals and students. Since 1980, in addition to highly educated Pakistani immigrants, lesser-educated Pakistanis from the lower middle class have immigrated.

percent of the people, followed by Sindhi (11 percent), Pushto, Gujarati, and Baluchi.

Customs

The favored sports of Pakistanis are cricket, squash, hockey, and polo. Pakistani television series are broadcast in some areas of the United States on cable networks, providing entertainment and a link with Pakistan.

Traditional Pakistani clothing varies according to region. In general, both men and women wear the *shalwar kameez* (baggy trousers and long tunic). While men dress in somber colors, women may dress extremely colorfully. Cotton and linen are preferred daytime fabrics, while silk is used for formal wear. Often these clothes are embroidered in gold and silver and made of brocade, velvet, or satin. Traditional wedding dress for a woman is a red *gharara* (elaborate culottes, short shirt, and long veil covering the face). Men wear a raw silk *sherwani* (long coat) and turban. Pakistani men who immigrate to the United States usually adapt to Western dress more than do Pakistani women.

Pakistani food is similar to the cuisine of north India. Curries are spicy and accompanied by *chapatis* or *nan*, leavened bread. Rice is a staple, along with lentils cooked with meat and spices. Rich, sticky sweets are a favorite wedding food. Mangoes eaten ice cold or in milkshakes and sherbets are summer fare. Tea is preferred to coffee.

Observance of ritual celebrations and national holidays is a unifying tradition for Pakistani Americans. For the Islamic holidays of Eid-ul-Fitr and Eid-ul-Azha, Pakistani Americans gather at local mosques to worship. On August 14 Pakistan Indepen-

Ten U.S. States with Highest Population of Thai Descent, 1990

State	Thai Population
California	32,064
New York	6,230
Texas	5,816
Illinois	5,180
Virginia	3,312
Maryland	2,578
Washington	2,386
Nevada	1,823
New Jersey	1,758
Georgia	1,608

Source: Susan B. Gall and Timothy L. Gall, editors, *Statistical Record of Asian Americans*, Gale, 1993, p. 689; see www.census.gov for state data from the 2000 census of population, scheduled for release in fall 2003.

dence Day is celebrated with a parade in cities with large Pakistani American populations, such as New York City.

Information about current affairs in Pakistan is communicated in America via the newspapers *Millat* and *Pakistani Calling*, published in New York City. *Newsline* and *Herald*, widely circulated magazines from Pakistan, are also sources of information about social, religious, and political events in Pakistan.

Thai Americans

History and Immigration

A little smaller than the state of Texas, the Kingdom of Thailand, formerly known as

Siam, covers an area of 198,456 square miles and is located in Southeast Asia. Bordered on the north and west by Myanmar (Burma), on the northeast by Laos, to the southeast by Cambodia, and to the south by Malaysia and the Gulf of Thailand, this country has a population of more than 62 million.

Under the dynasty of Rama I, begun in 1782, the country became known as Siam, and the capital was moved to Bangkok. In the late nineteenth century, Thai relations with Europe were strengthened and social reforms—such as the abolishment of slavery and the establishment of public education—were instituted.

In 1932, the Thai government was changed from an absolute monarchy to a constitutional monarchy and in 1939 the nation's name was changed from Siam to Thailand. In 1942, during World War II (1939–45), Thailand declared itself at war with the United States and Great Britain. From 1948 to 1963, Thailand was ruled by a military dictatorship. From 1965 through 1975, the U.S. influence in Thailand increased with the establishment of air bases there during the Vietnam War. In 1983, the Thai constitution was amended to allow for a democratically elected National Assembly. Elections were held in 1992 through the king's intervention and Chuan Leekphai, the leader of the Democratic Party, was elected.

Prior to the U.S. involvement in the Vietnam War, immigration to the United States from Thailand was almost nonexistent. However, by the 1970s 5,000 Thais had emigrated, mostly as wives of servicemen stationed in Thailand. Concentrations of Thai immigrants formed in U.S. towns located near military installations. During the 1980s, Thais immigrated at a rate of 6,500 per year,

Ten U.S. States with Highest Population of Vietnamese Descent, 1990	
State	Vietnamese Population
California	280,223
Texas	69,634
Virginia	20,693
Washington	18,696
Louisiana	17,598
Florida	16,346
Pennsylvania	15,887
New York	15,555
Massachusetts	15,449
Illinois	10,309

Source: Susan B. Gall and Timothy L. Gall, editors, *Statistical Record of Asian Americans*, Gale, 1993, p. 689; see www.census.gov for state data from the 2000 census of population, scheduled for release in fall 2003.

drawn by job and educational opportunities and the promise of higher wages. As of 2000, there were approximately 150,283 people of Thai ancestry living in the United States. The greatest Thai population concentration is in the state of California, particularly in the city of Los Angeles.

Assimilation and Acculturation

Thais have assimilated well into mainstream American society, maintaining their culture and traditions while also accepting American cultural norms. Thai culture is more closely related to Buddhist and Indian culture than to Chinese culture, although Americans commonly err in assuming that Thais are Chinese, Vietnamese, or Cambodian. Some Thais are offended by such misperceptions, because most Vietnamese and Cambodians in the United States are refugees. Thai Americans wish to be regarded as immigrants who chose to come to the United States, not as refugees.

Traditional Thai families are close-knit, highly structured clans in which each member has a role based on age, gender, and rank within the family unit. Relationships are strictly defined, and relatives' relational names (aunt, uncle) may be used in place of their given names. The extended family, while the norm in Thailand, is not the norm in the United States due to mobility and lifestyle changes that Thai Americans have embraced. Marriages of choice are desired by Thai Americans, although parental approval is customary. Education is valued by Thais, and achievement in this area enhances one's social status.

Language, Religion, and Food

The Thai language, one of the oldest tongues in Southeast Asia, may even predate Chinese. It is a tonal and monosyllabic language with only 420 phonetically different words. Meanings of words are determined by five different tones. Thus the word *mai,* depending on the inflection or tone, can mean either "widow," "silk," "wood," "burn," "new," "not?" or "not." The Thai alphabet, originally conceived in 1283 and still used today, is phonetic in nature and uses signs patterned from Sanskrit. A common Thai greeting, *Sa was dee,* can mean "Good morning," "Good afternoon," or "Good evening," as well as "Good-bye."

Ninety-five percent of all Thais practice Theravada Buddhism, the prevalent form of Buddhism in India. It is a religion that stresses three aspects of existence: *dukkha* (suffering, dissatisfaction, disease), *annicaa* (impermanence of all things), and *anatta* (impermanence of the soul). Most Thai men at some point in their lives become monks, either temporarily or permanently, although in the mid-1990s the tradition of entering Buddhist monkhood as a coming-of-age ritual was quickly dying out.

Thai cuisine is light, pungent, and flavorful, and has become popular in the United States. It is eaten with a spoon and fork. Rice is the staple. Presentation of food for Thais is considered an art form, with fruit often intricately carved in classic designs. A meal may consist of a soup, two or more dishes with sauces such as curry, and many side dishes such as a stir-fried dish, a deep-fried dish, and a dish with hot chili peppers.

Employment

In the United States, many Thai Americans work in small businesses or as skilled laborers, but no one profession is dominated by this ethnic group. Many educated or middle-class Thai women pursue professions in health care or real estate. Many Thai Americans are concerned with political, social, and economic issues in their home country of Thailand.

Vietnamese Americans

History and Immigration

Vietnamese Americans, numbering an estimated 1,223,736 in 1991, are the fourth-largest Asian American population, following the Chinese, Filipinos, and Koreans.

The Nguyen family in their coffee shop in Pittsburgh, Pennsylvania. The Nguyens, who left Saigon when it fell on April 30, 1975, still hope to be reunited with the two daughters they were forced to leave behind.

Located south of China on the Indochina peninsula, Vietnam is a predominantly agricultural country with a troubled history of occupation and domination by foreign powers.

Occupied for over 1,000 years by the Chinese (111 B.C.–A.D. 939) and then ruled independently by eight different dynasties until 1883, Vietnam endured 70 years of French colonial rule (1883–1945) followed by thirty years of continuous warfare (1945–75). During this period, the communist North Vietnamese fought a guerilla war against the anticommunist South Vietnamese to reunify the country, which had been partitioned along the seventeenth parallel in the 1954 Geneva Accords. After the United States entered the war in the early 1960s in an attempt to prevent a communist victory, involvement of American troops grew until Saigon, the South Vietnamese capital, fell to the communist North in April 1975.

Following the fall of Saigon, approximately 130,000 Vietnamese refugees immigrated to the United States under provisions in the 1975 Indochina Refugee Act. The early immigrants were in general more educated and wealthier than those who followed. Most were Roman Catholic, spoke English, and had ties with the U.S. military, political, or corporate establishments and were readily assimilated into U.S. society.

The former premier of South Vietnam, Nguyen Cao Ky, now runs a shrimp processing plant in Dulac, Louisiana.

The second wave of immigration from 1978 through 1982 was different. The harsh communist regime in Vietnam instituted severe economic reforms and launched an invasion of Cambodia (1978). Refugees by the thousands fled in boats—and thus came to be known as "boat people." Many found that, after risking a dangerous voyage, they were rejected for asylum by neighboring nations and pillaged by pirates. Many died when their boats sank, or from starvation or lack of water. Prompted by humanitarian concerns, the U.S. **Refugee Act** of 1980 was passed, which ultimately resulted in the immigration of 280,000 Vietnamese refugees between 1978 and 1982. Most of these refugees were fishermen, farmers, or ethnic Chinese who had owned small businesses. From 1982 to 1991, the regime in Vietnam allowed the direct legal emigration of 66,000 Vietnamese, of whom only a small number were Amerasian.

Beside the major waves of immigration, a secondary immigration among Vietnamese within the United States has occurred since 1975. Because government policy for the settlement of refugees in the United States originally prohibited more than 3,000 Vietnamese in any one area, Vietnamese immigrants were forced to settle in communities scattered throughout the country. As a result, kinship ties were broken, isolating families and inhibiting extended support systems. The quest to reunite clans and families and to seek better jobs, warmer climates, and better community services led many Vietnamese Americans to relocate. Today nearly half of all Vietnamese Americans reside in Texas and California.

Assimilation and Acculturation

The primary obstacle to acculturation of Vietnamese American immigrants is linguistic. Because Vietnamese is a language in which the meaning of a word is conveyed by the tone used, the word *ma* can mean either "ghost," "check," "but," "tomb," "horse," or "rice plant," depending on the tone given it. English, in contrast, is not a tonal language. Further, English is an inflected language, in which meaning is conveyed by emphasis on certain words or syllables, while Vietnamese is an uninflected language. Another linguistic difference involves names: with Vietnamese names, the family name precedes the surname and all surnames have a specific meaning. For example, *Loan*, a popular female name, means "great beauty." There are only 30 Vietnamese family names in all.

In addition to linguistic contrasts, Vietnamese Americans have encountered cultural differences. Vietnamese do not consider it good manners to express disagreement, a trait often misinterpreted by Americans as dishonesty. A traditional medical treatment—rubbing the sharp edge of a coin coated with tiger balm ointment on a baby's skin to combat a fever—often leaves red marks misinterpreted as child abuse in the United States. Some Vietnamese parents perceive their authority to be undermined when U.S. law prohibits them from physically dis-

ciplining their children, a cultural norm in Vietnamese society.

Family and Community

The importance of the family is the foremost value for Vietnamese, and family loyalty is paramount. It is common for two to four generations to live together in the same household and more than half of Vietnamese American households include extended family members. Many Vietnamese Americans support extended families in their homeland by sending money and hard-to-find goods or by sponsoring relatives to immigrate to the United States.

Ancestor worship—or honoring those who have died—is a common Vietnamese practice. Altars dedicated to deceased relatives are common in the home and many Vietnamese Americans celebrate the anniversary of an ancestor's death by a festive meal attended by the extended family. Tet, the celebration of the Vietnamese New Year, dedicates the first day to ancestors and Thanh-Minh, another holiday, is marked by visits to the graves of relatives with food, flowers, and incense.

Religion

In addition to the influence of the family, religion is a major source of cultural continuity and stability for Vietnamese Americans. Approximately 30 to 40 percent of the population is Roman Catholic. Most Vietnamese Americans practice Mahayana Buddhism, the form of Buddhism prevalent in China (as opposed to Theravada Buddhism, predominant in India). Other religions represented include Protestantism, Islam, Confucianism, Taoism, Cao-Dai (a combination of several Eastern belief systems), and Hoa-Hao (a meditative religion originating in the Mekong River Delta in Vietnam).

Employment

The Vietnamese often describe themselves with the phrase *tran can cu,* which means "hard working," "patient," "tenacious," and "relentlessly driven to succeed." First-wave immigrants, for the most part, were forced to accept a decline in status in employment from white- to blue-collar jobs. In time, however, most gained access to better jobs through retraining or passing licensure requirements. However, second wave immigrants with fewer job skills, less education, and a poor knowledge of English have remained in blue-collar or service jobs earning an average of $14,000 in 1987, which was $3,000 under the U.S. median income.

One group of Vietnamese workers—fishermen—was able to translate previous work experience directly into employment in the United States. Most of these fishermen settled in Texas and Louisiana. Vietnamese Americans have also succeeded in small business ownership. The top sectors for Vietnamese businesses are services, retail, fishing, manufacturing, and finance/insurance/real estate. These businesses are usually family run and often cater to other Vietnamese Americans. Over one-third of all Vietnamese American businesses are located in California.

Suggestions for Further Reading

Chan, Sucheng, *Hmong Means Free: Life in Laos and America,* Philadelphia: Temple University Press, 1994.

Cohen, Warren I., *The Asian American Century,* Cambridge, MA: Harvard University Press, 2002.

Daniels, Roger, *Coming to America: A History of Immigration and Ethnicity in American Life,* New York: HarperCollins, 1990.

Daniels, Roger, *History of Indian Immigration to the United States,* New York: The Asia Society, 1989.

Distinguished Asian Americans: A Biographical Dictionary, Westport, CT: Greenwood Press, 1999.

Fawcett, James T., and Benjamin V. Carino, *Pacific Bridges: The New Immigration from Asia and the Pacific Islands,* New York: Center for Migration Studies, 1987.

Fong, Timothy P., *The Contemporary Asian American Experience: Beyond the Model Minority,* Upper Saddle River, NJ: Prentice Hall, 2002.

Hayslip, Le Ly (with Jay Wurts), *When Heaven and Earth Changed Places: A Vietnamese Woman's Journey from War to Peace,* New York: Doubleday, 1989.

Kibria, Nazli, *Becoming Asian American: Second-Generation Chinese and Korean American Identities,* Baltimore, MD: Johns Hopkins University Press, 2002.

Kim, Hyung-chan, editor, *Dictionary of Asian American History,* Westport, CT: Greenwood Press, 1986.

Maira, Sunaina, *Desis in the House: Indian American Youth Culture in New York City,* Philadelphia: Temple University Press, 2002.

Mark, Diane Mei Lin, *A Place Called Chinese America,* Dubuque, IA: Kendall/Hunt, 1992.

Niiya, Brian, editor, *Japanese American History: An A-to-Z Reference from 1868 to the Present,* New York: Facts on File, 1993.

Takaki, Ronald, *Strangers from a Different Shore,* Boston: Little, Brown and Company, 1989.

Vida, Nina, *Goodbye, Saigon,* New York: Crown Publishers, 1994.

Zia, Helen, *Asian American Dreams: The Emergence of an American People,* New York: Farrar, Straus and Giroux, 2000.

2
Significant Documents

Laws, Speeches, and Other Chronicles
of Asian American History

FACT FOCUS

- *Asians were the targets of early laws to restrict immigration.*
- *The United States government annexed the Hawaiian Islands in 1898 and established a government there in 1900.*
- *In the 1930s, limits were established by country for numbers of immigrants admitted to the United States each year. Quotas for most Asian countries were set at 100.*
- *President Franklin D. Roosevelt's Executive Order 9066 authorized the internment of Japanese Americans from 1942 to 1945.*
- *In 1965, immigration quotas were eliminated, resulting in a huge increase in the number of immigrants from Asia.*
- *In 1980, laws were passed to provide for admission of large numbers of refugees from Cambodia, Laos, and Vietnam.*
- *In 2001, the USA Patriot Act broadened the government's power to deport noncitizen individuals for any activity related to terrorism.*

The text of all documents in this section has been abridged.

Chinese Exclusion Act, 1882

This act suspended the immigration of Chinese laborers to the United States for ten years. (The Geary Law of 1892 extended the act for ten years; further legislation kept the act in effect until its repeal in 1943.)

Whereas, in the opinion of the Government of the United States the coming of Chinese laborers to this country endangers the good order of certain localities within the territory thereof: Therefore,

Be it enacted by the Senate and House of Representatives of the United States of America in Congress assembled, That from and after the expiration of ninety days next after the passage of this act, and until the expiration of ten years next after the passage of this act, the coming of Chinese laborers to the United States be, and the same is hereby, suspended; and during such suspension it shall not be lawful for any Chinese laborer to come, or, having so come after the expiration of said ninety days, to remain within the United States.

Section 2

That the master of any vessel who shall knowingly bring within the United States on such vessel, and land or permit to be landed, any Chinese laborer, from any foreign port or place, shall be deemed guilty of a misdemeanor, and on conviction thereof shall be punished by a fine of not more than five hundred dollars for each and every such Chinese laborer so brought, and may be also imprisoned for a term not exceeding one year.

Section 3

That the two foregoing sections shall not apply to Chinese laborers who were in the United States on the seventeenth day of November, eighteen hundred and eighty or ninety days next after the passage of this act.

Section 4

That for the purpose of properly identifying Chinese laborers who were in the United States on the seventeenth day of November, eighteen hundred and eighty, and in order to furnish them with the proper evidence of their right to go from and come to the United States of their free will and accord, the collector of customs shall make a list of all such Chinese laborers, in which shall be stated the name, age, occupation, last place of residence, physical marks or peculiarities, and all facts necessary for the identification of each of such Chinese laborers ... every

such Chinese laborer so departing from the United States shall receive, free of any charge or cost upon application therefore, a certificate which shall contain a statement of the name, age, occupation, last place of residence, personal description, and facts of identification of the Chinese laborer. The certificate shall entitle the Chinese laborer to return to and re-enter the United States.

Sections 5–13 detail specific procedures for issuing and presenting certificates.

Section 14

That hereafter no State court or court of the United States shall admit Chinese to citizenship; and all laws in conflict with this act are hereby repealed.

Approved, May 6, 1882.

Joint Resolution Annexing the Hawaiian Islands to the United States, 1898

This joint resolution by both houses of the U.S. Congress gave control of the Hawaiian Islands to the United States government. The resolution also made it illegal for Chinese to immigrate to Hawaii. A later act, the Organic Act of 1900, outlined a government for the Territory of Hawaii.

Whereas the Government of the Republic of Hawaii having signified its consent, in the manner provided by its constitution, to cede absolutely and without reserve to the United States of America all rights of sovereignty of whatsoever kind in and over the Hawaiian Islands and their dependencies, and also to cede and transfer to the United States the absolute fee and ownership of all public,

Government, or Crown lands, public buildings or edifices, ports, harbors, military equipment, and all other public property of every kind and description belonging to the Government of the Hawaiian Islands, together with every right and appurtenance thereunto appertaining: Therefore,

Resolved by the Senate and House of Representatives of the United States of America in Congress assembled, That said cession is accepted, ratified, and confirmed, and that the said Hawaiian Islands and their dependencies be annexed as a part of the territory of the United States.

The existing laws of the United States relative to public lands shall not apply to such lands in the Hawaiian Islands; but the Congress of the United States shall enact special laws for their management and disposition: Provided, That all revenue from or proceeds of the same, except as regards such part thereof as may be used or occupied for the civil, military, or naval purposes of the United States, or may be assigned for the use of the local government, shall be used solely for the benefit of the inhabitants of the Hawaiian Islands for educational and other public purposes.

Until Congress shall provide for the government of such islands all the civil, judicial, and military powers exercised by the officers of the existing government in said islands shall be vested in such person or persons and shall be exercised in such manner as the President of the United States shall direct: and the President shall have power to remove said officers and fill the vacancies so occasioned.

The existing treaties of the Hawaiian Islands with foreign nations shall forthwith cease, being replaced by such treaties as may exist, or as may be hereafter concluded,

---

WORDS TO KNOW

alien: a person who came from or owes allegiance to another country or government

annex: to incorporate, or add, territory to an already existing state or nation

appurtenance: a secondary right, or something added on

asylum: shelter, protection

cede: to formally transfer or surrender

emigration: to leave the country of one's birth with the intention of living somewhere else

evacuation: to remove out of a zone of danger or military activity

humanitarian: promoting human welfare

immigration: to move to a country where one was not born for the purpose of living there

internment: confinement or imprisonment, especially during war

naturalize: to admit as a citizen

quota: numerical limit

redress: to make up for or compensate

refugee: a person who flees to another country to escape danger

repatriation: to return to the country of one's origin or birth

resettlement: establishing a home in a new location

resolution: formal expression of opinion by the Congress

---

between the United States and such foreign nations. The municipal legislation of the Hawaiian Islands shall remain in force until the Congress of the United States shall otherwise determine.

Until legislation shall be enacted extending the United States customs laws and regulations to the Hawaiian Islands, the existing customs relations of the Hawaiian Islands with the United States and other countries shall remain unchanged.

The public debt of the Republic of Hawaii, lawfully existing at the date of the passage of this joint resolution, including the amounts due to depositors in the Hawaiian Postal Savings Bank, is hereby assumed by the Government of the United States; but the liability of the United States in this regard shall in no case exceed four million dollars.

There shall be no further immigration of Chinese into the Hawaiian Islands; and no Chinese shall be allowed to enter the United States from the Hawaiian Islands.

The President shall appoint five commissioners, at least two of whom shall be residents of the Hawaiian Islands, who shall recommend to Congress such legislation concerning the Hawaiian Islands as they shall deem necessary or proper.

Approved, July 7, 1898.

Cable Act, 1922

After this act was approved, a female citizen of the United States who married a man ineligible for citizenship lost her own citizenship.

Be it enacted by the Senate and House of Representatives of the United States of America in Congress assembled, That the right of any woman to become a naturalized citizen of the United States shall not be denied or abridged because of her sex or because she is a married woman....

Section 2

That any woman who marries a citizen of the United States after passage of this Act shall not become a citizen of the United States by reason of such marriage, but if eligible to citizenship, she may be naturalized upon full compliance with all requirements of the naturalization laws.

Section 3

That a woman citizen of the United States shall not cease to be a citizen by reason of her marriage after the passage of this Act; provided that any woman citizen who marries an alien ineligible to citizenship shall cease to be a citizen of the United States.

Section 4 deals with marriages and citizenship issues that took place before passage of the Act.

Section 5

That no woman whose husband is not eligible to citizenship shall be naturalized during the continuance of the marital status.

Approved, September 22, 1922.

Immigration Act, 1924

This Act, with its specifications about "quota" and "non-quota" immigrants, denied immigration to virtually all Asians. The Act's two key provisions relating to Asians follow.

Section II. (a) The annual quota of any nationality shall be 2 per centum of the number of foreign-born individuals of such nationality resident in continental United States as determined by the census of 1890, but the minimum quota shall be 100.

Section 13. (c) No alien ineligible to citizenship shall be admitted to the United States unless such alien (1) is admitted as a non-quota immigrant, or (2) is the wife, or the unmarried child under 18 years of age, of an immigrant admissible under this Act.

Presidential Proclamation, 1938

On April 28, 1938, President Franklin D. Roosevelt made a proclamation establishing immigration quotas by country. Only a partial list of the national origin immigration quotas is included here.

A Proclamation

I, FRANKLIN D. ROOSEVELT, President of the United States of America, acting under and by virtue of the power in me vested by Congress, do hereby proclaim and make known that the annual quota of each nationality effective for the remainder of the fiscal year ending June 30, 1938, and for each fiscal year thereafter, has been determined in accordance with the law to be, and shall be, as follows:

Country or Area	Quota
Afghanistan	100
Albania	1,000
Australia	100
Belgium	1,304
Bhutan	100
Bulgaria	100
China	100
Czechoslovakia	2,874
Danzig, Free City of	100
Denmark	1,181
Egypt	100
Estonia	116
Ethiopia (Abyssinia)	100

Country or Area	Quota
Finland	569
France	3,086
Germany	27,370
Great Britain and Northern Ireland	65,721
Greece	307
Hungary	869
Iceland	100
India	100
Iran	100
Iraq	100
Ireland (Eire)	17,853
Italy	5,802
Japan	100
Latvia	236
Liberia	100
Liechtenstein	100
Lithuania	386
Luxemburg	100
Monaco	100
Morocco	100
Muscat (Oman)	100
Nauru (British mandate)	100
Nepal	100
Netherlands	3,153
New Zealand	100
Norway	2,377
Poland	6,524
Portugal	440
Romania	377
San Marino	100
Saudi Arabia	100
Siam (present-day Thailand)	100
South Africa, Union of	100
Spain	252
Sweden	3,314
Switzerland	1,707
Syria and Lebanon (French mandate)	123
Turkey	226
Union of Soviet Socialist Republics	2,712
Yugoslavia	845

The immigration quotas assigned to the various countries and quota areas are designed solely for purposes of compliance with the pertinent provisions of the Immigration Act of 1924 and are not to be regarded as having any significance extraneous to this object.

DONE at the City of Washington this 28th day of April, in the year of our Lord nineteen hundred and thirty-eight and of the Independence of the United States of America the one hundred and sixty-second.

Franklin D. Roosevelt

Executive Order 9066, 1942

This order, issued by President Franklin D. Roosevelt, led to the establishment of internment camps and the forced evacuation of people of Japanese ancestry from a defined area in the western United States.

Authorizing the Secretary of War to prescribe Military Areas.

WHEREAS the successful prosecution of the war requires every possible protection against espionage and against sabotage to national-defense material, national-defense premises, and national-defense utilities:

NOW, THEREFORE, by virtue of the authority vested in me as President of the United States, and Commander in Chief of the Army and Navy, I hereby authorize and direct the Secretary of War, and the Military Commanders whom he may from time to time designate, whenever he or any designated Commander deems such action necessary or desirable, to prescribe military areas in such places and of such extent as he or the appropriate Military Commander may determine, from which any or all persons may be excluded, and with respect to which, the right of any person to enter, remain in, or leave shall be subject to whatever restrictions the Secretary of War or the appropriate Military Commander may determine, from which any or all persons may be excluded, and with respect to which, the right of any person to enter, remain in, or leave shall be subject to whatever restrictions the Secretary of War or the appropriate Military Commander may impose in his discretion. The Secretary of War is hereby authorized to provide for residents of any such area who are excluded therefrom, such transportation, food, shelter, and other accommodations as may be necessary, in the judgment of the Secretary of War or the said Military Commander, and until other arrangements are made, to accomplish the purpose of this order. The designation of military areas in any region or locality shall supersede designations of prohibited and restricted areas by the Attorney General under the Proclamations of December 7 and 8, 1941, and shall supersede the responsibility and authority of the Attorney General under the said Proclamations in respect of such prohibited and restricted areas.

I hereby further authorize and direct the Secretary of War and said Military Commanders to take such other steps as he or the appropriate Military Commander may deem advisable to enforce compliance with the restrictions applicable to each Military area herein above authorized to be designated, including the use of Federal troops and other Federal Agencies, with authority to accept assistance of state and local agencies.

I hereby further authorize and direct all Executive Departments, independent establishments, and other Federal Agencies to assist the Secretary of War or the said Military Commanders in carrying out this

Executive Order, including the furnishing of medical aid, hospitalization, food, clothing, transportation, use of land, shelter, and other supplies, equipment, utilities, facilities, and services.

Franklin D. Roosevelt

The White House, February 19, 1942.

Public Proclamation, 1942

This proclamation outlines the wartime living and travel restrictions placed on Japanese, German, and Italian aliens and people of Japanese ancestry on the U.S. Pacific Coast, which was considered at high risk of attack by nations at war with the United States.

Headquarters Western Defense Command and Fourth Army, Presidio of San Francisco, California

TO: The people within the States of Arizona, California, Oregon, and Washington, and the Public Generally

WHEREAS, By virtue of orders issued by the War Department on December 11, 1941, that portion of the United States lying within the States of Washington, Oregon, California, Montana, Idaho, Nevada, Utah and Arizona and the Territory of Alaska has been established as the Western Defense Command and designated as a Theatre of Operations under my command; and

WHEREAS, By Executive Order No. 9066, dated February 19, 1942, the President of the United States authorized and directed the Secretary of War and the Military Commanders to prescribe military areas in such places and of such extent as he or the appropriate Military Commander may determine, from which any or all persons may be excluded, and with respect to which the right of any person to enter, remain in, or leave shall be subject to whatever restrictions the Secretary of War or the appropriate Military Commander may impose in his discretion; and

WHEREAS, The Secretary of War on February 20, 1942, designated the undersigned [General J. L. DeWitt] as the Military Commander to carry out the duties and responsibilities imposed by said Executive Order for that portion of the United States embraced in the Western Defense Command; and

WHEREAS, The Western Defense Command embraces the entire Pacific Coast of the United States, which by its geographical location is particularly subject to attack, to attempted invasion by the armed forces of nations with which the United States is now at war, and, in connection therewith, is subject to espionage and acts of sabotage, thereby requiring the adoption of military measures necessary to establish safeguards against such enemy operations:

NOW THEREFORE, I, J. L. DeWitt, Lieutenant General, U.S. Army, by virtue of the authority vested in me by the President of the United States and by the Secretary of War and my powers and prerogatives as Commanding General of the Western Defense Command, do hereby declare that:

1. The present situation requires as a matter of military necessity the establishment in the territory embraced by the Western Defense Command of Military Areas and Zones thereof as defined in Exhibit 1, hereto attached, and as generally shown on the map attached hereto and marked Exhibit 2.

2. Military Areas No. 1 and 2, as particularly described and generally shown

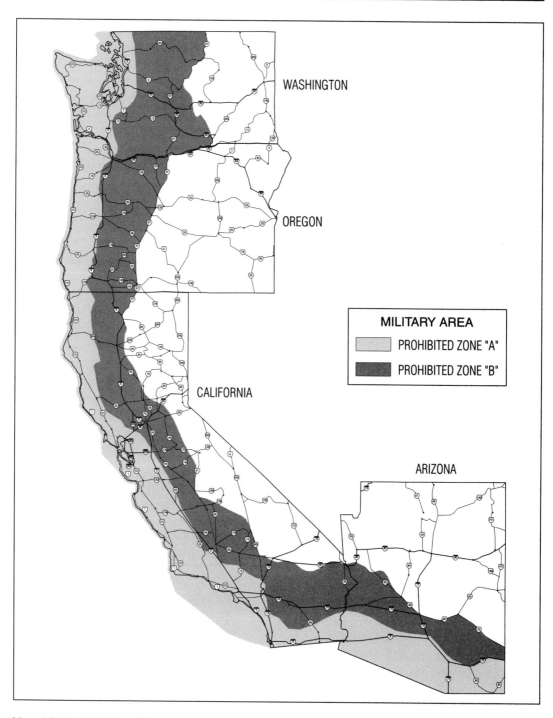

Map of California Military Zones.

hereinafter and in Exhibits 1 and 2 hereto, are hereby designated and established.

3. Within Military Areas Nos. 1 and 2 there are established Zone A-1, lying wholly within Military Area No. 1; Zones A-2 to A-99, inclusive, some of which are in Military Area No. 1, and the other in Military Area No. 2; and Zone B, comprising all that part of Military Area No. 1 not included within Zones A-1 to A-99, inclusive; all as more particularly described and defined and generally shown hereinafter and in Exhibits 1 and 2.

Military Area No. 2 comprises all that part of the States of Washington, Oregon, California and Arizona which is not included within Military Area No. 1, and is shown on the map (Exhibit 2) as an unshaded area.

4. Such persons or classes of persons as the situation may require will by subsequent proclamation be excluded from all of Military Area No. 1 and also from such of those zones herein described as Zones A-2 to A-99, inclusive, as are within Military Area No. 2.

Certain persons or classes of persons who are by subsequent proclamation excluded from the zones last above mentioned may be permitted, under certain regulations and restrictions to be hereafter prescribed, to enter upon or remain within Zone B.

The designation of Military Area No. 2 as such does not contemplate any prohibition or regulation or restriction except with respect to the zones established therein.

5. Any Japanese, German, or Italian alien, or any person of Japanese Ancestry now resident in Military Area No. 1 who changes his place of habitual residence, is hereby required to obtain and execute a "Change of Residence Notice" at any United States Post Office within the States of Washington, Oregon, California and Arizona. Such notice must be executed at any such Post Office not more than five nor less than one day prior to any such change of residence. Nothing contained herein shall be construed to affect the existing regulations of the U.S. Attorney General which require aliens of enemy nationalities to obtain travel permits from U.S. Attorneys and to notify the Federal Bureau of Investigation and the Commissioner of Immigration of any change in permanent address.

6. The designation of prohibited and restricted areas within the Western Defense Command by the Attorney General of the United States under the Proclamations of December 7 and 8, 1941, and the instructions, rules and regulations prescribed by him with respect to such prohibited and restricted areas, are hereby adopted and continued in full force and effect. The duty and responsibility of the Federal Bureau of Investigation with respect to the investigation of alleged acts of espionage and sabotage are not altered by this proclamation.

J. L. DeWitt
Lieutenant General, U.S. Army
Commanding.

The remaining pages of the proclamation (3–30) describe in detail the zones covered. The map described in this section illustrates the areas of the states of Washington, Oregon, and California that were designated "Military Areas." Zones A2–A99 represent bridges, power plants, and other locations considered to be important to the Western Defense Command Effort.

Public Law 503, 1942

This law provided penal sanctions (punishment or penalty) for those who disobeyed Executive Order 9066.

Be it enacted by the Senate and House of Representatives of the United States of America in Congress assembled, That whoever shall enter, remain in, leave, or commit any act in any military area or military zone prescribed, under the authority of an Executive Order of the President, by the Secretary of War, or by any military commander designated by the Secretary of War, contrary to the restrictions applicable to any such area or zone or contrary to the order of the Secretary of War or any such military commander, shall, if it appears that he knew or should have known of the existence and extent of the restrictions or order and that his act was in violation thereof, be guilty of a misdemeanor and upon conviction shall be liable to a fine not to exceed $5,000 or to imprisonment for not more than one year, or both, for each offense.

Approved, March 21, 1942.

Repeal of Chinese Exclusion Acts, 1943

Besides repealing the Chinese Exclusion Act of 1882 and its amendments, this act granted naturalization rights and a small immigration quota to the Chinese.

Be it enacted by the Senate and House of Representatives of the United States of America in Congress assembled, That the following Acts or parts of Acts relating to the exclusion or deportation of persons of the Chinese race are hereby repealed. . . .

Section 2

All Chinese persons entering the United States annually as immigrants shall be allocated to the quota for the Chinese. A preference up to 75 per centum of the quota shall be given to Chinese born and resident in China.

Approved, December 17, 1943.

Immigration and Nationality Act, 1952

This extensive act regulating immigration and naturalization grants the right of naturalization to all immigrants and establishes quotas by country of origin for immigrants. Quotas for immigrants from Asia are lower than those for European countries. This act is also known as the "McCarran-Walter Act."

Title I provides definitions of immigrant terminology and defines the powers and duties of the Attorney General, Commissioner, Secretary of State, and Bureau of Security and Consular Affairs.

Title II, Chapter 1—Quota system: This chapter establishes numerical limitations and annual quotas based upon national origin.

Section 201. (a) The annual quota of any quota area shall be one-sixth of 1 per centum of the number of inhabitants in the continental United States in 1920: Provided, That the quota existing for Chinese persons prior to the date of enactment of this Act shall be continued, and, except as otherwise provided in section 202 (e), the minimum quota for any quota area shall be one hundred.

Section 202. (e) Any increase in the number of minimum quota areas above twenty within the Asia-Pacific triangle shall result in a proportionate decrease in each minimum quota of such area in order that the sum total of all minimum quotas within the Asia-Pacific triangle shall not exceed two thousand.

The remainder of this act sets qualifications and procedures for admission of aliens, including regulations for exclusion and deportation.

Immigration and Nationality Act Amendments, 1965

Immigrants from Asian countries gained equal footing with those from other countries through this act, which abolished "national origins" as a basis for allocation of immigration quotas.

An Act

To amend the Immigration and Nationality Act, and for other purposes.

Be it enacted by the Senate and House of Representatives of the United States of America in Congress assembled, That section 201 of the Immigration and Nationality Act be amended to read as follows:

Section 201. (a) Exclusive of special immigrants and of the immediate relatives of United States citizens, the number of aliens who may be issued immigrant visas shall not in any of the first three quarters of any fiscal year exceed a total of 45,000 and shall not in any fiscal year exceed a total of 170,000.

(b) The "immediate relatives" referred to in subsection (a) of this section shall mean the children, spouses, and parents of a citizen of the United States.

Section 2

Section 202 of the Immigration and Nationality Act is amended to read as follows:

(a) No person shall receive any preference or priority or be discriminated against in the issuance of an immigrant visa because of his race, sex, nationality, place of birth, or place of residence, except as specifically provided in section 101(a)(27), section 201(b), and section 203.

Provided, That the total number of immigrant visas made available to natives of any single foreign state shall not exceed 20,000 in any fiscal year.

For the purposes of this Act the foreign state to which an immigrant is chargeable shall be determined by birth within such foreign state.

Refugee Relief Act, 1980

This act systematized admission of refugees to the United States. An Orderly Departure Program was established to enable Vietnamese people to emigrate legally.

Title I—Purpose

Section 101. (a) The Congress declares that it is the historic policy of the United States to respond to the urgent needs of persons subject to persecution in their homelands, including, where appropriate, humanitarian assistance for their care and maintenance in asylum areas, efforts to promote opportunities for resettlement or voluntary repatriation, aid for necessary transportation and processing, admission to this country of refugees of special humanitarian concern to the United States, and transitional assistance to refugees in the United States. The Congress further declares that it is the policy of the United States to encourage all nations to provide assistance and resettlement opportunities to refugees to the fullest extent possible.

(b) The objectives of this Act are to provide a permanent and systematic procedure for the admission to this country of refugees of special humanitarian concern to the United States, and to provide comprehensive and uniform provisions for the effective resettlement and absorption of those refugees who are admitted.

Title II—Admission of Refugees

The term "refugee" means . . . any person who is outside any country of such person's nationality or, in the case of a person having no nationality, is outside any country in which such person last habitually resided, and who is unable or unwilling to return to, and is unable or unwilling to avail himself or herself of the protection of, that country because of persecution or a well-founded fear of persecution on account of race, religion, nationality, membership in a particular social group, or political opinion. . . . The term "refugee" does not include any person who ordered, incited, assisted, or otherwise participated in the persecution of any person on account of race, religion, nationality, membership in a particular social group, or political opinion.

Annual Admission of Refugees and Admission of Emergency Situation Refugees. The number of refugees who may be admitted under this section in fiscal year 1980, 1981, or 1982, may not exceed fifty thousand unless the President determines, that admission of a specific number of refugees in excess of such number is justified by humanitarian concerns or is otherwise in the national interest.

The number of refugees who may be admitted under this section in any fiscal year after fiscal year 1982 shall be such number as the President determines is justified by humanitarian concerns or is otherwise in the national interest. . . .

Before the start of each fiscal year the President shall report to the Committees on the Judiciary of the House of Representatives and of the Senate regarding the foreseeable number of refugees who will be in need of resettlement during the fiscal year and the anticipated allocation of refugee admissions during the fiscal year. . . .

Asylum Procedure. Section 208. (a) The Attorney General shall establish a procedure for an alien physically present in the United States or at a land border or port of entry, irrespective of such alien's status, to apply for asylum, and the alien may be granted asylum in the discretion of the Attorney General. . . .

The Attorney General shall not deport or return any alien to a country if the Attorney General determines that such alien's life or freedom would be threatened in such country on account of race, religion, nationality, membership in a particular social group, or political opinion.

Title III deals with the establishment of the position of United States Coordinator for Refugee Affairs and Assistance for Effective Resettlement of Refugees in the United States. Title IV, Miscellaneous and Refugee Assistance, defines the role of the Office of Refugee Resettlement within the Department of Health and Human Service. This office is required to submit a report to the Congress annually on employment statistics for refugees and geographic distribution of refugees and outlines appropriations for refugee resettlement programs.

Approved March 17, 1980.

Commission On Wartime Relocation and Internment of Civilians Act, 1980

The commission established by this act was to conduct hearings about civilians, most of them of Japanese descent, who were detained in internment camps during World War II.

Section 2—Findings and Purpose

(a) The Congress finds that—

(1) approximately one hundred and twenty thousand civilians were relocated and detained in internment camps pursuant to Executive Order Numbered 9066, issued February 19, 1942, and other associated actions of the Federal Government;

(2) approximately one thousand Aleut civilian American citizens were relocated and, in some cases, detained in internment camps pursuant to directives of United States military forces during World War II and other associated actions of the Federal Government; and

(3) no sufficient inquiry has been made into the matters described in paragraphs (1) and (2).

(b) It is the purpose of this Act to establish a commission to—

(1) review the facts and circumstances surrounding Executive Order Numbered 9066, issued February 19, 1942, and the impact of such Executive order on American citizens and permanent resident aliens;

(2) review directives of United States military forces requiring the relocation and, in some cases, detention in internment camps of American citizens, including Aleut civilians, and permanent resident aliens of the Aleutian and Probilof Islands;

(3) recommend appropriate remedies.

Section 3—Establishment of Commission

(a) There is established the Commission on Wartime Relocation and Internment of Civilians (hereinafter referred to as the "Commission").

(b) The Commission shall be composed of seven members, who shall be appointed within ninety days after the date of enactment of this Act as follows:

(1) Three members shall be appointed by the President.

(2) Two members shall be appointed by the Speaker of the House of Representatives.

(3) Two members shall be appointed by the President pro tempore of the Senate.

(c) The term of office for members shall be for the life of the Commission. A vacancy in the Commission shall not affect its powers, and shall be filled in the same manner in which the original appointment was made.

(d) The first meeting of the Commission shall be called by the President within one hundred and twenty days after the date of enactment of this Act, or within thirty days after the date on which legislation is enacted making appropriations to carry out this Act, whichever date is later.

(e) Four members of the Commission shall constitute a quorum, but a lesser number may hold hearings.

(f) The Commission shall elect a Chairman and Vice Chairman from among its members. The term of office of each shall be for the life of the Commission.

(g) Each member of the Commission who is not otherwise employed by the United States Government shall receive compensation at a rate equal to the daily rate prescribed for GS-18 under the General Schedule contained in section 5332 of title 5, United States Code, for each day, including travel time, he or she is engaged in the actual performance of his or her duties as a member of the Commission. A member of the Commission who is an officer or employee of the United States Government shall serve without additional compensation. All members of the Commission shall be reimbursed for travel, subsistence, and other necessary expenses incurred by them in the performance of their duties.

Section 4—Duties of the Commission

(a) It shall be the duty of the Commission to—

(1) review the facts and circumstances surrounding Executive Order Numbered 9066, issued February 19, 1942 and the impact of such Executive order on American citizens and permanent resident aliens;

(2) review directives of United States military forces requiring the relocation and, in some cases, detention in internment camps of American citizens, including Aleut civilians, and permanent resident aliens of the Aleutian and Pribilof Islands;

(3) recommend appropriate remedies.

(b) The Commission shall hold public hearings in such cities of the United States that it finds appropriate.

(c) The Commission shall submit a written report of its findings and recommendations to Congress not later than the date which is one year after the date of the first meeting called pursuant to section 3(d) of this Act.

Section 5—Powers of the Commission

(a) The Commission or, on the authorization of the Commission, any subcommittee or member thereof, may for the purpose of carrying out the provisions of this Act, hold such hearings and sit and act at such times and places, and request the attendance and testimony of such witnesses and the production of such books, records, correspondence, memorandum, papers, and documents as the Commission or such subcommittee or member may deem advisable. The Commission may request the Attorney General to invoke the aid of an appropriate United States district court to require, by subpoena or otherwise, such attendance, testimony, or production.

(b) The Commission may acquire directly from the head of any department, agency, independent instrumentality, or other authority of the executive branch of the Government, available information which the Commission considers useful in the discharge of its duties. All departments, agencies, and independent instrumentalities, or other authorities of the Commission shall furnish all information requested by the Commission to the extent permitted by law.

Section 6 authorizes the Commission to hire personnel and buy supplies for its duties.

Section 7

The Commission shall terminate ninety days after the date on which the report of the Commission is submitted to Congress pursuant to section 4(c) of this Act.

Section 8

To carry out the provisions of this Act, there are authorized to be appropriated $1,500,000.

Approved July 31, 1980.

Civil Liberties Act, 1988
Public Law 100-383

An Act

To implement recommendations of the Commission on Wartime Relocation and Internment of Civilians.

Be it enacted by the Senate and House of Representatives of the United States of America in Congress assembled,

Section 1—Purposes

The purposes of this Act are to—

(1) acknowledge the fundamental injustice of the evacuation, relocation, and internment of United States citizens and permanent resident aliens of Japanese ancestry during World War II;

(2) apologize on behalf of the people of the United States for the evacuation, relocation, and internment of such citizens and permanent resident aliens;

(3) provide for a public education fund to finance efforts to inform the public about the internment of such individuals so as to prevent the recurrence of any similar event;

(4) make restitution to those individuals of Japanese ancestry who were interned;

(5) make restitution to Aleut residents of the Pribilof Islands and the Aleutian Islands west of Unimak Island, in settlement of United States obligations in equity and at law, for—

(A) injustices suffered and unreasonable hardships endured while those Aleut residents were under United States control during World War II;

(B) personal property taken or destroyed by United States forces during World War II;

(C) community property, including community church property, taken or destroyed by United States forces during World War II; and

(D) traditional village lands on Attu Island not rehabilitated after World War II for Aleut occupation or other productive use;

(6) discourage the occurrence of similar injustices and violations of civil liberties in the future; and

(7) make more credible and sincere any declaration of concern by the United States over violations of human rights committed by other nations.

Section 2—Statement of The Congress

(a) With Regard To Individuals Of Japanese Ancestry.—The Congress recognizes that, as described by the Commission on Wartime Relocation and Internment of Civilians, a grave injustice was done to both citizens and permanent resident aliens of Japanese ancestry by the evacuation, relocation, and internment of civilians during World War II. As the Commission documents, these actions were carried out without adequate security reasons and without any acts of espionage or sabotage documented by the Commission,

President George Bush signs a proclamation declaring May Asian/Pacific American Heritage Month on May 7, 1990. Attending the ceremony, from left: Taylor Wang, astronaut from Tennessee; Virginia Cha, 1989 Miss Maryland and Miss America first runner-up; I. M. Pei, architect from New York; Sammy Lee, Olympic diving gold medalist and physician from California; Nancy Kwan, actress from California; and Tsung-Dao Lee, Nobel Prize winner in physics from New York.

and were motivated largely by racial prejudice, wartime hysteria, and a failure of political leadership. The excluded individuals of Japanese ancestry suffered enormous damages, both material and intangible, and there were incalculable losses in education and job training, all of which resulted in significant human suffering for which appropriate compensation has not been made. For these fundamental violations of the basic civil liberties and constitutional rights of these individuals of Japanese ancestry, the Congress apologizes on behalf of the Nation.

Hate Crimes Statistics Act, 1990

This act established guidelines for maintaining statistical data on crimes motivated by prejudice.

An act to provide for the acquisition and publication of data about crimes that manifest prejudice based on certain group characteristics.

Be it enacted by the Senate and House of Representatives of the United States of America in Congress assembled, That

(1) this Act may be cited as the "Hate Crime Statistics Act."

(b)(1) . . . The Attorney General shall acquire data, for the calendar year 1990 and each of the succeeding 4 calendar years, about crimes that manifest evidence of prejudice based on race, religion, sexual orientation, or ethnicity, including where appropriate the crimes of murder, non-negligent manslaughter, forcible rape, aggravated assault, simple assault, intimidation, arson; and destruction, damage or vandalism of property. . . .

(4) Data acquired under this section shall be used only for research or statistical purposes and may not contain any information that may reveal the identity of an individual victim of a crime.

(5) The Attorney General shall publish an annual summary of the data acquired under this section. . . .

Section 2

(a) Congress finds that—

(1) the American family life is the foundation of American Society,

(2) Federal policy should encourage the well-being, financial security, and health of the American family,

(3) schools should not de-emphasize the critical value of American family life.

(b) Nothing in this Act shall be construed, nor shall any funds appropriated to carry out the purpose of the Act be used, to promote or encourage homosexuality.

Approved, April 23, 1990.

Asian /Pacific American Heritage Month, 1991 and 1992

President George Bush declared May Asian/Pacific American Month in May 1990 by this proclamation.

A Proclamation

With characteristic clarity and force, Walt Whitman wrote: "The United States themselves are essentially the greatest poem. . . . Here is not merely a nation but a teeming nation of nations." Those immortal words eloquently describe America's ethnic diversity—a diversity we celebrate with pride during Asian/Pacific American Heritage Month.

The Asian/Pacific American heritage is marked by its richness and depth. The world marvels at the wealth of ancient art and philosophy, the fine craftsmanship, and the colorful literature and folklore that have sprung from Asia and the Pacific Islands. Whether they trace their roots to places like Cambodia, Vietnam, Korea, the Philippines, and the Marshall Islands or cherish their identities as natives of Hawaii and Guam, all Asian and Pacific Americans can take pride in this celebration of their heritage.

By preserving the time-honored customs and traditions of their ancestral homelands, Americans of Asian and Pacific descent have greatly enriched our Nation's culture. They have also made many outstanding con-

On October 9, 1992, Attorney General Dick Thornburgh crouched on bended knee to present redress checks in the amount of $20,000 to elderly Japanese Americans who had been interned during World War II. The presentation took place at the Justice Department. Accepting checks were, from left, Kisa Isari of Ontario, Oregon; Hau Dairiki of Sacramento, California; and Mamoru Eto of Santa Monica, California. In addition to the checks, each received a signed apology from President George Bush for their wrongful imprisonment.

tributions to American history. Indeed, this country's westward expansion and economic development were greatly influenced by thousands of Chinese and other Asians who immigrated during the 19th century. Today recent immigrants from South Asia are giving our Nation new appreciation for that region of the world.

Over the years—and often in the face of great obstacles—Asian and Pacific Americans have worked hard to reap the rewards of freedom and opportunity. Many have arrived in the United States after long and arduous journeys, escaping tyranny and oppression with little more than the clothes on their backs. Yet, believing in America's promise of liberty and justice for all and imbued with a strong sense of self-discipline, sacrifice, courage, and honor, they have steadily advanced, earning the respect and admiration of their fellow citizens. Today we give special and long-overdue recognition to the nisei who fought for our country in Europe during World War II.

During one of America's darker hours, they affirmed the patriotism and loyalty of Japanese Americans and, in so doing, taught us an important lesson about tolerance and justice.

Time and again throughout our Nation's history, Asian and Pacific Americans have proved their devotion to the ideals of freedom and democratic government. Those ideals animate and guide our policies toward Asia and the Pacific today. The economic dynamism of the Pacific Rim is a crucial source of growth for the global economy, and the United States will continue working to promote economic cooperation and the expansion of free markets throughout the region. The United States also remains committed to the security of our allies and to the advancement of human rights throughout Asia and the Pacific.

The political and economic ties that exist between the United States and countries in Asia and the Pacific are fortified by strong bonds of kinship and culture. All Americans are enriched by those ties, and thus we proudly unite in observing Asian/Pacific American Heritage Month.

The Congress, by House Joint Resolution 173, has designated May 1991 and May 1992 as "Asian/Pacific American Heritage Month" and has authorized and requested the President to issue a proclamation in observance of these occasions.

Now, therefore, I, George Bush, President of the United States of America, do hereby proclaim the months of May 1991 and May 1992 as Asian/Pacific American Heritage Month. I call upon the people of the United States to observe these occasions with appropriate programs, ceremonies, and activities.

In witness whereof, I have hereunto set my hand this sixth day of May, in the year of our Lord nineteen hundred and ninety-one, and of the Independence of the United States of America the two hundred and fifteenth.

Joint Resolution on the 100th Anniversary of the Overthrow of the Hawaiian Kingdom, 1993

By this resolution the U.S. Congress acknowledged the significance of the illegal overthrow of the Kingdom of Hawaii and expressed its deep regret to the Native Hawaiian people.

To acknowledge the 100th anniversary of the January 17, 1893, overthrow of the Kingdom of Hawaii, and to offer an apology to Native Hawaiians on behalf of the United States for the overthrow of the Kingdom of Hawaii.

The first part of this resolution provides a lengthy history of the circumstances surrounding the overthrow of the Kingdom of Hawaii. A summary follows.

Whereas, prior to the arrival of the first Europeans in 1778, the Native Hawaiian people lived in a highly organized, self-sufficient, subsistent social system based on communal land tenure with a sophisticated language, culture, and religion; from 1826 until 1893, the United States extended full diplomatic recognition to the Hawaiian Government, and entered into treaties and conventions with the Hawaiian monarchs to govern commerce and navigation;

The Congregational Church (now known as the United Church of Christ), through its American Board of Commissioners for Foreign Missions, sponsored and sent more than 100 missionaries to the Kingdom of Hawaii between 1820 and 1850;

On January 14, 1893, John L. Stevens (hereafter referred to as the "United States Minister"), the United States Minister assigned to the Kingdom of Hawaii, conspired with a small group of non-Hawaiian residents of the Kingdom of Hawaii, including citizens of the United States, to overthrow the indigenous and lawful Government of Hawaii ... and caused armed naval forces of the United States to invade the sovereign Hawaiian nation on January 16, 1893, and to position themselves to intimidate Queen Lili-uokalani and her Government;

On the afternoon of January 17, 1893, a Committee of Safety that represented the American and European sugar planters, descendants of missionaries, and financiers deposed the Hawaiian monarchy and pro-claimed the establishment of a Provisional Government, and the United States Minister extended diplomatic recognition to the Pro-visional Government that was formed by the conspirators without the consent of the Native Hawaiian people or the lawful Gov-ernment of Hawaii and in violation of trea-ties between the two nations and of international law;

Soon thereafter, when informed of the risk of bloodshed with resistance, Queen Liliuokalani issued the following statement yielding her authority to the United States Government rather than to the Provisional Government;

"I Liliuokalani, by the Grace of God and under the Constitution of the Hawaiian Kingdom, Queen, do hereby solemnly pro-test against any and all acts done against myself and the Constitutional Government of the Hawaiian Kingdom by certain per-sons claiming to have established a Provi-sional Government of and for this Kingdom.

"That I yield to the superior force of the United States of America whose Minister Plenipotentiary, His Excellency John L. Stevens, has caused United States troops to be landed at Honolulu and declared that he would support the Provisional Government.

"Now to avoid any collision of armed forces, and perhaps the loss of life, I do this under protest and impelled by said force yield my authority until such time as the Government of the United States shall, upon facts being presented to it, undo the action of its representatives and reinstate me in the authority which I claim as the Constitutional Sovereign of the Hawaiian Islands."

Done at Honolulu this 17th day of Janu-ary, A.D. 1893. . . .

Whereas, on February 1, 1893, the United States Minister raised the American flag and proclaimed Hawaii to be a protectorate of the United States. . . .

In a message to Congress on December 18, 1893, President Grover Cleveland reported fully and accurately on the illegal acts of the conspirators, described such acts as an "act of war, committed with the partic-ipation of a diplomatic representative of the United States and without authority of Con-gress," and acknowledged that by such acts the government of a peaceful and friendly people was overthrown. The President fur-ther concluded that a "substantial wrong has thus been done which a due regard for our national character as well as the rights of the injured people requires we should endeavor to repair" and called for the restoration of the Hawaiian monarchy;

The Provisional Government protested President Cleveland's call for the restoration of the monarchy and . . . successfully lobbied the Committee on Foreign Relations of the Senate (hereafter referred to in this Resolution as the "Committee") to conduct a new investigation. . . .

The Committee conducted hearings in Washington, D.C., from December 27, 1893, through February 26, 1894, in which members of the Provisional Government justified the actions of the United States Minister and recommended annexation of Hawaii . . . [but were] unable to rally the support from two-thirds of the Senate needed to ratify a treaty of annexation;

On July 4, 1894, the Provisional Government declared itself to be the Republic of Hawaii, and on January 24, 1895, while imprisoned in Iolani Palace, Queen Liliuokalani was forced by representatives of the Republic of Hawaii to officially abdicate her throne;

The indigenous Hawaiian people never directly relinquished their claims to their inherent sovereignty as a people or over their national lands to the United States, either through their monarchy or through a plebiscite or referendum;

On April 30, 1900, President William McKinley signed the Organic Act that provided a government for the territory of Hawaii; on August 21, 1959, Hawaii became the 50th State of the United States;

The Eighteenth General Synod of the United Church of Christ in recognition of the denomination's historical complicity in the illegal overthrow of the Kingdom of Hawaii in 1893 directed the Office of the President of the United Church of Christ to offer a public apology to the native Hawaiian people and to initiate the process of reconciliation between the United Church of Christ and the Native Hawaiians; and

On the occasion of the impending one hundredth anniversary of the event, [U.S. Congress shall] acknowledge the historic significance of the illegal overthrow of the Kingdom of Hawaii, express its deep regret to the Native Hawaiian people, and support the reconciliation efforts of the State of Hawaii and the United Church of Christ with Native Hawaiians: Now, therefore, be it.

Resolved by the Senate and House of Representatives of the United States of America in Congress assembled,

Section 1—Acknowledgment and Apology

The Congress —

(1) on the occasion of the 100th anniversary of the illegal overthrow of the Kingdom of Hawaii on January 17, 1893, acknowledges the historical significance of this event which resulted in the suppression of the inherent sovereignty of the Native Hawaiian people;

(2) recognizes and commends efforts of reconciliation initiated by the State of Hawaii and the United Church of Christ with Native Hawaiians;

(3) apologizes to Native Hawaiians on behalf of the people of the United States for the overthrow of the Kingdom of Hawaii on January 17, 1893, with the participation of agents and citizens of the United States, and the deprivation of the rights of Native Hawaiians to self-determination;

(4) expresses its commitment to acknowledge the ramifications of the overthrow of the Kingdom of Hawaii, in order to provide a

proper foundation for reconciliation between the United States and the Native Hawaiian people; and

(5) urges the President of the United States to also acknowledge the ramifications of the overthrow of the Kingdom of Hawaii and to support reconciliation efforts between the United States and the Native Hawaiian people.

Section 2—Definitions

As used in this Joint Resolution, the term, "Native Hawaiian" means any individual who is a descendent of the aboriginal people who, prior to 1778, occupied and exercised sovereignty in the area that now constitutes the State of Hawaii.

Section 3—Disclaimer

Nothing in this Joint Resolution is intended to serve as a settlement of any claims against the United States.

Approved, November 23, 1993.

Executive Order 13216, 2001

By this Executive Order, President George W. Bush aimed to increase opportunities for, as well as improve the quality of life of, Asian Americans and Pacific Islanders.

By the authority vested in me as President by the Constitution and the laws of the United States of America, including the Federal Advisory Committee Act, as amended (5 U.S.C. App.), and in order to improve the quality of life of Asian Americans and Pacific Islanders through increased participation in Federal programs where they may be underserved (e.g., health, human services, education, housing, labor,

transportation, and economic and community development), it is hereby ordered as follows:

Section 1.

(a) There is established in the Department of Health and Human Services the President's Advisory Commission on Asian Americans and Pacific Islanders (Commission). The Commission shall consist of not more than 15 members appointed by the President, one of which shall be designated by the President as Chair. The Commission shall include members who:

(i) have a history of involvement with the Asian American and Pacific Islander communities;

(ii) are from the fields of health, human services, education, housing, labor, transportation, economic and community development, civil rights, and the business community;

(iii) are from civic associations representing one or more of the diverse Asian American and Pacific Islander communities; and

(iv) have such other experience as the President deems appropriate.

(b) The Secretary of the Department of Health and Human Services (Secretary) shall appoint an Executive Director for the Commission.

Section 2.

The Commission shall provide advice to the President, through the Secretary, on:

(a) the development, monitoring, and coordination of Federal efforts to improve the quality of life of Asian Americans and Pacific Islanders through increased participation in Federal programs where such persons may be underserved and the collection of data related to Asian American and Pacific Islander populations and sub-populations;

(b) ways to increase public-sector, private-sector, and community involvement in improving the health and well-being of Asian Americans and Pacific Islanders; and

(c) ways to foster research and data on Asian Americans and Pacific Islanders, including research and data on public health.

Section 3.

The Department of Health and Human Services shall establish the White House Initiative on Asian Americans and Pacific Islanders (Initiative), an interagency working group (working group) whose members shall be appointed by their respective agencies. The Executive Director of the Commission shall also serve as the Director of the Initiative, and shall report to the Secretary or the Secretary's designee. The working group shall include both career and noncareer civil service staff and commissioned officers of the Public Health Service with expertise in health, human services, education, housing, labor, transportation, economic and community development, and other relevant issues. The working group shall advise the Secretary on the implementation and coordination of Federal programs as they relate to Asian Americans and Pacific Islanders across executive departments and agencies.

Section 4.

The head of each executive department and each agency designated by the Secretary shall appoint a senior Federal official responsible for management or program administration to report directly to the agency head on activity under this Executive order, and to serve as a liaison to the Initiative. The Secretary also may designate additional Federal Government officials, with the agreement of the relevant agency head, to carry out the functions of the Initiative. To the extent permitted by law and to the extent practicable, each executive department and designated agency shall provide any appropriate information requested by the working group, including data relating to the eligibility for and participation of Asian Americans and Pacific Islanders in Federal programs. Where adequate data are not available, the Initiative shall suggest the means of collecting such data.

Section 5.

Each executive department and designated agency (collectively, the "agency") shall prepare a plan for, and shall document, its efforts to improve the quality of life of Asian Americans and Pacific Islanders through increased participation in Federal programs where Asian Americans and Pacific Islanders may be underserved. This plan shall address, among other things, Federal efforts to:

(a) improve the quality of life for Asian Americans and Pacific Islanders through increased participation in Federal programs where they may be underserved and the collection of data related to Asian American and Pacific Islander populations and sub-populations;

(b) increase public-sector, private-sector, and community involvement in improving the health and well-being of Asian Americans and Pacific Islanders; and

(c) foster research and data on Asian Americans and Pacific Islanders, including research and data on public health. Each agency's plan shall provide appropriate measurable objectives and, after the first year, shall assess that agency's performance on the goals set in the previous year's plan. Each plan shall be submitted at a date to be established by the Secretary.

Section 6.

The Secretary shall review the agency plans and develop for submission to the President an integrated Federal plan (Federal Plan) to improve the quality of life of Asian American and Pacific Islanders through increased participation in Federal programs where such persons may be underserved. Actions described in the Federal Plan shall address improving access by Asian Americans and Pacific Islanders to Federal programs and fostering advances in relevant research and data. The Secretary shall ensure that the working group is given the opportunity to comment on the proposed Federal Plan prior to its submission to the President. The Secretary shall disseminate the Federal Plan to appropriate members of the executive branch. The findings and recommendations in the Federal Plan shall be considered by the agencies in their policies and activities.

Section 7.

Notwithstanding any other Executive order, the responsibilities of the President that are applicable to the Commission under the Federal Advisory Committee Act, as amended, except that of reporting to the Congress, shall be performed by the Secretary in accordance with the guidelines and procedures established by the Administrator of General Services.

Section 8.

Members of the Commission shall serve without compensation, but shall be allowed travel expenses, including per diem in lieu of subsistence, as authorized by law for persons serving intermittently in the Government service (5 U.S.C. 5701-5707). To the extent permitted by law and appropriations, and where practicable, agencies shall, upon request by the Secretary, provide assistance to the Commission and to the Initiative. The Department of Health and Human Services shall provide administrative support and funding for the Commission.

Section 9.

The Commission shall terminate on June 7, 2003, unless renewed by the President prior to that date.

Sec. 10. For the purposes of this order, the terms:

(a) "Asian American" includes persons having origins in any of the original peoples of the Far East, Southeast Asia, or the Indian subcontinent; and

(b) "Pacific Islander" includes the aboriginal, indigenous, native peoples of Hawaii and other Pacific Islands within the jurisdiction of the United States.

George W. Bush
The White House, June 6, 2001.

A Proclamation by the President of the United States of America on the 100th Anniversary of Korean Immigration, 2003

Governor Linda Lingle (left) and Senator Paull Shin, both of Hawaii, participate in a banquet held in Honolulu on January 13, 2003, to commemorate the 100th anniversary of Korean immigration to Hawaii.

In this proclamation, President George W. Bush celebrates 100 years of Korean immigration.

From every corner of the world, immigrants have come to America to discover the promise of our Nation. On January 13, 1903, the first Korean immigrants to the United States arrived in Honolulu, Hawaii, on the SS *Gaelic.* Today, Korean Americans live throughout the United States, representing one of our largest Asian-American populations. As we commemorate the centennial anniversary of Korean immigration to the United States, we recognize the invaluable contributions of Korean Americans to our Nation's rich cultural diversity, economic strength, and proud heritage.

For the past century, Korean immigrants and their descendants have helped build America's prosperity, strengthened America's communities, and defended America's freedoms. Through their service in World War I, World War II, the Korean Conflict, the Vietnam War, and other wars, Korean Americans have served our Nation with honor and courage, upholding the values that make our country strong.

The American and Korean people share a love of freedom and a dedication to peace. The United States was the first Western country to sign a treaty of commerce and amity with Korea in 1882, promising "perpetual peace and friendship" between our nations. Since that time, the United States has built a strong friendship with Korea -- a friendship based on our common commitment to human dignity, prosperity, and democracy. In the coming months, more than 1 million Korean Americans throughout our Nation will celebrate the 100th anniversary of the arrival of the first Korean immigrants to the United States. During this time, we acknowledge and commend Korean Americans for their distinguished achievements in all sectors of life and for their important role in building, defending, and sustaining the United States of America.

NOW, THEREFORE, I, GEORGE W. BUSH, President of the United States of

America, by virtue of the authority vested in me by the Constitution and laws of the United States, do hereby proclaim January 13, 2003, as the Centennial of Korean Immigration to the United States. I call upon all Americans to observe the anniversary with appropriate programs, ceremonies, and activities honoring Korean immigrants and their descendants for their countless contributions to America.

IN WITNESS WHEREOF, I have hereunto set my hand this thirteenth day of January, in the year of our Lord two thousand three, and of the Independence of the United States of America the two hundred and twenty-seventh.

3

Landmarks

Significant Historical Sites for Asian Americans

FACT FOCUS

- Early sites in Asian American history are found in ethnic communities such as Chinatowns.
- California's Angel Island Immigration Station was the entry point for most of the 175,000 Chinese who immigrated between 1910 and 1940.
- The home of Philip Jaisohn, the first Korean to become a naturalized U.S. citizen, is a research center devoted to the history of Korean immigration.
- Many sites in Hawaii commemorate the royal family of Hawaii, overthrown by U.S. and other foreign interests in 1893.
- The imprisonment of 110,000 Americans of Japanese descent is remembered at the sites of the ten camps in western states where they were held.

The traces of early Asians and Pacific Islander settlers can be found throughout the United States in Chinatowns, temples, vineyards, and railroads. In these places, early Chinese immigrants worked and lived, often on the fringes of society and in relative obscurity. Their mark, though often faint, remains visible nonetheless. Darker memories are stirred at other places—massacre sites and incarceration camps. Though painful to revisit, they remind all Americans of the perils of intolerance. For good or ill, they are part of the fabric of U.S. history.

Given the diversity and relative youth of the Asian American population, a historic site is not determined by its age or culture, but by the events that occurred there. In the pages that follow, some of the major landmarks of Asian American culture and history are listed by state and briefly described.

Arizona

Gila River Relocation Center

The Gila River Relocation Center was one of ten internment camps in which Japanese

The barracks at Angel Island Immigration Station, San Francisco Bay.

Americans, most of them U.S. citizens, were incarcerated during World War II. Constructed on Native American reservation land, the facility was in operation from July 20, 1942, to November 10, 1945; its peak population reached 13,348.

Poston Relocation Center, Parker

The larger of Arizona's two internment sites, the Poston relocation center was one of ten camps in which Japanese Americans were incarcerated during World War II. Like the Gila River site, Poston was also established on Native American land. The camp opened May 8, 1942, and closed November 28, 1945; peak population reached 17,814. Today, a 30-foot-high single concrete column marks the site. Six memorial plaques around the bottom portion give a short history of the evacuation, the establishment of the Poston complex, its administration, the resettlement of the internees, and a tribute to Poston's 24 internees who perished in World War II.

Arkansas

Jerome Relocation Center

Jerome and Rohwer Relocation centers were the easternmost of the ten relocation camps where Japanese Americans, mostly U.S. citizens, were incarcerated during World War II. Jerome opened October 6, 1942, and closed June 30, 1944; peak population at the camp reached 8,497. Today, a ten-foot-tall granite monument commemorates the site.

Rohwer Relocation Center

One of ten Japanese American relocation camps, Rohwer opened September 18, 1942, and closed November 30, 1945; its peak population reached 8,475. Most of the internees were relocated from Los Angeles and Stockton. Today, the Rohwer Memorial Cemetery contains three monuments to honor the Rohwer internees who died serving their country and to commemorate the site.

California

Angel Island Immigration Station, San Francisco Bay

Angel Island was the entry point for most of the 175,000 Chinese immigrants who came to the United States between 1910 and 1940. Chinese immigration had been severely restricted by the Chinese Exclusion Act of 1882, which allowed only government officials, merchants, students, teachers, visitors, and those claiming U.S. citizenship to enter. All potential immigrants, both new arrivals and returning U.S. residents, if admitted, were subjected to medical scrutiny and an elaborate questioning process before being released. At any given time, between 200 and 300 males and 30 to 50 females were detained on Angel Island.

Evidence of the immigrants' ordeal is recorded in the form of poetry that was carved into the barrack walls. These poems expressed the immigrants' impressions of their voyage to the United States, their longing for families back home, and the outrage and humiliation they felt at the often unjust treatment they endured. Today, the detention center is the site of a picturesque state park in the middle of San Francisco Bay.

WORDS TO KNOW

assembly center: a temporary holding facility, such as a race track, where West Coast families of Japanese descent were taken when the U.S. military forced them to leave their homes; after a short stay at an assembly center, prisoners were moved to internment camps

Chinatown: neighborhood in a city where people of Chinese descent live and often operate businesses and restaurants

internment camp: remote, primitive camp where Americans of Japanese descent were held as prisoners during World War II, on the theory that they were risks to U.S. military security

---

Buddhist Church of Bakersfield, Bakersfield

This one-story, light gray clapboard structure is the United States's oldest Japanese Buddhist church building constructed by its congregation that is still used for religious services. Completed in June 1911, it cost $3,314.50. The church altar was shipped in pieces to Bakersfield from Japan and reassembled upon arrival.

China Camp State Park, San Rafael

This lush 1,600-acre park on San Pablo Bay is home to a Chinese fishing village that dates from the 1860s, when Chinese fishermen began shrimping in California. China Camp was one of the largest and longest lived fishing villages. Its peak population was 469 inhabitants, 368 of whom were directly associated with shrimp fishery,

Frank Quan, the last Chinese American in China Camp, near San Rafael, walked the wooden pier carrying a shrimp net in 1993.

according to the 1880 census. Records indicate that the village also had three general stores, one marine supply store, and a barber shop.

Today, China Camp is a near ghost town of tumbledown buildings. Frank Quan, a descendant of an early Chinese American shrimp fisherman, maintains the last standing pier and buildings. The camp is now surrounded by a wilderness park.

Chinatown, Los Angeles

Los Angeles's current Chinatown is actually its third, created by developers after the first and second Chinatowns were moved to make way for large construction projects.

Compared to San Francisco's Chinatown, Los Angeles's is small both in area and population. About 15,000 Chinese and Southeast Asians (mostly Vietnamese) live in the area, although many times that number frequent the area's shops, markets, and restaurants. Located in downtown Los Angeles near the intersection of the Pasadena Freeway and Highway 101, Chinatown's main street is North Broadway, where Chinese New Year celebrations are held.

Chinatown, San Francisco

Home to some 100,000, San Francisco's Chinatown is second only to New York City's. San Francisco's original Chinatown burned down in the fire that followed the 1906 earthquake. Today, this bustling, vital downtown area comprises approximately 24 blocks—a city within a city. Set on an incline, where San Francisco's famously steep streets begin their sharp ascent, Chinatown is located just south of North Beach. The green-tiled, dragon-crowned Chinatown Gate, at Bush Street and Grant Avenue, is the most obvious and most popular entrance.

Chinese Historical Society of America, San Francisco

Located at 650 Commercial Street in San Francisco's Chinatown, the society is the first of its kind in North America, founded on January 5, 1963. The society provides information about the history of Chinese immigrants and their contributions to California's rail, mining, and fishing industries. Exhibits trace the Chinese American experience from the 1850s to the present.

Harada House, Riverside

The Harada case (*The People of the State of California* v. *Jukichi Harada, et al*) was the first to confront the unconstitutionality of California's Alien Land Law of 1913, which prohibited Asian immigrants from owning property. (It was not abolished until 1952.) In December 1915, Jukichi Harada purchased a one-story saltbox cottage in a middle-class neighborhood in the name of his three U.S.-born children. Neighbors sued Harada, charging that he was an alien ineligible for U.S. citizenship and therefore not allowed to possess, acquire, transfer, or enjoy any real property in the state of California. The trial, which began December 14,

1916, was not resolved until September 17, 1918, when Judge Hugh H. Crain of the Riverside County Superior Court reached a favorable verdict for the Harada family. He ruled that although aliens who were ineligible for citizenship could not own land, their U.S.-born children had rights equal to those of any other U.S. citizen.

Japanese American National Museum, Los Angeles

The Japanese American National Museum, which opened in 1992, is the first museum in the United States dedicated to sharing the experiences of Americans of Japanese ancestry. The museum is located in Little Tokyo and is housed in the recently restored sanctuary of the former Nishi Hongwanji Buddhist Temple, which was built in 1925.

Japantown, San Francisco

Although some Japanese Americans had settled in the neighborhood known as the Western Addition before the 1906 earthquake in San Francisco, it was after the quake and its subsequent fire destroyed much of the city that many Japanese Americans moved to the Western Addition. By the 1930s, these pioneering residents had opened shops, markets, meeting halls, restaurants, and temples. During World War II, when many of the area's residents were unjustly incarcerated, the area was virtually deserted.

Japantown, or Nihonmachi, is centered on the slopes of Pacific Heights. One of the community's signature events is the Cherry Blossom Festival, which is celebrated over two weekends every April. At the heart of Japantown is the three-block-long, five-acre

Charles Toyooka, a Japanese American who served during World War II in the all-Japanese American 442nd Regiment, stood in San Francisco's Japantown in 1992.

Japan Center, a multimillion-dollar development created by Japanese American architect Minoru Yamasaki, which opened to the public in 1968 with a three-day festival.

In San Pedro harbor south of Los Angeles, overlooking the Catalina Channel in Angel's Gate Park, sits the Korean Bell and Belfry of Friendship. The largest bell of its type in existence, it was given by the Republic of Korea (South Korea) in 1976 to celebrate the United States Bicentennial, as well as to honor veterans of the Korean war. The bell weighs seventeen tons and was cast of copper and tin, with gold and lead added to improve the tone quality. The bell is rung three times a year—the Fourth of July, August 15 (Korean Independence Day), and New Year's Eve. The bell has no hammer. It is rung when a large wooden log strikes it from the outside.

The bell is patterned after the Bronze Bell of King Songdok, which was cast in 771 A.D. and is still on view in South Korea today. The pavilion housing the bell was constructed by thirty Korean craftsmen who traveled to California for the purpose of building the structure. They worked for ten months building the twelve columns repre-

Korean Bell of Friendship and Bell Pavilion in San Pedro, California.

senting the designs of the zodiac that support the pagoda's roof. Animals stand guard at the base of each column.

Koreatown, Los Angeles

Koreans are one of the newest and largest ethnic groups to settle in Los Angeles, where they constitute the single-largest Korean community in the United States. Located south of Wilshire Boulevard, along Olympic Boulevard between Vermont and Western Avenues, Koreatown has become a cohesive neighborhood with an infrastructure of active community groups and newspapers.

Little Tokyo, Los Angeles

Located in downtown Los Angeles, Little Tokyo was the Japanese community's original ethnic neighborhood in Los Angeles. The area today is less residential since many Japanese Americans have relocated to the suburbs of Gardena and West Los Angeles; Little Tokyo, however, remains a cultural focal point for the community.

Locke

The village of Locke in the Sacramento-San Joaquin Delta region has been declared a National Historic Monument as the only rural community in the United States to

Wood-frame buildings along block-long Main Street in Locke, California.

have been built solely by and for Chinese Americans. The town's original isolation resulted from alien land laws that barred early Chinese immigrants from owning land in California and prevented them from establishing permanent communities. They could only live in areas no one else wanted to be, and if the landowner wanted the property for other uses, the immigrants were forced to vacate.

Founded in 1915, the village of Locke gave Chinese farm laborers and their families social and recreational facilities, including schools, churches, temples, stores, community organizations, tea houses, restaurants, and a Chinese-run movie theater.

Today, many of Locke's fewer than 100 residents can trace their ancestry to the immigrants who mined the gold fields, built the transcontinental railroad, and constructed the delta's intricate levee system. The town is reminiscent of an outdoor museum. Along the ridgetops of the false-front buildings, one can still discern the outlines of hand-lettered signs for the Chinese Bakery and Lunch Parlor, the Star Theatre, or Waih and Co. Groceries & Dry Goods.

Los Angeles Massacre Site, Los Angeles

The Los Angeles Massacre, which occurred on October 24, 1871, left 19 Chinese Americans dead. The event that sparked the riot happened on October 23, 1871, when a quarrel between two Chinese Americans led to a shooting and consequent arrest. The dispute continued the next day, and when a police officer tried to step in, more gunshots were fired, and a bystander was accidentally shot and killed. Spectators began attacking the Chinese residents who sought refuge in a nearby adobe building. A mob began to gather and random shooting followed. The crowd forced its way into the building, torturing, hanging, and shooting the innocent Chinese inside. In addition, every Chinese building on the block was ransacked and robbed. Among the murderers, a few were imprisoned for a short period at San Quentin, but the mob leaders escaped punishment.

Manzanar Relocation Center

One of ten relocation camps where Japanese Americans, mostly U.S. citizens, were incarcerated during World War II, Manzanar opened March 21, 1942, and closed November 21, 1945. The peak population at the camp reached 10,046. Located between Independence and Lone Pine, Manzanar was originally established as one of thirteen temporary detention centers in California; three months later, the War Relocation Authority took over the site, and Manzanar became the first of ten permanent centers. Today, two stone entrance stations, a high school auditorium, and a 15-foot-high cemetery monument, interspersed with concrete barracks foundations, tea garden ruins, grave sites, and mess hall debris are all that remain of the camp.

Mo Dai Miu or Temple of Kuan Kung, Mendocino

This temple is the last remaining Chinese house of worship on the northern coast of California. The building dates from at least 1883, although oral history suggests that it may have been built as early as 1854. The temple is an important reminder of the contributions of early Chinese pioneers, especially since written records make little mention of them.

National Japanese American Historical Society, San Francisco

Founded in 1980, the mission of the National Japanese American Historical Society is to ensure that stories of the Japanese American experience are remembered. Through traveling exhibitions, publications, and educational programs, the society is a vital national and international resource for institutions and individuals.

Quick Ranch Stone Wall, Mariposa

Often referred to as a miniature Great Wall of China, this rock boundary wall is four miles long and four feet high. Quick Ranch records show that it was constructed in 1862 by Chinese builders, under the direction of a Chinese boss. Each worker had to complete a rod and a half (24¾ feet) every day to earn the $0.25 daily wage. The ranch's founder, Morgan Quick, provided food for the workers from a herd of hogs he had bought at about a cent and a half a pound. The Chinese overseer, who sat under an umbrella and kept count of each foot of wall on his abacus, was paid $1.75 per rod (16½ feet). Most of the original wall, constructed for a total cost of $6,000, is still standing.

Terminal Island, East San Pedro

Before World War II, Terminal Island was a fishing village where approximately 3,000 Japanese Americans lived and worked. It began as an all-male community, and by the summer of 1907, when canning companies began production on the island, was home to several hundred Japanese fishermen. The number of women and children soon increased, especially when women were hired to work in the canneries. The island's main language was Japanese and many cultural activities reflected Japanese influences.

In February 1942, however, the island's inhabitants were forcibly relocated to internment camps, the first of the more than 120,000 Japanese Americans to be imprisoned during the war. When the war ended, the residents of Terminal Island did not return to their homes.

Today there is no trace of the Japanese community—the fishermen's houses and shops have been destroyed. The only remaining structure is the Terminal School, once attended by Japanese schoolchildren and now used by the Marine Corps.

Tule Lake Relocation Center, Newell

The largest of ten relocation camps where Japanese Americans, mostly U.S. citizens, were incarcerated during World War II, Tule Lake opened May 27, 1942, and was the last camp to close on March 20, 1946. Its peak population reached 18,789. Located six miles south of the California-Oregon border, the camp encompassed 7,400 acres, most of it used for agricultural activities.

In July 1943, Tule Lake was designated as the segregation center for internees who wished to be repatriated to Japan or who had not responded to the satisfaction of the U.S. Government on its Loyalty Questionnaire. Due to its program of segregation, Tule Lake's history is more heavily marked by human tragedy and inner disturbance than other relocation camps. The Tule Lake Historic Monument marker, a large semicircular red stone, is located on California Highway 139 in Newell.

Yamato Colony, Livingston

In 1904, Kyutaro Abiko purchased 3,000 acres in Livingston and divided them into 40-acre units. He planned to establish Yamato Colony, an agricultural Japanese community in the Central Valley. There were two other Yamato colonies, one in Florida and one in Texas. Abiko was confident that the future of Japanese in California was in farming. In November 1906, the first Japanese purchased land in Yamato, and by 1908, 30 individuals had bought into the venture. From 1910 to 1915, the new farmers toiled at converting open land to productive fields.

Prior to World War II, 69 Japanese American families were reported to be farming more than 3,700 acres in Yamato. During the war and the internment years, 54 families from Livingston and the neighboring town of Cortex hired a land manager to oversee their property. Upon return, many of the first-generation farmers passed management of the farms to the next generation. In recent years, the Livingston Farmer's Association listed 65 members, of which 57 were second-generation Japanese Americans.

Colorado

Amache Relocation Center, Granada

One of ten relocation camps where Japanese Americans, mostly U.S. citizens, were incarcerated during World War II, Amache opened August 24, 1942, and closed October 15, 1945. The peak population at the camp reached 7,318. Today, the site of the camp is marked by Amache Remembered, a monument that commemorates the 31 internees who lost their lives in World War II as well as the approximately 7,000 stateside internees, 120 of whom died while incarcerated. In the cemetery stands a ten-foot monument, ten graves, and a small building housing another, smaller monument.

Florida

The Morikami Museum and Japanese Gardens, Delray Beach

The Morikami Museum and Japanese Gardens, founded in 1977, in Delray Beach in Palm Beach County, Florida, is the only museum in the United States dedicated exclusively to the living culture of Japan. The idea of the museum arose through an act of generosity by George Sukeji Morikami (1886-1975), a Japanese farmer who came to the United States in 1906 as a penniless 19-year-old indentured worker in the Yamato Colony, an experimental cooperative community settled by Japanese farmers in Boca Raton in the early 1900s. Morikami went on to build a million-dollar land empire from the sandy soil of southern Florida. Out of gratitude to the people of his adopted homeland, this last living pioneer of the Yamato Colony donated 35 acres of his land to Palm Beach County in 1974. Additional gifts in

1974 and 1975 increased the park to nearly its present size of 200 acres.

The original Morikami Museum building, Yamato-kan, is situated amid pine forests, lakes, waterfalls, and formal Japanese gardens. Modeled after a Japanese imperial villa and opened in 1977, it houses a permanent exhibition detailing the history of Yamato Colony. In 1993, the Morikami was expanded by the addition of a new 32,000 square-foot museum building designed in the Japanese style, which houses an array of exhibitions, special events, cultural activities, and educational programs for all ages to develop a deeper appreciation and understanding of Japanese art and culture.

Morikami Park is a picturesque reserve of pine forests surrounded by modern Palm Beach and suburban communities. An untamed nature trail winds through the forest, punctuated by picnic pavilions. In a novel blending of East and West, traditional Japanese gardening techniques and vegetation indigenous to Florida come together in the gardens, which host a wide range of native species of plants and animals.

Hawaii

The Alexander and Baldwin Sugar Museum, Puunene, Maui

Puunene is a working plantation village surrounded by sugarcane fields. The town's museum presents the story of sugar in Hawaii, beginning with Samuel Alexander and Henry Baldwin, who bought massive chunks of Hawaiian land. Also on display is a turn-of-the-century labor contract from the Japanese Emigration Company that set wages at $15 a month for 10 hours per day of field work, 26 days a month (less $2.50,

Iolani Palace in Honolulu, once the home for the royal family of the Kingdom of Hawaii, now serves as the seat of the state government.

which was deducted for return passage to Japan).

Aliiolani Hale, Honolulu, Oahu

The first major government building constructed by the Hawaiian monarchy, Aliiolani Hale ("House of Heavenly Kings") housed the Hawaiian legislature until it became the home of Hawaii's Supreme Court in 1874. Almost 20 years later, in January 1893, Sanford Dole, the son of a pioneer missionary, proclaimed the establishment of a provisional government and the overthrow of the Hawaiian monarchy on the steps of Aliiolani Hale.

Byodoin, Kaneohe, Oahu

The Byodoin, or Temple of Equality, is the main attraction in the Valley of the Temples, an interdenominational cemetery. The temple was dedicated in 1968 to commemorate the one hundredth anniversary of Japanese immigration to Hawaii. It is a replica of a 900-year-old temple of the same name in Uji, Japan.

Chinatown, Honolulu, Oahu

Located west of downtown Honolulu, Chinatown is bordered by Honolulu Harbor, Nuuanu Avenue, and River Street. It became a Chinese enclave around 1860, when Chinese sugar-plantation workers who had worked off their labor contracts settled in the area and opened small businesses there.

Today, Chinatown is home to a diverse group of Asian immigrants, with recent Vietnamese, Thai, and Filipino influences. Highlights of the area include Oahu Market, the heart of Chinatown and a local institution since 1904; Wo Fat, which was built in 1900 and is the oldest restaurant in Honolulu; the Izumo Taisha Shrine, a small wooden Shinto shrine built in 1923; and the Taoist Temple, which is the temple for the Lum Sai Ho Tong Society, first organized in 1889.

Duke Kahanamoku Statue, Waikiki, Oahu

On Waikiki Beach stands a larger than life bronze statue of Olympic swimmer and surfing legend Duke Kahanamoku. The statue was erected in 1990 to honor the father of modern surfing, and welcomes visitors to Waikiki. The statue has become an icon of Waikiki, with thousands of tourists snapping pictures of themselves with "the duke," and Kahanamoku's admirers adorn the native Hawaiian's statue with leis.

Iolani Palace, Honolulu, Oahu

The Iolani Palace is the only royal palace in the United States. From 1882 to 1891, it served as the official residence of Hawaii's last king, King Kalakaua, and his consort, Queen Kapiolani. Kalakaua's sister, Queen Liliuokalani, took residence in 1891 upon her ascension to the throne as Hawaii's last monarch. When the monarchy was overthrown in 1893, the palace became the capitol, first for the Republic of Hawaii, then for the U.S. territory, and later for the state of Hawaii.

Kamehameha's Birthplace, North Kohala, Hawaii Island

Located one-third of a mile from Mookini Heiau, near one of the oldest and most historically significant *heiaus*, or ancient stone temples, in Hawaii, lies a stone enclosure that marks the birth site of King Kamehameha I. The great king is said to have been born here in 1758 on a stormy winter night. According to local legend, the king's mother was told that her son would become a destroyer of chiefs and a powerful ruler. The prophecy was fulfilled when Kamehameha united all the Hawaiian islands under his rule in 1810.

Kamakahonu, Kona, Hawaii Island

The beach at the north end of Kailua Bay, named Kamakahonu (which means "eye of the turtle"), was the site of the royal residence of King Kamehameha I. Also known as King Kamehameha the Great, he united all of the Hawaiian Islands under his rule and called them Hawaii after his home island. The king died here in 1819. Today, the ancient sites have been incorporated into the grounds of the Hotel King Kamehameha. A few thatched structures and carved wooden statues that stand erect (called *kii* gods) have been reconstructed above the old stone temple. Nearby is the Ahuena Heiau, an ancient site of human sacrifice.

Pearl Harbor, Oahu

On December 7, 1941, a wave of more than 350 Japanese planes attacked Pearl Harbor, home of the U.S. Pacific Fleet. Approximately 2,335 soldiers died in the two-hour attack, 1,177 of them on the battleship U.S.S. *Arizona*, which suffered a direct hit and sank in nine minutes. The attack served as the catalyst for the United States entrance into World War II. Three months later, on February 19, 1942, claiming that Americans of Japanese ancestry posed a potential threat to national security, President Franklin D. Roosevelt signed Executive Order 9066, which unjustly incarcerated over 120,000 Japanese Americans in ten relocation centers throughout the West for the duration of the war. Over 1.5 million people "remember Pearl Harbor" each year by visiting the U.S.S. *Arizona* memorial run by the National Park Service, making it Hawaii's most visited site.

Puuhonua O Honaunau National Historical Park, Honaunau, Hawaii Island

Commonly called the Place of Refuge, the park encompasses ancient temples, royal grounds, and a *puuhonua*, a place of refuge or sanctuary. A temple in the park, called Hale O Keawe Heiau, was built around 1650. The bones of 23 royal chiefs are purported to be buried there.

Royal Mausoleum State Monument, Honolulu, Oahu

In the Royal Mausoleum, located at 2262 Nuuanu Avenue, lie the remains of Kings Kamehameha II, III, IV, and V, as well as King David Kalakaua and Queen Liliuokalani, Hawaii's last two reigning monarchs. The only monarch missing is King Kamehameha I, the mighty ruler who united the Hawaiian islands. He was the

The sidewalks are crowded in New York's Chinatown, where over 150,000 people live in an area of only two square miles in lower Manhattan.

last king to be buried in secret, in accordance with traditional Hawaiian beliefs.

Idaho

Minidoka Relocation Center

One of ten relocation camps where Americans of Japanese ancestry were incarcerated during World War II, Minidoka opened August 10, 1942, and closed October 28, 1945. The peak population at the camp reached 9,397. Located between Jerome and Eden, the site of the camp is marked by a wooden sign and by four memorial plaques, installed as part of the Idaho State Centennial Project in 1990, to commemorate the site.

Illinois

Chinatown, Chicago

During the 1880s, at the height of anti-Chinese campaigns on the West Coast, more and more Chinese workers began heading east. A small group of Chinese congregated in Chicago in a one-block Chinatown at Clark and Van Buren Streets, south of the downtown area. In 1910, due to rising rents, the need for expansion, and conflict between two rival organizations, a second Chinatown was formed five miles away in the ten-block area centered on Cermak and Wentworth Streets known today as Chinatown. While the new area prospered, the old Chinatown was eventually razed for new construction. A third small Chinatown was eventually established uptown on Argyle and Broadway Streets, where a number of Chinese already lived.

Massachusetts

Chinatown, Boston

In 1875, 75 Chinese workers from San Francisco were contracted to work in a shoe factory in North Adams, Massachusetts. A number of these workers later settled in Boston near the South Railway Station. They were soon joined by another group of West Coast workers who were under contract to build the Pearl Street telephone exchange. This was the beginning of what, in the 1970s, would become the fourth-largest Chinatown in the United States. Centered on Beech Street, Boston's Chinatown was originally a middle-class enclave that was abandoned by its white residents and then quickly taken over by Chinese immigrants, most of whom were poor.

With the advent of World War II and the repeal of the exclusion acts in 1943, immigration increased and the Chinatown population grew quickly. Families were finally reunited, women were allowed to immigrate, new families were formed, and a fresh generation of U.S.-born Chinese Americans grew up. The 1950s through the 1970s saw an increase of immigrants from Hong Kong and other cosmopolitan Asian cities. Today, only about 10 percent of Boston's Chinese American population lives in Chinatown.

New York

Chinatown, New York City

According to the 1980 census, New York's Chinatown has the largest Chinese American settlement in the United States. On July 10, 1847, the *New York Herald* reported that 35 Chinese had arrived in New York; they were the crew of the ship *Keying*. Not until the 1870s, however, spurred by growing anti-Chinese violence in the West, did significant numbers of Chinese immigrants begin arriving in New York.

In 1878, the same year that the U.S. government denied Chinese immigrants the right to become citizens, the first Chinese grocery store, Wo Kee, opened on Mott Street. Immigrants who had been forced out of a variety of occupations entered low-status service work, finding jobs especially in hand laundries. These workers frequented Wo Kee, cementing the New York Chinese community. Unfortunately, the Chinese Exclusion Act of 1882 and subsequent anti-Chinese immigration laws made it nearly impossible for Chinese women and children to enter the United States. This created an artificial "bachelor society" in New York and other Chinatowns across the country.

Old Chinatown, clustered in the lower Mott Street area, remains at the neighborhood's heart. In 1965, however, when immigration restrictions were lifted, an influx of Chinese and other Asian immigrants flooded the community. Today, with more than 150,000 residents, the area has grown from below Canal Street into Soho and the Lower East Side, with another 150,000 living in satellite communities in Brooklyn and Queens. Today's Chinatown has become the city's manufacturing center, as well as an important jewelry district.

Chinatown History Museum, New York City

The Chinatown History Museum's mission is to reclaim, preserve, and share Chinese American history and culture with a broad audience. Its core exhibit is an interactive, interpretive look at the Chinese-immigrant experience in the United States. Public programs include lectures, readings, symposia, and family events. The museum, located at 70 Mulberry Street, also houses a library whose extensive archives contain oral histories, photographs, documents, and artifacts.

Oregon

Chinatown, Portland

Just west of the Old Town area of Portland is a small Chinatown, no larger than a few blocks. The main serpent-adorned entrance is on Fourth Avenue, and fiery red and yellow lampposts decorate its streets. In 1989, the area north of Burnside between Third and Sixth Avenues was designated as a national historic district, making the area the oldest and the largest historic district in Oregon.

Gin Lin Trail, Applegate Valley

One of the most diligent Chinese-immigrant miners was Gin Lin, whose mining site is still visible south of Ruch, on the Gin Lin Trail in southern Oregon's Applegate Valley. Gin Lin began mining here in 1881, and throughout the decade deposited over a million dollars worth of gold dust in a neighboring Jacksonville bank before he returned to China. According to one source, as he got off the return ship in China, he was robbed and fatally beaten.

Pennsylvania

Chinatown, Philadelphia

The Chinese make up one of Philadelphia's oldest ethnic communities. Since their arrival in the late 1800s, they have made Chinatown the residential and commercial hub of the Chinese American community. Located just two blocks north of Market Street, centered on Tenth and Race Streets, Chinatown is a self-supporting community of small businesses.

Philip Jaisohn Memorial House, Media

In 1888, Philip Jaisohn (1864-1951) became the first Korean to become a naturalized U.S. citizen. Four years later, he became the first Korean American to receive a medical degree in the United States. A physician, businessman, civil servant, and newspaper publisher, Jaisohn played an important role in Korean reform and independence. The Philip Jaisohn Memorial Foundation, established in 1975, founded the Philip Jaisohn Memorial House in 1987 to preserve some of Jaisohn's possessions, including his books and writing. The home, located at 100 East Lincoln Street, is a research center that offers a collection of documents pertaining to Korean immigration; in the near future, it will house the oral histories of Korean immigrants on audio-cassettes.

Utah

Golden Spike National Historic Site, Promontory Point

On May 10, 1869, the Great Plains were linked by rail when spikes of Nevada silver and California gold were driven into a railroad tie made of California laurel. The hammer that drove the spike was connected to telegraph wires so that the sound would be carried across the country. The Union Pacific and Central Pacific Railroads had finally come together, creating the country's first transcontinental railway.

Topaz Relocation Center, Sutherland

One of ten relocation camps where Japanese Americans, mostly U.S. citizens, were incarcerated during World War II, Topaz opened September 11, 1942, and closed October 31, 1945. The peak population at the camp reached 8,130. Sixteen miles away in the city of Delta, the Topaz Monument stands in a park on the city's main street; the town's Great Basin Museum also houses an internment exhibit. At the camp itself, a five-and-a-half-foot monument is surrounded by dry, desolate, sagebrush land.

Washington

International District, Seattle

The area that comprises the International District, or "I.D." as locals call it, was also the site of two Chinatowns and a Japanese area called Nihonmachi. In the 1880s, Seattle's first Chinatown was centered in a much smaller area. The inhabitants had come to the area to work on railroads and in lumber mills or mines. White laborers, who resented the Chinese and their cheap labor, invaded Chinatown in February 1886 and herded almost all of the city's 350 to 400 Chinese toward ships bound for San Francisco. Not until after Seattle's Great Fire of 1889, when they were needed to provide the labor to rebuild the city, did they begin to return.

In the early 1900s, a second Chinatown sprang up, clustered around King and Jackson Streets. At the same time, large groups of Japanese laborers settled just north of the second Chinatown area. This community, which developed into Nihonmachi, had more than 6,000 residents by 1910. World War II took a drastic toll on both ethnic communities, especially because of the displacement of its Japanese residents to concentration camps throughout the West. Fortunately, during the 1970s a concerted effort to revitalize the area brought Chinatown and Nihonmachi together as the integrated International District. Families returned to the area; more businesses began to open; and I.D. became a pan-Asian melting pot filled with a rich mix of Chinese, Japanese, Filipino, Korean, and, most recently, Southeast Asian influences.

Nina Akamu created the 14-foot bronze sculpture depicting two cranes straining for freedom against barbed wire (right) that makes up the centerpiece of the National Japanese American Memorial located near the Capitol in Washington, D.C.

Washington, D.C.

National Japanese American Memorial

The National Japanese American Memorial, operated by the National Park Service, was dedicated on November 9, 2000, and officially opened near the Capitol in Washington, D.C., in June 2001. Described as a memorial to both World War II and civil rights, according to the sponsoring organization, the National Japanese American Memorial Foundation, the purpose of the memorial is "to preserve for posterity the story of a brave and loyal people. And, to tell this Nation that what happened during World War II to these people must never

again happen to any other people because of their race, creed or national origin."

The memorial is dominated by a 14-foot bronze statue of winged cranes struggling through barbed wire created by artist Nina Akamu.

One aspect of the National Japanese American Memorial, the text of an inscription, was controversial among Japanese Americans. Known as the Japanese American Creed, it was written in 1940 by Mike Masaoka, who was a leader of the Japanese American Citizens League during World War II. It reads "I am proud that I am an American of Japanese ancestry. I believe in this nation's institutions, ideals, and traditions. I glory in her heritage; I boast of her history; I trust in her future." Some Japanese Americans believed that Masaoka, in his effort to be cooperative with the government under extreme circumstances, did not speak out strongly enough in support of Japanese Americans' civil rights.

Chinatown, Northwest Washington

Primarily a commercial center, the current Chinatown was established in the early 1930s. This is one of the smallest Chinatowns in the United States. The Chinese Friendship Archway, which marks the entrance into Chinatown, was built by the District government in coordination with the Municipality of Beijing as part of a sister-city exchange program.

Wyoming

Heart Mountain Relocation Center

One of ten relocation camps where Americans of Japanese ancestry were incarcerated during World War II, Heart Mountain opened August 12, 1942, and closed November 10, 1945. The peak population at the camp reached 10,767. Today, the campsite is listed on the National Register of Historic Places as Wyoming #226. Located between Cody and Powell, it is marked by four memorial plaques and a visitor registering post that also provides information about the internment.

Rock Springs Massacre Site, Rock Springs

Rock Springs, located along the Overland Trail, was founded around 1862. The town was an important point on the Union Pacific Railroad and a coal mining center. Until 1875, only white laborers worked in the coal mines run by the Union Pacific. That year, however, the miners went on strike. The company fired them and hired 150 Chinese and 50 white strikebreakers.

By 1885, 331 Chinese and 150 whites worked in the mines, with racial tension building during the decade. On September 2, 1885, violence erupted when a group of whites went into Rock Springs' Chinatown and killed 28 Chinese, wounded another 15, and drove hundreds out of town.

One week later troops from nearby Camp Murray were called in to escort the fleeing Chinese back to Rock Springs. The Union Pacific put them back to work immediately. Sixteen men were eventually arrested and jailed for the attack. However, no indictments were brought against the men, and they were soon released. The surviving Chinese were never compensated for losses to their property.

Suggestions for Further Reading

Chen, Jack, *The Chinese of America*, San Francisco: Harper & Row, 1980.

Cohen, Warren I., *The Asian American Century*, Cambridge, MA: Harvard University Press, 2002.

Daws, Gavan, *Shoals of Time: A History of the Hawaiian Islands*, New York: The MacMillan Company, 1968.

Drinnon, Richard, *Keeper of Concentration Camps: Dillon S. Myer and American Racism*, Berkeley: University of California Press, 1987.

"Duke Kahanamoku Statue," *Hawaiiweb*, http://www.hawaiiweb.com/html/duke_kahanamoku_statue.html (April 28, 2003).

Iritani, Frank, and Joanne Iritani, *Ten Visits: Accounts of Visits to All the Japanese American Relocation Centers*, San Mateo, CA: Japanese American Curriculum Project, Inc., 1994.

Kim, Illsoo, *New Urban Immigrants: The Korean Community of New York*, Princeton, NJ: Princeton University Press, 1981.

Kinkead, Gwen, *Chinatown: A Portrait of a Closed Society*, New York: Harper Collins, 1992.

"Korean Bell of Friendship and Bell Pavilion," *San Pedron, A Whale of A City,* http://www.sanpedrochamber.com/champint/korenbel.htm (accessed May 28, 2003).

Lai, Him Mark, Genny Lim, and Judy Yung, *Island: Poetry and History of Chinese Immigrants on Angel Island, 1910-1940*, Seattle: University of Washington Press, 1980.

O'Brien, David J., and Stephen S. Fugita, *The Japanese American Experience*, Bloomington: Indiana University Press, 1991.

The Story of the National Japanese American Memorial, Washington, DC: National Japanese American Memorial Foundation, 2003.

Weglyn, Michi Nishiura, *Years of Infamy: The Untold Story of America's Concentration Camps*, New York: William Morrow, 1976.

4
Immigration

Immigration Patterns for Asian Americans

FACT FOCUS

- *Chinese immigrants were a key part of the labor force that built the railroads that cross the United States. At the height of construction, nine out of ten workers on the Central Pacific Railroad were Chinese.*
- *The Immigration Act of 1924 essentially ended all Asian immigration to the United States for twenty years.*
- *The McCarran-Walter Act of 1952 officially ended the exclusion of Asian immigrants to the United States.*
- *The 1965 Hart-Celler Act abolished immigration quotas based on national origin.*
- *In 1975, Congress passed the Indochina Refugee Act, exempting up to 200,000 Vietnamese and other Southeast Asians from normal immigration procedures and allowing them to enter the United States.*
- *In 1988, Congress passed the Amerasian Homecoming Act, which brought thousands of Amerasian children, usually the offspring of American servicemen fathers and Asian mothers, to the United States.*
- *By the end of 1993, the Humanitarian Operation Program had brought 70,000 former political prisoners and their families from Asia to the United States.*
- *California has become the home of 409,800 refugees since 1975, almost 40 percent of the total Southeast Asian refugee population.*
- *Almost three million Asian/Pacific Americans entered the United States in the 1980s.*
- *An estimated 500,000 illegal Chinese immigrants entered the United States between 1984 and 1994.*

Asian immigration to the United States began in significant numbers in the 1850s. Chinese and Japanese were the first to immigrate. Later, Koreans, Asian Indians, and Filipinos began to come to the United States also. Most sought to escape poverty by responding to U.S. demands for cheap agricultural and industrial labor. In the early

WORDS TO KNOW

aliens: persons who came from or owe allegiance to another country or government

Amerasian: a person of mixed American and Asian descent; this term is commonly used to describe children of American servicemen fathers and Asian mothers

backlash: a strong negative reaction to a recent social or political development

emigration: the act of moving away; a person emigrates *from* one country when he or she immigrates *to* another

exclusionism: depriving people of a right or privilege

extortion: to get money from someone by threatening them

harassment: persistent annoying or threatening behavior

issei: first-generation Japanese Americans, those who emigrated from Japan; second generation Japanese Americans (first generation born in the United States) are called nisei, and third generation, sansei

immigration quota: the number of immigrants legally allowed from a specific country or region

naturalization: the process of becoming a citizen of a country other than the country of one's birth

refugee: a person who flees his or her homeland to a foreign country to escape danger or persecution

1900s, recruiters representing U.S. employers such as the railroads traveled to Asian countries to court eager workers. Once these workers arrived in the United States, they faced a growing tide of bigotry fueled by white workers' fears of job competition. Adding to their stress and homesickness was the fact that the immigrant communities were mostly composed of men. Very few women from Asia immigrated, forcing the men to exist in what were called "bachelor societies." Some women managed to make the difficult passage, either to join other family members or to take a husband in an arranged marriage. But by the 1920s, the federal government had enacted a series of restrictive policies to virtually seal off the country to further Asian immigration.

Beginnings: 1850 to 1920

From China

The California Gold Rush first drew large numbers of Chinese to the United States. As the immigrants sent word back home of riches to be had on *Gam San* (or "Gold Mountain"), new arrivals joined them at a rate that grew rapidly from 450 in 1850, to 2,716 the following year, to 12,000 in 1852, the peak year. At first, most Chinese earned their living providing services to white miners. However, when Chinese sought the wealth of the gold fields for themselves, whites retaliated with harassment, discriminatory policies, and violence, all of which drove total immigration down to 4,000 by 1853.

In the 1860s, however, the United States once again beckoned to the Chinese, this time with work on the transcontinental railway. At the height of construction, nine out of ten

Sketch by A.R. Ward of "European and Asiatic" workers completing the last mile of the Pacific Railroad.

workers on the Central Pacific Railroad were Chinese. In 1882, the western states, in league with the South, pushed through federal legislation to respond to what they perceived as the growing Chinese "threat." The **Chinese Exclusion Act** banned immigration by Chinese workers and denied future citizenship to all Chinese already in the country. This act was broadened by the turn of the century and renewed indefinitely in 1902. The result was that the Chinese population in the United States decreased rapidly. (Text of this act appears in the **Significant Documents** chapter of this volume.)

From Japan

Japanese immigration to the United States was also set in motion in the 1850s, when American naval officer Commodore Matthew Perry opened Japan to diplomatic and economic relations after 400 years of isolation. Large-scale Japanese immigration to Hawaii began in 1868 with the recruitment of Japanese to work on the sugar and pineapple plantations. When the United States annexed Hawaii in 1900, and its Japanese residents gained the right to enter the United States without passports, thousands of issei, or first-generation immigrants from Japan, moved to the West Coast to farm. There were 70,000 Japanese in the country by 1910. Meanwhile, as the Chinese left, anti-Asian feeling started to focus on the Japanese. President Theodore Roosevelt was pressured into signing the 1907-1908 Gentlemen's Agreement, by which the Japanese government agreed to severely limit the number of passports issued for immigration to the United States. California's 1913 Alien Land Act denying land ownership to aliens ineligible for citizenship was also aimed primarily at the Japanese. It was later copied in other states.

From Korea

Hawaii's plantations also attracted large numbers of Koreans fleeing drought and the hardships imposed on them by Japanese rule. (Korea was dominated by Japan from the late 1800s until the end of World War II, 1945.) Many Koreans were recruited to go to North America by Christian missionaries. Between 1903 and 1907, 7,226 Koreans immigrated to Hawaii and the mainland United States. However, Korean immigration to the United States was abruptly cut off in 1905 when Japan, having declared Korea a protectorate, prohibited Korean immigration to Hawaii. Altogether, some 8,000 Koreans immigrated to the United States between 1903 and 1920, including "picture brides" who emigrated from Korea to marry Korean laborers overseas.

From India

Most immigration by Asian Indians occurred after 1905. The first immigrants were small farmers, mostly Sikhs who immigrated to countries all over the world, including the United States. Between 1906 and 1908, nearly 5,000 Indian contract laborers, mostly from the Punjab region of India, immigrated to Canada. When that country began turning them away, some migrated southward to Washington, Oregon, and California, where many worked on the railroad, in lumber mills, and in agriculture. Although 3,453 Asian Indians were denied entry into the United States between 1908 and 1920 due to exclusionist policies, 6,400 had been admitted by 1920.

Between the Wars: The Triumph of Exclusionism

Discrimination against Asian immigrants reached its peak around the time of World War I (1914–18). In 1910, the congressionally appointed Dillingham Commission issued a report on immigration, complete with "scientific" findings claiming the inferiority of recent immigrants—including both Asians and growing numbers of newcomers from southern and eastern Europe—compared to the original settlers from northern and western Europe.

Immigration Acts of 1917 and 1924

The Immigration Act of 1917, based on the findings of the Dillingham Commission, prohibited all immigration by laborers from the "Asiatic Barred Zone," which included India, Indochina, Afghanistan, Arabia, the East Indies, and other, smaller Asian countries. (China and Japan, already covered by previous measures, were not included.) The **Immigration Act** of 1924 reduced total annual immigration levels, set quotas that favored northern and western Europeans, and barred entry completely to

Sketch by H.A. Rodgers depicting a rally against Chinese laborers.

"aliens ineligible for citizenship." This reaffirmed Chinese exclusion and effectively ended all further Japanese immigration. In combination with the 1917 Act, the 1924 Immigration Act essentially ended Asian immigration to the United States for twenty years.

Filipinos—American Nationals

There was one group of Asians who remained untouched by the acts to restrict immigration. Filipinos, citizens of the Philippines, began arriving in the United States around 1910. They were not subject to immigration laws because they were not, technically, foreigners: the Philippines was a U.S. territory, acquired at the end of the Spanish-American War, and its inhabitants, while not U.S. citizens, were considered "American nationals." A rapid flow of immigrants in the 1920s brought a dramatic rise in the total U.S. Filipino population to 45,208 by the end of the decade. Like other Asian immigrants before them, Filipinos found themselves subjected to white working-class backlash and racist attitudes. The 1924 Immigration Act ending Asian immigration was not applicable to Filipinos. The 1934 Tydings-McDuffie Act, however, established the Philippines as a commonwealth and provided for its independence in ten years. This meant that Filipinos lost their exemption from restrictive immigration legislation; they were reclassified as aliens, with an annual immigration quota of only 50.

Post-World War II Liberalization

World War II (1939–45) bolstered Chinese immigration to the United States in a small but significant way. After China became a U.S. ally in its war with Japan, Congress finally repealed the Chinese Exclusion Act on December 17, 1943, and opened up U.S. citizenship to foreign-born Chinese. However, the Chinese received only a token quota of 105, and were the sole exception to the exclusion of Asian immigrants.

After the war, more laws liberalized Asian immigration. In 1946, the Luce-Celler Bill granted small immigration quotas and naturalization rights to Asian Indians and Filipinos. The following year, the War Brides Act of 1946 was amended to allow entry to Chinese war brides of Chinese American soldiers. By 1953, over 7,000 Chinese women had immigrated as war brides.

McCarran-Walter Act. The **Immigration and Nationality Act** of 1952 (the McCarran-Walter Act) officially ended the exclusion policies that had been directed at Asians in the past. However, the act remained discriminatory, according immigrants from northern and western Europe 85 percent of the total annual quota. Japan was given a quota of 185, China's quota remained at 105, and countries in the area designated as the Asia-Pacific Triangle received quotas of 100 each. The act removed all bans on the naturalization of foreign-born Asians; it also increased the number of non-quota immi-

Immigration to the United States, as Percent of U.S. Total Immigration	
Total Immigration from 1920 to 1960	
—from Europe	60%
—from Central and South America	35%
—from Asia	3%
Immigration in 1975	
—from Europe	19%
—from Central and South America	43%
—from Asia	34%

Source: Susan B. Gall and Timothy L. Gall, editors, *Statistical Record of Asian Americans*, Gale, 1993, p. 410.

grants (immigrants who were not counted in filling the annual quota), including immediate relatives of citizens and permanent residents.

Immigration and Nationality Act of 1965 (Hart-Celler Act). By the late 1950s and early 1960s, U.S. immigration policy was becoming increasingly incompatible with both the changing attitudes toward race at home and the country's Cold War reputation as "leader of the free world." Urged by presidents John F. Kennedy and Lyndon B. Johnson, Congress enacted a wide-ranging immigration policy reform. The **Immigration and Nationality Act** of 1965, known as the Hart-Celler Act, abolished the national origins quota system and the designation of the Asia-Pacific Triangle, finally terminating discrimination against Asian immigrants. The total annual immigration ceiling was raised to 290,000, with 170,000 visas available altogether for countries in the

President Lyndon B. Johnson chose the site of the Statue of Liberty for the signing of the immigration law repealing quotas by national origin.

Eastern Hemisphere and no limit for any one country. Applicants were to be approved on a first-come, first-served basis, with special preferences for family reunification and vocational skills.

The 1965 Immigration Act drastically changed the nature of immigration to the United States. Between 1920 and 1960, 60 percent of all immigrants to the United States came from Europe, 35 percent from Central and South America, and only 3 percent from Asia. By 1975 Europe accounted for 19 percent of all immigration, while the totals for Asia and the Americas had risen, respectively, to 34 and 43 percent. Chinese immigration rose from 1,000 quota and non-quota immigrants per year in the decade preceding 1965 to 9,000 in 1975.

Immigration by Asian Indians rose from 300 in 1965 to 14,000 in 1975; over three decades, Korean immigration would grow more than tenfold. The Immigration Act of 1965 also set the stage for the dramatic wave of immigration from Southeast Asia that would begin ten years later.

After the Vietnam War: Refugees from Southeast Asia

A mass exodus of refugees from Southeast Asia—Vietnam, Cambodia, and Laos—began in 1975, when the Vietnam War ended and power was seized by the Pathet Lao in Laos and the Khmer Rouge in Cambodia. The first wave of refugees, approximately 130,000 men, women, and children, arrived in the United States within a year. These early arrivals were temporarily housed in refugee camps set up by the U.S. government. Several charity organizations, working closely with and supported by the federal government, immediately began resettlement efforts. With the assistance of these private sponsors, the refugees were relocated to communities across the nation.

Indochina Refugee Act and Orderly Departure Program. Special legislation was necessary to admit such a large group of immigrants at one time. Congress passed the 1975 Indochina Refugee Act, allowing up to 200,000 Vietnamese and other Southeast Asians to enter the United States exempt from the normal immigration process and restrictions. Continuing repression in Vietnam—including reeducation camps, forcible resettlement, and privatization of businesses—led to a new wave of emigration in the late 1970s.

In late 1978, 85,000 Vietnamese took to the sea in rickety, overcrowded fishing boats. Turned away by neighboring countries, many were preyed upon by pirates in the Gulf of Thailand. Alarmed at the potential for loss of life created by this situation, the United States and the free world community called for international action. The Orderly Departure Program (ODP) was established in May 1979 to provide a safe alternative to clandestine escape by sea. Refugees were allowed to leave Vietnam directly for resettlement in one of two dozen countries, including the United States. In July 1979, President Jimmy Carter expanded the admission quota for Southeast Asian refugees from 7,000 to 14,000 per month. This brought large numbers of all Southeast Asian nationality groups into the country.

Among the 130,000 Southeast Asians who arrived in 1975, approximately 125,000 were Vietnamese. The 118,000 arrivals between 1976 and 1979 were ethnically more diverse, with about 60,000 Vietnamese, 49,000 Laotian (including a substantial number of Hmong), and 9,000 Cambodians. When Vietnam invaded Cambodia in 1979, hundreds of thousands of Cambodians fled. Over 100,000 were resettled in the United States by the end of the decade, as were a comparable number of Laotian refugees. Other Southeast Asian groups joined the refugee population in later years.

Amerasians, Unaccompanied Minors, and Detainees. Amerasians—children of American fathers and Asian mothers—benefited very little from the Orderly Departure Program. The Vietnamese government sharply limited their emigration to pressure the United States for recognition and aid.

Discrimination against these biracial young people limited their opportunities for education and employment in Vietnam. Under the provisions of the Amerasian Homecoming Act of 1988, over 56,000 Amerasian youths and their family members arrived in the United States.

Many children without parents or guardians, often referred to as "unaccompanied minors," found themselves among the refugees from Southeast Asia. From 1979 to 1992 a total of 10,638 unaccompanied minors were cared for in a federally funded program operated by volunteer agencies, private organizations, and state governments that cared for the children until they reached adulthood. As of September 30, 1992, 2,149 refugee children received care in projects throughout the United States.

In 1989, after many years of intense American diplomatic efforts, the Socialist Republic of Vietnam agreed to release its former "reeducation camp" detainees—or political prisoners—for immigration to the United States. Most of these were military or civilian officials of the former government of South Vietnam detained since 1975. By the end of 1993, the Humanitarian Operation Program had brought 70,000 of these former political prisoners and members of their families to the United States.

Results of Resettlement

From the beginning of its resettlement effort in 1975, the U.S. government wanted to disperse Southeast Asian refugees throughout the country, hoping to minimize their socioeconomic impact on any single community and to ease the refugees' adaptation to their new country. For a variety of reasons, the policy produced mixed results.

Hanh Huynh, left, Huong Huynh, center, and Thu Phan live in the neighborhood in San Diego known as "Little Saigon" because of the high concentration of Vietnamese refugees.

Many refugees wanted to live in a few selected states, with California leading the list. New arrivals joined their families in these states, significantly expanding the size of existing refugee communities. Despite government efforts to scatter the refugee population throughout the country, settlement patterns emerged. By 1980, Vietnamese and Cambodians were concentrated in the Southwest. In contrast, Laotians were more likely to settle in the northern and midwestern states.

California has become the home of 409,800 refugees since 1975, almost 40 percent of the total Southeast Asian refugee population in the United States. In 1991, close to 38 percent of arrivals from Southeast Asia settled in California, more than the number who settled in the next nine most populous states combined.

Secondary Migration. After being resettled initially in a community, a substantial number of refugees decided to move to another city or state. This process is called "secondary migration." A refugee may decide to migrate for any one of several reasons: warmer climate, availability of employment opportunities and better training programs, more generous welfare benefits, reunification with relatives, and the presence of a larger ethnic community. Many moved to California or other states with large refugee concentrations.

Anti-Immigration Trends

With total immigration in the 1980s reaching record levels of nearly ten million—including almost three million Asians and Pacific Islanders—a new wave of anti-immigrant feeling arose in the United States. Pressure to curb immigration was fed by a shaky economy, a conservative political climate, and a decline in federal aid to immigrants. As the federal government cut back on aid to new immigrants, more of the economic burden shifted to individual states. This issue is especially important to those states with large concentrations of illegal immigrants.

Proposition 187

In 1992, 86 percent of the United States's 3.4 million illegal aliens lived in seven states: California, New York, Texas, Florida, Illinois, New Jersey, and Arizona. One-third lived in California, which spent $1.3 billion on education for 300,000 children of illegal immigrants in 1992. Two years later, in 1994, California voters passed Proposition 187, denying health, education, and welfare benefits to illegal immigrants and their children. The controversial regulation triggered a number of legal actions. When Gray Davis was elected Governor of California in 1998, he stepped in to stop the appeals process on the proposition, and virtually eliminated it.

California's action fueled sentiment against illegal immigrants in other states. A week after the passage of Proposition 187 in 1994, a group called "Save Our State" announced a campaign to pass an anti-illegal immigration law in Arizona.

Legal immigration also came under attack in the 1990s. In 1994, a proposed bill in the U.S. House of Representatives was designed not only to crack down on illegal immigration, but also to reduce legal immigration by around 20 percent.

In 1996, the U.S. Congress passed the Immigration Reform and Immigrant Responsibility Act. The law states that noncitizens who have overstayed their visas can be deported. If the noncitizen has overstayed his or her visa for six months, he or she is barred from returning to the United States for three years. If the person had stayed in the United States longer than a year after the visa expired, he or she may be deported and barred from returning for ten years.

The law also made it easier for government officials to arrest and detain noncitizens while crimes are under investigation. Hyung Joon Kim, a citizen of South Korea who had been convicted of two crimes in

1996 and 1997, and the Immigration and Naturalization Service initiated deportation proceedings against Kim because of the convictions. Kim was detained without bond, because under the Immigration Reform and Immigrant Responsibility Act, it is legal to detain noncitizens who are waiting to be deported because they have committed certain crimes.

Suggestions for Further Reading

Asian Americans and Congress: A Documentary History, Westport, CT: Greenwood Press, 1996.

Chan, Sucheng, *Asian Americans: An Interpretive History,* Boston: Twayne Publishers, 1991.

Chinese Immigrants and American Law, New York: Garland Publishing, 1994.

Davis, Wendy M., *Closing the Borders,* New York: Thomson Learning, 1995.

Dixon, Edward H., *The Immigration and Naturalization Service,* New York: Chelsea House, 1990.

Gilmore, Rachna, *Lights for Gita,* Gardiner, ME: Tilbury House, 1995.

"History of Proposition 187," California Coalition for Immigration Reform, http://ccir.net/REFERENCE/187-History.html (accessed May 7, 2003).

National Immigration Law Center, http://www.nilc.org/new/index.htm (accessed June 4, 2003).

Odo, Franklin, ed., *The Columbia Documentary History of the Asian American Experience,* New York: Columbia University Press, 2002.

5

Civil Rights

Asian American Activism and Anti-Asian Violence

FACT FOCUS

- *In the 1960s Asian Americans joined other minority groups in organized activism for civil rights.*
- *The term "Asian American" replaced "Oriental" as activists worked to have Americans of Asian descent acknowledged as equal and part of American society.*
- *Activists campaigned for the establishment of Asian American studies programs at colleges and universities.*
- *Anti-Asian sentiment has been a factor in a growing number of violent crimes in the United States against Asians of all ethnic groups.*

In the early 1960s, many minority groups began to organize to assert their rights to equal treatment in U.S society. Formed in 1930 under the banner of loyalty, patriotism, and U.S. citizenship, the Japanese American Citizens League (JACL) was one of the groups that took an activist stand in the 1960s. JACL was a nisei (second-generation Japanese American) civic organization dedicated to gaining acceptance for its people. On August 28, 1963, more than 200,000 demonstrators—including representatives from JACL—were led by Martin Luther King, Jr., in a march on Washington, D.C., to protest civil rights violations.

Moved to action by the 1960s civil rights movement, Asian Americans focused on concerns they shared with other minorities: equal access to and treatment by the educational system; fair employment for farmworkers; and an end to discrimination in U.S. immigration policy. While these concerns were technically separate from the civil rights movement, they were similar in spirit. They triggered the Asian American movement of the late 1960s and early 1970s.

The Student Movement

In the 1960s, Asian Americans began to join together to form organizations dedicated to achieving equality, and sometimes to work toward a specific goal. Groups formed in major cities and on university campuses across the United States.

San Francisco State College Strike

At San Francisco State College, students formed the Third World Liberation Front (TWLF), a coalition of African American, Latino, and Asian American groups. TWLF demanded reforms in the school's curriculum and policies. After more than a year of negotiating and organizing, TWLF called a strike on November 6, 1968. It became the longest student strike in U.S. history. When it was finally settled in March 1969, many of the students' demands were met, including the establishment of a School of Ethnic Studies.

Intercollegiate Chinese for Social Action. One of the groups involved in the TWLF was the Intercollegiate Chinese for Social Action (ICSA). Formed in November 1967, ICSA worked in San Francisco's Chinatown, setting up a youth center, initiating tutorial projects for teenagers, volunteering at the office of the War on Poverty (a U.S. government program), and teaching English to Chinese immigrants.

Philippine-American Collegiate Endeavor. Another group that was active in the TWLF was the Philippine-American Collegiate Endeavor (PACE). Organized in the spring of 1968, PACE encouraged Filipino American students to fight for positive change in their community and on campus. They organized high school recruitment drives that encouraged Filipino youth to apply to college through the Equal Opportunity Program, held tutorials and counseling programs to help students stay in school once they were

---

WORDS TO KNOW

activist: a person who takes action supporting or opposing a political issue

assimilate: to become like or similar to, to join

audit: methodical examination or review

civil rights: the rights of an individual to equal treatment and equal access to the benefits of society, such as housing, free speech, employment, and education

coalition: two or more groups working together toward a common goal

manong: immigrant to the United States from the Philippines

---

admitted, and worked vigorously within San Francisco's Manilatown, where a large concentration of Filipino Americans lived. Out of the estimated 125 Filipino students on campus, close to 70 were PACE members.

Asian American Political Alliance. The Asian American Political Alliance (AAPA) was also involved with the TWLF. Formed in the summer of 1968, AAPA sought to organize around issues facing all Asian Americans and to recognize their common history of struggle in the United States. The group's name is believed to be the first use of "Asian" instead of "Oriental."

The legacy left by the Asian American activists in the San Francisco State strike cannot be underestimated. Besides establishing an ethnic studies program, which soon spread to other U.S. colleges, the students helped inspire a wellspring of activism that created Asian American community centers, self-help clinics, and other institutions that are still in operation.

The Labor Movement

Asian Americans built the transcontinental railroad, worked in the mines, farmed the plantations of Hawaii and California's Central Valley, worked in the fish canning industries along the Pacific Coast, and labored in sweatshops, laundries, and restaurants from Honolulu to New York.

Although Asian American workers toiled for generations to build the United States, the American labor movement historically opposed Asian immigration and union membership. The American Federation of Labor and the California Workingmen's Party forcefully demanded passage of the **Chinese Exclusion Act** of 1882, which curtailed immigration of Chinese workers and prohibited naturalization for Chinese in the United States. (Text of the act appears in the *Significant Documents* chapter of this volume.)

Labor unions blamed Asians for unemployment and other social ills. Union leaders feared that Asian labor would be used to lower wages and break strikes. They opposed the inclusion of Asian workers into unions, believing they could neither be assimilated nor organized.

In spite of the exclusion policies of labor unions, Asian American workers organized themselves. As early as 1867, thousands of Chinese American railroad workers led a strike to demand higher wages. From the plantations of Hawaii to the fields of California, Asian American workers took collective action to demand better living and working conditions. Asian American workers participated in numerous labor-organizing activities in the 1930s.

The Farmworkers Movement

Filipino Americans, since their arrival in the United States in the 1920s, helped build the farmworkers movement through leadership, backbreaking labor, and participation in numerous strikes against growers for fair wages and working conditions. On September 8, 1965, the largely Filipino American Agricultural Workers Organizing Committee (AWOC) voted to strike against the Delano, California, grape growers. In retrospect, some feel it was the most significant strike vote ever taken in the history of the farmworkers movement.

Before 1965, the farmworkers movement was organized along traditional trade union lines. AWOC found an important ally in the National Farm Workers Association (NFWA), a primarily Hispanic labor union led by César Chávez. As the strike progressed, AWOC and NFWA worked together to build support for their movement.

In March 1966, six months after the strike began, NFWA raised the stakes by organizing a 200-mile march from Delano to the California state capitol in Sacramento. Larry Itliong and several Filipino leaders in the union broke ranks with other AWOC leaders and joined the NFWA march under the AWOC banner. With camaraderie at a new high, the two unions merged in August 1966 as the United Farm Workers Organizing Committee (UFWOC), later shortening the name to the United Farm Workers (UFW). Chávez was named director of the new

Filipino farm workers on an asparagus ranch in California around 1950.

union while Filipino Americans Larry Itliong, Philip Vera Cruz, and Andy Imutan from AWOC were among those named vice presidents, essentially acting as part of a board of directors.

On July 29, 1970, the Delano growers were forced to recognize the UFW and signed labor contracts with the union. In 1971, Vera Cruz was elected second vice president, becoming the highest-ranking Filipino in the union.

Asian American Labor Union Participation

Since the 1960s, with the tremendous growth of the Asian American work force, the number of Asian/Pacific Americans in labor unions has also grown. Hundreds of thousands of Asian/Pacific Americans are union members, including New York garment workers in the International Ladies' Garment Workers Union; Seattle cannery workers in the International Longshoremen and Warehousemen Workers Union; Honolulu government workers in the American Federation of State, County, and Municipal Employees; San Francisco nurses in the Service Employees International Union; and Los Angeles supermarket workers in the United Food and Commercial Workers Union, to name only a few.

Asian/Pacific American Labor Alliance

In 1992, the Asian/Pacific American Labor Alliance (APALA) held its founding convention. Five hundred Asian American unionists participated, representing 35 unions from 22 states and a wide range of Asian and Pacific Islander heritages. For the first time, Asian American unionists from all over the country had an opportunity to meet one another, address common interests, and plan for the future.

At the founding convention, seven Asian/Pacific American labor pioneers were honored: educator Sue Kunitomi Embrey of the United Teachers of Los Angeles/American Federation of Teachers and the National Education Association; Morgan Jin, vice-chair of the newspaper guild unit at the *New York Times;* Ah Quon McElrath of the International Longshoremen and Warehousemen Workers Union Local 142 in Hawaii; Art Takei of the United Food and Commercial Workers Union (UFCW) Local 770 in Southern California; Philip Vera Cruz, a former vice president of the United Farm Workers Union; George Wong, founder and president of the Asian American Federation of Union Members in San Francisco; and Karl Yoneda of the International Longshoremen and Warehousemen Workers Union.

At its annual convention in 1993, APALA honored four more pioneers in the crusade for Asian American civil rights. Among them were Fred Korematsu, the civil rights proponent who called upon the U.S. Supreme Court to rule on the internment of Japanese Americans during World War II; Yuri Kochiyama, a peace and community activist from New York who died in 1994; David Trask, Jr., a noted Hawaiian labor

> ## WORDS OF PHILIP VERA CRUZ, FILIPINO LABOR ACTIVIST
>
> "When my mother asked me how long I planned to stay away, I told her three years. Well, I've been here in the U.S. almost 50 years now and I haven't been back yet. . . . I always just had enough money to send home but as far as having enough money for myself to return and lead my own life, it never happened. My life here was always just a matter of survival. . . . That's the way it has been for most of us Filipino old-timers."

leader; and Frank Atonio, who brought forward a complaint in the important labor discrimination case known as Wards Cove (see below).

Wards Cove Case. One civil rights campaign that APALA has actively pursued involves the Wards Cove cannery workers of Alaska. The Asian/Pacific Islander workers of Wards Cove Packing Company filed a discrimination suit in 1974 to protest the "plantation style" segregation at the cannery. All of the best jobs at the cannery were reserved for whites, while Asian and Pacific Islander workers were relegated to inferior job assignments as well as to separate dining and living facilities. This case went all the way to the U.S. Supreme Court, where it was used, unfortunately, to set a more difficult standard for proving employment discrimination. This misdeed was changed by Congress in the Civil Rights Act of 1991.

Filipino labor activist Larry Itliong.

future. From their perspective, even in the days of labor union glory, Asian American workers were largely excluded. In that sense, the formation of APALA reflects opportunities that may not have previously existed for Asian/Pacific Americans.

By building alliances between unions and Asian American communities, defending civil and workers' rights, and embracing a vision of unity among workers of all colors, APALA is striving to help build a new labor movement that reflects the hopes and aspirations of all working people.

In 1997, APALA launched the "Campaign for Worker Justice" to reach out into communities to organize workers. Through APALA's training programs, organizers—who can communicate with workers in their native Asian languages—including Cantonese, Korean, Hindi, Vietnamese, Tagalog, and Hmong—learn how to motivate workers to form unions and to participate in local politics. APALA has helped to bring over 500,000 Asian American and Pacific Islander workers into the labor movement.

However, due to an exemption proposed by Alaskan senators, the Wards Cove workers were excluded from protection by the very law that was enacted to correct the previous court ruling. The message from Congress was clear: the rights and interests of Asian and Pacific Island workers were vulnerable to shifts in attitude or circumstances.

The decades of the 1980s and 1990s were difficult times for the American labor movement. The percentage of workers who are members of unions declined from about 35 percent in the 1960s to about 17 percent in the mid-1990s. However, the leaders of APALA have an optimistic view of labor's

Anti-Asian American Violence

The first national audit of violence against Asian/Pacific Americans was conducted in 1994 by the National Asian Pacific American Legal Consortium (NAPALC). The goal of the audit was to motivate public and private leaders to address this widespread and serious problem. While acts of discriminatory violence have occurred throughout U.S. history, in the 1980s and 1990s violent threats and acts committed because of race, national origin, religion, sexual orientation, or other characteristics were recognized as a national problem.

Labor activists of all ethnicities join an Asian Pacific American Labor Alliance march in Washington, D.C.

The number of hate crimes increased in the late 1980s and early 1990s. Of the 4,755 hate crimes reported in 1991, acts against Asian/Pacific Americans comprised 6 percent of the total, an amount higher than the 2.9 percent that Asian/Pacific Americans represented in the U.S. population that year. The number of hate crimes may be even greater than reported, since many police departments around the nation did not report bias-incident statistics.

In 2002 NAPALC published *Backlash: When America Turned on Its Own,* which included the annual audit of hate crimes against Asian Pacific Americans. The report noted an increase in anti-Asian violence following the terrorist attacks on New York and Washington, D.C., that took place on September 11, 2001. In the last three months of 2001, the audit reported nearly 250 bias-motivated incidents targeting Asian Pacific Americans (APA) in general and South Asians (Asian Indian Americans, Pakistani Americans, and Bandladeshi Americans) in particular; this spike in anti-APA violence contributed to a 23 percent increase in total anti-Asian violence in 2001 compared to 2000. In the late 1990s and 2000, the number of anti-APA incidents reported averaged 400–500 per year. The states with the highest number of anti-APA incidents in 2001 were California (with 128 reported); New York (94); New Jersey (71); Maryland (47); and Massachusetts (39).

Harassment and Hate Violence: A Case Study. When Southeast Asian tenants moved into certain San Francisco Housing Authority (SFHA) housing projects, many were subjected to name-calling, physical and emotional intimidation, threats, assaults, and even beatings and killings. Children were harassed and assaulted on their way to and from school. Units were robbed and vandalized, with rocks and eggs thrown at windows. Tenants with limited English-speaking abilities, such as those from Southeast Asia, could not even report such incidents because there were no bilingual housing project staff.

A recognizable pattern in this harassment and hate violence developed. National Asian Pacific American Legal Consortium (NAPALC) and Asian Law Caucus (ALC) attorneys realized the problem was more than a few racist individuals. The antagonism toward these tenants arose from larger institutional dynamics, including economic and language issues, as well as from ignorance and prejudice.

As a result of a lawsuit on behalf of the tenants against the SFHA and U.S. Department of Housing and Urban Development (HUD), the agencies agreed to improve security, provide language assistance, institute staff training, provide support services for new tenants and community organizations, and change discriminatory assignment and transfer policies. This settlement offers a model for improving community relations and reducing racial hostility.

Suggestions for Further Reading

Asian Americans and the Supreme Court: A Documentary History, Westport, CT: Greenwood Press, 1992.

Asian Pacific American Labor Alliance, http://www.apalanet.org/ (accessed May 20, 2003).

Backlash: When America Turned on Its Own, Washington, DC: National Asian Pacific American Legal Consortium, 2002.

Banks, Jacqueline Turner, *A Day for Vincent Chin and Me,* Boston: Houghton Mifflin, 2001.

Banton, Michael P., *Discrimination,* Berkshire, England: Open University Press, 1994.

Everything You Need to Know About Bias Incidents, New York: Rosen Publishing Group, 1993.

Hate Crimes, San Diego: Greenhaven Press, 1996.

Hate Crimes: The Rising Tide of Bigotry and Bloodshed, New York: Plenum Press, 1993.

Nguyen, Viet Thanh, *Race & Resistance: Literature & Politics in Asian America,* New York: Oxford University Press, 2002.

United States Commission on Civil Rights, *Civil Rights Issues Facing Asian Americans in the 1990s: A Report of the United States Commission on Civil Rights,* Washington, DC: U.S. Government Printing Office, 1992.

6

The Legal System in the United States

Laws, Lawmakers, Lawyers, and Criminal Justice

FACT FOCUS

- Early laws prohibited immigration to the United States from Asian countries; they also targeted Asian residents for special taxes and license requirements.
- Asian Americans are nearly 3 percent of the total population, but make up less than 2 percent of the total number of lawyers in the United States.
- Thirty-three of the 50 states have no Asian American federal or state judges.
- Less that 1 percent of the population of prisoners in U.S. prisons is Asian American.
- Six percent of hate crimes were directed against Asian Americans in 1991.

Laws Against Asian Americans

Early Anti-Asian Laws

Anti-Asian sentiment and legal exclusion have been dominant factors in Asian American history. The influx of Chinese immigrants into California in the 1850s provoked an anti-Chinese backlash in California that was felt from union halls to the governor's office. Chinese, hearing news of gold mines and good wages for laborers, flooded onto ships headed for *Gum San,* or "Gold Mountain," as the United States was called. In response to the immigration wave, the California legislature passed a number of laws that were either explicitly prejudicial or effectively discriminated against the Chinese.

In 1850, the California state legislature passed a $3 tax on any foreign miner not intending to become a citizen. At the time, federal law prohibited Chinese from becoming citizens. Thus, an estimated $5 million,

WORDS TO KNOW

affirmative action: a program designed to remedy the effects of past discrimination and to end such discrimination

alien: foreign-born resident of a country

backlash: a strong negative reaction to a recent social or political event

bilingual: speaking two languages with equal fluency

discrimination: treatment or judgment of a person based on something other than merit

exclusion: barring from participation in an activity or group

hate crime: illegal acts committed against a person because of the victim's characteristics, such as race, religion, or sexual orientation

internment camp: remote, primitive camp where Americans of Japanese descent were held as prisoners during World War II, on the theory that they were risks to U.S. military security

miscegenation: marriage between two races, especially between a white person and a person of another race

multilingual: speaking three or more languages with fluency

naturalization: admission as a citizen

redress: compensation for a loss

segregation: the enforced separation of a race, ethnic group, or social class in education, housing, and other social arenas

about half of the state's revenue, was collected from Chinese miners before the tax was voided twenty years later. In 1854, perhaps the greatest discriminatory act to the Chinese was implemented when the state of California barred any Chinese from testifying in court against white people. In the case of *Hall* v. *People,* a white man had been convicted of murder by the testimony of Chinese witnesses. Judge Charles J. Murray reversed the verdict, citing the Criminal Act of 1850, which provided that "No Black, or Mulato person, or Indian, shall be allowed to give evidence in favor of, or against a White man." Murray declared Chinese equally ineligible to give testimony. For the next 18 years, crimes against Chinese in California (including murder) were committed on a daily basis, with very few arrests.

In 1882, in an attempt to "protect Free White Labor against competition with Chinese Coolie Labor, and to Discourage the Immigration of the Chinese," California passed the monthly Alien Poll Tax, a head tax of $2.50 per month for most Chinese living in the state. At the end of the century, hard economic times inspired many more discriminatory laws affecting Asians in both the economic and social arenas. Ship captains faced fines and imprisonment for bringing Chinese to the Pacific coast; California schools were segregated to separate Chinese, Native American, and African American children from white children; and the state legislature passed an anti-miscegenation law prohibiting the marriage of whites to persons "negro, mulatto, or Mongolian."

Cries of "Yellow Peril" also reached the nation's capital. In 1882, Congress overwhelmingly passed the **Chinese Exclusion Act,** barring all Chinese laborers from entering the United States and prohibiting naturalization of those already here. This act marked the first time a specific group was restricted from immigrating. Several Chinese immigrants challenged the constitutionality of the act, but the Supreme Court of the United States rebuffed their claims in a series of cases beginning in 1889. The Court deferred to the government's sovereign (supreme) right to exclude or deport alien residents. It also recognized national security concerns as a justification for restricting the "scourge of yellow people" entering the labor market. In 1917, Congress created the "Asiatic barred zone," which excluded emigration from most Asian countries other than Japan. The **Immigration Act** of 1924 effectively barred all Asian immigration by prohibiting admission of any "alien ineligible [for] citizenship." (The text of these acts appears in the **Significant Documents** chapter of this volume.)

Asians and Pacific Islanders mobilized and brought challenges to such laws in state and federal courts as early as the nineteenth century. Not surprisingly, court records do not tell the complete story, because most grievances were unreported and, if reported, were judged under laws and by courts that routinely allowed discrimination against Asian/Pacific persons. In one court's view, the Chinese were "a race of people whom nature has marked as inferior, and who are incapable of progress or intellectual development beyond a certain point."

Despite such setbacks, Asian Americans continued to appeal to the courts for legal protection. In *Yick Wo* v. *Hopkins* in 1886, they won a major victory when Chinese laundry owners challenged a San Francisco

---

TIME LINE

1882 Chinese Exclusion Act barred all Chinese laborers from entering the United States and prohibited naturalization of those already here.

1924 Immigration Act effectively barred all Asian immigration by prohibiting admission of any "alien ineligible [for] citizenship."

1943 Congress repealed the Chinese Exclusion Act of 1882.

1990 Hate Crimes Statistics Act was passed to begin recording incidences of hate crimes nationwide.

1991 Civil Rights Act was passed providing for damages in cases of intentional employment discrimination.

---

ordinance that prohibited operating laundries in wooden buildings without the consent of county supervisors. The Supreme Court of the United States struck down the ordinance because it enabled local officials selectively to drive out Chinese businesses, even though the law did not literally target any racial class. In addition, the case extended the constitutional protection of equal treatment under the laws to non-citizens.

Overall, however, anti-Asian legislation and legal defeats were common through the turn of the twentieth century. Alien land laws passed in Washington and California in the early 1900s prohibited persons ineligible for citizenship from purchasing land. These laws specifically targeted newly arriving Japanese farmers and, like earlier anti-Chinese laws, were used to discourage immigration. Judicial tolerance of anti-Asian laws reached its most significant expression in World War II (1939–45) when detention and curfew laws against the 120,000 Japanese American citizens confined in internment camps withstood constitutional challenges.

The Legacy of Anti-Asian Laws

The legacy of exclusion and anti-Asian sentiment continues to appear in laws affecting Asian Americans. Record immigration of Asians and Pacific Islanders to the United States reached almost three million people in the 1980s. This is more than twice the number of the previous decade, and will likely aggravate controversy over immigration and immigrants. Two issues, "English only" rules and conflict among minority groups, illustrate some of the racial tensions that continue to challenge Asian Americans.

Official English Movement

United States English, a national lobbying group claiming more than 500,000 members in 1993, has spearheaded most of the Official English campaigns underway today. The organization lobbies for the exclusive use of English in government, the restriction of bilingual education, the elimination of multilingual ballots, and the ratifications of an amendment to the United States Constitution confirming the officiality of the English language in the United States.

Some of the goals of United States English have become reality. In 1984, 70 percent of voting Californians passed an initiative to rescind (remove) bilingual ballots and voting materials. Two years later, they returned to the polls and approved an English Language Amendment to the State Constitution to "preserve, protect and strengthen ... English." The amendment is largely symbolic since it does not require the elimination of any currently existing multilingual government services. It has, however, been used to justify "English only" rules in the workplace and to stop further creation of multilingual programs. Similar amendments were passed in Colorado, Florida, and Arizona in 1988. In 1990, however, a federal court declared that the Arizona amendment violated the First Amendment of the United States Constitution (freedom of speech), thereby casting doubt on the legal status of other such measures.

The number of people with limited English proficiency is growing; immigration now outstrips new births as the leading source of Asian American population growth. According to 1990 census figures, the five largest Asian ethnic groups in the United States, comprising three-fourths of all Asians in the country, are Chinese, Filipino, Japanese, East Indian, and Korean. Sixty-three percent of each of these groups, except the Japanese, are foreign-born, and 55 to 73 percent of each of the non-Japanese groups speaks a language other than English at home. In response to this population growth, Congress passed the Federal Voting Rights Language Assistance Act of 1992, broadening the availability of bilingual ballots. The 1992 standard should allow at least sizable populations of Asian language speakers to qualify for bilingual ballots.

Interethnic Conflict

A second illustration of a recent anti-Asian law arises from conflicts among minority groups. Tensions between Korean American and African American communities were apparent in the aftermath of the riots in South Central Los Angeles following the 1992 acquittal of four white police officers charged with the beating of African American motorist Rodney King. In the consequent rebuilding, the Los Angeles City Council passed an ordinance to speed up permit procedures for those businesses damaged in the riots that were not "materially detrimental" (that is, businesses that were not harmful) to the neighborhood. Thus, swap meet concessions, auto repair shops, gun stores, second-hand stores, and businesses selling alcoholic beverages were required to apply for relicensing through a public hearing. While the new city ordinance did not explicitly target them, many Korean Americans felt it was used to drive them out of business. Some African American community members argued that Korean American businesses made conditions worse in a community that was overwhelmed by alcohol-related violence and was saturated with the city's highest concentration of liquor stores, about 1 for every 700 residents. By the end of 1993, 45 percent of the Korean American-owned businesses in the area still had not reopened.

Mobilization Against Anti-Asian Laws and Judicial Decisions

Asian Americans developed political power in the United States despite, or perhaps as a necessary response to, prevalent public and private discrimination. Over the years, Asian American communities grew, consolidated, and organized in response to anti-Asian laws. This section examines three examples of national efforts for redress by Asian

Americans: first, the movement to repeal the Chinese Exclusion Act; second, the campaign for reparations for the wartime internment of Japanese Americans; and finally, the shaping of the Civil Rights Act of 1991.

Repeal of the Chinese Exclusion Act

An early victory for Asian Americans in Congress was the repeal of the Chinese Exclusion Act of 1882. Although the first legal challenge to the act had proven unsuccessful, Chinese Americans seized a new opportunity to overturn it 61 years after its passage.

The Japanese attack on Pearl Harbor that brought the United States into World War II (1939–45) transformed the relationship of white Americans with Chinese in the United States. China became an important ally of the United States. On December 22, 1941, a few weeks after the bombing of Pearl Harbor, a *Time* magazine article described how to distinguish Chinese "friends" from Japanese "enemies." Sensing the shift of attitudes, Chinese American groups sought congressional repeal of the Chinese Exclusion Act. They received vital political support from the "China Lobby," a small group of Congressmembers and Chinese sympathizers. After many deals and international negotiations, Congress repealed the Chinese Exclusion Act in 1943. Although it set a quota on Chinese immigration far below that of Europeans, repeal of the Act was nevertheless a substantial achievement.

Reparations for Wartime Internment of Japanese Americans

While wartime improved the standing of Chinese Americans, the status of Japanese

Americans deteriorated. Following the bombing of Pearl Harbor, President Franklin D. Roosevelt authorized the evacuation of Japanese Americans living in certain areas to "relocation centers." With often less than a few days to evacuate their homes, Japanese American families were forced to give up their jobs and sell their properties at far below market value. One citizen, Fred Korematsu, disobeyed the evacuation order and was convicted in 1943. In the nation's highest court, he and two other Japanese Americans, convicted under wartime curfews, argued that singling out Japanese American citizens for such harsh deprivations was unconstitutional.

In the 1944 decision *Korematsu* v. *United States*, the Supreme Court upheld the convictions in all three cases, based on government evidence of "wartime necessity." After the war, under the Evacuation Claims Act of 1948, Congress granted token financial redress amounting to only ten cents on every dollar lost to internees.

A generation later, the Japanese American Citizens League (JACL), the National Committee for Redress and Reparations (NCRR), and grassroots groups of former internees and academics renewed the call for redress and reparations. In 1984, Fred Korematsu himself, backed by a coalition of Asian American attorneys and advocacy groups, returned to court with newly declassified evidence to challenge his conviction. The evidence established that the government had known Japanese Americans did not pose a threat to national security as it had claimed and that the government had misled the Court in the earlier proceedings. The federal judge rehearing Korematsu's case overturned his conviction and the two curfew convictions.

After the legal victory in *Korematsu II*, JACL and NCRR returned to Capitol Hill to lobby for redress for all surviving internees. The facts uncovered in the new court proceedings aided Congress in passing House Resolution 442, which provided an official apology for the internment and set aside $20,000 for each surviving internee or internee's survivors. Over $1.5 billion has been paid to Japanese American claimants. The act also created a $50 million trust fund for educating people about the internment.

Wards Cove and the Civil Rights Act of 1991

Asian Americans have continued to file legal challenges to change other discriminatory conditions. In the case of *Wards Cove Packing Co.* v. *Atonio*, for example, 2,000 Filipino and Native Alaskan cannery workers sued their employer for discriminatory employment practices that one Supreme Court justice characterized as "a kind of overt and institutionalized racism we have not dealt with in years." The workers claimed that they were systematically steered away from higher paying jobs in favor of white workers, that they were segregated in on-site living quarters and dining areas, and that they were assigned badges according to race and sex. Even so, in 1989 a majority of the Supreme Court rejected the workers' claims, applying new standards that made it extraordinarily difficult for employees to prove illegal race discrimination. The Civil Rights Act of 1990 would have overturned the *Wards Cove* decision, but President George Bush vetoed the legislation. Consequently, the Civil Rights Act of 1991 corrected the damage done by the *Wards Cove* decision to antidiscrimination laws, but provided no relief to Wards Cove workers themselves. The *Wards Cove* case inspired new efforts in the unfolding history of Asian Americans' challenges to discrimination.

Both President Bill Clinton and United States Attorney General Janet Reno publicly stated that they supported repeal of the section of the Civil Rights Act of 1991 that excludes Wards Cove workers. Although developments in employment law since 1991 reduced the practical significance of repeal, acknowledging the injustice to Wards Cove workers still has symbolic importance.

Lawmakers and Lawyers

Voting and Political Representation

Assuring justice for Asian Americans begins not with lawyers, but lawmakers. The noticeable absence of Asian American local, state, and national government officials, even in highly populated areas such as California and New York, merits close examination. Asian Americans have long been regarded as apolitical (not interested in politics) or unsuited for the aggressiveness of American politics. This assumption is, to a degree, supported by low voter registration and turnout from Asian American communities. Some analysts explain the lack of political involvement as the product of a large immigrant population that either cannot or does not know how to vote. Voting rights advocates point to the legacy of disenfranchisement (many Asians emigrated from non-democratic nations, such as those ruled by monarchs or military regimes), language barriers in the electoral process, and the dilution of Asian Americans' voting power in general elections, where many believe their numbers may be too low to have an effect on the outcome.

Whatever the explanation, the proportion of Asian American elected officials is lower than the presence of Asian American persons in the general population. In California, where Asian Americans account for more than 10 percent of the population, there were only 46 elected Asian representatives out of 2,861 statewide in 1990, less than 2 percent of elected officials.

Some political analysts suggest that Asian American political power is wielded in ways that cannot be measured by voter registration or turnout. For example, politicians have long sought campaign contributions from Asian Americans, although some contributors complain that politicians accept their support yet remain unresponsive to community concerns. Regional Asian American community groups also have a significant presence in local politics. At the national level, several prominent groups consistently lobby on issues of importance to the community.

Finally, Asian Americans have made significant gains at the appointive level. At the end of the Bush Administration in 1992, Asian Americans held 124 appointed federal government offices. Under the Clinton Administration, Asian Americans obtained 150 substantial appointments. Under President George W. Bush, more than 80 Asian Americans were appointed to cabinet and sub-cabinet positions, more than under any president before him. Among the notable appointments was Debra W. Yang to U.S. Attorney for the Los Angeles, California, office. Upon Yang's unanimous confirmation on April 22, 2002, she became the first Asian Pacific American U.S. Attorney.

Federal Judicial Officers by Court and Race/Ethnicity

Court/Status	Total	Asian	Percent Asian
Total	1,477	9	0.6%
Circuit Courts[a]	156	1	0.5%
District Courts[b]	555	4	0.7%
Bankruptcy Judges	294	1	0.3%
U.S. Magistrates			
Full-time	325	2	0.5%
Part-time	143	1	0.7%
Percent change			
1990 to 1991	-0.3%	-10.0%	
1989 to 1991	1.5%	-18.2%	
1988 to 1991	-0.2%	25.0%	
1987 to 1991[d]	3.1%	-25.0%	
1988 to 1991[c]	5.6%	-18.2%	

Source: Susan B. Gall and Timothy L. Gall, editors, *Statistical Record of Asian Americans,* Gale, 1993, p. 730. Notes: (a) Includes the temporary emergency Court of Appeals. (b) Includes the Territorial Courts; Claims Court; Court of International Trade; Special Court, Regional Rail Reorganization Act of 1973; and Judicial Panel on Multidistrict Litigation. (c) Excludes judicial officers in senior status. (d) 1987 figures reflect 15-month reporting period.

The Judiciary

The United States judiciary also does not fully reflect the presence of Asian Americans in the country. Among more than 27,000 federal and state judges in the United States in 1993, only 204—less than 1 percent—were Asian Americans. Only 20 sat in federal courts. California had the largest number of Asian American judges at 89. This figure is still far from reflecting the proportion of the group in the state. Hawaii had the second highest number of Asian American judges (58), followed by Washington State (14), and New York and Pennsylvania (8 each). In 1993, thirty-three states had no Asian American state or federal judges. Almost a decade later, in 2002, with the appointment of Korean American Jeanne Hong, Maryland, Washington, D.C., and Virginia all gained their first Asian American judge, according to the National Asian Pacific American Bar Association.

Asian Americans have much less familiarity with the courts than any other racial or ethnic group and hold a significant distrust for the judicial system. Seventy-six percent of Asian Americans surveyed believed that the courts treat people with a good understanding of English better than people who speak little or no English. All racial and ethnic groups surveyed agreed that the courts should guarantee adequate numbers of foreign-language interpreters. Although Congress has passed a Court Interpreters Act that mandates certified interpreters to translate courtroom testimony, certification is available only in Spanish. Asian-language interpreters are still requested on an *ad hoc* (as needed) basis and accurate interpretation of testimony is not guaranteed.

The Legal Profession

The almost 10,000 Asian American lawyers made up only 1.4 percent of lawyers nationwide in 1990. Although this is barely half the percentage of Asian Americans in the general population, it is a significant increase over the 3,776 Asian American lawyers identified ten years earlier. Despite a late entry into the profession, Asian Americans are now the fastest-growing ethnic group in the bar.

On the whole, Asian Americans are on a more equal level with whites in the legal profession than are their African American, Hispanic American, and Native American colleagues. Minority attorneys have disproportionately entered public interest law or government; according to some observers, this is due in part to discrimination in large law firms, forcing minorities into these less lucrative areas of practice. However, statistics on the graduating class of law students in 1993 show only a 1 percent gap between the rate that white and Asian American law graduates entered private practice; Asian Americans entered private practice at higher rates than other minority groups. Indeed, the median starting salary of Asian American lawyers in 1993 was $43,000, $7,000 higher

Judicial Officers by State	
State	**Asian/Pacific Americans**
Arizona	2
Arkansas	2
California	46
Massachusetts	1
New York	2
Washington	4

Source: Susan B. Gall and Timothy L. Gall, editors, *Statistical Record of Asian Americans*, Gale, 1993, p. 731.

than the median of all other ethnic groups, including whites.

A 1988 survey commissioned by the Bar Association of San Francisco found that racial and ethnic minorities faced both objective and subjective disadvantages in the city's law firms, a problem borne out by the low number of minority attorneys. The report concluded that minority attorneys were much more likely than whites to be asked inappropriate and offensive questions during hiring interviews, earned less than white attorneys at similar points in their careers, and were twice as likely to be passed over or denied promotion. Perhaps because of their greater ability to penetrate large law firms, however, Asian Americans in San Francisco perceived less discrimination in the profession than African Americans and Hispanic Americans who were surveyed.

Legal Education

The future of Asian American representation in the legal profession will be shaped by the recent surge of applicants to law schools. Asian American applicants to law schools increased steadily in the 1980s. By 1992, Asian Americans submitted nearly 5.7 percent of the 86,500 total applications to accredited law schools. This may reflect the fact that Asian Americans finish college at a higher rate than any other racial group, a success rate attributed in part to the selective immigration of educated Asians and Pacific Islanders.

The number of Asian law school graduates in 1993 was almost 300 percent more than the graduating class in 1983; in the same period, the total number of law degrees conferred annually grew by only less than 10 percent. Nonetheless, Asian Americans are still a relatively small part of graduating classes in absolute numbers. In 1993, only 1,554 J.D. (juris doctorate, a law degree) graduates from accredited law schools were Asian American, compared to more than 34,000 whites, 2,368 African Americans, and 1,682 Hispanic Americans. And Asian Americans and other minorities also appear to lag behind whites in passing state bar examinations required for practice. In a study of 15 New York law schools, the pass rate of white applicants on the July bar exam in the early 1990s averaged 73 percent, more than Asian Americans at 62 percent, Hispanic Americans at 41 percent, and African Americans at 31 percent.

The Criminal Justice System

As if locked into stereotypes of old Asian gangster movies, police in many communities have focused on high-profile gang-related crime. They have neglected less visible problems within Asian American communities, such as hate crimes and domestic violence. Language barriers and community distrust of police further hinder law enforcement and raise a host of obstacles in the criminal courts.

Criminal Defendants

The U.S. Justice Department reports that Asian Americans comprised less than 1 percent of the population in state and federal correctional facilities and prisons in 1990. The largest concentration of Asian American prisoners—3.5 percent of the inmate population—was in the western states, where more than half of the country's Asian Americans live. According to the same report, there were 14 Asian Americans on death row as of 1990, only 0.5 percent of the death row population nationwide.

The arrest rates for Asian Americans are also lower than their presence in the population. In 1991, Asian Americans accounted for 0.8 percent of all arrests of persons 18 years and over and 1.6 percent of arrests of persons under 18. The largest number of arrests of Asian Americans were for property crimes and for driving under the influence. The highest rate of arrest by far was for illegal gambling. Asian Americans accounted for 8.2 percent (1,024) of the total gambling arrests in 1991. Some critics believe this is due to a police emphasis on this activity in Asian American communities. The higher arrest rates of Asian American juveniles may suggest a focus on youth gangs.

Victims of Crime

Like most Americans in the early 1990s, Asian Americans ranked crime second only to jobs as the more important political issue of the day. But the justice system's current focus on overseas organized crime and on Asian gang activity diverts resources away from protecting Asian Americans who are targets of other types of crime. Many Asian Americans suffer from high crime rates that plague poor neighborhoods. Criminals both in and outside the community also target Asian American immigrants, since they may be susceptible to theft and fraud and are unlikely to report criminal activity. Hate crimes and domestic violence have remained virtually invisible in Asian American communities because of underreporting and ineffective police responses.

Hate Crimes

Hate crimes are illegal acts committed against a person because of the victim's characteristics, such as race, religion, or sexual orientation. Hate crimes include vandalism, assault, intimidation, or murder. Asian Americans, even those who have grown up in this country, are often still regarded as "foreigners" who "look different."

Hate violence has become an increasingly important issue for ethnic minorities, particularly with the rise of neo-Nazi groups in the United States, who proclaim the superiority of the white race. In 1990, the United States Congress passed the Hate Crimes Statistics Act to begin recording incidences of hate crimes nationwide. The U.S. Department of Justice reported that in 1991 bias against Asians/Pacific Americans inspired 6 percent of the 4,755 hate crimes reported by law enforcement agencies in 32 states. Asian Americans at that time made up only 2.9 percent of the national population. Still, the incidence of reported hate crimes against them was below the proportion of similar

crimes against African Americans at 35.5 percent and Jews at 19.3 percent. The same report found that whites made up 36.8 percent of the offenders in hate crimes, while Asian Americans accounted for 1 percent of the perpetrators. The race of offenders in 43.3 percent of the incidents was unknown. The National Asian Pacific American Legal Consortium (NAPALC) began tracking both hate crimes and hate violence, defined as any verbal or physical act that intimidates, threatens, or injures a person or person's property because of membership in a targeted group. In 1993, the Consortium documented 335 incidents against Asian Americans. At least 30 Asian Americans died in these incidents. The Consortium's efforts paid off, and by 2000, the rate of hate crimes against Asian/Pacific Americans had dropped to 2.9 percent while their percentage of the total population rose to over four percent. However, in the aftermath of the terrorist attacks on New York and Washington, D.C., on September 11, 2001, hate crimes again were on the rise.

NAPALC's publication, *Audit of Violence Against Asian Pacific Americans: Backlash–Final Report,* detailed 507 incidents of hate crimes, a 23 percent increase in hate violence against Asian Americans nationwide over 2000. Selected incidents included in the report were the murder of Thung Phetakoune, a 62-year-old Laotian American, on July 14, 2001, in Newmarket, New Hampshire. In a statement to police, the attacker said that he hated Vietnamese people and was seeking revenge against Asians for the deaths of Americans in the Vietnam War. In Mesa, Arizona, Balbir Singh Sodhi, a 49-year-old South Asian American, was murdered by an assailant, who shouted, "I stand for America all the way," as he fired several shots into Sodhi, who was working at landscaping at the time of his murder.

While civil rights groups have struggled, in some cases successfully, for legislation against hate violence, criminalizing hate speech raises complex problems. Hate speech against Asian Americans ranges from vicious epithets to more subtle forms of anti-Asian bias, such as the anti-Asian images perpetuated in the popular media or in rhetoric about the nation's economic competitiveness. Some legal scholars argue that racist epithets are the equivalent of racially motivated violence and should be criminalized. In a 1992 decision, however, the Supreme Court declared that regulation of speech solely because of its hostility or favoritism to groups was inconsistent with the guarantee of freedom of speech provided by the First Amendment of the U.S. Constitution.

Other Crimes

Crimes committed by Asian Americans against people in their own communities are particularly resistant to prevention by authorities. One example is the growing phenomenon of home invasion robberies, where Asian American intruders, often gang members, break into homes of other Asian Americans, tie them up, torture, and rob them. These intruders tend to target victims that speak their language, who are known or likely to have valuables stored in their homes, and who are unlikely to report even serious crimes to the police. The intruders often intimidate their victims by killing one person or by threatening to return if the victims go to the police. For similar reasons,

Asian American businesses are often the targets of extortion.

Domestic violence is another serious crime that plagues Asian American communities, yet poses uniquely complicated barriers to prevention and prosecution. It is one of the most underreported crimes in the United States, the primary cause of injury to women, and linked to one in three homicides.

Both Asian American communities and society at large have, for the most part, turned their backs on domestic violence by accepting the problem as a "traditional" part of Asian culture, or by denying its existence. Language barriers and distrust of the police often deter women from seeking official intervention and fewer than half a dozen shelters for battered women in the United States are designed to aid Asian Americans.

Organized Crime, Gangs, and Immigrant Smuggling

The vast majority of Asian Americans are law-abiding citizens; however, a small percentage are involved with criminal activity. Asian-organized crime and youth gangs are becoming significant crime problems, according to law enforcement experts. The three main types of Asian American criminal activity—much of which targets members of their own immigrant community— are adult organized crime syndicates, adult-directed juvenile crime units, and youth gangs. Extortion, auto theft and burglary, residential robbery, prostitution, and gambling top the list of illegal activities.

Organized Crime. In seventeenth-century China, a number of secret organizations called Triad Societies were formed to attempt to overthrow the ruling Ch'ing

U.S. Coast Guard personnel in a raft approach a boat off the shore of San Diego, California. The Chinese travelers on board, who do not have the documents necessary to enter the United States, hold up signs proclaiming their interest in freedom in the United States.

dynasty (which conquered China in 1644) and restore the native Chinese Ming dynasty. When the British invaded and colonized Hong Kong in 1841, these societies gained membership and power because citizens were distrustful of the foreign British government. The Triad Societies gradually used their influence in society to make or extort money through illegal activities. Triads continue to exercise powerful crime rings in China and now infiltrate (join or enter an organization for purposes of spying or taking it over for other purposes) and direct criminal activity in Chinese American communities in the United States.

The triads' first American victims were the tongs. Tongs were established by Chinese American businessmen in the late 1800s and early 1900s as benevolent or fraternal organizations. Tong members supported each other and other Chinese Americans in the community by helping people to cope with racial discrimination, language problems, and difficulties assimilating into U.S. society.

The tongs' wide influence made them attractive targets for members of triads. Triad members infiltrated some of the tongs, using them to extort "protection" money from local businesses. Often a business owner, under threat of robbery, vandalism, or arson, was forced to pay these criminals a sum of money, usually weekly, for "protection." This practice is common even today, and even large businesses can be affected: computer chips have been stolen from California high-tech firms by gang members attempting to extort "protection" money.

Crimes such as these are difficult to solve, because the victims are often afraid to report them to the police. They fear that the crime syndicate will retaliate and will cause further damage. Also, crime syndicates often recruit young people through gangs to maintain control over their territories by using intimidation and violence. If a young person is arrested and convicted, the sentence for his or her crime will be less than that for an adult committing the same crime.

Youth Gangs. Groups of poor immigrant youths began banding together to form gangs in the 1970s. Members ranged in age from fourteen to the mid-twenties and were predominantly male until the 1990s, when some female Asian American gangs were formed. Many teenagers join gangs to rebel against traditionally strict parents and to achieve a sense of belonging.

Gangs are typically composed of members from one ethnic group, such as Vietnamese, Cambodian, Laotian, Filipino, Chinese, and Vietnamese Chinese. Unlike African American and Hispanic American gangs, most Asian American gangs aim at generating profit rather than protecting neighborhood turf.

In areas with high concentrations of one particular Asian ethnic group, such as New York's Chinatown, the gangs eventually became associated with tongs. Since the mid-1980s, new gangs, with names like the Green Dragons and Born to Kill, have begun to operate independently of the tongs. More ethnically diverse—and considered by many to be particularly dangerous—these gangs and their activities have expanded from Chinatown to include neighboring parts of New York, notably the borough of Queens. In 1992, a wing of one gang, the Flying Dragons, robbed the entire congregation of a church at gunpoint.

Immigrant Smuggling. The connection between immigration and gangs has taken a new turn since the late 1980s, as smuggling illegal aliens into the United States has grown into a multi-million-dollar underworld industry. An estimated 90 percent of the 500,000 Chinese illegals who arrived in the United States between 1984 and 1994 came from Fujian province in southeastern China, a stronghold of Asian organized crime. The smugglers charge $25,000 to $30,000 per person, most of it paid in installments once the immigrant arrives in the United States.

The two international smuggling rings that were initially responsible for much of this massive wave of illegal emigration recruited gangs in the United States to collect payments for them. As the gangs became more independent, they began running smuggling operations themselves through connections of their own in China. By 2003, there were nearly twenty different smuggling networks in operation.

Having scraped together a few thousand dollars in China as an initial down payment, the Fujianese, once in the United States, practically become indentured servants, working up to 20 hours a day and handing over most of their pay to the gangs. Desperate to meet their payments, some in turn victimize others; the Fujianese now have their own gang called Fuk Chang, or Fujianese Youth.

Law Enforcement

The California Attorney General estimates that less than 50 percent of crimes against Asian Americans are reported to the police. In addition to distrust of the authorities, many Asian Americans, particularly recent immigrants, are reluctant to turn to the police for help because of language barriers. According to the attorney general, more than half of California's police departments reported they did not have a sufficient number of Asian language interpreters. Incidents nationwide of police harassment and brutality against Asian Americans and other minorities tend to encourage avoidance of any contact with the police.

Meaningful law enforcement requires much more than national policies that target gangs of young men in Chinatowns. Much work remains to be done to create ties between local law enforcement and Asian American communities. The different ethnic composition of police forces from the communities they serve has hindered effective law enforcement in residential areas for minorities. Affirmative action and recruitment by local law enforcement agencies have only begun to close this gap.

The Criminal Courts

Distrust of state authority affects not only the relationship of Asian Americans and the police, but also the interaction of Asian Americans with the court system. The New York State Judicial Commission on Minori-

ties found that Asian Americans are generally distrustful of the judicial process. California's Committee on Racial and Ethnic Bias in the Courts also heard complaints from minorities maintaining that they "could not get a fair shake" from the system. Some attribute distrust to historical prejudice against Asian Americans in the courtroom, recalling *People* v. *Hall*, for example, when the California Supreme Court barred Chinese Americans from giving testimony against white people in court.

Into the twenty-first century, barriers persist. Asian Americans are often disadvantaged by lack of English-language skills, deterring many from using the court system because of difficulty in reporting crimes or in testifying, especially when foreign-language minorities are not provided with trained interpreters to help them talk to their lawyers and to the courts. In criminal trials, Asian Americans must also contend with the same difficulties that other minority defendants, victims, witnesses, and personnel often face. These include racial overtones in the investigation and prosecution of cases and stereotyping in the selection and deliberation of juries.

Suggestions for Further Reading

American Bar Association, *A Review of Legal Education in the United States*, spring 1993.

Asian Indians, Filipinos, Other Asian Communities and the Law, New York: Garland, 1994.

Asian Law Caucus, http://www.asianlawcaucus.org/ (accessed May 28, 2003).

Chiu, Christina, *State of Asian America: Activism and Resistance in the 1990s,* New York: South End Press, 1994.

Gall, Susan B., and Timothy L. Gall, eds., *Statistical Record of Asian Americans*, Detroit: Gale Research, 1993.

National Asian Pacific American Legal Consortium, http://www.napalc.org/ (accessed May 28, 2003).

National Asian Pacific American Legal Consortium, *Audit of Violence Against Asian Pacific Americans: Backlash–Final Report, 2001,* Washington, DC: 2002.

O'Hare, William, and Judy C. Felt, "Asian Americans: America's Fastest Growing Minority Group," *Population Reference Bureau Bulletin*, No. 19, February 1991.

Takaki, Ronald, *Spacious Dreams: The First Wave of Asian Immigration,* New York: Chelsea House, 1994.

Takaki, Ronald, *Strangers from a Different Shore: A History of Asian Americans,* Boston: Little, Brown and Company, 1989.

"2000 Hate Crime Statistics," *U.S. Department of Justice,* http://www.fbi.gov/ucr/cius_00/hate00.pdf (accessed May 9, 2003).

U.S. Commission on Civil Rights, *Civil Rights Issues Facing Asian Americans in the 1990s*, February 1992.

7
Population

America's Fastest-Growing Minority

and Where They Live

FACT FOCUS

- *Over 2.7 million immigrants came from Asia to the United States between 1991 and 2000, a number greater than the total Asian American population in 1970.*
- *Six Asian American subgroups, Chinese, Filipino, Japanese, Asian Indian, Korean, and Vietnamese, made up 84 percent of the total Asian American population in 1990.*
- *Pacific Islanders constitute only 7 percent of the Asian American total.*
- *Hawaiians comprise two-thirds of the total Pacific Islander population.*

The 2000 census indicated that the Asian American population was one of the fastest-growing population segments in the United States. Both the Asian and the Hispanic populations grew at an extremely high rate in the 1990s. The Asian American population more than doubled between 1980 and 1990, and grew by nearly 50 percent between 1990 and 2000, to approximately 11.9 million. The dramatic growth of the Asian and Pacific Islander population is due to three factors: the elimination of exclusionary immigration policies directed at Asian immigrants between 1882 and 1964; refugee resettlement policies for Southeast Asians since 1975; and special attention paid by the U.S. government to get a complete count of this population when conducting the decennial census (done every ten years). About three-fourths of the growth in population each year among Asian Americans is due to new immigration, rather than birth rate.

Population Trends

Though it is a fast-growing population group, in 2000 the Asian American population was the second-smallest racial/ethnic group in total numbers in the United States. Only the American Indian/Alaskan Native population is smaller.

Projections for the year 2050 indicate that the Asian and Pacific Islander population will continue to be one of the fastest-growing groups in the United States, increasing to 40 million or 11 percent of the total population. This will still be smaller than the projected Hispanic and black populations. The Hispanic population, projected to be 81 million in 2050, is expected to constitute 21 percent of the total population. The black population is expected to rise to 62 million, or 16 percent of the total U.S. population. The non-Hispanic white population is expected to number 202 million and still constitute a majority of the population at 53 percent. The indigenous population of American Indians/Alaskan Natives is expected to double by 2050, remaining the smallest group.

Asian Americans and the Census

Some Asian and Pacific Islander population groups grew faster than others between 1970 and 1990. In 1970, the federal government wanted a more accurate and comprehensive analysis of the U.S. population. Although government agencies collect information on the population continuously, once every ten years the Bureau of Census attempts to count every person living in the United States. The data collected by the government have become more detailed with each census since 1970.

Pacific Islanders

Pacific Islanders are a special subgroup in the category of Asian American. They are, like Native Americans, indigenous peoples of the Americas. For the most part, they are not immigrants to this nation but preceded the founding settlers of the United States. Hawaiians and Guamanians are U.S. citizens; American Samoans are nationals. Hawaii was an independent monarchy before becoming a United States territory in 1898 and the fiftieth state in 1959. Guam was ceded to the United States after the Spanish-American War in 1898; it became a U.S. territory in 1950 and American citizenship was conferred on the Guamanian population. By contrast, the Samoan island chain consists of American Samoa, a U.S. territory, and Western Samoa, an independent nation since 1962.

In 1993, Hawaiians, a native people, requested federal designation as Native Americans along with American Indians and Alaskan Natives. While such a change is numerically and proportionally small, it sets a precedent that specific groups may choose to be included or excluded from major racial and ethnic categories.

1790 to 1890

The Constitution of the United States requires that the government count the population every ten years. Since 1790, data from the census of the American people have been used, among other things, to determine each state's appropriate number of seats in the House of Representatives. Data have been collected on the Chinese population since the 1860 census, and on the Japanese since 1870. No census data were available for Pacific Islanders until Pacific territories were acquired by the United States after the Spanish-American War of 1898.

Early censuses documented a low proportion of Asian American females. In 1860, the ratio was 33 Chinese males to 1 Chinese female; in 1870, 29 to 2; and, in both 1880 and 1890, 25 to 1. The disproportionately low number of Chinese females was reinforced by an 1884 federal court ruling that excluded the wives of Chinese laborers from immigrating to the United States. This decision kept the Chinese population in the United States overwhelmingly male through the end of the century.

1900 to 1960

In 1900, at the dawn of the twentieth century, the Asian and Pacific Islander popula-

Asian American Ethnic Groups Included in the Census, 1970 to 1990

1970	1980	1990
Chinese	Chinese	Chinese
Filipino	Filipino	Filipino
Japanese	Japanese	Japanese
	Asian Indian	Asian Indian
Korean	Korean	Korean
	Vietnamese	Vietnamese
	Laotian	Laotian
	Thai	Thai
	Cambodian	Cambodian
	Pakistani	Pakistani
	Indonesian	Indonesian
	Hmong	Hmong
		Malayan
		Bangladeshi
		Sri Lankan
		Burmese
		Okinawan
Hawaiian	Hawaiian	Hawaiian
	Samoan	Samoan
	Tongan	Tongan
	Micronesian	Micronesian
	Guamanian	Guamanian
	Melanesian	Northern Mariana Islander
		Tahitian
		Palauan
		Fijian

Source: Susan B. Gall and Timothy L. Gall, editors, *Statistical Record of Asian Americans*, Gale, 1993, p. 567.

Asian Pacific Islander Immigration by Country of Origin, 1850 to 2000

Decade	Chinese	Japanese	Asian Indian	Korean	Filipino	Vietnamese
1850–1860	41,397	—	43	—	—	—
1861–1870	64,301	186	69	—	—	—
1871–1880	123,201	149	163	—	—	—
1881–1890	61,711	2,270	269	—	—	—
1891–1900	14,799	25,942	68	—	—	—
1901–1910	20,605	129,797	4,713	7,697	—	—
1911–1920	21,278	83,837	2,082	1,049	869	—
1921–1930	29,907	33,462	1,886	598	54,747	—
1931–1940	4,928	1,948	496	60	6,159	—
1941–1950	16,709	1,555	1,761	—	4,691	—
1951–1960	9,657	46,250	1,973	6,231	19,307	—
1961–1970	34,764	39,980	27,198	34,526	98,376	3,788
1971–1980	124,326	49,775	164,134	271,956	360,216	179,681
1981–1990	366,622	43,248	261,841	338,824	295,271	201,419
1991-2000	419,114	67,942	363,060	164,166	503,945	286,145

Note: Beginning in 1982, Taiwan was no longer included in the Chinese total. Immigration from Taiwan to the United States from 1982 to 1990 was 118,105. These immigrants are not included in the total for Chinese that appears in the table. Sources: *Statistical Yearbook of the Immigration and Naturalization Service*, various years. U.S. Commission on Civil Rights, *The Economic Status of Americans of Asian Descent: An Exploratory Investigation*, 1988.

tion was about 0.03 percent of the total U.S. population. The 1900 census included the territory of Hawaii for the first time. The Asian American population grew numerically, but proportionally remained less than 1 percent of the total population. After World War II (1939–45), several laws removed immigration restrictions for Asian Americans. These included the 1946 War Brides Act, the Displaced Persons Act (1948–54), and the 1952 **Immigration and Nationality Act,** commonly known as the McCarran-Walter Act. Immigration quotas were still quite low at 100 persons each for countries of the Asia-Pacific Triangle, but the sum of such a modest immigration allocation was sufficient to raise the 1960 census count of Asian American population to 878,000, a 75-percent increase from the 1940 census count of 500,000. (Text of the act appears in the **Significant Documents** chapter of this volume.)

Chinese. Within specific Asian American groups, Chinese population growth stagnated until the end of World War II. Chinese

Asian and Pacific Islander Population, 1900 to 2000			
Year	Total U.S. Population	Total U.S. Asian/Pacific Islander Population	Asian Pacific/Islander, Percent of Total
1900	76,212,168	204,462	—
1910	92,228,531	249,926	—
1920	106,021,568	332,432	—
1930	123,202,660	489,326	—
1940	132,165,129	489,984	—
1950	151,325,798	599,091	—
1960	179,323,175	877,934	—
1970	203,211,926	1,429,562	0.7%
1980	226,545,805	3,466,421	1.5%
1990	248,709,873	7,273,662	2.9%
2000	281,421,906	10,242,998	3.6%

Note: A dash (—) indicates that the percentage is less that 0.5. Source: U.S. Bureau of Census, *Decennial Censuses of Population.*

generally came to the United States with the idea that their stay in this country was temporary. One came to "Gold Mountain" (as the United States was known), a land of economic opportunity, to earn one's fortune and to return to China. During World War II, however, China was an ally of the United States and Chinese Americans joined the armed forces. By 1950, growth was on the rise due to immigration; that year's census showed an increase of 46,000 persons over 1940 with an overall count of 150,005 Chinese. By 1960, Chinese Americans numbered 237,292.

Japanese. The Japanese population, by contrast, increased consistently in all decades and was the largest of all Asian American groups in this period. Between 1900 and 1910, the Japanese population grew from 86,000 to 153,000. By 1920, there were roughly two males for each female, a ratio not attained until 1950 for the Chinese and 1960 for Filipinos. The Japanese were the first Asian American group to shift from a society of single male sojourners (temporary travelers) to a permanent resident population of family units. By 1960, the Japanese population had grown to 464,250 and maintained the majority of the Asian American population at 53 percent.

Filipino. In the 1910 census, the Filipino population was counted for the first time. Unlike the Japanese and Chinese who were subject to exclusionary immigration laws, Filipinos were American nationals, since the Philippines had been ceded to the United States following the Spanish-American War of 1898.

The number of Filipinos increased dramatically when Hawaiian plantations and California agriculture began recruiting Filipino males as laborers. Their numbers grew between 1910 and 1920 from 2,800 to 27,000. Between 1920 and 1930, they quadrupled to 108,000. The ratio of Filipino males to females in 1930 was eleven to two.

Alarmed by the growing numbers of a mainly single male population, the U.S. government initiated a repatriation movement (a program to return members of a certain group to their country of origin) to the Philippines. In 1940, the Filipino population of 99,000 reflected a decrease of 9 percent from the 1930 count of 108,000. However, Filipino and American cooperation during World War II and the establishment of the Republic of the Philippines were followed by relaxed immigration restrictions. By 1950, the Filipino population had increased to 123,000 and in 1960 stood at 176,310.

Koreans and Asian Indians. Between 1900 and 1960, the sizes of the Korean and Asian Indian populations were small, about 9,000 Koreans and fewer than 3,000 Asian Indians.

Post-1965 Immigration and Refugee Resettlement

The passage and subsequent implementation of the 1965 immigration act brought tremendous growth and diversity to the Asian American population. Earlier immigrants were primarily from working-class backgrounds. New immigrants were from varied backgrounds: affluent entrepreneurs, working-class relatives of earlier immigrants, highly educated middle-class profes-

sionals, and illiterate war refugees with no material possessions.

Refugees are people who leave their homeland, not by choice, but to escape some condition that makes it impossible to stay. In 1975, the end of the war in Southeast Asia left many Vietnamese, Cambodians, and Laotians without a safe or livable home. Between 1977 and 1978, the number of Vietnamese immigrants increased from 4,600 to 89,000. Cambodian and Lao immigrants also began to increase in 1977, ranging from 10,000 to 20,000 per year.

Trends in Population Growth

The Asian American population was less than 1 percent of the total U.S. population, but growing, in 1970. Japanese, Chinese, and Filipinos in the United States numbered 1,369,000, an increase of 56 percent over 1960. By comparison, the total population in the United States increased only 13 percent during this period.

Two-thirds of the increase in the Japanese population was due to natural increase (births). Chinese and Filipinos could credit two-thirds of their growth to immigration. Koreans totaled 70,000, a tenfold increase from their 1950 total of 7,000.

Geographic Distribution

As recently as 1940, almost 100 percent of Asian Americans lived on the West Coast of the United States. By 1970, the percentage of Japanese, Chinese, Filipinos, and Hawaiians living in the West had dropped to 72 percent. Over one-fourth (27 percent) of Chinese were residing outside the west coast, with almost 20 percent of all Chinese living in the state of New York.

By 2000, a further decrease—to just under half of all Asian Americans (49 percent) lived in the West. In 2000, the majority of Asian Americans lived in only three states—California, New York, and Hawaii.

Urban versus Rural

In 1970, 90 percent of Asians living in the United States were urban residents, compared to 73 percent of the total population. However, this varied by individual groups. From 1960 to 1990, about 97 percent of the Chinese population lived in cities. In contrast, over one-fourth of Filipinos lived in rural areas in 1960, but this proportion sank to 14 percent by 1970. This decrease was due to the deaths of first-generation single males, many of whom were rural farm workers. At the same time, the numbers of new Filipino immigrants, primarily professional, began to grow. These Filipinos settled in metropolitan areas. Japanese also moved from rural to urban areas as second- and third-generation Japanese Americans migrated to metropolitan areas. While 18 percent of the Japanese population resided in rural areas in 1960, this proportion was down to 11 percent by 1970.

Nationally, 31 percent of the total population lived in cities, but 37 percent chose to live in surrounding suburbs. Asian Americans do not follow this trend, however: the proportion of Asian Americans living in central cities in 1970 was greater than the proportion in the suburbs. Almost one out of two (48 percent) Japanese and Filipinos lived in central cities. Among the Chinese, over two out of three (68 percent) lived in central cities, and just one-fourth lived in the suburbs.

The 1990 census revealed that more Asian Americans—95 percent—were living in urban areas (cities) than any other racial or ethnic group. By comparison, 75 percent of the total U.S. population lived in urban areas.

1980 Census

The 1980 census was the first census to identify and provide data on the total Asian American population and its subgroups in all 50 states.

The civil rights movement of the 1960s focused attention on the unequal treatment of people in U.S. society because of their racial or ethnic background. Between 1970 and 1980, the government started many new programs and procedures to correct these inequities. To be able to measure the progress being made by ethnic groups, the government needs data. Therefore, the Office of Management and Budget, a powerful government agency, asked all federal agencies to collect racial and ethnic data by five major categories: white, black, Asian American, American Indian/Alaskan Native, and Hispanic.

Geographic Distribution

By 1980, the shift of Asian Americans from the West Coast to other regions was noticeable. While the majority—almost three out of five (58 percent)—of this population still lived in the West, this was less than the almost three out of four persons (72 percent) from 1970.

Seventy percent lived in just five states: California, Hawaii, New York, Illinois, and Texas. California was the place of residence for over one-third (35.2 percent) of all Asian Americans, and had the highest concentration of Chinese, Japanese, Filipino, and Vietnamese of the 50 states.

Asian and Pacific Islander Population Projections, 1990 to 2050		
Year	Asian and Pacific Islanders in Millions	Asian and Pacific Islanders as a Percent of Total Population
1990	7.3	2.8%
1995	9.6	3.7%
2000	11.9	4.5%
2010	14.2	5.9%
2030	16.3	8.4%
2050	18.4	10.1%

Source: U.S. Department of Commerce, "Population Projections of the United States by Age, Sex, Race, and Hispanic Origin: 1992–2050," *Current Population Reports,* 1993.

The largest population of Asian Indians—18 percent—was in New York.

Urban versus Rural

In 1980, 90 percent of the Asian American population lived in urban areas and were about equally divided between central cities and suburbs. Over 45 percent resided in just five metropolitan statistical areas (MSAs): Los Angeles, San Francisco, New York, Chicago, and Honolulu.

Refugee Resettlement

Refugees—mainly Vietnamese, Cambodians, and Laotians—began arriving in the United States in significant numbers in the mid-1970s. The Vietnamese were the first wave of immigrants to arrive in large numbers. Initial U.S. government policy was to settle them in communities across the country to minimize their impact on any one location. However, the Vietnamese refugees chose to move within the United States not long after their arrival. This secondary migration occurred almost immediately, as Vietnamese moved to join other refugees in warmer climates and in Asian American population centers.

1990 Census

The 1990 census reinforced the dramatic growth rate of all racial and ethnic minorities, first noted in the 1980 census. Growth rates were impressive for all groups, but the Asian American population had almost quadrupled in 20 years, growing from less than 1 percent to 3 percent of the American population. Between 1980 and 1990, the total American population grew at the rate of 9.8 percent, while the growth rate for Asian Americans was 107.8 percent, greater than any other group.

Asian American Ethnic Groups

The 1990 census made available detailed data for 17 Asian groups—Chinese, Filipino, Japanese, Asian Indian, Korean, Vietnamese, Laotian, Cambodian, Thai, Hmong, Pakistani, Indonesian, Malayan, Bangladeshi, Sri Lankan, Burmese, and Okinawan—and eight Pacific Islander groups—Hawaiian, Samoan, Guamanian, Tongan, Tahitian, Northern Mariana Islander, Palauan, and Fijian. The six largest groups—Chinese, Gilipino, Japanese, Korean, Asian Indian, And Vietnamese—accounted for 84 percent of all Asian Americans in 1990, down from 90 percent in 1980.

Between 1981 and 1990, almost two million immigrants arrived in the United States from Asian countries. This is over one-quarter (27 percent) of the Asian American population in 1990.

Geographic Distribution

Over half (56 percent) of all Asian Americans lived in the West in 1990. The U.S. Immigration and Naturalization Service asks each immigrant where he or she intends to live in the United States. Approximately 36 percent of the two million Asian immigrants who entered the United States between 1982 and 1989 said that they planned to live in California, 11 percent in New York, and about 5 percent in either Texas or Illinois. Seventy percent of all Asian Americans lived in just five states—California, New York, Hawaii, Texas, and Illinois. Thirteen states had an Asian American population of 100,000 or more in 1990, compared to only seven in 1980.

Within groups, several shifts occurred from 1980 to 1990. For example, there were more Asian Indians in California (160,000) than in New York (141,000). Vietnamese had replaced Chinese as the largest Asian American group in Texas. Filipinos were the largest group in California, followed by Chinese and Japanese.

Almost half (44 percent) of Pacific Islanders in the United States in 1990 resided in Hawaii. Fewer than one-third (30 percent) lived in California, and 4 percent were in Washington state. Two out of three Hawaiians lived in Hawaii. About half of all Samoans and Guamanians and four out of five Fijians lived in California. Due to their relationship with Mormon missionaries, one out of four Tongans lived in Utah.

Urban versus Rural

While 75 percent of the U.S. population lived in urban areas, Asian Americans continued to be the most urban of all racial and ethnic groups at 95 percent in 1990. Chinese were the most urban at 97 percent. In 1990, over half (about 54 percent) of all Asian Americans lived in one of five metropolitan areas: Los Angeles/Anaheim/Riverside, California; San Francisco/Oakland/San Jose, California; New York City/northern New Jersey/Long Island, New York; Honolulu, Hawaii; and Chicago/Gary, Indiana/Lake County, Illinois. (The government groups urban areas together when gathering statistics on the U.S. population. These groupings are called metropolitan statistical areas, or MSAs.)

2000 Census

The 2000 census added the category of "Other Asian" so that Asians whose ethnicity was not listed already on the questionnaire could identify themselves. The census also allowed individuals to report one or more races that they considered themselves to be. For the first time, people of mixed racial descent could claim multiple races. For this reason though, the numbers from the 2000 census are not directly comparable with earlier censuses.

The Asian population continued its growth, growing at over five times the rate of the general population. The Asian population in total reached 11.9 million, increasing by 72 percent over its 1990 total.

Asian American Ethnic Groups

The 2000 census continued the trend towards inclusiveness, as it provided information on 24 Asian groups—Asian Indian, Bangladeshi, Bhutanese, Burmese, Cambodian, Chinese, Filipino, Hmong, Indo Chinese, Indonesian, Iwo Jiman, Japanese, Korean, Laotian, Malaysian, Maldivian, Nepalese, Okinawan, Pakistani, Singaporean, Sri Lankan, Taiwanese, Thai, and Vietnamese. Chinese, Filipino, Korean, Japanese, Indian, and Vietnamese continued to be the largest groups.

Geographic Distribution

A large portion of Asians in the United States continue to live in the west. In 2000, 49 percent of them reported living in the West, making up 9.3 percent of its total population. The Northeast accounted for 20 percent of the nation's Asian population, the South had 19 percent, and the Midwest 12 percent. Though the Asian population was more geographically diverse than in the 1990 census, the majority of Asians, 51 percent, still lived in three states, California, New York, and Hawaii.

Population Projections

The Asian American population is expected to continue to be one of the fastest-growing population segment in the United States. By the year 2050, the Asian American population is projected to almost quadruple to 11 percent of the total population.

One factor to consider in projecting the future for Asian Americans is the increasingly interracial composition of this population. In 1991, interracial marriages accounted for only 2 percent of 53 million marriages in the United States. However, among married Asian Americans, 25 percent had spouses outside their race.

A related factor is interracial birth. According to the National Center for Health Statistics, the total births of mixed parentage to Asian Americans and whites almost doubled between 1978 and 1989.

When counting the U.S. population, the addition or subtraction of Asian Americans of mixed origins will affect the increase or decrease of this population. The term "Asian American" represents a rapidly growing, heterogeneous, interracial population. By 2050, the term "Asian American" may be replaced by something new to reflect the changes the group will undergo.

Suggestions for Further Reading

Gall, Susan B., and Timothy L. Gall, eds., *Statistical Record of Asian Americans*, Detroit: Gale Research, 1993.

Odo, Franklin, ed., *The Columbia Documentary History of the Asian American Experience,* New York: Columbia University Press, 2002.

Raatma, Lucia, *Chinese Americans,* Chanhassen, MN: Child's World, 2003.

Springstubb, Tricia, *The Vietnamese Americans,* San Diego, CA: Lucent Books, 2002.

U.S. Bureau of Census, *The Asian Population*, February, 2002.

8

Jobs and Money

Entrepreneurship and Workforce Participation

FACT FOCUS

- *About 12 percent of all Asian American workers between the ages of 25 and 64 were self-employed in 1990.*
- *Korean Americans and Asian Indian Americans experienced the largest growth in business ownership between 1977 and 1987.*
- *Asian American businesses provide many newly arrived immigrants with a starting place in the U.S. economy.*
- *In the early 1990s, Asian Americans owned nearly one-third of all minority-owned businesses in the United States.*
- *Rotating credit associations operating within ethnic communities have provided financial assistance to new Asian American enterprises.*

Businesses owned by Asian Americans make up one of the fastest-growing areas of the U.S. economy. From 1987 to 1997, Asian American businesses grew by 257 percent. In 1987, Asian Americans owned 355,311 firms, or 27 percent of all minority-owned businesses. By 1997, this number had risen to 912,960, representing 30 percent of all U.S. minority-owned enterprises.

The ratio of businesses to population shows the significance of Asian American entrepreneurship. In the Asian American community, the ratios are: Chinese American, 1 business owner for every 18 Chinese; Filipino American, 1 for every 35 Filipinos;

Japanese American, 1 for every 16 Japanese; Asian Indian American, 1 for every 16 Asian Indians; Korean American, 1 for every 12 Koreans; and Vietnamese American, 1 for every 24 Vietnamese. Comparatively, the ratios for African Americans is 1 business owner for every 71 African Americans, and for Hispanic Americans, 1 for every 53 Hispanic Americans.

The six largest Asian American population groups are Asian Indian, Chinese, Filipino, Japanese, Korean, and Vietnamese. Korean Americans and Asian Indian Americans experienced the greatest growth in business ownership between 1977 and 1987.

145

WORDS TO KNOW

enclave: a distinct territorial or cultural unit, such as Chinatown

entrepreneurship: organizing, starting, and running a business

ostracize: to keep a person or persons from participating in a group by agreement among the members of the group

stereotype: an oversimplified image based on one characteristic of a group

Asian American workers generally show a higher self-employment rate than the national average. According to the 1990 census, about 12 percent of all Asian American workers between the ages of 25 and 64 were self-employed. Koreans were most likely to be self-employed (27 percent), followed by Chinese (12 percent), Japanese (10 percent), Vietnamese (10 percent), and other Asians (9 percent). Filipinos had relatively fewer self-employed workers: their rate of self-employment (5 percent) was roughly similar to the rate of self-employment found among non-Asian, U.S.-born individuals.

Why do Asian Americans go into business? Why are immigrants more likely to be entrepreneurs than U.S.-born members of the same ethnic groups? Why do Asians from different national backgrounds have different rates of entrepreneurship?

Immigration and Entrepreneurship

Chinese. Asian American business ownership dates back to the nineteenth century.

The first significant wave of immigrants from Asia came from China in the mid-1800s. Their distinct physical appearance, dress, and religious and cultural practices made them stand out from mainstream society. Many Chinese were discriminated against and ostracized. As anti-Chinese violence and discrimination intensified, the Chinese took refuge in their own Chinatowns. Early Chinatowns were mainly male enclaves, consisting largely of workers who had immigrated to the United States to earn money for their families in China. They would seek fellowship in tea and coffee houses or restaurants after long hours of work. These meeting sites were the first Asian-owned businesses, and Chinatowns became environments of opportunity for Chinese Americans.

Chinese Americans were so successful in the laundry business that the Chinese laundry became a stereotype. By 1920, for example, well over one-third of Chinese workers in New York (37.5 percent) were occupied in laundry work.

Many Chinese immigrated through family networks, and clan and district associations made high levels of cooperation and networking possible. For example, a loan for starting a small laundry or restaurant could be sought through the assistance of rotating credit associations (see box, p. 147) or other types of mutual aid societies among Chinese American communities. In 1997, the U.S. Census Bureau reported that Chinese Americans owned 252,577 businesses with total gross annual sales of $106,196,794

Japanese. Japanese immigrants to the United States were usually rural people, dis-

ROTATING CREDIT ASSOCIATIONS

Chinese American and Korean American communities (and some others) organize rotating credit associations to provide financial assistance to their members. These associations are similar to the more formal credit unions operated, for example, by employee groups and labor unions. The rotating credit association provides loans without interest to its members. Many recent immigrants have problems when applying to a bank for a loan: they are unfamiliar with American banking practices, they may not speak English, and they lack credit history. Most banks would not consider giving a loan to such an applicant.

In the rotating credit association, individual members contribute an amount of money to a collective pool. These contributions may range from less than $100 to several thousand dollars. Associations may accumulate hundreds of thousands—or even millions—of dollars to help members with their financial needs. These credit associations frequently are the only available source of financing for immigrant group members who do not have established credit.

Credit associations have helped many enterprising Asian Americans to open the doors of their first business, or to overcome unexpected financial problems. The key to success of these associations is the trust shared among the members of the group. Because the associations are made up of family members and friends, it is rare that a member does not fulfill his or her commitment to the group. Even more important, the associations provide emotional support and friendship to the members. This can be even more valuable than economic support when new immigrants are adjusting to their adopted homeland of the United States.

located from their native land by Japan's rapid modernization. While the Chinese started commercial enterprises in response to their difficulties in the mainstream labor market, many Japanese sought agricultural self-employment as tenant farmers, small landholders, and contract gardeners. In urban areas of the West Coast, Japanese businesses were concentrated in hotels and boardinghouses, restaurants, barber shops, poolrooms, tailor and dye shops, supply stores, laundries, and shoe shops. These businesses provided services to the Japanese community and created job opportunities for Japanese workers. Between 1900 and 1910, for every twenty-two Japanese workers, there was one Japanese business.

In the West, farmers were threatened by the Japanese entry into agriculture, and organized in an attempt to force the Japanese out. A series of laws, called alien land laws, were passed to prohibit the ownership or leasing of land to Asians in California and in other states. In 1997, the U.S. Census Bureau reported that Japanese Americans owned 85,538 businesses, with total gross annual sales of $43,741,051

Filipinos and Asian Indians. Filipinos and Asian Indians have had different immigration experiences than the Chinese and Japanese. Since 1965, Filipino and Asian Indian immigrants have tended to be highly educated professionals, such as physicians, nurses, educators, and engineers. This reflects the trend of Filipino and Asian

Indian immigration in which a disproportionate number of health professionals have immigrated under the employment-based provisions of U.S. immigration policy for skilled foreign workers needed in the U.S. labor market. Indeed, Asian Indian American doctors were the largest group of foreign-born doctors in the United States in the mid-1990s. Thus Filipinos and Asian Indians have been less likely to take up self-employment than members of other Asian groups. They come from countries where English is an official language and is widely spoken, and therefore are more likely than other groups to have English-language proficiency. This makes it easier for them to get jobs.

Asian Indian immigrants from the Gujarati region of northwest India are an exception to the generalization that Asian Indians do not become business owners in the United States. Asian Indians from this region, approximately 90 percent of whom have college degrees, often invest in hotel/motel franchises in the United States. An estimated 6,000 hotels and motels are owned by Asian Indian Americans. In 1997, the U.S. Census Bureau reported that Asian Indian Americans owned 166,737 businesses, with total gross annual sales of $67,503,357. and that Filipino Americans owned 84,534 businesses, with total gross annual sales of $11,077,885.

Koreans. Koreans arriving in the United States have generally had high levels of education in Korea, but they lack the proficient English-language skills of Filipinos and Asian Indians. Thus newly arrived Koreans have the skills to manage businesses, but they have difficulty finding employment and

sources of capital. Many rely on other members of the Korean American community for financial assistance. Korean Americans join together to form rotating credit associations, called *kyes,* that provide financial assistance to start a business, pay for a wedding or funeral, or meet other significant financial needs of members. In 1997, the U.S. Census Bureau reported that Korean Americans owned 135,571 businesses, with total gross annual sales of $45,936,497.

Vietnamese. Almost all Vietnamese Americans have arrived in the United States since 1975, as a result of the fall of U.S.-supported South Vietnam in the Vietnam War. Most arrived under U.S. government resettlement programs and were initially channeled into entry-level employment in existing U.S. businesses. The Vietnamese in the 1990s are beginning to move into self-employment and to establish their own ethnic economies. The 1990 census showed that their self-employment rate increased from less than 4 percent of the labor force in 1980 to close to 10 percent in 1990. In 1997, the U.S. Census Bureau reported that Vietnamese Americans owned 97,764 businesses, with total gross annual sales of $9,322,891.

Entrepreneurs and Ethnic Firms

Major Industry Groups of Asian-Owned Businesses

The largest concentrations of Asian American entrepreneurs are in retail trade and services, which together make up almost three-quarters of all Asian American firms. Chinese and Korean entrepreneurs are more highly concentrated in retail trade than others. Chinese and Japanese enclave economies have noticeable export industries. Chinese export industries are composed mainly of apparel or garment manufacturing, while Japanese export industries involve agricultural activities. Other common industries are restaurants and food stores (close to two-thirds of Chinese and about one-third of Japanese- and Vietnamese-operated businesses are restaurants or other eating establishments), retail, repair, hospital and health services, and personnel, professional, and social services. There is greater diversity of economic activities in Chinese, Japanese, and Korean economies than in Filipino and Asian Indian economies. The last two groups are highly concentrated in hospital and health services and other professional services.

Geographic Concentration of Asian American-Owned Businesses

A large number of businesses owned by Asian Americans are located in states where the Asian American population is rapidly growing. Ten states account for 80 percent of all Asian American firms. California ranks number one in the scale of Asian American entrepreneurship, followed by New York, Texas, Hawaii, New Jersey, Illinois, Florida, Washington, Virginia, and Maryland. California alone is home to 48 percent of Chinese firms, 46 percent of Filipino firms, 46 percent of Japanese firms, 20 percent of Asian Indian firms, 41 percent of Korean firms, and 46 percent of Vietnamese firms in the United States. Approximately one-half of all Chinese, Filipino, Japanese, Korean, and Vietnamese entrepreneurs reside in California.

In general, Asian American entrepreneurs cluster around long-standing ethnic communities such as Chinatowns, Koreatowns, Little Tokyos, and Little Saigons. However, in recent years, many Asian American businesses have dispersed to other communities in urban and suburban areas. Korean-run fruit and vegetable stores are seen on almost every street corner of residential neighborhoods in New York and Los Angeles, particularly of poor, minority neighborhoods where other entrepreneurs are unlikely to conduct business. The Chinese restaurant business is another example. Chinese-owned restaurants serving Chinese food can be found in every region of the United States, even in rural towns.

Secrets of Success

What enables Asian Americans to become successful entrepreneurs? Asian American immigrants have some key advantages over other ethnic groups in establishing small enterprises. The first advantage is education and work experience. Immigrants from Asia are from a variety of socioeconomic backgrounds and often have clear intentions of settling in the United States to achieve success for themselves and their families. Many have come with strong educational and occupational backgrounds and with lifelong family savings to begin life in the United States. College graduates are roughly twice as common among Asian immigrants as among the rest of the U.S. population. Asian Indian immigrants are more than four times more likely to have a college degree than the overall U.S. population.

Many Asian immigrants share the value of thrift and stress the importance of saving money for later purchases. Even for some low-income immigrant families, this emphasis on saving money makes it possible to

Cardiologist Zachariah P. Zachariah in the heart catheterization control room at a hospital in 1994. According to the American Medical Association, about 24,000 of the 650,000 doctors in the United States were born in India.

start a small business. Startup costs for small businesses such as small garment factories and grocery stores range from $2,000 to $30,000. It is possible for a family to build up this amount in savings.

Asian American entrepreneurs raise resources to establish businesses in several ways: through family savings, through investment from people in their home country, and through close ties to the ethnic community in the United States. Through the ethnic community, entrepreneurs have access to low-interest (or interest-free) loans and to family and low-wage immi-

grant labor. Many immigrant enterprises—especially labor-intensive grocery and food stores, restaurants, and garment factories—depend on unpaid family labor and low-wage immigrant labor. Even though these jobs pay low wages and have long working hours and sometimes poor working conditions, immigrant workers have a familiar work environment. They speak their native language with their coworkers and are shielded from the unfamiliar American workplace. They are able to work longer hours to quickly accumulate family savings. Working for an entrepreneur can give the

Percentage of Self-Employed Asian American Workers by Top-Ranking State: 1990

State	Chinese	Filipino	Japanese	Asian Indian	Korean	Vietnamese
California	47.0	46.6	50.3	20.0	43.7	49.4
New York	13.1	6.8	3.9	15.4	12.2	1.9
Hawaii	4.4	7.8	26.3	.1	2.6	2.6
Texas	4.8	2.9	.8	8.6	3.2	15.7
Illinois	2.4	5.0	1.4	6.7	5.2	.9
New Jersey	3.7	5.3	1.2	8.0	6.2	.8
Florida	3.2	2.9	.9	6.6	1.6	2.5
Washington	2.4	2.5	3.4	.7	2.9	1.8
Virginia	1.1	2.2	.8	3.0	3.3	4.2
Maryland	1.6	1.8	.4	3.6	5.0	1.5
Other States	16.3	16.2	10.6	27.3	14.1	18.7
Total	100.0	100.0	100.0	100.0	100.0	100.0

Note: Number includes persons aged 25 to 64 and in the labor force. Source: U.S. Bureau of Census, *1990 PUMS.*

new immigrant job training and expose him or her to the entrepreneurial spirit. Workers will be prepared for the transition to running businesses of their own.

For many new immigrants, low-wage menial work is a part of the time-honored path toward economic independence and the upward mobility of their families in the United States.

Consequences of Entrepreneurship

Benefits of Entrepreneurship

Entrepreneurship can create job opportunities for immigrant group members. Through entrepreneurship, Asian immi-

grants can achieve a sense of accomplishment and position as new arrivals in the United States. Furthermore, immigrant entrepreneurs can bypass the harmful psychological and social consequences of racial discrimination by creating conditions for their own economic mobility. Without exception, self-employed workers are much more likely than their salaried group members to own homes.

In New York City, the decline of the manufacturing sector has caused severe unemployment among minority workers. Immigrant Chinese women who have low English proficiency, minimal education, and little work experience display exceptionally high rates of labor force participation: 74 percent are in the labor force as compared to only 22 percent of Puerto Rican women. More than half of these Chinese women are employed in Chinatown's garment industry. Without Chinatown's garment industry, many Chinese immigrants might be jobless.

Entrepreneurship accounts in part for the high labor force participation rate and particularly low unemployment rates among foreign-born Asian American workers. Asian American immigrants have unemployment rates ranging from 2 to 5 percent, as compared to over 10 to 14 percent for other minority workers. It is true that workers in ethnic firms generally work for lower pay. However, this may be an alternative to possible joblessness.

The Downside of Entrepreneurship

There are some negative aspects of Asian American entrepreneurship. Relations with other U.S. racial groups poses a growing problem. Some Asian American businesses are operated in poor, inner-city, minority neighborhoods. The Asian American entrepreneur often avoids living there. Relations between business owners and community residents are often fragile; when Asian American business owners do not make special efforts to establish links with the communities of their customers, they may be viewed as invading strangers.

Asian Americans have been portrayed as indifferent to U.S. politics and uninterested in assimilation, differing sharply from other immigrant groups. Most Asian immigrants have instead remained closely connected with events in their home country. This type of political isolation reinforces negative stereotypes of Asian Americans as clannish.

Asian American entrepreneurs frequently think of themselves as "foreign." By

A seamstress works at a garment shop in New York City.

hiring only members of their own ethnic group, they never get to know members of mainstream society except as customers.

Asian Americans have gone into small business in large numbers because entrepreneurship can provide the best economic opportunity for them. Although there is some basis to the stereotypical view of Asian American businesses as small, family-operated firms, in recent years these businesses have grown in size and diversity.

Both workers and entrepreneurs may receive benefits from Asian American businesses. For employers, relatively inexpensive labor can provide a competitive advantage. Although the owners benefit more from this situation than employees, Asian American businesses provide newly arrived immigrants with a starting place in the U.S. economy. They also give new immigrants a familiar work environment in which they can slowly amass savings, develop skills, and prepare children for careers in the fields of their choice.

Suggestions for Further Reading

"America's Top Asian Entrepreneurs," *Gold Sea 100,* http://goldsea.com/Profiles/100/100.html (accessed May 28, 2003).

Asian American Alliance, http://www.asianamericanalliance.com/aasbdc (accessed May 28, 2003).

Chan, Sucheng, *Asian Americans: An Interpretive History,* Boston: Twayne Publishers, 1991.

Daniels, Roger, *Asian America: Chinese and Japanese in the United States since 1850,* Seattle: University of Washington Press, 1988.

Kwong, Peter, *The New Chinatown,* New York: Hill and Wang, 1987.

Light, Ivan H., *Ethnic Enterprise in America: Business Welfare among Chinese, Japanese and Blacks,* Berkeley: University of California Press, 1987.

Mangiafico, Lusiano, *Contemporary American Immigration: Patterns of Filipino, Korean, and Chinese Settlement in the United States,* New York: Praeger, 1988.

Odo, Franklin, ed., *The Columbia Documentary History of the Asian American Experience,* New York: Columbia University Press, 2002.

Parillo, Vincent N., *Strangers to These Shores: Race and Ethnic Relations in the United States,* New York: MacMillan, 1990.

Takaki, Ronald, *Strangers from a Different Shore: A History of Asian Americans,* New York: Penguin Books, 1989.

Wong, Bernard, *Patronage, Brokerage, Entrepreneurship and the Chinese Community of New York City,* New York: AMS Press, 1984.

Zhou, Min, *Chinatown: The Socioeconomic Potential of an Urban Enclave*, Philadelphia: Temple University Press, 1992.

9

Women and Families

A Look at Women and Family Life

FACT FOCUS

- Most Asian American families experience separation at some point during the process of immigrating to the United States.
- Thousands of Asian women married U.S. servicemen during and after World War II (1939–45), the Korean War (1950–53), and the Vietnam War (1965–75) and came to live in the United States.
- Many Asian families send one member to the United States first; once he or she has found employment and housing, other family members are sent for.
- Asian American women (except Vietnamese) have fewer children than women of any other racial or ethnic group.

There is no umbrella that will cover all Asian American families. In adjusting to life in the United States, families of Asian ancestry have been buffeted on all sides by discriminatory laws, wars, social and economic changes, and uprooting. Family types include separated families, relay immigrant families, native-born and foreign-born families, war-bride families, intermarried families, and refugee families.

Historically, many Asian American families have shared a common experience. Both husband and wife had to work to help add to family income, even after their children were born. This was very difficult for the women, particularly, because they did not have the extended family support they relied on at home in their native countries. They had to work at their jobs as farmers, cooks, seamstresses, laundresses, and shopkeepers and take care of their husbands and children all by themselves. Some women also took in boarders, adding even more to their work load.

Social and moral customs kept many Asian women from immigrating to the United States in the past. Although some of these customs are changing, some still restrict Asian women, even in the late 1990s. In some Asian cultures, it is not considered proper for a woman to travel alone. Women are expected to stay at home and take care of their families.

Confucianism

From the late 1800s through the 1940s, many people in China, Japan, Korea, and Vietnam followed the teachings of the Chinese philosopher Confucius. Under Confucianism, each person has a relative place in society and in the family.

Confucian society was patriarchal, that is men were dominant and held in higher esteem than women. Women had to submit to the authority of men. Families were patrilocal, which meant that when a woman married, she joined her husband's family. Her own family had little or no significance.

The cornerstone of Confucius's teachings is that children must honor and obey their parents, always putting their parents' comfort, interests, and wishes above their own. This is known as filial piety. A man is judged by how he treats his parents; a woman, by how she treats her in-laws.

Family Life Before World War II

Separated Families

For the earliest Asian groups to come to the United States—the Chinese— family life was almost nonexistent. When able-bodied males came to the United States, they left wives behind to care for the husband's parents, per Confucian teachings. A nineteenth-century Chinese folk song expresses the sadness of these broken families:

> *Flowers shall be my headdress once again*
> *For my dear husband will soon return from a distant shore.*
> *Ten long years did I wait*
> *Trying hard to remember his face*
> *As I toiled at my spinning wheel each lonely night.*

Thus Chinese American communities were characterized as "bachelor societies," although most of the men were married with children. Almost none of the early Chinese immigrants were women. Of the nearly 12,000 Chinese immigrants counted in the United States in 1852, only 7 were women. In 1900, only 5 percent—or about 4,500— of the 89,863 Chinese living in the United States were women. Most of these women were prostitutes who had been kidnapped, tricked, or sold to brothel owners or others who treated them like slaves. (A brothel is a house where prostitutes live and work.) Even very young girls could be sold—often by their own families—to brothel owners.

Japanese Families and the Picture Bride System

In the late 1800s, the Japanese government allowed only healthy and well-educated Japanese to leave the country. To prevent groups of men living alone from becoming lonely and turning to alcoholism or prostitution for comfort, Japan encouraged women to emigrate too. As a result, many more Japanese women immigrated to the United States than did Chinese women. Between 1911 and 1920, 39 percent of Japanese immigrants were women (as opposed to about 5 percent for Chinese). The Japanese women who came to the United States were well educated, and many found work in shops or in the clothing industry.

Japanese families arranged marriages for their children. If a son were in America, however, the arrangements could not be made in person. Instead, the families sent pictures and made matches by mail. Many Japanese women came to the United States as "picture brides."

The Japanese government made rules for the picture bride system to protect the women involved and to protect Japan's reputation in the world. In 1915, the rules allowed any man with at least $800 in savings to send for a picture bride. Husbands, who could not be more than 13 years older than their brides, were required to meet their wives at the docks.

Even with the Japanese government's protections, some women found shocking disappointments when they reached America. Their husbands were much older or much less attractive than the pictures had

---

Two Chinese Immigrants' Stories: Sold into Slavery

Lilac Chen remembers being sold into sex slavery by her father when she was six. Historian Ronald Takaki records her words: "And that worthless father, my own father, imagine ... sold me on the ferry boat. Locked me in the cabin while he was negotiating my sale."

Another young woman, Wong Ah So, was tricked into prostitution by a man who said he wanted to marry her: "I was nineteen when this man came to my mother and said that in America there was plenty of money. He was nice to me, and my mother liked him, so my mother was glad to have me go with him as his wife. I thought that I was his wife, and was very grateful that he was taking me to such a grand, free country, where everyone was rich and happy." When she got to America, she was forced to sell herself sexually to make money for her "husband."

—*Oral history provided by Betty Lee Sung*

---

shown. Their married lives were much poorer and more difficult than they had been led to believe. For these women, being a picture bride was not much different from being sold into slavery like their Chinese sisters. On the other hand, some Japanese couples found good marriages and productive lives this way.

The Japanese were the only Asians with American-born children in any numbers until after World War II (1939–45). Japanese Americans used special terms to

Wedding photo of Mr. and Mrs. Lee Yoke Suey around 1900. Mrs. Suey was detained by immigration authorities for 16 months before being allowed to enter the United States.

distinguish among generations. First-generation Japanese were called issei, second-generation nisei, third-generation sansei, fourth-generation yonsei, and fifth-generation gosei. By the 1940s, nisei outnumbered the issei two to one.

Korean Families

Korean men and women were recruited by business interests in Hawaii in the early 1900s. Hawaiian plantation owners were afraid that the mostly Japanese work force was going to organize into labor unions, so they began to recruit workers from Korea. (The owners hoped that an ethnically mixed group of workers would have a harder time getting organized. This was true, at first.) Many of the Koreans who came to Hawaii were Christian and wanted to settle with their families in what they had heard was a Christian country. Others brought their families with them because they were afraid they would never be able to return to Korea, which had been taken over by Japan. Some Korean women came as picture brides, like their Japanese sisters.

Filipinos

The culture found in the Philippines and Indonesia is referred to as Malayan. In Malayan culture women were accorded a respectable status, with some restrictions.

Thousands of Filipinos began to move to America when the Philippines became a U.S. territory in 1898. Most of these early immigrants were young men; it was considered immoral for a young woman to travel without a father or husband. Some women came with their husbands; others came later as students when the *pensionado* program was begun in 1903. In the *pensionado* program, the United States government gave financial aid to young Filipino men and women who wanted to study in America.

Filipino families were likely to settle in Hawaii, where they could have steady income from work on the plantations. On the United States mainland, most of the jobs available to them were for migrant farm workers. (Migrant workers do not establish a home in a community. Instead, they move from farm to farm, following the planting and harvesting seasons for different crops.) Also, Hawaiian plantation owners encouraged women to immigrate, believing family men to be more reliable than single men.

In California, where large numbers of Filipino men eventually settled, they found an affinity with Mexicans because of their common Hispanic heritage. (The Philippines had been ruled by Spain for 400 years.) Filipino men married Mexican women, and most of the children from these marriages assumed a Mexican American identity.

Family Life from World War II to 1965

War Brides

After World War II, the War Brides Act of 1946 enabled the women who married U.S. servicemen during the war to immigrate to the United States. Both European and Asian women were included in the act.

China was one of the U.S. allies during World War II, and many Chinese servicemen decided to remain in the United States after the war. From 1948 to 1953, almost every Chinese immigrant (90 percent) who disembarked at an American port of entry was a young Chinese woman with or without young children in tow. This marked the beginning of Chinese American family life in the United States.

In the period that followed the war (1946 to 1952), more than two million U.S. servicemen were stationed in Japan. An estimated 55,000 to 60,000 Japanese women married U.S. servicemen during this time. From 1950 to 1953, U.S. troops fought in the Korean War, and more than 40,000 of them married Korean women. About the same number of servicemen stationed in Manila, the Philippines, married Filipina women. And after the Vietnam War, the Vietnamese brides of U.S. troops who fought there also

> ## WORDS TO KNOW
>
> **bachelor society:** community comprised primarily of men; usually refers to an immigrant community where only men have immigrated
>
> **internment:** holding and confining a group of people, against their will, away from society
>
> **outmarriage:** marriage to a spouse outside one's own ethnic group
>
> **picture bride:** a woman whose marriage is arranged through the exchange of letters and photographs
>
> **refugee:** one who leaves his or her homeland to escape a dangerous or unlivable condition
>
> **war bride:** a woman who meets and marries a soldier from another country serving in her country during wartime

accompanied their husbands when they returned to the United States.

These families are quite different from any of those known before. The Asian women had experienced war and upheaval in their homelands. The American soldiers, sailors, and marines—GIs as they were known—were fighting a war or stationed abroad under hostile conditions. They were lonely and far away from their loved ones at home. Even though they came from totally different backgrounds and were of a different race, many friendships with local women developed into marriage.

Huge cultural differences as well as other tremendous difficulties have confronted these couples. Many brides had already undergone tremendous conflict and psychological strain generated by their families and communities to the interracial marriages. One Japanese bride revealed: "I felt like a traitor. I knew my family was deeply hurt and ashamed that I was dating an American G.I." The grooms' families often were not accepting either.

Many of these couples could communicate in only the simplest phrases in each other's language. Customs and traditions were different. Compelled to move to their husbands' hometowns, the brides often met with a hostile reception. Adjustment to life in America was reportedly easier for European war brides, since their racial and cultural heritage was similar to their husbands'—and their physical appearance allowed them to blend into the small towns of America more easily.

Family Life after 1965

The 1965 **Immigration and Nationality Act** did away with national quotas and allowed up to 20,000 immigrants to be admitted to the United States from any one country. Prior to passage of this act, quotas ranged from 100 to 185 people per country. In addition, Taiwan and Hong Kong—formerly counted with China—were granted separate quotas, 20,000 for Taiwan in 1980 and 10,000 for Hong Kong in 1990. Vietnamese and Southeast Asians entered under the 1980 **Refugee Relief Act** and separate immigration quotas.

"Relay Immigration"

Most Asian families do not enter the United States together when they immigrate.

As a rule, one member of a family will arrive first, find employment and housing, and then send for other members. A fairly common practice is to send the wife abroad with the children, while the husband continues his business back home. Another practice is to send the children to college in the United States. The parents remain in the home country until the child secures employment or acquires permanent residency status and can apply for the parents to immigrate too. This is known as "relay immigration."

When the family is reunited and established in the United States, they may send for the grandparents, generally on the husband's side, so that sons can fulfill their obligation of taking care of their parents. About five years after an immigrant arrives in the United States with "permanent resident" status, he or she can apply for U.S. citizenship.

American-Born Families

There is a growing percentage of Asian American families whose members were all born in the United States. The children of immigrants, known as the second generation, usually grow up observing the customs and values of their homeland culture. By the third generation, U.S. customs often prevail in issues of dating, choosing a mate, following wedding customs, role expectations, child rearing, and care of the elderly.

If the family resides in an ethnic community like a Chinatown, the traditional customs of the homeland will have a heavier influence because they are also the community tradition in the United States. But if a family lives in a multicultural community, it is likely that it will follow American practices more closely. Cultural roots run deep and even many American-born Asian American families remain close to their heritage.

Marriage

In Asian countries, marriage is very important. It is the obligation of parents to find a mate for their sons and daughters. But in the United States, many Asian American young people want to date and choose their own marriage partners. This presents a unique challenge, since their families do not understand this process. Parents who are recent immigrants often have no experience with setting dating rules, or with building a relationship before marriage.

Outmarriage

Interracial marriage is called outmarriage by most Asian Americans. These marriages involve an Asian American man or woman and a spouse of another race. More Asian women marry outside their race than do Asian men.

Not limited to Asian Americans, in the 1990s interracial and interethnic marriages were becoming more common in the United States. In fact, many government agencies that gather statistics on race and ethnicity are considering adding a new category—multiracial—to the established categories of white or Caucasian, black or African American, Hispanic, Native American, and Asian or Pacific Islander. Beginning in the fall of 1995, school districts in Florida provided their students with the option of "multiracial—or M" on enrollment forms.

Family Size

The cost of bringing up children in the United States and the lack of relatives nearby to help in child rearing may deter Asian American couples from having large families. In most Asian countries, large families are considered a blessing; in the United States, large families are often viewed as a financial burden. With the exception of Vietnamese, Asian American women have fewer children than women of other racial and ethnic groups. In fact, the Japanese and Chinese fertility rates are extremely low—less than one child per woman.

Children and Child-Rearing

The Asian American family tends to be strict. Parents demand respect and obedience, and they often encourage dependency upon the family instead of independence. Immigrants who arrive as children usually absorb U.S. ways of thought and behavior as they acquire English at school and play. As they observe American customs and patterns, many Asian children begin to question their parents' ways.

When parents don't speak English, many rely upon their children to be intermediaries in their contact with the outside world. With the children leading and the parents following, a reversal of parent-child role ensues. In their dealings with a new culture and language, Asian parents often become dependent upon their children.

Asian children growing up in the United States often lose—or never learn to speak—the language of their parents. Asian American children may feel pulled in two directions if they observe their schoolmates and playmates living by different standards. Witnessing the freedom that some of their peers seem to enjoy may distance them from their parents and grandparents.

Women's Resource Groups

The National Asian Pacific American Women's Forum (NAPAWF) was launched in 1996. It is a grassroots organization based in Washington, D.C., dedicated to economic justice and political empowerment of Asian and Pacific American women and girls. NAPAWF reports that, as of 2000, about 59 percent—or 2.5 million—of all Asian Pacific American women were working outside the home, with just under 4 percent unemployed.

Suggestions for Further Reading

Asian American Alliance, http://www.asianamerican alliance.com/aasbdc (accessed May 28, 2003).

"Asian American Women," *National Women's History Project,* http://www.nwhp.org/new_catalog/asian /asian1.htm (accessed May 30, 2003).

Asian Pacific American Women's Leadership Institute (APALI) http://www.apawli.org/ (accessed May 28, 2003).

Barringer, Herbert, Robert Gardner, and Michael Levin, *Asians and Pacific Islanders in the United States,* New York: Russell Sage Foundation, 1993.

Chan, Sucheng, *Asian Americans: An Interpretive History,* Boston: Twayne Publishers, 1991.

"Fact Sheet: Asian Pacific Islander Women in the Workplace," *National Asian Pacific American Women's Forum,* http://www.napawf.org/ (accessed May 25, 2003).

Kibria, Nazli, *Becoming Asian American: Second-Generation Chinese and Korean American Identities,* Baltimore: Johns Hopkins University Press, 2002.

Kuklin, Susan, *How My Family Lives in America,* Minneapolis: Bradbury Press, 1992.

Making More Waves: New Writing by Asian American Women, Boston: Beacon Press, 1997.

Making Waves: An Anthology of Writing By and About Asian American Women, Boston: Beacon Press, 1989.

10

Languages

Native Languages of Asian Americans

FACT FOCUS

- *There are thousands of languages and dialects spoken by the people of Asia.*
- *Romanization is the process used to write many Asian languages in a form English-speaking people can read.*
- *Words derived from English, called* gairaigo *(words of foreign origin), are becoming more common in Japanese.*
- *Written Chinese uses characters to represent words rather than a phonetic alphabet; after six years of elementary school, most students can read and write about 3,000 characters—enough to read a newspaper.*
- *The Korean alphabet is called Han'gul, or "great letters"; it was created in 1443.*

The native languages spoken by Asian Americans are even more diverse than the population groups themselves. For example, India has over 2,000 languages and dialects. Fourteen of them are recognized by the government as official languages. Many Asian languages use tones to give their language meaning. English speakers also use rising and falling tones. For example, if a teenager tells her father that she just smashed up the car, he may reply, "You *what?*" Or if a teacher questions someone suspected of causing a disruption in class, the student's response may be "*Me?*" These are both rising intonations. The falling tone in English is illustrated in this example: A young child is about to touch a hot stove, and his mother says "*No!*" This is the falling tone.

Presented here are a few widely spoken Asian languages.

Bengali

Bengali (also known as Bangla) is the official language of Bangladesh, and is spoken by almost all Bangladeshis. In the 1950s, Bengali and Urdu were given equal status as official languages. Bengali is the language of instruction in Bangladesh

---

CHINESE LANGUAGE

Numbers	Pronunciation
one	yī
two	èr
three	sān
four	sì
five	wǔ
six	liù
seven	qī
eight	bā
nine	jiǔ
ten	shí

Expressions	Pronunciation
hello	mi hǎo
good evening	wǎn ān
how are you?	mi hǎo ma?
you're welcome	búkèqi
no	búshì
yes	shì
please	qiňg
thank you	xie
pardon me	dùibu qí

Rabindranath Tagore, began composing poems. He was awarded the Nobel Prize for literature in 1913, the first Asian writer to be so honored.

(*See also* sections on Hindi and Urdu.)

Chinese Languages

More than one billion people speak some form of Chinese. The most common form is Mandarin. In Hong Kong, Cantonese or Yùe is the Chinese dialect most people speak. The Cantonese and Taiwanese dialects, like many other Chinese dialects, are not understood by Mandarin speakers. However, many speakers of Cantonese and Taiwanese do speak and understand Mandarin. In fact, Cantonese, Taiwanese, and Mandarin are the most commonly heard Chinese dialects in the United States and Canada.

Other major Chinese dialects include the Wu dialect in Shanghai (80 million speakers); Xiang in Hunan (45 million speakers); Hakka in both southern China and in Taiwan (35 million speakers); and Gan in Jiangxi (22 million speakers). There are also hundreds of minor dialects throughout China.

The Chinese language does not have a phonetic alphabet, so all people who learn to write Chinese must learn one word, which is represented by a single character, at a time. After six years of elementary school, most students can read and write about 3,000 characters—enough to read a newspaper.

Tones

Mandarin Chinese has four stressed tones, plus an unstressed one. (Cantonese has nine tones.) The first tone is the high level tone, *mā* ("mother"). Next, is the second tone:

schools, but English is widely understood among the educated population.

Bengali is the language of well over 100 million people. One-third of them live in the Indian provinces of West Bengal and Tripura; the remainder live in Bangladesh. The language is used for religious purposes.

Bengali script contains curving strokes. There are no capitals. Verse was the first form written in Bengali. In the nineteenth century, the most famous Bengali poet, middle level and rising, *má* ("hemp"). The third tone is the low level and rising, *mǎ* ("horse"). And the fourth tone is the high level and falling, *mà* ("to scold").

Romanization

To write a Chinese character in English, the writer first needs to sound out the word phonetically. Then the character can be written in the Roman alphabet, which English uses. This process of writing Chinese in the English-language alphabet is called "romanization."

Several systems of romanization are used in China. Hànyǔ Pinyin is the official romanization system of the Chinese government, the United Nations, the U.S. Library of Congress, and the U.S. Postal Service. *Hànyǔ* means "Chinese language" and *Pinyin* means "spelling and sound."

Family Names

The Chinese say and write the last name first, then follow it with the first name, which is usually comprised of one or two characters. For example, Deng Xiaoping is not Mr. Ping, but rather Mr. Deng; Xiaoping is his first name. Some common Chinese last names are Chen, Dai, Feng, Lu, Qian, Wang, and Zhang.

Japanese

Since Japan did not have its own writing system, educated Japanese used Chinese characters, called "kanji," to write ideas in Japanese. Around the tenth century A.D., a unique Japanese syllabary derived from the Chinese written characters developed. A syllabary is different from an alphabet. Each

> ## WORDS TO KNOW
>
> **dialect:** a regional variety of a language
>
> **inflection:** the change of form words undergo to make distinctions pertaining to case, gender, number, tense, person, mood, or voice
>
> **phoneme:** a single, distinct speech sound, one of the smallest units of speech that distinguish one utterance from another, for example, the *g* sound and *h* sound
>
> **phonetic spelling:** using the alphabet of one language to represent the sounds of another
>
> **stress:** to place emphasis on, to accent
>
> **syllabary:** a set of symbols or characters, each representative of a syllable
>
> **tone:** the pitch of a word, often used to express different meanings

symbol represents a syllable rather than a letter. The invention of these symbols, called "kana," allowed the Japanese to express themselves in their own form of writing for the first time in their history.

Kana

Kana take two forms: katakana and hiragana. Katakana characters are rigid or straight, and originated by abbreviating or simplifying some part of Chinese characters. Katakana is usually used for communicating foreign names, concepts, and inventions. Many words written in katakana may be recognized by anyone who knows English. *Jon-sumisu, ká-puru,* and *rajio* are

JAPANESE LANGUAGE

Numbers	Pronunciation
one	ichi
two	ni
three	san
four	shi (yon)
five	go
six	roku
seven	shichi (nana)
eight	hachi
nine	kyū
ten	jū

Expressions	Pronunciation
hello	konnichiwa
good evening	kombanwa
how are you?	ogenki desu ka?
you're welcome	dō itashimashite
no	iie
yes	hai
please	dōzo
thank you	arigatō
pardon me	sumimasen

Romaji, another form of Japanese writing, is based on the Roman alphabet, hence its romanized characters (*roma*—"Roman"; *ji*—"characters or words").

The Japanese Sentence

The Japanese sentence is written in a combination of different symbols. Kanji, the characters adopted from the Chinese language, are used to represent basic ideas (e.g., nouns, verbs, adjectives) and Japanese names. Kana (hiragana and katakana) are the phonetic symbols that represent sounds; each symbol begins with a consonant and ends with a vowel. Altogether there are 46 sounds; this is the Japanese "alphabet."

Although a large percentage of Japanese vocabulary words are derived from Chinese, more and more English words are coming into the Japanese language. These are called "gairaigo" ("words of foreign origin"). Examples of gairaigo are *kóhí kappu*, *terebi*, and *kamera*—"coffee cup," "television," and "camera" in English.

Japanese is written either vertically with columns running from top to bottom and right to left or horizontally with text running from left to right. Most books, newspapers, magazines, and formal letters are written vertically; word processing and informal writing is usually done horizontally.

Grammar

The sentence structure in Japanese is different from the sentence structure of English. The sentence, in English, "John ran to school" is, in Japanese, "John to school ran." Word order in Japanese is subject-object-verb.

three words in katakana that come from English. They are "John Smith," "car pool," and "radio," respectively.

Hiragana employs soft, cursive, flowing symbols, and has been called "the soul of the Japanese." Many culturally important terms such as *wa* ("harmony") and *giri* ("duty or obligation") were originally written in hiragana.

Politeness

Many levels of politeness are used in Japanese. When speaking to someone older or to a supervisor, a polite, formal form of speech is used. A humble or modest form of speech is also used. *Onegaishimasu* is an example of this, meaning, "Would you do this for me, please?"

Names

In Japanese, the last name is spoken before the first name. *San* is added to the last name to show respect. This is equivalent to Mr., Mrs., Miss, or Ms. Some common last names are Kato, Sato, Nakamura, and Tanaka. Some common male given names are Hiroshi, Kiyoshi, Taro, and Yoshio. Typical female given names are Kazuko, Keiko, Michiki, and Yoko. Thus, Nakamura Yoshio would be Mr. Yoshio Nakamura in English and Nakamura-san in Japanese. Kato Michiko would be Miss, Ms., or Mrs. Kato in English and Kato-san in Japanese.

Korean Language

Koreans have a strong national identity, in part because they all speak and write the same language. But both written and spoken Korean have been influenced by the Chinese language, due largely to China's immense political and cultural impact on Korea over the centuries.

The Korean language is written with a largely phonetic alphabet called Han'gul, or "great letters." Han'gul was created in 1443 by a group of scholars and is considered to be one of the most efficient writing systems in the world. The Korean alphabet originally had ten vowels and fourteen consonants.

KOREAN LANGUAGE

Numbers	Pronunciation
one	hana
two	tul
three	set'
four	net'
five	taso`t'
six	yo`so`t'
seven	ikop
eight	yo`to`l
nine	ahop
ten	yo`l

Expressions	Pronunciation
hello	annyo`ng-haseyo
goodbye	annyo`nghi gaseyo
how are you?	o`tto`ke chinaeshimnika?
you're welcome	cho`nmaneyo
no	anio
yes	ye
please	chebal
thank you	komapsu`mnida
pardon me	choesong-hamnida

Five consonants and eleven vowels have been added. Han'gul is simple and easy to learn, print, and apply to computer systems.

Romanization

To convert Han'gul symbols to a form using the English-language alphabet (Roman alphabet), the sounds are written phonetically. There are two systems for romanizing Korean: the McCune-Reischauer system developed in 1939 and now conventional in English, and an ROK (South Korea) Ministry of Education system developed in 1959. In 1984, the ROK system was modified to align with the McCune-Reischauer system.

Since 1949, the Democratic People's Republic of Korea (DPRK), or North Korea, has used only Han'gul (calling it *Choson Muntcha*) for writing. In 1964, Korean leader Kim Il-Sung called for purification of Korean by replacing borrowed words from English and Japanese with native Korean or familiar Chinese terms. The Republic of Korea (ROK), or South Korea, has undertaken similar "language beautification" drives designed to eliminate borrowing from Japanese and other languages.

Names

Korean names almost invariably consist of three Chinese characters that are pronounced with three Korean syllables. The family name comes first and the remaining two characters form the given name. One of these often identifies the generation.

There are about 300 family names in Korea, but most people have one of the common last names. These are Kim, Lee or Yi, Park or Pak, An, Chang, Cho, Ch'oe, Cho'ng, Han or Hahn, Kang, Yu, and Yun.

Korean women do not change their names when married. Koreans do not refer to others by their given, or first, name except among very close friends. Even among siblings, the younger ones do not address the older ones by given names. A girl calls her older sister *o'nni* and her older brother *oppa*. A boy calls his older sister *nuna* and his older brother *hyo'ng*.

Pilipino

In the Philippines there are two official languages, Pilipino and English. The national language, Pilipino, is based on another Filipino language, Tagalog. Pilipino is mandatory in public and private schools, and was adopted as the national language in 1946. The English language, which is widely used in schools, is also spoken and understood by the majority of Filipinos.

Although Spanish was an official language in the Philippines prior to 1973, it is now spoken by a small minority of the population. More than 80 indigenous (native) languages and dialects (primarily of Malay-Indonesian origin) are spoken in the Philippines. Besides Tagalog, which is spoken around Manila, the principal languages include: Cebuano, spoken in the Visayas; Ilocano, spoken in Northern Luzon; and Panay-Hiligaynon.

Urdu and Hindi

Hindi and Urdu are essentially two forms of the original Hindustani language. Although the speaker of one can usually understand a speaker of the other, their scripts are different. Hindus adopted the Sanskrit script and Muslims (Urdu speakers) used the Persian or Arabic script.

Urdu

Urdu is the national language of Pakistan. Although native speakers account for only 9 percent of the total population, it is now spoken and understood by over 100 million people.

Because it developed in India, the Muslims called it Hindi or Hindavi, the language of India. Over the years this language assumed various names like Zaban-e-Dehli, Zaban-e-Hindustan, Zaban-e-Urdu-e-Mualla, Zaban-e-Urdu and, finally, Urdu. Urdu is a word derived from the area of Mughal Delhi, known as *urdu-e-mualla,* or "the exalted camp." Urdu was taken to different parts of the Indian subcontinent by travelers from the north.

Urdu script (the written language) is an adaptation of Persian and Arabic script. By 1800, the phonetic writing system or alphabet of the language had been fully developed.

Modern Urdu has fifty phonemes, or distinct sounds, including thirty-eight consonants, ten vowels, one nasal, and one phoneme of juncture (joining), reflecting Indic, Persian, and Arabic influence. Urdu has two genders, masculine and feminine.

Hindi

Hindi is the official language of modern India. It is written in the Sanskrit, or Devanagari, script. English is also widely used as a means of conversation and for administrative purposes. India also recognizes 14 regional languages (or *bhashas*) in addition to Hindi and English.

In the late 1800s and early 1900s, British authorities in India encouraged Urdu as an official language. The underprivileged Hindu majority began to oppose the use of standard Urdu. This became an important factor in the conflict leading to the eventual partition (division) of India and Pakistan in 1947.

The 1948 Indian constitution made Nagari the standard script of Hindi, the national language of India. However, Arabic numerals continued to be used, and English remained an official language over the next 15 years. Although standard Hindi has become more widely used since the 1948 partition of India and Pakistan, it has not completely overtaken English. The mass media, particularly the film industry, uses a mixture of languages intelligible to Hindi and Urdu speakers alike.

The Hindi Sentence

Basic Hindi word order is subject-object-verb. Hindu men are usually addressed by their last name with a polite term *ji* added to it. For example, Mr. Sharma would be *Sharma ji.* Hindu women, however, are usually known by their first name. As in Urdu, Hindi has two genders, masculine and feminine.

Throughout India, English continues to be the language of the elite; in fact, private schools teach only an elementary form of Hindi.

Suggestions for Further Reading

Crystal, David, *The Cambridge Encyclopedia of Language,* New York: Cambridge University Press, 1987.

Lehonkoski, Ritva, *Describing East-Asian Grammar: An Application of Role and Reference Grammar,* Helsinki: Finnish Oriental Society, 2000.

Mazumdar, B. C., *The History of the Bengali Language,* New Delhi: Asian Educational Services, 2000.

Nakanishi, Akira, *Writing Systems of the World: Alphabets, Syllabaries, Pictograms,* Rutland, VT: Charles E. Tuttle, 1980.

Scurfield, Elizabeth, *Beginner's Chinese: An Easy Introduction,* London: Teach Yourself Books, 2002.

11

Education

Asian American Students

From Elementary to Graduate School

FACT FOCUS

- *From 1980 to 1990, Asian American enrollment in higher education doubled in 36 of the 50 states.*
- *In 1999, Asian Americans made up almost 3 percent of the total U.S. population, about 5 percent of elementary and high school enrollment, 7 percent of college enrollment, but only 1 percent of the teaching force.*
- *Differences between Asian and U.S. cultures may cause conflicts for Asian American students.*
- *In 1999, of all ethnic minorities, Asian American students were most likely to have at least one foreign-born parent.*

Asian Americans

In the early 1900s, children of immigrants from Asia, like other children of minority groups, were not permitted to attend schools with white children in many communities. In California, there were "Oriental Schools" for Asian American children—mostly Chinese, Japanese, and Korean. In the 1990s, Asian Americans were one of the fastest-growing racial/ethnic group in the United States. There are more students of Asian descent than ever in schools, colleges, and universities. Many newspaper and magazine articles and television segments have focused on the success of Asian American students in school, especially in science, engineering, and medicine. But, given their cultural diversity, it is impossible to categorize Asian Americans into a single group and unfair to stereotype them as science "whiz kids."

The academic performance of some Asian Americans overshadows the difficulties faced by others. Asian Americans in different ethnic groups show significantly different high school completion rates. In 1980, only 22 percent of the Hmong population and 43 percent of Cambodians in the United States completed high school, compared with more than 80 percent of Asian Indians, Japanese, Indonesian, and Pakistani individuals. Further, the Asian American high school dropout rate was 7.4 percent in 1991; by 1992, the rate had risen to 14.5 percent, doubling in one year, while dropout rates for other major ethnic groups remained relatively unchanged. By 1999, the dropout rate had declined to 4.8 percent (representing about 25,000 Asian American high school dropouts).

Elementary through High School

Language Abilities and Challenges

The number of families in the United States that speak a language other than English at home is increasing. In 2000, a total of 2,022,143 lived in homes where Chinese was spoken, more than double the 769,000 who lived in homes where Chinese was spoken in 1990. Some 1,224,241 lived in homes where Tagalog (Pilipino or Fili-

pino) was spoken, compared to 713,000 in 1990. Homes where Vietnamese was spoken included 1,009,627 people in 2000.

Because the United States is an English-speaking country, English is the primary tool for succeeding in school and securing employment. Yet many experts in bilingual education argue that schools do children and their families a disservice if they foster the loss of the home language. Losing the ability to speak their home language can sever cultural roots and family connections,

> ## WORDS TO KNOW
>
> **bilingual:** able to speak, read, and write two languages with equal skill
>
> **Oriental:** belonging to the countries of Asia. This term was used until the 1950s, when it was replaced by the term "Asian"; many Asian Americans consider "Oriental" an offensive term

Language Spoken at Home by Top Five States, 1991

State	Only English	Chinese	Japanese	Korean	Tagalog (Pilipino)	Vietnamese
California	18,764,213	575,447	147,451	215,845	464,644	233,074
Hawaii	771,485	26,366	69,587	14,636	55,341	4,620
Illinois	9,086,726	41,807	13,174	33,973	46,453	7,572
New York	12,834,328	247,334	29,845	80,394	46,276	11,531
Texas	11,635,518	52,220	11,898	26,228	22,256	57,736
Total all US states	187,346,912	1,302,665	420,533	617,207	835,785	496,677

Source: Asian/Pacific Islander Data Consortium (San Francisco: Asian and Pacific Islander Center for Census Information and Services, 1993). Primary source: U.S. Census Bureau, Summary Tape Files 1 and 3; consult www.census.gov for updates. State data from the 2000 census was scheduled for release in fall 2003.

traditionally of great importance in Asian American families.

In addition to language differences, Asian American students observe classroom and school values that often contrast with values they're taught at home. Their efforts to adapt to the values and behavior of their U.S. peers may cause conflict with their parents or family members. For example, Asian children struggle with the fact that in the United States authority figures in schools are not always shown great respect by students. Asian children are raised to avoid behaving aggressively, and to turn away when they are the targets of someone else's aggression. Because many in the United States favor tougher, more "masculine" behavior, being aggressive at certain times is often a positive trait in U.S. classrooms. Asian American students, who come from cultures in which talking a lot is considered rude, find this a problem. Also, Asian children are often quick to report wrongdoing to teachers; their U.S. peers view reporters as "tattlers."

These and other conflicting cultural characteristics affect some Asian American students profoundly. An effort has been made to understand and explain these differences through a growing number of books written for children and young adults that focus on Asian Americans in the United States.

Higher Education

As a group, Asian Americans are the most-educated ethnic population in the United States. The 2000 census reported that 87.4 percent of Asian Americans over 25 had completed high school, compared with 84.8 percent of whites and 84.1 percent of the total U.S. population.

Asian Americans are also more likely to have completed four years of college than any other ethnic group including whites. In 2000, 47.2 percent of Asian Americans age 25 and over had at least four years of college, compared to 27.2 percent for whites, and 26.7 percent for the total U.S. population

Because data on more than 30 different ethnic groups—Asian Indian American, Chinese American, Filipino American, Japanese American, Korean American, Vietnamese American, to name the six largest groups—are lumped together into the Asian American category, it is not possible to examine the differences in participation and achievement of the individual Asian ethnic groups.

Scholastic Assessment Test (SAT)

Many colleges require that applicants take the Scholastic Assessment Test (SAT) in order to be considered for admission. The numbers of Asian Americans who take the SAT are increasing: in 1993, 83,096 Asians took the SAT, up from 68,824 in 1988, a 20.7 percent increase in five years. Asian Americans are less than 3 percent of the total U.S. population, but they were 7.5 percent of the total of SAT-takers in 1993; by 2002, Asian Americans represented 10 percent of all SAT-takers. Of those Asian American and Latino (Hispanic) students who took the test in 1999, 39 percent did not list English as their first language. To compare, fewer and fewer white students are taking the SAT, declining from 75 percent of all SAT-takers in 1989 to 65 percent in 2002.

The College Board is the organization that administers the SAT test, and it gathers information on all test takers. It published these interesting facts about Asian American test-takers in the class that graduated from high school in 2002:

—Thirty-seven percent had parents who did not earn college degrees, compared to 31 percent for white students.

—The average high school grade–point average (GPA) of Asian American SAT test-takers was 3.41, compared to 3.35 for white students.

—The overwhelming majority—83 percent—attended public schools. Only 11 percent went to religious-affiliated high schools, and 6 percent attended independent (private) schools.

—Only 57 percent of Asian American test-takers were U.S. citizens, compared to 98 percent of whites and 92 percent of the national sample. Twenty-eight percent were permanent residents and 15 percent had nonresident status.

The SAT consists of two parts: the verbal (language) portion and the math portion. In 2002, Asian American SAT takers scored a little below the national mean (average) on the verbal portion of the SAT while performing well above the national mean on the math portion of the test. From 1992–2002, Asian Americans made significant gains in SAT test scores. Average Asian American verbal test scores increased by 14 points (from 487 to 501), while whites gained 8 points in the same period (519 to 527). Average math scores achieved by both Asian American and white students increased by 18 points (from 551 to 569 for Asian Americans and 515 to 533 for whites).

Asian college-bound seniors of both genders took more years of mathematics and natural science courses than did all other college-bound seniors. Eighty-two percent of Asian test applicants completed at least three years of natural sciences and almost all (94 percent) took at least three years of mathematics. They also took more years of foreign and classical languages, and their total years of study overall were higher. Their years of English study were the same as the national average, but they lagged slightly behind the national average in hours of arts, music, social science, and history courses.

College Major and Degree Aspirations

Asian students are likely to choose to major in biological sciences, engineering, and health in college. Asian college-bound students are more likely to aspire to a doctorate than all other college-bound students (34 percent versus 23 percent). An equal proportion of Asian males and females plan to earn a doctorate.

Higher Education Enrollment

In the 1980s, the Asian American population increased in every state and doubled in 31 states. Asian American enrollment in higher education during this time doubled in 36 states. In 1990, for every 100 students attending U.S. colleges and universities, 4 were Asian Americans; by 1999, the number had increased to 7 of every 100 college students. (Their total number rose from 286,000 in 1980 to 573,000 in 1990, to more than one million in 1999.) By contrast, 10 percent of college students in 1999 were African Americans; 4 percent were

Asian College-Bound Seniors: 1993 SAT Profiles Intended College Major and Degree-Level Goal

	Number of SAT Takers	Percent	% Male/Female
Intended College Major			
Agriculture/Natural Resources	340	0	45/55
Architecture/Environmental Design	2,337	3	61/39
Arts: Visual and Performing	3,258	4	39/61
Biological Sciences	4,680	6	45/55
Business and Commerce	12,860	17	46/54
Communications	1,699	2	25/75
Computer/Information Sciences	2,994	4	71/29
Education	2,210	3	23/77
Engineering	11,703	15	82/18
Foreign/Classical Languages	400	1	24/76
General/Interdisciplinary	216	0	37/63
Health and Allied Services	19,456	25	41/59
Home Economics	136	0	23/77
Language and Literature	679	1	26/74
Library and Archival Sciences	23	0	48/52
Mathematics	462	1	53/47
Military Sciences	247	0	81/19
Philosophy/Religion/Theology	177	0	60/40
Physical Sciences	1107	1	62/38
Public Affairs and Services	917	1	50/50
Social Sciences and History	6,244	8	33/67
Technical and Vocational	486	1	70/30
Undecided	3,879	5	50/50
Degree–Level Goal			
Certificate Program	1,152	2	54/46
Associate Degree	873	1	45/55
Bachelor's Degree	13,129	17	50/50
Master's Degree	21,611	29	52/48
Doctoral/Related Degree	25,822	34	50/50
Other	654	1	45/55
Undecided	12,358	16	47/53

Source: The College Board, *College-Bound Seniors, Asian Report: 1993 Profile of SAT and Achievement Test Takers* (New York: The College Board), unpublished data.

Asian American GRE General Test Examinees by Broad Intended Graduate Major Field, 1990 to 1991
(U.S. Citizens Only)

Field	Number	Percent	% of Total
Business	159	19	6
Education	555	65	1
Engineering	1,741	205	10
Humanities/Art	611	72	2
Life Sciences	1,390	164	3
Physical Science	939	111	6
Social Science	1,141	135	3
Other fields	767	90	3
Undecided	1,177	139	3
Total	8,480	1,000	3

Source: Graduate Record Examination Board, *Examinee and Score Trends for the GRE General Test: 1989-90, 1990-91* (Princeton, NJ: Educational Testing Service), unpublished data.

Hispanic; 84 percent were non-Hispanic white.

Increases in Asian American participation in higher education continued to outpace other ethnic groups in the 1990s. From 1990 to 1991, total enrollment increased by 3.9 percent, while Asian American enrollment grew more than 11 percent, the largest increase among all ethnic groups. Much of the increase occurred at community colleges (19.1 percent). Asian Americans were still more likely to attend four-year institutions than two-year colleges. In 1999, seven percent of students enrolled full time at both two- and four-year institutions were Asian-American. The 2000 census revealed that among Asian Americans who were at least 25 years old, over 40 percent had earned a bachelor's degree or higher, compared to about 27 percent for the total population.

Indeed, after earning a bachelor's degree, many Asian American students chose to continue their studies, entering graduate programs to earn a master's degree or doctorate. In 1999, Asian Americans reported the largest graduate enrollment increase, 9.4 percent, among all ethnic groups. By comparison, African American graduate enrollment increased by 6.0 percent, Hispanic by 8.5 percent, white by 2.4 percent, and total graduate enrollment by 3.3 percent. Asian Americans accounted for 3.5 percent of all graduate enrollment in 1991, and nearly 13 percent by 1999.

More than half (59 percent) of Asian American graduate students planned to earn master's degrees. Since 1980, engineering has consistently ranked as the top field (and education as the bottom) of intended graduate study. Asian Americans are participating in increasing numbers all along the educational pipeline. Growth in their numbers in high school, college, graduate, and professional schools in the 1980s and early 1990s was dramatic.

Graduate Study. Many graduate schools require applicants to take the Graduate Record Examination (GRE) as part of the application process. Asians made up 3 percent of all GRE test takers in 1987, but represented 4 percent of those who had majored in science and engineering at the undergraduate level. Although they generally scored lower than whites on the verbal and analytical sections of the GRE, Asian American test takers scored higher on the quantitative (math) section, where their average scores were 63 points higher than those of their white counterparts (604 versus 541) and 73 points higher than the total GRE test-taking population. On the verbal section, the overall score of Asian American test takers was 476, 40 points lower than that for whites and 29 points lower than all test takers.

The majority of Asian American GRE test takers were biological or physical sciences majors as undergraduates (64 percent), by far the highest percentage in these fields of any of the other racial/ethnic groups. In terms of intended major of graduate study, 56 percent of Asian Americans responded that they intended to major in biological or physical sciences, again, by far, the largest racial/ethnic group pursuing these fields.

Teaching and Teacher Education

The increasing diversity and multiracial complexion of American society is particularly apparent in the nation's schools. According to estimates, by the year 2020, 40 percent of school children will be nonwhite. In the 1990s, at least 30 percent of students in schools are children of color. (Children of color may be African American, Hispanic American, Asian American, or Native American.) In 20 of the largest school districts in the United States, over 70 percent of total school enrollments are children of color. Despite these statistics, teachers, college faculty training teachers, and school administrators continue to be largely white.

In the 1990–91 school year, the number of Asian American elementary and secondary public school teachers had reached 25,952, or 1 percent of the teaching force.

Asian Americans in Teacher Education

Although Asian Americans are well represented in colleges and universities in many disciplines, they are still largely absent from undergraduate teacher preparation programs. In fact, Asian American registration in schools and colleges of education hovers at about 1 percent. In 39 states, Asian American enrollment in schools and colleges of education is negligible (less than 1 percent). The largest percentages of Asian American teacher education students are clustered in only eight western states—Alaska, California, Hawaii, Idaho, Nevada, New Mexico, Oregon, and Washington.

Similarly, Asian Americans constitute only one percent of education faculty. Asian American doctorates are concentrated in engineering and computer science; thus, Asian Americans who hold doctorates join teacher education faculties at rates lower than the national average. In total, less than 4 percent of Asian American college students prepare for teaching careers, unlike nearly 12 percent of all college students.

Summary

The number of Asian American students at all levels of education is growing. Asian American college-bound high school seniors show greater participation rates in higher–level mathematics and science courses than the average U.S. student. They often score higher on the SAT and have higher degree aspirations. They are more likely to choose majors in biological sciences, engineering, and health than the average U.S. degree student. They are also more likely to aspire to earn a doctorate.

Suggestions for Further Reading

Asian American Higher Education Council, http://www.aahec.org/events/ (accessed June 2, 2003).

Banks, J. A., "Teaching Multicultural Literacy to Teachers," *Teaching Education* 4, No. 1 (1991): 135-144.

Crew, Linda, *Children of the River*, New York: Dell, 1989.

Goodwin, A. Lin, *Asian Americans and Pacific Islanders in Teaching,* ERIC Digest 104.

Hamanaka, S., *The Journey: Japanese Americans, Racism, and Renewal,* New York: Orchard Books, 1990.

Hirabayashi, Lane Ryo, *Teaching Asian America: Diversity and the Problem of Community,* Lanham, MD: Rowman & Littlefield, 1998.

Hsia, Jayjia, *Asian Americans in Higher Education and at Work*, Hilldale, NJ: Lawrence Erlbaum Associates, 1988.

Le, C. N., "Immigrants in the Postindustrial Economy," *Asian-Nation: The Landscape of Asian America,* http://www.asian-nation.org/postindustrial.shtml (accessed May 5, 2003).

Lortie, D., *Schoolteacher*, Chicago: University of Chicago Press, 1975.

Takaki, Ronald T., *A Different Mirror: A History of Multicultural America*, Boston: Little, Brown and Co., 1993.

Takaki, Ronald T., *Raising Cane: The World of Plantation Hawaii,* New York: Chelsea House Publishers, 1993.

Takaki, Ronald T., *Strangers from a Different Shore: A History of Asian Americans*, New York: Penguin Books, 1990.

Uchida, Yoshiko, *The Bracelet*, New York: Philomel, 1993.

Yep, Laurence, *The Star Fisher*, New York: Morrow, 1991.

Yoo, David. *Growing Up Nisei: Race, Generation, and Culture Among Japanese Americans of California, 1924–49,* Urbana: University of Illinois Press, 2000.

12

Science and Engineering

Asian Americans in Science and Engineering

FACT FOCUS

- In 1988, 5 percent of scientists and engineers in the United States were of Asian descent, although Asian Americans represented only 2 percent of the overall workforce.
- More Asian students are well prepared academically for science-related majors than any other group of college-bound students.
- Asian Americans received 4.4 percent of all science and engineering doctorates awarded to U.S. citizens in 1992.
- Asian Americans are more likely to choose majors in biological sciences, engineering, and health than the average U.S. degree student.

Many Asian Americans pursue careers in science and engineering. In 1988, for example, Asians made up 5 percent of those employed in science and engineering fields in the United States, although they represented only 2 percent of the overall workforce and 3 percent of those employed in professional fields. In contrast, African American and Hispanic American professionals represented 2.6 percent and 1.8 percent, respectively, of the pool of employed scientists and engineers. Their representation in the general workforce is much higher, at 10 percent for African Americans and 7.2 percent for Hispanic Americans.

Sometimes data that are collected about the workforce do not separate citizens and noncitizens with U.S. permanent resident status. This presents a problem, since many Asians studying and working in the United States are not citizens.

Anti-Asian American Bias: Fear or Reality?

In December 1999, Dr. Wen Ho Lee, a Taiwanese American scientist at the Los Alamos National Laboratory in New Mexico was charged 59 counts of mishandling nuclear secrets, and was sent to prison. He remained in prison for over nine months, where he was held in solitary confinement because he was deemed to be a "clear and present danger" to national security. After a thorough investigation, authorities concluded that there was no evidence that Dr. Lee was involved in espionage. However, Lee pleaded guilty to improperly downloading classified material. He was given a sentence that equaled the time he had already served in prison. After his case was closed, scientists prepared for a backlash of anti-Asian American action, especially against scientists.

After the terrorist attacks on New York and Washington, D.C., in September 2001, national security became an issue of importance to all U.S. citizens. In December 2001, the American Association for the Advancement of Science (AAAS) convened a symposium to study whether heightened security measures would affect the conduct of scientific research in the United States. Since the new security measures had only been in place for a short period, most scientists presented papers concluding that neither the Wen Ho Lee case nor the terrorist attacks had affected Asian American scientists directly. However, international students studying on U.S. campuses were finding it more difficult to get visas, with new security measures causing a backlog in processing applications.

On its Web site, the American Association for the Advancement of Science expressed concern about the possibility that xenophobia (fear or suspicion of foreigners) could result in repression of scientific inquiry and research at U.S. universities.

Success Factors

What factors contribute to Asian American success in science and engineering? What do the scientists and engineers have in common in their home environments, attitudes, and educational experiences? Data from large-scale databases such as the National Assessment of Educational Progress (NAEP), the Student Descriptive Questionnaire (SDQ) of the Scholastic Aptitude Test (SAT), the National Research Council's Survey of Earned Doctorates, and others will help to answer these questions.

Data was collected and published on students in the fourth, eighth, and twelfth grades by the NAEP Science Assessment of 1990. These data include information on demographic characteristics, educational experiences, background (including home environment and attitudes), and achievement in science of the students surveyed.

Demographic Information

The group of students the NAEP surveyed was approximately evenly divided between boys and girls. Among the Asian American students in the sample, most reside in the western region of the United States. The majority of Asian American students had parents who had graduated from college. (In the case of fourth graders, 46 percent did not know their parents' educational level.)

Overall, Asian American students' parents had higher educational levels than did any other racial ethnic group in the sample. This sample of Asian American students, during their elementary and middle school years, attended private or Catholic schools at a greater rate than their peers from other racial/ethnic categories.

Home Environment

The home environment influences a student's proficiency in science. In general, students who live in homes with more reading material perform better than those with access to fewer materials. Students who watch six or more hours of television daily have lower performance than students who watch less television.

With the exception of Hispanic American students, Asian American students at all three grade levels are much more likely to come from homes where a language other than English is spoken "sometimes" or "always" than other students surveyed. Even though Asian American homes have fewer newspapers, encyclopedias, books, and magazines than do their white counterparts, Asian American students generally do not turn to television. By twelfth grade, they are the most likely of all groups to watch no television at all.

Study Habits

The amount of time students spend doing homework is another indicator of achievement in school. At grades eight and twelve, Asian American students are much more likely to spend two or more hours daily on homework than are any of their counterparts; they are also more likely to read more than eighth and twelfth graders in the other racial/ethnic groups.

Students and Science

Students who report liking science achieve at a higher level in the subject than

those who do not like science. When asked if they liked science, Asian Americans were more likely than African American and Hispanic American students to reply "yes" at the fourth grade. By the twelfth grade, Asian Americans were more likely to report that they liked science than did any other students.

Another factor contributing to success in science is having the opportunity to conduct experiments. By grade twelve, only white students reported having performed science experiments at a greater rate than Asian Americans. A majority of Asian American fourth graders reported spending between half an hour to one hour doing science homework each week, the largest percentage reporting this across racial/ethnic categories. By the twelfth grade, Asian American students report spending more than two-and-a-half hours a week on science homework.

Science Achievement

At the fourth grade, white students score nine points higher than Asian American students on standardized tests in science; at the eighth grade, the gap, with whites leading, is two points; by the twelfth grade, Asian

ASIAN AMERICAN MILESTONES IN SCIENCE

1901 Dr. Jokichi Takamine isolates pure epinephrine (adrenaline) at Johns Hopkins University.

1951 An Wang founds Wang Laboratories. Wang invented the magnetic core memory, a key component of early computers, and built Wang Laboratories from a $600 investment to one of the giants in the computer industry.

1957 Chen-Ning Yang and Tsung-Dao Lee share the Nobel Prize for physics for their work contradicting the long-held scientific belief in the conservation of parity theory. Chien-Shiung Wu worked with them and corroborated their research findings. Wu went on to become the first woman awarded the Comstock Award from the National Academy of Sciences and the seventh woman elected to the National Academy of Science.

1968 Har Gobind Khorana wins the Nobel Prize for medicine/physiology for his work on the genetic code.

1976 Samuel C.C. Ting shares the Nobel Prize for physics with Burton Richter for discovering the existence of a new particle called j/psi.

1980 Safi Qureshey, Thomas Yuen, and Albert Wong found AST Research, which will become the fourth largest producer of personal computers behind IBM, Apple, and Compaq.

1981 Before the disease was given a name, Dr. David Ho was treating and researching what would become known as AIDS. In 1990, he was named to head the Aaron Diamond AIDS Research Center in New York City, and in 1994 he was appointed to President Bill Clinton's Task Force on AIDS. Ho gained celebrity when he began treating basketball star Ervin "Magic" Johnson, who is infected with the virus that causes AIDS.

1983 Subrahmanyan Chandrashekhar wins the Nobel Prize for physics for his theories on white dwarfs, medium-sized stars that collapse into dense, white-hot balls about the size of the Earth.

1985 Lieutenant Colonel Ellison Onizuka becomes the first Asian American astronaut in space on January 24, when he flies as a specialist on a space shuttle mission. Dr. Taylor Wang, a Chinese American, is the second to fly on the shuttle, on April 29 to May 5.

1986 Onizuka perishes with the crew of the space shuttle *Challenger* when it explodes after takeoff on January 28; Yuan T. Lee wins the Nobel Prize in chemistry for research into the nature of chemical reactions.

1990 Flossie Wong-Staal becomes chair of AIDS research at the University of California at San Diego after more than a decade of working at the National Cancer Institute.

1992 Lillian Gonzalez-Pardo becomes the first Asian American to head the American Medical Women's Association; Dr. Reginald C. S. Ho becomes the first Native Hawaiian to head the American Cancer Society.

1993 Arati Prabhakar, an Asian Indian American scientist, is appointed by President Bill Clinton to head the National Institute of Standards and Technology (NIST). She is the first Asian American to hold the post.

1994 Leroy Chiao becomes the third Asian American scientist in space when he flies aboard the space shuttle *Columbia*. He will make a second shuttle flight in 1996.

1997 Kalpawna Chawla becomes the first Indian-American woman to go in to space, aboard the space shuttle *Columbia*. Sadly, Chawla will die in 2003 on a later mission, when the shuttle *Columbia* breaks up upon re-entry to Earth's atmosphere.

American students outperform their white counterparts in science by five points.

College Education in Science and Engineering

How prepared are Asian American students to study science or engineering at the undergraduate level? Information the Student Descriptive Questionnaire (SDQ) of the Scholastic Achievement Test (SAT) collected from college-bound high school seniors shows that Asian American students participate in higher-level mathematics and science courses in high school than the average U.S. student and express higher degree aspirations. They also earn higher scores in the math section of the SAT.

The survey indicated that more Asian American students are well prepared academically for science-related majors than most other college-bound students. For example, while almost all students have taken biology courses, a larger portion of Asian students have taken chemistry and a much higher proportion have taken physics courses. A similar pattern emerges for coursework in mathematics. Large percentages of all students have taken algebra and geometry, but much larger proportions of Asians have taken trigonometry, precalculus, and calculus courses.

Asian American college-bound students are more likely to aspire to a doctorate than either white or all other college-bound students (34 percent versus 20 and 23 percent, respectively). While a greater proportion of females than males in the white and national categories have doctoral degree goals, an equal proportion of Asian males and females plan to earn a doctorate.

Bachelor's Degrees

Six percent of all science and engineering bachelor's degrees went to Asian graduates in 1989, almost tripling the number for 1979. Approximately 35 percent of the undergraduate science and engineering degrees awarded to Asian graduates were in engineering; 20 percent were in the social sciences; 15 percent were in biological sciences; and 11 percent were in computer science. The 2000 census revealed that among Asian Americans who were at least 25 years old, about 33 percent were employed in an information-related job, compared to 26 percent of the total population.

Graduate Study

Asians made up 3 percent of all Graduate Record Examination (GRE) test takers in 1987, but represented 4 percent of those who had majored in science and engineering at the undergraduate level. Although they generally scored lower than whites on the verbal and analytical sections of the GRE, Asian American test takers scored higher on the quantitative (mathematical) section.

The majority of Asian American GRE test takers were biological or physical sciences majors as undergraduates (64 percent), by far the highest percentage in these fields of any of the other racial/ethnic groups.

Compared to their white counterparts, Asian science and engineering degree recipients (U.S. citizens and permanent residents) were much more likely to pursue graduate study. Approximately 28 percent of Asian baccalaureate degree holders who had received their degrees in 1988 or 1989 were in graduate school full time, and 10 percent attended on a part-time basis. Of their white counterparts, on the other hand, only 19 percent attended full time and 11 percent part time.

In 1990, Asian Americans represented 5.8 percent of total enrollment in graduate science and engineering programs, almost doubling their 1983 enrollment. Their representation in engineering programs was double that in science programs (9.5 versus 4.7 percent). Of all Asian Americans enrolled in science and engineering graduate programs in 1990, 30 percent were in engineering, 13 percent in biological science, and 16 percent in computer science programs.

Master's Recipients in Science and Engineering

In 1989, Asians (U.S. citizens and permanent residents) represented about 6 percent of science and engineering master's degree recipients. The increase in master's degrees in engineering awarded to Asians over a ten-year period—1979 to 1989—was 138 percent. In comparison, the number of engineering degrees earned by whites in the same period increased by 33 percent.

Doctorates Awarded in Science and Engineering

The number of science and engineering doctorates awarded to Asian Americans (U.S. citizens) in 1992 increased by 94 percent in a ten-year period, from 327 to 634. Asian Americans received 2.5 percent of all science and engineering doctorates awarded to U.S. citizens in 1982 and 4.4 percent in 1992. In 1990, the largest percentage of these Asian American degree recipients were in engineering fields (34 percent); 22 percent earned doctorates (PhDs) in agricultural/biological

sciences and 17 percent in the physical sciences.

At this level, it is important that the distinction be made between Asian Americans (U.S. citizens and permanent residents) and noncitizens on temporary visas. In 1990, 80 percent of the total doctorates in science and engineering were awarded to noncitizens.

Postdoctoral Appointments

Asians (including both citizens and noncitizens) held 16 percent of all science and engineering postdoctoral appointments in 1989, while whites held 82 percent. The increase in these appointments for Asians between 1979 and 1989 was 104 percent, compared with a 40-percent increase for whites.

Medical School

From 1974 to 1999, Asian American applicants to medical school grew from 986 to 7,622, with the percentage of women growing from 20 percent in 1974 to 45 percent in 1999.

Suggestions for Further Reading

American Association for the Advancement of Science (AAAS), *"The War on Terrorism: What Does it Mean for Science?"* December 18, 2001, http://www.aaas.org/spp/scifree/terrorism/report.shtml (accessed May 5, 2003).

Crew, Linda, *Children of the River*, New York: Dell, 1989.

Hsia, Jayjia, *Asian Americans in Higher Education and at Work*, Hilldale, NJ: Lawrence Erlbaum Associates, 1988.

"Kalpawna Chawla Biographical Data," *National Aeronautics and Space Administration*, Lyndon B. Johnson Space Center, Houston, Texas, 2003.

Le, C.N. "The Demographics of Asian America," *Asian-Nation: The Landscape of Asian America,* http://www.asian-nation.org/demographics.shtml (accessed May 5, 2003).

Min, Pyong Gap, *Struggle for Ethnic Identity: Narratives by Asian American Professionals,* Walnut Creek, CA: Alta Mira Press, 1999.

Takaki, Ronald T., *Strangers from a Different Shore: A History of Asian Americans*, New York: Penguin Books, 1990.

Yount, Lisa, *Asian-American Scientists,* New York: Facts on File, 1998.

13

Religion

Asian American Religious Practices

FACT FOCUS

- Hinduism in the United States is practiced primarily by Asian Indian Americans.
- Buddhism is no longer widely practiced in India where it originated; Vietnam, Cambodia, Laos, and Tibet are now the main areas where Buddhism thrives.
- Islam is the fastest-growing religion in the world.
- Confucianism, more a philosophy than a religion, is widely practiced in China.
- Taoism has as its central tenet the quest for spiritual immortality.
- Shintoism, or "the way of the gods," is the oldest religion still practiced in Japan.

Asian American religious practices are as diverse as those of any population segment. Many Asian Americans are Christians, and can be found in all denominations, from Catholic to Baptist. According to a City University of New York study done in 2001 on religious affiliations in the United States, an estimated 36 percent of Asian Americans identified themselves as Christian. About 6 percent of those responding to the survey did not list a Christian denomination, but 20 percent identified themselves as Roman Catholic and 10 percent reported adhering to various Protestant denominations. Another 20 percent reported no religious affiliation, and 9 percent

identified themselves as adhering to Buddhism. The Asian American Muslim population in the survey represented 5 percent of respondents. Although the respondents were not further identified by specific Asian ethnicity, analysts report that Filipino and Vietnamese Americans are likely to be Roman Catholic. Many Asian Americans observe cultural aspects of various Asian religions, celebrating holidays and ceremonies of passage, while also participating as active members of Christian congregations.

The major Asian religions, each of which has specific tenets, teachings, and customs, are described in the sections that follow.

Hinduism

Hinduism, or "the eternal religion," is the primary religion of the Indian people. Based upon ancient mythology, it has evolved over thousands of years. Unlike Christianity, Islam, and Buddhism, Hinduism has no founder and its exact history is not known. It has several books of sacred writings, although none of them is considered to be definitive of the beliefs common to all Hindus.

The oldest and most sacred of Hindu writings are the Vedas, a Sanskrit word meaning "knowledge," or "sacred teaching." These works, which Hindus consider to have been divinely revealed, are vastly longer than the holy scriptures of Western religions—six times the length of the Old and New Testaments together—and predate them by centuries, with most estimates dating their origin no later than 1500 B.C.

One of the basic tenets (beliefs) of Hinduism is the immortality of the soul and its reincarnation after the death of the physical body. Hindus believe that the soul is on a timeless journey toward perfection, and that during each lifetime the soul is afforded the opportunity to live in accordance with spiritual principles. Those who choose to reject Hindu principles are returned to life in an inferior life form after their death, while those who embrace them and live a pure life are reborn into a higher or improved life form. These reincarnations continue until the soul achieves perfection and enters a new realm of existence called *moksha,* after which it is united with Brahman, the underlying force in the universe.

Hinduism also has a pantheon (a group of recognized gods) of hundreds of gods, which the faithful worship in a variety of ways. The three most important gods—referred to as the Hindu trinity—are Brahma, the creator of the universe; Shiva, the destroyer of the universe; and Vishnu; the preserver of the universe.

Hinduism teaches the existence of a grand, harmonic interdependence among all living things. It is a view of life in which human action has a higher meaning than can be known in the present, and Hindu practices promise greater understanding of the nature of reality and, ultimately, communion with Brahman.

Buddhism

Buddhism was founded in the sixth century B.C. by Siddhartha Gautama, a prince in India who abandoned his life of wealth and prestige to seek enlightenment as a wandering monk. His faith in Hinduism had been shaken by his observation that life was full of meaningless suffering, and that if the Hindu doctrine of reincarnation were correct, this suffering would continue after death into the next life.

Siddhartha pondered this dilemma during his six years of wandering in poverty. In an instant of enlightenment, he is said to have discovered the solution, called the Four Noble Truths. According to Gautama's truths, life is fraught with suffering brought about by ignorance and craving, and to remedy this existence one must follow the Eightfold Path, a series of laws geared toward living a more virtuous life.

As Siddhartha began to teach his new insights, called the dharma, or "saving truth," he obtained a wide following and earned the name Buddha, meaning the "enlightened one." Over time, Buddhism spread throughout India and then into other parts of southern Asia, especially Southeastern Asia, where today variations of Buddhism are the predominant religion. In India, where the religion was born, it is no longer a major force.

The major schools of Buddhist thought in existence today are Theravada, Mahayana, Mantrayana, and Zen. Theravada Buddhism is based upon the Pali canon (sacred Buddhist texts) and supports a nontheistic universe (a universe that was not created by and is not governed by one supreme God) in which salvation is reserved for a limited number of people. While it too is based upon the Pali canon, Mahayana Buddhism is more liberal than Theravada Buddhism, stressing universal salvation. Mantrayana Buddhism and Zen Buddhism are closely related religious branches, which chiefly focus on meditation. Buddhism is one of the world's great religions, with over 300 million adherents worldwide.

Buddhist doctrine is contained in a collection of scriptures called the Tripitaka, or "Three Baskets," often referred to as the dharma. Its basic tenets, called *samsara,* are that existence is a cycle of life, death, and rebirth and that one's circumstances in the present life are largely a consequence of one's behavior in a previous life. To attain higher and higher states of existence ultimately leading to nirvana—a condition of perfect peace and freedom from samsara— one must follow the Middle Way and the Noble Eightfold Path.

The Middle Way is a life void of extremes, not given entirely to satisfying human desires nor to complete self-denial and self-torture. The Noble Eightfold Path is made up of: (1) perfect view, which involves understanding the Four Noble Truths; (2) perfect resolve; (3) perfect speech; (4) perfect conduct; (5) perfect livelihood; (6) per-

WORDS TO KNOW

adherents: followers of a leader, an idea, a church, or political party

canon: accepted rules and standards

deity: a god or goddess

enlightenment: achievement of spiritual insight; complete understanding

immortality: a state of eternal life without vulnerability to death

meditate: to focus thoughts; to enter a state of deep contemplation

pantheon: official gods of a group of people; supreme beings

reincarnation: rebirth of a soul in a new body

revelations: teachings revealed by a god or supreme being to humans

ritual: ceremony or pattern of behavior, often used in religious worship

scripture: sacred writings

sect: a group within a larger religious body that follows specific teachings or rules

tenet: a belief held to be true

theism: belief in the existence of a god or gods

theology: the study of religious faith and practice

fect effort; (7) perfect mindfulness; and (8) perfect concentration.

Zen Buddhism

Zen Buddhism is a Buddhist sect that is predominant in East Asia, particularly Japan, where it has had a deep cultural influence. Zen is also popular in the United States and is practiced by both Asian and non-Asian Americans. Like Buddhism itself, Zen has several schools of thought, two of which are most prominent. The Rinzai emphasizes meditation on *koans,* or unsolvable riddles, and the Soto relies upon emptying the mind through meditation. The ultimate goal of Zen Buddhism is the attainment of inner peace and spiritual enlightenment, called *satori.* Zen, more than any other form of Buddhism, teaches its followers to rely upon meditation when seeking enlightenment, while downplaying the importance of ritual and philosophical inquiry that mark other Buddhist schools.

Buddhism in America

Of the major East Asian religions, Buddhism is perhaps the most prominent in the United States. Historically, it has been associated with numerous intellectuals in the United States and elsewhere. In more recent times Zen and Tibetan Buddhism have become popular among a wider range of people. The Dalai Lama, the spiritual leader of Tibetan Buddhism who lives in exile in India, has become somewhat of a celebrity in the United States as he seeks to loosen China's colonial grip on Tibet, which it has occupied for decades.

Islam

Islam is the fastest-growing religion in the world today, and its followers can be found on all inhabited continents. Founded by the prophet Muhammad in the seventh century, Islam has much in common with the Jewish and Christian religious traditions based in the Old and New Testaments. Like Judaism and Christianity, Islam is an Abrahamic faith, which means that its original followers are descendants of Abraham, a major figure found in the Old Testament and the Koran, the holy book of Islam. Followers of Islam consider Jesus a prophet, but, as do followers of Judaism, deny the claim to his divinity found in the New Testament— the cornerstone of Christianity. According to Islam, Muhammad is also a prophet, but his teachings are considered the final revelations of God, thus superseding all teaching that came before them.

Muslims (the name for adherents of Islam) believe that God revealed the Koran to Muhammad, who, although he was believed to have been illiterate, transcribed it. Muslims use the Koran as a guide for nearly every aspect of their lives. Islam teaches that God is just and merciful and that followers can attain paradise after death if they obey God's laws. Islam commands a strict moral code on its adherents, emphasizing honesty, kindness, brotherly love, and obedience to God. Islam is a highly ritualized religion that imposes duties on its followers, which are called the Five Pillars of Faith. These pillars are: (1) belief in the unity of God and the prophethood of Muhammad; (2) prayer; (3) fasting; (4) almsgiving; and (5) pilgrimage.

TIME LINE OF ASIAN RELIGIONS

1500 B.C. Most scholars estimate that the Vedas, the sacred texts of Hinduism, were written around this time

660 B.C. First Japanese emperor ascends the throne; believers in Shintoism claim he is descended from the sun-goddess

6th century B.C. Lao-tzu, founder of Taoism, lived

551–479 B.C. Confucius, the founder of Confucianism, lived

1st century B.C. Religious Taoism, known as Tao-chiao, dates from this period

A.D. 570–632 Muhammad, the prophet and founder of Islam, lived around this time

1727 First recorded use of the word "Shintoism" in English

1800s Christian missionaries arrive in Asia

1954 The Unification Church was founded in Korea by Sun Myung Moon; it has become a worldwide church ministry

1977 The government of China officially lifted its ban on Confucianism; it had been in effect since the communist takeover in 1949

Many Americans associate Islam only with the Middle East, but it is the dominant religion in Pakistan, parts of India, Bangladesh, Indonesia, Malaysia, and parts of Africa. Immigrants from these areas, as well as those from the Middle East, combined with American converts, have contributed to the significant spread of Islam in the United States and throughout the world.

Confucianism

Confucianism is not strictly a religion, but a set of moral beliefs taught by the Chinese philosopher Confucius (K'ung-tzu; c. 551–479 B.C.), who himself adapted them from ancient philosophers. The tenets of Confucianism center around the concepts of *jen* and *li*. *Jen* is a combination of the characters for "human being" and for "two"; it embodies the most important aspect of Confucianism, the compassion and sensitivity to others that should be at the foundation for human relations. *Li* is a combination of morality and etiquette, custom and ritual. Confucianism does not have a clergy, nor does it address the metaphysical aspects of religion, such as the life of the soul or the meaning of death and suffering.

Confucius was born into a noble family in 551 B.C. in what is now the Shantung province of China during a time of social upheaval. He spent his working life as a civil servant in various posts and studied China's ancient philosophers with a variety of teachers. He began to revive the teachings and ideas of the ancients in an attempt to restore social and civil order in the country through philosophical enlightenment. Confucius died in relative obscurity in about 479 B.C.

Scholars of Confucius have not been able to determine with any certainty if the philosopher wrote any books; however, several books have been attributed to him. A collection of his teachings, the Analects, was compiled by his disciples. Confucianism teaches that successful individual human relations form the basis of society. To bring order to society, one must first bring order to the family, which will ultimately bring order to the community, which will bring order to the government.

Another Confucian belief is that roles have to be clearly stated and fulfilled to avoid civic chaos. In other words, a prince must be princely, a mother must be motherly, and a son must behave with filial reverence, that is, respect his parents.

Confucianism heavily influenced Chinese, Korean, and Japanese life for more than two thousand years. Its influence varied throughout Chinese history, but it fell into official disfavor with the communist takeover of China in 1949. However, in acknowledgment of the people's continued reliance on its teachings, the communist government lifted its official ban on Confucianism in 1977.

Taoism

While Taoism is often considered a religion, like Confucianism it is a philosophy as well. The word Tao means "the way," and was used by Lao-tzu, its founder, to describe the way the universe functions: the path taken by natural events.

Taoism as a philosophy (called Tao-chia) originated in China and dates from the third century B.C. Its teachings are found in the writings of Lao-tzu, called the *Tao-te-ching*. Recent scholars of this text, however, believe that it may have been written by more than one person. Like Buddhists, philosophical Taoists use meditation to achieve enlightenment, which they define as a mystical union with the Tao.

Religious Taoism, or Tao-chiao, dates from the first century B.C. Its central tenet is the quest for spiritual immortality. There are many schools of religious Taoism, each with its own path to immortality. Among them are the Inner Deity Hygiene School, the Way of Right Unity, the School of the Magic Jewel, Five-Pecks-of-Rice Taoism, and the Way of Supreme Peace. All use meditation, breathing and physical exercises, alchemy (a process by which something common is made into something valuable, meaningful, or spiritual), sexual practices, fasting (not eating), confession, and spiritual healing.

Shintoism

Shintoism, or "the way of the gods," is the oldest religion still practiced in Japan. Adherents worship a large number of gods, called *kami,* several of which are believed to form the essence of nature and all of its parts, including mountains, trees, oceans, and rocks. It is believed that the Japanese imperial family is descended from Amaterasu, the sun-goddess. *Kami* are thought to determine human creativity, illness, and healing.

While Shintoism has no actual canon of scripture, elements of the religion can be traced back to ancient Japanese mythology. Shintoism places heavy emphasis on morality and rituals, as well as on matters of immediate concern. Unlike other religions, which tend to concentrate on the meaning of life or the nature of death, followers of Shintoism are far more likely to pray for good health, a bountiful harvest, or the end of a drought. Shintoism has a strong link to Japanese society and even to the government.

For many years, it was used to cultivate loyalty and devotion to the state.

The origin of Shintoism is not known, although many of its tenets and practices date back thousands of years to pre-agricultural Japan. No one person is credited with its founding and no human is venerated as a deity, although during the nineteenth century and through the end of World War II (1939–45) the emperor was considered a god.

Shinto priests often lead large ritual prayers such as the Great Purification Ceremony, in which followers give a mass confession and plea for forgiveness. Historically, Shinto priests came from noble clans or families and served the local lord. They acted as mediators between the people and the *kami* and directed the ritual offerings that were made to the spirits.

Today only large Shinto shrines have full-time priests; the smaller ones are served by part-time priests chosen from local families. After World War II and the consequent occupation of Japan by the United States, many Shinto shrines were dismantled. Since that time, however, Shintoism has been revitalized and has come to be regarded as one of the most important religions in Japan.

The Unification Church

Founded in 1954 after the Korean War, the Unification Church of Sun Myung Moon has become a worldwide ministry, noted as much for its fabled assets and behind-the-scenes power politicking as for its spiritual message.

According to church accounts, the beginnings can be traced to Easter 1936, when Jesus and other religious figures from world religions appeared to sixteen-year-old Moon, conferring on him a mission to establish the kingdom of heaven on Earth. After schooling in Seoul and a course of study in electrical engineering in Japan, Moon returned to Korea and, legend has it, was imprisoned, by the Japanese occupation forces in Korea in 1943 for subversive religious and political activities. In 1946, after the end of the World War II, Moon established his first church in northern Korea at Pyong-yang. He was then imprisoned and tortured in a communist forced labor camp until his liberation by United Nations forces in 1950.

Moon's theology reached its present form in the 1957 publication *The Divine Principle,* the 536-page basic text and bible of the Unification Church. The essence of the *Divine Principle*'s message, and the foundation of the Unification Church, is the unstated assumption that Moon is the Messiah, the actual Lord of the Second Coming. Much of the *Divine Principle* is devoted to demonstrations and scriptural "proofs" of the suitability of Korea as the birthplace of Moon and his movement, pinpointing the timeframe within which the final Messianic birth (the birth of a savior) and action should take place.

In outline, the revelations of the *Principle* deny that the crucifixion of Jesus Christ was a part of God's plan, instead characterizing this central event of traditional Christianity as a sort of historical blunder, partly the fault of John the Baptist (who is believed to have failed to have recognized Jesus as the Messiah), and partly of the Jews as a nation.

The accomplishment of the true divine plan, according to Moon, was delayed until the present time, and must involve an acting out of the original scheme of redemp-

Reverend Sun Myung Moon conducted a mass wedding of 28,000 couples at the Robert F. Kennedy Stadium in 1997.

tion. Moon says that Eve had sexual relations with Lucifer in his serpent form, giving birth to Cain and polluting the bloodline of humanity. Had Jesus, considered by Moon to be the second Adam or incarnation of the "True Father," not been executed and his mission prematurely ended, he would have married his counterpart, the second Eve, and thus redeemed the first parents, saving and renewing mankind. This consummation, then, is part of Moon's task on Earth, his role as the Third Adam. Moon describes his fourth marriage in the mid-1950s to Hak Ja Han as finding the Third Eve.

The Unification Church, headquartered in New York City, currently operates 55 large centers of worship in the United States, at least one in every state, plus 206 smaller churches. Moon's politically oriented operations and holdings include the American Freedom Coalition, Professors World Peace Academy, Washington Institute for Values in Public Policy, and CAUSA USA (Confederation of Associations for the Unification of American Societies), an organization specializing in anticommunist activities, from congressional lobbying to support of the Nicaraguan *contras*.

Suggestions for Further Reading

Graduate Center at the City University of New York, "American Religious Identification Survey 2001," http://www.gc.cuny.edu/studies/aris.pdf (accessed May 2, 2003).

Hoobler, Thomas, *Confucianism,* New York: Facts on File, 1993.

Larson, Bob, *Larson's Book of Cults,* Wheaton, IL: Tyndale House, 1987.

Mann, Gurinder Singh, *Buddhists, Hindus, and Sikhs in America,* New York: Oxford University Press, 2001.

Maxwell, Joe, "New Kingdoms for the Cults," *Christianity Today,* January 13, 1992, pp. 37-41.

Pandel, Karen, *Learning from the Dalai Lama: Secrets of the Wheel of Time,* New York: Dutton Children's Books, 1995.

Prebish, Charles S., and Kenneth K. Tanaka, eds., *The Faces of Buddhism in America,* Berkeley: University of California Press, 1998.

Takahashi, Kazuko, "Media Madness Mirrors Mass Moonie Marriages," *Japan Times,* September 14, 1992, pp. 6-7.

Unification Church, http://www.unification.org/ (accessed May 2, 2003).

U.S. Department of State, International Information Programs, "Islam in the United States," http://usinfo.state.gov/usa/islam/ (May 2, 2003).

14

Literature

Asian American Writers

FACT FOCUS

- Asian American literature has won mainstream popularity since the 1970s.
- Amy Tan, Maxine Hong Kingston, Gus Lee, and Bharati Mukherjee have published works of fiction that explore the lives of Americans of Asian descent.
- Works of fiction by Asian American authors are being made into major theatre and film productions in the 1990s.
- Chinese writer Ha Jin, who lives in the United States and writes in English, won the 1999 National Book Award for his novel, Waiting.
- Award-winning children's authors of Asian descent include Dhan Gopal Mukerji, Allen Say, Ed Young, Laurence Yep, Jose Areugo, and Linda Sue Park.

Since the 1970s, Asian American writers have been producing a body of work that is revolutionizing the way Asian Americans are viewed by the mainstream culture and the way they view themselves. In describing the experiences of Asian Americans, these writers are sweeping away the stereotypical images of the past as well as starting to define a new literary field.

Asian American literature remained relatively unpublished until the 1970s. The few hangouts for Asian American writers and artists were known only by word of mouth in the overlapping artistic and social change communities. They included the Kearney Street Workshop and Japantown Arts and Media in San Francisco, Visual Communications in Los Angeles, and the Basement Workshop in New York's Chinatown.

By the mid-1980s, the types of Asian literature had grown considerably, reflecting the arrival of newer communities of South Asians and Southeast Asians to the established communities of Chinese, Japanese, Korean, and Filipino Americans. Asian American women's literature had begun to take shape as well, and works in Asian languages were being added to the Asian American literary canon.

In the mid-1990s, literary works by Asian American authors were being published in record numbers. The commercial success of

WORDS TO KNOW

assimilate: to become like or similar to, to join

ceded: formally transferred or surrendered, usually under the terms of a treaty

internment: forcible confinement of individuals against their will

mainstream society: the majority or dominant group in a culture, which shares certain customs, assumptions, and ways of interacting

Maxine Hong Kingston (*The Woman Warrior, Tripmaster Monkey*), Amy Tan (*The Joy Luck Club, The Kitchen God's Wife*), and other best-selling authors proves not only that Asian Americans can write, but that their work has mass-market appeal.

In this chapter, only writings in English will be discussed, although Asian American literature in Asian languages is an increasingly important field of study, since recent immigrants' thoughts are expressed best in letters, poems, and diary entries in their native languages.

Asian American Literary History

By the late 1800s, Asian Americans had already spent decades in the United States, most picking crops or hauling railroad ties for the transcontinental railroad. Their lives were made harder by state and federal laws that were designed to restrict their freedoms and business opportunities. Therefore, it is noteworthy that the earliest surviving piece of Asian American literature deals not with the trials and tribulations of life in the United States, but with life in China. *When I Was a Boy in China*, published by Lee Phan Phou in 1887, is an autobiographical account of daily life in China, including food, ceremonies, and games.

Other early works include autobiographies such as Etsu Sugimoto's *A Daughter of the Samurai,* Younghill Kang's *East Goes West*, Pardee Lowe's *Father and Glorious Descendant*, and Jade Snow Wong's *Fifth Chinese Daughter*. Many of these early works were written by first- and second-generation Asian Americans longing to be accepted in white Christian society.

During World War II (1939–45), the United States government unjustly removed over 120,000 Japanese Americans from their homes and sent them to internment camps. The shared anguish of the experience of internment —and the shattered illusion that Asian Americans were as "American" as their European peers—resulted in an eloquent outpouring of literary works. John Okada's novel *No No Boy,* Wakako Yamauchi's story and play *And the Soul Shall Dance*, Mine Okubo's pictorial essay *Citizen 13660*, Hisaye Yamamoto's short story "The Legend of Miss Sasagawara," and Toshio Mori's *Woman from Hiroshima* are but a few of the works informed by this tragic episode in U.S. history.

In the early 1970s, Asian Americans, caught up in the growing social change movement, began to challenge many fundamental beliefs and practices of mainstream American society. As they strove to present to American society a more realistic view of cism of Asian American texts, a new stage has been reached in this growing field.

Since the 1970s, Asian American stories have appeared on television, in the movies, and on the stage. As Asian American literary works more and more become part of the American mainstream, Asian American writers will continue to share their experiences with others.

Asian American Writers of Adult Literature

Lynda Barry (1956–)

Cartoonist Lynda Barry, whose mother was Filipino, first recognized the value of her artistic talent in second grade when one day she drew an orange grove to illustrate the letter O and gained instant recognition in her class. It's a story, in short, that could have come straight out of her popular comic strip "Ernie Pook's Comeek," published weekly in more than 60 alternative publications throughout the United States and Canada. The four-panel serial strip, drawn in a scratchy childlike style, follows the adventures of Arna, Arnold, Freddie, Maybonne, and Marlys, a group of children growing up in the 1960s.

Barry's 1992 collection of strips, *My Perfect Life,* takes on issues like race, sex, alcoholism, and religion. In 1994 she released her eighth book, *It's So Magic.* Barry has also tried other artistic media. In 1988, she published her first novel, *The Good Times Are Killing Me,* which won the Washington State Governor Writer's Award. In 1990, she became a commentator for National Public Radio's *Morning Edition.* In 1994, Barry released a CD, *The Lynda Barry Experience,*

Lynda Barry.

Asian Americans, they celebrated their unique cultures in a variety of literary works.

The emerging awareness that Asian Americans have a literature of their own, combined with growing numbers of post-1965 immigrants (Asian Indians, Southeast Asians, and others educated in U.S. schools), have resulted in even more Asian American writing. Authors such as Amy Tan and dramatists such as David Henry Hwang (see *Theatre* chapter) have brought some aspects of the Asian American experience into the mainstream of U.S. culture. And with the publication of literary criti-

Jessica Hagedorn.

featuring readings of her short stories, and completed her first television special, *Grandma's Way-Out Party.* Despite her busy schedule, she has remained loyal to her first love, cartooning.

Carlos Bulosan (1913–1956)

Carlos Bulosan, a Filipino American poet and author, was one of America's most prolific writers. His autobiography *America Is in the Heart,* published in 1946, was hailed as one of the 50 most important U.S. books. In it, he told of his search for an ideal United States he had learned of in school, and the real, often harsh United States he found when he immigrated. The book captured the Filipino American experience during the 1930s and 1940s. Bulosan, however, was involved in left-wing politics and labor union activities. In the conservative post–World War II climate, many Americans turned their backs on his writings, and his work was largely forgotten for decades.

Born in the Luzon province of Pangasinan, Bulosan was 17 when he came to the United States at the beginning of the Great Depression, and experienced the racism and violence other Filipinos suffered during the period.

Bulosan considered himself, above all, a poet and built his literary reputation on the genre. In 1943, he published the historically significant collection of poems *The Voice of Bataan,* dedicated to the memory of the Filipino, American, and Japanese soldiers who died in that crucial World War II battle. The following year he published *The Laughter of My Father,* his first collection of short stories. An instant wartime success, it was translated into several European languages and was transmitted worldwide over wartime radio.

Frank Chin (1940–)

Frank Chin is an award-winning playwright, critic, novelist, and short-story writer who is highly visible in Asian American literary circles. He has published three novels: *Donald Duk, Gunga Din,* and *Gunga Din Highway;* a collection of short stories, *The Chinaman Pacific and Frisco R.R. Co.*; and several plays and essays. He coedited, in 1974, *Aiiieeeee! An Anthology of Asian American Writers,* and, in 1991, *The Big Aiiieeeee! An Anthology of Chinese American and Japanese American Literature.*

Ben Fong-Torres (1945–)

Ben Fong-Torres, a founding editor of the music magazine *Rolling Stone,* has interviewed some of the biggest names in the history of popular music, such as Bob Dylan, the Beatles, and the Rolling Stones. He also worked as a disk jockey in San Francisco. He has published three books, including his 1994 autobiography, *The Rice Room: Growing Up Chinese American, From Number Two Son to Rock 'N' Roll.*

Jessica Hagedorn (1949–)

Jessica Hagedorn's first novel, *Dogeaters,* was nominated for a National Book Award when it was published in 1990. Born in the Philippines in 1949, Hagedorn is hailed as the creator of a literary tradition whose works represent some of the most exciting new concepts in contemporary literature. In addition to writing novels, Hagedorn has written poetry and plays. One of her collections of poems and short works, *Pet Food and Tropical Apparitions* (1983), received an American Book Award.

Le Ly Hayslip (1949–)

Le Ly Hayslip is the youngest of six children in a close-knit Buddhist family that was torn apart by the war in Vietnam during the 1960s and 1970s. She was only 12 years old when helicopters landed near her village in central Vietnam. For the next four years, she suffered near-starvation, rape, torture, and the deaths of many family members. In 1989, while living in California, Hayslip published *When Heaven and Earth Changed Places,* an autobiographical account of her childhood in Vietnam during the war that ravaged her country. It was later made into a

Le Ly Hayslip.

major motion picture directed by Oliver Stone and starring Joan Chen. In 1992, writing with her eldest son, James, she published a sequel, *Child of War, Woman of Peace.* In this work, she recounts how she exchanged the horrors of war for a challenging and insecure life in the United States.

Garrett Hongo (1951–)

Garrett Hongo edited *Open Boat, Poems from Asian America,* published in 1993. Hongo was born in Volcano, Hawaii, and grew up on Oahu and in Los Angeles. Included in his published works are *Yellow*

Light and *The River of Heaven,* which was the Lamont poetry selection of the Academy of American Poets and a finalist for the 1989 Pulitzer Prize in poetry. He is a professor of English and director of creative writing at the University of Oregon.

Jeanne Wakatsuki Houston (1934–)

In 1971, Jeanne Wakatsuki Houston's nephew asked her about her experiences in the internment camps—the remote prison camps where Americans of Japanese descent were held against their will during World War II (1939–45). The flood of memories that this question stirred inspired Houston, writing with her husband, James D. Houston, to write *Farewell to Manzanar,* about life in the camp where the Wakatsuki family was interned. This book gave voice to the family, and also reflected the experiences of the 120,000 Americans who had silently endured the internment experience. Published in 1973, the book still appears on many school and university reading lists.

Lawson Fusao Inada (1940–)

Lawson Inada was born in 1940, a third-generation Japanese American. He is the author of *Before the Way* and the recipient of two fellowships from the National Endowment for the Arts. A teacher of multicultural literature and creative writing classes at Southern Oregon State College since 1966, Inada has served on the commission on racism and bias in education for the National Council of Teachers of English.

He is one of four coeditors of *Aiiieeeee! An Anthology of Asian American Writers* (1974) and its sequel, *The Big Aiiieeeee!* (1991). In 1978, with Garrett Hongo and Alan Chong Lau, he wrote *The Buddha Bandits Down Highway 99.* Much of his work deals with his experiences in an internment camp during World War II (1939–45). Inada writes a monthly column for the *International Examiner,* a Seattle-based Asian American community newspaper.

Gish Jen (1955–)

Born in Queens, New York, on August 12, 1955, to immigrant parents from Shanghai, China, Lillian Jen was the second of five children. She would later adopt the name "Gish"—as in the actress Lillian Gish. In 1983 she graduated from the University of Iowa's Writer's Workshop, and married David O'Connor. Married life for Jen was initially trying. "I was married to a very successful businessman and I didn't know what it meant to be a wife." When she finally freed herself—with her husband's supportive encouragement—from the pressure of trying to be a dutiful wife, Jen threw herself wholeheartedly into writing. But she was still uncertain about her future. "I was writing, but nothing particularly was happening for me as a writer." Her uncertainty turned to success though, and her first novel, *Typical American* (1991), was a finalist for the National Book Critic's Circle Award. Her subsequent works, *Mona in the Promised Land* (1996) and *Who's Irish* (1999), received critical and popular acclaim as well.

Ha Jin (1956–)

After the Tiananmen Square Massacre in 1989, Xuefei Jin, who was then a graduate student at Brandeis University in the United States, decided not to return to his native China. Instead, he decided to seek a teaching position in the United States. When none were forthcoming, using the pen name Ha Jin, he turned to writing to make a living and found his niche. By the beginning of the twenty-first century, Ha Jin had become an award-winning novelist and poet, even though he had only begun writing in English in 1988. Since then, he has written several collections of poetry and short stories, including *Oceans of Words* (winner of the 1996 PEN/Hemingway Prize); *Under the Red Flag* (winner of the 1997 Flannery O'Connor Award for Fiction); and *The Bridegroom* (winner of both the 2001 Asian American Literary Award and the 2002 Townsend Prize for Fiction). Jin's novel *Waiting* (1999) won both the 1999 National Book Award and the 2000 PEN/Faulkner Award for fiction. After *Waiting,* he published *Crazed* (2002), a novel about academic life in China in the late 1980s.

Jin was born in 1956 in the rural province of Liaoning, China. At the age of fourteen, he joined the army, where he served for five years. Jin completed the Creative Writing Studies curriculum at Boston University in 1994, and joined the faculty there in 2002 as professor of English and creative writing.

Ha Jin.

Maxine Hong Kingston (1940–)

Maxine Hong Kingston, a highly acclaimed writer of fiction and nonfiction, was one of the first Asian Americans to make it to the top of the U.S. literary world. Her first book, a memoir published in 1976 called *The Woman Warrior: Memoirs of a Girlhood among Ghosts,* won the National Book Critics Circle Award and made her a literary celebrity at the age of 36. In 1980, Kingston published a sequel, called *China Men,* which also earned the National Book Critics Circle Award. She published her first novel, *Tripmaster Monkey: His Fake Book,* in 1989.

Gus Lee (1946–)

Lawyer Gus Lee began writing as a second career, publishing his first novel, the semiautobiographical *China Boy,* in 1991 when he was 45 years old. It was followed in 1994 by *Honor and Duty,* which also became a bestseller, in addition to being selected by the Book of the Month Club and recorded as a Random House AudioBook. In 1993, following the success of *China Boy,* he left the law to become a full-time

Ruthanne Lum McCunn.

writer. In 1996, Lee published *Tiger's Tail*, a novel about Chinese Americans.

Ruthanne Lum McCunn (1946–)

Born on February 21, 1946, in San Francisco's Chinatown to a Scottish American father and a Chinese mother, Ruthanne Lum McCunn was educated through high school in Hong Kong. She traveled to the United States for college, where she has lived ever since. Her first book, *An Illustrated History of the Chinese in America,* was published in 1979, and has been used as a college text. Her second book, *Thousand Pieces of Gold,* was published in 1981 and became the basis for an American Playhouse film. It tells the story of Lalu Nathoy, a Chinese woman who was shipped to the United States as a slave and became Polly Bemis, a well-loved pioneer woman in Idaho. McCunn's next book was a children's story, *Pie-Biter,* a Chinese American folktale.

In 1988, McCunn published *Chinese American Portraits: Personal Histories, 1828–1988. Chinese Proverbs,* a collection of bits of Chinese wisdom, followed in 1991. And in 1995 McCunn published *Wooden Fish Songs,* the true story of one Chinese American man told by three different women.

Ved Mehta (1934–)

In 1957, Ved Mehta published the autobiographical work *Face to Face,* which was acclaimed by critics and the public alike. His numerous novels, books of nonfiction, screenplays, and autobiographical studies reflect his sense of himself as an Indian living outside his native country. Permanently blinded by spinal meningitis at the age of three, Mehta's early life was spent in boarding schools, hospitals, and institutions. His 1982 book *Vedi* chronicles the four years he spent in the Dadar School for the Blind in Bombay.

In 1960, Mehta published *Walking the Indian Streets*, recounting a trip to India and Nepal. In 1961, *New Yorker* editor William Shawn, who had encouraged Mehta in his writing, invited him to join the magazine staff, a post he still held in the 1990s. Some of Mehta's other works include *Delinquent Chacha, Portrait of India, Sound-Shadows of the New World,* and *The Stolen Light.*

Anchee Min.

Anchee Min (1957–)

Anchee Min, the author of the critically acclaimed 1994 memoir *Red Azalea,* was born in Shanghai, China, in 1957. The book details her life in China during the Cultural Revolution. During the decade-long Cultural Revolution, from 1966 to 1976, Chinese leader Mao Zedong attempted to instill his communist ideology in the minds of all Chinese youth. The anti-intellectual, anti-middle class movement turned violent, and hundreds of thousands of people were killed. In the midst of the revolution, at the age of 17, Min was sent to a labor camp, where she endured brutal living conditions. In 1984, the actress Joan Chen intervened in her case and helped her to get permission to come to the United States. In 2000, Min published *Becoming Madame Mao,* a work of historical fiction based on the life of the wife of Mao Zedong.

Bharati Mukherjee (1940–)

Bharati Mukherjee's writings reflect the Asian Indian community in North America and her own experiences as an immigrant. A professor of English at the University of California at Berkeley, she is the author of more than a dozen novels and several short stories.

Mukherjee's first book, *The Tiger's Daughter,* was published in 1972. It is the story of an Indian woman who returns to India after having lived for many years in the West. In 1985, Mukherjee published a collection of short stories, *Darkness,* exploring Canadian prejudice against South Asians. In 1994, she published her novel *The Holder of the World.* Her 1988 collection, *The Middleman and Other Stories,* won the National Book Critics Circle Award for best fiction.

Linda Sue Park (1960–)

Linda Sue Park launched her career as an author for young readers with *The Seesaw Girl* (1999). Since then, she has written three more novels, including *A Single Shard,* which was awarded the 2002 Newbery Medal, the highest award for American children's literature. The characters and plots of Park's novels are inspired by her Korean heritage, as she is the daughter of Korean immigrants. She was motivated to pursue Korean themes by her desire to share her heritage with her own children. Since she grew up in Illinois, Park didn't know much about Korean culture and traditions. Her research about Korean history eventually led to the writing of her novels. Park's *When My Name was Keoko* (2002) is the story of a Korean family living under the Japanese occupation of Korea.

Cathy Song (1955–)

Poet Cathy Song was born and raised in Honolulu, Hawaii. In 1983, her poetry collection *Picture Bride* won the Yale Series of Younger Poets Award and was nominated for the National Book Critics Circle Award. Her second book, *Frameless Windows, Squares of Light*, was published in 1991. She is active in Hawaii's Artists in the Schools program, teaching poetry to students—from kindergarten through high school—throughout the Hawaiian islands. Song's poetry has been included in a number of anthologies.

Vikram Seth (1952–)

With the publication of his novel *The Golden Gate* in 1986, Vikram Seth became a literary sensation—so much so that he left his job as an editor at Stanford University Press to return to his native India to escape the attention, and to continue writing. Six years later, in 1993, Seth offered the draft of a novel of epic proportions, *A Suitable Boy,* to publishers. Seth's story was one of the longest English-language novels to be published in the twentieth century, and Harper Collins eventually won the right to publish it by offering Seth a $600,000 advance.

Seth was born in 1952 in Calcutta, but spent most of his early childhood in Lon-

Amy Tan.

don. In 1980 he published a collection of poems, titled *Mappings,* and in the following year, he hitchhiked to Delhi, India, via Tibet, keeping a journal which he later published as *From Heaven Lake.* After completing his massive novel, Seth turned his energies toward writing plays.

The English National Opera commissioned Seth to adapt the Greek legend of Arion and the Dolphin. In 1994, the opera was performed, and later a picture book version of the opera, with Seth's words accompanied by illustrattions by Jane Ray, was published.

Amy Tan (1952–)

Amy Tan is one of the most successful new writers of serious fiction to emerge in the last decade. Her first novel, *The Joy Luck Club,* remained on the *New York Times* best-seller list from April to November 1989 and was the basis for a major feature film. Her second novel, *The Kitchen God's Wife,* was a success with the public and critics as well. Tan was born in Oakland, California, to first-generation Chinese Americans. In 1992, Tan published a children's book, *The Moon Lady.*

Another highly acclaimed novel, *The Hundred Secret Senses* (1995), is the story of a young woman who leaves China to join her half-Chinese, half-American family in San Francisco and imparts to her younger sister the mystery and spirit of her Chinese heritage.

Michiko Nishiura Weglyn (1926–)

In the 1950s and 1960s, Michiko Nishiura Weglyn was a successful costume designer for many popular television variety shows such as the *Jackie Gleason Show, The Tony Bennett Show,* and *The Dinah Shore Show.* But in the late 1960s, she was moved to explore the internment of Japanese Americans, having been a prisoner herself for two years. The resulting book, *Years of Infamy: The Untold Story of America's Concentration Camps,* exposed to the general public the U.S. government's unconstitutional imprisonment of 120,000 Americans of Japanese descent in remote prison camps. Weglyn's book was the first to expose the U.S. government's role and is considered a landmark work in Asian American history.

Jade Snow Wong (1922–)

Jade Snow Wong came to national prominence in 1950 with the publication of *Fifth Chinese Daughter*, a memoir of her childhood in San Francisco's Chinatown. In 1951, it was awarded the Commonwealth Club's Silver Medal for Non-Fiction and was made into an award-winning special for public broadcasting in 1976. Her second book, *No Chinese Stranger*, was published in 1975. In addition to being regarded as a pioneer Asian American writer, Wong is also an accomplished ceramist with works at the Chicago Art Institute and the Metropolitan Museum of Art.

Hisaye Yamamoto (1921–)

Hisaye Yamamoto is one of the pioneering writers in Asian American history. Her short stories were first published in the 1930s in such publications as *Kenyon Review, Harper's Bazaar, Fuioso, Asian America,* and *Partisan Review.* Yamamoto worked for several years as a journalist and even wrote for the camp newspaper when she was imprisoned at the Poston Internment Camp during World War II (1939–45) with other Japanese Americans wrongly removed from their homes. She was presented with the American Book Award for Lifetime Achievement from the Before Columbus Foundation in 1986.

Children's Literature

Jose Aruego (1932–)

Jose Aruego holds a law degree from the University of the Philippines, but he practiced law for only three months—just long enough to lose one case. He left his native

Jose Aruego.

country and moved to New York, where he attended the Parsons School of Design. After graduation, Aruego worked at various magazines and advertising agencies before becoming a full-time cartoonist. In the 1970s, he turned his talents to children's book illustration. He first illustrated *Whose Mouse Are You?* by Robert Kraus, and it was named an American Library Association's Notable Book. He then began to illustrate *and* write his own books. Aruego won the Outstanding Picture Book of the Year Award from the *New York Times* three times for his self-illustrated works in *Juan and the*

Asuangs (1970), *The Day They Parachuted Cats on Borneo* (1971), and *Look What I Can Do* (1972). In 1972 and 1973, three of Aruego's works were chosen as Children's Book Council Showcase Titles: *Look What I Can Do, The Chick and The Duckling,* and *A Crocodile's Tale.*

Dhan Gopal Mukerji (1890–1936)

Dhan Gopal Mukerji wrote children's books about animal life, frequently including Hindu folklore and philosophy in his work. His family, members of India's Brahmin priest caste, managed the temple in his native jungle village near Calcutta, India. In 1910, Mukerji immigrated to the United States. A poet and playwright, in 1922 he published his first work for children, *Kari, the Elephant,* which was followed in 1923 by *Jungle Beasts and Men,* a collection of stories. Next came *Hari, the Jungle Lad,* followed by *Gay-Neck: The Story of a Pigeon,* his most acclaimed work. *Gay-Neck* was selected by the American Institute of Graphic Arts as one of the 50 best books of 1927; it also won the American Library Association's Newbery Medal in 1928. In the same year Mukerji's work *Ghond, the Hunter* was named to the American Institute of Graphic Arts list of 50 best books.

Allen Say (1937–)

Allen Say's award-winning books for children often explore the experience of being an immigrant in the United States. He illustrated his first children's book, *A Canticle of Waterbirds,* in 1968. Four year later he wrote and illustrated *Dr. Smith's Safari.* In 1979 *The Inn-Keeper's Apprentice,* which he also wrote and illustrated, received the

Allen Say.

Yoshiko Uchida.

American Library Association's Notable Book Award and Best Book for Young Adults. The book tells the story of a young Japanese man who apprentices himself to a great comic-strip artist.

In 1989, Say wrote *The Lost Lake* and in the same year won the Caldecott Honor Medal for his illustrations in *The Boy of the Three-Year Nap,* written by Diane Snyder. In 1990, he published the critically acclaimed *El Chino,* followed by *The Tree of Cranes* in 1991. In 1993, Say produced *Grandfather's Journey,* which tells the story of his grandfa-

ther's life in Japan and the United States; the book won the Caldecott Medal for most distinguished picture book the following year.

Yoshiko Uchida (1921–1992)

Between 1948 and 1991, Yoshiko Uchida wrote 29 books, all but two of them for children. She is generally credited with creating a body of literature for children about the Japanese American experience. Her books dealing with the internment of Japanese Americans during World War II (1939–45) by the U.S. government include *Journey to Topaz* (about the internment camp where she and her family were kept) and *Journey Home.* Her trilogy, containing *A Jar of Dreams, The Best Bad Thing,* and *The Happiest Ending,* recounts the life of a Japanese American girl growing up in California during the Great Depression (1929–33). In 1991, Uchida published her last work, *The Invisible Thread,* an autobiography for teens.

Laurence Yep (1948–)

In 1970, a friend who worked in the children's division of a large publishing house asked struggling writer Laurence Yep to write a science fiction novel for children. Three years later Yep published *Sweetwater,* the first in a string of highly acclaimed works. *Dragonwings,* published in 1975, and its sequel, *Dragon's Gate,* both were named Newbery Honor books, the highest distinction awarded to children's books in the United States.

Dragonwings tells the true story of a Chinese American aviator who built and flew a flying machine in 1909. Yep's stage adaptation of *Dragonwings* was produced at Lincoln Center in New York and the Kennedy Center in Washington, D.C. *Dragon's Gate* is about the Chinese immigrants to America who built the transcontinental railroad.

In addition to the more than 15 novels for children he has published, Yep has written a number of plays, including *Age of Wonders, Pay the Chinaman,* and *Fairy Bones,* and has retold Chinese American folktales in two collections, *The Rainbow People* and *Tongues of Jade.*

Laurence Yep.

Ed Young (1931–)

Ed Young writes and illustrates picture books for children. Among works he has written and illustrated are *Night Visitors* (1995), *Little Plum* (1994), *Moon Mother: A Native American Creation Tale* (1994), and *Red Thread* (1993). In 1992 his book *Seven Blind Mice* was a Caldecott Honor Book.

Young has also illustrated works by other authors, including *Bitter Bananas* by Isaac Olaleye (1994); *Iblis* by Shulamith Oppenheim (1994); *Bo Rabbit Smart for True: Tall*

Tales from the Gullah by Priscilla Jaquith (1993); *Dreamcatcher* by Audrey Osofsky (1992); *The Rime of the Ancient Mariner* by Samuel Taylor Coleridge (1992); *What Comes in Spring?* by Barbara Savadge (1992); and *While I Sleep* by Mary Calhoun (1992).

Suggestions for Further Reading

Asian American Literature: An Annotated Bibliography, New York: Modern Language Association, 1988.

Asian American Portraits, New York: Macmillan Reference USA, 2001.

"Biography," *Linda Sue Park Website,* http://www.lspark.com (accessed March 18, 2003).

"Biography of Ha Jin," *Bookbrowse,* www.bookbrowse.com/index.cfm?page=author&authorID=368 (accessed April 15, 2003).

Bloom, Harold, ed., *Asian-American Writers,* Philadelphia, PA: Chelsea House Publishers, 1999.

Cheung, King-Kok, *Words Matter: Conversations with Asian American Writers,* Honolulu: University of Hawai'i Press, 2000.

Chin, Frank, et al, eds., *Aiiieeeee! An Anthology of Asian American Writers*, Washington, D.C.: Howard University Press, 1983.

Chin, Frank, et al, eds., *The Big Aiiieeeee! An Anthology of Chinese American and Japanese American Literature*, New York: Meridian Books, 1991.

Goshert, John Charles, *Frank Chin,* Boise: Boise State University, 2002.

Huang. Guiyou, editor. *Asian-American Poets: a Bio-Bibliographical Critical Sourcebook,* Westport, CT: Greenwood Press, 2002.

Ishizuka, Kathy, *Asian-American Authors,* Berkeley Heights, NJ: Enslow Publishers, 2000.

Jones, Malcolm, and David Gates, "Newsmakers," *Newsweek*, January 13, 2003, p. 71.

Kim, Elaine, *Asian American Literature: An Introduction to the Writings and Their Social Context*, Philadelphia: Temple University Press, 1982.

Kim, Elaine H., Lilia V. Villanueva, and Asian Women United of California, editors, *Making More Waves: New Writing by Asian American Women,* Boston: Beacon Press, 1997.

Lim, Shirley Geok-lin, compiler, *Asian-American Literature: An Anthology,* Lincolnwood, IL: NTC Publishing Group, 2000.

Lim, Shirley Geok-lin, and Amy Ling, eds., *Reading the Literatures of Asian America*, Philadelphia: Temple University Press, 1992.

Nelson, Emmanuel S., ed., *Asian American Novelists: A Bio-Bibliographical Critical Sourcebook,* Westport, CT: Greenwood Press, 2000.

Nguyen, Viet Thanh, *Race and Resistance: Literature and Politics in Asian America,* New York: Oxford University Press, 2002.

Srikanth, Rajini, and Esther Y. Iwanaga, eds., *Bold Words: A Century of Asian American Writing,* New Brunswick, NJ: Rutgers University Press, 2001.

Wong, Sau-ling Cynthia, *Reading Asian American Literature: From Necessity to Extravagance*, Princeton: Princeton University Press, 1993.

Wong, Sau-ling Cynthia, and Stephen H. Sumida, eds. *A Resource Guide to Asian American Literature,* New York: Modern Language Association of America, 2001.

15

Theatre

Asian American Theatres, Playwrights, and Actors

FACT FOCUS

- Flower Drum Song *by C.Y. Lee was the first successful Broadway musical written by an Asian American; it was staged in 1958. In October 2002, a new production based on the original but adapted by David Henry Hwang and starring Lea Salonga, opened on Broadway.*
- *Six Asian American actors and actresses founded East West Players in Los Angeles in 1965; this was the first Asian American theatre in the United States.*
- *The second Asian American theatre was the Kumu Kahua Theatre in Honolulu, Hawaii, founded in 1971.*
- *The Asian American Theatre Workshop was founded in San Francisco in 1973 by writer Frank Chin.*
- *Pan Asian Repertory Theatre was founded in 1977 in New York City.*

Throughout the history of American theatre, film, and television, Asians and Asian Americans have been portrayed in stereotypes: the silent servant, the exotic geisha, the evil prison camp commandant, or the brainy geek. Not only were Asians denied accurate depictions, but for decades they were not even allowed to play the few Asian roles available. For instance, the 1902 musical *Chinese Honeymoon,* imported from London to Broadway, featured Caucasian chorus girls in exaggerated slant-eyed makeup. Many New York stages flourished after World War II (1939–45) with shows that focused on Asian characters created by non-Asian writers, such as *The King and I* with Yul Brynner and *The Tea House of August Moon* with David Wayne. In these plays, both of which were later made into movies, Asians—the exotic king, the Japanese peasant—always remained foreigners in foreign settings.

Early Asian American Theatre

In 1958, with *Flower Drum Song,* the public witnessed a major production (it was a Rodgers and Hammerstein musical) that was about Asian Americans, performed by

Asian Americans, and based on a novel by an Asian American, C.Y. Lee. But the play was not much of an improvement from earlier plays written by non-Asians. Audiences felt that the stereotypes—the wise Confucian father, the China-doll female lead, and the submissive bride, all in a postcard-perfect setting of Chinatown—did little to reveal the real story of life in Asian America. (In 2002, David Henry Hwang adapted the original production. The new version opened in October starring Lea Salonga, and ran until March 2003.)

In the mid-1960s and early 1970s, the founding of several theatres devoted to the work of Asian Americans—playwrights, actors, set designers, directors—gave Asian American theatre increased national recognition as an important, living, growing form of artistic expression. The five theatre groups that struggled to bring Asian American theatre to the mainstream are discussed in the following section.

East West Players

When veteran Asian American actor Mako returned from New York to Los Angeles in 1960, he got to know many Asian American actors. "All we talked about," remembers Mako, "was the lack of decent roles for Asian Americans. . . . Eventually it came down to a group of seven of us who were totally committed to forming an organization." These seven—Mako, James Hong, June Kim, Guy Lee, Pat Li, Yet Lock, and Beulah Quo—founded East West Players in Los Angeles in 1965. Their first production, *Rashomon,* a play based on the short story by Japanese writer Akutagawa Ryunosuke, was staged in a small church basement in 1966. By 1968, East West Players found a perma-

Asian American actor and theatre pioneer, Mako.

nent home in Los Angeles's Silverlake area, and for the first time, Asian Americans had a place to perform rewarding roles in a realistic setting.

Under the artistic direction of Mako, East West Players initially staged adaptations of novels by Asian writers, Western classics, and plays written by Asian Americans, which provided Asian American actors with the opportunity to try roles that had been previously inaccessible to them due to their skin color. They premiered an original work almost every season.

More than two decades in the position—and a number of Los Angeles Drama Critics' awards—later, Mako was succeeded as artistic director in 1989 by actress Nobu McCarthy. In 1993, she passed the reins to actor/director/producer Tim Dang, who had been involved with East West since 1980.

Dang plans to add dance concerts, classical music performances, poetry readings, a visual arts gallery in the lobby, a bookstore featuring Asian American literature, and a performing conservatory of classes throughout the year. He also hopes to move East West Players to a larger theatre in the Los Angeles neighborhood known as "Little Tokyo." After almost 30 years, the oldest Asian American theatre is still a vital part of the arts community.

Kumu Kahua Theatre

Founded in 1971, the Kumu Kahua Theatre in Honolulu, Hawaii, whose name means "original platform or stage," is the second-oldest Asian American theatre in the United States. Self-described as "home-grown theatre," Kumu Kahua is dedicated to staging plays about past and present life in Hawaii, plays by Hawaii's playwrights, and plays for Hawaii's people.

Kumu Kahua was started by a group of University of Hawaii students and University of Hawaii professor Dennis Carroll. Five productions per season are staged there. In the more than 30 years since its founding, Kumu Kahua has offered well over 100 productions reflecting Hawaii's multiethnic community. The company's performances are not limited to Honolulu, but, each year in May or June, productions travel to the islands of Kauai, Maui, and Hawaii.

> ## WORDS TO KNOW
>
> **multiethnic:** reflecting two or more ethnic groups
>
> **playwright:** the author of a work for performance on stage
>
> **repertory:** several different plays produced over the course of a season
>
> **stereotype:** oversimplified image based on a characteristic or trait of group members

In addition to a statewide reach, Kumu Kahua productions also tour the mainland United States and beyond. In 1990, the company traveled to Edinburgh, Scotland; Washington, D.C.; and Los Angeles. Kumu Kahua also helps to develop local writers through an annual playwriting contest and workshop productions of three new plays a year.

Twenty-two years after its inception, Kumu Kahua finally acquired a permanent home in time for its 1993-94 season. The new 100-seat theatre is housed on the lower floor of the historic Kamehameha V Post Office in downtown Honolulu. With a new home and a full-time administrative staff for the first time, Kumu Kahua looks forward to continuing to serve the community as Hawaii's local theatre company.

Asian American Theater Company

The Asian American Theater Company (AATC) was originally established as the Asian American Theater Workshop (AATW) in San Francisco, California. Sponsored by the American Conservatory Theatre, the San Francisco Bay area's oldest and largest regional repertory theatre, AATW began in 1973 as a personal vision of writer Frank Chin: "I founded the Workshop as the only Asian American theatre that was conceived as a playwright's lab."

As AATW grew and evolved, the focus shifted from the writers to the actors. In mid-1977, Frank Chin left the group, and it became the Asian American Theater Company. AATC has been a testing ground for playwrights such as Philip Kan Gotanda and David Henry Hwang, and a training facility for actors including Dennis Dun, Kelvin Han Yee, Amy Hill, Brenda Wong Aoki, and others who have moved on to star in films and television. Since 1989, AATC has been operating in the Asian American Theater Center, with a 135-seat main stage, a 60-seat second stage, dance and rehearsal studios, and offices.

Northwest Asian American Theatre

The Northwest Asian American Theatre (NWAAT) began as two separate arts groups, both founded in 1973 and both dedicated to serving the Asian American arts community in Seattle, Washington.

The Asian Multi Media Center (AMMC) began in 1973 as an acting group that expanded into a multimedia production center. It included photography, graphic arts, and journalism with a training program that encouraged inner city youth to enter the mass-communication field.

Simultaneously, a group of students from the University of Washington formed the Theatrical Ensemble of Asians (TEA). They were concerned about the negative stereotyping of Asian Americans in mass media, the use of non-Asian actors to portray Asian

Frank Chin.

characters, and the lack of local performance opportunities for Seattle's Asian American actors, directors, and playwrights. TEA produced their first play, Carlos Bulosan's *Philippine Legends, Folklore, and American Impressions,* in 1974.

In 1975, TEA and AAMC together began to provide a showcase for such notable Asian American playwrights as Frank Chin and Wakako Yamauchi. In 1978, the two groups merged and became the Asian Exclusion Act, which evolved into Northwest Asian American Theatre in 1981. Soon NWAAT was able to produce two or three major shows a year, including such works as David Henry Hwang's *FOB*, Philip Kan Gotanda's *Song For a Nisei Fisherman,* and Rick Shiomi's *Yellow Fever.*

NWAAT opened the doors of its permanent home, Theatre Off Jackson, in 1987, after several years of fundraising and renovation of what had been a vacant parking garage in the International District of Seattle's downtown. The opening was marked by the world premiere of *Miss Minidoka 1943,* about a beauty pageant held in a Japanese American internment camp.

NWAAT has added a children's series and the annual Winterfest to its season. Winterfest presents Asian American entertainers from all over the United States, including jazz musicians, improvisational comedy groups, and solo performers.

Pan Asian Repertory Theatre

"My earnings on Broadway literally made it possible to fund my first production," says Tisa Chang, founder and artistic director of Pan Asian Repertory Theatre in New York City. In May 1977, Chang was playing Al Pacino's Vietnamese girlfriend on Broadway in *The Basic Training of Pavlo Hummel,* and she launched Pan Asian Repertory Theatre that year.

Pan Asian Repertory Theatre had the assistance of LaMama E.T.C., a leading New York stage for nontraditional, ground-breaking theatre. Its productions ranged from adaptations of Chinese classics to original works by new Asian American voices. Throughout its history, Pan Asian's focus has been on the actor.

In 1981, Pan Asian moved from LaMama into the 28th Street Theater. During its four years there, highlights included a trilogy of plays on the Japanese internment experience written by new Asian American writers. In addition, Pan Asian produced Rick Shiomi's detective-story spoof, *Yellow Fever.* It was so successful that it transferred off-Broadway where it remained for six months.

Pan Asian moved into Playhouse 46 in time for the 1985–86 season. In 1986 the company presented *Shogun Macbeth,* an original adaptation of the Shakespeare classic. In the 1990s, Pan Asian settled comfortably into financial stability, having received a number of grants including a $100,000 grant from the Ford Foundation and a multiyear grant from the Lila Wallace-*Reader's Digest* Foundation Theater for New Audiences Program.

New Generation of Theatres

National Asian American Theatre Company

Richard Eng and Mia Katigbak together founded the National Asian American Theatre Company, Inc. (NATCO) in 1988 in New York City. Their goal is to provide performance and production opportunities for skilled Asian American actors, directors, technicians, and designers. The company performs European and American classics.

NATCO stages productions of classic plays by William Shakespeare and Anton Chekhov, among others, with cast members who just happen to be Asian American. "As Asian American actors, it's nearly impossible to get cast in classical productions," explains Katigbak. Limited by budget constraints, NATCO attempts to mount one major production a year.

Angel Island Theatre Company

Chicago, Illinois, did not have an Asian American theatre company until 1989 when eight local Asian American community leaders and theatre artists banded together to form Angel Island Theatre Company (AITC). Their stated goal was "to present high-quality professional theatre that accurately depicts the Asian American experience, creates positive Asian role models, shatters narrow and negative stereotypes, preserves our cultural heritage, and enhances understanding between East and West through the arts." Due to funding restrictions, AITC has not yet established a regular season plan.

What makes AITC different from other Asian American theatre companies is that in spite of Chicago's sizable Asian American population, the city does not have a history of Asian American activism or even the same level of political organization or movement that is present on the West and East Coasts. When AITC staged its first production, David Henry Hwang's *FOB,* Adachi noted the need in Chicago for the theatre. "The play was so well received by the Asian American community. They made it absolutely clear that they were happy to have a theatre with Asian American actors who were playing something besides soldier number four."

Theater Mu

One of the younger Asian American theatres was founded in Minneapolis, Minnesota, by four individuals—Rick Shiomi, Dong-il Lee, Diane Espaldon, and Martha Johnson—who first met in May 1992. Minnesota has the largest population of Koreans adopted by U.S. families in the United States. It also includes the fastest-growing Asian American minority group of any state, with the population almost quadrupling from 1980 to 1990. Theater Mu committed itself to "giving voice to Asian Americans . . . to share our personal experiences, distinct cultures, and Asian American vision, creating and producing theatre works that can draw on both Asian and Western traditions."

The name of the group comes from the Korean pronunciation of a Chinese character. The character symbolizes the shaman/warrior/artist who connects the heaven and earth through the tree of life. Theater Mu believes that "performance is a ritual in which the shaman/warrior/artist takes the audience on a spiritual journey of transformation. This act of transformation changes the audience's perception of time, space, and reality, transforming their awareness of themselves and society."

In 1993, the group established an annual playwriting festival called *New Eyes* that showcases short new works by Asian American writers.

Emerging Companies

During the 1990s, several new Asian American theatres opened, with the aim of increasing opportunities for Asian Americans in theater, as well as dispelling racial stereotypes.

Lodestone Theatre Ensemble

In 1992, the idea for the Society of Heritage Performers/Lodestone Theatre Ensemble was born, as a response to racial rioting that disrupted the Los Angeles community and perpetuated racial stereotypes. In 1995, the vision was realized, and the performance

Kelly Miyashiro, Tony Lee, Elaine Kao, and Rachel Morihiro star in Lodestone Theatre Ensemble's *Refrigerators.*

troupe was born. The troupe was founded by Alexandra Bokyun Chun, Philip W. Chung, Chil Kong, and Tim Lounibos, and seeks to provide a forum for Asian Americans in theater. Committed to dispelling the limited perception of Asian Americans in the mass media, Lodestone provides workshops, full productions, and a Youth Outreach and Asian Teen Theatre program to reach at-risk youth.

Here and Now

Here and Now is another Asian American theater company based in Los Angeles that was receiving critical acclaim in the early twenty-first century. It has been staging performances since the 1990s, "the collective voice of its diverse cast to reach out to the audience through universal themes of the show; that everyone comes from a unique experience, and that all people have stories to share."

Contemporary Asian Theatre Scene

Contemporary Asian Theatre Scene, based in San Jose, California, is devoted to advancing theater of Asian American theater. It was formed in 1995 "to present works

Sab Shimono (right) and Kelvin Han Yee in a performance of Philip Kan Gotanda's *Yankee Dawg You Die* at the Berkeley Repertory Theatre, Berkeley, California.

dealing with Asian Pacific American issues and concerns of the community at large, while contributing to the cultural enhancement of the City of San Jose and beyond."

Community Asian Theatre of The Sierra

CATS, or Community Asian Theatre of the Sierra, is another nonprofit multicultural theater organization based in the Sierra foothills of northern California. In a community that is 92 percent white, CATS has been exploring the Asian influence on American history since 1994.

18 Mighty Mountain Warriors

In 1994, the 18 Mighty Mountain Warriors premiered their unique brand of comedy. The group confronts prevailing stereotypes through humor, using their comedy to promote positive images. 18 Mighty Mountain Warriors grew out of an ensemble that spent a year in residence at the Asian American Theater Company from 1993-1994. The group's strategy is to "push the envelope," with both their performance and content. Though the troupe focuses on Asian American themes, their appeal is universal, and they have established themselves as a force in comedy.

Playwrights

Wakako Yamauchi

Undeniably one of the classic Asian American plays, Wakako Yamauchi's *And the Soul Shall Dance* began as a short story. Although Yamauchi could not find a publisher among mainstream magazines, her story was selected for the pioneering anthology of Asian American writers, *Aiiieeeee!* Mako, the artistic director of East West Players, decided to turn it into a play and produce it. The story of two Japanese families, farmers in Southern California's Imperial Valley in the 1930s, *Soul* became one of the most-produced Asian American plays.

Yamauchi continues to write for the stage. Some of the works she has authored are *The Music Lessons,* (1980 New York Shakespeare Festival Public Theater premiere), *12-1-A* (1982 East West Players premiere), *A Memento* (1984 Pan Asian Repertory premiere), and *The Chairman's Wife* (1990 East West Players premiere).

Momoko Iko

In 1970 and 1971, Momoko Iko's plays, *Gold Watch* and *Old Man,* won the playwriting contests sponsored by East West Players. *Gold Watch* has been her most-produced work. Premiered in 1970 at the Inner City Cultural Center in Los Angeles, *Gold Watch* was produced for television by PBS.

Iko's other works include *When We Were Young* (1974 East West premiere), *Flowers and Household Gods* (1981 Pan Asian premiere), and *Boutique Living and Disposable Icons* (1988 Pan Asian premiere).

Frank Chin

Fifth-generation Chinese American Frank Chin was the first Asian American playwright to have his work produced in New York. In 1972, *The Chickencoop Chinaman* was staged at The American Place Theatre in New York City. In this work, Chin introduces three unpredictable, often comic characters that defy generalizations and challenge stereotypes of Asian Americans. The play opened to glowing reviews from such publications as the *New Yorker* and *Newsweek.* Chin wrote: "That this play is the first play by an Asian American to, in any sense, make it, that people should be surprised at our existence, is proof of the great success white racism has had with us. America might love us. But America's love is not good. It's racist love. I don't want it."

Chin's next play, *The Year of the Dragon*, was also presented at The American Place Theatre in 1974. The play's theme was the disintegration of the Chinese American family. The play went on to be filmed as a PBS production in 1975.

Chin left the Asian American Theater Workshop in 1977. "I am out of theatre," Chin said in the mid-1990s. "I will not work with any theatre, producer, writer, director, or actor who plays and lives the stereotype. So I write fiction, essays, and articles."

Genny Lim

San Francisco native Genny Lim is best known for her ground-breaking one-act play, *Paper Angels,* which premiered at Asian American Theater Company in 1980. The work focuses on the experiences of Chinese immigrants detained on Angel Island in the San Francisco Bay. Lim's detainees in *Paper Angels* are of different generations and various backgrounds. They represent the approximately 175,000 Chinese immigrants who entered the United States between 1910 and 1940 through Angel Island. In 1985, *Paper Angels* was produced by American Playhouse for PBS.

Since writing *Paper Angels,* Lim has produced other historically based, realistic works such as *Bitter Cane,* which focuses on the virtual imprisonment of laborers by Hawaiian sugar cane plantations.

Valena Hasu Houston

Born in Japan to an American G.I. father and Japanese mother, Valena Houston's ethnic background is half-Asian, a quarter Native American, and a quarter African American. Her multicultural identity has been pivotal to her works, which include *Asa Ga Kimashita* ("Morning Has Broken"), *American Dreams,* and *Tea,* a trilogy based on her family's experiences. The first play of the trilogy, *Asa Ga Kimashita,* is a work based on Houston's mother's decision to marry an American soldier. It premiered in 1981 at the Studio Theater, University of California at Los Angeles.

Houston refers to *Tea,* the final play of the family trilogy, as "a poem to my mother." *Tea* received its world premiere at the Manhattan Theatre Club in 1987. The play reveals the struggles of five Japanese-born wives of U.S. servicemen who are brought together after one of them commits violent suicide.

Philip Kan Gotanda

Philip Kan Gotanda's first theatrical endeavor, a musical called *The Avocado Kid,* was staged at East West Players in 1980. The following year, Gotanda wrote the nonmusical *Song for a Nisei Fisherman.* It is a Japanese American family saga, first produced at Asian American Theater Company. In 1984, Gotanda's fairy-tale-like work set in ancient Japan, *The Dream of Kitamura,* premiered at AATC.

Gotanda's next play, *The Wash,* a poignant depiction of the troubled marriage of an older Japanese American couple, brought him national acclaim and moved him into the mainstream. First staged at San Francisco's Eureka Theatre in 1987, the play was made into a 1988 PBS American Playhouse film (which starred East West founder, Mako, and second artistic director, Nobu McCarthy).

The Wash was followed by the acclaimed *Yankee Dawg You Die,* which began at the Berkeley Repertory Theater in 1988 and went on to New York's Playwrights Horizon in 1990. The play features two actors arguing. The older one has survived as an actor by doing small, character parts. The younger

Philip Kan Gotanda.

is idealistic and believes he will be able to find substantial roles.

In 1992, Gotanda's *Fish Head Soup* also premiered at Berkeley Repertory. In early 1994, *Day Standing on Its Head* premiered at Manhattan Theatre Club in New York City and made its West Coast debut at the Asian American Theatre Company in San Francisco later the same year. It tells the story of law professor Harry Kitamura who, on the verge of middle age, embarks on a journey toward his true self.

Gotanda has been very successful in mainstream theatres and has been awarded fellowships from many prestigious organizations. In the 1990s he began working on films as well as plays.

David Henry Hwang

As a senior at Stanford University, David Henry Hwang turned in a play called *FOB*. (The term *FOB* refers to a new immigrant, someone who is "fresh off the boat.") It tells the story of the clash between a new immigrant and a westernized Asian American. From its first production in 1979 in a Stanford dormitory to a 1981 Obie for Best New Play, *FOB* propelled Hwang toward stardom at an age when most young adults have not even decided on a career.

Hwang's second work, *Dance and the Railroad,* inspired by the experiences of Chinese railroad workers in the United States in 1867, was nominated for a Drama Desk Award. His next play, *Family Devotions,* was a semiautobiographical work in which Hwang questioned the Christian tradition that obstructed his journey into his cultural past.

Hwang became interested in a story he heard about a French diplomat who was involved in a 20-year love affair with a male Chinese spy whom he believed to be a woman. His interest evolved into the 1988 Tony Award-winning play, *M. Butterfly.* It became one of the most successful nonmusical works in Broadway history, grossing over $35 million. In addition to the Tony Award, the play also garnered the Drama Desk, Outer Critics Circle, and John Gassner awards in 1988, followed by a 1991 Los Angeles Drama Critics Circle Award.

David Henry Hwang.

A few months after the opening of *M. Butterfly*, Hwang and avant-garde (an artist who develops new and experimental forms or ideas) composer Philip Glass produced *1000 Airplanes on the Roof*, a multimedia extravaganza about a close encounter with aliens.

In 1992, Hwang premiered another one-act, *Bondage,* at the Humana Festival of New American Plays at the Actors Theatre of Louisville. The play is a gender-bending, race-changing, label-challenging work that confronts the inherent racism and sexism

Lea Salonga, star of the the 2002 revival of *Flower Drum Song*, reviews costume sketches in September 2002, a month before the show opened on Broadway in New York.

Behind the Scenes in Theatre

Phyllis S. K. Look, Director

Trained at Yale University Drama School, Phyllis S. K. Look had many years' experience as an actress before her seven-year stint directing at the Berkeley Repertory Theatre in Berkeley, California. While she is one of the few Asian American directors working today in a major mainstream regional theatre, Look still finds "something very special about directing Asian American plays." She remembers Laurence Yep's *Dragonwings* as the play that originally propelled her career forward and gained her national recognition. More than that, the play helped her to find her voice as a theatre director. Look explained: "There are few opportunities in one's lifetime where a piece *really* uses all of you. That's how I felt about this work. I felt so connected emotionally, aesthetically, and politically to it."

At the end of the 1994 season, Look left the Berkeley company to start a freelance directing career.

Ming Cho Lee, Set Designer

Ming Cho Lee has been described as the most influential figure in the history of theatre set design. (A theatre set designer creates the state setting, or scenery, for a play.) Lee has spent 11 years designing for the New York Shakespeare Festival, 14 years for the New York City Opera, and 20 years for the Metropolitan Opera. He has designed productions in probably every major regional theatre in the United States and in many international venues as well. Lee balances his design career with teaching. In

rampant in society. Hwang's next production was a second Broadway opening. *Face Value*—a farce inspired by the controversy over the casting of a white man in the lead role of the blockbuster musical *Miss Saigon*—was extremely short-lived.

In October 2002, Hwang's new rendition of the Rodgers and Hammerstein musical *Flower Drum Song* opened on Broadway. Starring Lea Salonga, it ran through March 2003.

Ming Cho Lee.

2003 Lee was in his thirty-fourth year at Yale University, and was chair of the design department at the Drama School.

Willa Kim, Costume Designer

Willa Kim designs costumes for theatre productions. She has won Tony Awards (given for Broadway theatre productions) for Duke Ellington's *Sophisticated Ladies* (1981) and *The Will Rogers Follies* (1991). She has received Tony nominations for Peter Allen's *Legs Diamond* (1988), Andrew

Lloyd Webber's *Song and Dance* (1985), Bob Fosse's *Dancin'* (1978), and Joel Grey's *Goodtime Charley* (1975). She won an Emmy for the San Francisco Ballet's production of *The Tempest* (choreographed by Michael Smuin, 1981). She has also received Drama Desk awards for Maria Irene Fornes's *Promenade* (1969), Sam Shepherd's *Operation Sidewinder* (1988), and Jean Genet's *The Screens* (1971), and an Obie (an Off-Broadway award) for Robert Lowell's *The Old Glory* (1976).

Credited with being the first designer to use thin stretch fabric for dancer's tights as well as the first to paint designs onto fabrics, Kim continues to design for dance, opera, and theatre, and holds a special preference for musicals.

Victor En Yu Tan, Lighting Designer

Victor Tan shares his more than 20 years of experience in designing lighting for theatre with graduate students at the University of Michigan. He also manages to do lighting design for about 8 to 12 stage productions each year. Tan's first design opportunity in New York was for the 1974 production of Frank Chin's *The Year of the Dragon* at the American Place Theatre. Since 1979, Tan has been a freelance lighting designer and has completed over 400 productions in the United States and abroad, including over 25 productions at New York's Public Theater. Notable among these are: David Henry Hwang's *FOB* and *Dance and the Railroad*, and George Wolfe's *The Colored Museum*. Tan's regional theatre credits include designs for the Actors Theatre of Louisville's annual Humana Festival of New American Plays, the Mark Taper Forum, American Repertory Theater, and Pasadena Playhouse.

Since 1980, Tan has been the resident lighting designer for Pan Asian Repertory, where he recently designed the revival of *FOB*, directed by David Henry Hwang. He won an Obie in 1985 for sustained excellence in lighting and most recently a Dramalogue for *The Colored Museum*.

Asian American Theatres

Asian American Theater Co.
403 Arguello Blvd.
San Francisco, CA 94118
(415) 751-2600

Community Asian Theater of the Sierra
228 Commercial Street #88
Nevada City, California 95959
(530) 273-6362

East West Players
4424 Santa Monica Blvd.
Los Angeles, CA 90029
(213) 660-0366

Eighteen Mighty Mountain Warriors
P.O. Box 590356
San Francisco, CA 94159-0356
(415) 646-0868

Great Leap, Inc.
244 S. San Pedro St., Ste. 408
Los Angeles, CA 90012
(213) 687-3948

Here and Now
244 S. San Pedro St., Ste. 403
Los Angeles, CA 90012
(213) 628-7018

Lodestone Theatre Ensemble
P. O. Box 1072
Studio City, CA 91614
(323) 993-7245

Ma-Yi Theatre Ensemble, Inc.
P.O. Box 661
New York, NY 10159-0661
(212) 662-0079

National Asian American Theatre Co.
200 W. 20th St., Ste. 211
New York, NY 10011
(212) 675-0767

Northwest Asian American Theatre
409 7th Ave.
Seattle, WA 98104
(206) 340-1445

Pan Asian Rep
47 Great Jones St.
New York, NY 10012
(212) 505-5655

Ping Chong and Co.
47 Great Jones St.
New York, NY 10012
(212) 529-1557

Theater Mu
1201 Yale Place, Ste. 911
Minneapolis, MN 55403
(612) 332-5763

Theatre of Yugen
Noh Space
2840 Mariposa St.
San Francisco, CA 94110
(415) 621-0507

Wise Fool Productions
125 Seaman Ave., Ste. 6G
New York, NY 10034
(212) 569-1836

Suggestions for Further Reading

Chin, Frank, *The Chickencoop Chinaman and The Year of the Dragon*: *Two Plays by Frank Chin,* Seattle: University of Washington Press, 1981.

Chin, Frank, et al, eds., *Aiiieeeee! An Anthology of Asian American Writers,* New York: Mentor, 1974.

Chin, Frank, et al, eds., *The Big Aiiieeeee! An Anthology of Chinese American and Japanese American Literature,* New York: Meridian, 1991.

Eighteen Mighty Mountain Warriors, http://www.18mmw.com (accessed April 28, 2003).

Feng, Peter X., *Identities in Motion: Asian American Film and Video,* Durham, NC: Duke University Press, 2002.

Hagedorn, Jessica, *Charlie Chan Is Dead: An Anthology of Contemporary Asian American Fiction,* New York: Penguin Books, 1993.

Here and Now Theater, http://www.blacklava.net/hereandnow/temp.html (accessed April 28, 2003).

Houston, Valena Hasu, *The Politics of Life: Four Plays by Asian American Women,* Philadelphia: Temple University Press, 1993.

Hwang, David Henry, *"FOB" and Other Plays,* New York: Plume, 1990.

Odo, Franklin, ed., *The Columbia Documentary History of the Asian American Experience,* New York: Columbia University Press, 2002.

"The Solid Past," *Lodestone Theatre Ensemble,* http://www.lodestonetheatre.org (accessed April 28, 2003).

Uno, Roberta, *Unbroken Thread: An Anthology of Plays by Asian American Women,* Amherst: University of Massachusetts Press, 1993.

16
Sports and Athletics

FACT FOCUS

- Martial arts, with roots in Asia, are enjoyed by Americans of all racial and ethnic groups.
- Native Hawaiian swimmer Duke Kahanamoku was the first Asian American Olympian, competing in the 1912 Olympics in Stockholm, Sweden.
- Sumo wrestling was a popular way to celebrate important events and keep up the spirits among Japanese workers on Hawaiian sugar plantations.
- Beginning at the turn of the twentieth century, youth clubs in the Japanese American community stressed sports and good citizenship and were the springboard for Japanese American athletic leagues.

Asian immigrants brought new sports to the United States. The various kinds of martial arts were some of the most notable new athletic activities brought to the Americas by immigrants from many Asian/Pacific Island nations. Surfing was a native Hawaiian sport, and sumo wrestling was introduced to Westerners by Japanese immigrants to Hawaii.

Asian Americans have also excelled at mainstream American sports and are represented in all the professional athletic organizations. Until the turn of the twentieth century, however, Asian American participation in professional sports was not as common as it is today. One of the reasons for this was that many early immigrants were too busy working to learn American games. Another reason was that American sports organizations were prone to racial discrimination. It was noteworthy, therefore, when in the 1850s a Chinese student, Yung Wing, made a remarkable touchdown playing football at Yale, and a fellow Cantonese student was a coxswain (the steerer of a racing boat who directs the rowers) on Yale's rowing team. In the following one hundred years, however, there were few Chinese American athletes in public competition.

For Japanese immigrants, both "Japanese" sports—that is, sports with historical roots in Japan—and "American" sports— sports with historical roots in the Americas—played an important role in adapting to

Chinese American youngsters participate in an Olympics sponsored by the local chapter of the Organization of Chinese Americans in San Jose, California.

a new country. Sports helped them to maintain a strong sense of a Japanese community, while also helping them to assimilate (adopt the mainstream U.S. culture). The two most important sports to the issei (first-generation Japanese Americans) were sumo and baseball.

Sumo

Sumo is a type of wrestling that has been practiced in Japan for two thousand years. It involves two participants who face each other and try to force each other down or outside of the ring. Although it is a sport involving great strength and athletic skill, sumo is also quasi-religious in nature and is generally practiced with many rituals. Most sumo wrestlers are extremely large males, weighing from 300 to 400 pounds.

The first official immigrants from Japan arriving in Hawaii in February 1885 celebrated their arrival with a sumo match in front of the Hawaiian king. As Japanese immigrants arrived in large numbers over the next two decades to work on Hawaiian sugar plantations, sumo's popularity grew. Sumo tournaments—held to determine the best sumotori of each plantation camp—evolved into inter-camp and inter-island tournaments, and the first Hawaii Grand Sumo Tournament was held in Honolulu on June 25, 1896. From the turn of the century through the 1930s, sumo was practiced in

SOME ASIAN AMERICAN BASEBALL STARS

Player	Position	Team(s)	Awards/Achievements
Ron Darling (1960–)	Pitcher	New York Mets (1982–1991) Oakland Athletics (1991–)	National League All-Star Team, 1985 National League Golden Glove Award, 1989
Sid Fernandez (1962–)	Pitcher	Los Angeles Dodgers (1981–1983) New York Mets (1984–)	National League All-Star Team, 1986 and 1987
Wendell Kim (1950–)	Coach	San Francisco Giants (1989–)	First Korean American to wear a major league uniform
Masanori Murakami (1944–)	Pitcher	San Francisco Giants (1964–1965)	First Japanese player in U.S. major league baseball
Len Sakata (1954–)	Utility Infielder	Milwaukee Brewers Baltimore Orioles Oakland Athletics New York Yankees	In 1982, hit .259 in 136 games
Makoto "Mac" Suzuki (1975–)	Pitcher	Seattle Mariners (1993–) San Bernardino Spirit (CA League)	Pitches measured at 96 mph
Chan Ho Park (1973–)	Pitcher	Los Angeles Dodgers (1994–2001) Texas Rangers (2002–)	First Korean to play in the major leagues
Ichiro Suzuki (1973–)	Outfielder	Seattle Mariners (2000–)	American League Most Valuable Player (2000)
Kazuhisa "Kaz" Ishii (1973–)	Pitcher	Los Angeles Dodgers (2001–) Texas Rangers (2002–)	Over 15 wins in 2002 season
Hideki Matsui (1974–)	Outfielder	New York Yankees (2003–)	First draft pick in Japan (1993)

Hawaii by church groups, by young and old men, and even by women. It was used to celebrate Japanese victories in wars and to raise spirits during the bitter 1909 plantation strike by Japanese laborers.

Although sumo was already losing its popularity by the 1940s, the coming of World War II was nearly the end of the sport in the United States. In an atmosphere where all things Japanese were considered suspect, sumo was virtually stamped out in Hawaii. (It was, however, practiced in some of the mainland internment camps during the war.) There are some followers of sumo in the United States today, but few Japanese Americans participate in the sport anymore. In the late 1980s however, an American of Samoan descent became an internationally known sumo star. Konishiki, as he is known professionally, became the first non-Japanese to be elevated to the rank of *ozeki* (champion).

Japanese Athletic Leagues and Clubs

The first Japanese American baseball team, called JBS, was formed in 1901 by

Reverend Takie Okumura and was made up of students from his boarding school. Baseball soon became a favorite pastime among issei and nisei (first- and second-generation Japanese Americans) from both Hawaii and the mainland. In Hawaii, baseball was encouraged by the sugar plantations as a healthy recreation that would occupy the workers and keep them out of trouble. Rivalries soon developed between different plantation teams. Similarly, Japanese American communities on the mainland formed teams that played one another.

In Los Angeles, home of the largest Japanese American community since the 1910s, the roots of nisei athletics can be traced to a Caucasian school teacher named Nellie Grace Oliver, who formed the Japanese Boys Club and the Japanese Girls Club on November 21, 1917, after observing nisei youngsters playing on the streets of Little Tokyo. The club and its many successors became known as the Olivers, the first of the nisei social clubs. The Olivers stressed sports and emphasized good citizenship and education.

As the Japanese American community in Los Angeles continued to grow in the 1920s, similar youth clubs formed in outlying areas. As early as 1926, a YMCA basketball league was operating in Los Angeles. Soon these groups were challenging each other in various sports. Contests took place in a haphazard and unregulated manner. In an attempt to regulate the proceedings, the Japanese Athletic Union (JAU) was formed in June 1932. The similar Japanese Amateur Athletic Union (JAAU) had formed in the San Francisco Bay area around 1929. By 1934, a basketball championship game was taking place between the Southern California JAU champion and the Northern California JAAU

champion. In the next few years, participation boomed among nisei Americans. According to Isami Waugh, there were over 400 nisei clubs in Southern California by 1938.

Though the scale was different, nisei sports seemed to develop along more or less similar models elsewhere on the mainland. Samuel Regalado described an eight-team Central Japanese (Baseball) League that formed in Central California from 1934 to 1941 and noted the particularly bitter rivalry between the Livingston Dodgers and the Cortez Wildcats, for instance. In his study of baseball in the World War II internment camps, Jay Feldman notes that by the 1930s, "every community had a nisei team, ardently supported by issei immigrants." In his ground-breaking study of the Japanese American community, Harry H. L. Kitano notes the presence of "the ambitious all-Japanese athletic leagues."

Though most of the teams and leagues in the mainland United States were segregated, in the multi-ethnic society of Hawaii teams of various ethnic groups played against each other. The most famous Japanese American team was the Asahis, formed as a sandlot team in 1905. The team became dominant in the multi-ethnic Oahu Junior League, winning titles from 1911 to 1914. The Asahis became a founding member of the Hawaii Baseball League in 1925, which was made up of segregated teams of various ethnic groups. In addition to the Asahis, the Japanese team, there were also the Braves, Portuguese; the All-Chinese; the Wanderers, Haole; the All-Hawaiian; and others. There was also the case of the Wapato Nippons, a nisei team competing in the mostly white leagues of eastern Washington, whose success made them the pride of the Japanese American community there.

SOME ASIAN AMERICAN FOOTBALL STARS

Player	Position	Team	Awards/ Achievements
Walter Aichu	Running back/ punter	Dayton Triangles (1927–1928)	First Asian American to play professional football
Eugene Chung (1969–)	Offensive tackle	New England Patriots (1992-1994) Jacksonville Jaguars (1995) Indianapolis Colts (1997) Kansas City Chiefs (1998)	First Asian American drafted in first round to NFL; Sports Award of the Mainstream American Award for Excellence, Asian Pacific Coalition
Leo Goeas (1966–)	Offensive lineman	San Diego Chargers (1990–1992) Los Angeles Rams (1993–)	Ed Block Memorial Award; All-Rookie honors
John Lee	Placekicker	St. Louis Cardinals (1986) Los Angeles Raiders (1987)	One of the most prolific kickers in NCAA history
Alfred Pupunu (1969–)	Tight end/ halfback	San Diego Chargers	Caught 13 passes for a total of 142 yards gained, 1992–1993
Ron Rivera (1962–)	Linebacker	Chicago Bears (1984–)	Consensus first-team All-American; finalist for the Lombardi Award; Pac Ten co-Defensive Player of the Year (CA); Traveler's Man of the Year Award
Jesse Sapolu (1961–)	Offensive lineman	San Francisco 49ers (1983–)	Prominent fixture on San Francisco offensive line
Junior Seau (1969–)	Linebacker	San Diego Chargers (1990–)	1993: co-Most Valuable Player; NFL Players Association Linebacker of the Year; voted All-Pro by Associated Press
Dat Nguyen (1975–)	Linebacker	Dallas Cowboys (1999–)	First Vietnamese American to play professional Football.

Segregation and Assimilation in the Leagues

Like the role it played in other ethnic communities, sports activity was a vehicle for assimilation in U.S. society. Harry Kitano explained that participating in baseball and other sports provided Japanese Americans with a kind of model for life in the United States: "The Nisei were free to develop in the American pattern. The play, the rules, the goals and values were all American; only the players were Japanese." However, the segregation (the separation of a race, class, or ethnic group by discriminatory means) of the leagues and the intergenerational support they received served to increase the bonds within the Japanese

American community. Given the difference in experiences and ideas between issei and nisei, sports was a means of finding common ground between the generations and cultures. For the nisei, sports was a form of recreation and a chance to be a star. For the issei, the segregated leagues insured that nisei would associate with other nisei, increasing ties among Japanese American communities and serving as a convenient forum for betting and spectatorship. Successful teams became focal points of great pride for their communities.

The mass removal and incarceration of West Coast Japanese Americans during World War II brought an end to the nisei sports leagues. In Hawaii, the Asahis became the Athletics and added non-Japanese players. Sports, however, still played an important role in the concentration camps that housed the uprooted Japanese Americans, and baseball continued to be the most popular sport among issei and nisei alike. At some camps, as many as 100 teams existed, with leagues for various age groups. In other camps where the populations of existing communities remained intact, teams were able to remain together and compete as before. Teams were also organized by block, or, in the case of Tule Lake, by former camp. Nisei also competed in basketball, girls' volleyball and softball, and touch football, while issei busied themselves with *go*, cards, or baseball. As the title of a recent children's book on baseball in internment camps states, "baseball saved us."

The postwar era saw the rebuilding of Japanese American athletic leagues along the same lines as before the war, with basketball replacing baseball as the most popular sport. In 1946, the Nisei Athletic Union was formed in both southern and northern California, and play began in January 1947. The "resettlement" strategy of the War Relocation Authority led to the formation of postwar Japanese American communities in many places outside the West Coast where there had been no such communities before. It was not long before similar leagues emerged in places like Chicago, where the Chicago Nisei Athletic Association was formed. The coming of age of the sansei in the 1950s and 1960s led to increasing popularity for these leagues, with participation probably peaking in the 1970s. The still segregated leagues continue to this day, though participation is falling with the declining population of young Japanese Americans.

Surfing

Surfing is the sport of riding the ocean's waves. A surfer swims out into the ocean to the point where the waves begin to form. He or she then mounts the board and begins to paddle toward shore. When a wave catches the surfboard, the surfer stands on the board and rides the breaking wave into the beach. Early surfing was done on a long wooden board; in modern times there are lightweight synthetic boards that glide more easily through the waves.

No one knows for certain how it came into being, but surfing originated in Hawaii, where it was popular in the nineteenth century. It is thus a native American sport, although Hawaii was a separate nation until 1898. At that time, surfing was unknown to the mainland. It spread as a popular sport in the Americas and throughout the world largely due to the efforts of Olympic swimmer Duke Kahanamoku, a full-blooded

SOME ASIAN AMERICAN OLYMPIC CHAMPIONS

Tiffany Chin (1967–)	1984 Olympics, Sarajevo, Yugoslavia	4th place: Women's Figure Skating
Duke Kahanamoku (1890–1968)	1912 Olympics, Stockholm, Sweden	Gold Medal: Men's Swimming (100-meter freestyle)
	1920 Olympics, Antwerp, Belgium	Gold Medal: Men's Swimming (100-meter freestyle)
	1924 Olympics, Paris, France	Silver Medal: Men's Swimming (100-meter freestyle)
Tommy Kono (1930–)	1952 Olympics, Helsinki, Finland	Gold Medal: Weightlifting, Lightweight
Sammy Lee (1920–)	1948 Olympics, London, England	Gold Medal: Men's Platform Diving and Bronze Medal: Men's Springboard
	1952 Olympics, Helsinki, Finland	Gold Medal: Men's Platform Diving
Greg Louganis (1960–)	1976 Olympics, Montreal, Canada	Silver Medal: Men's Diving
	1984 Olympics, Los Angeles, California	Gold Medals: Men's Springboard and Men's Platform Diving
	1988 Olympics, Seoul, South Korea	Gold Medals: Men's Springboard and Platform Diving; Olympic Spirit Award
Victoria Manolo Draves (1924–)	1948 Olympics, London, England	Gold Medals: Women's Springboard and Women's Platform Diving
Kristi Yamaguchi (1971–)	1992 Olympics, Albertville, France	Gold Medal in Women's Figure Skating
Michelle Kwan (1980–)	1998 Olympics, Nagano, Japan	Silver Medal in Women's Figure Skating
	2002 Olympics, Salt Lake City, Utah	Bronze Medal in Women's Figure Skating
Apolo Anton Ohno (1982–)	2002 Olympics, Salt Lake City, Utah	Silver Medal in 1000-meter Speed Skating; Gold in 1500-meter

Hawaiian and the descendant of the early-nineteenth-century king Kamehameha.

Kahanamoku became an international sensation after winning the 100-meter freestyle race at the Olympic games in Stockholm, Sweden, in 1912. When the 1916 Olympic games were cancelled because of World War I, Kahanamoku spent eight years traveling, defending his swimming titles at meets all over the world. While he was traveling, he delighted observers with his demonstrations of surfing. His 1915 visit to Australia is remembered by today's Aussie surfers as nothing less than the appearance of a prophet. During a 1916 Red Cross fundraising tour through the East Coast, Kahanamoku stopped to do surfing exhibitions in Atlantic City and Coney Island. In New York, officials even named a Brighton Beach thoroughfare after him.

Kahanamoku and his surfboard have become legendary in Hawaii and Kahanamoku is remembered as a true hero. In 1925, he and a group of friends saw a boat capsize during a fierce storm off the coast of southern California. Without hesitation, Kahanamoku grabbed his surfboard and, making three trips through violent waves, personally saved eight people in a disaster that claimed seventeen out of twenty-nine lives. The local chief of police was later quoted in newspapers: "Kahanamoku's performance was the most superhuman rescue act and the finest display of surfboard riding that has ever been seen in the world."

Surfing caught on in California during the 1920s. In the 1960s surfing became a subculture and lifestyle among a young and nonconformist group of dedicated surfers in the United States. Although people surf in many Pacific nations, Hawaii is still the world's center of the sport.

Martial Arts

The martial arts encompass a number of systems of self-defense and self-discipline that grew out of early Asian fighting methods. These techniques are used today for fitness and sport as well as self-defense. Prominent among these systems are aikido, judo, karate, kung fu, and tae kwon do, along with many others.

History

Scholars disagree on the exact origins of the martial arts, since unarmed methods of combat were known in many early civilizations, some dating from 2000 B.C. The Asian styles, however, almost certainly came to China from India and Tibet, where they were used for centuries by unarmed monks, who were prime targets of bandits flourish-

ing in those lands. These fighting styles, which eventually spread to all of Asia, began, according to legend, with an Asian Indian Buddhist monk named Bodhidharma (A.D. 470-543).

In the year 527, the story goes, Bodhidharma traveled to China as a Zen Buddhist missionary and later founded the Shaolin temple in Honan province. Finding his disciples unable to withstand the intensity of Zen's strict discipline and self-denial, he is said to have developed a series of exercises to toughen them both mentally and physically. With or without Bodhidharma's influence, the Shaolin monks eventually transformed these techniques into a martial way called *kempo* that became known throughout China.

Unarmed combat in Korea has been documented in tombs and paintings that date from A.D. 37. By the period of the Koro Dynasty (963-1392), a system of martial arts called *soo bahk* was taught to members of the Korean military. During the Japanese occupation of Korea (1907–1945), the Korean arts were suppressed—until the Japanese found that Korean troops fought much better when allowed to use the national style. During this time, many Japanese styles, such as judo, aikido, and karate, were adapted to Korean techniques.

Isolated and far to the east, Japan was the last Asian nation to develop martial arts. As early as A.D. 220 a collection of primitive fighting skills called *chikara kurabe* was used in battle, and an ancient warrior's training included both armed and unarmed combat. The invention of armor was a temporary stumbling block, but combatants soon discovered that it was far more effective to wrestle an armored opponent to the ground than it was to hit him. Fighting styles were quickly adapted. By the seventeenth century these early martial arts, known as *ju-jitsu* in Japan, were so effective that knowledge of them was limited by law to feudal warriors. The tradition continued through World War II, when Japanese soldiers were trained in ju-jitsu methods. Although their instruction was banned after the war, by the mid-1950s they were again legalized.

Martial Arts in the United States

The history of the martial arts in the United States can be traced to the presidency of Ulysses S. Grant, who attended a demonstration of judo techniques by a young master while on a state visit to Japan in the late 1800s. Later, a professor from Yale traveled to Japan to study judo; by the early 1900s, President Theodore Roosevelt had arranged a judo demonstration at the White House. There were soon a number of judo clubs in the United States, and the sport had attracted a moderate following.

It was not until World War II, however, that the martial arts became more widely known and practiced in this country. U.S. service personnel in occupied Japan were fascinated by the arts and began studying them in large numbers. Upon returning to the states, a few of them set up schools and invited Japanese masters to come and teach. Some *dojos*, or practice halls, did exist before this time, but they were little known and hard to find; both teachers and students were almost exclusively Asian. After the war, however, a wave of popularity made the martial arts a part of mainstream U.S. society. Similarly, the Korean War led to the importation of the Korean art of tae kwon do.

Aikido

Aikido means "way of harmony" or "way of the spirit." It is an essentially nonviolent martial art that emphasizes meditation and cultivation of the *ki*. The ki, the center of the body's strength and source of mental energy, is located in the abdomen, approximately 1½ inches above the navel.

Practitioners of this art strive to develop themselves in four ways: increasing physical strength; practicing a disciplined, nonviolent attitude; increasing suppleness in their joints through stretching exercises; and developing a more refined posture. Beginning-level aikido students concentrate on its physical aspects.

Judo

Judo, roughly translated as the "gentle way," is a system of barehanded fighting that combines throws and holds, along with hand and foot blows. The objective is to unbalance or immobilize opponents, using their own weaknesses and the bulk of their bodies against them. Students of the art are called *judoka*.

Judo matches are based on strict rules of performance and ritual. The combatants are either *tori*, the thrower or aggressor, or *uke*, the one who falls. The tori earns points for his or her throwing technique, for pinning or immobilizing the uke, or for a combination of throws and holds. Judo is one of the most widely practiced of the martial arts in the United States. It received Olympic recognition in 1964.

Judo first came to the United States when President Theodore Roosevelt (1901–1912) became interested in the sport and arranged a demonstration at the White House. A judo expert fought the wrestling coach of the U.S. Naval Academy, pinning him easily several times. Roosevelt was very impressed and began to study the sport himself, earning a brown belt after leaving the presidency. At the same time, judo was also being taught in areas that had been heavily settled by Japanese immigrants, mainly the West Coast and Hawaii.

The first recorded judo competition in U.S. collegiate athletics was in the early 1930s, when students from the University of California at Berkeley fought exhibition matches in San Francisco.

Karate

Karate, literally meaning "empty hand," is the most popular martial art worldwide. It has more than 100 styles, with varying degrees of emphasis on the sporting and artistic or spiritual aspects.

Karate techniques, whether offensive or defensive, are made up of hand and foot moves. Defensive moves, known collectively as *uke-waza*, block or deflect an opponent's weapon. Offensive techniques are divided into striking and punching. Punches are usually delivered in a straight line and are generally a closed fist thrown from the attacker's hip to the target. Strikes usually follow a circular path and are what people generally think of as a "karate chop."

Karate first came to the United States in the 1920s, when it was practiced among Japanese immigrants in Hawaii. Karate remained a largely secretive ethnic practice until after World War II, when U.S. service personnel in occupied Japan brought it back to the United States with them.

Jhoon Rhee.

In 1946, the first karate school in the mainland United States was established in Phoenix, Arizona, by Robert Trias, who had served in the navy. In 1948, Trias established the United States Karate Association, the first such organization in the country.

In the late 1960s, full-contact karate, or American kick-boxing as it is sometimes known, emerged.

Tae Kwon Do

Tae kwon do, meaning the "art of kicking and punching," is a martial art native to Korea that is closely related to Japanese karate. Tae kwon do's emphasis is on the kick, which is elevated to an art form. Kicking techniques are divided into the circular and the linear.

Tae kwon do was introduced in the United States in 1957 by Jhoon Rhee, who is known as the father of U.S. tae kwon do. In 1958, he established the country's first tae kwon do school in San Marcos, Texas. In November 1967, the United States Tae Kwon Do Association was formed. In 1974, the Amateur Athletic Union (AAU) accepted it as an official sport and established as its governing body the AAU National Tae Kwon Do Committee.

Kung Fu

Kung fu is a generic term applied to several hundred forms of unarmed Chinese martial arts. Literally translated, the term refers only to skill or ability and can just as easily be applied to a potter or chef as it can a practitioner of a martial art. Kung fu has been practiced in the United States since the beginning of Chinese immigration in the mid-nineteenth century. It was an integral part of the mining towns and labor camps of the old West. In 1957, the first known school of kung fu opened in Honolulu, Hawaii. In 1964, Ark-Yueh Wong opened a school in Los Angeles, California, that was the first to offer kung fu training to non-Asians.

Suggestions for Further Reading

Buck, Ray, *Tiffany Chin: A Dream on Ice,* Chicago: Children's Press, 1986.

Corcoran, John, *The Martial Arts Companion: Culture, History, and Enlightenment,* Mallard Press, Lombard, IL, 1992.

Dell, Pamela, *Michael Chang,* Chicago: Children's Press, 1992.

Donohue, Shiobhan, *Kristi Yamaguchi: Artist on Ice,* New York: Lerner Publishing Company, 1994.

Franks, Joel S., *Crossing Sidelines, Crossing Cultures: Sport and Asian Pacific American Cultural Citizenship,* Lanham, MD: University Press of America, 2000.

Hawaii Sports Hall of Fame, http://www.alohafame.org (accessed May 2, 2003).

Lewis, Peter, *The Martial Arts,* Edison, NJ: Chartwell Books, 1987.

Lieber, Jill, "Hard Charger," *Sports Illustrated,* September 6, 1993, p. 64.

"Michelle Kwan," *United States Figure Skating Association,* http://www.usfasa.org (accessed May 2, 2003).

Milton, Joyce, *Greg Louganis: Diving for Gold,* New York: Random House, 1989.

Mochizuki, Ken, *Baseball Saved Us,* New York: Lee & Low, 1993.

"Player Profile," Dallas Cowboys Official Website, http://www.dallascowboys.com (accessed March 19, 2003).

Rambeck, Richard, *Kristi Yamaguchi,* Chicago: Child's World, 1994.

Savage, Jeff, *Kristi Yamaguchi: Pure Gold,* San Diego: Dillon, 1993.

Soet, John Steven, *Martial Arts Around the World,* Burbank, CA: Unique Publications, 1991.

17

Military

Asian Americans in the Military

FACT FOCUS

- *Americans of Asian descent have served in the U.S. military since the Spanish-American War in 1898.*
- *During World War II, the Japanese American 100th Infantry Battalion, 442nd Regimental Combat Team, was the most decorated unit for its size and length of service in the history of the United States.*
- *By the 1990s, Asian American men and women were entering all branches of the U.S. military, at all levels and ranks.*
- *In 2002, President Bill Clinton presented the Medal of Honor to 22 Asian American veterans of World War II.*

Asian Americans have fought in America's wars since the Spanish-American War of 1898. Despite nearly constant adversity and frequent violence against them, Asian Americans have served loyally and contributed significantly to the national security goals of the United States. Chinese, Japanese, Koreans, Filipinos, Vietnamese, and, to a lesser degree, Pacific Islanders, all have significant representation in the armed forces of the United States. The accomplishments of Asian Americans in America's military service are well documented and have established a place for this minority group in the military history of the United States.

Before World War II (Pre-1939)

The initial participation of Asian/Pacific Americans in America's wars was during the Spanish-American War when seven issei men, or first-generation Japanese, and one Chinese man were reported to have been among the crew members killed during the sinking of the USS *Maine* in Havana Harbor in 1898. In addition, Filipino Army units fought side by side with the U.S. Navy against the Spanish in Manila. Ironically, those same soldiers would eventually fight against the U.S. Army in the fierce Philippine struggle for independence from the United States from 1898 to 1902.

Active Duty Personnel by Service Branch, 1993

Service	Chinese	Japanese	Korean	Filipino	Vietnamese	Other Asian	Total Asian	All Personnel
Army	362	451	1,198	3,046	425	1,412	6,894	571,619
Navy	440	685	672	18,096	669	1,028	21,590	503,886
Air Force	383	717	438	3,925	6	2,285	7,754	441,578
Marines	120	148	240	1,002	174	360	2,044	179,160
Total	1,305	2,001	2,548	26,069	1,274	5,085	38,382	1,696,243

Source: Defense Manpower Data Center, Arlington, VA, December 1993.

Active Duty Personnel by Service Branch, 2003

Service	Chinese	Japanese	Korean	Vietnamese	Other Asian	Total Asian	All Personnel
Army	659	534	2,382	650	2,031	6,256	487,078
Navy	749	678	1,017	862	1,559	4,865	376,057
Air Force	335	451	915	140	2,712	4,553	364,830
Marines	265	161	433	272	775	1,906	175,832
Total	2,008	1,824	4,747	1,924	7,077	17,580	1,441,993

Source: Defense Manpower Data Center, Arlington, VA, April 30, 2003.

Following Spain's defeat and the quelling of the Philippine insurrection, the United States formed the Philippine Scouts within the United States Army. Filipino officers, however, could only be assigned to the Scouts and were limited to the rank of major. The Philippine Scouts remained in existence through World War II and were an integral part of the U.S. Army in the Philippines. General Douglas MacArthur served with the Scouts on several occasions and was their division commander in the late 1920s.

In 1903, the United States Navy listed nine Filipinos in its ranks. By 1905, the number was 178. Filipinos were restricted to the steward rating until the late 1970s, but were found throughout the navy on ships, at shore stations, and wherever senior navy officers were assigned. Between World Wars I and II, the number of Filipinos in the armed forces remained at roughly 4,000. Despite their restrictions, duty in the navy was far more desirable to some than the low wages or unemployment they faced in civilian life.

Philippine Scouts, around 1900.

World War II (1939–45)

Japan's attack on the U.S. naval base at Pearl Harbor, Hawaii, on the morning of December 7, 1941, had a positive as well as a tremendously negative impact on Asian Americans. It resulted, on the one hand, in the internment and economic deprivation of 120,000 Japanese Americans. On the other hand, the rapid expansion of the war effort opened the U.S. armed forces to immigrants who had previously been denied enlistment. Many Asian Americans saw the war as a chance to prove their loyalty as Americans.

Korean Americans in World War II

Since 1910, when Japan officially annexed Korea, Korean Americans as a community had focused strongly on Korea's independence from Japan. In fact, in 1939 Korean Americans picketed against U.S. supply shipments to Japan, organizing the first public demonstration in the United States against Japan's invasion of China. When Japan attacked the naval base at Pearl Harbor, the Koreans acted quickly to show their solidarity with the U.S. government's decision to enter the war against Japan.

On the evening of December 7, 1941, Korean residents of Los Angeles congregated at the headquarters of the Korean National Association and passed three resolutions:

- *Koreans shall promote unity during the war and act harmoniously.*
- *Koreans shall work for the defense of the country where they reside and ... should volunteer for National Guard duty, should purchase war bonds, and... volunteer for appropriate duties.*
- *Koreans shall wear a badge identifying them as Koreans, for security purposes.*

The formation of a Korean Guard unit soon followed. On December 4, 1943, Military Order Number 45 was issued, exempting Koreans from enemy alien status and granting them the right to enlist in any of the armed services.

Chinese Americans in World War II

The Japanese attack on Pearl Harbor initiated a series of profound changes for Chinese Americans, who already felt tremendous animosity toward the Japanese because of Japan's brutal invasion and occupation of China. America's entry into the war provided Chinese Americans the opportunity to take action.

They worked in defense industries, frequently in scientific and technical positions that commanded higher wages. The navy waived its alien restrictions and recruited 500 Chinese Americans as apprentice seamen immediately after the bombing of Pearl Harbor. Chinese community leaders urged young Chinese to enlist as a demonstration of the loyalty of all Chinese Americans. This call was widely heeded; the New York Chinatown community, for instance, cheered enthusiastically when the first draft numbers included Chinese Americans. Of the eleven Chinese Americans of draft age in Butte, Montana, all had enlisted prior to being drafted. And, in battle, Chinese Americans fought side by side with white Americans whose ancestors, ironically, had attempted to expel the Chinese from America.

During the war, over 20 percent of the 59,803 Chinese adult males in the United States in 1941 enlisted or were drafted into the U.S. Army. Smaller numbers also served in the navy and air corps. The known Chinese American death total from the war numbered 214 servicemen. World War II unmistakably altered America's image of the Chinese, just as Chinese self-image also changed.

Filipino Americans in World War II

The Filipino American experience roughly paralleled that of the Koreans and Chinese. Thousands of Filipino Americans volunteered for military service immediately after the bombing of Pearl Harbor, but were refused due to the United States citizenship requirement for enlistment. However, by December 20, 1941, Congress had passed resolutions allowing virtually unlimited enlistment and employment of Filipino Americans in the war effort.

The Secretary of War issued a statement on February 19, 1942, inaugurating the First Filipino Infantry Battalion, U.S. Army.

This new unit is formed in recognition of the intense loyalty and patriotism of those Filipinos who are now residing in the U.S. It provides for them a means of serving in the Armed Forces of the United States, and the eventual opportunity of fighting on the soil of their homeland.

The Filipino American units played a significant role in the change of attitude in the U.S. Congress that led to the July 12, 1946, legislation that granted Filipinos the right to become citizens. Once citizens though, these same Filipino Veterans were not awarded the same benefits as American veterans. They formed a group called the Fil-AmVets Foundation, and met in January of 2003 to ask President George W. Bush to issue an executive order "to restore the full U.S. veterans benefits to all Filipino World War II Veterans who served under the U.S. Army Forces and the American Flag regardless of their present citizenship and residence."

Japanese Americans in World War II

After Japan attacked Pearl Harbor, the Selective Service reclassified all Japanese Americans as 4-F (physically, mentally, or morally unfit) and later as 4-C (not acceptable

Awards and Citations Earned by the 442nd Regimental Combat Team

1 + 18*	Congressional Medal of Honor
52	Distinguished Service Crosses
1	Distinguished Service Medal
560	Silver Stars plus 28 Oak Leaf Clusters
22	Legions of Merit
15	Soldier's Medals
4,000	Bronze Stars with 1,200 Oak Leaf Clusters
9,486	Purple Hearts
18,143	Individual decorations for personal valor

*In June 2000, President Bill Clinton presented the Medal of Honor to 22 Asian American veterans of World War II, 18 of whom had served with the 442nd Regimental Combat Team.

for military service because of nationality or ancestry). The Selective Service only relaxed its rules to allow some Japanese Americans to enlist to serve as translators.

The Fourth Army Intelligence School was created in San Francisco in November 1941. Japanese American instructors taught Japanese to Japanese American soldiers. These soldiers used their skills to interrogate prisoners, analyze documents, and familiarize others with Japanese geography and map reading. The program was expanded and reorganized as the Military Intelligence Service Language School on June 1, 1942.

Japanese American translators were assigned to nearly every unit in all major engagements in the Pacific. General Joseph

Stilwell paid tribute to the Japanese American translators (and soldiers) under his command in the China, Burma, and India theater of operations by stating, "The Nisei bought an awful big hunk of America with their blood." Over 6,000 Japanese Americans were trained to serve in the Pacific.

100th Infantry Battalion, 442nd Regimental Combat Team

In the European Theater of Operations, the exploits of the Japanese American 100th Infantry Battalion, 442nd Regimental Combat Team, stand at the forefront of Asian American military achievements. The 100th Infantry Battalion was created in 1942 from interned Japanese Americans in Hawaii, who were sent to Shelby, Mississippi, for training. In 1943, three thousand more men from Hawaii and 1,500 from the mainland joined the 100th Battalion. Many had families held in internment camps. The 100th Battalion was sent to Europe, where it was engaged repeatedly in fierce fighting. Over 100 Purple Hearts were awarded, earning the 100th the name "Purple Heart Battalion." In less than two years, the 100th Infantry Combat Battalion and the 442nd Regimental Combat Team successfully fought in seven major military campaigns: Naples, Foggio; Rome, Arno; Southern France (Operation Anvil); Rhineland; North Apennines; Central Europe; and the Po Valley. They suffered 9,486 casualties, including 650 soldiers who were killed in action.

Overall, more than 33,000 Japanese Americans served in World War II. Besides translators and combat soldiers, some served as nurses, doctors, therapists, and pharmacists in unsegregated combat units in all theaters and in the Women's Army Corps. Following World War II, Asian Americans were fully integrated into the armed forces. Segregated units were no longer formed, although some units, such as the 100th Battalion Hawaii National Guard, maintain a predominantly Asian American membership.

Korean War (1950–53)

In 1950, communist forces clashed with noncommunist forces in Korea, a nation divided during World War II. When the United Nations condemned communist North Korea, U.S. president Harry S Truman committed American forces to aid South Korea. But the outbreak of war in Korea found U. S. forces unprepared. The draft was expanded and few groups were exempted from service.

The severe shortage of frontline combat soldiers led to the foundation of the Korean Augmentation to U.S. Army (KATUSA) Program, which was still operating in the mid-1990s. KATUSA soldiers normally remain within the same company or battery for the duration of service. In addition to military specialty duties, they act as interpreters and are invaluable in helping Americans adapt to Korean customs. As of 1995, there were approximately 6,200 KATUSA soldiers assigned to the Eighth Army.

Japanese Americans also served with distinction in the Korean War. One veteran of the 442nd Regimental Combat Team during World War II, Sergeant Hiroshi Miyamura, was recalled to active duty. He received the Congressional Medal of Honor for action near Taejon-ni, Korea, on April 24–25, 1951, when he ordered and covered the withdrawal of his squad against a numerically superior enemy force. He received his

Congressional Medal of Honor from President Dwight D. Eisenhower in 1954. Sergeant Leroy A. Mendonca and Private First Class Herbert K. Pililaau, who both died in the conflict, also won the Congressional Medal of Honor for valor.

Asian/Pacific American Service Personnel

After World War II, African American service personnel took up the struggle against segregation and discrimination in the U.S. armed forces. By the time of the Vietnam War, official policies of racial or ethnic discrimination were a thing of the past, although many instances of unofficial racial discrimination have been documented. Asian Americans now serve in the armed forces without being restricted by military policy.

Asian/Pacific Americans in military service can be found in most ranks, from enlisted personnel to officers. Despite the gains Asian/Pacific Americans have made in the military, however, the number of Asians, as a percentage of the whole, decreases as rank increases. That means that promotions, particularly in the upper ranks, have not been as easy to obtain as the right to enlist and serve. With the rapid growth of the Asian American population, the number of military personnel from this minority group is almost certain to rise at all levels.

In 2003, American Samoan Iuniasolua (Iuni) Savusa received a promotion to Installation Command Sergeant Major at Fort Polk, Louisiana. Eni Faleomavaega, U.S. Congressman from American Samoa, met with Savusa to congratulate him, stating, "It is my understanding that Iuni Savusa is the

Congressman Eni Faleomavaega (representative from American Samoa) met with Command Sergeant Major Iuniasolua Savusa in Washington, D.C., in 2003, after Savusa's promotion made him the first Samoan enlisted in the U.S. army to achieve his rank.

first Samoan enlisted in the U.S. Army to ever achieve the position of Command Sergeant Major in a military installation or post, and I am proud of him for it." CSM Savusa has also received the Bronze Star Medal for valor, among other commendations.

Asian Pacific Military Heroes

Since the Spanish-American War, the United States has awarded the Congressional Medal of Honor (CMH) to the fol-

Private First Class Herbert K. Pililaau.

lowing nine Asian Americans. (The men are listed in the order in which they received this award. An * indicates that the award was given posthumously.)

Private José B. Nisperos
34th Company, Philippine Scouts, U.S. Army

Born in San Fernandos Union, Philippine Islands, José Nisperos was the first Asian American to win the Congressional Medal of Honor. He was cited for valor for his efforts in the Spanish-American War. On September 24, 1911, while fighting Spanish forces at Lapurap, Basilan, Philippine Islands, Nisperos was badly wounded. (His left arm was broken and lacerated, and he had received several spear wounds in the body so that he could not stand.) Nisperos continued to fire his rifle with one hand until the enemy was repulsed, thereby aiding materially in preventing the annihilation of his party and the mutilation of their bodies.

Fireman Second Class Telesforo Trinidad
U.S. Navy

Born in New Washington Capig, Philippine Islands, Telesforo Trinidad displayed extraordinary heroism when a boiler exploded aboard the U.S.S. *San Diego,* on January 21, 1915. Trinidad was driven out of fireroom no. 2 by the explosion, but immediately returned and rescued an injured shipmate. While bringing his shipmate out, he was caught in another explosion. After ensuring the safety of the sailor and without regard for his own life, Trinidad assisted in rescuing another injured man. He suffered burns on the face by the blast from the second explosion.

Sergeant José Calugas
Battery B, 88th Field Artillery,
Philippine Scouts, U.S. Army

Born in Barrio Tagsing, Leon, Iloilo, Philippine Islands, José Calugas was cited for bravery during hostilities that took place during World War II near Culis, Bataan Province, Philippine Islands, on January 16, 1942. While under heavy Japanese artillery attack, he ran 1,000 yards to a partially destroyed gun position whose cannoneers were either killed or wounded. Upon reaching the position, Calugas organized a volunteer squad that put the guns back in commission and fired effectively against the enemy.

Private First Class Sadao S. Munemori*
Company A, 100th Infantry Battalion,
442nd Regimental Combat Team, U.S. Army

Born in Los Angeles, California, Sadao S. Munemori fought with great gallantry in a World War II battle near Seravezza, Italy, on April 5, 1945. When his unit was pinned down by fire from the enemy's strong mountain defense, command of the squad fell to him after its leader was wounded. Munemori singly made frontal assaults through direct fire and destroyed two machine guns. While withdrawing under heavy fire from other enemy emplacements, he had nearly reached a shell crater occupied by two of his men when an unexploded grenade rolled into the crater. Immediately Munemori, exposing himself to withering fire, dove on the grenade and smothered the blast with his body. By his supremely heroic action, Munemori saved two of his men at the cost of his own life.

Corporal Hiroshi H. Miyamura
Company H, 7th Infantry Regiment,
3rd Infantry Division, U.S. Army

Born in Gallup, New Mexico, Hiroshi H. Miyamura distinguished himself during the Korean War by conspicuous gallantry against the enemy near Taejon-ni, Korea, on April 24 and 25, 1951. On the night of April 24, the enemy attacked and threatened to overrun the defensive position occupied by Company H. Aware of the imminent danger to his men, Squad Leader Miyamura immediately engaged the enemy with a bayonet in hand-to-hand combat. He killed about ten of the enemy. Returning to his position, Miyamura administered first aid to the wounded and directed their evacuation. As the enemy attacked again, he provided machine-gun fire until his ammunition was expended and then ordered the withdrawal of the squad while he stayed behind to render the gun inoperable. Next, Miyamura covered the withdrawal of a second gun position, killing more than 50 of the enemy before running out of ammunition and being severely wounded. Despite his wounds, Miyamura continued to fight the enemy until the position was finally overrun and he was captured.

Private First Class Herbert K. Pililaau*
Company C, 23rd Infantry Regiment,
2nd Infantry Division, U.S. Army

Born in Waianae, Oahu, Hawaii, Herbert K. Pililaau was engaged in heavy combat near Pia-ri, Korea, on September 17, 1951, during the Korean War. Pililaau's platoon held a key terrain feature on "Heartbreak Ridge" against wave after wave of enemy troops. The unit repulsed each attack until its ammunition was almost exhausted and it was ordered to withdraw. Pililaau volunteered to cover the withdrawal. He first engaged the enemy with automatic fire and grenades and then fought in hand-to-hand combat until being overcome and mortally wounded. When the position was subsequently retaken, more than 40 enemy dead were counted in the area Pililaau defended.

Sergeant Leroy A. Mendonca*
Company B, Seventh Infantry Regiment,
3rd Infantry Division, U.S. Army

Born in Honolulu, Hawaii, Leroy Mendonca was cited for conspicuous gallantry against the enemy near Chich-on, Korea, on July 4, 1951, during the Korean War. After his platoon had captured Hill 586, the enemy counterattacked during the night with superior forces. When Mendonca's unit was outflanked and under heavy pressure, it was ordered to withdraw to a secondary defensive position. Mendonca volunteered to cover its withdrawal. After using all of his ammunition and grenades, he fought on with his bayonet until he was mortally wounded. Mendonca was credited with an estimated 37 enemy casualties and with enabling his unit to repel the enemy's attack and retain possession of the vital hilltop.

Sergeant First Class Rodney J. T. Yano*
Air Cavalry Troop, 11th Armored Cavalry
Regiment, U.S. Army

Born in Kealake Kua, Hawaii, Rodney Yano was a crew chief during the Vietnam War on the Air Cavalry Troop's command-and-control helicopter during action against enemy forces entrenched in the dense jungle of Bien Hao, Republic of Vietnam, on January 1, 1969. Exposed to intense small-arms and anti-aircraft fire, Yano delivered suppressive fire upon the enemy and marked their positions with smoke and white phosphorous grenades. A grenade exploded prematurely, covered him with burning phosphorous, and left him mortally wounded. The flaming fragments also caused the supplies to burn and ammunition to explode. Despite having the use of only one arm and being partially blinded by the initial explosion, Yano began hurling blazing ammunition from the helicopter. In doing so, he suffered additional wounds, but he persisted until the danger had passed. His action, at the cost of his life, averted loss of life and additional injury to the rest of the crew.

Technical Sergeant Yeiki Kobashigawai, left, and Senator Daniel K. Inouye, right, both of Hawaii, listen as President Bill Clinton addresses Medal of Honor recipients on June 21, 2000, at the White House.

Corporal Terry Teruo Kawamura*
173rd Engineer Company,
173rd Airborne Brigade, U.S. Army

Born in Wahiawa, Hawaii, Terry Kawamura was cited for risking his life above and beyond the call of duty at Camp Radcliff, Republic of Vietnam, on the evening of March 20, 1969, during the Vietnam War. An enemy demolition team had infiltrated the unit quarters area and opened fire with automatic weapons. When an explosion tore a hole in the roof of a room full of American servicemen, Kawamura grabbed his gun and, while running to the door to return fire, saw another explosive charge being thrown through the hole in the roof. Disregarding his own safety, Kawamura unhesitatingly hurled himself on the charge.

A Special Presentation

In June 2000, President Bill Clinton made a special presentation of the Medal of Honor to 22 Asian American veterans of World War II. The recipients were selected from those awarded the Distinguished Service Cross, and may have been overlooked for the Medal of Honor due to wartime prejudice. Most of the recipients were members of the 442nd Regimental Combat Team, whose motto was "Go for Broke!"

Staff Sergeant Rudolph B. Davila
7th Infantry Division, U.S. Army

On May 28, 1944, Staff Sergeant Rudolph B. Davila distinguished himself by performing above the call of duty in battle. During an offensive near Artena, Italy, he provided heavy weapons support for his rifle company, despite the risk of death. Staff Sergeant Davila was caught on an exposed hillside by fire from the Germans, with his machine gunners unwilling to risk themselves. Taking control of the situation himself, Davila crawled to the nearest machine gun and proceeded to set it up alone. After opening fire on the Germans, he then ordered a gunner to take over, and crawled to a vantage point where he directed the gun battle with hand signals. His gunners were able to bring the enemy into a reserve position, but Davila was wounded in the leg. Despite this, he climbed into an abandoned tank and continued the battle. Davila then advanced—by dashing and crawling—to the house where the Germans were firing from. Using a hand grenade he forced them out of the house and continued shooting at them from the attic of the house.

Though the house was crumbling, Staff Sergeant Davila continued to attack the enemy.

Private Barney F. Hajiro
100th Infantry Battalion, 442nd Regimental Combat Team, U.S. Army

While standing on guard as a sentry on October 19, 1944, Private Barney F. Hajiro assisted Allied troops in attacking a house in eastern France by exposing himself to fire and directing fire to the enemy. Later, on October 22, Private Hajiro and a comrade ambushed a heavily armed enemy patrol, killing two, wounding one, and taking the remainder prisoner. On October 29, Hajiro would again perform heroically under fire, when he ran 100 yards (110 meters) under fire up "suicide hill." He spotted two machine-gun nests and destroyed them single-handedly. Because of Hajiro's heroic efforts, the attack was successful.

Private Mikio Hasemoto*
100th Infantry Battalion, 442nd Regimental Combat Team, U.S. Army

Near Cerasuolo, Italy, a force of nearly 40 enemy soldiers approached Private Mikio Hasemoto's platoon on November 29, 1943. Private Hasemoto, an automatic rifleman, challenged the approaching machine gunners, until his weapon was shot and damaged. He then ran 10 yards to find a new weapon, which subsequently jammed. Not to be deterred, Hasemoto ran through enemy fire to pick up an M-1 rifle. Along with his squad leader, he charged forward, killing most of the attacking platoon. The next day, Hasemoto continued his heroism, and was killed by enemy fire, defending his squad.

Private Joe Hayashi
100th Infantry Battalion, 442nd Regimental Combat Team, U.S. Army

Private Joe Hayashi distinguished himself in action in April of 1945 near Tendola, Italy. Private Hayashi and his unit were ordered to attack a well-defended hill, when they were fired upon. Hayashi dragged his wounded comrades to safety, but then returned to the hill and attacked with his remaining men, obtaining their objective. Two days later, during battle, Hayashi crawled under intense fire to eliminate several enemy machine guns with a grenade and forcing others of the enemy to flee. Sadly, on this courageous mission, he was mortally wounded by a burst of machine-pistol fire.

Private Shizuya Hayashi,
100th Infantry Battalion, 442nd Regimental Combat Team, U.S. Army

On November 29, 1943, near Carasuolo, Italy, during an enemy assault, Private Shizuya Hayashi alone bravely rose to confront the grenade, rifle, and machine-gun fire. He retuned the fire with his rifle, and took over an enemy machine-gun position. Hayashi fought on bravely, now with the help of his platoon, forcing the remainder of the enemy force to retreat.

Second Lieutenant Daniel K. Inouye
100th Infantry Battalion, 442nd Regimental Combat Team, U.S. Army

Daniel K. Inouye was born in Hawaii, and would later become a U.S. senator, but on April 21, 1945, he was a military hero. Attacking a defended ridge in San Terenzo, Italy, Second Lieutenant Inouye directed his platoon under enemy fire in a maneuver that brought them to within 40 feet of the enemy, where they were halted by continued fire. Inouye risked his own life and crawled up the hill to throw a grenade, destroying the enemy's advantage. Wounded by a sniper's bullet in the process, he continued to fight, until a grenade shattered his right arm. He refused to give up, though, and continued directing his platoon, enabling them to capture the ridge.

Technical Sergeant Yeiki Kobashigawa
100th Infantry Battalion, 442nd Regimental Combat Team, U.S. Army

During an attack on June 2, 1944, in Lanuvio, Italy, Technical Sergeant Yeiki Kobashigawa encountered enemy machine-gun fire. Kobashigawa and a comrade crawled forward to throw a grenade at the gunners. Kobashigawa then provided support while a soldier charged, capturing four enemies. Kobashigawa then discovered and eliminated several more machine-gun nests, enabling his unit to advance.

Staff Sergeant Robert T. Kuroda*
100th Infantry Battalion, 442nd Regimental Combat Team, U.S. Army

Leading his men to destroy snipers and machine-gun nests on October 20, 1944, in Bruyeres, France, Staff Sergeant Robert T. Kuroda encountered heavy enemy fire. Once he located the source of the fire, he fired off ammunition, killing at least three of the enemy. He took a gun from a downed American officer, and continued to fight and destroy machine-gun positions. While turning to fire on additional enemy soldiers,

Kuroda was killed by a sniper. His heroic actions, though, ensured the destruction of the enemy.

Private First Class Kaoru Moto*
100th Infantry Battalion, 442nd Regimental Combat Team, U.S. Army

While on a scouting mission, Private First Class Kaoru Moto noticed a machine gun hindering his platoon. Alone, he approached and killed the offending gunner. The gunner's assistant, however, opened fire on Moto, but Moto was able to approach the assistant from the rear and take him prisoner. With the prisoner in tow, Moto took up a position guarding a house and engaged a machine-gun team, driving them away, but sustained an injury in doing so. He applied first aid to his wound and changed position, encountering more machine gunners along the way, and taking them prisoner.

Private First Class Kiyoshi K. Muranga*
U.S. Army

Near Suvereto, Italy, on June 26, 1944, Private First Class Kiyoshi K. Muranga's company encountered enemy fire. Many of the men dispersed, but Muranga's company was ordered into action. Because of casualties, Muranga was forced to attempt to neutralize the enemy weapon alone. By his third round of ammuniton, Muranga's shots were hitting directly in front of the weapon. The enemy perceived his position, however, and fired shots on him, killing him instantly. Because of the accuracy of Muranga's shots, his company was forced to abandon its position and not risk further exposure.

Private Masato Nakae*
U.S. Army

Private Masato Nakae performed heroically in action on August 19, 1944, near Pisa, Italy. When his gun was damaged by a shell, Nakae picked up a wounded comrade's rifle, and continued shooting at the advancing enemy. To deter their advance, Nakae then threw six grenades, forcing them to withdraw. Nakae was seriously wounded, though, by mortar fire. Nonetheless, he refused to surrender his position and continued firing, inflicting heavy casualties that caused the enemy to withdraw.

Private Shinyei Nakamine*
100th Infantry Battalion, 442nd Regimental Combat Team, U.S. Army

During an attack on June 2, 1944, near La Torreto, Italy, Private Shinyei Nakamine's platoon became trapped by enemy crossfire. On his own initiative, Nakamine approached an enemy machine-gun nest, killing three enemy soldiers and capturing two. Later that day, under cover from his platoon, he crawled toward an enemy machine-gun nest and threw a grenade, wounding one and capturing four. While charging toward yet another machine-gun nest, Private Nakamine was killed.

Private First Class William K. Nakamura*
100th Infantry Battalion, 442nd Regimental Combat Team, U.S. Army

On July 4, 1944, Private Fist Class William K. Nakamura crawled toward a hostile machine-gun nest on his own initiative, with enemy fire barely missing him. At a distance of 15 yards from the nest, Nakamura raised himself to his knees and threw four hand grenades. With the weapon neutralized, Nakamura crawled back to his company which was able to advance because of his courage. Later that day, while his company withdrew from a hill, he volunteered to remain in place and cover his comrades' withdrawal. During the withdrawal, the platoon was pinned down by machine-gun fire, but Private Nakamura was able to accurately pick off the gunner, so that his platoon could withdraw safely. Doing so, Nakamura lost his life, heroically.

Private First Class Joe M. Nishimoto*
100th Infantry Battalion, 442nd Regimental Combat Team, U.S. Army

After his company attempted to dislodge the enemy in La Houssiere, France, for three days, Private First Class Joe M. Nishimoto decided to take things into his hands on November 7, 1944. Acting as squad leader, he crawled through an area laced with mines to destroy the enemy embankment with a grenade. Circling to the back of another machine-gun position, Nishimoto destroyed several more enemy gunners. With these strategic points taken, the enemy was forced to withdraw.

Staff Sergeant Allan M. Ohata
100th Infantry Battalion, 442nd Regimental Combat Team, U.S. Army

On November 29 and 30, 1943, Staff Sergeant Allan M. Ohata performed heroically on the battlefield in Cerasuolo, Italy. Having been ordered to protect the flank of his platoon, Ohata fired effectively against the enemy. When the man to Ohata's left called for assistance with a broken firearm, Ohata left his position and advanced 15 yards

through machine-gun fire to assist his comrade. Ohata and an automatic rifleman then held their position, killing 37 of the enemy in the process. Later Ohata and the rifleman would stop an attacking force of 14 enemy soldiers. The next day, the two comrades would hold their position again, and hold off all attacks.

Technician Fifth Grade James K. Okubo
100th Infantry Battalion, 442nd Regimental Combat Team, U.S. Army

As a medic, Technician Fifth Grade James K. Okubo exhibited extraordinary courage in late October and early November 1944, in the Foret Domaniale de Champ, Eastern France. Okubo crawled to within 40 yards of enemy lines amid grenades being thrown at him, to carry back wounded comrades. He treated 17 men under constant fire on October 28, and eight more the next day. On November 4, Okubo again risked his life when he ran 75 yards under machine-gun fire to treat a wounded crewman from a burning tank. Without Okubo's help, the crewman would have died.

Technical Sergeant Yukio Okutsu
100th Infantry Battalion, 442nd Regimental Combat Team, U.S. Army

On April 7, 1945, on Italy's Mount Belvedere, Technical Sergeant Yukio Okutsu's platoon was caught in the crossfire of three machine guns. Bravely, Okutsu crawled through heavy fire and destroyed the enemy position with hand grenades. Dashing from cover to cover, he threw another grenade, which hit its mark. While charging toward a third machine gun, Okutsu was stunned by rifle fire that grazed off his helmet. He was able to recover, though, and capture the machine-gun crew single-handedly. His actions enabled his platoon to continue on with their assault.

Private First Class Frank H. Ono*
100th Infantry Battalion, 442nd Regimental Combat Team, U.S. Army

Caught in enemy fire on July 4, 1944, in Italy, Private First Class Frank H. Ono eliminated an enemy machine gunner, and a sniper. While the rest of his platoon was reorganizing, Ono alone defended their position. Even after his weapon was destroyed by fire, Ono continued to stand his ground, hurling grenades and taking a wounded friend's weapon. Then, seeing his platoon leader and a rifleman wounded, Ono ran through fire to assist them. Even after that, as the platoon was forced to withdraw, Ono volunteered to cover as the men withdrew. From an unprotected vantage point, he faced enemy fire, and defended his platoon, allowing them a safe escape.

Staff Sergeant Kazou Otani*
100th Infantry Battalion, 442nd Regimental Combat Team, U.S. Army

In July of 1944, in Italy, Staff Sergeant Kazuo Otani performed heroically in battle. When his platoon became endangered, Staff Sergeant Otani left his cover to shoot the sniper who was harming them. Then, dodging bullets, he helped his platoon find cover under a cliff, by exposing himself further and distracting the enemy while the platoon moved toward the cliff. Seeing a wounded man, Otani crawled toward him, though he was in plain view of the enemy, and brought him back to a ditch where he began to give first aid. In the process, though, Otabi was mortally wounded by the enemy. Nonetheless, his bravery allowed his platoon to seek cover.

Private George T. Sakato
100th Infantry Battalion, 442nd Regimental Combat Team, U.S. Army

After Private George Sakato's unit had defeated two enemy platoons in France on October 29, 1944, they came under further enemy fire. With no regard for his personal safety or the enemy fire, Sakato charged ahead alone, encouraging his unit to follow suit and destroy the enemy. Sakato then took over leadership of his squad, as the leader had been killed, and inspired his platoon to reorganize and halt the enemy's counter attack. His bravery and leadership allowed his platoon to turn near-defeat into victory.

Technical Sergeant Ted T. Tanouye*
100th Infantry Battalion, 442nd Regimental Combat Team, U.S. Army

On July 7, 1944, in Molino A Ventoabbto, Italy, Technical Sergeant Ted T. Tanouye led an attack on a hillside. During the attack, Tanouye killed several enemy machine gunners. In doing so, he was hit by a grenade which wounded his left arm. He continued to fight, though, and shot at an enemy-held trench. When Tanouye ran out of ammunition, he crawled 20 yards on the ground to get more from his nearest comrade. With the new ammunition, Tanouye was able to silence three more machine guns before he took his objective. It was only after he had organized a defensive position on the hill that Tanouye would accept any first aid for his wound.

Captain Francis B. Wai
U.S. Army* 34th Infantry Regiment, 24th Infantry Division

When Captain Francis B. Wai landed at Red Beach in Leyte, Philippine Islands, on October 20, 1944, he encountered fiercely accurate enemy gunfire. Four waves of American soldiers had landed before Wai. When Wai landed, the soldiers already there were leaderless and pinned down. Wai took control of the situation, issuing orders, and began to move the men inland. Wai risked his own life several times in the action, as he exposed himself to determine the location of the enemy. Wai was killed in an attack on the last remaining Japanese station. His actions and his leadership inspired the men to continue and destroy the enemy, even after his death.

Suggestions for Further Reading

"Asian American Medal of Honor Recipients," *The United States Army,* http://www.army.mil/cmh-pg/ap-moh2.htm (accessed April 29, 2003).

Goodsell, Jane, *Daniel Inouye,* New York: Crowell, 1977.

"Hot Topics," *Asian American Politics,* http://www.asianam.org (accessed April 21, 2003).

Lee, Gus, *China Boy: A Novel,* New York: Dutton, 1991.

Lee, Gus, *Honor and Duty,* New York: Knopf, 1993.

McGowen, Tom, *Go For Broke: Japanese Americans in World War II,* New York: F. Watts, 1995.

Tanaka, Chester, *Go for Broke: A Pictorial History of the Japanese American 100th Infantry Battalion and the 442d Regimental Combat Team,* Sacramento, CA: Go for Broke, Inc., 1982.

Wright, David K., *Causes and Consequences of the Vietnam War,* Austin, TX: Raintree/Steck-Vaughn, 1996.

INDEX

A

AAAS. *See* American Association for the Advancement of Science
Affirmative action 7
Agricultural Workers Organizing Committee (AWOC) 113
Ahuena Heiau 91
Aichu, Walter 233
AIDS 182
Aikido 26, 237
Air Force 241
Akamu, Nina 96–97
Alexander & Baldwin Sugar Museum 89
Alexander, Samuel 89
Alien Land Act, California's 1913 102
Alien land laws 121, 147
Alien Poll Tax 120
All-stars, baseball 231
Amache Relocation Center 89
"Amache Remembered" 89
Amateur Athletic Union (AAU) 239
Amerasian Homecoming Act of 1988 107
Amerasians 106
America Is in the Heart, 200
American Association for the Advancement of Science 180
American Conservatory Theatre (ACT) 215

American Dreams 221
American Federation of Labor 113
American Federation of State County and Municipal Employees 114
American Federation of Teachers 115
American Freedom Coalition 194
American kick-boxing 238
American Library Association
  Best Book for Young Adults 209
  Newbery Honor Books 210
  Newbery Medal 205, 208
  Notable Book Award 209
  Notable Books 208
American Place Theatre 221
American Playhouse 204, 221
American Samoans 136
American-born families 161
Analects 191
And the Soul Shall Dance 220
Angel Island Immigration Station, 16, 80–81
Angel Island Theatre Company 218
Aoki, Brenda Wong 216
APALA. *See* Asian/Pacific American LAbor Alliance
Army 241
Arno 246
Aruego, Jose 197, 207–208
Asa Ga Kimashita (Morning Has Broken) 221

Asahis 232
Asian American, definition 1
Asian American Federation of Union Members 115
Asian American Political Alliance (AAPA) 29, 112
Asian American Theater Company 215, 221, 222, 226
Asian American Theater Workshop (AATW) 215
Asian Exclusion Act 27, 216
Asian Indian Americans
  education 5
  entrepreneurship 148, 151–153
  fertility 161
  immigration 5, 102, 104, 106, 138
  1990 population 5, 143
  political participation 5
  professions 5
Asian Law Caucus (ALC) 118
Asian Multi Media Center (AMMC) 216
Asian/Pacific American Heritage Month, 1991 and 1992 69
Asian/Pacific American Labor Alliance 115, 117
Asian Pacific Islanders
  active duty military personnel 241
  arrest rates 128
  civil rights 111–116
  crime victims 128

on death row 128
education 2, 171–185
entrepreneurship 145, 148–153
exclusion from free immigration 241
families 155–152
fertility 161
geographic distribution 139
high school dropout rate 172
judges 126
in law enforcement 133
lawmakers 125
lawyers 125
legal issues 119–134
literature 197–211
marital status 161
political power 123
population 1, 135, 139, 142
in prison 128
in science and engineering 179
sports 229–239
in U.S. military 241–256
veterans organization 250
writers 197–211
"Asiatic Barred Zone," 102
Asylum Procedure 64
Athletic leagues, Japanese 231
Athletics, Oakland 231
Atonio, Frank 115
The Avocado Kid 222

B

Bachelor societies 14, 94, 156
Backlash: When America Turned on Its Own 117–118
Baldwin, Henry 89
Baltimore Orioles 231
Bangladesh 163
Bar Association of San Francisco 127
Barry, Lynda 199–200
Baseball 230–234
    Asian American baseball stars 231
    in internment camps 232
The Basic Training of Pavlo Hummel 217
Basketball 232, 234

Bears, Chicago 233
Becoming Madame Mao 205
Bengali language163
Berkeley Repertory Theatre 220
Bicultural conflicts 161
Bilingual ballots 122
Biracial births 161
Bitter Bananas 210
Bitter Cane 221
Bo Rabbit Smart for True 210
Boat people 49
Bodhidharma 236
Book of the Month Club 203
Bordallo, Madeleine A. 39
Boutique Living and Disposable Icons 221
The Boy of the Three-Year Nap 209
Boys Club, Japanese 232
Brewers, Milwaukee 231
The Bridegroom 203
Brynner, Yul 213
Buddha 188
Buddhism 188–190
    among Cambodian Americans 11
    among Chinese Americans 17
    Mahayana 50
    Theravada 37, 47
Buddhist Church of Bakersfield, Bakersfield, CA 81
Bulosan, Carlos 200, 216
Bush, George 71, 124
Bush, George W. 74–76, 77–78, 125
Business ownership 145–153
Byodoin (Temple of Equality) 90

C

Cable Act, 1922 56
Caldecott Honor Book 209, 210
California Committee on Racial and Ethnic Bias in the Courts 133
California Gold Rush of 1848 14
California League 231
California Workingmen's Party 113
California's Alien Land Law of 1913 83

Calugas, Jose 248
Cambodian Americans 9–13
Camp Radcliff, Vietnam 250
Cardinals, St. Louis 233
Carroll, Dennis 215
Carter, Jimmy 30, 106
CATS. *See* Community Asian Theatre of The Sierra
Centennial of Korean Immigration 77–78
Central Europe 246
Central Japanese (Baseball) League 232
Central Pacific Railroad 15, 101
Chan Ho Park 231
Chandrashekhar, Subrahmanyan 182
Chang, Tisa 217
Chargers, San Diego 233
Chavez, César 113
Chawla, Kalpana 182
Chen, Joan 205
Cherry Blossom Festival 83
Chiao, Leroy 182
Chicago Bears 233
Chicago Nisei Athletic Association 234
The Chick and the Duckling 208
The Chickencoop Chinaman 221
Chikara kurabe 236
Child of War, Woman of Peace 201
Child-rearing practices 161
Children's Book Council Showcase 208
Children's literature 207–210
Chin, Frank 200, 216, 221, 225
Chin, Tiffany 235
China (quotas, 1938) 57
China Boy 203
China Camp State Park 81–82
Chinatown Gate 83
Chinatown History Museum, New York City 94
Chinatowns 82–83, 90–92, 93, 94, 97
Chinese American Portraits 204
Chinese Americans 17, 149, 165

active duty personnel by service branch 241

Confucianism 191

entrepreneurship 146, 151–153

immigration 14–16, 53–54, 58, 137, 138, 221

intermarriage 161

in World War II 244, 245

Chinese Exclusion Act 16, 53–54, 62, 81, 101, 104, 113, 120

   repeal 62, 123

Chinese export industries 149

Chinese Friendship Archway 97

Chinese Historical Society of America 83

Chinese Honeymoon 213

Chinese language 164

Chun, Alexandra Bokyun 219

Chung, Eugene 233

Chung, Philip W. 219

Citizen 13660 198

Civil Liberties Act of 1988 30, 115–116

Civil rights 29, 111–118

   labor movement 113–116

   student movements 111–113

Civil Rights Acts 115, 123–124

Cleveland, Grover 72

Clinton, Bill 125, 182, 250, 251

Coaches, baseball 231

Cold War 104

Commission on Wartime Relocation and Internment of Civilians (CWRIC) 30, 65–67

Commonwealth Club's Silver Medal for Non-Fiction 207

Community Asian Theater of the Sierra 226

Confucianism 17, 34, 191

Congregational Church (United Church of Christ) 71

Congressional Medal of Honor (CMH) 247–256

Contemporary Asian Theatre Scene 219–220

Cook, James 41

Cortez Wildcats 232

Court Interpreters Act 127

Cowboys, Dallas 233

Crain, Hugh H. 83

Crazed 203

Criminal justice system 128–134

A Crocodile's Tale 208

Cultural Revolution 205

D

Dalai Lama 190

Dallas Cowboys 233

Dance and the Railroad 223, 225

Dan, Tim 215

Darling, Ron 231

A Daughter of the Samurai 198

Davila, Rudoph B. 251

Day Standing on Its Head 222

The Day They Parachuted Cats on Borneo 208

Dayton Triangles football team 233

Demographics 1–51

Deportation 64

DeWitt, J. L. 59

Dharma 188

Dillingham Commission 102

Displaced Persons Act 138

The Divine Principle 193

Diving, Olympic 235

Dodgers, Livingston (California) 232

Dodgers, Los Angeles 231

Dogeaters 201

Dojos, martial arts 237

Dole, Sanford 90

Domestic violence 130

Donald Duk and Gunga Din 200

Dragon's Gate 210

Dragonwings 210

Drama Desk award 225

Dramalogue 226

The Dream of Kitamura 222

Duke Kahanamoku Statue 91

Dun, Dennis 216

E

East Goes West 198

East West Players 214, 222, 226

Education 171–185

   college majors 175

   elementary through high school 172–173

   graduate school 176

   higher education 173–177

   independent schools 174

   public schools 174

   religious-affiliated high schools 174

18 Mighty Mountain Warriors 226

Eisenhower, Dwight D. 247

Embrey, Sue Kunitomi 115

Emergency Situation Refugees 64

Emmy award 225

Employment 145–153

Eng, Richard 217

Entrepreneurship 145–149, 151–153

"Ernie Pook's Comeek" 199

Espaldon, Diane 218

Eureka Theatre 222

European Theater of Operations 246

Evacuation Claims Act of 1948 124

Exclusion 62

Exclusionism 102

Executive Order 9066 27, 30, 59, 62, 65, 92

Executive Order 13216 74–76

F

Face Value 224

Faleomavaega, Eni 42

Families 20, 155–162

Family Devotions 223

Farmworkers movement 113–114

Father and Glorious Descendant 198

Federal Bureau of Investigation 61

Fernandez, Sid 231

Fifth Chinese Daughter 207

Figure skating, Olympic 235

Fijians 39–41, 143, 241

Filipino Americans

   active duty military 241

   citizenship 245

   education 19

employment 20
entrepreneurship 147–148, 151–153
immigration 18, 57, 138
language 20
population statistics 18
religion 21
in World War II 243–244
First Filipino Infantry Battalion 245
Flower Drum Song 213, 214, 224
Flowers and Household Gods 221
FOB 217, 223, 225
Fong-Torres, Ben 201
Football 229, 233
Ford Foundation 217
Foreign-born families 155
Foreign miner's tax 119
Forty-Niners, San Francisco 233
442nd Regimental Combat Team 29, 241
Fourth Army Intelligence School 245
Frameless Windows, Squares of Light 206

G

Gam Saan (or "Gold Mountain") 100
Gangs 130, 132
Guamanians 40–41
Gautama, Siddharta 188
Gay-Neck: The Story of a Pigeon 208
Generation gap 161
Gentlemen's Agreement 102
Ghond, the Hunter 208
Giants, San Francisco 231
Gila River Relocation Center, AZ 79–80
Gin Lin Trail (Oregon) 94
Girls Club, Japanese 232
Glass, Philip 223
Goeas, Leo 233
Gold Mountain 139
Gold Watch 221
Golden Glove Award, baseball 231

Golden Spike National Historic Site, Promontory Point, UT 95
Gonzalez-Pardo, Lillian 182
Gotanda, Philip Kan 216, 217, 222
Graduate Record Examination 176
Graduate study 176–177
Grandfather's Journey 209
Grant, Ulysses S. 237
GRE. See Graduate Record Examination
Great Basin Museum 95
Great Fire of 1889 95
Great Leap, Inc. 226
Great Purification Ceremony 193
Guamanians 40, 143

H

Hagedorn, Jessica 201
Hajiro, Barney F. 251
Hale O Keawe Heiau 92
Han, Hak Ja 194
Hanyu Pinyin 165
Harada House, Riverside, CA 83
Harada, Jukichi 83
Harassment 118
Hart-Celler Act (Immigration Act of 1965) 104
Hasemoto, Mikio 251
Hate crimes 118, 129
Hate Crimes Statistics Act, 1990 68, 121, 129
Hawaii Baseball League 232
Hawaii, Kingdom of 71, 73
Hawaii, Republic of 56, 73, 91
Hawaii, state of 41, 91
Hawaiian Postal Savings Bank 56
Hawaiians 41, 137
Hayashi, Joe 252
Hayashi, Shizuya 252
Hayslip, Le Ly 201
Heart Mountain Relocation Center, WY 97
"Heartbreak Ridge" 249
Hercules Powder Plant, Hercules, CA 83
Here and Now 219
Higher education

degree goal 175
fields of study 175
Hill, Amy 216
Hinduism 7, 188
Historic landmarks 79–97
Hmong Americans 21–23
Hmong, customs 22
Ho Chi Minh 36
Ho, David 182
The Holder of the World 205
Holidays 45, 50
Hong Kong 160
Hong, James 214
Hong, Jeanne 126
Hongo, Garret 201
Honor and Duty 203
Hotel King Kamehameha 91
Houston, Jeanne Wakatsuki 202
Houston, Valena Hasu 221
Humana Festival of New American Plays 223
Hwang, David Henry 214, 216, 217, 223, 225

I

Idaho State Centennial Project 93
Iko, Momoko 221
Immigrant smuggling 131, 132–133
Immigration 99–106
Asian Indian Americans 102
Chinese Americans 53–54, 58, 137, 221, 239
Filipino Americans 57
Japanese Americans 102, 137
Korean Americans 102
post-World War II liberalization 104
quotas for refugees 106
refugees 64

Immigration Act(s)
  of 1917 102
  of 1924 16, 27, 56–58, 102, 121
  of 1952 62–63, 104
  of 1965 19, 32, 44, 104, 106, 140
Imutan, Andy 114
Inada, Lawson Fusao 202
Income 2
India, 57
Indochina Migration and Refugee
  Assistance Act 37
Indochina Refugee Act 48, 106
Indonesian Americans 24–25
Inner Deity Hygiene School 192
The Inn-Keeper's Apprentice 208
Inouye, Daniel 30, 250, 252
Intercollegiate Chinese for Social
  Action (ICSA) 112
Interethnic conflict 122
International District, Seattle, WA
  95
International Ladies' Garment
  Workers Union 114
International Longshoremen and
  Warehousemen Workers
  Union 114–115
Internment
  reparations for 123–124
Internment camps 29, 58
  Amache 89
  baseball in 232
  Gila River 79–80
  Heart Mountain 97
  Jerome 80
  Manzanar 87
  Minidoka 92–93
  Poston 80
  Rohwer 81
  Topaz 95
  Tule Lake 88
Interracial marriage 161
Ishii, Kazuhisa "Kaz" 231
Islam 190
  among Indonesians 25
  among Pakistanis 44
Issei 29, 101, 158
Itliong, Larry 116
Izumo Taisha Shrine 91

J

Jaisohn, Philip 31, 94–95
Japan Center 84
  Kana 165
Japanese Amateur Athletic Union
  (JAAU) 232
Japanese American Citizens
  League (JACL) 30, 124
Japanese American National
  Museum, Los Angeles, CA
  83
Japanese Americans
  active duty military 241
  athletic leagues and clubs 231–
  234
  first in baseball 231
  discrimination 241
  distribution (percent) of self-
  employed workers by state,
  1990 151
  entrepreneurship 146–153
  fertility 161
  immigration 26–27, 102, 137–
  138
  internment during World War II
  58, 59, 65, 217, 243
  in Korean War 246
  redress movement 65, 67
  religion 192
Japanese Athletic Union (JAU) 232
Japanese Boys Club 232
Japanese Emigration Company 89
Japanese enclave economies 149
Japanese export industries 149
Japanese Girls Club 232
Japanese language 165
Japantown, San Francisco, CA 83–
  84
JAU. *See* Japanese Athletic Union
JBS baseball team 231
Jen, Gish 202
Jerome Relocation Center, AR 80
Jin, Ha 197, 202–203
Jin, Morgan 115
Jin, Wuefei. *See* Jin, Ha
John Gassner award 223
Johnson, Martha 218

Joint Resolution Annexing the
  Hawaiian Islands 54
Joint Resolution on the 100th
  Anniversary of the
  Overthrow of the Hawaiian
  Kingdom, 1993, 71–74
The Joy Luck Club 198, 207
Judges 126
Judo 237, 238
Ju-jitsu 237

K

Kahanamoku, Duke 91, 229, 234–
  35
Kalakaua, David 92
Kalakaua, King 91
Kamakahonu, Kona 91
Kamehameha I 91
Kamehameha II–V 92
Kamehameha V Post Office 215
Kami 192
Kana, in Japanese language 165–
  166
Kang, Younghill 198
Kao, Elaine 219
Kapiolani, Queen 91
Karate 236, 238
Katigbak, Mia 217
KATUSA 246
Kawamura, Terry Teruo 250
Khmer Empire 36
Khmer Rouge 10, 106
Khorana, Har Gobind 182
Ki 237
Kick-boxing. *See* karate
Kim, June 214
Kim, Wendell 231
Kim, Willa 225
The King and I 213
King Kamehameha I 92
King, Martin Luther 111
King, Rodney 123
Kingston, Maxine Hong 197, 198,
  203
Kitamura, Harry 222
Kitano, Harry H.L. 232
The Kitchen God's Wife 198, 207
Kobashigawai, Yeiki 250, 252

Kochiyama, Yuri 115
Kono, Tommy 235
Kong, Chil 219
Koran 190
Korean Americans
  active duty military 241
  centennial of immigration 77–78
  Confucianism 191
  distribution (percent) of self-employed workers by state, 1990 151
  employment 34
  entrepreneurship 148, 151–153
  fertility 161
  first in baseball 231
  immigration 30, 102, 106, 138
  language 167
  population distribution 32
  relations with African-Americans 122
  religion 33
  in World War II 243
Korean Augmentation to U.S. Army (KATUSA) Program 246
Korean Bell and Belfry of Friendhip 84–85
Korean Guard 244
Korean language 167
Korean names 168
Korean National Association 243, 244
Korean War 31, 246
Koreatowns 32, 84, 85, 94, 149
Korematsu v. United States 124
Korematsu, Fred 124
Kumu Kahua Theatre 215
Kung fu 236, 239
Kuroda, Robert 252–253
Kye 34

L

Labor unions 113–116
Landmarks 79–98
Languages 163–169
  Bangladesh 163–164
  Bengali 163–164
  Cantonese dialect164–165
  Chinese 164–165
  Gan dialect 164
  Hakka dialect 164
  Hindi 168–169
  Hmong 23
  Japanese 165–167
  Korean 167
  Khmer 10
  Korean 35, 167–168
  Lao 37
  Mandarin dialect 164–165
  Pilipino 168
  pinyin 164
  romanization of Chinese 165
  romanization of Korean 167–168
  the Philippines 168
  Pilipino 168
  spoken at home 172
  Thai 47
  Urdu 44, 163, 168–169
  Xiang dialect 164
  Yùe 164–165
  Wu dialect 164
Laotian Americans 37
Lao language 37
Lao-tzu 192
Lapurap, Basilan, Philippine Islands 248
Lawmakers 125
Law school enrollment 128
Laws, anti-Asian American 119–122
Lawyers 127
Lee, C. Y. 214
Lee, Dong-il 218
Lee, Gus 197, 203–204
Lee, Guy 214
Lee, John 233
Lee, Ming Cho 224
Lee, Sammy 235
Lee, Tony 219
Lee, Tsung-Dao 182
Lee, Wen Ho
Lee, Yuan T. 182
Li 191
Li, Pat 214

Lila Wallace-Reader's Digest Foundation Theater for New Audiences Program 217
Liliuokalani, Queen 72, 73, 91, 92
Lim, Genny 221
Lin, Gin 94
Lingle, Linda 77
Literature 197–210
Little Plum 210
Little Saigon 149
Little Tokyo 85, 149, 215, 232
Livingston Dodgers 232
Livingston Farmer's Association 88
Lock, Yet 214
Locke, CA 85–86
Lodestone Theatre Ensemble 218–219
Look, Phyllis S.K. 224
Look What I Can Do 208
Los Alamos National Laboratory 179–180
Los Angeles Dodgers 231
Los Angeles Drama Critics' Circle Award 223
Los Angeles Massacre Site, Los Angeles, CA 86
Los Angeles Raiders 233
Los Angeles Rams 233
Louganis, Greg 235
Lounibos, Tim 219
Lowe, Pardee 198
"Loyalty Questionnaire" 88
Lum Sai Ho Tong Society 91

M

Magellan, Ferdinand 40, 42
Mahayana Buddhism 189
Mako 214, 222
Manhattan Theatre Club 222
Manila Galleon Trade 18
Manzanar Relocation Center 87
Mao, Zedong 205
Mariners, Seattle 231
Marines 241
Marriage 161
Martial arts 236–240
  aikido 236, 237
  judo 236, 237

karate 236, 238
kung fu 236, 239
tae kwan do 236, 238
Masaoka, Mike 96–97
Matsui, Hideki 231
Ma-Yi Theatre Ensemble, Inc.
    address and phone number 226
M. Butterfly 223
McCarran-Walter Act 62, 104, 138
McCarthy, Nobu 215, 222
McCunn, Ruthanne Lum 204
McElrath, Ah Quon 115
Mehta, Ved 204
Melanesians 39
Mendonca, Leroy A. 247, 249
Mets, New York 231
Micronesians 39
The Middleman and Other Storie
    205
Military 241–256
    active duty personnel 242, 247
    air force 242
    army 242
    before World War II 214–242
    Congressional Medal of Honor
        247–256
    442nd Regimental Combat
        Team 245–246
    Korean War 246–247
    marines 242
    military heroes 247–256
    navy 242
    World War II 243–246
Military Intelligence Service
    Language School 245
Military Order Number 45 244
Military zones, California 61
Milwaukee Brewers 231
Min, Anchee 205
Minidoka Relocation Center, ID
    92–93
Miss Minidoka 1943 217
Miss Saigon 224
Miyamura, Hiroshi H. 249
Miyashiro, Kelly 219
"Model Minority" 4
Mohammed 190

*Moon Mother: A Native American
    Creation Tale* 210
Moon, Sun Myung 193, 194
Mori, Toshio 198
Morihoro, Rachel 219
Morikami Museum and Japanese
    Gardens 89
Morikami, George Sukeji 89
Mormons 143
Moto, Kaoru 253
Mukerji, Dhan Gopal 197, 208
Mukheree, Bharati 197, 205
Munemori, Sadao S. 249
Murakami, Masanori 231
Muranga, Kiyoshi K. 253
Music 9, 11
The Music Lessons 220
Mutual aid societies 146

N

Nakae, Masato 253
Nakamine, Shinyei 253
Nakamura, William K. 253–254
Names 165, 167, 168
Naples 246
NAPALC. *See* National Asian
    Pacific American Legal
    Consortium
National Asian American Theatre
    Company (NATCO) 217,
    226
National Asian Pacific American
    Bar Association 126
National Asian Pacific American
    Legal Consortium
    (NAPALC) 116, 118, 129
National Asian Pacific American
    Women's Forum
    (NAPAWF) 162
National Book Critic's Circle
    Award 197, 203, 205, 206
National Committee for Redress
    and Reparations (NCRR)
    124
National Education Association
    115
National Farm Workers
    Association (NFWA) 113

National Football League (NFL)
    233
National Japanese American
    Historical Society 87
National Japanese American
    Memorial 96–97
National League All-Star Team,
    1985 231
National League All-Star Team,
    1986 and 1987 231
National League Golden Glove
    Award, 1989 231
National origins 63
National Public Radio 199
Native Hawaiians 72
Navy 241
Nepal 57
New England Patriots 233
New Eyes 218
New York Mets 231
The New York Shakespeare
    Festival 224
New York Times 115
New York Yankees 231
Newbery Honor Book 205, 208,
    210
Newspaper guild 115
NFL. *See N*ational Football League
Nguyen, Dat 233
Night Visitors 210
Nihonmachi 83, 95
1965 Immigration Act 160
Nippon Hospital, Stockton, CA 87
Nirvana 17, 37, 189
Nisei 29, 158, 246
Nisei Athletic Association, Chicago
    234
Nisei Athletic Union 234
Nishi Hongwanji Buddhist Temple
    83
Nishimoto, Joe M. 254
Nisperos, Jose B. 248
Nobel prize
    Chandrashekhar,
        Subrahmanyan 182
    Khorana, Har Gobind 182
    Lee, Tsung-Dao 182
    Lee, Yuan T. 182

Tagore, Rabindranath 164
Nobel prize *continued*
   Ting, Samuel C.C. 182
   Yang, Chen-Ning 182
Noble Eightfold Path 189
No No Boy 198
North Apennines 246
Northern Mariana Islanders 41–42
Northwest Asian American Theatre
   (NWAAT) 216, 226

O

Oahu Junior League (baseball) 232
Oahu Market 91
Oakland Athletics 231
Obie Award 223, 225, 226
Oceans of Words 103
Office of Management and Budget
   141
Ohata, Allan M. 254
Okada, John 198
Okuba, James K. 254
Okuba, Mine 198
Okumura, Reverend Takie 232
Okutsu, Yukio 254–255
Old Man 221
Oliver, Nellie Grace 232
Olivers social clubs 232
Olympic games
   Asian American champions 235
   1912, Stockholm, Sweden 229,
    235
   1920, Antwerp, Belgium 235
   1924, Paris, France 235
   1948, London, England 235
   1952, Helsinki, Finland 235
   1976, Montreal, Canada 235
   1984, Los Angeles, California
    235
   1992, Albertville, France 235
Olympic Spirit Award 235
100th Anniversary of the
   Overthrow of the Hawaiian
   Kingdom, 1993, 103rd
   Congress Joint Resolution
   71–74

100th Battalion Hawaii National
   Guard 246
100th Infantry Battalion, 442nd
   Regimental Combat Team
   29, 246, 249, 251
   awards and citations earned
    246–256
1000 Airplanes on the Roof 223
Onizuka, Ellison 182
Ono, Frank H. 255
*Open Boat, Poems from Asian
   America* 201
Orderly Departure Program (ODP)
   106
Organic Act 73
Organized crime 130–132
Orioles, Baltimore 231
Otani, Kazou 255
Outer Critics Circle 223
Outmarriage 161
Outstanding Picture Book of the
   Year Award 208
Overland Trail 97

P

Pa, Chay 21
Pacific Islanders 39–43
Pakistan 6
Pakistani Americans 43–44
Paluans 42
Pan Asian Repertory Theatre 217,
   226
Paper Angels 221
Park, Chan Ho 231
Park, Linda Sue 197, 205–206
Park, Yong-man 31
Patriots, New England 233
Pearl Harbor, attack on 27, 41, 91–
   92, 123, 243
PEN/Hemingway Award 203
Pensionados 19
Pet Food and Tropical Apparitions
   201
Phetakoune, Thung 129
Philip Jaisohn Memorial
   Foundation 94–95

Philippine-American Collegiate
   Endeavor (PACE) 112
*Philippine Legends, Folklore, and
   American Impressions* 216
Philippines, annexed by the United
   States 19
Philippine Scouts, U.S. Army 243,
   248
Philippines, Republic of 140
Phou, Lee Phan 198
Pia-ri, Korea 249
Picture Bride 206
Picture brides 27, 31, 102, 157–158
Pililaau, Herbert K. 247, 249
Pilipino 18
Pilipino language 168
Ping Chong and Co. 226
Place of Refuge 92
Playhouse 46 217
Playwrights 220
Po Valley 246
Political isolation 152
Population 135–144
   American Samoans 136
   Asian Indians 5
   Asian Pacific Islanders 142
   by country of origin 138
   Cambodians Americans 10
   Filipino Americans 18
   Gaumanians 136
   Hawaiians 137
   historical statistical record 137
   Hmong Americans 22
   Indonesian Americans 24
   Korean Americans 31
   Laotian Americans 37
   1980 Census 141–142
   1900 to 1960 137–140
   1900 to 2000 139
   1990 Census 142–143
   Pacific Islanders 136
   Pakistani Americans 43
   population projections 142, 144
   population trends 135–136
   post-1965 immigration 140
   refugee resettlement 140, 142
   1790 to 1890 137
   2000 Census 143–144

Vietnamese Americans 50
Poston Internment Camp 80, 207
Prabhakar, Arati 182
Presidential Proclamations 57–58, 61, 77–78
President's Advisory Commission on Asian Americans and Pacific Islanders 74–76
Professors World Peace Academy 194
Public Law 503, 1942 62
Public Proclamation, 1942 59–61
Pupunu, Alfred 233
Purple Heart Battalion 246
Puuhonua O Honaunau National Historical Park 92

Q

Quan, Frank 82
Quick Ranch Stone Wall 87
Quick, Morgan 87
Quo, Beulah 214
Quota system, immigration 57, 58, 62, 102, 106, 137
Qureshey, Safi 182

R

Racial and Ethnic Bias in the Courts, California Committee on 133
Raiders, Los Angeles 233
Rams, Los Angeles 233
Rangers, Texas 231
Red Azalea 205
Red Thread 210
Redress movement 30, 123
Refrigerators 219
Refugee Relief Act 49, 63–65, 160
Refugee resettlement policies 135
Refugees
    adjustment of status 64
    Cambodian 10
    definition of 64
    deportation 64
    Hmong 106

Orderly Departure Program (ODP) 106
    resettlement 107, 142
    secondary migration 108
    unaccompanied minors 107
Relay immigration 160
Religion 41, 187–194
    Buddhism 188–190
    Confucianism 191–192
    Hinduism 188
    Islam 190–191
    Shintoism 192–193
    Taoism 192
    Tibetan Buddhism 190
    timeline of Asian religions 191
    Unification Church 193–194
    Zen Buddhism 190
Relocation camps 29
    Amache 89
    baseball in 232
    Gila River 79–80
    Heart Mountain 97
    Jerome 80
    Manzanar 87
    Minidoka 92–93
    Poston 80
    Rohwer 80, 81
    Topaz 95
    Tule Lake 88
Reno, Janet 125
Repeal of Chinese Exclusion Acts, 1943 62
Republic of Korea (ROK) Army 246
Rhee, Jhoon 238, 239
Rhee, Syngman 31
The Rice Room: Growing Up Chinese American, From Number Two Son to Rock 'n' Roll 201
Rime of the Ancient Mariner 211
Rinzai 190
Rivera, Ron 233
Rock Springs Massacre Site, Rock Springs, WY 97
Rohwer Relocation Center 80, 81
Romanization 165, 167
Rome 246

Roosevelt, Franklin D. 27, 57, 58, 92, 124
Roosevelt, Theodore 237
Rotating Credit Associations 147
Royal Mausoleum State Monument, Honolulu 92
Ryunosuke, Akutagawa 214

S

St. Louis Cardinals 233
Sakata, Len 231
Sakato, George T. 255
Salonga, Lea 214, 224
Samoans 42, 57, 143, 247
Samsara 189
San Bernardino Spirit 231
San Diego Chargers 233
San Francisco 49ers 233
San Francisco Giants 231
San Francisco Housing Authority (SFHA) 118
San Francisco State College 112
Sansei 29, 158
Sapolu, Jesse 233
Sari 8
SAT. *See* Scholastic Assessment Test
Satori 190
Savusa, Iuniasolua 247
Say, Allen 197, 208–209
Scholastic Assessment Test (SAT) 173–174
School of the Magic Jewel 192
Science and engineering 179–185
    Asian American milestones 182
Seattle Mariners 231
Seau, Junior 233
Secondary migration 108
The Seesaw Girl 205
Selective Service System, Japanese Americans 245
Self-employment rate 145, 148, 151
Separated families 155, 156
Seravezza, Italy 249
Service Employees International Union 114
Seth, Vikram 206

Seven Blind Mice 210
Shawn, William 204
Shimono, Sab 220
Shin, Paull 77
Shintoism 192
Shiomi, Rick 217, 218
Shogun Macbeth 217
Sikhs 102
A Single Shard 205
Social class 152, 161
Sodhi, Balbir Singh 129–130
Song for a Nisei Fisherman 217, 222
Song, Cathy-Lynn 206
Soo bahk martial arts system 236
Soto 190
Southern France (Operation Anvil) 246
Spanish-American War 19, 42, 103, 136, 137, 139, 241
Spirit, San Bernardino 231
Sports 229–239
    aikido 237
    baseball stars 231
    football stars 233
    Japanese athletic leagues and clubs 231–234
    judo 237–238
    karate 238
    kung fu 239
    martial arts 236–239
    Olympics 235
    sumo 230–231
    surfing 234–236
    tae kwon do 238–239
Stereotypes 2, 4, 213
Stevens, John L. 72
Stilwell, Joseph 245
Studio Theater 222
Sugar plantations 19, 26, 41, 232
Sugimoto, Etsu 198
Suh Jae-pil 31
Suharto 24
A Suitable Boy 206
Sukarno 24
Sumo wrestling 229, 230–231
Surfing 229, 234
Suzuki, Makato "Mac" 231

Suzuki, Ichiro 231
Swimming, Olympic 235

T

Tae kwon do 236, 238–239
Taejon-ni, Korea 246, 249
Tagore, Rabindranath 164
Taiwan 160
Takamine, Jokichi 182
Takei, Art 115
Tan, Amy 197, 198, 206, 207
Tan, Victor En Yu 225
Tanouye, Ted T. 255
Taoism 17, 192
Taoist Temple 91
Tao-te Ching 192
Taxes
    Alien Poll Tax 120
    foreign miners' tax 119
    head tax, California 120
The Tea House of August Moon 213
Teacher education 177
Terminal Island, East San Pedro, CA 88
Terminal School 88
Texas Rangers 231
Thai Americans
    assimilation 46–47
    employment 47
    family life 47
    immigration 46
    language 47
    1990 census population distribution 46
Thai language 47
Theater Mu 218, 226
Theatre, Asian American 213–227
    addresses 226
    American Conservatory Theatre (ACT) 215
    The American Place Theatre 221
    Angel Island Theatre Company 218
    Asian American Theater Company (AATC) 215, 221, 222

Asian American Theater Workshop (AATW) 215
Asian Exclusion Act (AEA) 216
Asian Multi Media Center (AMMC) 216
behind the scenes 224–226
Chinese Honeymoon 213
Community Asian Theater of the Sierra 226
Contemporary Asian Theatre Scene 219–220
Drama Desk award 225
Dramalogue 226
East West Players 214, 222
18 Might Mountain Warriors 220
Emmy award 225
Eureka Theatre 222
Flower Drum Song 213, 224
Here and Now 219
Humana Festival of New American Plays 223
The King and I 213
Kumu Kahua Theatre 215
Lodestone Theatre Ensemble 218–219
Los Angeles Drama Critics' Award 215, 223
National Asian American Theatre Company (NATCO) 217
New York Shakespeare Festival 224
Northwest Asian American Theatre (NWAAT) 216
Obie awards 223, 225, 226
Pan Asian Repertory Theatre 217
Playhouse 46 217
playwright pioneers 220
Rashomon 214
Ryunosuke, Akutagawa 214
stereotypes portrayed 213–214
The Tea House of August Moon 213
Theater Mu 218
Theatre Off Jackson 217
Theatre of Yugen 226

Theatrical Ensemble of Asians (TEA) 216
Tony Awards 223, 225
28th Street Theater 217
Theatre Off Jackson 217
Theatrical Ensemble of Asians (TEA) 216
Theosophy 7
Theravada Buddhism 189
Third World Liberation Front (TWLF) 112
Thousand Pieces of Gold 204
Tibetan Buddhism 190
Ting, Samuel C.C. 182
Tongans 43, 143
Tony Awards 223, 225
Topaz Relocation Center 95
Transcontinental Railroad 113
Trask, David Jr. 115
Triad Societies 130–132
Trias, Robert 238
Trinidad, Telesforo 248
Tripitaka 189
Tripmaster Monkey: His Fake Book 203
Tule Lake internment camp 88
    baseball in 234
28th Street Theater 217
Tydings-McDuffie Act 57, 103

U

Uchida, Yoshiko 209
Unification Church 193–194
United Church of Christ 73
United Farm Workers Union 115
United Food and Commercial Workers Union 114, 115
U.S. Constitution 56
United States English 122
U.S. government's "Loyalty Questionnaire" 88
United States Karate Association 238
U.S. military 241–256
    Asian American heroes 241–256
    rank titles by service branch 241
    segregation 246

veterans organizations 250
U.S.S. *Arizona* 92
U.S.S. *San Diego* 248
United States Tae Kwon Do Association 239
United Teachers of Los Angeles 115
University of California at Berkeley 238
University of Hawaii 215
University of Washington 216
Urdu language 44, 163, 168–169

V

Vedas 188
Vedi 204
Vera Cruz, Philip 115
Vietnamese Americans
    active duty military personnel 241
    employment 51, 151
    entrepreneurship 151–153
    family life 50
    fertility 161
    immigration 48, 106, 138
    linguistic difficulties 49, 50
    population 47, 143
    religion 50
    self-employed workers 151
Violence
    against Koreans 34
    anti-Asian American 116–118
    audit of anti-Asian/Pacific American 116–118
    in Chinatowns 15
Voting rights 125
Voting Rights Language Assistance Act, 1992 71

W

Wai, Francis B. 256
Waiting 197
Wakamatsu Tea and Silk Colony 27
Walking the Indian Streets 204
Wang, An 182
Wapato Nippons, Washington 232
War Brides Act 138, 155
War Relocation Authority 87, 234

Wards Cove Packing Co. v. *Atonio* 115–116, 124–125
The Wash 222
Washington Institute for Values in Public Policy 194
Washington State Governor Writer's Award 199
Washington state, baseball in 232
Way of Right Unity 192
Way of Supreme Peace 192
Wayne, David 213
Weglyn, Michiko Nishiura 207
Weightlifting, Olympic 235
Western Defense Command 59
What Comes in Spring? 211
When Heaven and Earth Changed Places 201
When I Was a Boy in China 198
When My Name Was Keoko 206
When We Were Young 221
While I Sleep 211
White Point, San Pedro, CA 88
Whose Mouse Are You? 208
Wildcats, Cortez (California) 232
Wing, Yung 229
Wise Fool Productions 227
Wo Fat 91
Wo Kee 93
Woman from Hiroshima 198
The Woman Warrior: Memoirs of a Girlhood among Ghosts 203
Women's Army Corps 246
Wong, Ark-Yueh 239
Wong, George 115
Wong, Jade Snow 198, 207
Wong-Staal, Flossie 182
World War II 16, 27, 41, 42, 46, 140, 243
Wrestling, sumo 229
Wu dialect 164
Wu, Chien-Shiung 182
Wyoming #226 97

Y

Yale Series of Younger Poets Award 206
Yamamoto, Hisaye 207
Yamasaki, Minoru 84

Yamato Colonies 27, 88
Yamauchi, Wakako 216, 220
Yang, Chen-Ning 182
Yang, Debra W. 125
Yankee Dawg You Die 222
Yankees, New York 231
Yano, Rodney J. T. 250
The Year of the Dragon 221, 225

Years of Infamy: The Untold Story of America's Concentration Camps 207
Yee, Kelvin Han 216, 220
Yellow Fever 217
Yellow Light 201–202
"Yellow Peril" 15, 27
Yep, Laurence 197, 210

Yick Wo v. Hopkins 121
Yoneda, Karl 115
Young, Ed 197, 210–211
Youth gangs 130, 132

Z

Zen Buddhism 190

RAMPAGE

Also by Susan Taylor Chehak

THE STORY OF ANNIE D.
HARMONY
DANCING ON GLASS
SMITHEREENS

RAMPAGE

Susan Taylor Chehak

DOUBLEDAY

New York   London   Toronto   Sydney   Auckland

PUBLISHED BY DOUBLEDAY
a division of Bantam Doubleday Dell Publishing Group, Inc.
1540 Broadway, New York, New York 10036

DOUBLEDAY and the portrayal of an anchor with a dolphin are trademarks of
Doubleday, a division of Bantam Doubleday Dell Publishing Group, Inc.

Library of Congress Cataloging-in-Publication Data

Chehak, Susan Taylor.
Rampage / Susan Taylor Chehak. — 1st ed.
p.   cm.
I. Title.
PS3553.H34875C37   1998
813′.54—dc21   97-40826
CIP
ISBN 0-385-48452-6

1   3   5   7   9   10   8   6   4   2

To Mom and Dad
To Betty
To the memory of John

What is this crying that I hear in the wind?
Is it the old sorrow and the old grief?
Or is it a new thing coming, a whirling leaf
About the grey hair of me who am weary and blind?

—*Fiona Macleod*

PROLOGUE

Carried Away

IN A SQUARE WHITE HOUSE AT THE END OF A LONG MUD road there is a four-year-old girl who is supposed to be asleep. She can hear the mom and the dad arguing in another room. They aren't angry with her, she knows that. They're angry with each other, but for reasons that make no sense to her, and that by itself is enough to keep her up, wondering, worried, afraid. They're off in their own bedroom down the hall and around the corner on the very far other side of the house. She was put to bed hours ago, and now if they think of her at all, what they think is that she is asleep. She's always been good that way. Or tried to be. Or hoped to make them think she is.

But in fact Jolie is awake. She's wide-eyed with her sleepless-ness. Twisty and turny is what the mom calls it whenever she sees the child get like this. So twitchy and itchy that she can't lie still. She's squirming inside her skin. She's hot, her body is damp and sticky and warm, and she has thrown her blanket off. It lies in a crumpled heap near her on the floor. She stands up and then sits back down again. She bounces on her mattress. She rocks her body back and forth. She sings to herself. The rocking seems to soothe her some. And the singing does drown out anything else that she maybe would rather not have to hear. Such as their voices on the other side of the house, raised.

Jolie's bedroom isn't really a room. It's a closet off the kitchen, with a window and a bed. The bed isn't really a bed. It's a mattress on the floor. The window has star-shaped stickers pressed onto its glass—she's put them there herself. The door has been pulled as tightly shut as it will go, which isn't much. It's warped and sagging on its frame so that it never can be closed up all the way, not tightly enough to please her anyway, because it has been bent out of shape by the damp and also from the time when the dad in his anger slammed it off its hinges one night so it never would be right again. There is a crack at the side where the light comes to her and that's how the sounds come to her too, even when the lights are off. She can always hear them, no matter how much she might want not to; the voices have a way of traveling and finding her, they wing to her and hover, picking at her head, snagging in her hair—listen listen—so she has to hum out loud to herself to block out their constant noise.

She is sitting in her bed, rocking back and forth, holding on to her feet and squeezing them. She has on her shortie cotton pajamas, green-striped with just one button at the back and curly lace around the cuffs and a hole under one arm and a green-and-yellow turtle on the front. She wiggles her toes inside her hands. She bounces her knees. Her legs are bruised like a bad banana— that's what the mom said, holding a cigarette between her fingers and tapping the ashes off its end to sizzle in the toilet bowl, frowning at the little girl who was sitting bare-naked in the bathtub with her hair wet and slimy from laying her head back in the soapy water to silence again in another way the kinds of noises that she would rather not have to hear.

She is singing, "And then another one's here and the next one's here and then another one's here." It isn't really a song, just some words that she's put together and likes to say to herself over and over again, "and the next one's here and then another one's here," counting on her fingers with it because that is one way for her to keep track and it seems to be something like a story to her, one that might go on and on forever if that is what she thinks she wants from it, with everybody getting there and nobody ever going off to anyplace else. She can hum this and hear it in her head and then whatever else there is isn't anymore. Silence is what she is after. The sounds of them drowned out.

And besides, it is a story that seems like maybe it has some kind of a promise in it, doesn't it? Some sort of a hope that something else might be just about to happen? Though she knows that she has no idea what that something else might be. People piling up in one place like bottles on a shelf and then . . . what? They all fall down.

She is aware of the rain outside. And of the wind, rising. It has been raining all day and now on into the night, not a hard rain, only a slow and tired-seeming one, and the wind keeps on bumping into the house, it swims through the branches of the trees and there is a movement at the window, a shadow, but when she looks up, she sees that it isn't only the wind that's out there, and it isn't just the rain either. It's him.

This little girl, four years old, this smallish, thin-limbed, long-haired, dark-eyed child, is not afraid. She knows who the man outside her window is. She's seen him before, and she recognizes him now. He's peering through the window glass, past the stars, with his hands cupped around his face.

She stops rocking. She stops humming. She looks at his face, into his eyes. Like two blue stones, like the string of blue beads that the mom keeps in the carved wood box that Jolie has been told not to touch. The only thing she knows about him is his name. Rafe. He's been here with the dad once or maybe twice. Outside on a Sunday afternoon after they all came back home from church. When the sun was shining and it was hot. The grownups were standing around a smoking barbecue drinking glasses of cold lemonade and iced tea. The mom yanked her back from the fire—because she'd been drawn to it, was trying to poke at it with a stick that she'd found—and whapped her one with her bare hand on the back of her bare leg. He saw this, she saw him see it, and she saw him start to say something but then decide not to and just wink at her instead. Later he pushed her in the tire swing. And he tickled her, with his fingers in her ribs, and he made her laugh so hard that she piddled in her pants.

His hand slams against the window glass, smashing it like stomping on the thin skin of ice over a puddle. There is an explosion of star stickers, and then he is reaching in like groping in a fish tank and he's found the latch and he's lifting the window up and open and then he is climbing in. He stands in that small room that is really only a closet; he seems to fill it with himself. He is wet from the rain, and water drips onto the rug and won't that make the mom mad when she sees it? He kicks at the door to open it and then the sound of their argument is louder, like the volume on the TV set turned up high because the dad's hearing is not so good. He looks back at her, one hand in his pocket, one finger to his lips. He smiles at her because they share a secret now and the secret is that she is not alone because he is there. Then he's gone. And then it's quiet and then the mom's voice is rising up like the soprano's solo song in church, and a groaning, then there are three loud bangs and then one more and then nothing again. Silence.

This must be the silence that Jolie has been after all along.

She stands up on the mattress, her feet sink into it as if it were mud. He's come for her, she knows. She raises her arms and he is reaching for her. He lifts her up close to him and takes her with him out into the night, into the rain that's cold and soft, enfolding her, carrying her away. The smell of him. His warmth. The sounds of his feet against the ground.

He carries her then for a long time, it seems, across the field and into the woods. The house, a dark shape behind them, shrinks away, smaller and smaller. The front porch light winks out between the trees. And then there are only the two of them. And the bounce of his body. And the slop of his boots through the leaves and grass. His breathing, heavy. Over a fence. Woods and shrubs. To a road, a car.

He shifts her in his arms to get the door open. Then he puts her down on the seat and closes the door and goes around to the other side and climbs in next to her. She looks at the road in front of them, then at him, his profile sharp like a paper cutout of a face.

She is rocked and lulled by the car as it moves. She is slumped against him. His body is warm and the warmth makes her drowsy, so she lies down on the seat and closes her eyes and drifts off toward sleep. With his hand on her head and with his fingers in her hair.

———

Later, when he pulls the car off into the bright glass-and-chrome oasis of a roadside way station and stops it there, the sudden stillness wakes Jolie up, and at first she can't be completely sure about where exactly she is.

She looks down at herself and recognizes the green-and-yellow turtle on the front of her pajama top. When she rolls over onto her back she sees him, and at the same time she remembers too where she is. She understands that he's been watching her, with his blue eyes that look like stones. He doesn't scare her. She is not afraid. She thinks she likes his face.

She sits up and wipes her mouth with the back of her hand. She rubs with her fingertips at her eyes. Outside the car, beyond the flickering high arches of the lights, the sky is black with night. She can see too the gleaming glass windows of a convenience store—its sentry row of gas pumps, stacks of merchandise, the bright mysterious numbers and letters of the advertisement signs. The rain has stopped, or they've gone far enough already that they've managed to move out of it, but the highway behind them is still black and damp, silky-looking as a velvet ribbon, and the trailer trucks whoosh past—they seem to swoop down the hill like giant dark birds, then they roar on and rise away again, their red taillights a diminishing shimmer, like something half-forgotten in the mist.

He gives her clothes—a pair of faded blue jeans with an elastic waist and one knee frayed and torn, a green T-shirt with a pocket, a hooded sweatshirt jacket with a zipper up the front, a pair of gray socks in a ball, and black tennis shoes—and he helps her put them on. He fills the car with gas and pays the attendant inside the store and then he pulls forward and around, out onto the highway between the soaring trucks, and then they are driving again. He steers the car with just his one hand, his palm flattened against the bottom half of the wheel.

The radio is on, but after the news is over, he turns the volume down so low that she can hardly hear the music anymore.

The car moves through the dark, and out the windows on both sides and behind them there is nothing but blackness. Jolie doesn't want to guess at what might be out there in it, hiding from her or waiting for her, so instead she tries turning her thoughts to how the world might as well include nobody else except for the two of them, just Rafe and only Jolie, and there they are, moving along their way through it in this safe bubble that is made up of the greenish light that's cast over them from the dials and the numbers on the dash and also of the dry warmth that is blowing over her legs from the heater out of the vents. The headlights feel out the way, probing forth into the darkness, casting twin cones of light against the road as it ribbons off away, forward on and on. There are no other cars, not even trucks, and so the road seems to be unfolding this way for them alone, and she watches it as if it might be the unknown future of her life and also, by the way, his.

Whenever the music on the radio is interrupted by the news, he reaches over and turns it up to listen. When he sees that she is watching him, he smiles and looks away, back at the road again. She climbs over the seat into the back and sits for a while that way behind him, studying his face, which fills up the slender slice of glass that is the rearview mirror.

Jolie watches Rafe toss her frog pajamas into a trash can on an unlit street in some dark and empty-seeming city she doesn't know where. She notices that another man in a torn black jacket with the collar turned up has stepped out from the shadows of a doorway and is watching him too. She points this out to him and he digs down into his pocket and gives the other man a crumpled-up dollar bill and the other man thanks him, says God bless and touches his forehead, then drifts off into the shadows again and is gone.

She holds on to his hand; her fingers feel small and cold inside the warm pocket of his curled fist. He is talking on a pay phone. He hangs it up when he's finished and looks down at her, then bends toward her and lifts her up onto his shoulders and carries her that way while she squeezes her knees on his neck and holds on to his head with both hands. Because, she knows, what would be worse would be if he were to go off and leave her here alone.

In the morning they're parked in an empty rest stop by the side of the road. Jolie is sitting on the car's hood while he bends over her and cuts her hair so close to her scalp that it curls. There are mountains all around them, huge and still. The air is cold. When he's finished he stands back and studies her. He scoops her loose hair up with his hands and puts it in a trash bin. What of it he's missed is lifted by the wind, and she watches it as it wafts away. When he sets her down on her feet on the ground again, she feels lightheaded, as if she's lost some part of herself to which she has been until now bound. He reaches into his jacket pocket and pulls out a pair of child's sunglasses, round with red plastic frames. She puts them on and feels the muscles of her face relax behind the dark lenses. She is surprised at how dim the world around her has become. Something like the sky before a thunderstorm, she thinks. Or after dinner, when it's time for her to go to bed. But when she lifts the glasses and looks again, there still aren't any clouds and the sun is still bright and the sky is still wholly clear.

Maybe for one lucid moment Jolie is remembering something, maybe she sees some quick bright flash of her former self, maybe she relives some small bit of her other life, the one that she had before. Maybe she had another haircut once, and this one has reminded her of that one: when the mom carried her bare-naked out into the yard and she stood there on the prickly brown carpet of grass while the dad leaned down and hacked at her tangled hair with the sharpened blade of his opened pocket knife.

In the bathtub afterward, the soap that the mom used smelled like what the dad squirted on the barbecue to get it to light, and its fumes stung her eyes and made her breath catch in her throat.

"Bugs," the mom said, and then she dunked the girl's head down into the water and held her there under it until Jolie kicked and fought and finally struggled her own way free.

Or maybe now that she's with Rafe she isn't able to remember anything of her other life before this anymore at all.

When it's dark again they stop again. He pulls the car off the road into the dimly lit parking lot of a motel. It's a flat low building painted white and green with a row of numbered red doors and a flashing sign on a tall pole. The town around them is so small it isn't much of anything at all, not even railroad tracks or telephone poles, just a simple intersection it looks like, one road crossing over another one, a blinking yellow light, fields at two corners, a store on one side and the motel there on the other. He'll have already tried to figure out what might be safer—to stick to the back roads, end up out of the way here in a little place like this, where no one is apt to be looking for him but where he's maybe more likely to be noticed and remembered, or to try to lose himself and her in someplace larger, where theirs would be only two faces among thousands, but two faces that are already being circulated and seen. He's decided that his chances will be better here.

Jolie follows him into the office and hears him say out loud that he's her father to the woman at the front desk, who is thin and hard-looking like a long splinter of stone and wears a shiny turquoise dressing gown with gold birds on it and a row of silver buttons that look like nickels up its front. Jolie is dizzy from the driving and glad to have, for the moment, stopped.

An old man in a pair of worn-out overalls is coming into the motel office then, just at the same time that Rafe and Jolie are going out. His face, in the shadow of his feed cap's bent bill, is gray and wrinkled, coarsened by a silvery sandpaper beard. He shuffles when he walks, head down, his eyes making a study of the ground. He stops when he looks up and sees the younger man and his child—hard to tell if it's a boy or a girl—and he nods first, then he winks at the kid and excuses himself, steps back outside, holds open the door. He's friendly. Says it sure was a terrible winter, wasn't it? Good to see some sunshine now, for once.

He doesn't get an answer to this, but he will remember the encounter later. He'll look at the photograph that is printed on the front page of the newspaper, and he'll recall this child's face. He will remember too this man who only frowns and nudges at his kid to move her on.

There are two beds in the room. When Rafe falls asleep in his,

Jolie gets up out of hers and creeps over to the window. She pulls back a corner of the drapes and peeks out at the flat land that seems to be rolling off forever in every direction all around underneath a vast sky that's like a black bowl overturned and pinpricked by glittery holes. Stars—she does at least know that much. But these ones are real.

His boots are on the floor near the door where he's left them, set side by side just so. She kneels next to them and slips her small hands down inside to feel for the linger of his warmth. He is sleeping on his back, with one hand on his belly and the other arm folded behind his head. She climbs back into her own bed again, next to his. She slides her small self down under the covers. She puts on the sunglasses that he's given her and lays her head on her pillow and gazes into the darkness that is all around her now. She's listening to his breathing, trying to memorize it, trying to see if maybe she can match it up exactly with the quick and shallow rhythm of her own.

The old limestone barn emerges from the trees like a hidden picture. Near it is a stone house whose walls are crawling with creeping ivy. A hobbled truck has been left parked in the driveway, up on blocks, two of its tires flat. Rafe stops behind it and turns off the engine, then just sits there for a minute, looking over at the shadow of the barn, at its blank and empty windows and the ragged black stains on the stone. To anyone else, he supposes, the place might look like something quaint. A piece of the past maybe, better days gone by, preserved here in what could seem to somebody who doesn't know better to be the permanence of stone. But he is taking some satisfaction from the fact that it has been let get rundown, and he can see that it is starting to crack and crumble in some places, that its windows are broken and its roof has begun to sag, that in time it will of its own accord and without any help from anyone, without even any interference from him, wear away and finally fall down. He's been away from this place for a long time.

He looks over at Jolie, unsmiling again—the doubt in his eyes darkens them, grays their blue and grows, looming like the hard foreboding of a storm. Then he's leaning forward and peering through the windshield at the house. He honks the car's horn by slamming at it with his curled fist. He sits back. She watches him; he watches the house. But nothing happens. He presses the ball of his hand against the horn again, and this time it howls, louder and longer.

With that the front door opens and a woman is stepping out onto the wide porch. She is barefoot; she stands solidly, spread-legged. She is a large woman, huge, she billows, her dress balloons out all around her; its colorful cloth, printed with pictures of flowers and fruit, looks like an exotic flag or a huge flowing scarf. She holds a tall thin glass in one hand; she raises the other hand up to her face, shading the sun from her eyes.

He tells Jolie to wait, and then he opens the car door and climbs out, leaving her there where she is, alone. She sees him lift his foot, rub the toe of his boot against the back of his pant leg, polishing it, first one and then the other. He runs a hand over his hair, smoothing it.

The woman on the porch is calling out to him. She plods down the steps heavily, her big dress flowing out around her, full of air, and she steps off onto the grass, holding her glass aloft as she moves, laughing, careful not to spill. She takes him in her arms and engulfs him in a hug, turns him, turns with him. Her hugeness seems to envelope him, and then she lets him go and stands back.

Rafe has turned, red-faced and squinting, and he is saying something, pointing at Jolie and waving, beckoning for her to come on and get out now, come on over there next to him. So she works the handle and she leans her weight against the door and she climbs down from his car. She hears him say again that she is his daughter. She's heard him mention this two times now, and she's begun to wonder if maybe it just could be that it is true.

The big woman has swooped to her and is stooping over her. The colorful cloth of her dress ripples silkily; it swishes softly, makes a drowning water sound. Her face is ample, full-cheeked, dimpled and round. Her body gives off a smell of flowers and soap and dust. Still holding on to her drink, this woman takes Jolie's hand and squeezes it, burying it in the flesh of her own. Her big moon face grins and wags. Jolie looks up into her eyes, she inhales that reckless fragrance, and she smiles.

A four-year-old girl whose full name was Joliet Anne Ray was taken, snatched in the middle of the night from her closet-sized bedroom in the little town of Monarch, Oregon, not far from Eugene. The mom and the dad were both of them shot dead. It was a crime that the local papers were full of for a while. They howled about a double murder and a kidnaping, in bold print, outraged not just because she'd been taken but maybe even more so because the residents of Monarch had been so prone to smugness over the safety of their streets.

"They gave her what they could," one neighbor told a reporter, wincing. Those people weren't her real parents. It was a foster family. They'd been paid to take her in.

There were two bodies, a man and a woman, and each had been shot twice. By the time they were found they'd been dead for a week already, maybe even more. The mom didn't have many friends. The dad was unemployed. They'd only had the girl there with them for a few months. They'd kept to themselves mostly. Except for church on Sundays, which for two weeks in a row by then already they'd missed.

There was a broken window, glass on the floor, a rain-soaked rug. And no sign of the little girl that another neighbor described for the papers as "quiet, but sweet."

The police secured the crime scene with yellow plastic tape. The windowsill in the girl's room was dusted for fingerprints. Search parties were sent out into the surrounding woods and fields. Cold sandwiches and hot coffee were provided by the church, and a flask of bourbon was discreetly passed from hand to hand among the men out in the yard. It almost seemed like a party, in a way. People gathered just to stand and stare at the house, as if maybe they were thinking that they might be able to take something for themselves from the sight of it, as if some kind of a serious lesson might be about to be learned.

A roadblock was set up on the highway. Search dogs scrambled in the ditches. Straining at their leashes, they nosed the piled leaves. Bulletins came up on the radio and updates were aired on the news and flyers were stapled to telephone poles all up and down the streets of that town as well as of others nearby. But already by then the girl was long gone. She'd been taken, and that was about as much as anybody knew.

———

Jolie followed Rafe into the house, and he sat down at the kitchen table and popped open a beer that he'd helped himself to out of the refrigerator. She stood near him; she touched his knee with her fingertips; she studied the round toe of his boot. She was afraid to move.

"You can stay here," the fat woman was telling him. "For as long as you need to," she went on. "I guess I owe you at least that much."

Her gestures were expansive. She reached out and pressed her soft white hand, dimpled, to the side of his face; her palm cradled the curve of his jaw, and at the same time she weaved the fingers of her other hand into the slight fall of his straw-colored hair.

He lifted his bottle of beer and took a long swallow. His eyes filled, tearing from the beer's sudden hard bite. He lit a cigarette and blew out smoke, which Jolie waved away with the flat of her open hand.

Jolie was given her own room to sleep in upstairs. It was not next to the kitchen. It was bigger than a closet. There was a bed with tall, carved posts and there was a window above and behind it, framed on the outside by a sprawl of climbing vines. There were two paintings on the wall; one was of an ocean and a beach, the other was of mountains and turning trees. The old carpet on the floor was thin, its backing worn through brownly, as if the ground itself were seeping and rising up into the dark green pile and faded rose pattern on top. There were fresh flowers nodding in the blue glass of a fluted vase on the dresser. There was a radio. There was a mirror, crazed with silvery, glittery cracks like worm tracks. There were glass knobs on the drawers in the dresser. The curtains at the window were delicately patterned lace. The window was open; there was a hole torn in the screen.

She considered this; she poked the tip of one finger through. A June bug on the inside sill jumped once, scrabbling, and then within its hard brown shell it was still. Jolie lay in the dark under a thin summer quilt in the bed in that room that she'd been told would be her own now, in that house in the shadowed woods. She studied the gloom beyond the dark lenses of her sunglasses as she listened to the voices of the two grownups in the yard outside her window.

He was telling the woman his story, it seemed. Explaining to her how he'd come to be back here again, but Jolie wasn't hearing what he said. The woman was quiet as she listened, and then her voice chimed. She asked him a question. His answer was brief. He laughed once. She laughed back, a yelp. She struggled to her feet, groaning, and she came inside for a moment, then went back out into the night again. The screen door slapped shut after her, twice. Once coming, once going. There was music playing softly, a fluid trill of piano notes that drifted lazily on the warm night air.

The two adults were sitting close together in chairs on the grass. The old broken-down barn building loomed in the shadows behind them. Their voices rose up to Jolie's ears and they were no more than a murmur, soft and low, broken only now and then by the wild high whacking sound of the woman's sudden laugh. The creaking of the crickets seemed like something soothing to Jolie. The woods all around on every side and overhead too, their branches arching, closed in, and she was grateful for their shadow, for their darkness and their cover, where it seemed to her now that she belonged.

ONE

Amok in Rampage

IT WAS IN THE SWELTER OF THE SECOND SUMMER AFTER their father's death, when Glen was ten and his sister Claire was just about to turn thirteen, that an elderly woman ran amok in Rampage, Iowa. At least that was how Madlen Cramer described it to her children, and those were the words she used—running amok. At first Glen thought that what his mother was talking about was the mud, because that was how the old woman's body was found—she was curled up in the ditch like a sleeping child, nestled into the hammock of wet ground with one hand fisted in the grass against her cheek, her quilted bathrobe filthy and sopping, her legs and feet bare, her hair snarled and mud-caked, and the whole of her blanketed by enough weeds and leaves and debris that she might have been overlooked altogether. It was Claire who explained to her brother that no, it was just that the woman went crazy in the storm, that was what the amok part was.

The woman's name was Evelyn Frye. She wasn't anyone that Glen and Claire Cramer knew; they'd neither one of them ever talked to her, not even to say hello. They'd only seen her from a distance once, standing in her side yard with her hands on her hips, her bony bare arms bent outward and a thin cotton dress hanging limply from her frame as if she were a wire hanger. When they drove past she was looking upward at the sky, watching the chalky contrail of a jet that coursed across it and moving Claire to comment that that was probably the most exciting thing that had happened there in Rampage all that day. All that week, in fact. All that year.

Behind Mrs. Frye a line of tangled sheets flapped like the frantic wings of wild white birds, and Madlen tried to counter her daughter's sarcasm with the observation that there were few pleasures greater than sleeping on a bed made up with sheets that had been dried outside in the sun and fresh air.

Claire only sniffed and looked away. She was not about to let her mother think for even a minute that she could be so easily cajoled into acting happy about having to spend a month at her grandfather's house in Iowa instead of off at sleepaway camp in the high sierras with her friend Anne Pence.

Anne had groaned in commiseration when Claire told her about the change in plans, even though the truth that Claire was not ready to admit to anyone yet was that she had been in a way partly grateful for it. She hadn't been so sure that she was going to be able to tolerate the commotion of what Anne had been telling her camp life was like. Sleeping in a cabin in the midst of so many unknown girls seemed somehow treacherous to her, for one thing. And for another, the mere thought of so complete a separation from her mother and her brother had filled Claire with a dark feeling of dread that pounded in her blood and threatened to strangle her with fear.

Although on the other hand the one thing that Claire desperately wanted, almost as much as she wanted not to be left alone, was to be allowed to pick herself up and get on with her life again, to move forward into it and put the hard fact of her father's accident and absence behind her, let it become just as much a part of her past as her first day of kindergarten and the day he taught her how to swim. Because since that night when her father died, time had seemed to Claire Cramer to have somehow stopped. And there she was, stuck, an ant in amber, standing still and locked in place, because she wasn't able to see how it might be possible for her to go forward. And there was no way either to go back. Overnight, it seemed, Claire had lost track of herself. She wasn't who she'd always been anymore. Now she was someone else, a stranger, a girl whose mother was a widow—spidery word—a girl whose father had not only died but had been killed, in a car accident that was not altogether not his fault, a girl whose family had by this fact been forever and all time harmed, marked as clearly as if they'd had scars that marred their faces.

Claire would say that the worst of it for her was that she wasn't sure she knew much at all about this new girl that she'd become—the one who had her name, the one who looked away, who avoided questions, who avoided eyes, liable to be either sullen and sarcastic or suddenly strangled by indifference and at the same time fighting back an inexplicable rising fear. But, she reasoned, if Claire herself didn't know who she was, well then, who in the world did?

When she'd told Anne's mother that she'd be going to Iowa

instead of to camp, she hadn't mentioned her father, or that her parents had grown up together there. She'd only said that she and her mother and brother would be staying for a month in the house they called the Riverhouse with her grandfather, who was called Deem although his real name was Tim, and Ruth, who was his new wife and was younger than Claire's mother and was expecting a baby soon. Mrs. Pence's response had been to raise an eyebrow and comment that surely no one could blame Madlen for wanting to get out of California for a few weeks, for wanting to go home. Anne herself had simply looked puzzled, her frizzed red hair framing her freckle-splattered face, as if she didn't know what Claire was talking about.

"Iowa?" she'd said. "Potatoes?" she'd asked.

"No," Claire had answered, frowning, "pigs and corn."

To get from the airport in Linwood to the Riverhouse in Rampage, you have to skirt the larger city, drive past the car lots and the strip malls on the northeast side of town, into the black fields along Highway 16, east toward Chicago, until you hit the four-way stop signs at Highway 10. There you turn north and keep on going, up and down the small hills and across the rolling creeks until you come to the unmarked county road near the little gated Rampage cemetery, where you take a right, heading east again now, and at the fork just past the sign that points to a sandy area of the river known as Sugar Bottom, you hold to the left. In a while you will be crossing over the old iron bridge at the Rampage River, and by then the town of Rampage itself will begin to be in sight.

Madlen knew the way without having to think about it—along that winding asphalt road toward what she still, in spite of how many years she'd lived elsewhere, called and thought of as home.

"The river, the river, the roaring Rampage River. If you can't sing a rhyme and sing it on time, we'll throw you in the river."

It was hard to tune in to any good radio stations so far outside of Linwood, and in the silence of the rented car the old half-forgotten chorus that she and Haven and Rafe used to sing was rattling insistently in her head.

"Old King Cole was a merry old soul and a merry old soul was he. He called for his pipe and he called for his bowl and he threw them in the river."

Glen, in the front seat next to his mother, looked at her, startled, when she began to sing the song out loud, softly. Claire, in the back, frowned and squeezed her eyes shut as if the sound of Madlen's voice pained her, then turned and gazed out the window, with the book that she'd been reading closed in her lap, one gnawed finger tucked in to keep her place, her gaze distant, attention lost, her chin cupped in her hand.

"Do you remember the song, Claire?" Madlen asked, catching her daughter's eye in the rearview mirror. In places the highway ran right up alongside the river, but it flowed the other way, so they were traveling against the current, and it seemed to Madlen that she was having to struggle and fight to make her way back.

Claire turned and raised one eyebrow in her Pence-appropriated way. "I don't think so, Mom," she answered, her face infuriatingly placid, covering up the roil of her fear and expressing her disdain by way of her indifference, without either a smile or a sneer. And then she turned back to gazing out her window again, as if the passing flat fields and bowed fences and sunsplashed farmhouses and silos and barns might be together the most absorbing scenery she'd ever encountered in the world and she didn't want to miss a bit of it. Her sigh fogged the window glass for a moment, then it was gone.

"The river, the roaring Rampage River. If you can't sing a rhyme and sing it on time, we'll throw you in the river." Madlen was picturing Haven's hands grasping her legs at the ankles and Rafe with a hold on her wrists as together they swung her back and forth between them over the grass, while she laughed and screamed for them to stop.

She'd been driving so fast that the scenery was a blur, and when Glen shut his eyes it felt as if they'd maybe left the ground. With the radio off there was hardly any sound, only the engine's steady hum and a whistle of the wind that was blowing through the cracked-open window as they skimmed along the rolling road, over the flat black-topped surface on its long straight infinite-seeming line, sailing between the blurred fields—grass and hay and neatly rowed plantings of soybeans and corn.

Madlen slowed to bump up over the rugged hump of the railroad tracks, and then they were crossing the river on a black steel webwork bridge that arched up high between two stone-strewn banks. It was Glen who saw the sign first, white letters on black: RAMPAGE. POP. 1498.

Claire didn't think she'd ever been in anyplace so small.

Sunlight glared on the white concrete streets; heat was a shimmer on the surface of the road. Glen rolled his window down and leaned his head out into the hot wind, felt it ruffle his lank black hair. Shop windows along a brief block of stores reflected the sun's white light in the squares of their wavery glass. Outside one house a couple of old men were sitting heat-dazed in a pair of chairs, gazing at the road, and they turned their heads together to watch and consider as the Cramers' car crawled by.

When they drove past what looked like it might be a castle—blocks long, with high stone windowless walls, machicolated parapets, rounded turrets, and wind-furled flags—Glen craned to see.

"What is it?" Claire asked her mother.

"The reformatory," Madlen answered. Then shook her head and added, "Never mind."

The streets of the town were shady, quiet, lined with houses and sidewalks, tall trees, straight cement driveways split by rectangles of wild grass. Some bare-bottomed small children played in the high bright rainbow-sparked fan of a sprinkler's glittery spray, squealing, legs churning, hands waved up over their heads high. A man out mowing his lawn looked up and shaded his eyes to watch as the car cruised slowly by, through the town and out of it, and then they were on blacktop again.

There was Mrs. Frye's small white house, set up like a cake on a plate at the top of its rise of grassy lawn and shaded on one side by a huge, shaggy willow whose switches swept the ground. And there was Mrs. Frye, standing in her yard. The sheets were flapping on the line behind her. A jet plane arced across the sky.

Mrs. Frye lived alone, and she'd kept mostly to herself after her husband passed away—dead of a heart attack at forty-five—many years earlier. Unlike his wife, Mr. Frye went peacefully, in his sleep, sometime in the middle of the night, without a struggle, without even a cry, with the result that Mrs. Frye slept right through it. Later she spent some time trying to remember what her dreams had been that night. As well as wondering why she hadn't known what was happening to him until hours after it was over, when she woke, disoriented because it was already light outside the windows, full daylight, long into the morning, and he was still there in the bed beside her, he hadn't moved. In the twenty-five years of their marriage to each other, this would have been the first time that such a thing had happened; not even on the morning after their wedding night had Mr. Frye slept in past dawn. Because there was always work to be done and he'd be up and dressed and on his way outside to do it. It wasn't until she tried to rouse him, pulled on his shoulder and rolled him over onto his back, that she realized her husband was dead. He lay there next to her unmoving, his eyes open, jaw hanging, as if he'd looked at his own death coming for him in the dark and been amazed by what he'd seen. But the doctor explained to Mrs. Frye later that it was only a reflex she was seeing, a tightening of the man's stiffened muscles—Mr. Frye's eyes had opened and his jaw had dropped sometime after he was already dead and not at the instant before.

It had taken a moment for the understanding of what was wrong with her husband to sink in, and when it did Mrs. Frye panicked, reared away from him, struggled to free herself from the twisted sheets. She gasped for breath, horrified not only by the fact that he was dead but even more by the knowledge that he'd been dead for a while, while she was asleep, oblivious, beside him.

She was left childless and without much else to call her own either, only what little was left over of their meager savings after the funeral expenses, some personal possessions, clothes and furnishings, along with the seven hundred acres of farmland that had been the sole source of their modest livelihood. She wasn't able to work the land by herself, and so over the years she sold all of it off, parcel by parcel, until the only thing that she owned outright was her house, not even the land that it stood upon. After Mrs. Frye's death the place would go unclaimed—it would stay abandoned and neglected, sagging steadily groundward over time until one winter it would collapse altogether and have to be bulldozed away in the spring.

Right now the awnings on the upstairs windows made them look to Glen like a pair of hooded eyes, watching him. Their glass panes glared back the sunshine at him, flashing light at the moment that Madlen's rental car swept past.

The woods on both sides of the road thickened, dark with leaves and undergrowth closing in. Madlen turned off at the limestone pillar with its brass plaque that read THE RIVERHOUSE and stopped. She looked through the windshield down the long driveway at the house—its broad brick face, tile roof, and dormer windows—watching it, expecting . . . well, she wasn't sure what. She rolled her window down and listened, heard the chitter of squirrels, birdsong, wind stirring in the trees.

Madlen and Haven had moved away from Iowa when the children were small, and she had not been back to visit since then. Now it seemed as if nothing about this place where she'd grown up had much changed. Her father was in the yard. His figure was so familiar to her—from that distance she could imagine that Deem was still a young man. Except that standing at the top of the porch steps was his new wife, Ruth, with her arms wrapped around herself. She was watching their car where it was stopped at the top of the drive. She said something to Deem, and he turned and looked and saw them there. He raised his hand and, grinning, waved.

Claire was impatient. "Mom, what are you doing?" she asked, her voice rising. Their eyes met in the rearview mirror.

"We're here," Madlen answered, and let her foot up off the brake. After everything that had happened, there she was now, finally: home.

You can feel it when a storm is coming; even before they start to mention it on the radio or over the television news, you know inside yourself it's on its way. A storm is not a sudden thing. It doesn't blow up out of nowhere. It starts slow and then it builds. It grows into something larger than itself and then it begins to move toward you and it gets even bigger, gathering up its strength as it nears. This is some of its appeal.

The storm that killed Evelyn Frye that summer came into Rampage from the southwest, brushing the edges of the old quarry cliffs, swirling out across the river and then bringing itself up high, traveling fast, so that when it got to her house up on its rise of land just this side of the limestone bridge, it was as severe as it was ever going to get.

First there is a hollowed-out-seeming stillness, a silence that's started to seem like a sound by the time you notice it, an emptiness that hums and roars and makes your teeth ache in your head. By then the sky will have begun to darken. It will close itself down over the land like an upturned bowl, glower bluish and yellowish, then start seeping purple and green. It's best to crack your windows to it, everybody knows this, it's the advice they always give you on the news, between the watches and the warnings. That's supposed to keep the whole house from exploding out against the low pressure that's been brought on by the full-blown blast of the wind.

Evelyn Frye knew this. She'd lived in Rampage all her life,

and so she knew what to do. She knew that she should go down into her basement and take shelter in the southwest corner there, but that isn't what she did. She stayed put upstairs instead, and she listened to the thing as it approached her. Like a train coming, is what people who live to tell it always seem to say—a steady, growing roar. She raised the shades in the front room and pulled back the curtains in the bedroom, maybe to try to get a look at it. Then, wresting open the latches, she lifted up every single one of those old-fashioned double-hung windows front and back all over the whole house. Mrs. Frye didn't only crack a couple of them for safety's sake, she went ahead and opened each window wide, and she knocked out all the screens besides, so that later what it looked like was that instead of trying to keep her house from blowing up in the storm, maybe what she was actually doing was inviting the wind right inside.

And inside it came to her, too. It surged around in the rooms, knocking over furniture and toppling lamps and breaking dishes, while outside in Rampage the sirens wailed and the trees were tossed and cracked and some of them altogether brought down. The rain swooped in next, following along like an afterthought to the wind. It splattered Evelyn Frye's bedroom curtains, drenching them. It puddled on the linoleum in the kitchen and flooded the dining room and soaked into the hallway rug. Outside, lightning lacerated the sky and the thunder rolled along on top of it, echoing off and dying out across the far fields like a barrage of bombs.

Sheriff Tom Nicholls speculated afterward that most likely what happened then was that there in the midst of the worst of the storm, Mrs. Frye became confused. After a while it must have got so bad inside her house that she couldn't tell the difference anymore, in the dark and with all that noise, between what was outside and what was in. Maybe she was trying to get her windows shut again. Maybe she'd changed her mind. Maybe she'd realized the seriousness of her mistake.

She struggled with the door, in her bathrobe and her slippers, trying at the same time to keep the robe from flapping open— she would have been naturally discreet that way, the way that older women often are. Her hair would have been blown free from the pins and curlers on her head, and the rain would have been drumming in at her. She was deafened by it, made blind.

She was on the porch and thought she was inside the house. She went down the steps, believed it to be the cellar. She flailed and staggered outside in the yard, was turned around and around, disoriented and lost.

By the time it was all over, by the time the storm had moved on and the wind had died down, its pure fury spent, when it was only the rain still pouring and the thunder distant and low, by then Mrs. Frye was not able to understand anymore where she was or why. The trees around her didn't seem to be the same, the land did not look right to her, she couldn't see her house anymore, she wasn't able to find it in the dark with no lights, no moon, not even stars because they were all of them hidden from her by the overcast, the thunderclouds, the fog, and the rain.

All the electricity for miles and miles around had popped out, and the only light that came to her was from the Rampage Reformatory, which had its own generator. Mrs. Frye tried to head for that glow, thinking that at least it was something, even if she could no longer be sure exactly what.

As the Rampage weekly paper quoted Sheriff Nicholls after-ward, "She didn't make it far." She slid off the road into the ditch and lost her slippers in the mud. She was tired, maybe. She was old. What reason did she have left to live? She let herself fall back against the ground, she allowed it to hold and cradle her, she closed her eyes and she opened her mouth and she drowned.

Madlen was in her old room upstairs in the Riverhouse, and she was listening to the radio, trying to keep track of the weather bulletins—tornado watches and warnings that were out all over the state—trying to remember which counties were where—Polk, Johnson, Keokuk, Linn—when the storm hit. Deem had gone back out to Cedarcrest after dinner, and Glen and Claire were downstairs watching television. Ruth, looking weary, had already gone to bed. When the electricity snapped off and the sirens in town started to howl, it was Ruth who led the way through the house, with Madlen and the children stumbling along after her in the dark, through the dining room and into the kitchen, then on down farther, to the basement. Glen had a flashlight with him, and he was shining it into his own face, widening his eyes and baring his teeth, hoping to make his sister screech. After everyone had settled into what had been decided was most likely the southwest corner—Madlen standing in the middle of the room turning around and around with her hands on her hips, trying to remember and get her bearings, and Ruth next to her looking up at the ceiling, pointing out that the front door was that way and so Indian Hill Road must run that way, north and south, right?—then Glen said that he'd like to see a real tornado, face to face. Madlen's mouth hardened, and Claire whacked at her brother's head with the back of her hand, but he ignored them both.

The windows in the Riverhouse basement were high up in the wall, at the level of the ground, and the window wells were filled with leaves, so it was hard to see out. They could hear the rain pouring down, and the wind was making the house creak and groan above their heads. Claire had burrowed herself in snug between her mother and Ruth. Glen was on the end, and Madlen had an arm around him, but still he struggled free. He thought he'd like to try standing outside in the wind, he said, just to see how long he could maybe take it, how long he'd last before he was lifted up and tossed, like the tree limbs that got caught in the river and were carried off by its current. That was stupid, Claire said. But no, Glen answered, it was brave. It was liking how it felt to be afraid. Not just being afraid, but relishing the feeling of the fear itself. He just wanted to have a look at the storm, that was all. Probably he was only bluffing.

"Will you listen to that wind?" Ruth said.

It was blowing in three notes, one a high-pitched howling sound, another shrieking in the middle range, and the last a low deep rumbling noise, like the engine of a truck on the highway as it approaches the crest of a hill. Glen clambered up onto the shelf where his grandfather kept his tools. He just wanted to be at the window, he said, so he could look outside for a second and see. But Madlen didn't like the idea of that at all, and she was standing up behind her son, pulling at him and telling him to get down again before somebody got hurt. When he tried to kick her away with his foot, he knocked a jar of nails down onto the floor, and it shattered on the cement with a loud explosion at her feet. Then there was the crunch of her shoes on the glass and the rain still slamming down outside, and the wind's wild chord being sounded out all around them. Ruth was screaming and

Glen was whooping until finally Madlen found a way to wrestle him away from the window and back down into the corner again with her.

He sat between her and Claire then, but he had trouble keeping still and he kept squirming around and poking at them both with his elbows while they all four cowered against each other, listening to the wind as it finally began to die down.

The basement of the Riverhouse was dank and dark and it smelled like mildew and mud. The light from Glen's flashlight skimmed the slick cement floor, shining on the scattered nails and bits and pieces of glass from the shattered jar.

"What in the world, Glen?" Ruth kept asking. "What did you think you were going to do?"

She had one hand spread out over her swollen belly, was palming it like a pumpkin. Ruth was almost eight months pregnant, and her baby was going to be an uncle, ten years younger than his own nephew and thirteen years younger than his niece. Madlen still had some trouble accepting the fact that her stepmother was more than two years younger than herself.

"I just wanted to see it, is all," Glen said.

The limestone wall of the basement was cold and sweating at their backs. Over their heads the big house seemed to be swaying, rocked by the wind and creaking like a boat. Glen was running his light over the shelf of garden preserves on the side wall, and the jars winked back at him, packed with dark and floating pickled things. He scanned the whole of the cellar, throwing shadows, illuminating the washing machine and the dryer and the clothesline and pins and the toilet in the corner and the laundry basket on the floor, and the rickety-seeming stairs with some junk piled up underneath—canvas cots and the tent that he would find later and set up outside in the back yard and some broken lamps and empty picture frames and what looked like an old camp stove.

"I think the worst is over, maybe?" Ruth asked more than said, hopefully.

They all held still and listened. There was a bang and some thumping. Then the door at the top of the stairs was thrown open and filled with light, and Madlen could see her father's heavy shadow and his big shoes on the steps. He had one hand on the railing, and in the other hand he was holding a flashlight of his own.

Deem was calling out, "Hey, are you there? Ruth? Madlen? Everybody okay?"

The beam from his flashlight found them, first Madlen, then Glen, and when it came to Claire, Ruth gave another scream. Claire had her hand up covering her face, and when she brought her fingers down into the light, they were wet and dark with blood.

"Some storm," Ruth said after it was all over and they were upstairs in the kitchen again. The electricity was back on, and she was at the stove, warming some milk to help her calm down and get to sleep.

Deem had poured himself a glass of scotch. A film of sweat was shining on Glen's face. Madlen had cleaned out the cut on Claire's forehead and then given her a towel wadded around ice chips to hold against it, to keep the swelling down. There'd been some debate about whether she needed to have stitches, and Claire was relieved when she heard Deem decide not, even though she suspected that his conclusion had been drawn more for his own personal convenience than for any long-term well-being of hers.

He lit a cigarette and sipped at his drink and sat back. On a napkin on the table was the tiny moon-shaped sliver of glass that he'd extracted with the tweezers from her brow. She looked at him, her grandfather, from under hooded eyes. She noted his broad wrists and gnarled hands, the black lines of dirt under his nails. He wore the wedding ring that Ruth had so recently given him, a thin gold band whose simple luster seemed oddly elegant in contrast to the rugged knuckles of his battered hand. His smell was of wet grass and sour sweat, cigarettes, and the amber-colored whisky that he drank. Claire decided right then that she didn't trust him, not completely.

He was talking about dead birds. Sparrows, to be exact. Small brown feathered bodies that he and his assistant, a young man named Scott, had been finding in the grass and the gardens where he worked, at Cedarcrest Retreat. They didn't know yet what was killing the creatures, but something was. Poison? Disease? Maybe it was the wind, Ruth suggested. Maybe the storm had blown them down out of their nests in the trees. Which Claire thought was a stupid suggestion, since Deem had already said that they'd been finding the bodies before tonight, since even before last week.

It was a puzzle and a problem, and Deem seemed to be taking it personally. If the birds were being poisoned, then by what? Or whom? And if it was disease, then how far was it likely to spread? To other animals? To humans? The grounds at Cedarcrest Retreat were Deem's responsibility, he said, and that included not only the grass on the lawns and the trees in the orchard, the flowers and vegetables in the gardens and the seedlings and plants in the conservatory, but also the birds and squirrels and rabbits and gophers and whatever other indigenous wildlife might have chosen to make those grounds their home. The doctors took care of the patients who came to the retreat to be cured of whatever it was that ailed them, and it was Deem's job to take care of the natural surroundings that were to be an integral part of that cure. At least, that was what the arrangement had been for more than thirty years. Until recently, when it had slowly, almost imperceptibly, started to change.

In the dark it was hard to tell, Deem said, just how much harm had been done outdoors by the storm. He'd have to go back out there first thing in the morning to see, before he'd know for sure. He could get Scott to help him with the cleanup. A couple of branches down maybe, at the worst. Some of the newly planted seedlings might have to be replaced.

It hadn't looked like there was any damage to the buildings, though, and that seemed to be a relief. The patients and the staff had taken refuge in the basement, same as here. Deem had begun to wonder, though, whether anyone but him would have really minded it all that much if the wind from this storm had been strong enough to blow the conservatory down. They'd probably have been glad to be rid of it that easy, Deem said. The maintenance on it had got to be almost more than it was worth.

Ruth resisted this. She waved a hand at her husband and said that that was only Deem's pride talking now, not anything that was in any way the truth. Because the conservatory was beautiful, wasn't it? Nobody could deny that. It was an architectural work of art, first of all. Like a wedding cake, three rounded tiers of white mullion and beveled glass. It was valuable as a landmark, at the very least. And, she argued—cheeks reddened, green eyes bright as grass—no one who had really seen the place, no one who had walked along the strange meander of its brick paths, no one who had experienced the thriving leafy greenness of it, could want to see it destroyed. Could they? By man or nature or God, any one. There was God there in it, wasn't there? And nature? And man?

But that was precisely what the problem of it was—this was what Deem insisted that the doctors, with their charts and pills and dosages and blood work, would have said. A problem complicated by humanity instead of simplified by science. The Cedarcrest conservatory had been built by psychiatrists who believed in analysis—whose faith was in talk, in composure, in beauty, as a cure. It was a huge and green and thriving place, and with its labeled flowers and plants in pots and trays, it was a place of edification, meant to bring beauty and serenity and health to the patients. But lately the doors to the conservatory were kept locked most of the day and the patients were told to stay out. The doctors seemed to have abandoned the idea of analysis. They didn't find anything concretely palliative about beauty or tranquillity or peace anymore. They'd changed their tack. Now they seemed to be ready to put their faith in the firm results that they had been getting with medication. The patients were slower, calmer, more controlled. The problem seemed to be merely a matter of chemicals. Deficiencies. Diet. Drugs.

And so all that left for Deem to do was simple grooming: he was to mow the lawns and keep the dandelions and the crabgrass from taking over, and that was pretty much it. Maintenance. He hated it. And, he admitted, he was having trouble finding a way to accommodate himself comfortably to such a profound philosophical change. It seemed to be the end of an era, and maybe he should just admit it: his time at Cedarcrest Retreat was past. He was beginning to wonder whether what was required of him now was that he gracefully retire, before they had a chance to fire him or ask him to quit. Maybe he ought to let Scott take over, he said. Stay at home with Ruth and the baby. Be a full-time husband and father. Take life easy for a while.

With this Ruth, smiling, sipping at her mug of warm milk, didn't disagree.

The next morning Deem drove out to Cedarcrest to check on the gardens and grounds while Glen went down into the cellar to rummage around in the junk that he'd seen piled and forgotten under the stairs and bring up the old pup tent. He wanted to pitch it at the edge of the yard, in the shade of the trees, right then, but Madlen held him back. He'd have to wait for Deem to get home and help him with it.

It was Ruth who suggested that they pass the time until then by going to the river. She'd been thinking that this was something Glen might enjoy. They might find the river on the rampage that it had been named for, swollen and out of control, running fast and hard from the downpour that had been brought in by the storm the night before.

"That would be something to see, wouldn't it?" she asked.

Claire already had on her bathing suit and she'd dragged an aluminum lounge chair out onto the grass of the side yard, where the sun would be best at that time of the morning. She'd rubbed a mixture of baby oil and iodine onto her arms and legs, and her skin glistened with it. She had a portable radio and her book and a glass of iced tea. She was not about to go on a walk.

"Oh, go on and get dressed and come with us, why don't you?" Madlen said, standing over her. "It might be fun."

Claire looked at her mother. "Because I don't want to, okay?" She put on her sunglasses and closed her eyes and lay back. The bathing suit was one piece, dark blue, and it was an old one, too small for her that summer—its straps pinched her shoulders, its neckline was low across her breasts, and its legholes rode high, snug on her buttocks and hard hips.

It was late July, and hot already, even in the morning. In summer in Iowa it was likely to be hot in the middle of the nighttime, too, didn't matter that there'd been a storm.

Ruth was standing on the porch with her hands folded over her belly. She narrowed her eyes at the sky. "We'd love to have your company, Claire," she said. She was smiling, or still squinting into the sun in such a way that it made her expression look like it might be a smile.

Claire lifted her glasses and gave Ruth a look, then let them fall back down on her nose again. Glen was making monkey faces behind Ruth's back, but Claire didn't respond.

Madlen followed Ruth inside, to put on shoes.

Glen sat in the grass near his sister and fiddled with the radio until Claire sat up and snatched it from him. "Fuck off, okay? Just leave me alone?" She tugged at the tight crotch of her suit.

"You ought to come along with us, you know," he said. "It's something to do. And you can get a suntan while you walk, instead of just lying here."

"You got any cigarettes?" she asked.

He grinned. "Maybe."

"Let me have one, then."

"What'll you do for me?"

She sighed and rolled over onto her stomach, rested her head on her folded arms. "Nothing," she told him. She bent her knees and entwined her feet up in the air behind her.

He reached into the pocket of his shorts and brought out a plastic bag with several partially smoked cigarettes in it. He'd found them in the woods. There had been a whole pile of them on the path just past the back yard. Seemed like somebody had stood there smoking, watching the house or something, he thought, but when he said so to his sister she answered that it was probably just Ruth sneaking off into the woods for a smoke so Deem wouldn't know that she hadn't really quit.

He dangled the bag in front of her face. "Come on with us, Claire, and you can have some of these," he said.

"That's disgusting," she answered, and turned her head away.

He shrugged. "It's better than nothing," he told her. "Take 'em or leave 'em."

Claire hoisted herself up onto her elbows and took the bag from him and examined it. Some were almost whole. "All of them, then," she told her brother, sitting up and wrapping the bag in her towel.

Glen bounded up onto the porch and picked up her sneakers and her shorts. "Deal," he said, and dropped the clothes down on the grass beside her chair.

She stepped into the shorts, stood, and zipped them up. Her legs were long and straight. She slipped her feet into her canvas shoes, ran her fingers through her short white hair, and, hip cocked, folded her arms across her stomach. "Why are we doing this again?" she asked.

"Dad helped build that bridge," Glen said. "The one we're going to."

She shrugged. "So what?"

"Well, don't you want to see it?"

He clambered up onto the porch rail and balanced himself there. He was going to stand in the middle of the bridge and lean out over the water, he told his sister. Get lost and dizzy from the sheer power of the current, from the sight of its wild flow.

"You're crazy, Glen," Claire said, adjusting her sunglasses again.

"Thanks." He grinned. And then let go, pushed off from the railing, arms raised, hands high, as he flew, fell, was caught by the solid ground.

The darkened rooms inside the Riverhouse where Madlen had gone to get her shoes were silent and chill. The drapes had been drawn shut against the sun outside, and a fan was blowing somewhere—its deep hum was distant and soft, as if maybe it belonged to someone who was distracted and lost in thought. The house itself had always seemed to Madlen to be poised, watching, as if it might have been expecting in its stillness that something was just about to happen, some action was just about to be taken, and the place only had to wait for it, like a darkened stage, patient and unmoving, suspended in the breathless pause between events.

When she mentioned this to Ruth, the younger woman just looked at her, blankly at first, and then she shrugged and shook her head and frowned.

"But don't you ever feel it, Ruth?" Madlen wanted to know. "It's always so quiet in here, isn't it?"

Ruth misunderstood. "I don't know what you're trying to tell me," she said. "What do you want me to do?"

Surprised, Madlen answered, "Do?"

"Did you want me to change it? Get some new furniture? Put down some different rugs?"

"No, I—"

"Because your father wouldn't stand for that, you know. He likes it how it is."

Madlen nodded. "I know."

"There isn't any reason for me not to give Deem what he wants, is there?" Ruth asked.

"Nothing that I can think of," Madlen replied.

She supposed that her family's visit must seem like an intrusion to Ruth, but hadn't this house once been her home, too? She tried to explain it, how when she was a little girl growing up here, the objects in this house had sometimes felt to her to be alive. How she'd often thought that when she turned her back on a room, its furnishings conspired against her, tried to tease and trick her so that when she looked again the placement of her mother's things in it would be ever so slightly altered, just ever so subtly out of place. She could close her eyes and hear the whisper of movement, she thought—fabric rustling, springs creaking. She was able to imagine a commotion that was being carried on out of her sight whenever she looked away.

"Is that crazy?" she asked Ruth.

Ruth wrinkled her nose and nodded. "Yes, Madlen," she answered. "You know, I think maybe it might be."

Beyond the beveled glass of the front door was the foyer, with its polished parquet floor and hanging chandelier. Madlen's reflection gazed back at her from the mirror above the table on the opposite wall. She'd lost weight since Haven's death, and her face had begun to seem too angled and sharp—the high cheekbones and strong jaw of what she'd always been told was her good bone structure looked more like an aging gauntness to her now, a hardening of her features that felt ugly and caused her to grimace at herself and turn away.

Ruth had stepped out of the foyer and into the dining room to the right, where the old marble-topped breakfront stood solidly against one wall and the huge walnut table, opened up and gleaming and surrounded by a careful placement of frail cane-bottomed chairs, took up the whole rest of the room. Ruth had arranged a large vase of flowers from the Cedarcrest conservatory on a doily at its center, bringing a wanton splash of color into the otherwise dreary room. As she walked past it, her leather sandals clapped against the bare wood floor. Even pregnant, Ruth was graceful in her short skirt and sheer flowered blouse. Although, Madlen noted with some satisfaction, the baby's weight was causing her to waddle some. She pushed through the swinging door into the kitchen and was gone.

To the left of the front foyer was the living room, with its green velvet sofa and high-backed wing chairs and a glass-topped coffee table littered with trinkets—bits and pieces of breakable bric-a-brac that Ruth had collected and put there. Looking at this, Madlen realized that what was really irking her about the situation with her father and Ruth was not that there was a baby on its way but that Ruth seemed to think that nothing else in their lives was going to have to change.

Just past the living room was the cozy alcove that Madlen's mother had dubbed the music room because its bit of floor space was just large enough to hold the upright piano and its bench against one wall. Sunshine streamed in through the uncurtained panes of the bay window. Its seat was cushioned and cozy, and Grinnell had liked to nap there in the afternoons.

To one side of the music room was the screened porch, where the only sign of daily clutter was—newspapers and magazines and coffee cups and cereal bowls. On the table were spread the scattered pieces of the jigsaw puzzle that Ruth had brought out for Claire and Glen to work on. It was a scene of snow-capped mountains and a flower-strewn meadow and a running stream, and Madlen had looked up from the paper just that morning to see Ruth sitting with her chin in her hand, staring dreamily into its broken landscape.

"Maybe after the baby comes Deem will take some time off and we can travel," she'd said, and sighed.

I doubt it, Madlen had wanted to respond, but didn't. She'd never known her father to take time off from his work willingly.

She started up the stairs. The walls were lined with photographs—tintypes and black-and-whites in heavy square and oval frames, all of them of people from some branch of the family on Deem's side. They were all Maleks and Browns, many of them relatives who were only dimly remembered, if at all, even by Deem, and whose names and relationships Madlen didn't know. They stood posed with one foot up on the running board of an old car, or seated in a grinning half-circle around a fully laden picnic table, or lined up with all seriousness in front of an imposing brick building—a dark-haired man in spats and white pants and a broad-shouldered, double-breasted jacket, a frowning woman in a fur coat and black cloth hat, a pair of babies in matching eyelet-and-lace christening gowns, a grinning boy in baggy dark shorts, suspenders, and a wide-collared shirt. Madlen's grandfather, Robert Malek, stood behind his wife, Rose Brown, who sat in a chair with a baby, Deem himself, cradled in her arms. There were no pictures of Madlen or of Haven, none of the children, none of Grinnell.

But at the top of the stairs there was one last photo, which had been most recently added: in a plain black frame, it was the only full-color photograph in the bunch. This was a honeymoon shot of Ruth and Deem, and in it they'd been posed together at the railing of a covered bridge, by an accommodating passerby, Madlen supposed. They had their arms around each other, and their heads were turned toward the camera, cheeks pressed, faces smiling, hair recklessly windblown. Mr. and Mrs. Tim Malek. Ruth and Deem. This was one that Ruth herself must have hung.

The Riverhouse had always been called the Riverhouse, but it was only after Claire started talking that Madlen's father became Deem. Before that he was Tim Malek, and that was all. Madlen's mother had still been alive then and she'd insisted on being called by her given name, so she'd spent some time teaching Claire to say it correctly. Grinnell. Then Claire had toddled around the Riverhouse, calling out for Deem and Grinnell, disturbing all those quiet rooms in a way that Madlen herself had never dared to—upsetting tables, pulling down books, knocking over knickknacks, and standing in the hard heels of her thick-soled leather shoes on the delicate weave of her grandmother's antique cane-bottomed chairs—and Deem had got such a kick out of his new name, as well as of the sound of Claire's small voice saying it, that after a while he just naturally began to refer to himself as Deem too, and by now the name had stuck.

At first after Grinnell's death, Deem said he liked his solitude, but it wasn't very long before it got to him, the loneliness. What happened was that as much as he and Grinnell had not got along over the years that they were married, after she was gone Deem found that he couldn't help himself, he missed her. He was the first to admit it—he just did not like living alone.

So it was lucky for him that he met Ruth when he did. At the Knight Life, a bar in Rampage, where she was working as a waitress. He'd gone in for a beer after work, something that he never did when Grinnell was alive. Putting off going home to the empty house, he guessed. And she was so nice, interested in what he had to say about flowers. He started bringing them to her, even in the middle of winter, some bright bloom that would seem to take her breath away. Gardenias were her favorite. They'd filled up the whole bar with their smell.

And he would also say that he was lucky she agreed to marry him when he asked her to. And he was lucky again now that she was pregnant, too, because it seemed to him that he might be about to start his life all over again, fresh from square one. It was as if he had been granted the pleasure and the privilege of being able to live two lives in one, wasn't it? He'd been given a second chance, he liked to say. So what if there were thirty years between them? If she was only just being born in the year that he first went to work in the gardens at Cedarcrest? If when he and Grinnell bought the Riverhouse and moved into it, Ruth had hardly started school? So what?

Madlen stepped into the upstairs hallway. The door to the master bedroom at the top of the landing stood open. The bed had been left unmade. Under the window on Ruth's side, Madlen saw, was the old bentwood cradle that had once held Claire and after her Glen and years before that had held Madlen, and even longer ago than that had held Deem. It was an heirloom that had been in the Malek family for a whole stairwell wall's worth of generations.

Madlen turned away from this, toward what had always been her own room at the far end of the hall, passing along the way the empty bedroom that was meant to be the nursery for the new baby when it came. Already there was a crib set up in the corner near the door that led out to the sleeping porch, and a changing table stood against the wall, but for the moment the nursery was still a guestroom, and it was there that Glen and Claire had settled in for their stay, with cots out on the screened porch for them to sleep on. Clothes and shoes and books and bedclothes had been strewn around in such a mess that Madlen didn't want to have to look at it. She reached out and pulled the door shut, then hurried on past the black-and-white penny-tiled bathroom with its old-fashioned clawfoot tub and freestanding sink to the end of the hall, to the farthest back side of the house, where her room was.

Madlen didn't remember that she had ever been afraid, squirreled away so far from her parents. She could only recall feeling as if she'd been somehow trapped, held captive inside this house as she lay tucked under the covers in the dark, watching the clock on the table by her bed, waiting for it to get late enough and dark enough outside that she could slide her window open and, unseen, unmissed, slip away. Madlen's getting out of the house at night had only been made easier by the fact that her room was on the opposite side from her parents', just as her parents' absorption in themselves and in each other had made it simpler for her to get away with just about anything she wanted to.

Madlen had lied, and no one had caught her at it. She'd gone places she'd been forbidden to go, done things she'd been specifically told that she was not in any way to do. Such as swimming in the quarry. Such as wading in the river. Such as slipping onto the Rampage Reformatory property and venturing in as close as the last chainlink fence to try to get a glimpse of the prisoners there, maybe Haven's dad among them. And such as simply sneaking out in the middle of a summer night to meet up with Haven and Rafe in the woods. How often she'd opened the window and swung out onto the trellis and climbed down, dropped to the ground, and run off in the mere moonlight to find her two friends, who had hidden themselves away and were waiting for her at a designated spot amid the lacework shadows at the edges of the trees.

Madlen found a pair of socks in her suitcase and her running shoes on the floor beside the bed, and then she hurried back out of the room and downstairs and outside into the air.

They called it the Riverhouse, always had, even the brass plaque on the limestone pillar at the end of the driveway said so, but the house wasn't on the river, it was only close by, within walking distance—one mile straight out the back door and through the woods to the swinging bridge, farther than that if you were to take the road that rolled over the rise of land in front of the old Frye place. Longer that way, maybe, but easier going too, especially on a summer morning like that one, after there'd been a big blowing storm to clutter up the paths and make a mess of the woods.

They were out on the straight dirt access road that stitched a shortcut through the fields between Old Indian Road and Highway 10 at the easternmost edge of Rampage, within sight of the reformatory but still just shy of the driveway and the mailbox outside Mrs. Frye's place, far enough away that they hadn't noticed yet that all the windows in the little farmhouse had been thrown wide open. No gleaming glint of glass winking back the sunshine at them. Not even the shadowing of screens. Only empty space, gaping blank and blind. Like the eyes of Glen's turtle when it died, Claire thought.

Later Ruth would say that her baby came early because of the shock of what she saw, but the medical fact of it was that she had a weak cervix. At least, that was what Madlen believed.

Gnats swarmed in black clouds so you had to keep your mouth closed or maybe you'd by accident breathe them in. Pure protein, Glen said, smiling, hoping to shock the others with the idea that he might like eating bugs. Claire lagged behind, slapping at mosquitoes and waving off the gnats. The bugs were drawn to the cut on her eyebrow, Ruth said. Every now and then Madlen turned and waited for Claire to catch up.

"Come on, slowpoke," Glen called out to his sister.

She looked up at him and frowned, then began to run, all legs and knees, her head back and arms pumping at her sides, shoes squelching in the road's mud. Glen took off after her to catch up. Ruth crossed her arms over her belly and shook her head while Madlen smiled.

At almost thirteen, Claire Cramer was still a towhead blonde, just the same as her mother had been when she was a kid, but Claire was taller, leggier, than Madlen had ever been. The sun had bleached her hair almost to white, her skin was clear and easily tanned, her eyes were gray to almost colorlessness, and her eyebrows were so soft and fair that hardly any trace of them was to be seen there on her face at all. That summer her hair was as light as it had ever been. Before they left California, Madlen had suggested that she get it cut, because she knew it would be hot in Iowa, and Claire had come home with a trim that was at once boyish and chic, shorter even than Glen's.

According to Deem, his grandchildren were like two sides of the same coin, just the same as their parents had been before them. When Glen smiled he showed his teeth, white and small, gleaming in his face against a year-round brown that was further deepened now by exposure to the sun. His hair was black and straight, as Haven's had been, and he wore it parted on one side. Every time he leaned forward it fell into his eyes and he'd snap it back out of the way again, so often that it seemed to have become a nervous gesture. His eyes were blacker even than his hair.

He was wearing cut-off denim shorts with a white fringe that he fiddled with and one of Haven's old blue-and-black plaid flannel shirts, which had been washed so many times it was thin as a rag and faded and soft. He wore it unbuttoned over his hairless bare belly and chest. Somebody had torn the sleeves off and Glen's naked arms were brown and thin, stringy and strong but not exactly muscular yet. He was a scrawny kid. He wore rubber-toed hightop tennis shoes on his bare feet, untied so the laces were worn down and dragged the ground, wet and blackened by dirt. The smell of her son made Madlen catch her breath. Like old leaves or old fruit, sweat and dirt and ear wax and bug spray and sometimes, although he was more than likely to deny it, cigarette smoke.

They were at the top of the hill that rolled down to the river, above the place where the road crossed over it on the arched stone bridge that Haven and Rafe had both of them together helped build when they were kids. Ruth's reddish curls were like a halo of light around her head; the skirt of her yellow maternity dress billowed around her. The farm fields rolled off toward the horizon on both sides and behind her; the corn was silky and green. The trees in the distance were moving in some wind, gesturing gently and kindly, with a friendliness that was nothing at all like the fury that had been at the heart of last night's storm.

The road had dried to dirt at its crown, but there was still nothing but mud and muck at the shoulder and in the ditches on either side. Clouds bloomed on the horizon, white and cottony and without threat, as if maybe the storm's high wind had only been a dream and nothing at all that was ever real.

Claire stood in the road and waited for the others to catch up. She could see the mass of the reformatory building in the distance. With its limestone walls and turrets and its iron-barred windows, it looked like a castle or a fortress of some kind. She wondered what the storm must have been like for the inmates in their cells.

Glen had spotted a bottle half buried in the deeper weeds, and he scooted down to get it. He'd taken off his shirt and tied it around his waist. He was rummaging through the wet leaves and weeds for more bottles, and then his eye was caught by something shining and he was stepping toward it. Claire had started to get impatient; it was hot and getting hotter out there in the shadeless sun.

"Glen!" she called out.

But he seemed not to have heard her. He was bent over at the waist and poking at the mud with the toe of his shoe. He stood up straight then, with his hands on his hips, and he looked up at the road, and then he looked back down at the ground again, shaking his head.

"Shit," he said. "Shit. Shit."

"Glen!" Madlen shouted.

"What is it?" Ruth asked.

Claire put one hand up to shade her eyes, but all there was for her to see was Glen standing in the weeds and the grass and the leaves and the muck.

"Just come down here," he called. He was squatting now, with his hands on his knees. He reached out and picked up a stick and poked it at the ground. "Shit," he said again.

Ruth stayed up on the road while Claire followed her mother down the incline into the ditch. Her sneakers slid on the mud, and she put her arms out straight from her sides to keep her balance.

"What is it?" Madlen was asking Glen again.

He turned to her, squinting. "Just look," he said.

So Madlen and Claire looked, but at first they couldn't tell what it was that they were looking at. Some weeds. Some leaves. Some cloth. A slipper maybe. A foot and a leg and a robe, quilted, pink and blue. It was a woman, Claire realized then. Evelyn Frye, Madlen would tell her later. She was lying there on the ground, curled up as if she might have been sleeping, embraced by the earth with her bathrobe bunched up to her hips, her bare white legs mud-spattered and blue-veined. Her hair was snarled, muddied, and a mess. Dead, she was pressed against the earth, she was snuggled up and hugging it, her bony body seemed to have been folded into it. Glen poked at her with his stick again, but she didn't much budge.

Claire looked away, past Ruth, up toward Mrs. Frye's house where it sat perched there on its rise of lawn, and it was only then that she noticed that all its windows were agape. A tree had fallen through the roof of the narrow front porch, smashing it as if it had been nothing much more than a dollhouse toy. Ruth would say later that she guessed it was unlikely that Mrs. Frye would ever have been able to find her way back inside there again.

She ran amok. It happens sometimes, Madlen said. Deem could tell them, he'd seen it for himself firsthand at Cedarcrest, plenty of times. In fact, that was exactly why some of the patients had been sent there by their families in the first place, and it was also why some of them were kept there by their doctors in the second.

Evelyn Frye had died by drowning, within throwing distance of her own front door. And Glen and Claire agreed that what was most amazing about it was to think that you didn't need a river or a lake or a pond or even a puddle to drown in—you could just as easily be strangled lifeless by the simple-seeming rain.

TWO

That Drowning Sound

DEEM HAD SET THE PUP TENT UP ON THE FAR SIDE OF THE grass, in the shadows at the hem edge of the skirted trees. Glen had tried to talk Claire into sleeping out there with him, but she'd refused to take up his challenge, thereby proving herself to be what he accused her often of being—with a sneer borrowed from what he'd seen on the faces of some of the older boys in his class at school—which was a girl. What this meant, in the way that he said it, was that she was something other than what he himself was, she was something less than that, something soft and weak and easily damaged, a flower, maybe, fragile and frail and mysterious and strange, all turned in on herself and without any outward courage of her own. But she had managed to defy and outdo him, in her own most beautiful and mysterious and strange and inward-turned and infuriating way, because her sub-lime indifference was double again what his arrogant daring was.

She didn't care where she slept, she told him, matching his sneer not with a sullen twist of her lip but with the look that she'd spent time practicing in front of a mirror—her chin lifted, one eye fluttered half shut, the other open and its eyebrow arched. And she didn't care what he thought about it, either. She picked up her book and said goodnight and trudged upstairs to bed.

Now, standing at the back porch door of the Riverhouse and peering out through the screen at the darkness of the yard which sprawled out toward the trees beyond it, Madlen was trying to remember what it had been like to be a child here, with parents to be got away from and friends who waited for her to come to them in the woods. She leaned her forehead against the screen; she smelled its dusty metallic scent, touched and tasted it with the tip of her tongue. She thought that summer's flavor would always have to be this for her: rust.

Glen had his flashlight on, and when he shifted his position, turned over or raised himself up on an elbow, his shadow seemed to loom there against the slanted canvas tent wall, like a moth inside a lampshade, drawn to the light, about to be trapped there maybe by the sheer sear of its white heat.

"You think Glen'll be all right out there all night by himself?" Madlen asked.

Deem was slumped down in his big cushioned wicker chair, completely at ease, smoking a cigarette and sipping at his glass of whisky and ice. He had on a worn and wrinkled old pair of khaki work pants, grass-stained at the knees, big at the waist, and frayed at the hems, held up by a braided brown leather belt, and a blue work shirt with its sleeves rolled back against his wrists. Grinnell had hated to see him sitting around the house in his work clothes like that. She'd made him go upstairs when he came home and change into something clean before he sat down to dinner. But Ruth didn't seem to mind. His hand was curled around his highball glass. He leaned forward and tapped the ash off the end of his cigarette into the crystal ashtray on the table near his feet.

"Why wouldn't he be?" he asked.

"Sure isn't something he'd be likely to do in L.A.," Ruth said. "Is it?" She'd hardly ever been much farther away from Rampage than Linwood, except when she and Deem went to Los Angeles for a couple of days to be with Madlen after Haven's death. Southern California had seemed to Ruth then to be the altogether other side of the world. Far away and foreign. Hot and bright and crazy, teeming with immigrants and criminals.

Deem rattled the ice in his glass and studied it for a while before he took another swallow. Madlen wondered whether she should ask her father to make her a drink. Maybe it would help her get to sleep later, when she had to.

"Too bad Claire didn't want to stay outside with him," Deem said.

Madlen shook her head. "She's better off in here, I think," she said. She was exhausted. Her eyes burned and watered, felt burnished by grit.

"Well, I wish you'd come and help me with this, Madlen," Ruth said.

She was leaning forward over the glass-topped table and frowning at the fractured jigsaw puzzle's depiction of mountain, meadow, and stream. She held her chin in her hand. Her fingertips tapped at her teeth. She'd combed her hair off her face, swooped it up and pulled it back and fastened it into a twist with pins. She crossed her legs and flexed her bare foot and considered the pleasant sight of her polished toenails.

"No thanks," Madlen answered.

Claire had always been a bad sleeper. She'd been a colicky baby, and when she was a toddler she'd been awakened often by night terrors. As a young girl she'd been racked by wild dreams. Sometimes she'd get up out of her bed and roam the house in the dark, but since Haven's death that habit seemed to have stopped. Once Madlen had found Claire standing downstairs at the front door in her flowered flannel nightie and her bare feet, with her hair a wild white tangle on her head, and it looked as if she'd been trying to get the door unlocked so that she could open it and go outside. She was hunched over with her back bent like an old crone's, squinting like a blind woman in the pitch black, working at the door's lock with her thumb pressed against her fingers as if she were holding a key, turning her fist back and forth and back and forth. She didn't seem to know that it wasn't working for her, or to have any understanding of why. Madlen had whispered to her, reached out and turned her and without a struggle led her back upstairs to her bed, where she settled down, suddenly and deeply asleep.

When she was four she woke up screaming and gasping, shrieking when Madlen came hurrying into the room to get her. She flailed and screeched that she couldn't lie down on the sheets on her bed, she couldn't touch them, they couldn't touch her, the cloth was burning her skin or freezing her or scraping or bruising, it wasn't clear what, only that the feel of it hurt her in some impossible and indefinable way and she wouldn't wake up or settle down until Haven had scooped her into his bare arms and carried her down the hall to their own room, brought her into their own bed. He held Claire there, let her spread her small body out flat upon his—the breadth of his torso, his ribs, his chest, his skin cool and smooth—and only then did she calm and go back to sleep again. She lay sprawled upon her father with her flushed cheek pressed against the smooth flat surface of his skin, her mouth open, her eyes closed. Her breathing deepened and slowed. Haven had turned and looked at Madlen and he'd smiled and folded his hands in the small of Claire's back and closed his eyes and gone to sleep again himself. While Madlen curled up against him on his other side and listened to the two of them breathe.

Another time—later, she must have been almost ten—Claire found her way into her parents' bedroom without waking them. She crawled into her mother's closet and curled down inside behind the hanging skirts and dresses to bury herself in a pile of carelessly tossed shoes. When Madlen found her in the morning, Claire was sleeping with her hands slipped inside a pair of her mother's red patent-leather pumps. When Madlen said her name, Claire raised her head, and her face was blank, her eyes wide and mystified, and she lifted her hands up with those red shoes on them like flowers blooming on stems, and there was such an awkwardness, but still no recognition in her face at all, as if her mother were a stranger, as if Claire didn't know her, didn't recognize her, as if the girl didn't understand anything at all about what she was doing or where she really was.

Sparks of firefly flame blinked on and off in the deep shadows of the looming trees. Madlen glanced at Deem and saw that he'd been watching her, and she held his look for an instant before he drew on his cigarette and exhaled a cloud of smoke that engulfed his face and hid his expression from her again. He shifted in his chair, then settled back.

"Like mother like daughter, eh, Madlen?" he said. He turned to Ruth. "She used to wander around the house at night too when she was a kid."

Grinnell had called what Madlen sometimes did in the middle of the night sleepwalking, but the truth is, that wasn't what it was. Madlen had walked, but she hadn't been asleep. She'd been sneaking out, and most of the time she hadn't been caught. She'd learned which doors squeaked, which floorboards to avoid, which steps to skip. Her feet had moved so quietly from one room to the next that her parents almost never heard. She slipped into the music room and stood in the pool of moonlight that spilled in through the bay window's glass panes. She crept into the kitchen and helped herself to a snack of soda crackers and peanut butter and milk. All in silence. All so her mother wouldn't know. Then she mustered her courage, got braver and ventured farther, outside. Where she stood in the yard and stopped and looked back at her house and felt as if she might be outside herself in a way, like an observer of her own being, separated and apart. She'd had the uneasy idea then that she might be able to climb the trellis on the side of the house and peer into her own window upstairs to see her own self asleep and peaceful in her own bed there.

Madlen looked down at herself now—her white blouse and blue jumper dress, her long legs, slim ankles, bare feet—and it occurred to her that how she'd felt then was something like how she'd begun to feel about herself since Haven's death. As if she were an outsider to that event, and to her family, to her house, even to herself. As if she might look out the window right now and, without surprise, see her own smaller, younger self drop down onto the grass and run across the lawn and disappear into the shadows of the trees.

"You want something to drink, Madlen?" Ruth was asking.

Deem rattled his glass and handed it to her. "I'll have one more," he said.

"Maybe a weak one," Madlen said. "To help me get to sleep."

She looked up to see that her father was watching her again as, glasses in hand, Ruth padded out of the room. She frowned at him, annoyed. Asked, "What?"

He leaned forward, crushed out his cigarette, and sat back.

"I thought you'd want to know . . . ," Deem began, then shook his head, stopped.

Madlen watched him. Waited. "Know what?"

He sighed. "That Rafe Ramsay's back. He's got a little girl, and he brought her with him. There doesn't seem to be a wife. He's staying over there with Hannah Daggett, in the house at the Old Barn."

Madlen peered out at the lit tent and the dark trees beyond it. Her father wasn't telling her anything that she didn't already know. But she wasn't ready to tell him about Rafe yet, about how he'd written to her and called. Or that he'd sent her a necklace, a thin gold chain with an emerald pendant, and that she was wearing it now, hidden inside her dress because she didn't want her father to see it and ask questions but she didn't want to take it off either. Or that she'd stood naked in front of the full-length mirror of her bedroom and hooked the clasp at the back of her neck, then considered herself, worrying over her aging body, softened breasts and thickened thighs, her bare skin seemingly lined by the cracks in the crazed surface of the antique mirror.

"Madlen," Deem went on. He sat up, leaned toward her. "I think I know what you're thinking."

She smiled, shook her head. "What am I thinking, Daddy? Please tell me, because I'd sure like to know."

How like her mother she was, he thought. "Some things can't be changed," he said. "That's all. Some things can't be gone back on. Best just let what's been be."

"Now that's what you're thinking. That's not what I'm thinking."

"That's what I want you to be thinking."

"Oh, well, I'm not sure I can do that."

"Why not?"

She crossed the room and sat down on a chair near his. "You don't even believe in what you're saying. Why would you expect me to?"

"What's that supposed to mean?"

"It means, if you thought things couldn't be changed or started over, then what are you doing here, married to Ruth, about to have yourself another child?"

He looked at her, held her gaze. "You knew he'd be here."

She nodded. "He wrote."

"And you're planning to see him?"

"Why not? Why shouldn't I? He was one of my best friends once, wasn't he? Rafe and Haven. And now . . ." Her voice trailed off. She picked at the thin fabric of her dress, let it settle in the hollow of her lap. She had not been able to confide in her father that there had been any kind of trouble in her marriage to Haven before he was killed. But the fact was that what had once been the grace of their intimacy had grown awkward and bulky between them, had turned into a many-armed, clod-footed, jagged-edged contraption that they each kept bumping into, stumbling along, tripping over words and intonations as they went. That it had seemed simpler to Haven to avoid her altogether, to leave the house early and come home late, as he had done on the night when he was killed. This was the piece of information that Deem didn't have, because Madlen had not wanted to explain. It was the one part of the whole that she thought he wouldn't want to understand.

Ruth came back onto the porch with a tray in her hand. She handed out the drinks, then stood next to Deem's chair. He settled his hand on the shelf of her hip. As always, Madlen was struck by how unlike this her father's marriage to her mother had been. Or hers to Haven. Maybe because this one was still new.

In the years before his death, Haven and Madlen had seemed to be drifting apart, and she'd thought for a while that she could understand how this was natural and probably to be expected, because they'd known each other for so long. They'd been friends as children first and then lovers since they were in college. There had only been a few years, after Haven and his mother moved back to Linwood, when they'd lost touch. By then she hadn't seen Rafe anymore either. Daggett was dead, and Rafe had already been sent away to live somewhere else.

It wasn't until she was taking classes at Foster College in Linwood that Madlen ran into Haven again. He came to her like something from a dream then, emerging from a cloud of sidewalk steam and bus exhaust one frigid February afternoon—a tall, thin figure in a long dark coat hurrying through the busy late-afternoon traffic on Burlington Street, dodging cars as he crossed toward her against the light. She recognized him immediately, with his snow-powdered ink-black hair and the one long lock of it that still gashed his broad forehead and fell into his eyes. He snapped his head to toss it back, grinned and waved a fist at a honking car, then strode on without seeing or recognizing Madlen bundled up in a parka with her face veiled by the scrim of fur around its hood. She'd followed him for a few blocks, then stopped across the street to watch him turn up a walk and let himself into a square brick house whose rooms had been converted into student apartments. She wasn't sure why she didn't call out to him before the door closed and he was gone. Or why she didn't go up and knock and show herself and say hello. The timing wasn't right, she reasoned. She'd have to explain that she'd followed him. He might wonder why. She wasn't the same person that she used to be, when he had known her before, and neither, she supposed, was he. It just seemed too awkward. And what if he didn't remember her?

But then a few weeks later she was eating breakfast in the cafeteria of the student union and she looked up to see him at another table with his coffee cup poised halfway between its saucer and his lips, an expression of pleased disbelief and amazement on his face. How happy he'd been to see her. How eager he was to hear all about her: how she was and how she'd been, how long she'd been here, what she was studying, how her family was. His mother had a house on Forty-second Street in Linwood. Yes, she was still doing hair—she had a chair in a shop downtown. No, she hadn't remarried. He didn't know about his father—didn't care to know, to be frank about it. Ten years later, when he received a letter from the warden saying that the old man had been killed in a knife fight in the yard, he wrote back and told them to go ahead and bury him there, in the little cemetery on the Rampage Reformatory grounds.

Madlen had been drawn immediately to Haven's friendliness and openness, amazed at how easy it was to be with him again, as if no time had passed at all. They skipped their classes and spent the day together, trying to remember everything and recount it all, as if they thought they'd found in each other, like a scrap-book or a photo album, something of the essence of their own childhood, preserved. Their pairing had seemed so natural, there had seemed to be no friction in it: they'd fit together like a pair of puzzle pieces. They enjoyed telling their friends that they'd been playmates when they were kids.

He was studying mathematics and computers, which to Madlen was strange and mysterious stuff. The books he read and the ideas that he tried at first to share seemed unintelligible to her. After a while he didn't bother. It didn't matter. She didn't need to know.

After he graduated, Haven started sending off resumes to the data processing departments of companies in Southern California. That would be a nice place to live, wouldn't it? How strange it was to think now that when he'd first asked her to marry him, she'd said no. They'd been living together for a year already by that time, sharing a studio apartment above the Web, a down-town bar that was across the street from Haden's Furniture Store, within walking distance of the Foster College campus. A blue neon spiderweb spanned the broad space above the front door, and the light from it seeped up through their bathroom window so that if the door was left open, everything inside the place looked unreal, as if it were merely a projection of black-and-white TV.

Haven had been working part-time as a bartender at the Web and sometimes Madlen waited tables there. Two years behind Haven, she was still in school, but in a way it felt to her as if they were married already, living a real life, getting up to go to work or classes every day, bringing home their separate paychecks, paying bills and going grocery shopping and sleeping in on Sunday mornings. They had only had one thing that they fought about then, an argument that they got into with each other over and over again, until finally it turned out to be strong enough to just about break them up. Haven hated Linwood. He called it Deadwood, Iowa, and said it was the end of the world. Or the beginning, depending on how you looked at it. If you stayed here and died, then it was the end, but if you took what it had to give you as a kid, then grew up and moved on, it was the beginning. This was what Haven had in mind for himself. And for Madlen too, if she would go with him.

But she liked Linwood. And she liked the life that she and Haven had been living in it at the time. She would lie there in their bed with the lights turned off and she'd listen to Haven talk about the sunshine and the mountains and the ocean and the desert in California and she'd try her best to see what it was that he was hoping to show her, but even though the picture that he painted should have been tempting, still she'd had a hard time understanding his need to get away. She couldn't see why he had to want more than what they already had. Why couldn't he get a job in Linwood? Why couldn't they just stay put?

They were going to the movies one night, driving across town to a theater complex that had just opened up out on Centerpoint Road. He was trying to get her to agree to go with him out to L.A. at least for a weekend, just for a glimpse of it, he said, and she was still dragging her feet, trying to come up with reasons why that wouldn't work—she couldn't get away, she had classes, it would cost too much, it was a bad idea. She realized later that probably she was the one who was in the wrong, but it didn't seem that way to Madlen at the time. In the end, she decided that she'd had enough. She was tired of arguing and she just didn't want to talk about it anymore, so when Haven pulled to a stop at a red light, she opened the car door and got out and started to walk back downtown by herself, home to their apartment again. He honked at her. He called out the window. He swore and told her to stop acting like a baby, to get back in the car. But she ignored him. And after a while he realized that she was serious and he gave up and peeled off.

Madlen took the bus home. She sat there at the back window and she looked out at the comfort of Linwood's familiar neighborhoods passing by her and she was wondering then whether maybe Haven was right and she was the one who was wrong. Maybe she did need to get out and see the world some. Bring a little bit of risk into her life that way. She still didn't want to do it and she still couldn't see why she should, but Haven was making her doubt herself about it and that felt bad. Maybe she didn't love him enough, she thought. Because if she loved him more, then it wouldn't matter where they went, would it? As long as they were together?

Haven had gone on to the movies that night without Madlen. He did get up in the middle to call and see whether or not she'd been able to make it back downtown to the apartment okay. She hung up on him. Of course she'd made it back. This was Linwood, wasn't it? It was small and safe here, for one thing. And for another, she knew her way around those streets like she knew her way around her own house. If they'd been in Los Angeles, though, that would have been another story. If they'd been in Los Angeles, then she would have been altogether lost.

One of the reasons, maybe the real reason, that Madlen hadn't wanted to leave Iowa and go off to California with Haven was that her parents were still in Rampage. She would never have said this to them herself—they would not have wanted to think that she had decided to stick around on account of them. They would have told her that she could go anywhere she wanted to, that she shouldn't let her considerations for them stop her from doing what she wanted with her life. They'd get along all right without her. Because hadn't they always?

Haven hadn't seemed to know what Madlen was talking about when she tried to explain to him how she felt about this. It wasn't like this was Rampage. It was Linwood. She hardly saw her parents anymore anyway. So what difference did it make? He was leaving his mother behind, wasn't he? They'd come back to visit now and then. They weren't going to live on another planet, after all, just in another state.

Madlen didn't see any reason for her to go on trying to explain herself to him. Because what was the point?

After the movie was over that night, Haven came right home. He hadn't enjoyed himself, he said. It was a lousy movie anyway, and she was lucky that she'd missed it. He was sorry and ashamed. "I love you, Madlen," he said, and she could have accepted his apology, but she didn't. She was lying in bed in the blue-gray blear that passed for darkness in that place, pretending to be asleep. She didn't feel like getting up and talking to him. They'd had the same argument so many times, why repeat it all over again now?

Looking back on it later, Madlen realized that it could have been that she was trying to make him mad enough at her that he'd just leave, go off to California by himself so that then she could be done with it, with him and with the whole question of going and staying and how uneasy it made her feel. So maybe she was trying to sabotage their relationship on purpose. Because she was afraid of leaving. Because she was afraid of marrying him. Because she was afraid of growing up. And the fact of it was that it came to her as a big relief at first, when Haven finally gave up on her and moved out. She couldn't deny it. She'd been, in a way, glad.

When she gave him the cold shoulder that night after the movie that she didn't see, he slammed out and went downstairs to drink, even though it was his night off. He drank tequila shooters and chased them with beer from the tap until the place closed and then he came upstairs and slept the rest of the night passed out on the sofa. The next morning Madlen left early for her classes and she didn't see him all day, although she kept thinking he was going to show up at any minute with an apologetic smile on his face and an offer to drive her home. Maybe with flowers or something like that. Instead what happened was that he wasn't there, and after her classes were over she walked— empty-handed, she walked. And when she got up to the apartment, she could see right away that Haven was gone. He'd taken his clothes and his stereo and his tapes and his books and moved back home to live with his mother for a while. A few weeks after that she heard that he'd done it, gone off to California on his own.

His mother and Madlen's parents hadn't objected when Haven and Madlen moved together into the apartment above the Web, because they'd figured that it would be only a matter of time before the two of them were married. Grinnell and Doreen had been close friends at one time, and everyone was modern enough now to accept a premarital cohabitation, as long as it was truly premarital. But when Haven left and the implicit wedding plans looked like they were off, then Madlen was no longer a potential daughter-in-law to Doreen but just another in a long line of girlfriends used up and discarded by her son. It was so unfair, Madlen had protested to her mother. She was still the same person she'd been before. She hadn't changed, the situation had. Grinnell had raised an eyebrow in disdain and said but wasn't that just like Doreen, to take a moral high road.

Having the apartment to herself made up somewhat for Doreen Cramer's hard rejection of her, though. Madlen enjoyed the solitude and the self-reliance of it. After only a few days, she'd settled into a good routine of classes and coming home and going to class again that felt even more like a real life to her than the one that she'd had with Haven. The apartment itself wasn't anything much, with its small rooms and the blue-gray tint that pervaded them if she left the bathroom door open even a crack, but it was decent and she kept it clean. The bar downstairs was noisy sometimes, but she was already used to that.

Haven had stayed on bartending at the Web after he moved out, during those weeks before he took off, and she went down one night to see him because she was feeling a little bit lonely, for one thing, and for another she didn't want him to go away forever without at least a last goodbye. They shared a beer, and he gave her some money to help out with the rent, and that was decent of him, she thought. He said she should give him a call if she changed her mind and decided that she wanted to join him in Los Angeles after all—his mother would know how to find him. But she still held her ground and insisted that that wasn't likely. If he ever decided he wanted to come back to Linwood to live, she said, well, then he should consider calling her.

She left and went upstairs. She lay there in the bed alone and listened to the noise of the music and the drunks trying to make themselves heard above it downstairs. After a while she opened the bathroom door all the way and thought about how the light from the sign outside made it look like she might be underwater. She fell asleep that way, and when she woke up later the place was dark and silent, and so she knew that Haven was gone.

It took only two weeks of living back at the Riverhouse with her parents again for Madlen to realize that she'd made a mistake. Doreen gave her Haven's phone number in Los Angeles. She called him there and told him that she'd changed her mind—she wanted to join him, if he still wanted her to.

The wedding was small—only the two families and some friends from the bar—at a little Episcopal church in Linwood. Doreen wove a garland of white roses into Madlen's hair; Grinnell wore a lavender chiffon dress and sat straight-backed and straight-faced in the front pew while Deem walked his only daughter down the aisle and handed her over to Haven. The reception was in the basement of the church. Doreen hugged Grinnell and told her how happy she was, how lucky they were to have such children, to be such friends. The marriage had made them almost sisters, hadn't it? They could spend holidays together, as a family, now. They could travel together too, to go visit their kids. Grinnell had stiffened, nodded, murmured—yes, she supposed so.

But then Haven didn't get a job in Los Angeles after all. Instead they bought a house on Foxridge Road in Linwood. He went to work as a programmer for a small data processing company and used the connections that he made there over the years to position himself for an offer from a comparable firm in Los Angeles. That time he was hired and that time they went and that time they stayed. By then Madlen had forgotten altogether why she'd ever been reluctant to leave.

There were some unhappy times before Haven's accident when Madlen had tried to imagine what it might be like if they had never married, and sometimes she'd wondered whether he did the same. She'd supposed that he must. Maybe he would decide to leave her, she'd thought. And then, what if he did? What if he had an affair and thought he was in love with someone else and decided to move out? Would she mind? Or would she be grateful for the release, just as she had been when she found herself alone in the blue light of the apartment above the Web?

Madlen would never have been the one to end their marriage herself, she knew. Because she hadn't really wanted it to be over, she'd only wanted it to be changed. Because she'd begun to feel oppressed by him and by his presence and by the self-reflecting sameness of their two similar selves. There seemed to be so little adventure, so little spontaneity, so little interesting otherness in the way that they were living, and the tiresome sameness of the days often left her feeling stunned. What if she were to pack her bags and leave the children and move out? Madlen tried to imagine what that might be like, but found she didn't even know how to begin.

For a while she'd had a sort of fantasy crush on Glen's soccer coach, and she felt guilty about it even now, although nothing had ever happened. His name was Paul something—she couldn't even remember what anymore—and he was a jeweler, and he drove a black Mercedes. He wore a Rolex watch and gold rings. His hair was long, dark, combed back from his face and curled behind his ears. When she saw him in the late afternoon, his beard was a bluish shadow on his jaw. Sometimes he came to the games dressed in a square-shouldered expensive-looking suit and almost dainty tasseled leather shoes. He worked the practices in shorts and a T-shirt, with his long hair pulled back into a ponytail. She'd sit in her car and watch him run the field with the boys, trying to make up a scene of herself with him: in a wood-paneled booth in a restaurant on the Westside somewhere, a bottle of white wine between them, his hand under the table, gold-ringed fingers skimming the skin on the inside of her thigh, her face close to his, her lips pressed against the warm sinew of his throat, the soft pound of his jugular pulse against her tongue. That was as far as she ever went with it, though, because she couldn't get past the banal details of what would have to happen next: paying the check and going outside, waiting for the valet to bring his car around, driving to a hotel, checking in at the desk, the elevator ride, the bellboy, the undressing and the getting into bed. It was all too clumsy, she thought. He'd telephoned once when Haven was out of town, not to talk to Madlen but to check on Glen, who'd been knocked down by a bigger kid during a game that afternoon. It was late, and she could hear talking, laughter, music in the background—she guessed he must be at a party somewhere, or a club. It was nice of him to think of Glen, she said. His voice, low and quiet, had seemed to fill her darkened bedroom. When she thought about this now, she was embarrassed and ashamed. How foolish she had been.

And how easily irritated by Haven—at home at night after dinner, when the kids were upstairs in bed and the two of them had a few quiet moments alone, when he'd be reading or watching television and she'd sit down with him, to ask a question or to tell him about something that had happened or something that she'd done, but he'd be so distracted, so lost in himself, that she'd have to repeat what she'd said a few times before he'd answer or before he understood. It had been a joke for a while, Haven's self-absorption and his absentmindedness—a joke that stopped being funny because it got to be uncomfortably too true.

It had started to seem to her that they were living in two different worlds. She had the house and the children and their schools and her everyday routines. And he had his work, which she didn't even really understand completely, and his office, which always seemed like a foreign place to her, no matter how many times she went there. It seemed that Madlen and Haven had allowed themselves to become so accustomed to each other over the years that it was hard to see themselves clearly and remember again what exactly it was about the other that each of them had for so long, practically all their lives, loved.

That Haven had always had another self and a secret-seeming life, of work and office and people that she met but never knew, recognized but made no effort to be friends with, made it possible for her to look at him and still see something of a stranger there, she thought. She had tried to believe that not knowing exactly what Haven did all day kept a sort of mystery about him—a place in him where she didn't ever go. Because otherwise he was too well known. This was what she'd worked to make herself believe, anyway.

But, she'd wondered, what place in herself did she have that was like that? Nothing that she could think of, until after Grinnell's death when Rafe started to write, and later when his letters came more and more often. Then that became her secret. She hid the letters, for no reason, really, except that she didn't feel like sharing them with Haven. She felt like keeping them to herself. She suspected that he would have disapproved.

So maybe it shouldn't have surprised her to find out that he was renting an apartment without her knowledge. And maybe in a way, in fact, it hadn't. When she discovered the lease among the things that were sent home from his office, she felt as if she'd always known, even that she'd been there before somehow, although of course she hadn't. She had to guess that there was a woman involved, possibly someone that Madlen had met and then forgotten.

There had been so many people at his office. Of course they had all come to the funeral, where their faces had seemed at once familiar to her and utterly unknown and strange, and she knew she should have known them better, at least have remembered their names, if only because of how well they all seemed to know her. They'd taken her hand or kissed her cheek, said something to her about Haven—about how brilliant he was, or how kind, how generous with his talent and his time, how well-respected by his colleagues and how well-liked by his friends— but to hear these strangers saying these personal things about this man who had been both her husband and her best friend . . . she'd found it irritating, offensive even, because it made her realize finally how much of him had not belonged to her. Madlen thought of those women and tried to guess which one of them had been his lover. Or, she wondered, had there been more than one? And which of the men were close enough to him to have known the truth, which ones had always known, even when she didn't, which ones had he confided in, which ones had gone home and told their own wives? How many people knew?

Before Haven died, Madlen thought that at least she could console herself with the belief that what had seemed to be happening in her marriage was a far cry from what had happened to her parents in theirs. Deem and Grinnell had been two people who did not drift quietly apart and then back together again, the way that she and Haven had. At least, not in the beginning. In fact, they'd been so busy fighting that they never had much time left over to worry about anybody else around them, including Madlen.

What was it that they had fought about? Money, for one thing. How much they needed, how little they had. How much Grinnell spent at the grocery store every week. How little Deem gave her to buy the things she thought she needed for herself and for Madlen and for the upkeep of the house. They were living in Linwood then, where he was working as a greenskeeper at the country club. His salary wasn't much and so money was tight. When he got the job at Cedarcrest Retreat there was more, but then he had to drive all the way out there and back every day, and he was also working longer hours. Grinnell complained about the long days and sometimes nights that he spent there that spring, getting the gardens ready for summer, tending the flowers and the seedlings in the conservatory, cleaning up the debris of winter from the grounds. But that was his job, what was he supposed to do?

Finally, when Madlen was ten, they bought the Riverhouse and moved to Rampage so that at least he wouldn't have so far to drive to work and back every day. At first Grinnell was lonely. She was bored, stuck all by herself in the middle of nowhere— they never went out, they never saw anyone, they never did anything, she'd always expected more in her life than this. What more? She didn't know. She couldn't say exactly. Just something. Just anything.

When Madlen heard them begin with this, she hid herself away in her room, not knowing how seriously she should be taking what they said or what they did, only doing what she could in her own way to drown out the sounds of their raised voices by talking or humming or singing out loud to herself. Sometimes she would creep out into the hall and huddle in the shadows outside their door, and she'd watch them, could feel the tension that sang between them—it was as tangible to her as if it were an actual electrical current, arcing over empty space. And she was sure that if she were to stand up and step into the light of their room she would expose herself to their anger, would bring its focus down on her and then she would be zapped, slapped back by the force of their feelings just as one time she could remember when she'd curled her hand around the frayed cord on a plugged-in table lamp. She believed that what she'd feel would be an electric thrill something very much like that one, that it would take hold and shake her, the same only stronger, harder, sharper, so powerful that she'd be burned up and turned into ashes and carelessly blown away. So mostly she stayed quiet and kept herself safely hidden out of their sight. And mostly they were quick to forget that she was there.

But the fact she was beginning to realize now was that instead of driving her parents apart, all that arguing had served to rev them up. It had turned them on, as if it were possible for them to take some sexual thrill from the fury of their fighting, rekindling something between them with the sparks of their anger and frustration and disappointment and pain. Maybe if she and Haven had quarreled more, the air between them would not have been left to get so stale and dead. Madlen remembered how Grinnell had stood in the bedroom in only her bra and slip on a hot summer night, how her jaw had clenched, how her bare shoulders had shone, how the wisps of her hair had curled against her skin, dampened by her sweat. How she'd held a book in one hand, how she'd waved it, shaken it, slammed it down, until finally he said something to her that was more than she was willing to take and then she let go and she threw the book at the wall behind him. Just missed his head. Didn't throw it in a way that would have broken anything anyway. Not with the dead aim or the hard strength to do any real damage. Only just enough to make the point, that was all. And Madlen remembered too how her father had fought back, face red and throat corded, a black vein throbbing in his temple. How he'd slammed his hand against the wall, how he'd approached Grinnell with his fists clenched, then turned away from her again, stopped himself before it maybe got taken too far.

But then summer came and Grinnell met Doreen Cramer and after that everything changed.

Madlen was ten years old when she first saw the two boys who for the next three years would be her best friends. She'd been waiting up for her father to come home, late. It was the beginning of summer, the first warm day, and they'd only been living in the Riverhouse for a few weeks. Grinnell had already put her to bed and then gone to her own room and closed the door. Madlen waited for a while and then she got up and went downstairs and outside to the porch. The sun had set and the shadows had grown and darkened the woods around the house with their black wash. He was too late for dinner, Madlen knew, but probably he'd have already eaten something by that time anyway. She and her mother had shared a meal of baked chicken and green beans, sliced tomatoes and white rolls with honey butter, in silence at the kitchen table. Grinnell hadn't bothered to set anything aside for him to find in the refrigerator later. Jaw set, she'd grimly washed the dishes and rinsed the sink and sponged the counter, then she'd turned off the lights and gone upstairs to sip at a glass of gin and read her book in bed.

Madlen was sitting outside on the porch by herself, fiddling with a length of string whose ends had been tied together for a cat's cradle, and she was listening and watching for her father's big pickup truck to bounce off the road and come barreling toward her down the rutted narrow drive. When at last she saw his lights turn in, she slipped off into the shadows to hide. She watched him stop the truck and turn it off, get out and walk across the yard up to the house.

His white T-shirt was bright, even in the dusky twilight. When he came to the steps she popped out into the light, startling him. Laughing, he bent and swooped her up and hugged her close to him. He smelled sweet, like flowers. Sour, like lemons. And alcohol. And smoke.

"Where's your mom?" he asked.

Madlen nodded up at the house. "In bed already," she said.

The light was on in the bedroom upstairs, but the window was closed and the shade was down and the curtains had been yanked shut. He took a deep breath, then bent and set her down on her own two feet on the ground again.

"She know you're out here?" he wanted to know.

Madlen nodded, unsure. "I think she does," she said.

"Not sleepy?" he asked.

"No," she told him, although she was.

"Want to sit up with me some, then?"

She did.

He told her to wait there, and he went into the house and came back out a minute later with a bottle and a glass of ice. He sat down on the top step and she placed herself beside him and watched while he poured his amber whisky into the glass. She leaned sideways against the porch post and peered up at the spangle of stars that had begun to twinkle down from overhead. They were bright and clear in the black sky, so perfect, so cold, so far away. Madlen reached over and dipped her finger into his glass and then sucked on it, enjoying the smoky taste. He pulled off his boots and his socks, then flattened the soles of his bare feet against the rough and paint-peeled boards of the step. He smoked a cigarette, and when he was finished with it he lit another one from its end and flicked the first off into the grass, where it glowed for a moment and then, in the moisture, died.

The shadows at the edge of the yard deepened when the bedside lamp was turned off in Grinnell's room upstairs. Madlen and her father sat together in the dark and they didn't speak anymore. He smoked and sipped at his drink. She closed her eyes and listened to the sizzle of his cigarette and the chiming of the ice in his glass, the whisper of his bare feet when he shifted them against the worn floorboards of the porch and the high hum of the crickets in the woods.

After a while he got up and went into the house to fill his glass with more ice. The screen door creaked when he opened it, and then it creaked again as it swung back shut behind him.

When she woke up later, Madlen was alone. He'd left her

there—forgotten her, it seemed. The night was warm and wet. The light in the bedroom upstairs had been turned back on again, and its glow spilled out onto the grass. She could see her mother's moving shadow outlined against the drawn shade. She could hear her father's voice, a murmur, soft and deep. And then Grinnell's, louder, rising. And then his again, a sharp hard bark.

Madlen dropped down from the porch step onto the grass. She crossed the lawn, away from the house, toward the woods, and then kept on going down the path as far as it would take her, past the old fire pit, all the way to the river and the swinging bridge. Madlen sat and scooted down the bank. She waded into the water to where it was knee deep and stooped down in it, leaning forward to soak her arms and dunk her face. She came up sputtering and stood shivering with cold. Her wet clothes clung to her body. In the trees on the other side of the river she could see the strings of white twinkle lights and she could hear the talk and the music that rolled toward her from a party that seemed to be going on there, sound that was punctuated now and again by a man's loud voice and the startling ring of what she recognized as a woman's laugh.

There was movement, and the bridge above her creaked as it was crossed. There was whispering, shadows shifting, and the boys' two forms materialized there, up on the bank on the far side. The flare of a match lit their faces—a pair of hollow-eyed masks—for a moment and then was out. The burning end of their cigarette glowed, passing from one to the other before they turned away and moved on, following the path alongside the river away from her, merging into darkness, disappearing into the night again, gone now as suddenly as they'd appeared.

———

Headlights from the road at the end of the Riverhouse drive swam over the walls, scanned the room, and then drifted off. There was a long, hollow-sounding screech as the car's tires hugged the tight curve, and Madlen held her breath, listening, waiting for more, a *thunk* as it hit the bank, maybe, but there was nothing and the car went on unharmed, the sound of its engine droning off and then dimming into silence when it was gone.

"Damned drivers," Deem growled.

She heard the slur in his speech and guessed that he might be a little bit drunk, but she didn't hold that against him—rather envied him for it, in fact.

Indian Hill Road, where the Riverhouse was perched, had always been a good shortcut for getting out of Rampage and onto the highway on the way to Linwood, but it was slow to be discovered, mud at first and then gravel sometime after that and, until the time when it was paved, little used. It was Jack Daggett who had pressed for the improvement, because he thought it would help him lure more people out to the summer parties and dances that he put on at the Old Barn on Friday and Saturday nights. But over the course of the summer after they laid the blacktop down there was some kind of an accident just about every weekend, it seemed. Drivers who'd been used to being slowed by the road's deep ruts and washboard bumps found that the smoother asphalt made the trip fast and fun, but the tight curves had not been regraded or more sharply banked, and the drivers who were drunk or tired or maybe simply didn't know any better didn't compensate by slowing down on their own, so they often lost control and went off the road, into the ditch if they were lucky, into a tree if they were not.

In one of the worst of them, a young couple from Linwood was killed. Like the others, they'd been on their way home after a night of dancing and drinking at the Old Barn. The next morning the car was still there, a crumpled blue convertible Corvette pressed up against a tree. It looked like it had lost the curve, flown off the road, skimmed under a wire fence, and then slammed into the tree. There was blood to be seen on the road and gore smeared into the grass. A piece of cloth—some bit of the boy's shirt, Rafe suggested, or a tatter from the girl's dress— had been snagged in the fence. It flapped and waved, rose and fell in the breeze.

A few people who had heard about what happened came by for a look at the spot, because it was a Sunday, a nice morning for a slow drive, and then somehow the word must have spread because pretty soon there was a long line of cars, all of them slowing, faces pressed up to the windows, eyes craning for a look, some stopping and pulling over to park and get out, to stand and stretch and squint, with their arms folded or their hands in their pockets, talking quietly to each other, shaking their heads at what they could see was the utter waste of it, what was the utter shame.

And there had been Madlen and Haven and Rafe standing together with the others, tight-lipped and wide-eyed, fidgety and flushed, gaping at the gore.

Had that been the beginning of the end of her own innocence? she wondered now. And of Haven's? And of Rafe's too? And did Haven's death mark what would be looked back upon and seen as the end of her children's innocence? The closing chapter of their childhood? There was Claire, already growing into her adolescence. And Glen, struggling to shrug off his boyishness.

She'd always tried her best to protect her children, as any mother would. From the moment of their birth, Madlen had

done everything she could think of to keep her babies safe, untouched by what she thought she already knew to be the world's
hardness, unharmed by what would come to seem to her to be
the unavoidable violence of life. But now it turned out to be
Haven himself who had done the most damage to them. By
being their father. By leaving them. By dying when they still
loved him and still needed him, when they were still young.

Madlen thought of what everybody always said was supposed
to be the purity and the simple innocence of childhood, and she
thought she could see now that she hadn't ever really understood
its value for herself, that simplicity, or at least she hadn't been
able to see it clearly for what it was until after it was taken from
her, until after it was altogether gone. The summers that she had
spent with Rafe and Haven together in the woods alongside the
Rampage River had seemed to her then to be nothing extraordinary, nothing less than what she should have expected, nothing
but what they, being children, naturally deserved.

After Haven's death a huge hole had seemed to open up all
around her, threatening to swallow her altogether, she thought.
It had left her breathless and yawning, as if there weren't enough
oxygen in the air. At first she was able to fill that vacuum with
the mundane daily business that death had dredged up—the lawyer and the accountant, the minister, the funeral director, the
people from Haven's work. There were papers to sign and decisions to be made.

All because of a singular, momentary bad choice. Madlen had
tried to guess what must have gone through Haven's mind in
those last seconds. Had he thought of her? Probably not, she
thought. Probably he had thought of himself, and who could
blame him? Struggling with the wheel, trying to hold the curve,
trying to slow down, but already it was too late. She'd imagined

it so many times that in the beginning she was afraid to drive, because the small quick fright of a close call kept expanding in her mind into the detailed atrocity of a full-blown wreck. What would happen to her children if something happened to her? Where would they go? How would they live? Or, worse, what if she lost them? Madlen gulped at her drink, gasping.

Deem stood up. He raised his arms high over his head, stretching so his belly was flattened and smooth, his hipbones sharp against the ragged waistband of his khaki pants.

"I'm in," he said, and turned to look at Ruth.

She nodded. "Me too," she agreed.

He left his empty glass on the table, but Madlen carried hers with her as she followed him up the stairs. Ruth lingered behind, turning off lights and checking locks and latches as she went.

On the sleeping porch, Claire seemed to be asleep. She was on her cot, curled in on herself with her knees tucked up. Madlen leaned and pressed her lips to the round mound of her daughter's bare sunburned shoulder, and Claire murmured, stirred, then settled into stillness again as Madlen headed down the hall to her own room.

She undressed in the dark. Put on a shirt that had belonged to Haven. Looked at herself in the mirror. She couldn't help but think of Grinnell and of how beautiful she'd been when she was young, with her clear skin and fine bones and glossy straight hair, none of which had ever in her own opinion seemed to do her any good. For all the hours Grinnell spent at her dressing table fixing her face, fussing with her hair, getting herself dressed up for a night of dancing at the Old Barn, still she always complained that her husband didn't notice. He took her for granted

that way, she said. Partly she'd been flirting, trying to tempt him
with herself. Standing at the top of the stairs in a bright dress that
flattered her figure and high heels that showed off her legs, her
hair cut short, her long slim neck bared, but he hardly looked at
her. He preferred to stay at home.

Madlen would wait until Grinnell was gone, then she'd creep
out onto the porch, drop down onto the grass, take off into the
woods to meet Haven and Rafe under the twinkle lights in the
trees at the end of the swinging bridge. From there they spied on
the adults. Stole up into the yard and swiped leftovers off the
piled plates. Fished beer bottles out of the trash and drank the
warm, flat dregs. Smoked cigarettes behind the house. Watched
the men and women dance and talk, swim in the river, sometimes slip off into the trees to be alone. Madlen had stood on the
bridge with Haven and Rafe and watched the couples whose
bare limbs were white streaks that stitched the surface of the dark
water as they flipped and turned and flashed like silvery fish.
She'd seen that Daggett was watching too, his shadow outlined
in the light that was on in the barn's loft window, where his
office was. And she'd been shocked to hear her own father's
voice, calling out to her mother as Grinnell scrambled up the
bank, laughing, slipping in the mud. He took off his jacket,
wrapped her in it, and then yanked her after him, along the edge
of the woods to the parking lot and his truck. He pushed her up
onto the seat and slammed the door after her, got in himself, and
backed out and pulled away.

Madlen raced back along the paths and was upstairs in her bed
again when they came in, but it didn't matter. She supposed she
could have stayed out all night if she had wanted to, because they
didn't even stop to look into her room and make sure that she
was there.

———

Deem was already in bed when Ruth came in. In his under-wear—T-shirt and boxers—he sat propped up against the pillows and watched her step out of her shoes and slip out of her dress. Her breasts were heavy in a lace-trimmed silky brassiere, her belly round and full, panties tucked down low beneath its firm swell. She spread her hands out on her hips, looked at him, and frowned. She shuddered. "That poor old woman . . . ," she began, then stopped.

He shook his head. "I'm sorry you had to see it."

"Well, I didn't see much. Anyway, I tried not to look."

She turned to the mirror on the dressing table and leaned forward and squinted at her reflection as she unpinned her hair. She shook her head and the curls flew, then settled around her face.

"I guess you must think I'm getting uglier every day," she said. "Like a big old cow."

"No," he told her, and meant it. "You're still beautiful, Ruth." And she was. Legs long and slim, buttocks firm, back gently curved, shoulders silky, arms muscled and brown.

She shrugged a negligee over her head and sat at the table rubbing cream onto her face with her fingertips. She worried about the weight that she'd been gaining, he knew. She worried about stretch marks. She worried that her breasts would soften and fall. She'd told him that she didn't know what she'd do without her looks and the sense of physical grace that went with them, but Deem knew that this just was not worth worrying about. She was going to lose it all eventually, and by the time she did she might not even notice anymore that she had.

That was how it had happened with Grinnell. How beautiful

she had been, and how wild, when they first met. He'd thought he was in love with her extravagance, her drama, at first. But then later, after they'd moved here, when Madlen was a child, he'd been embarrassed by her. That she drank too much and her laughter was too loud. That her clothes revealed too much of her body. When she and Doreen Cramer got to be friends, it had only got worse. Then she'd wanted to go out all the time, to the weekend parties at the Old Barn, with their drinking and dancing and food, and he'd only wanted decorum and dignity, to be at home, to be quiet, to live a life that was simple and steady and calm. When he married her, he expected Grinnell to be something like the flowers in his gardens, beautiful but contained. Not like the woods that rose up around the house here, too lush and too wild, untended and overgrown.

"Do you think Madlen's going to be all right?" Ruth asked.

Deem frowned. "I think she's glad she's back here."

"Do you think she'll stay?"

"They never should have left. But Haven had big ideas. He thought he could go to California and be a big shot there."

He recalled the night when Madlen and Haven told them that they were leaving, taking Claire and Glen and moving to Los Angeles, this time for good. The news, delivered over drinks before dinner, had ambushed Grinnell and left her reeling. By the time they'd finished eating, she'd had to be helped upstairs to bed. It wasn't that she cared so much about Madlen or Haven or where they went or what they did, Deem knew—it was the fact that she was going to be losing touch with Claire. Bad enough already that Grinnell had had to give up her driver's license and the kids were living all the way away in Linwood, where she could hardly find a way to get to them. But California, that was worse. Impossible. Madlen had been hoping that Grinnell would come to visit, and at one time she maybe would have done that, Deem thought, but by then she'd already given up on those kinds of plans for herself. And as it turned out, she didn't even last the summer. She was gone before they were.

So saying goodbye to them then, waving them off, standing on the porch and watching as they pulled out onto the highway in their little car with the babies in the back seat and the U-Haul trailer hooked up behind—that had been hard. Almost as hard as Haven's funeral was, except that by that time Deem had Ruth to help him get through the misery of what had happened. They'd flown out from Linwood to Los Angeles together—and it was such an unusual thing for them to be traveling that it was hard not to appreciate some of the novelty of it. Drinks and a movie on the plane, the layover in Denver, the cab ride from the airport to Madlen's house. But when they got there and saw the children, it was plain to them again why they were there.

They stayed in a bedroom downstairs, near the kitchen; it seemed to have been put there for a maid, although Madlen didn't have one. The house was in the hills, up high in a canyon with a view of the city spread out far and wide below—pretty at night, when the lights were on, but cloaked in an ugly smudge of brown smog during the day. It was a hell of a place for a person to live, Deem thought, but not as bad as some of the houses they saw. At least Madlen's had a yard and even a swimming pool. It wasn't propped up on stilts and thrust out from the edge of the hill so that if you stepped up close to the windows, all you had below you was empty space. The street up to it was treacherous, worse even than Indian Hill Road, steep and narrow and winding and blind. And even though it was warm and sunny all day, in the morning and the late afternoon the wind turned bad, blowing hot and dry and dusty—like the breath of the devil himself, Ruth said.

Deem had never felt so out of place. All of Haven's colleagues and Madlen's friends had been strangers to him. They were successful people, he knew, with big houses and expensive cars and beautiful clothes that Ruth couldn't stop herself from admiring. Lawyers and businessmen, doctors and accountants and real estate brokers—professionals with good money coming in on a regular basis. But then at the service itself, up at Forest Lawn in a little chapel in the shade, when a couple of them got up to give a eulogy for Haven—well, it hadn't sounded to Deem like they were talking about Haven Cramer at all. Not the boy that he had known, anyway, and that had made him angry. Doreen Cramer had been out of her mind, didn't even know what was happening, and those other people, all of them strangers to him, they didn't know the first thing about who his son-in-law had been. Or who Madlen was either, for that matter. So he was glad that she was back here again, where she was known, where she belonged. And he was hoping that now maybe she was going to make up her mind to stay.

At least, he had been hoping so. Until he found out that Rafe Ramsay had come back too. Deem guessed that he must have heard about Haven—maybe he was still in touch with Hannah, maybe she had told him. And then it looked as if he wrote to Madlen and she let him know that she'd be here for a couple of weeks this summer. He'd be figuring that he might finally have some kind of a chance with her, Deem guessed, now that Haven was out of the way.

When Deem thought of Rafe, he was picturing Jack Daggett, even though the boy was not his son and wasn't even related to him but had only been a foster child there, not even formally adopted, only taken in for a few years. Chances were that Rafe was nothing at all like Daggett had been, but still, when Deem thought of Rafe, that's what he saw. Jack Daggett at the Old Barn. Coming down from his office up there in the loft, stepping out onto the grass and across it to the ballroom-size platform that had been constructed in the yard. A small combo was playing easy dance tunes from a raised stage under the trees. Paper lanterns were swinging in a breeze, casting their soft colored lights against the crystal glasses and linen cloths on the dinner tables and the heavy silver chafing dishes lined up along the buffet. Daggett had taken Grinnell's hand and pulled her to her feet. She'd followed him out onto the floor, looking back over her shoulder to cast a quick smile at her husband before she disappeared, seemed to be swallowed up by the chaotic jostle of the dancing crowd.

Deem reached across Ruth's pillow to turn off the light. He could smell her perfume in the sheets as he slid down flat on the bed to wait for her to come to him, to climb in and curl up close against him, soft and fragrant and warm.

The lights were off and her eyes were closed and everybody else in the Riverhouse was in bed, but Madlen had known before she went upstairs that she wasn't going to be able to sleep, and she was right, she couldn't. The room was too hot. The scotch in her glass was almost gone.

She was having trouble getting rid of the clear picture she still had in her head of the body they'd found nestled in the weeds at the bottom of the ditch that morning. When she closed her eyes, she could see again the childish curl of Mrs. Frye's sullied fingers. The fine spray of mud-spatter on the backs of her bare legs. Glen's stick prodding the piled leaves, his thin legs bent and folded like hairpins, his dirt-smudged face, the strength of his struggle as he kicked and climbed up toward the window so that he could get a better look at the storm. Claire's cropped white hair, the pale lifted line of her arched eyebrow. The gape of a thin gash against the crisp corner tip of a napkin, blood seeping, blooming, flowering on white, the crystal glint of a glass splinter stabbed into the soft white buttery surface of a child's skin.

Almost as bad as the sight of Mrs. Frye's body had been what the ruined insides of her house had looked like, Madlen thought, with the opened windows and soggy drapes, the murky pooled water on the floor and the windblown splatter of mud and sticks and leaves on the carpet and the walls and the pretty flowered cushions of the chairs.

She sipped her scotch and tried to think of Haven instead. And of herself. And Rafe. Of three children running one after the other along a sinuous path in the stately blue shadows of the trees. Three children dropping like stones from the railing of the swinging bridge into the warm green depths of still river water below. Three children sneaking up out of the woods and over the lawn and into the shelter of bushes at the back side of a house.

Jostling for a place at the window, standing up on tiptoe to see Evelyn Frye napping in only her underpants on the sofa in her living room. It was summertime and hot, and Mrs. Frye had been a younger woman then.

They watched her lying there on her side for a while, asleep it looked like, and that was a disappointment, because there wasn't much of anything at all to see until Haven got smart and stepped back to heave a handful of dirt at the side of the house. Then she was awake all right and sitting up and looking around, groggy-eyed. She leaned forward and picked up the half-bottle of gin that was on the floor, pushed back out of sight underneath the table near her. She tilted her head back and swallowed. Then she closed her eyes and swiped at her mouth with the back of her hand, which made Rafe laugh so Madlen had to pinch him to get him to shut up.

But it didn't matter anyway, because Mrs. Frye didn't seem to have heard. There was a small portable record player on top of the table, and she leaned over toward it in such a way that her bare belly was bunched up into an accordion row of soft folds. She turned the machine on and set the needle down and cranked the volume up loud enough that they could hear it from outside the window. A man crooned a love song in a deep soft balmy voice. Mrs. Frye listened to this for a minute, head cocked and eyes closed, and then, maybe a little unsteadily, she stood up. Her feet were narrow and high-arched and fine-boned. Her dark hair was damp, and it curled against her long neck and down onto the stretch of her back. Her shoulders were freckled and browned and her bare breasts were not the white droopy things that Madlen had seen on her own mother's body, pale and soft and hanging on Grinnell's chest like a feather tick. Mrs. Frye's breasts were small and firm, with nipples as hard and round as raw peas. She stood there in the late afternoon sunlight that was streaming in through the window and she gathered her hair in her hands and twisted it around and bobby-pinned it up on top of her head.

Strains of the man's song drifted outside. Overhead the sky was bright and blue and still; it seemed to Madlen that the boys on either side of her had both stopped breathing, that the whole world all around them had somehow paused, and it was waiting and watching and listening too, until Mrs. Frye began to dance. Her hips swayed with the movement of her feet; the muscles of her legs tightened like strung ropes on the long insides of her thighs. She swung her head from side to side and waved her arms and hands out in the empty air around her. Her belly was smooth and flat and tight; a wedge-shaped shadow of dark hair lurked below the elastic trim and behind the silky white fabric of her panties there in the V between her legs. When she shrugged her shoulders her breasts were lifted, and when she turned in circles on her toes and raised her hands and waggled her fingers up high above her head, her breasts were stretched and flattened, and when the song was over abruptly she stopped.

She dropped her arms down to her sides and she turned her head to look straight across the room, past the window and the bushes outside it, through the screen of twigs and leaves right straight into the children's peeping eyes, exactly as if she'd known all along that they were there.

Mrs. Frye was smiling then, and cradling her bottle of gin, she seemed to pooh-pooh her performance with an ironic wave of her hand.

Haven, howling, scrambled across the lawn and tore off down the path into the trees, followed first by Rafe, who was whooping and clapping his hands, and then by Madlen, who came shrieking after them both. The three of them sat together breathless on the riverbank, and the boys claimed to have been disappointed by the meagerness of Mrs. Frye's bosom, but Madlen had been charmed. Later she tried standing in her underpants and moving that same sexy way in front of the mirror in her bedroom at home, but it was absurd, and she was ashamed of her own flat chest and pink nipples, her own skin, pale and white, with its sickly-seeming bluish sheen of skimmed milk, her own hair pallid and straight and thin and cropped short, her own fingernails ragged and chewed, her own knees grimy and skinned and scabbed.

She turned and slithered out of bed, across the room, into the hallway and down. Along the way she passed the closed door at the top of the stairs, but she didn't pause to listen to the hushed voices of her father and Ruth as they talked quietly to each other in the dark in their shared bed.

In the kitchen she poured herself another drink, and then she walked silently, barefoot, out onto the side porch. She took a swallow of the scotch, wincing at its bite, took another swallow and another one after that. The jigsaw puzzle was still laid out on the table. Madlen ran her fingers over its surface, the surprising bits and pieces of its mountain scenery fitted together and beginning to make a more mundane whole.

She could see that Glen had left his flashlight on inside the tent. She studied the tangled shadows of the trees and the thick underbrush beyond, then put her glass down and let herself out through the screened door. The grass was cold and wet against her bare feet as she crossed the lawn. She lifted the tent flap and peered in to see the shape of Glen there, asleep on his back, with his hair spread, his mouth open, his arms and legs outflung. He looked so much like Haven had when he was a kid. His dark brows, furrowed in his sleep. His tanned arms, long and thin. His wrists, his hands, his smooth brown skin, marred by the whitened scars of mosquito bites and picked-at scabs. She reached in and turned the flashlight off. She let the tent flap drop shut.

And when she stood up she was confronted by the trees. And the path, the one that she used to follow when she crossed these same deep woods that lay between the Riverhouse and the Old Barn, gone off to meet up with Haven and Rafe.

Where the three of them had played their games of ghost and tag and king snake. She recalled the mottle of the green leaves and yellow sunshine, the seeming magic shiver in the air, glints of silver dew and black bark and gold light. There had seemed to her then to be a built-in wonder to their games. She remembered Haven's black eyes, his dark hair, the mud that he'd smeared with two fingers over his cheeks and under his eyes—war paint, god mask, camouflage. He'd looked so oddly unfamiliar to her then that suddenly it was as if he'd become an animal, dangerous and beautiful and strange. It had scared her, seeing him that way, watching the change that had seemed to come over him like a cloud across the sun. He had scared her sometimes, just as he'd meant to, with his monster growls and narrowed forest-beast eyes. And she'd loved him for that too.

But then would come Rafe to frighten them both—he'd burst from the underbrush, waving his arms and howling out their names. Rafe Ramsay, blond-haired and blue-eyed and boy-wild.

They weren't supposed to go swimming in the river, but they did it anyway, whenever they could. The best spot was at Sugar Bottom, an expanse of soft sand at a wide bend beneath the swinging bridge, where the water was dark and deep. Upstream were the more perilous palisades, with their high cliffs that cast cold shadows and were said to be riddled with dangerous caves. But there at Sugar Bottom the river was still and wide and its banks were gentle and low. Rafe and Haven had worn themselves out by racing each other across from bank to bank, and they were lying on their backs on the grass in the sun. Madlen was out in the middle by herself, treading water, feeling the changes in temperature, cold and warm swirls around her hanging feet. It was Rafe who slipped in like a snake and swam up behind her and grabbed hold of her ankles and yanked her down. She saw his face floating before her, his hair drifting; she saw his hands and his arms, his waist and hips and legs, his narrow bony knees, his long flat feet. She felt the bones of his shoulders under her hands as she struggled to push herself free, away from him. But his hands clenched her arms, they tightened, and he held her down. His eyes were the color of the water, gray and flat. She couldn't breathe. She fought for a moment, then quit, felt herself surrender to him, to the pain that was swelling in her chest, to the roar that was surging in her ears. She might have allowed herself to be drowned, she thought, if Haven hadn't swum out and torn Rafe away, freed her from him and pulled her up. She remembered the sound, a low drone that rose up loud and howling—like the sound of the wind, it had whistled through her head, singing. It had been the sound of drowning, she thought.

Madlen peered up into the branches above her, watching the shadows that loomed and moved, stirred by some wind. Beyond them the sky was, as ever, black and impassive. She held her breath, and before she let it go and gasped again for air, she thought that maybe she could hear that sound again—it roared in her ears, that drowning sound, and it occurred to her that it seemed that this was just what she had begun to hear in her head lately almost all of the time.

THREE

The Uphill Choice

CLAIRE WAS ON THE SLEEPING PORCH OF THE RIVERHOUSE and the lights were off and her eyes were closed but she was still awake. She was lying as perfectly still as she possibly could, on her back on top of the quilt on top of the cot. She was naked. It was an experiment. She was trying to see if she could figure out what it maybe felt like to be a person who was dead. She held her hands cupped and crossed, fingers entwined against her chest and under her chin. She held her breath and studied the stillness that seemed to have settled in all around her. Her legs, out-stretched, were thin and weightless; in the darkness her skin looked white, as translucent as firefly light.

Claire was thinking that she might like to be able to believe in the reality of ghosts. There seemed to her to be some kind of a hope for the future of things, or at least of herself, in that, and she thought she'd like to know what it might be like to be a ghost herself. She let her breath go, slowly, felt the whisper of it leave her lips. What she was wondering was whether death might be like this, if it could be as simple as a measured exhalation, a warm moist draft of air rising up and out of the body, and she wondered too, if she really did happen to be dead, would she be tempted to linger afterward, would she be held back and hovering there somewhere in the air above herself and above what she would have become—a clump of flesh lifeless and left behind, looking limp and used up, not necessary to anything or anyone anymore, no longer even useful, like an old wrapper or a torn bit of paper, something thoughtlessly discarded, an empty bottle tossed from a passing car, half sunk in the mud in the weeds in the ditch by the side of an out-of-the-way field road?

Would she feel sorry for herself, would she be reluctant to go, would she want to stay close and watch what might happen to her body next? Swarmed by flies. Burrowed by worms. Poked at with the point of a boy's stick. One eye open, glazed over. Black gnats in her ears and up her nose and crawling on the inside of her opened mouth. One hand outstretched, palm flattened, fingers entangled in a mat of mud-soaked grass.

They'd climbed the slope across the road, up to the empty house with its gaping windows and ruined front porch. Glen and Claire waited in the yard while Ruth and Madlen went inside and used the phone to summon the Rampage County sheriff, Tom Nicholls, who'd then come barreling up the road with his lights flashing, their shine made dim-seeming by the high sun, and when he'd pulled his car over onto the shoulder, the sound of his tires skidding on the wet gravel had seemed to add some real seriousness to the emergency of what Glen had happened to find.

Tom was a hump-shouldered and red-faced man, and he climbed out of his cruiser and clomped along the dirt in his boots, handcuffs and keys and club and gun all holstered to his belt and clanking as he moved. He wore his hat pulled down low over his eyes, and he seemed to take some look of importance and authority from that. He fiddled with its brim, then stumbled down into the ditch, looked at the body, then away, then down at it again. Sucked on his teeth, shook his head. Said later that he'd never seen anything like it. That it sure was a goddamned shame.

Claire herself stayed put, watching this, standing with her brother in what shade there was under the willow tree on the hill outside Mrs. Frye's wrecked house. The soles of her sneakers slid on the wet grass, and she rubbed them back and forth against it until she'd worn right through to the raw dirt. Gnats swarmed around her. She hugged her arms to herself and cupped her elbows in her palms. She watched the fluttery shadows of the blowing leaves, and she heard the stirring of the willow switches, and she wondered then whether the woman's spirit wasn't around there somewhere still. Hovering. Watching. Amused, maybe, by the serious-seeming business that her death had turned out to be for everybody else.

After a while the coroner's black windowless van had come and pulled up at an angle behind the sheriff's car. Down in the ditch the men were rolling the body over onto its back. One arm flopped across, hand back-slapped the dirt. One leg was bent, knees were parted, had to be brought together, pulled straight. The bathrobe had got hitched up. Skin was white and soft-looking, dimpled and soggy, like wet bread. Fabric was picked at by fingertips reluctant to touch, the hem drawn discreetly down.

The men stooped down close, and one of them, not Sheriff

Nicholls but the other one, reached out and swept the woman's hair away from her face with the back of his hand. Then they hoisted her up. They took her by her shoulders and her feet and slung her body between them—roughly, not the way that Claire's father used to lift her to carry her upstairs to bed, where he'd set her down and brush his lips against hers, whisper goodnight, sleep tight, and tuck the blankets in around her snug.

The head lolled, the arms were hanging. The men dropped Mrs. Frye on the stretcher. They arranged her there, brought her hands close to her sides, placed her feet together, then pulled the sheet all the way up over her face.

Later, Glen said, they'd zip her up inside a black rubber bag. They'd lay her out on a metal table and poke holes to drain out all her blood. Poke holes where? Claire had wanted to ask him, but she didn't dare, for fear of sounding ignorant. In her hands? Her fingertips? In the bottoms of her feet? Then they'd pump her veins full of chemicals to preserve her. After you're buried, your hair keeps growing, everybody knows that. Longer even than Grinnell's had been. And your fingernails too. They'd crack her head open like an egg, then they'd suck her brain out with a vacuum-cleaner kind of thing; they'd carve into her chest and gather up her insides and throw them away in the trash. They'd leave her hollowed out that way, and then they'd get her dressed up and they'd fix her hair, wash and set it, powder her face, and finally, after everybody was done crying, they'd bury her. Unless, Glen said, she'd already told her lawyer that she wanted to be burned. Maybe then they'd scatter her ashes in the fields.

How did Glen know all of this? He shrugged. He wasn't sure. Just did, that's all. Somebody else must have said so. Or else he'd seen it on TV.

Michael Parry, who was in Glen's class at school and had

played on his Little League team one season, had lost his dad too, the year before Haven was killed. But that man had been sick and in the hospital for a long time already and so everyone had known what was coming, even though they'd all been hoping and praying against it. Flowers were sent to the house and the mothers baked dinners for the family and arranged for the care of the children, so that by the time the man died, it was almost a relief. Then the night before the funeral the family, who were Catholic, held a wake, which Madlen went to with Glen. The casket had been open, Glen said, and Michael had been standing by it, stiff and serious and dressed in a suit and tie. Sometimes he'd turned around and straightened something on his dad—his glasses or a picture that had been slipped into the casket next to him. Now that was real courage, Glen told Claire afterward. To actually touch a person who was dead.

When their own father was killed, though, no one got to see the body. It was more like one day he was there and then the next day he wasn't. They'd used dental records to identify him. And so for a long time afterward Claire kept having trouble believing that he was really gone.

She'd seen enough car crashes in the movies and on TV to know something about what it might be like for a person to die in a burning car. She could close her eyes and imagine her father's old convertible MG crawling up the hill toward their house, like a beetle or a bug. Making its way through a maze of curves and switchbacks, past darkened houses set close to the curb, cars parked with their wheels cramped, garbage cans set out for pickup the next day. Somewhere near the top, the car slowing and pulling off onto a dirt turnout. Haven Cramer a mere shadow climbing out and standing and looking down into the black folds of the canyon below him and the panoramic array of city lights spread out starlike beyond. What might he have been thinking? Standing by his car in the dark, the engine purring. He'd been drinking. He shouldn't have been driving. But he couldn't stay there. He was almost home, and yet for some reason he stopped there on the turnout for a moment. At least, that was what the police report had said—someone had seen him, a neighbor or another car driving past. But then the MG was moving again. Following the road's labyrinthine curl and turn, climbing higher, picking up speed on the straightaways, braking at the curves. He was drunk, and he was driving too fast. Who knows why? The car plunged through the guardrail and took flight, soared then fell, tipped and turned and crashed down onto the brush, rolled, stopped. Then, nothing. Dust settling. A face at a window in a stilt house across the way, peering out into the darkness—what was that sound? The headlights bright against the dry brush. A coyote nearby, watching, crouched, wary. The sky overhead, silent, dark. And then, inside the car, heat. Fuel seeping. Wood interior, rag top.

The old MG would have caught fast, Claire supposed, and burned hard. It would have exploded quickly into brutal flame. And then its fire had caught the canyon, burned through the dry grasses, set the brush all around it viciously ablaze.

What Claire knew about fire was that it's usually the smoke that kills, not the flame. And Haven had been drunk, might have passed out at the wheel, unaware that he'd even left the road, gone flying off into the bare air. Or he would most likely have been knocked unconscious by the impact anyway, after the car hit and rolled, before the fire started, before his body was burned. He might not have felt it, Claire thought. Probably her father didn't ever even know.

And, she wondered now, what if Glen, who thought he knew

everything, was wrong about Mrs. Frye? Maybe the woman's soul had been separated from her body, maybe she'd been released by her death in the middle of the storm, maybe she'd been blown out or breathed out or sucked out, maybe she'd gone soaring off through some black and starless void toward an itty-bitty pinprick of aching white light, and maybe she'd passed on her way there all the dead people that she'd ever known, and all of them would have been applauding and cheering her on, everybody who had ever lived and who now was ever dead, there'd have to be crowds and crowds of them, flat as a farm field, rolling off as far as the naked eye could see. Famous people and ordinary ones, both. Old people and young people, babies even. And animals too. Most of them would be strangers probably, folks that you'd never seen. But some you'd maybe recognize, at least fleetingly. All those people in the picture frames in the Riverhouse stairwell, for example. Or the boy at the high school who'd been shot down by some gang members last fall. People had put flowers and burned candles on the exact spot on the sidewalk near the bus stop where he'd died. Some of the girls had left notes for him, white pieces of notebook paper with lipstick kisses on them, weighted down on the cement by black stones. Bobby pins and shoelaces and ribbons from their hair. They loved him, Claire realized, because he was dead. When he was alive, no one thought about him twice.

The only thing Claire knew to compare any of this to was the long black dream of anesthetic. What it had felt like when she'd had her tonsils taken out, how they'd brought the black rubber mask down over her face and the doctor had told her to close her eyes and just relax, to breathe in deeply, and when she had there'd come a sinking feeling, a wallowing, and the darkness had closed down over her, she'd been drawn deep into a sleep that was without dreams, blacker and more silent than anything she'd ever known.

It had been an endless-seeming blankness, an emptiness that in a way she'd welcomed, such a complete shutting up of sound and sight and sense that it had come to her as a relief almost. Like when the wind stops. Like when a motor is turned off. She'd been plunged into that stillness, into that silence and that nothingness, and she'd liked it, and she was trying to find something similar to it again now, but it evaded her.

In the darkened master bedroom down the hall, Ruth lay next to Deem and listened to the rhythmic rise and fall of his breathing near her. It was a sound that warmed and soothed her, made her feel cared for and safe. She hoisted herself up onto one elbow and leaned over him and looked into his face, lined at the corners of his eyes and mouth and pouched in his cheek and along the line of his jaw. She could smell the cigarette smoke and whisky on him. His hand was curled into a loose fist beneath his chin—childlike, she thought, smiling. His eyes moved under his closed lids. He was dreaming, she supposed, and she realized that she didn't know anything at all about what. It was true that there was much that she didn't know about him, but this didn't worry her—she was, after all, carrying a piece of him inside herself. Right now it was enough for her to know that he loved her, and of that she was certain. She wasn't going to be the one to question why, or how.

She put a hand on her belly, and as if in answer to her thoughts the baby inside her stirred, fluttered, then knocked her back, left her gasping at the force of its sudden heavy kick and strong turn. Her own body responded by clamping down hard around it. She closed her eyes and held her breath, waiting, as a trickle of hot fluid began to seep from between her legs.

Instead of death, what Claire was feeling was the wet heat of the evening as it flowed in through the open mesh of the screens and rolled over her bare skin like the liquid surge of a rising tide. The sunburn on her shoulders was a small nudging soreness, and it kept distracting her from what she was attempting to do—to understand what it might feel like to be dead. The cut on her eyebrow ached. And she had a mosquito bite on the back of her neck, too, and it itched—she'd already scratched it into a scab, twice. She tried hard to concentrate, to make the feeling, all sensation, leave her, go away. The only way to do this was to let the itch seep over her, surround her body, and waft off. A fly had got itself caught on the inside of a raised window and was frantically slamming itself against the glass.

Claire opened her eyes. The screens all around her were black with the moonless summer night. How dark it was there in that old house of her grandfather's, deep in the woods—it made her feel as if she might not be herself anymore, as if she could maybe be somebody else, as if that place had become someplace completely strange and unfamiliar, not Los Angeles certainly, but not Rampage either, not Iowa even. As if that night might be a different kind of night altogether from any that she'd ever known when she was home.

Outside the window of Claire's bedroom in the house in California, a streetlamp stood on the corner, old-fashioned, wrought iron and smoked glass, and it flickered and sizzled sometimes, as if it might be alive, like a big insect, humming. You could hear the freeway in the distance, and planes went by overhead sometimes, their engines a far-off murmur. Or heli-copters, clattering. Sometimes a truck would come up the hill, its gears grinding.

One time Claire had been awake and at her window after dark—it was late, past midnight already, she'd been promised a dollar an hour to baby-sit Glen—and some older boys from down the hill came by on bicycles. There were three of them, in shorts and dark T-shirts and baseball caps—Dan Moorehead and Tim Casey and his little brother, whose name Claire didn't know. They sat on their bikes and looked up at her house, then threw stones at the streetlamp until finally they managed to break it, with a bang and then a chime of scattered glass. Laughing, shocked by their own daring, they chased each other, unaware, Claire thought, that she was there watching them from the dark-ness of her room. But then Dan stopped and looked up and seemed to see her for a moment before he raised his fist and shook it at her, cursing, threatening, then turned, shrieking, and wheeled away.

Anne Pence told her later that that meant he must like her, but Claire wasn't so sure that this was true.

She sat up on the cot. She looked down at her body, bare belly as pale as smoke. Around her the high screened windows and the deep night outside them loomed; shadows seemed to separate and deepen as her eyes adjusted to the dark. The clothes and blankets and junk piled on Glen's cot next to her made it look as if a person might be there sleeping. She poked at it with her foot, was relieved when it didn't stir.

Claire was used to sleeping by herself, and she was glad that Glen had decided to spend the night outside in the tent instead of upstairs there with her, where she would have kept hearing him, wouldn't have been able to help but be aware of him near her all night long. He didn't know how to stay still, even when he was asleep. He turned and twisted, kicked out, moaned. He smelled, too. He was messy. He was reckless. His grin was goofy, his ears poked out, that black fan of hair always fell into his eyes so he had to toss his head to shake it away.

Glen's room was across the hall from hers in the house in California. It was filled with his boyish things, which sometimes she thought she maybe envied and sometimes she was sure she was glad weren't hers. Like plastic airplanes and model cars and the soccer trophies that he'd won.

Claire pictured their house—white stucco, with a red tiled roof and balconies and awnings, perched on a granite hillside up above Beachwood Drive; from the inside the nighttime panoramic view of the basin would be spread out like a blanket of stars far below. The house was empty now, Claire knew. Its windows from the outside would be black, the rooms behind them silent and dark and still. Dust gathering on the furniture and the polished hardwood floors. Cobwebs hanging from the high corners of the cathedral ceilings. Rats scuttling in the ivy outside her window. A skunk nosing the dirt below the eucalyptus. Coyotes prowling along the curves of the darkened street. She'd been away for only a few days, not even a week yet, and already Claire was imagining the house as if it had been abandoned for years.

She closed her eyes and tried to picture instead how it had been that last summer, almost exactly two years ago, before Haven's accident had changed everything. She tried to see him there, inside, standing at the refrigerator in the kitchen, fixing himself a drink, or sitting in his chair in the living room, flipping through the channels on the television, biding his time until they were finished with whatever it was that they were doing there at the Riverhouse with Deem and Ruth in Rampage, waiting for his family to come back home where they belonged. He'd have eaten his dinner at the kitchen table, alone. Maybe had a hamburger or a steak that he cooked outside on the grill, or some eggs that he fried on the stove. He might have stayed up late working, or maybe he sat in his chair in the den with a drink by his side and a magazine or the newspaper in his lap and the television on, or maybe the radio was playing. Claire would have sat with him, she thought. She'd have been good and kept quiet, she wouldn't have tried to talk or ask questions, she'd have stretched herself out on the sofa across from him and looked at one of her books, turned the pages slowly to keep from making noise. She would have said goodnight to him when it was time, kissed him on the cheek, winced at the stink of alcohol on his breath, maybe, but said nothing at all about it, gone on upstairs instead, quietly, to her room.

Even though Claire knew that of course this scenario was impossible, it was what she was wishing for. Even though she understood that of course her father wasn't there at all, not really, wouldn't be and couldn't have been, still the idea of it appealed to her, and she was having a hard time resisting it. So she didn't. She let herself hold on to it for a little while. She considered the possibilities. What if he was there after all? What if there had been some big mistake made by someone—it didn't matter who, or why—what if her dad just simply was not dead? What if he'd only been . . . and she fished for something, tried to drag it up out of herself, a solution that would make some sense, no matter how remote, an answer that might be plausible, however slightly so, just for that moment, just for then. Well, all right then, what if he'd only been gone? For a while. All that time. So maybe he'd been lost. Maybe he'd had an accident of some other kind, something simpler, something less drastic. Maybe he'd taken a fall, a knock on the head, and when he'd come to he had forgotten who he was and had wandered around, lost, until somebody found him and put him in a hospital, and then he didn't know who he was or where he was from, he couldn't tell them who to call, so they left him there, let him get better, and now he was, he was fine again, and he'd only just a few days ago got it all back, his memory, he'd only just now been able to find his way up the canyon and home again, so he was in a taxicab and he was winding his way up the hillside, slowly, along its curved and crooked streets, leaning forward on the seat to point out to the driver just exactly which way. Take the uphill choice, he used to say, instructing guests on how to get to the house. And there he was, he was doing exactly that himself now, on his way back home again. Wherever the road forked, going up.

But, Claire wondered, what if he did come back, and what if he found that his family had left? He would know where to find the key, there where they'd always kept it, inside the pocket of a gray hollow stone that Madlen had hidden under the bushes near the steps. He'd unlock the front door and he'd let himself in. Call out. Go into the kitchen and make himself a drink. Sit down in the living room and look out at the view, sit back and patiently wait.

He might think that they'd forgotten him, the way his mother had even before he died. But Doreen had forgotten all of them, after all, not only him. She lived in a home for old people who were sick, and she didn't have any memories at all, only an awareness of the moment—you had to keep explaining to her who you were, and even then she couldn't remember it for very long. Madlen said that when Doreen was told about what had

115

happened to Haven, she didn't even know who he was. Claire had thought at the time that that was a pretty good way to avoid the whole thing, by forgetting enough to make it not matter to her anymore. But then she'd thought again, considering what a crime it was against her father that his own mother didn't know him and so didn't care one way or another that he was dead. When she died, she wondered, would her mother know? Or would she be too old, too, to care?

Under her pillow Claire had a mirror and a silver lighter wrapped in a lace hankie that she'd swiped from a box she found at the back of the linen closet, behind a pile of folded quilts. The hankie used to belong to Grinnell, she knew; it had her initials embroidered in blue thread in a corner. The lighter she'd found last night, in a drawer in the table in the living room where the TV was, next to Deem's leather reclining chair. She snapped it open and struck it with her thumb—the bare skin of her legs and stomach looked buttery in the glow of the flame—and then she lit one of the cigarettes that Glen had given her, drew in deeply, blew out a billow of smoke. The mirror was silver too, with flowers and leaves engraved on the stem of its heavy handle. Claire held the lighter up to her face and looked at herself in the mirror. She bit her lip and checked her chin for pimples. Ran her finger over the thin pink line of the cut above her eye. Examined the spots of sunburn on her cheeks. She opened her mouth and looked at her teeth. Pulled at her ear and thought about asking if she could get her ears pierced like Ruth's. She touched her hair with her fingertips. She'd let them cut it so short that she was thinking she looked like a boy now. That was the fashion, Anne had said. Anne's own hair was longer and full of curls and soft waves.

Grinnell had had blond hair that was long and coarse and

straight. When Claire had known her, she'd worn it pinned up on her head, and she'd only taken it down at nighttime, when she slept. Then it had hung to her waist like a horse's tail, wavy from being braided, kinked from being wound up.

Claire remembered a visit here when Grinnell had sat at her dressing table and let Claire brush her hair for her; she'd held the hand mirror up close and peered into it at her face. Smoothed a finger over the fan of fine lines at the corner of her eye. Sighed and told her granddaughter, "I was beautiful once, you know that?"

The lighter was hot in Claire's hand. She snapped it shut and the darkness surged back over her again. She felt the weight of the mirror's silver handle in her palm. She ran her thumb over the intricate bumps of its small flowers and leaves.

Claire had regarded Grinnell—her gray eyes and rounded cheeks, the hard defiant flair of her nostrils, the compliant soft curve of her chin, her skin, which seemed as transparent and fragile as a dragonfly wing. "But you're beautiful now too, Grinnell, aren't you?" Claire had asked, and Grinnell had frowned and snatched the brush away from her and scolded her, said sharply, No.

Claire snapped the lighter back on again and held it up close to her face, letting the flicker of the flame play up over her features. She took a drag on the cigarette, tipped her chin up, and watched herself blow two long ribbons of smoke out of her nose. She bared her teeth, grinned. Pursed her lips, frowned.

Grinnell was an old bag, that's what Glen said. And Deem had married Ruth because she was beautiful and she wore short dresses and he liked to look at her naked.

Claire opened her knees and brought the bottoms of her feet together. She held the mirror aslant in her lap. The lighter

glowed yellow in her hand; she held its flame up closer to herself
and studied the reflection of her own folded flesh in the glass—
the petal-like lips, the inward swirl, the fleshy mound of her
pubis, cleft and fuzzed with blond down. She touched herself
with her fingertip, then covered herself with her flattened hand
and let the lighter go out.

Just about everybody Does It, that's what Anne Pence had
told her. At one time or another. You have to, she said, if you
want to be normal. Otherwise you'll turn out to be a nut. Or
worse. And it's not just kids who Do It, either. Even your parents Do It, Anne had insisted. Even your grandparents. Claire
understood that this was true, but it had been impossible anyway
to imagine Grinnell letting Deem Do anything like It to her. It
was even hard to think of Deem and Ruth Doing It, but obviously they had, because Ruth was pregnant, after all.

She thought about her father's body, how it had been, long
and lean, hard and brown. And her mother's, softer, pouched
and pillowy. And her brother's, stringy and stinky, sweaty and
dirt-smudged. With that silly small thing of his that poked out
like a mushroom between his legs. As hard as it was maybe to
believe, that was the Do part of the It, she knew.

Downstairs, hinges squeaked as the porch door opened, and
Claire sat up and crushed out against the screen what was left of
her cigarette, red embers burned down into the filter. She leaned
forward and craned to see outside. Below her the porch door
slapped shut again, and then there was her mother stepping
down and crossing the grass toward the woods. Madlen stumbled, stopped, and caught herself, then went on more slowly, as
if, it occurred to Claire, she might be drunk. She stopped at the
tent and peered in and turned off Glen's flashlight. Then she was

standing at the edge of the woods, with her hands on her hips, leaning forward, peering down the path.

It was so dark out that Madlen's shadow seemed to be blending her into nothingness, smearing her into the trees. So it wasn't right away that Claire realized that her mother was gone. She'd slipped away, she'd disappeared, she'd been absorbed, as if maybe she hadn't even ever been there at all.

Madlen's bare feet had softened with shoe-wearing, so she could feel every step she took, one and then another until she came to the swinging bridge and then the clearing and finally the familiar structure of the big limestone barn. Its windows were dark. It sprawled in the woods, rose up between the trees. Its stone face was rugged and old, and it seemed to have sagged some over the years. The woods all around shaded it, hovered over it, almost protectively, it seemed. There were no twinkle lights tonight. No music. And no laughter either.

Behind the barn was the house. On its far side would be whatever was left of the tiered flower gardens that Ivy Daggett used to keep. And the flat rectangle of the vegetable garden. Limestone walls. Fruit trees. An arbor and a chicken coop and the lawn where Jack Daggett's guests once had danced.

Bats flapped overhead. An owl called. Leaves whispered. Something scrabbled in the brush nearby.

A light went on in the window of the front room. The screen door squeaked open, and Rafe stepped out onto the front porch. Later Madlen would wonder whether it was possible that she'd dreamed him. Maybe she was sleepwalking after all, and was seeing only what she wanted to see, not what was really there. It was like a dream image to her, it could have been something that she'd merely conjured up in her mind, wishful thinking: the broad shadow of a man, outlined in light. There was such a familiarity to his form and his shape, to the way he walked, the way he held his shoulders, the way he carried his head. And when the light was in his face as he turned and closed the door, slowly so that it wouldn't slap shut, she understood at once who he was.

He was standing on the porch and he'd turned toward the woods; he seemed to be peering into the trees. His face had thinned and his jaw had hardened; his hair had darkened and his eyes had narrowed, but even though he was no longer the boy that she had known, still Madlen recognized Rafe. He'd stopped at the top of the steps and was fishing in his shirt pocket for a cigarette. Then he was snapping his lighter, and its flame momentarily brightened his face. He blew smoke and turned again and looked out at the shadowed woods where Madlen stood, breath held.

He seemed to be looking right at her, and she thought for a moment that he was going to smile and step forward, reach out for her, maybe pronounce her name, but instead he merely drew again on his cigarette and then sat down on the step with his elbows on his knees, lost in thought, it seemed, as he gazed down toward the grass and pondered the rounded toes of his boots.

She looked up at the window on the second story of the house and saw a girl's face there, framed by the light of the bedroom behind her. The small, dark-haired, dark-eyed child had been watching Madlen, but when she realized that she'd been seen she ducked away.

Madlen put her fingers to her lips and whistled, two long low notes followed by a higher, sharper squeak. Rafe's head snapped up, and he peered into the trees. He stood and stepped down into the yard.

"Madlen?" he asked.

She could have gone out into the light and shown herself to him, but she didn't. She wasn't ready yet. Instead she turned away and ran.

Claire continued to watch the woods. It was like watching the surface of water to see if the person who had just dived in was going to come up for air again soon. Like when Glen jumped off the palisade into the river, the way he'd been told not to do by Madlen and by Deem and by Ruth too, and Claire hadn't tried to stop him, had maybe even encouraged him some and then stood at the edge of the bank looking down stupidly, helplessly, waiting for her brother to come up again, imagining that he'd shattered his legs on rocks the way they'd all warned him that he would and now was drowning, broken to bits and pieces down there on the bottom. She'd held her own breath until her chest hurt, and then, just when she was beginning to think that she wasn't going to be able to stand it anymore, just as she was trying to decide whether she should go in after him or tear off back to the house for some help, his head had bobbed up, black and sleek as a seal's, a little ways off downstream. Glen came up sputtering and splashing, so proud of himself and of the stunt he'd pulled that he couldn't talk, he could only whoop with his delight, and then he swam to shore and stood there in the shallow mud, panting, his dark skin glistening, shaking his head, throwing the water off his hair just like a dog.

She stood up, and her knees cracked. She pulled on her shorts and a shirt, then slipped across the room and took hold of the knob and turned it. The door opened slowly and quietly, and Claire peeked out. Her mother's room was dark, its bed empty, its door standing agape.

She moved down the hall toward the stairs. A bar of light was shining out from under Ruth and Deem's door, so she figured they must still be awake. Doing It probably, she was thinking, although she was going to have ask Anne to know for sure; she was doubtful that It was possible with Ruth already as far along with her baby as she was. And wouldn't they have turned the light out, anyway? She wondered if she should knock and tell them that her mother was up and had gone outside, seemed to have disappeared. But then the door opened and Ruth was standing there, her belly huge and round under the skim of her peach-colored negligee. Her face was white, her eyes wide.

Claire could see into the room behind her. Deem was standing by the bed, talking on the phone. He looked up and peered at her over the top of his reading glasses.

"Go back to bed," he told her.

Ruth pushed past, went into the bathroom, and closed the door.

Deem had turned away and was listening carefully to whoever was on the other end of the phone. He hung up and looked again at Claire.

"Get back in bed," he said, his voice rough and his mouth hard.

She turned and stepped back into her room and closed the door behind her. She went to the window, sat on the edge of the cot again, and looked out at the trees, which seemed even darker to her now. She watched the woods, but still her mother didn't reappear.

———

Alone in his tent, sleeping and dreaming, Glen Cramer was running. He'd broken out, slipped off, was getting away. He slid in a ditch. He dodged a barrage of thrown stones. He stumbled over the brick and concrete rubble of fallen castle walls. Under a hover of brown-cloud sky, he was picking his way through blinding glitter in a field of bent nails and shredded metal and shattered glass.

A sound roused him—wood noise, bird scurry, animal squeak—and the vision was gone.

Glen was lost; he was falling, in a void. He didn't know where he was or even who. The dark was tangible to him; it had caught him in its net, and it was settling over his face like an opaque black gauze. His heart was pounding; blood roared in his ears; its thunder deafened him. His body was frozen by fear, his muscles were stiff, his limbs were crippled, and when he opened his eyes what he saw was nothing, only that same wave of blackness surging over him, all around. Like the blind man down on Franklin Avenue whose eyelids had been sewn shut.

Glen let his breath out slowly. He didn't dare move, was afraid he might fall farther, might sink down even deeper into the hollow murk that cradled him, cold. He listened. Pricked his ears and heard a rustling of leaves, movement deep in the trees, someone tromping on brush, someone coming—sounds that seemed to bring the natural world outside him swirling back into its proper place again.

The sleeping bag. The tent. The yard. The Riverhouse. Rampage. He lifted his hand and held it up in front of his face, could almost see it there, wiggled his fingers, curled his fist—a faint shadow, but substantial enough. His own hand. Glen's own hand. He put it down on the ground next to him and knuckled the earth—hard, solid, rugged, sure. Still listening. Still hearing. Leaves set astir down the path, deep down in the woods, someone running, someone coming.

Glen was out of the bag and up on his knees. He scooted to the front of the tent and cautiously lifted its flap just enough to peek out.

Behind him the trees were dark, their leaves and branches entwined like a tangle of black string. Across the yard the Riverhouse loomed, a refuge; the porch light was on, the back windows were black. He thought he saw Claire's face upstairs at the screen, watching the woods, but he wasn't sure.

He'd brought his slingshot and bag of marbles into the tent with him—he kept them close by, his only weapons of defense—but they seemed meager to him now, boyish there in the face of the possibility of a genuine threat. He should have something better, like a knife. He was trying to figure how long it might take him to cross the yard to get to the house. A few seconds was probably all, but for that time he'd be exposed. Could be picked off. Too slow. Clumsy. Mired by fear. He'd be caught up with. Reached out for, grabbed hold of, and dragged down from behind. Then what? Well, he didn't know.

He might have gone ahead and made a run for it anyway, he maybe would have risked it, could have, but already by then it was too late. He saw movement in the trees, a stirring, a flurry of leaves, and then Madlen burst forth from the deepest shadows. Her hair was wild, her legs and arms were white as steam, and her bare feet seemed to skim the damp grass as she flew across the lawn, up the steps, onto the porch.

The door slapped shut after her. Glen looked up at the house again and then he did see Claire's face there, framed in the black oblong of the screened window of the sleeping porch. He recognized the shock of his sister's white hair.

He slid back down into his sleeping bag and lay still while he waited for the pounding of his heart to slow. He wouldn't go inside the house now. How could he? Why should he? Nothing had happened, not really. And so there wouldn't be any believable excuse for him to make. Not after he'd bragged to everyone about how he'd be staying in the tent all night all by himself. It was only his mother that he'd seen anyway, nothing worse than that—not a monster or a killer, not even a bear. He patted the ground around him with the flat of his hands; he kicked his feet down toward the end of the bag, felt around inside the tent until he found his slingshot and marble pouch, and he brought them up and clutched them to himself.

The woods were quiet again now. Glen lay back and closed his eyes. There he was, he thought. Glen Cramer. Son of Haven and Madlen, grandson of Deem and Grinnell and Doreen, brother of Claire, these hands, these feet, this body, this head, this boy, in a tent in the yard of a house on a river in Rampage in Iowa, U.S.A., North America, Western Hemisphere, planet Earth, solar system, Milky Way. He was boggled, as always, by the enormity of the world and the insignificance of his own self, by the aloneness of his own being, by the singularity of who he was—merely Glen. There was something frightening about that, but something comforting in it too. That he wasn't much, but he was something. He was here, and he was alive.

When he opened his eyes again, it was dawn and it was raining. He sat up and looked out past the lifted flap to see the Riverhouse looming on the far side of the yard like a big ship riding waves of drizzle and mist. Voices floated toward him from the drive, and he saw Deem come out of the house and guide Ruth slowly down the porch steps with his hand on her arm. Her hand on her belly. Her head bowed. Her face hidden. Deem helped her into Madlen's rented car, then closed the door and went around to the driver's side and climbed in himself. The headlights popped on. The car backed out of the driveway, turned, and was gone.

There was a stirring in the leaves nearby. Glen looked and saw a toad there, sitting goggle-eyed, its sides pulsing. He reached for his slingshot, slipped a marble in, pulled back, and let go. The marble hit the toad with a soft *thunk*—green skin, pop and squeak. The toad sat still for a moment, and then it hopped away, unharmed, but the marble had been lost.

FOUR

Number-One Cause of Death in America

T

HE NEXT MORNING CLAIRE WAS SITTING AT THE BREAK-
fast table in the Riverhouse kitchen, hunched over in her usual
sullen pose, chin in hand, nose in her book. It was a concise
history of the world, called *The Story of Man,* that she was reading; it was something that she'd found among her father's things.
In the middle there was a hand-drawn zigzag time line, with all
the big events of history laid out one after the other—as if,
Claire thought, there were an order to what happened to people
as it happened and not just after the fact, when someone thought
about it later, when everything was over, and tried to find a way
to explain. She studied the line as it jogged down one page and
then started up again at the top of another. She was looking for
what might be the place on it where the definition of her own
life would show up if the line were to be extended to include the

present moment, but she guessed that that was not even a dot, less than that, barely an invisible speck, signifying the mere thirteen years that Claire Cramer had been alive on the planet, and she had a sense that her life in its entirety had been and would be nothing at all compared to the rest of what had been and would continue to be occurring over time and in different places since it had all of it begun.

She didn't look up when Madlen put a plate of eggs and toast down on the table in front of her, or when Glen banged in through the back door, stirring the still air. He was swaggering, full of himself for having spent the night in the tent. His hair, slept on, stood up in the back, black and thick and straight as a paintbrush. He took a seat at the table.

"All night long," he said. He was trying to prod Claire for some response. "All by myself."

Claire folded over the corner of the page in the book and closed it. She looked at Glen then, studied his startled hair, his smudged face, his grimy hands. She sniffed at the pungent boy-sweat smell of him.

"All night long, Claire," he said again, grinning. "In the dark. Outside."

She picked up her napkin and smoothed it out in her lap before she turned to him again.

"So what, Glen?" she asked. "Who in this world do you think gives a shit?"

"Don't swear, Claire," Madlen said.

Glen made a face and reached across the table for the milk, but Madlen's hand snapped out and stopped him.

"Wash up first," she told him.

Claire gave him a good smirk as he backtracked away from the table. He had to stand on tiptoe at the sink to reach and turn on the tap.

"How's the cut, Claire?" Madlen asked.

"It's fine," she answered. Madlen reached and touched Claire's chin, tipped her face to see the thin crescent-shaped scab above her eye. Claire shook her mother's hand away.

"Deem and Ruth aren't here," Glen said, stating the fact.

"I know it," Madlen replied.

Claire was squinting at her, in her way, waiting for an explanation.

"They went someplace in our car," Glen went on.

Madlen nodded. Watched Claire.

"So where'd they go?" Glen asked. The chair squealed as he pulled it away from the table and sat down.

"Linwood," she answered him.

She set a plate down. He took a piece of toast and bit into it.

"Ruth's going to have her baby early," Claire said, because she'd already figured that out. "Isn't she?"

"I don't know," Madlen answered. "I hope not. Maybe not."

"Will it die?" Glen asked, chewing.

Madlen frowned. "No. It isn't going to die."

Claire shrugged. "But it could, couldn't it?" She was poking the tines of her fork at the eggs on her plate, prodding their slimy yolks. She set the fork down and folded her napkin and sat back. "I mean, we might as well be honest about it. Might as well face the facts."

"Or maybe it'll be blind or retarded or deformed or something," Glen put in.

Madlen's face was flushed with heat and anger. "Eat your eggs before they get cold, Claire," she said.

"I'm not hungry."

Glen made another face at his sister, his mouth full of food.

"Glen, stop it!" Madlen scolded him.

Claire's voice was low, calm, quiet. "I saw you go out last night, Mom," she said. She was watching her mother carefully, again waiting for an explanation.

Glen nodded. "Me too."

"I took a walk," Madlen said. "That's all."

Claire's eyebrow went up again. "In the middle of the night?"

"I couldn't sleep," Madlen explained. "Glen, don't tip your chair." She reached out and nudged his shoulder, pushed at him harder than she meant to, so his chair whacked back down onto its front legs loudly, jarring him.

The two children were staring at her. It all seemed to have gone too far already, but still Claire couldn't leave it alone.

"What are we doing here, Mom?" she asked, her voice low, almost a whisper. "Why can't we just go home?"

Madlen picked up Claire's full plate and turned to the sink, her shoulders squared. "We're on vacation," she said, vigorously scraping the uneaten eggs into the trash. "We're here to have fun." She yanked at the door to the dishwasher and let it drop open, but the spring was broken and so the door fell heavily, scraping the side of her bare leg as it went down and landed with a crash on the cracked linoleum floor. She moaned. And turned back to see Claire's pale face and white hair, her mocking look and folded arms.

"I hate this place," Claire said, her voice quiet.

Madlen leaned down and lifted the door up and smacked it shut.

"Well, we're not going home," she said. "And it's about time the two of you started pitching in to help me here."

She reached under the sink for the scouring powder and sprinkled it over the grayed porcelain. She picked up the sponge and leaned forward and began to scrub fierce circles into the grit. Glen and Claire exchanged a quick glance, but it wasn't quick enough.

"Go pick up your room upstairs," Madlen snapped, turning on them both.

"I thought you said this was supposed to be a vacation," Claire answered, her voice louder now, challenging, her chin lifted, her cheeks flushed, her lip curled.

Madlen was across the room and had hold of Claire's arm. She yanked her up out of her chair and shook her. Claire let herself go limp, allowed herself to be shaken.

"Get upstairs," Madlen snarled. "Now." And then she turned to Glen. "Both of you," she said.

Glen was already up and on his way out the door. Claire pulled herself free and followed him, stomping. Madlen reached out and brought the back door around, taking some kind of strength for herself, it seemed, from the solid sound of its loud and resounding slam.

Claire didn't go straight upstairs. She lingered on the second-floor landing and listened to the thunder of her mother's fury working itself out in the kitchen as Madlen pulled pots and pans and dishes and glasses down from their shelves and yanked spoons and spatulas out of their drawers, then crashed them down onto the table and the counters and the floor. What was she so mad at? More, it seemed, than only Glen and Claire.

The door to Deem and Ruth's bedroom was standing ajar, and Claire nudged it open more, then peered in past it at the unmade bed, Ruth's nightgown a puddle of peachy silk on the floor, Deem's shirt draped over the chairback, and the empty antique cradle on the far side of the bed.

Claire didn't really want Ruth's baby to die. And she didn't want it to be a monster, either. She wanted it to be okay, normal and fat. She toed the negligee, half expecting to see a smear of blood on it, evidence of something gone wrong, but there was nothing.

In the room that she and Glen had been sharing, with its screened-in sleeping porch beyond, there was a white dresser and a matching padded changing table with ducks and umbrellas printed on its terrycloth cover, a rocking chair with a price tag still tied to its arm, and a crib with a mobile of paper fishes and real seashells suspended above it. Inside the crib the mattress was still wrapped in plastic, and on that were a box of diapers and some folded baby clothes and a blanket and a small square quilt. If the baby did die, Claire wondered, what was Ruth going to do with all that new stuff that she'd already bought? Take it back? Sell it? Give it away?

And then would there be a funeral? Would they dress the baby up and lay it down inside a coffin, nestled in satin like a doll in a box? Or would they even bother to bury it at all? Maybe they'd just bundle it up in a bag and toss it out with the rest of the trash. Like what Glen said they'd done to Mrs. Frye's innards.

Next to the bed was the old wooden cradle. If she were only smaller, Claire thought, she'd climb into it and, body curled, eyes closed, fill it with herself.

Madlen stood trembling in the echo of the door that she'd slammed, shaken by her own rage as well as by what she could feel to be her children's rising dread. On the table was the book that Claire had been reading. She picked it up, thumbed through it. Haven's name was written on the flyleaf in his boyish handwriting. She ran her finger over this and struggled to bring to mind some kind of a picture of her own self as she had been at Claire's age. Twelve going on thirteen. What had she looked like then? She couldn't remember. What had she done? Run wild in the woods all day and into the night. Listened to mournful swoony pop songs over and over again. Read lurid stories in the magazines that she bought or sometimes swiped off the rack at the General and then smuggled into the house and hid in the corner under her bed. *True Confessions* and *Detective Tales,* which she pored over with a flashlight, eating potato chips and sipping from a bottle of Pepsi-Cola to help keep herself awake until it was time to sneak out. But the history of the world? The story of man? No, that had been what school was for. Boring and pointless. It had not been anything that Madlen, twelve going on thirteen, would ever have considered engaging herself in by choice.

She understood that she was going to have to take control now, of herself and of her children. Of everything around her, or as much, anyway, as she could. She'd just have to do her best, that was all. She'd do whatever she could. Starting right there. Starting right then. With all that mess that Grinnell had left behind and Deem had kept and Ruth was afraid to touch.

Oh hell, leave it alone, her father would have been the first to tell her. He liked it the way it was. But she couldn't do that. Just could not. Simple as that. She would empty all the cupboards and drawers and throw out what was not worth keeping, or at least what she believed was not going to be missed, and then she would wash and wipe and polish all that was left. Upstairs the children were quiet, and outside, in the woods, it rained.

Glen's filthy clothes were piled up on the floor out on the sleeping porch, and he was kicking at them again and again, dancing on one foot, swinging the other back hard. His hair was damp with sweat. His dark face shone.

"Cut it out, Glen," Claire told him, coming into the room.

He turned to her, glowering, then kicked out again, once more for good measure.

She walked past him and climbed onto her cot. She fished the lighter out from under her pillow. Lying down flat on her back, she smoked the last of the cigarettes that Glen had given her, savoring each bitter exhalation, watching the cloud of gray smoke and thinking through the list of swear words that she knew, saying them over and over again to herself like a litany. Fuck. Shit. Piss. Cock. Suck. Cunt. Like a poem. She wondered what Anne Pence was doing just then. Getting ready to leave for camp probably. Or Dan Moorehead. She could just picture him on his bicycle, soaring down the hill past her house, his shirttails flying, his hair blown back flat. Beyond the screens the woods, trees and weeds, seemed compacted, and they crowded the Riverhouse yard like a solid living wall of dense dark green.

Glen sat down on the floor near her, with his back propped up against the wall under the screened window. He raised his slingshot and aimed a marble at the baby's fish-and-seashell mobile.

"You'll break it," Claire said.

"I know," Glen answered. "So what?" He fired, missed. "Might not be a baby for it anyway."

Claire sat up, her irritation washing over her. She dropped the spent cigarette into an empty can of Coke. Downstairs all was quiet—Madlen's mad banging had stopped. Claire crossed her legs and closed her eyes and folded her hands in her lap. She took a deep breath.

"I hate it here," she said. And murmured further, "This fucking place." Under her breath, "Cunt. Suck."

Glen sent a marble soaring across the room and this time hit one of the paper fish with a pop that put the whole mobile into a wild, string-tangling spin.

"Bull's-eye!" he cried.

Claire was up on her feet, digging into her clothes, picking up and folding each piece—a T-shirt, a blouse, a pair of shorts, a sweatshirt, a jacket, jeans, a skirt. She rolled a pair of socks into a tight ball and tossed them onto her cot.

"What are you doing?" Glen asked.

"What does it look like I'm doing?" Fuckhead.

"Packing."

She looked at him, then went back to work.

"So you think she'll take us home now?" he asked.

Claire shrugged. No. "I hope so. I doubt it." No fucking way.

Glen was standing so close to her that she could smell him. Like piss and shit, fuck and suck. Pussy.

"Well, anyway, I think you're wrong, Claire," he said.

"Probably. She'll want to stay here now to help take care of Ruth." Fucking bitch.

"No, I mean about this place. I mean, I like it here."

Claire scowled at him, her eyebrows at their sharpest angle.

"And I don't want to go home," he went on. "I mean, I'm not ready to. Not yet."

"Then stay if you want to." She was pulling her suitcase out from under her cot.

Glen leaned forward and pressed his forehead against the screen. His fingers found the latch and lifted it; he gave it a push, and the screen fell open. He knew that Claire was lying. Full of herself. Full of shit. How was she going to get there, for one thing? And where was it, home, anyway?

"What are you doing?" she asked.

He turned around and grinned, mimicking and mocking her. "What does it look like I'm doing?" he said. "Shitface." His grin widened. "Cuntmouth," he said.

And then he pulled himself up onto the sill and was stepping through. The smooth rubber soles of his sneakers skimmed the rain-slick tiles as he crossed them gracefully, his arms outstretched, hands raised for balance. He came to the peak and stopped and squatted there, rocking on his heels for a moment before he sat, straddling the roof's ridge. Below and all around him the land spread out under a furled cascade of breaking clouds. His eye followed the string of road that ran between the fields to the highway, the dark mass of the woods sloping down toward the water, then up and away from it again, the huddle of houses and storefronts on the main street of Rampage, and the machicolated stone walls of the reformatory, its many windows darkened by a mean crosshatch of wires and bars. A chainlink fence rambled along the far-flung perimeter of the reformatory property; it humped with the hill, then skirted a knot of trees. The morning's rain had diminished to a drizzle. When the sun broke through the clouds, its sudden heat beat against the red roof tiles.

A glint of white light winked out from the far side of the grove. Glen leaned on his hands and craned forward to catch it again—a sunlit blaze of metal, or maybe it was glass, flashed out at him as the trees stirred and parted, then was gone when they settled and closed down over it again.

Claire was at the window, calling out to him. Softly first, then louder. "Glen, get back in here."

His back, bent under the thin fabric of his T-shirt, looked suddenly too fragile to her, the narrow line of his spine like the curve of a china cup handle, the sharp blades of his shoulders poking out like stunted wings.

"Glen!" she called to him again.

She had no trouble picturing his fall—the slow roll and tumble down the roof's steep slope, feet scrabbling on the tiles, arms flailing, fingers grasping at the empty air, his eyes wide, mouth open, breathless, his hair blown outward from his head—and then how he'd land, hard, and bounce, crunch of bones and joints, crash of hip and head, and then the still flat sprawl of his body outspread in the grass down on the ground below.

He liked to think that he was brave—Claire knew this about her brother. But he seemed so small to her. She wanted to take hold of him right now. Yank him back into the room and stand him up on his feet and shake him.

"Glen!" She grasped hold of the window frame and put one foot up on the sill. "Get the fuck inside."

He stood up at that, slowly, and turned to her. His face was shining, damp from the last of the drizzle. His black hair was pressed to his head. Claire would have stepped up and out of that window, walked across the rooftop to get him and bring him back, and her heart had already begun to pound at the thought of herself doing this, but before she could begin to move toward him, he was coming back, one foot, then the other, to her.

———

Madlen started with the drawers, pulled them out and examined their contents—bottle caps and wine corks mixed in
with the flatware and utensils. A burned wooden spoon. A broken cheese slicer. A spatula with a melted plastic handle. Mismatched and crumpled paper cocktail napkins. Used plastic bags.
Folds of aluminum foil. What had Ruth been thinking of? Living here like this, putting up with all the old junk that had
belonged to, been bought and kept and accumulated by, Grinnell. The stuff that no one had bothered to throw away, thinking
of frugality and practicality, supposing that some little thing
might someday be found to have been worth keeping. Well, that
was just foolish and stupid, clinging to what was there just because of the fact that it was there.

But who was Madlen to complain, because wasn't her own
house in California just as bad? At least, it seemed just about as
old and cluttered up, its smaller rooms filled almost to bursting
with what they'd bought or been given and didn't want or need
or care about anymore. Some of it she guessed she didn't even
know she had. Broken things. Useless junk. Things that had
belonged to Haven that she didn't know what to do with now
that he was gone. Madlen had long ago realized that any attempt
she might begin to make to straighten out their own things was
going to be beyond her. There had just been too much between
them, and she wanted to be clear of it all, she wanted nothing to
do with any of it, wanted to start all over again from scratch.

Outside the Riverhouse the rain had stopped and the heat had
begun to well up from the woods again. How could it be so hot?
she wondered. The air was wet and warm and still, and it seemed

to be closing in around her like a fist. The house itself had grown disturbingly quiet.

She was sorry that she'd started this now. Sorry too that she'd sent the children away, that she'd shouted at them and banished them upstairs. How much better it would have been for everybody if she'd been able to think of something for them all to do together instead. Something fun. An inside rainy-day game of some kind. Make a fort in the dining room, for example. But Claire would never have gone for that, Madlen knew. She would have sneered at such a thing. Given that cold look and then turned away and tromped off upstairs to her cot again to be alone with her book. The history of the world? Of man?

The ceiling overhead thumped once. Madlen stopped and looked up, listening. She heard Claire's voice. And Glen's reply. Then silence.

What was she going to do? Madlen wondered. Where could she go? How could she live?

She thought of Deem and Ruth at the hospital in Linwood. How frightened Ruth must be. And how weary Deem. She considered the pile of silverware, tines and blades and bowls glinting in the overhead light. What next? she wondered, and understood even as she asked the question that she didn't know the answer and that she didn't know either how to find it. And then, before she was aware of what she was doing, or why, the phone was in her hand and she was dialing, calling her own house in California. She knew it was crazy, but she needed Haven. She needed to talk to him, he was the only one who could help her figure out what she should do now, even if the cause of her uncertainty was his very absence and if he'd been there she wouldn't have had to ask. What would she have said to

him, if she could? I saw Rafe again last night. He's back. He's
here. It wouldn't matter what they talked about, would it? She
only wanted to speak to him, she only wanted to hear his voice
again, that was all—as if by some strange miracle he might be
there still, might be waiting for her, might answer the phone.
But of course he wasn't. Of course he didn't.

She was just setting the receiver down into its cradle again
when she looked up to see the children standing in the doorway,
watching her.

"We want to go home," Claire said. Glen was behind her,
waiting to see what might happen next.

"We can't," Madlen answered.

"Why not?"

She shook her head, turned away.

Claire stayed put, but Glen pushed past her into the room,
then stopped.

"Jeez, what'd you do, Mom?" he asked, looking around at the
mess that she'd made of the kitchen—the cupboard doors hanging open, their shelves empty, wiped clean, the drawers gaping,
empty too. Dishes and pots and pans and knives and forks and
spoons in piles on the table and the counters and the floor. And
Madlen was standing in the middle of it all, her face flushed, her
hair undone and wild with damp curls, her expression bewildered and lost.

Claire smirked, in her best, most practiced way. "It looks
worse now than it did before you started," she said.

"I'm not done. I just need to get some new shelf paper, that's
all," Madlen told them. "Then I'll put everything back." She

picked up a saucer, turned it in her hand, then set it down again. "It's all clean, anyway," she added.

The children stared at her.

She sighed, stepped toward them. "Nothing is going to bring your father back, you know," she said. "I'm sorry, but it's the truth. We have to go on with our lives now. Without him. You have to grow up, go to school, get married, have children of your own. And I have to go on with my life now too."

Claire's scowl was deep. She took a step away. "You would do that?"

"Claire . . ."

"But how?"

Madlen didn't know. She couldn't say. She reached for her bag on the counter near the door. "Come on with me," she said, forcing cheerfulness into her voice. "We'll go into Rampage and get some lunch there."

Claire rolled her eyes. The last thing she wanted to do right now was to go into Rampage. She wanted to go home. Hadn't she made that clear? But Glen was already out the door.

"Deem took our car, Mom," Claire said, a last resort.

Madlen looked out the window at the old pickup that was still parked there in the driveway. "Well, then we'll have to take his truck."

Claire snorted. "You know how to drive a truck?"

A flame of anger brightened Madlen's face. She looked at her daughter and saw a cold judgmental stranger looking back at her. She resisted the urge to lash out and slap her, to burn her own rage into Claire's pale cheek, emblazon upon it the rosy imprint of her own opened palm. She sidled past her instead.

"Yes, I know how to drive a truck," she said, and she turned away and stepped outside, into the blinding midday fire of the early summer's sun.

Just outside the razor-wired chainlink fence that traced the outermost edge of the Rampage Men's Reformatory property, behind a moss-grown stone wall on a sandstone bluff above the river and at the far back side of a huddled grove of stunted apple trees, a battered aluminum camper squatted on a square of poured concrete at the end of a short mud drive. Its curved sides gleamed in the afternoon sunshine, throwing back a blinding dazzle of reflected light. The woman who was sitting in her wheeled chair at the top of the ramp in the open doorway was Ivy Daggett, and she was listening to what she supposed to be the sound of water beyond the wall and below the bluff—the river, she thought, hoped that it was. She closed her eyes and tilted her head back to envision its reckless swirl and flow, its seductive surge and pull. Calling out to her, she believed.

At eighty-six, Ivy was nearly blind, but she would not have cared to admit that fact to anyone, not even to herself. Or that she was just about deaf, too. She heard what she needed to hear, was how she would rather have had it put. And she'd seen more than she'd ever wanted to see. Her own son's death, for one thing—a handsome, intelligent, graceful man who'd died before he reached his prime, in her opinion. He'd only been just half as old as she was now.

Ivy's blindness was not an inability exactly, it was not an absence of sight, not murk, not even an inadequacy of light. It was only a failure of focus—a blurring at the edges, a smudging out of subtlety, a fuzzing-over of detail. And her deafness was not quite a silence either. In fact, it had a sound, unmelodic and continuous, like the watery mutter of a current. Like the low cold roar and liquid hiss of the Rampage River wending its way between its banks, she guessed. She coasted closer to it, to hear it better—down the ramp and over to the edge of the concrete near the wall.

A comparison of Ivy's face as it was now, in the flesh, and as it had been captured in the framed photograph that sat on the bookshelf inside the crowded bedroom of the camper behind her would show that she'd been a young and beautiful girl once, but not so anymore. The luminous complexion had become blotched and seamed, and the glassine skin had softened and loosened. It sagged off withered muscle and deteriorated bone; it hung in folds and wattles along her jaw and under her chin and around her throat. The full waves of her blond hair had dwindled to smoky wisps. The blue eyes had gone pink-rimmed and gray. The straight white teeth were decayed and nicotine-stained, some missing altogether. The full lips had hardened, shriveled, and thinned.

She'd been living in this camper ever since her son Jack opened up the old limestone barn and turned it into a dance hall. There'd been so much noise and commotion every night that first summer that she didn't have any choice but to find a way to escape from it. And even now she was glad that she had. Ever since Jack's death, Hannah had been trying to talk her into moving back into the house with her, but Ivy wasn't budging. Not yet, anyway. Not until she had to. With Jack not there, it couldn't be the same. What it was like without him, she didn't want to know.

In her cupped hands Ivy cradled a jelly jar with a cartoon picture of a grinning cat outlined on its side. She lifted it to her mouth shakily and lapped at the syrupy dark sherry; then she tipped it back and swallowed the rest down. She grimaced first, then sighed—with pleasure maybe, or maybe it was merely with relief. Maybe she was in some pain sometimes. The pills she took seemed to help that a bit, but the sherry she drank worked better, did more. It eased the pain, and it made her happy too. She nestled the empty glass in her lap and with some difficulty lit the cigarette that she'd pulled from the pack in the pocket of her sweater. She exhaled a long stream of smoke and then peered up past it, through the canopy of dripping leaves on rain-wet trees toward the clearing sky.

She would sit just so, just that way, for hours. She'd smoke and blink. Ashes would drop from the end of her cigarette into her lap, and absently she'd brush them away. What she would be doing was simply listening, hard. She'd crane closer, wishing to hear it all more clearly—the birds, the wind, and that sound that she took to be the roaring of the river, as it seemed to be ringing in her ears.

The truck's door screamed on its rusted hinges as Madlen opened it and then climbed awkwardly up. She slid in behind the wheel of the old pickup, with its high cracked leather seats and big red plastic steering wheel, which had always made her feel unpleasantly girlish and childlike, too helpless, too fragile, too small. When she looked in the rearview mirror, she could see the top of Glen's head framed in the back window. She winced. With that straight black hair of his, he looked all too much like Haven had sometimes.

Just how it was that Glen had been able to talk her into letting him ride in the back like that, Madlen wasn't sure. He'd just bounded up into it and taken his place there under the rear window before she could stop him, while Claire stood on the porch, frozen in place by her own unkindness, leaning on the railing, watching them. At first Madlen had resisted—it was against the law, for one thing, she told him, and too dangerous besides—but then she realized how many countless times she'd done the same thing herself, and nobody had minded it then, had they? With Haven and Rafe sitting up on either tire well. With Grinnell at the wheel, driving, and Doreen Cramer next to her. With the radio turned up high. With Grinnell smiling and having a good time, shouting out something so funny that it made Doreen howl and throw her head back hard to laugh. Madlen slowed and stopped at the end of the drive, saw Glen turn and grin at her; then she pulled out onto Indian Hill Road and headed down toward Rampage.

From the railing of the Riverhouse front porch, Claire watched her mother work to turn Deem's truck around, wrenching the wheel first one way and then the other, inching forward and back and forward again until she'd got it clear, then lurching off down the drive toward the road. Claire was regretting her own sullenness, sorry now that she hadn't decided to go along with them after all.

She hadn't meant to sound so hateful or so spiteful, not really. She'd just never thought that her mother might know how to drive a truck, that was all. It didn't seem like her to know something so practical as that, Claire thought. That was all she'd meant. And she hadn't realized either that her mother was going to let them ride there in the back like that. But Glen had gone ahead and done it—without even asking, he'd hopped right up and then hadn't even really had to argue very much before

Madlen simply shrugged and gave in. Just looked at him and said, Well, all right, I guess.

Claire might have changed her mind by that time, she might have decided to go along with them, if only her mother had turned back and looked at her and asked her again, You sure you don't want to come? But she hadn't done that. She had merely climbed up and closed the door, started the engine and gone on. Which left Claire standing there with no way to back down and give in gracefully.

She didn't want to screech out and run after them. Didn't want to make a big scene of it. She crossed over to the steps, running her fingertips along the railtop and palming the ball at the porch post, and she wondered if maybe what she ought to do was drop down onto the lawn and start out along the driveway after them. Glen would see her, all right. And he'd be glad to have her with him, she knew. He'd bang on the window glass with his fist to get Madlen to notice, to slow down and stop and wait for Claire to catch up. Then she could be hoisting herself up and over the back gate and into the bed and taking her place right there beside her brother where she belonged.

It might not have been so bad, might even have been fun in a way. She teetered there at the edge of the porch.

Glen was on his knees, sitting back on his heels and holding onto the truck's side with both hands. He let go to wave to his sister, whether goodbye or urging her to come on and run after them, she couldn't be sure. She'd just started down the steps when a bump in the driveway rattled Glen and bounced him loose so he lost his balance and tumbled backward. Then he righted himself again and held on that much harder. The brake lights flashed and the truck turned, and then it was gone.

Claire waited, motionless, in the yard. Maybe they'd forgotten something, but she couldn't imagine what. Maybe they'd change their minds, but she didn't know why. Maybe there would be some unexpected reason that came up and so her mother would have to turn back. Behind Claire, the Riverhouse, empty, seemed to loom. Overhead in a tree somewhere a squirrel was scolding her.

The rain had stopped and the sun's glare was sharp. The woods were damp and steaming with heat, trees dripping, bark black.

Claire kept still, didn't move. She waited, breath held, her eyes on the convergence of lines, their clear pinpoint of intersection at the faraway end of the drive. She could feel the slow seep of water from the wet grass soaking into her canvas shoes. The truck was not going to come back—she knew that, and she let the truth of it sink into her. Not yet, anyway, not just now. She knew it all right, but she still couldn't stop herself from continuing to wish for it to happen. She ought to have gone with them, she knew that too. She was wishing that she had. And she was wishing further that she didn't have to be who she was, wishing that it could be easier for her to give in and go along with whatever might be happening around her, wishing that she'd kept her mouth shut, that she hadn't made trouble for her mother, that she could have been more understanding, that she didn't always feel compelled to complain. That she didn't always have to be the one who said no. That she didn't always have to be the one who ended up making everybody else feel bad or get mad.

Deem's pickup truck was the same old rusted rattly thing that he'd had for as long as anybody in Rampage could remember.

He'd kept it, Madlen guessed, partly out of spite, because of the known fact that Grinnell had so disliked it. She wanted something nicer, she said, and after Madlen and Haven were married, she bought her own car. When she came into Linwood to visit them at the house on Foxridge Drive, before they moved to California, that was what she drove. It was smaller and simpler and easier to park, she said. It also wasn't a truck.

She'd been likely to drop in at just about any old time, back then. She'd show up uninvited and out of the blue, without calling first, acting as if she just happened to be in the neighborhood, was passing by and decided to pay a visit. It wasn't such an inconvenience, because she didn't stay long, only for an hour, at the most maybe two. It was as if Grinnell couldn't stay away, she had to come over and see her daughter, and yet when she got there she was uncomfortable and uneasy in Madlen's house. Out of control, it seemed. Lost and out of place.

Madlen had tried to convince her to stay overnight sometimes, but Grinnell wouldn't ever do it. There wasn't room, she'd say, even though of course there was. Where would she sleep? She didn't want to put her daughter out. And besides, she didn't care for Linwood. Said it was too noisy there, she wasn't used to all the coming and going, and it was bright outside at night, too. All those lights. The streetlamps bothered her; she could hear the trucks out on the nearby highway and they were bound to keep her awake.

What she never mentioned was the possibility that Deem might have wanted her to be at home, and her excuse was never that she might have preferred to be there in the Riverhouse with him.

There had been some times when Grinnell wouldn't even come inside Madlen's house at all. She'd just sit there in her car in the driveway and honk the horn until finally somebody heard her and went outside. Then she might take Claire off to play for a few hours at the park playground, or maybe they'd just walk around and look at things in the stores. They'd shop for a while, maybe Grinnell would even buy herself something, a scarf or a pair of shoes, and a toy or a trinket for Claire, and then the two of them would have lunch in the basement of Altman's department store.

Madlen and Claire had both welcomed these visits from Grinnell, for different reasons but with equal enthusiasm. They'd both looked forward to them, too—Claire with more anticipation than her mother—even though Grinnell never called first and her appearance most often came unannounced and therefore unexpectedly. Like a gift, it seemed. And it seemed to be the surprise of it that made it delicious for her too. But, Madlen wondered later, what about the times when Grinnell must have come by to visit and been disappointed to find nobody home? She would have sat there in the drive and honked her horn and waited and then honked again. She would have given up after a while, sighed, and turned her car around and headed straight back home, leaning forward with her lips pursed, both hands gripping the wheel, a frown of concentration and determination digging a pair of vertical folds into her brow between her eyes.

After Glen was born, it got to be that Madlen was more likely to go out to Rampage to visit with Deem and Grinnell there. She'd sit downstairs in the music room or on the back porch with Glen while Claire went along with her grandmother up into her bedroom to look at all her things. Photos and jewelry. Letters and invitations. Pocketbooks and sequined shoes. Grinnell had taken Claire into her private world; she'd talked to the girl, sometimes for hours at a time. Told her stories that Claire later forgot. Bathed her in her own old memories—about her childhood in Minneapolis, baseball games and parties where the rugs were rolled back and everybody danced, about her parents and the house they'd lived in, even about her brother, who had been killed in the war.

It was from these visits and this exchange between her mother and her daughter that there developed for Madlen an intimacy with Grinnell that she'd tried so hard but never managed to bring into being between them before. And at the same time that Madlen had been watching her mother start to change, without recognizing what she was seeing until later, when she thought back and remembered the fragile-seeming boniness of Grinnell's wrists, the transparency of her skin, the thinning of her hair, what she'd also been seeing without seeing was her children getting older too and becoming more independent— Glen weaned and on a bottle, Claire stronger and more stubborn, wanting to do everything for herself and in her own way. "I can do it," Claire would say, frowning. "Let me."

Just as she'd also insisted that everything that was done for her had to be executed exactly so: food placed on the plate in a certain way, arranged by texture or color or category, clothes put together and then put on in a particular order. Claire had begun to recite memorized poems and songs, she'd begun to talk, she'd begun to ask why.

And while she was working so hard to learn and to remember, her grandmother had been beginning to forget. There were phone calls. Grinnell wanted to talk to Claire in the middle of the night. She had a question for Madlen, and no, it couldn't wait until morning. She wanted to know something. What was the name of that song? she asked her daughter. You know, the one that we used to dance to? She said to Madlen, do you remember? How did it go? And what was it that Jack Daggett used to say? she asked.

If Madlen didn't have the answer, if she wasn't able to understand, if she couldn't recognize what it was that her mother was talking about, then Grinnell might be angry, she might snap at Madlen, say something nasty, slam down the phone. But then again, by the next day she was likely to have forgotten completely that anything had happened at all. It was the medication, Deem explained—the doctors never could seem to get the dosage exactly right.

When Grinnell came home with her third traffic ticket in a month, this one for running through a red light that she continued to insist had not changed, Deem put his foot down and took away the keys to her car, drove it into Linwood and sold it to a dealer there. He couldn't let her drive, he told her, it was too dangerous—not only for her, which was bad enough, but, even worse, for anybody who might have the distinctive bad luck to be out on the road at the same time. "What if you kill somebody, for God's sake?" he argued, thundering in his large and loud way. And Grinnell, as she'd always done, turned her back on him. She went upstairs to their bedroom and closed the door.

After that, when Madlen bundled her children into the station wagon and drove them to Rampage to visit, Grinnell and Claire went outside and sat in the car, pretending that they were on the road, on their way somewhere, going places. If they went too far or were gone too long, then Madlen had to go outside and bring them in.

Until the time came when she looked out the window to check on them and saw that they really were gone. She'd been frantic. She hadn't known what to do. She hadn't wanted to call Deem. She'd been afraid of what his response would be. So Madlen had merely waited. She'd paced the rooms of the Riverhouse, she'd peered out the windows, she'd kept her dread to herself, and she'd been hopeful, and she'd waited.

When at last they came back, her mother was only irritated by Madlen's concern.

"Just don't make it mean anything," she warned, her mouth hard. "Please."

And Claire laughed, delighted by the naughtiness of what she was only half aware they'd done.

"We ran away," she said. "I liked it," she added. She didn't seem to be scared. And she wasn't unhappy, either. She was holding a stuffed dog with a red collar that Grinnell had bought for her.

Madlen asked her where her grandmother had taken her, but Claire didn't know, or wouldn't say.

"We drove" is all that she would tell her. "We ran away," she said again.

And then, two weeks later, Grinnell was dead.

On the afternoon of Grinnell's funeral, after everything was all over and everybody had gone home, Madlen and Haven sat outside on their back porch, neither one of them knowing what to say, to each other or to themselves. The house behind them felt oddly empty, eerie, silent, muffled, as if, Madlen thought, it knew that the children were napping and so it had absorbed all their sound and ruckus into itself, was holding its breath for a time that would come later, when the children were up and life had inevitably and of necessity begun all over again.

They would be moving to California soon. A job in Los Angeles. A house in the canyon. Their lives forever changed.

"What are you thinking?" Haven asked finally.

Madlen looked at him. The air was hot and humid, without a whisper of a breeze. He'd loosened his tie and unbuttoned the collar of his white shirt. His dark skin glistened with sweat. He hadn't made love to her in a week.

"That I should have known," she said.

"How could you know?"

She shrugged. Fiddled with the clasp on her watch. "She wasn't herself. She looked bad. We should have known."

The last time Madlen had seen her mother alive, Grinnell was sitting at the kitchen table smoking a cigarette. She hadn't bothered to dress but still had on her nightgown, and her hair was snarly and uncombed, her face sagging and sallow without makeup; no jewelry, no shoes. She looked terrible, Madlen had thought. But she didn't care, Madlen knew. She watched talk shows and soap operas, and that was her day. She read paperback novels and she played solitaire and she drank icy glasses of gin until it was late enough for her to go back to bed again. She still polished her toenails, Madlen had noted, even though her legs were scabbed and flaked with psoriasis around the ankles and one once gracefully rounded knee was swollen with what she said the doctor had called gout. The nightgown had been pretty, a shimmery pink satin thing with a girlish ribbon at the neck. Her hair had been a mass of madness on her head.

"I don't think there's anything you could have done," Haven said. "Even if you did know."

They sat in silence with each other then, listening to the sounds of cars whooshing by on the street out in front of the house. A boy on a bicycle swooped by. A young mother passed, pushing a baby stroller, its wheels squeaking; the baby sitting in it looked stunned as it gazed out at the sun and the broad blue expanse of the blank summer sky.

"She was still in love with Jack Daggett," Madlen said.

Haven stared at her, his black eyes shining like buttons. "I can't believe that," he said.

Madlen shrugged. "But it's true. Your mother thinks so too."

"With what she remembered of him, you mean."

"Or with what she remembered of herself."

Haven turned away and said nothing. He had no answer for that.

And then among the notes of sympathy that came in the mail over the next few weeks was a letter addressed to Madlen, and it was from Rafe.

Claire was in the Riverhouse kitchen, on the phone, calling Anne Pence. She wanted to tell her friend that she didn't like it, not any of it, and she didn't want to be in Rampage anymore, she wanted to come home. She felt this fact with a desperation that was like a knot of panic tightening in her chest, growing inside her painfully, and if she didn't do something, if she didn't take care of it right now, right this minute, well, she didn't know, she wasn't sure what would happen, but she was pretty much certain that whatever it was, it wouldn't be good. Maybe Ruth's baby would die. Or maybe whatever had happened to Mrs. Frye just before she left her house and stepped out into that storm, maybe that would happen to her.

Claire gripped the receiver and bit her lip and waited, body tense, breath held, as the telephone rang in her ear. She looked around her at the mess that her mother had made of the kitchen, and she wanted to know again what she was doing here. Why was she in this place now?

Anne didn't hesitate. She told Claire that she had to come home as soon as she could, before it all went too far, before it was too late and Madlen did something stupid like decide to move back to Iowa for good. "You have to run away."

"How do I do that?" Claire asked.

Anne sighed. "Well, you have your plane ticket, don't you? Just tell them at the airport that you have to change your flight. Say it's an emergency. Say your father's sick or something." She paused, lowered her voice. "Say your father died."

Claire didn't answer. She looked around at the shabby kitchen, felt again that pang of pain in her stomach, rising up like a hard fist into her throat.

"Well, it's the truth, isn't it?" Anne continued. "You can stay here at my house with me for as long as you want. You know my mom won't care."

Claire shook her head. She wanted to go home, but she didn't think she could do what Anne was telling her to do. There seemed to be too many obstacles in the way. She swallowed hard to hide the tremble in her voice. "How am I supposed to get to the airport?" she asked.

The line was silent as Anne thought this over. "Can you get a cab?"

Now Claire laughed. "This isn't New York, you know." She looked out the window, past the lawn, at the trees. "It's fucking Iowa, all right?"

Anne sighed. "Well, then," she said, "I guess you'll just have to walk."

Claire tried to imagine what that would be like. She'd have to
sneak out, use the same trick that she'd heard her mother say
that she had played on Deem on those hot nights when she'd
slipped off into the woods to the river and the Old Barn, to be
with Haven and Rafe. Pillows under the blankets, bunched up to
make it look like there was a girl's body there, curled up, asleep.
Towels, clothes, whatever it took. Then out the window, down
the trellis to the ground, up the driveway to the road, down the
road to the highway, hitchhiking to the airport, on her way back
to what she considered to be her home. A driver grinding his
truck to a stop just past where she stood, pulling up onto the
shoulder with his hazard lights flashing, waiting while she ran to
catch up. She knew she couldn't do it.

"I'll figure something out," she told Anne, but she didn't have
any idea what. Outside the window, there was a stirring in the
trees.

"Just get your skinny ass back here," Anne was saying, but
Claire's attention had been drawn to that movement in the
woods.

She watched a man emerge from the shadows and step past the
tent into the yard. He had a child with him, and she was following him, struggling to keep up, clinging to his hand. Claire
slipped the receiver down into its cradle and moved away from
the window as Rafe Ramsay crossed the grass and came closer to
the house.

On his knees in the back of the pickup truck, Glen turned his
face into the wind as it blew over him and gasped as his breath
was sucked off. He lifted his chin and closed his eyes. His face

was brown from the sun and from dirt, and it gleamed with his sweat. The river flowed alongside the highway. Mrs. Frye's house sat up on its hill, with its windows still open and the tree fallen across its smashed front porch, but Glen saw none of this because his mind was focused on that shine he'd glimpsed from the height of the Riverhouse roof. There'd been something out there, he was sure of it. But when he'd told Claire about it, she'd scoffed.

"What are you thinking?" she'd sneered.

Glen had struggled for an answer, something that might intrigue her enough so maybe she'd want to know too.

"What if it's a crashed plane?" he'd ventured. Or maybe a spaceship. A UFO?

Claire hadn't bought into any of it, this fantasy of his, he could tell. Why couldn't she just go along anyway and pretend? Or maybe it was a pile of diamonds, he'd suggested, his voice shrill with wanting her to join him, figuring that no matter what else was going on, she'd at least have to find some attraction in the idea of that—a hidden treasure of gems and jewels, shining in the deep woods. But Claire hadn't budged. She'd only kept on looking at him.

"You're nuts," she'd told him, and then turned away.

Okay, he thought, if he couldn't find a way to get his sister to go with him, maybe he'd just have to slip off into the woods alone and find out all by himself what that shining thing he'd seen out there was.

The General sat smack dab in the middle of the two blocks of storefronts that passed for downtown Rampage. Madlen pulled

Deem's truck into one of the unmetered parking spaces out
front, taking up more room than she really needed to but willing
to risk an angry side-door dent if she must. Then she remembered where she was—in Iowa, where people were supposed to
be more patient and more considerate than that.

She climbed down from the truck. On the sidewalk outside
the store she caught a short and sudden and unwanted glimpse of
herself reflected in the wide front window. She stopped and
blinked, taken aback for a moment, because there she was,
Madlen Cramer, widow, mother, already past her mid-thirties,
shadowed by her half-grown son. Of course, she'd seen herself
there before, reflected just about that same way, in fact, and in
just that same window, but then she hadn't looked anything at all
like she looked now. Then she had been someone else; then had
not been now. Of course.

Then she'd been ten years old and new to Rampage, brought
into town by her mother to get her hair cut at a little place called
the Clip 'n' Curl. Grinnell had parked the truck in front of the
shabby single building on the corner next to the Sinclair gas
station. Madlen would have thought that her mother had made a
mistake if it hadn't been for the hand-painted sign on the wire
fence that encircled the small yard—in smaller letters across the
bottom, DOREEN CRAMER, STYLIST. The front door was open.
Inside, a ceiling fan circled slowly, doling out a slight uncertain
breeze that stirred the scattered hair clippings on the black-and-
white tiled floor. Against one wall had been arranged a rickety-
seeming rattan sofa with brightly flowered cushions and a
matching glass-topped coffee table littered with fashion and film
magazines. Across the room a single salon chair faced a sink,
countertop, and broad mirror. A hooded hair dryer lurked in the

corner. From behind a curtained doorway drifted the sound of a radio playing classical piano and a scent of fried food that mingled uneasily with the more expected and pervasive odors of perfumed shampoo and permanent solution.

Grinnell stepped toward the curtain and called out, "Hello?" but there was no answer. She looked at Madlen doubtfully, then reached out and with one hand pulled the curtain back to reveal a windowless room with a kitchen and a single bed. Beyond, stairs led up to a second story, and it was from there that the piano music came.

"Hello?" Grinnell called out again, but still no one replied.

After a moment of indecision, Grinnell dropped the curtain and let it fall across the doorway again. She looked at her watch and frowned. They had an eleven o'clock appointment with Doreen, and already it was ten minutes past. She sat on the sofa and picked up a magazine and leafed through it. Madlen climbed up into the salon chair and watched her mother in the mirror. They waited that way for twenty minutes before Doreen Cramer burst in through the front door, carrying a basket piled high with folded laundry, which she took into the back room and deposited there. She was full of apologies and explanations—something about the laundromat, one dryer on the blink, something about a dead car battery and an unexpected delay at the post office—all given as she pumped the chair with her foot, turned it around and tilted it back, cradled Madlen's head against the sink, and began to give her a shampoo. If she was intimidated at all by Grinnell's stern expression, she didn't show it. She was a blur of movement and talk—a small woman in a short sleeveless shift, with pink sandals on her feet, strong thin legs, narrow hips, flat belly, modest breasts. Her own hair was dark, straight, parted in the middle, cut short and blunt so that it fell in a clean line against her jaw and around the back of her neck. Next to the studied stateliness of Grinnell, Doreen looked like a child.

Madlen's white hair floated like feathers around her as it was cut. Doreen marveled at its pale color and downy texture, smiling in the mirror and saying over and over again how fine it was, so that Madlen thought she meant that there was something special about it, not that it was merely thin. Doreen talked and snipped and wouldn't let Grinnell get a word in edgewise, even if she wanted to, which likely she didn't.

Doreen lived there in the shop with her son, if you could believe it. That was only a temporary arrangement, though, just a transition phase, until they could get back on their feet again. It had been a good year in some ways—she had been able to open her own shop, after all—and a lousy one in others, what with her husband's situation.

What exactly that situation was, she didn't say. Later Madlen found out from Rafe that Haven's father was locked up in the reformatory, serving a life sentence because he'd killed a man in Linwood, where they had lived. Doreen had moved to Rampage two years before so that she and her son could be closer to where he was, but it wasn't clear to any of them anymore why. It wasn't that she loved him, it was only that he was her son's father and so she felt this sense of obligation and connection to him that Haven—who was, if anything, ashamed—didn't share. She didn't go to visit him anymore, because when she tried to he had the guards turn her away. He said she should forget about him now. Find somebody else to be a father to the boy. Pack up, move on.

When she finished Madlen's trim she turned to Grinnell, whose long hair had been wound and wrapped up on her head, held in place there by a pair of tortoiseshell pins. Doreen offered to give her a shampoo and condition as a compensation for having made her wait. Grinnell refused at first, but Doreen pressed and finally Grinnell had no reason not to give in. What else did she have to do, after all? Go home and do housework until her husband came home wanting dinner?

She sat in the chair in front of the mirror. She raised her hands up to the pins, exposing the soft white undersides of her bare arms and lifting the weight of her breasts beneath the silky fabric of the lavender blouse she wore. She pulled out one pin and then the other, and her hair came undone, cascading down the back of the chair in a long golden stream that, had she been standing, would have fallen all the way down to her hips.

She'd never had it cut, she said, not since she could remember, not since she'd been a little girl. Doreen reached to touch it, take hold of it, weigh it in her hand. It was so heavy, she said. It must be hot, especially now. Grinnell nodded. Sighed. It was. She hadn't taken her eyes away from the mirror, where the childlike image of Doreen's face seemed to be floating next to her more elderly-seeming own.

"Cut it," Grinnell said. Her voice sounded to Madlen like a growl.

At first Doreen didn't understand. She thought she meant she wanted the ends trimmed.

"No," Grinnell said. "I want you to cut it. All of it. Make it look like yours."

Doreen tried to wave the notion away. "Oh, honey," she said, "you don't mean that."

Grinnell's hand snapped out, gripped Doreen's wrist. "Yes, I do," she said. Her mouth was a tight thin line.

Still Doreen protested. Grinnell didn't mean it, she didn't

know what she was saying, she would regret it later, what would her husband think?

Grinnell's eyes glistened with tears. "He won't notice," she said. And as it turned out, she was right, he didn't—at least, not at first.

Doreen turned Grinnell away from her reflection and tipped the chair back so that her hair spilled into the sink and filled it.

Grinnell's eyes were closed. "Please," she said.

Later Doreen would say that she didn't really have any choice. She did what her clients asked, she did her best, they paid her for it, and what was wrong with that? It was Grinnell's hair. She could cut it all off if she wanted to. Who was Doreen, or Tim, or Madlen, or anybody, to try to talk her into doing anything otherwise?

Sometime in the middle of this, the boys had come in—Rafe and Haven. They dropped their bicycles in the yard and burst in through the door, all noise and dirt and sweat. They'd been out taping up flyers for Daggett, advertisements about the upcoming summer opening of the Old Barn. They disappeared behind the curtain and came back with bottles of pop. Doreen told Haven to go and get one for Madlen, and he did.

It was a memory that now seemed to be scattered in her brain in only tantalizing bits and pieces, as if it were a prism scattering shards of color and light: the bright flash of scissor blades, the chime of Doreen's laughter, the squeak of the boys' sneakers against the floor, piano music drifting down from the radio upstairs, the ponderous slow circle of the ceiling fan overhead. Grinnell's hair, wet, toppled like mown wheat. Her face relaxed, softened, as if a great weight were being lifted from her. That was the moment, Madlen thought, when everything changed.

For years old Mr. Sanford used to sit behind the register with his chin down and his hands folded over his chest, dozing with one eye shut and keeping close scrutiny of the candy counter and the book and magazine racks with the other. Madlen would distract him by seeming confused about the sum total of her dimes and nickels and the awkward bulk of how many of them she had while Haven and Rafe slipped rolls of chocolates and packs of bubble gum and dirty paperback books into their pockets or under their shirts.

Now there was a younger man there. He was perched on the same stool, but he was smoking a cigarette and leafing through a magazine, and he didn't look up when Madlen and Glen came in, and he was no one that she was able to recognize or know, and that unsettled her even more.

Mr. Sanford used to brag about how his Rampage General Store carried everything that anybody who was reasonable might ever be likely to want, in some form or another—socks and string, canned soups and vegetables and meats, soda pop and soap, envelopes and gloves, toys and puzzles and discount books. Anything that anybody needed, as long as it wasn't perishable, the General was likely to have. Including shelf paper.

At the back of the store, the young man said, pointing. Over toward the right.

Madlen left Glen examining an open display of pocket knives. He picked up one with an ink-black handle, pried out its blade, and held it up to the light, squinting at its pleasing glint. The man at the cash register looked up from his magazine and watched him. Glen smiled, then snapped the blade shut again with his thumb and balanced the knife in his open palm for a moment before he put it back and reached for another, larger, jewel green.

Claire could see through the crack in the curtain that the man in the yard had stopped there and was looking up at the house in much the same way that she had, as if he too were thinking that it might be alive. His face was long and thin. His hair, wet from walking in the woods, was blond, slicked back. His jeans were baggy on him, his shirt tucked in and buttoned down to its cuffs, up to his throat. He combed his fingers through his hair and then seemed to square his shoulders, as if he'd maybe come to a decision of some kind. He crossed the lawn, walking up closer to the house. Claire ducked farther back into the shadows of the room and listened to his footsteps on the stoop at the back door. He knocked twice and waited. Then knocked again.

When Rafe told Hannah that he was going to go over to the Riverhouse, she warned him, said that he shouldn't expect too much, things had changed. Like what? Well, Grinnell was dead, for one. And Tim had a new wife now, for another. Name was Ruth. Good thirty years younger than Tim. Could have been his daughter, was pregnant with his kid.

Rafe had only smiled at this. There was nothing new at the Riverhouse that he didn't know about already.

"Things have changed, all right," he said, and looked over at Jolie and grinned and winked at her. And she'd winked back, slowly, deliberately, as if she understood.

But then, crossing through the woods to get there, he wondered whether anything had changed after all. So much seemed to him to be the same. He had to lift Jolie up over the fallen tree that crossed the path near the fire pit, felt its moss brush against him like an animal's fur, and remembered that feeling from before. That downed tree had always been there, hadn't it? Too big for anybody to go to the trouble it would have taken to clear. And the rest of the woods seemed still the same too. Madlen and Haven might be running along the path ahead of him. They might all of them be children still. The only real difference that he could feel was maybe in himself.

He came to the clearing that was the Riverhouse yard, and there it seemed to Rafe as if maybe time had in fact been stopped. It could have been then instead of now. One of those hundreds of times when he'd gone there and stood there and looked up at her house, watched her window, waited for Madlen to climb down to the ground and join them. He could believe for a moment that it all might still be just the way it had always been, which—he knew better—it wasn't, and he was glad in a way for the reassurance of that fact too.

Because Haven was dead. And now there were only the two of them left, Madlen and himself.

A pup tent had been set up under the trees, near the path, and Jolie was stooped over, peering into its insides with her hands on her knees and her bottom in the air while he crossed the lawn, bold as ever, and climbed the steps up to the back door. He was recalling how many times he'd thought about doing just this very same exact thing again, and how he'd for a long time supposed, taken it for granted, that he never was going to be able to. That part of his life was over and done with, he'd thought. It was all of it as long gone as if it had never happened at all. Except that now she was here again, and here he was too, banging at her same old back door, standing back to wait for somebody to come.

There was nothing. No car in the driveway. It looked like no one was home.

He leaned forward to the window, cupped his hands around his face, and looked in. He thought he maybe saw somebody there, but it could be that he was mistaken. He knocked on the door again and called out, "Hello?" then stood back and looked up at the windows above him.

Jolie had gone inside the tent and was down on her hands and knees, with her head just poking out of the flap and her face turned to watch him, making sure, as always, that he was still there.

He knocked again, harder this time, thinking he'd give it one more try, and he was about to turn away when a girl was at the door, opening it, and standing at the screen. She looked just as he'd expected her to, with her white hair and gray eyes, like Madlen's.

"Hi," he said.

She seemed to shrug. Held one hand up to shade her eyes and squint at him. "Hi."

He cleared his throat and squared his shoulders again. "I was looking for Madlen Cramer?" he said.

Claire dropped her hand, shook her head. "Well, she's not here," she said.

He considered this. "You happen to know when she'll be back?"

"No," she answered, then thought. "Maybe any minute."

The child in the yard had tired of the tent and was pecking at the grass like a little brown bird.

"Think you could give her a message for me?" Rafe asked. "Tell her Rafe Ramsay stopped by?"

Claire shrugged again. "I suppose I could," she said.

Jolie had found Glen's lost marble, and she brought it over to show it to Rafe. He told her it was a cat's-eye, and she seemed to marvel at the bare idea of that, held it up to her own eye, sniffed at it, cupped it in the pocket of her palm. Rafe turned back to Claire, grinned, put his hand on the slim shoulder of the child.

"This is my daughter, Jolie," he said.

Claire took in the badly cut hair, the red sunglasses, the boy's clothing on the girl's slim frame. "Hi, Jolie," she said.

Rafe was looking at her. He seemed to be expecting something more. "And you're . . . ?" he asked.

"Claire," she told him. She waved her hand in front of her face, fidgeting, as if to swat at a gnat.

He sucked on his cheek and nodded. Shuffled his feet. "Claire."

"Claire Cramer," she said, wondering what business it was of his.

Rafe grinned, looked away, looked back at her, and shook his head and laughed.

Claire's face reddened. "What's so funny?"

"You're her kid."

Claire shrugged. Raised an eyebrow. "So what?"

"So nothing. I know your mom, that's all. And I used to know your dad. Days past. Long time ago." He pulled back, looked her over, nodded. "I should have figured it out sooner. You look like her," he said. "I mean, the way she used to look. When she was a kid."

Claire smiled, scratched at a bug bite on her knee.

"Well, you're as pretty as she was, anyway," he went on.

This embarrassed her. "You want me to tell her you were here?"

He looked away, squinted at the woods for a moment, then turned back to her again, his eyes steady and hard, like two blue stones.

"I'm real sorry about what happened to your dad, Claire," he said.

She blinked. He frowned, waited. She rubbed her hand on her head, scrubbed at her scalp with her fingers. He closed his eyes, exhaled, then looked back at her again. She fiddled with the handle on the door.

"Listen," he said, "you think you could maybe spare me a glass of water?"

She hesitated, unsure of what she should do. Here was a strange man and he was asking her to let him come inside the house. But he wasn't a stranger really, was he? He knew her mother. And he'd been a friend of her dad's too. Plus this was Iowa, and it was supposed to be safe—wasn't that what Ruth kept saying? Claire stepped back, held the door open. "Sure," she said. "I guess."

She let the screen slap shut after him. The mess that the kitchen was in embarrassed her. She found a glass and filled it with water at the sink, then turned to him. He was looking around at the empty cupboards, the piles of dishes and cups and glasses and utensils on the counters and the table and the floor.

"My mother's been cleaning," Claire told him.

She pushed some plates and saucers aside and set his glass down on the table. He pulled out a chair and sat down.

"You visiting here for long?" he asked.

She winced. "I hope not," she said.

He rubbed his chin with his thumb and looked at her askance. "Why's that?" he asked. "You don't like it here?"

She shrugged again. "Not much."

He nodded, as if he understood. He found an ashtray among the piled plates and pulled it toward him. Patted his shirt pocket. "You mind if I smoke?" he asked.

She shrugged. "I guess not."

"You smoke?" He held the pack out, offered it to her with one cigarette poked up.

She blushed. "No."

He eyed her long legs, bare feet, toes curled against the linoleum. She tugged at the hem of her shorts, then leaned back against the counter on her elbows and considered him back—his blue eyes, blond hair stiff as straw, white shirt pressed and creased and buttoned up at the collar and the cuffs. There was something familiar about him, she thought; he reminded her of someone. An actor, maybe. Somebody in a movie that she'd seen. It was hot, but he didn't seem to mind. He lit the cigarette, shook out the match, blew smoke.

"So," he asked, "is your mom still as pretty as she used to be?"

Claire shrugged. "I guess maybe she is," she said.

He smiled. "Now that was a stupid question," he said. "How would you know?" He picked a bit of tobacco off his tongue, paused, looked at her. His face had hardened, was suddenly serious again. "You know what they say, don't you, Claire?"

"No, what do they say?"

"It's always the good ones end up dying young. The rest of us, we go on and on."

She looked away from him.

"That's why the world's so bad." He cleared his throat.

He tapped his ashes, rolled the end of his cigarette against the edge of the ashtray. She watched a drop of sweat thread a trail down along the line of his jaw. He looked away from her, dropped his head, then suddenly slammed his fist down on the tabletop. Cups rattled, dishes jumped.

"Number-one cause of death in America," he said. "You know that?"

She shook her head. "I thought it was murder," she said.

"Naw," he said. "Fucking automobile. Shit."

She smiled. "Yeah. Shit." She rubbed her hands together, looked around the kitchen. Her eyes stung. She turned back to the sink, poured a glass of water for herself, and drank it down.

"So where'd everybody go?" he asked.

"Deem's in Linwood. His wife is having a baby."

"Deem?"

"My grandfather. We call him that. My mother went into Rampage."

"And she left you here all by yourself?"

She shrugged. "I'm old enough."

He considered her. "How old is that?"

"Thirteen. Almost."

He smiled. "Well, I guess that's old enough, all right."

He ran his fingers through his hair and smiled crookedly. She cleared her throat, tossed her head, took a breath.

"So you knew my dad when he was a kid?" she asked.

"I said I did."

She studied his blue eyes. "What was he like?"

Rafe smiled. He held his hand up, fingers spread, palm flat. "See this?" he asked.

A diagonal slash, white line, raised scar, ran straight down the mound of the ball of his thumb toward his wrist.

"Blood brothers," he said. He seemed to be shrugging himself free of something. "That's what we were, me and Haven—your dad and me."

Claire looked at the scar on Rafe's palm and thought she recognized it as something like the one she remembered seeing on her father's hand. She looked at Rafe's face and thought she recognized that too—he seemed to be someone that she'd seen before. He seemed to be someone she knew.

Jolie was at the door with her face pressed up to the screen. She was looking at him, her eyes wide, her face solemn. Rafe crushed his cigarette out in the ashtray, pushed his chair back, and stood up. His boots seemed heavy on the floor. He dug down into his pocket, pulled out a folded piece of paper, and set it on the table. "Give this to your mother for me, will you?" he asked.

She nodded. He came around the table to her, reached and cupped her chin in his hand, and lifted her face up closer to his. She could smell the citrus scent of his cologne. He leaned toward her, took a deep breath, pressed his lips to her forehead, and held them there for a moment before he let her go and turned away.

When she opened her eyes again, the door was slapping shut after him. The sun had broken down the morning's clouds; it hit the wet grass, raising steam. Rafe swooped Jolie up onto his shoulders and carried her down the steps, across the yard, and back into the deep cool shadows of the woods again.

Claire sat at the table in his chair. She thought of the scar on his palm and of the fine white line that she'd traced with her fingertip across the flat of her father's hand. Blood brothers, Rafe had said. She fished the butt of his cigarette out of the ashtray, smoothed it straight, and lit it. The glass of water that she'd given him sat untouched beside the note that he'd left for her mother, and Claire watched the world fracture as tears welled up in her eyes.

Madlen had found the shelf paper, rolls of it wrapped in plastic and stacked in a bin on a table at the back, and she was digging through them, trying to find some with patterns that matched, when she heard the sound of a woman's voice, loud and shrill, carrying through the store. She peered around a counter to see Hannah Daggett arguing with the young man at the register about the price tag on the little girl's sundress that she was holding in her hand. Glen was nearby, still studying the knives. Hannah shook the dress at him, and the gaudy flowered fabric of her own skirt billowed out around her as she moved.

"It's too much money," she complained.

The young man only shrugged. He reached past her to straighten the display of breath mints and matches next to the register.

"And there's a button missing. And I see a loose thread right here on the strap," Hannah went on, stepping up closer to the counter.

The young man sighed and smiled in resignation at her. He took the dress and examined it.

"Listen, it costs what it says, okay?" he said finally. Feebly. "That's all I can tell you, Miz Daggett. Now if you don't like it, well, I guess then maybe you don't want to buy it. What do you need with a dress like this one anyway?"

Hannah reached forward and furiously yanked the dress back. "None of your damn business," she said. She opened her purse and dug around inside it, then slapped a bill down on the counter. The young man took his time. He picked up the bill, studied it, and then punched at the buttons on the cash register as Madlen drew back into the shadows at the back of the store, to avoid being seen and recognized and greeted by Hannah Daggett. Glen slipped the green-handled knife into his pocket, then stepped out the door and into the blinding dazzle of sunlight on the street.

If Ivy Daggett had been sitting in her wheelchair in the doorway of her camper, or even on the concrete near the wall at the bottom of its ramp, she might have seen the car's approach; her attention might have been caught by the sparks of sunlight glinting on its glass and chrome and flashing through the trees as it rolled down the mud road, tires squelching.

Hannah pulled up and stopped. This wasn't much of a car that Rafe had brought with him and was letting her use for her errands in town, but at least it was a car. It started when you wanted it to, and it went where you drove it to, and there was definitely something to be said for that.

The interior of the camper was small and cramped and dark. Its layout was simple: there was a kitchenette and table at one end, a sitting room in the middle, and a bedroom and a bathroom at the other end. The place was a clutter of battered furniture and broken-looking junk that had been collected and piled up in corners and against the walls to maintain a path for Ivy's chair. The blond carpet, where it was exposed, was threadbare, mildew-splotched, and spill-stained, damp still in places near the open windows where the rain had been free to splatter in. The kitchen cabinets were loose at the hinges, their handles were broken, their paint was battered and chipped; the stovetop was grease-spattered and crumb-crusted; the countertop Formica had been worn through in places all the way down to the bare white bone of the wood. Plants hung in the windows, green and leggy, allowed to grow aimless and wild.

Ivy was sitting with her chair pulled up close to the kitchen table, and she was playing a game of solitaire. She held the deck of cards in her hand and squinted at each one before she set it down. Across the room the television set was on, but its picture rolled and its sound droned on without meaning. An almost full bottle of sherry sat within reach near Ivy's left hand. She turned over a card, peered at it, then placed it on a pile on the tabletop as best as she could.

Hannah's entrance seemed to raise the accumulated dust, a demented swirling sparkle within the long shafts of sunlight that streamed in through the gaps between the slatted windowpanes. Ivy put down the cards.

"What's in that bag?" she wanted to know.

Hannah smiled, pleased. "It's for Jolie," she said.

The old woman had been hoping that maybe it was something for her. A gift, for no reason, maybe. Something pretty. Something with some extravagance for once. She didn't know anybody named Jolie. Disappointed, she turned away. Picked up the cards and slapped at them. Reached for the bottle and poured more sherry into her glass.

Hannah, thrown by her enthusiasm, circled the room, swinging the dress from its hanger, raising her voice, explaining everything, talking about the young man at the General, how mean he'd been about the price of the dress. A button was missing and there was a loose thread, but she could fix that, no problem.

And also, listen to this, she'd seen Madlen Malek-I-mean-

Cramer in the store and guess who she'd had with her? Her son. It had to be. Couldn't be anybody else.

"He looks just like his father did," Hannah said. "Might be the exact identical spitting image of Haven when he was that age. You'd think you stepped back in time, to see the kid. You'd wonder if maybe somebody had found a way to turn back the clock."

And, Hannah went on, she'd also watched him shoplift, had seen with her own two eyes how he swiped a pocket knife from off the counter and didn't that just serve the young man right, after he'd already been so rude to her about the dress and what was obviously wrong with it?

Hannah's bulk seemed to fill the room. Ivy sank down into her chair. Hannah's voice was loud. She talked and talked, and the sound of her went on and on, in a garble of words that her mother-in-law was no longer able entirely to discern. Something about Haven, it seemed. Something about that boy Rafe.

FIVE

A Pitiful Sort of Solace

WHEN MADLEN AND GLEN GOT BACK TO THE RIVERHOUSE, Claire was waiting for them, sitting on the porch step, chin in hand, face crumpled into a frown that deepened at her mother's approach. Glen had brought a sandwich and a can of pop and a package of chips in a bag for her.

"A man was here," Claire told her mother. "He came by while you were gone."

Madlen was holding the shopping bag of shelf paper in her arms. "A man," she said, shifting the awkward bundle. "What man?"

Claire examined the sandwich. Egg salad, which she liked. Corn chips, which she didn't. She shrugged. "He said his name was Rafe and that he knew you. Daddy too."

Madlen set her bundle down. Her face was flushed with heat,

damp with sweat. She pushed her hair off her forehead with the back of her wrist while Claire pulled the tab of the pop can, grimacing. She sipped at it, nostrils flaring at the fizz.

"Did you talk to him?" Madlen asked. She supposed that she should have expected him to come by today, after he'd heard her whistle in the woods last night.

Claire shrugged again. "A little. But he didn't really come here to see me, I don't guess."

Madlen merely stared at her daughter, and she thought that what she saw in the girl's coolly returned look was something like her own long-gone insolence.

Claire stood up and hopped down the steps. "He left you a note," she said. "It's on the counter."

With a toss of her head, she turned and crossed the lawn and crawled into Glen's tent. She pulled the flap down and zipped it, with a certain finality, shut.

When Deem phoned from the hospital later to say that Ruth was all right and the baby hadn't come, Madlen mentioned to him that she'd seen Hannah Daggett at the General that morning. There was a pause, so at first she thought that maybe he didn't remember, maybe he didn't even know who it was she was talking about—when she was sure that of course he did, he had to, didn't he? Until it dawned on her that probably he hadn't been paying any attention at all to what she was telling him, he didn't care, he wasn't listening, and so she didn't go on to say that she'd also seen Rafe at Hannah's house the night before. Or that he'd come by the Riverhouse looking for her while Claire was home alone.

Deem only asked her, "What were you doing in town?"

She'd needed something at the store, she answered. Shelf paper. And again he hesitated, his thoughts on Ruth, and he didn't ask her what for. Which she was glad of, because she didn't want to have to tell him the truth, which was that his house was, had become, in her opinion, an almost hopeless mess. That this big brick behemoth of his was worse than only old now, it was close to getting to be rundown too. It needed work, a lot of it—not just a good scrubbing, but also some serious refurbishing and repair. It had been let go for too long was what Madlen thought, and Ruth just didn't seem to be very much of a housekeeper, either, although she was likely to have defended herself by arguing that she didn't want to change things unnecessarily, out of respect for Deem, and that was why.

Madlen didn't have any sympathy for this attitude of Ruth's, because what she was wanting was for everything around her to be fixed. Once and for all. And she'd do it herself if she had to, starting right then. She'd patch up all the holes, clean out all the drawers and all the closets and all the cupboards, sort through and throw away every bit and piece of old and worthless junk that had accumulated in her life over the years. Get rid of it all, each used-up and broken and battered thing she owned, and start over again, brand-new. Blank canvas. Clean slate. Empty room. Even if that meant leaving everything she'd ever had of her own behind.

"Are you okay?" she asked her father.

"I'm fine," he said, but his voice was brittle with fatigue.

"Get some rest," she told him.

He would. He was going to stay in Linwood overnight, at the Unique, a motel across the street from the hospital. Just in case;

he wanted to be close. He'd call her again in the morning. Or, if anything happened, before.

Madlen hung up the phone and looked around her at the Riverhouse kitchen, tidied now, its sink and stove and counters scrubbed, floor polished, walls wiped. Behind the closed cupboard doors the shelves were clean and newly papered and the dishes were neatly stacked and the glasses had been carefully arranged, overturned to keep them spotless and dust-free. Still it all looked too shabby to her. Maybe worse, even, than before she'd cleaned it up, that much more rundown-seeming for the exposure that its bareness gave it now. The tiles around the sink were loose, their grouting chipped and cracked. The knobs on the cupboards needed tightening. The garbage disposal didn't work at all.

She should have left it alone, she thought. Shouldn't have bothered, she knew. Sometimes maybe it's better to let what is be.

She crossed the kitchen to the back door. She looked at the tent and wondered whether she should go out and get Claire and bring her inside. Try to mend whatever breakage there'd been between them, even though she wasn't sure just what exactly that was and so she didn't know either how or where to begin.

Upstairs, Glen had climbed back up onto the sill of the open window and stepped out through it to the roof. He scuttled on all fours down to the end, then planted his feet and stood, leaning forward, trying to see something of that shine again out there in what had become the dusk of the trees. But the light had changed, and whatever the shining thing had been, it was hidden from him now. He squatted on his heels and unfolded the map that he'd begun to draw of the paths that coursed through the woodland between the house and the river, and he studied it, matching up what he could make out of the landscape from there with the marks that he'd made on the paper already. He turned it over and smoothed it carefully over the mound of his knee. Glen tossed his hair back out of his eyes, and he chewed at his lip as he began to chart what he could see now of the pasture that spread out farther, toward the reformatory grounds and the fence and the trees around the twinkle that he meant to go out tomorrow, with his sister or without her, and find.

It was hot inside the tent, where Claire lay sleeping and wildly dreaming. She was walking down a narrow road, scuffing through the dry dirt on purpose, soiling the toes of her new white canvas shoes.

The lights of Los Angeles were shining brightly in the distance; they were a beckoning shimmer on the horizon that she knew enough to head for, following the old dirt road that led there, because that was where her home was, wasn't it? And that was where she wanted to go, to be, to stay, didn't she?

There was a puddle in the middle of the road. She saw her own image reflected in its glassy surface before she stepped on it, before her face was shattered by the disturbance of her passage through it.

On both sides of the road, the ditches were full of water, tangled with weeds and mud and bloated floating things. A dog loped toward her, its nose down and tail up and tongue hanging. It stopped and lifted its head and looked at her and barked. Up on the hill above her, a house was falling silently inward. Like a long slow inhalation, it was collapsing down, board by board and brick by brick, upon itself.

After dinner Madlen poured herself a glass of scotch from the bottle that Deem kept on the bottom shelf of the cupboard above the kitchen sink. She held the glass up to her face and turned it against her cheek. She felt flushed and feverish, and she wondered for a moment whether she might be coming down with something. A summer cold, maybe, although it was probably nothing more than the heat. She guessed she just must not be used to how humid it was here anymore.

She'd picked up Ruth and Deem's bedroom, stripped the bed and changed the sheets, measuring the unexpected pang of resentment that struck her at that intimate glimpse into her father's second life. There wasn't much to it. On the table by the bed on Deem's side, a book about birds, a package of batteries, a portable radio, a jar of Vicks, almost gone. On Ruth's side, a box of tissues, a broken gold barrette, a silk flower pin, a pencil, and a pad of paper with Deem's name and Ruth's written over and over again, with hearts and arrows—Ruth's love doodles, Madlen guessed. In the closet, their clothes, fragrant with the smell of them. His foot powder. Her perfume. On the floor, their shoes, lined up. His boots, mud-spattered. Her high heels, open-toed.

She unfolded the note that Rafe had left and read it over again. "When can I see you?" was all that it said. She recognized his handwriting from the notes and cards and letters that he'd been sending her over the years since Grinnell's death—a correspondence that she'd kept hidden from Haven, who would have been baffled if he'd found them, maybe even angry with her if he'd known.

Grinnell's old writing desk was still in its place in the living room, under the window in the corner. Above it, in pots on glass shelves, her hoyas twined and bloomed. Madlen rolled the desktop open. Its pigeonholes were still stuffed with old letters and envelopes, receipts and canceled checks, worn pencils, leaky pens. The rubber band around the bundled photos snapped and broke when she pulled at it. She shuffled through the pictures: Grinnell on a porch step; a young man, her brother, in a uniform; Deem in his garden; Madlen on a bicycle; Haven and Rafe making faces, waving from a boat.

The small wooden box had been tucked away as if deliberately hidden in the shadows at the back. On its top was the inlaid body of a hawk, its wings extended, talons reaching out. Madlen traced the outline of the bird with her fingertip. She shook the box and listened to the papers inside it shift. She rattled the lid. Poked a paper clip into the clasp and jiggled it until the latch turned and the lock popped open and the lid was up and the box turned over, spilling its contents out onto her lap. Papers and envelopes; a crushed white flower; a place card with Grinnell's name on it; a paper napkin from the Old Barn, folded, crumpled, then folded again. And another photograph, this one of Grinnell and Daggett—his thin, crooked smile, his white shirt, narrow tie, felt hat. Her cropped blond hair. Her lips darkened, pursed, her flowered blouse unbuttoned and open at the top. His arm around her shoulders, hand at her throat, fingers brushing her skin. And the newspaper clipping recounting the events surrounding his death: at Saint Anne's Hospital in Linwood, in the early morning hours of Sunday, August 17, after he'd suffered a stroke the day before while out fishing on the Rampage River near his home. With him at the time of the incident were his foster son, thirteen-year-old Rafe Ramsay, and his friend, Haven Cramer, fourteen. Survived by his wife, Hannah, and his mother, Ivy. Owner and proprietor of the Old Barn, a popular summer nightspot outside the town of Rampage, just off Highway 10.

Madlen looked out at the woods, alive now with firefly flame. She had always supposed that her mother must have been sorry afterward for what had happened and for what she and Daggett had done. She must have wished that she hadn't loved him. She must have realized that it was a mistake, and yet even though there would have come a time when Grinnell had wanted to change it all somehow, find the place where it had started and go back again to the simple innocence of what had been before, how could she? Once she'd already been with him. Once she already knew.

And, Madlen thought now, what if you could somehow recapture what was gone, lost long in the past? Step behind yourself into an earlier moment, reclaim what had been forgotten, change what had gone wrong, make happen what hadn't, undo what you'd done? Make the other choice? Start everything all over again, fresh? Just as Deem had done.

And just as Doreen Cramer had tried to do too, when she finally gave up on her husband, divorced him and moved with Haven back to Linwood. That was after Daggett's death. The Old Barn had been closed down and Rafe had been sent away, so what reason was there anymore for them to want to stay? Doreen told Grinnell that she only wanted the opportunity to try to find her way back to where she'd been before, and was that so much to ask?

Apparently it was, until now, all these years later, when she was old and sick and in a home, hardly able to remember much of anything at all anymore. Now Doreen didn't need to find a way back, because without memory there could be no past to get to. When everything had been forgotten, there were no mistakes to be corrected and no deeds to be undone.

Madlen put the picture and the papers back, refastened the clasp, and returned the box to where she'd found it. She sat in her father's wicker chair out on the porch and probed again the black hole that had been left inside her in the place where Haven had been, a crater of despair that his death had plunged her down into as if it were itself the crevice of the canyon where his car had landed and caught fire. Darkness all around her. An utter emptiness into which Madlen had been grateful, at first, to disappear. A chaotic tumble of days where she'd gone through the motions of being who she was supposed to be, of doing what was expected of her, seeing to small tasks, getting the kids dressed and fed and off to school, answering letters, writing thank-yous for the flowers and gifts and donations, with nothing to discern the time that passed, one moment from the next. And after all the business of it was over, then had come the genuine void. A blackout, altogether. Days that she'd spent in bed, sleeping, with the curtains drawn and the blankets pulled up over her head.

What had brought her out of it was pain. They'd sent boxes of his things home from his office, and she'd dragged herself up, intent on going through them, on finishing this one last task. And in an unmarked manila envelope she'd found the lease agreement for an apartment in Los Feliz, with Haven's signature clearly at the bottom. The key was on the ring that the police had returned to her after the rest of the car's remains were hauled away; he'd tucked an extra one away under his socks in his dresser drawer. She wasn't going to believe it until she saw his name on the directory beside the security gate, first, and then again on the mailbox inside the apartment complex itself.

Even though she had the key, she rang the bell, as if she suspected that maybe he was there, hiding out from her, the accident and everything that went with it all just some elaborate hoax. When no one answered, she unlocked the door with trembling hands and let herself in, expecting . . . she didn't know what. Guessing at and not wanting to think too closely about what might have gone on in those rooms, away and apart from the children and from her. Afraid of what evidence he might have left behind there, in the cupboards and the drawers, in the bathroom and the kitchen, in the closets, in his bed, in his sheets.

But there wasn't much of anything—not enough, anyway, for her to understand clearly what he'd been doing there, or with whom. Shirts and pants on hangers in the closet. Some new underwear and T-shirts, still in their wrappers, in the dresser drawer. A pair of old tennis shoes that she'd thought he'd thrown away. Towels in the bathroom. A stack of mismatched china plates in the kitchen. A soup pan and a skillet. Cups, saucers, glasses. Knives and spoons and forks. A bottle of orange juice in the refrigerator. Cereal in the cupboard. A box of crackers. Cans of soup. He hadn't settled in yet, that was obvious, and there didn't seem to be anyone sharing the place with him.

What had been his plan? she wondered. To leave her? To live a dual life? To suggest a trial separation? To ask for a divorce? And when had he meant to tell her?

It was an utter mystery. She felt then as if maybe she'd never really known her husband at all, and because that meant that she had not clearly understood herself or her life with him either, it seemed to be a greater loss somehow even than his death.

She had opened the sliding door in the living room and stepped onto the balcony that reached over a covered central courtyard in the complex. A boy was there throwing a ball against a wall, catching it with one hand, then throwing it back again with the other. He was completely absorbed by the rhythm of what he was doing, and he didn't seem to notice that he was being watched. His obliviousness enraged her.

What had happened next Madlen would let herself forget. The fury that had overcome her—slamming doors, tearing out drawers, overturning chairs, smashing dishes and glasses, taking a knife to his clothes. The tears. The look of shock and fear and disbelief on the apartment manager's face. The policeman's calm voice, his firm grip on her arm. The gape of the strangers who had gathered in the courtyard to watch as she was led away.

But anyway, that was all over now, wasn't it? It was time to put the past behind her, time to look to the future, time to go forward and move on. Just as she had said that morning to Claire and Glen.

Madlen sipped at her scotch. She thought of Rafe standing on the porch of Hannah's house, no longer the boy that she had known but now a man, with a man's body, a man's face. The way he'd looked up and seemed to be expecting her. And she felt in this a first faint glimmer of hope. As if she were being pulled up and out, into some kind of lightness and air, some kind of life, once more. She folded her legs up under her, felt girlish again. She picked up the phone on the table and she dialed the number that she could remember at one time had been Rafe's.

Inside the house at the Old Barn the telephone was ringing.
Rafe let the screen door bang shut after him as he went in.

"Hello?" he said, but was met with silence. Then, faintly, the
sound of someone breathing.

He looked up and out the window. Hannah was down in the
grass, bent over Jolie, pressing firefly light to the girl's bare arms
and bare legs, smearing it across her skin, her knees, ankles, feet,
her toes and her face.

"Hello?" he said again, and heard the quick intake of breath.
"Madlen?"

His voice shook her, seemed to resound within her as she
pictured him and pictured the inside of that house, the way it
had been before.

She asked him, "How did you know it was me?"

He smiled. "A guess."

"I got your note," she told him.

"I'm sorry I missed you," he said.

"I had to run into town."

"So your daughter said."

"I saw Hannah at the General."

"I know it."

"Oh, well. I didn't think she saw me."

"She did."

"I wasn't sure she'd know me, or I would have said hello."

"I need to see you, Madlen."

Startled by his directness, she looked around as if she thought
maybe someone was watching. The living room was filled with
all her mother's old things. She felt her stomach tighten, knotted
up with shyness and embarrassment and guilt. She shook those
feelings off. She looked down at her hand, at her fingers twisting
the coiled telephone cord. This was not the hand of a young girl

anymore. It was a woman's hand. She was thirty-eight years old. Her husband was dead. She was not betraying Haven, she told herself. He had planned to leave her. She was not being unfaithful to him.

"Why don't you come on over?" Rafe was asking.

"I can't tonight," she said. It was late. The kids were already upstairs in bed. She'd been drinking. She didn't want to have to drive the truck at night. "Tomorrow would be better."

Rafe smiled. "All right then," he said. "Tomorrow."

Outside in the yard, Jolie, giggling, turning circles, was aglow.

Deem had seen Hannah Daggett that morning too. He hadn't wanted to talk about it, though, so he didn't mention it to Madlen when he called her from Ruth's hospital room to tell her that he'd be staying in Linwood overnight. But the fact was that he'd seen her. Passed right by her as they drove out from the Riverhouse on Old Indian Road toward the highway just after dawn. Ruth sitting in the car with her hands clenched in her lap, trying hard to hold on to the baby, telling Deem that she was doing her best but even so it seemed to keep leaking out of her and she didn't know how to stop it. Her eyes had been shut and so she hadn't seen the dark and twisted shape there in the misted early morning half-light—Hannah Daggett stooped over a stand of raspberry bushes with a child beside her, holding a basket in her arms. At first he'd thought the two of them to be a tree, but then as Hannah straightened and turned to watch his approach, he recognized her, and when he realized who it was, he honked and waved in a friendly way. But Ruth had frowned and Hannah had shaded her eyes and looked after him as he went past without smiling and without waving back, as if she didn't recognize him, had no idea who he was, which, he realized later, she more than likely didn't, because he was driving Madlen's rental car instead of his own more recognizable truck. The kid had waved back at him, though. Lifted her hand and wagged it at him slowly, back and forth.

All the rest of the day that one image of Hannah had stayed with him, and he couldn't get rid of it. Through the waiting and the checking into the hospital, the examinations and the blood tests and the sonograms and the doctor's discouraging frown.

There were Ruth's hands in her lap, fingers entwined, or at her sides, fists clenched. There was her jaw working, a pulse of tension in her temple. Tears streaking her cheeks, then willfully wiped away.

And there was Hannah's dress, a billow of bright fabric in the gray light. The big boots on Hannah's feet. The basket of berries on the girl's arm. Hannah straightening, lifting her head, turning her face, raising her hand up to shade her eyes in the early-morning murk.

So when Madlen mentioned it, the fact that she'd seen Hannah in the General that afternoon, Deem did not know what to say and just held still, listening to her. He looked over at Ruth, sedated, peacefully asleep in her hospital bed, with her hair curled against the pillow and her face sheened with sweat. Her small hands were upturned on the blanket and gently cupped. Her mouth was slightly open, damp at the corners. Her breathing was steady, if shallow. Her eyes, behind closed lids, were still. So she must not be dreaming, he guessed, but only sleeping peacefully, and that, he knew, was more than likely for the best. Oh, he did not want to lose her.

Her simplicity—that was what Deem loved about Ruth, he realized. It wasn't that she was younger. It wasn't even that she was beautiful, although she was, he thought. It was that she seemed to be uncomplicated and easy, in a way that Grinnell had surely never been. Deem knew what Ruth wanted, which wasn't much, and he understood what she expected of him, which was enough. It was Ruth's very innocence that had drawn and held him, her clarity—which might be mistaken for ignorance and stupidity, he realized, and thought he'd seen as much in his daughter's look when she spoke to Ruth. He'd heard the condescension in her voice, as if Madlen felt she had to talk louder to get the younger woman to understand whatever strange meandering thing it was that she meant to say.

He thought of the quiet of the conservatory at Cedarcrest, and he wished that he could be there instead of here, with the windows cranked open to the sky. He'd have been tending to the seedlings. Weeding between the flowers. Riding the mower in a circle around the long front lawn.

Deem followed the walkway that led away from the hospital's entrance, past the scantily planted flower beds that if they'd been his to care for would have been filled to the edges with a kaleidoscope of summer blooms. The lamps on the bridge over the river were just beginning to blink on. Out on the island, the courthouse squatted like a woman with her big skirts outspread, its steps flowing down to the street. Behind the courthouse was the bland rectangle of the police station and the city jail, with its row of small windows all lit.

Sometimes, Deem had heard, if you were lucky, you could maybe get a glimpse of a woman on the opposite bank, down at the edge of the old rundown neighborhood that was known as Rompot, standing in the grass with her blouse open, blowing kisses and showing herself off to her man, who'd been unlucky enough to get himself locked up for a few nights in the Linwood jail. That seemed like a pitiful sort of solace to Deem just then, for man and woman both, and he wasn't sure whether it ever really happened anyway. He'd never seen it for himself, although he always, by habit, looked.

He crossed the street to check into a room at the Unique. He had no baggage with him, which was an embarrassment because he thought it might seem suspicious to the woman behind the desk, and he wasn't sure that he had within him the strength to explain to her the innocent truth of his situation, but she didn't ask him any questions anyway, only glanced at the card that he filled out for her, then handed over the key and went back to the crossword puzzle that she'd been working on in her lap. He walked around the corner to a drugstore, where he bought a toothbrush, and then on down the block to a liquor store, where he bought a pint bottle of scotch.

When he was alone in the dim light of his motel room, drinking the scotch and worrying about Ruth, he couldn't help it, he was thinking of Hannah again. From there his mind went naturally to Daggett and from there back to Grinnell. He turned out the light and lay on his back on the hard mattress of the bed with his eyes closed and his hands folded on his chest. He had to try to get some sleep, he knew, for Ruth's sake if not for his own.

Maybe he was drunk. Maybe he was dreaming when he saw again that same form that had been haunting him all day—Hannah Daggett on the roadside, bent first, then straightening, turning to look at him, shading her eyes. And that image brought with it another, one that no amount of whisky could burn from his memory, here, now, as close and clear as it had ever been: Grinnell walking down the center of the tracks outside Rampage, her back to the train. She didn't seem to see it. Didn't seem to hear it. Was looking through a small bundle of snapshots, shuffling them through her hands like cards. Her head bent down, her shoulders hunched. Afterward the engineer admitted that he had seen her, and he testified that his horn blared for sixty seconds at least. But she didn't turn, didn't look up, didn't step out of the way. She must have felt it coming; she had to have sensed its solid approach. She must have heard it: the screaming of the brakes, the horn's long hard howl.

The train hit so hard that it tore off her clothes—the thin print dress, pink and black, with its velveteen collar and three-button cuffs—and it tossed her shoes, the black satin pumps. Grinnell's body was carried off, a tangle of arms and legs, mangled and dragged. The snapshots that she'd been studying were scattered—of herself as a girl, with her parents and her brother, of Deem standing next to her, of Daggett and Hannah and Ivy and Rafe, of Doreen and Haven, of Madlen and her babies, of everyone in her life. They rose up and floated on the air like ash, they drifted through the white smoke, they settled on the gravel, tattered, blurred beneath a film of powdery white dust and soiled by the fine dark drizzle of her blood.

SIX

All Under Control

DEEM AWOKE IN THE PITCH-BLACK VOID OF HIS ROOM AT the Unique Motel, and at first he didn't understand where he was, or why. He sat up and ran his hand over his face, through his hair. He was perched at the edge of the bed as if at the edge of an abyss. His body stemming out under him, bare legs long and pale, feet flat against the matted pile of the stained brown rug—all this seemed unfamiliar and strange. A bilious yellow seepage of light from the bathroom. The drapes across the window pulled shut. The sound of a woman coughing somewhere outside. He held himself still until the world was brought back to him again, painfully, by the stink of mildew from the carpet and the sound of water dripping in the sink.

He didn't want to be here, that much he knew for certain. What he was longing for instead was to be home, in his own house, with his family—his wife, at least, and even the trouble-some inconvenience of his daughter and her children too, if that had to be. Deem wanted to be done with breakfast and off to work, knowing that all was well and as usual behind him at home. He wanted to be outside working on an ordinary day, even if it was too humid and too hot.

He would not, he thought, have minded his own sweat-drenched shirt, or the gnats; not even the mosquitoes. There was plenty for him to get to—trimming the roses and picking back the suckers on the tomato plants, mowing the storm-fed grass on the long lawns, tending to the fruit trees and watering the flow-ers and pulling up the weeds. He should be there. It was his responsibility. He didn't like it that he'd had to entrust it all to Scott.

But he had had no other choice, and so here he was instead, thrown back into this impossible situation of uncertainty, with-out person and without place, forced to spend the day here at the hospital with Ruth. Only waiting. Only wondering. Help-less, and not sure what exactly might be about to happen next.

Not sure, either—and this was the greater, more troublesome uncertainty—what might be going to be expected of him in it. Not knowing even what exactly was wrong. How could he find a way to react with any sort of reasonableness when he'd been left only to wonder, and to wait? A shake of the head from the doctor. A shrug. A warning that they all should just hold on and sit tight here, let nature take its course, be patient, wait and see. A sympathetic smile from a nurse, the offer of a cup of coffee maybe—why not go outside for a while, take a walk, get some air?

He ate breakfast in the cafeteria, made more miserable by the gray color of the eggs, the saltiness of the bacon, and the bitter pulpiness of the unstrained juice. What was bothering him more than anything else, he was beginning to realize, was the fact that he was not sure even what the doctor had been trying to tell him about what was wrong with Ruth. About her cervix. A weakness there of some kind, it seemed. He wasn't even sure where her cervix was. Someplace unspeakable. Someplace deep, somewhere far and dark inside. And if it were to give way? Like a dike, he imagined, floodgates spilling over, a dam built up across the impossible force of the river, broken down, flooded over, pushed past, beaten and collapsed. And then what? If the baby were to come early, if it were to come now, precisely what was that likely to mean? Well, that was something else that was a mystery to Deem, something that they had not yet begun to mention or explain to him, something that they hadn't—yet—taken him aside and said.

And so, listening carefully and doing his best to try to comprehend, idiotically mouthing the words even as they were spoken out loud to him, Deem felt coming to him from all of it what turned out to be only a certain kind of filth. As if he'd been exposed somehow. Or at least as if Ruth had. Riverbottom mud.

He went into the gift shop, and he bought deodorant and razor blades, shaving cream, and a T-shirt there. Trying to seem clean. Trying to maintain control. He paid for all of it with some of the cash that he had left in his pocket, and he wondered for a moment whatever in the world he might be able to do next. The girl behind the register smiled at him. She shook out the T-shirt, looked at him, and said, "This is nice. Cheery. A good choice. I mean, here." The blush of her embarrassment filled up her whole face. She gave him two rolls of quarters in exchange for the last of his twenty-dollar bills.

The T-shirt was too bright—the brazen yellow of raw yolk, with the slick black imprint of an idiotic happy face emblazoned on its front. But it was clean, and that was something, Deem thought. And too, it was encouraging for him to believe that there was maybe some hope in it after all, even on his large frame, when Ruth saw it and she recognized him in it and she reached her hand out to touch him and she shook her head at him and, loving him, groggily, she smiled.

He sat in the chair by the window while Ruth slept and did her best to hold on.

Her dreams were full of birds. Of flocks that lifted up from the trees like swirled leaves, swarms of feathers that left the limbs and branches bare. That swooped out across the sky, billowed blackly in the air like thunderclouds above the spread lawns of Cedarcrest Retreat in the spring. She took this as a sign that everything was going to turn out all right.

The birds would stop dying. The baby would be fine.

She was aware of where she was, and why. That she'd been leaking. She felt it still, that slow and steady seepage, hot, between her legs. The padding on the mattress underneath her seemed to be sopped. Sometimes a nurse would come into the room and rouse her, take her blood pressure and her temperature, lift her hips to change the pad, give her a warm towelette to reach down and wipe herself clean. She lay in the bed, trying to hold herself completely still, but the baby seemed to be turning and rolling within her with a life and a will of its own, moving hugely, as if it had somehow grown, was growing, becoming something larger even than she was, as if she might be no more than a slim and fragile vessel holding it, a sheer shell encasing it, dispensable that way, like the unfixable damaged shell of a cracked egg.

She wanted to tell Deem what she knew—that anyway it was going to be all right. She tried to sit up. Within her the strong hard rolling feeling mounted. Her body clenched itself around it, closed over it like a fist, and she groaned. A crackling sound seemed to be rising up and echoing off from deep inside, some huge and heavy breakage, and then the water began to come. It spilled out hot and fast, more than only a leakage now, an agonizing gush. The mess of it embarrassed her, and she tried to roll herself away from her own filth, the soaked mattress already turning cold. Her hand flailed out and knocked a water glass off the near table. It shattered on the floor, and with that sound the pain condensed, sharpened, brightened, and it held Ruth, shook her, lifted her, until she couldn't help but cry out. Across the room, Deem stumbled to his feet.

And still there wasn't really anything for him to do but wait, awkwardly, self-consciously, in the brightly lit, spanking clean, tiled corridor outside the scuffed aluminum door of the delivery room. He stood by the window and looked out over the tops of the trees that lined the streets of Linwood. When Madlen had been born, he hadn't been there for Grinnell at all. Not even close by. Not in the delivery room or the waiting room. Not even outside in the hall.

This was a fact that Grinnell had forever afterward, in every situation that came up to support it, held against him. It was, for one thing, a good hard useful solid bit of ammunition that she'd been able to hold always at the ready to bring out and hurl at him at a crucial time during any one of their many arguments.

And it also served her as a mean swift pin to jab him with in public—on Madlen's birthday, for example, when, after the cake and candles were finished with, Grinnell was likely to tell the story of how, when her only daughter was born, with huge struggle and in inconceivable pain, she'd been left alone for all those long hours to endure it by herself.

But that was how they'd done it back then, wasn't it?

He folded his arms across his chest to cover up the silly-looking happy face on the front of his shirt. He was tired, feeling his age—joints aching, head pounding, eyes burning, neck stiff.

They'd told him that he could go into the delivery room with Ruth if he wanted to, but Deem had demurred. Would rather not, he said, if that was all right with Ruth. Her head back, eyes wide with fear, small smile of understanding, hand squeezing his one time hard before she let it go. Understanding, and loving him anyway. In fact, maybe even because.

Deem figured that he'd just have to go ahead and show how old he was then, stay old-fashioned and behind the times that way. So he stood outside in the hallway for as long as he could bear it, not wanting to see what might be happening beyond that door and not wanting to hear the sounds of it either. Her cries, if there were to be any. The fluorescent lights overhead were too bright and they burned his eyes, seemed to be searing directly into his brain, so that he had to get away and walk—head down, hands pocketed, shoulders hunched—along the hall to the waiting room at its far end, which was empty, and he was grateful for at least that.

He used the pay phone there to call Scott at Cedarcrest, leaning with his forehead against the wall, one hand in his pocket jingling quarters, the other holding the receiver to his ear while he waited through the rings for the boy to answer and then was startled upright when finally he did. He looked at his watch to see to his surprise that already it was past noon—Scott would have come into the work shed to eat his lunch. Deem figured he was lucky the boy didn't have his headphones on and so had been able to hear the ringing phone. He could picture him there at Deem's own desk, sitting in the chair with his long legs folded under him. Scott was tall and thin, like a grasshopper, all knees and elbows and knuckles and wrists, the gangle of his body exaggerated by the big T-shirts and baggy shorts he liked to wear. He was almost never without a baseball cap pulled down over the hard knob of his skull; his hair was buzzed so short that when he didn't have the hat on, his scalp shone through, pink and raw. He had a row of silver studs and hoops pierced along the long lobe of one ear. But he worked hard, and he was reliable, and he had a way with plants.

"Everything's copacetic, Mr. Malek," he said. "All under control."

Deem closed his eyes. Copacetic?

"Cool," Scott said. "Everything's cool." Deem should just chill. Be here now.

A few days ago Scott had asked him if he'd thought about maybe keeping the placenta and burying it in the vegetable garden to superfertilize the soil.

"Rosemary says it'll be a girl, Mr. Malek. And that you shouldn't worry. Everything'll be okay."

Rosemary was Scott's girlfriend. They were an odd-looking pair, because she was plump, loose-breasted, heavy-thighed, and half his height—vertically challenged, Scott said. Her hair was long and coarse and curly, brown as dirt, often dulled by a delicate dusting of dried white clay, because when she wasn't working at Cedarcrest changing beds, she was an artist. Or a potter, anyway—she made pots and vases and wall hangings out of white porcelain that she fired and then glazed with muted colors that streaked and soaked the fine porous surface of the clay. Sometimes Deem suspected that she and Scott wore each other's clothes.

"What about the birds?" he asked.

Scott sighed. "Well, I haven't found any more of them today. Rosemary says it's over."

"Over?"

"Yeah. Whatever it was. A plague or something. It's over."

"What does that mean?"

"You got me. You want me to ask her?"

"You mean she's there?"

"Uh."

Now it was Deem's turn to sigh. He tried not to picture their two incongruous bodies sweating in the heat, naked on a blanket on the worn wood floor of the shed. "Get to work now, Scott, all right?"

"Hey, Mr. Malek, no problem. It's cool. Chill. I got it all under control."

"Copacetic."

"Right!"

Deem dug some more change out of his pocket and dialed the number of the Riverhouse. The quarters had seemed to him to be a signal of his own optimism at the time that he'd asked for them from the girl in the gift shop downstairs. After the baby was born, he'd thought, there would be people that he would need to call. But now he couldn't come up with anyone except for Madlen, and it looked as if she wasn't home.

He didn't want to think about where she might have gone, what she might be doing, who she might be with. She was his daughter, sure, but she was a grown woman now, and she ought to be able to look out for herself. He had Ruth to worry about, after all. And the new baby that was about to be born. That should be enough, he thought. He didn't believe that anyone had a right just then to expect anything more from him. Deem lifted his hand, snagged the pay phone's chrome hook with his fingers, and hung up.

Glen liked the sound of himself walking. The clank and clatter of his equipment—canteen, flashlight, compass, binoculars, camp shovel, tin cup, pocket knife. And the crunch of his shoes on the footpath, how that sound worked to make him seem like he might be somebody bigger and more important than maybe just the ten-year-old boy he really was. He reminded himself of the cop who'd come when they found that old lady's storm-battered body in the ditch. How the tires of his car had sprayed up gravel when he stopped. How his hat had sat squarely on his head. How the badge on his shirt pocket had gleamed.

"He's not a cop, for fuck's sake. He's a sheriff," Claire had said, but Glen wasn't sure why that distinction was important, or what the bottom-line difference of it was.

He was on his way through the woods to the pasture that he'd seen and mapped from the aspect of the roof. He planned to climb the fence there, then cross the field and duck into the woods on its other side. He believed that he knew where he was going. He was pretty sure he could find the way there, all right. And then, after that, the way back. He'd set up markers to help him keep track. A small pile of stones. A broken branch. A notch carved into a tree.

He'd told his mother that he was going out to look for bugs.

She'd believed him readily. Didn't ask any questions. Had seemed to be thinking about something else, and he was, just this one time, grateful for her distraction. Any other time he would have wanted her to pay attention to him, but right now this was better. He'd found a kind of freedom in it, in fact. He could have been anyone, he thought. He could have gone anywhere, and no one would have known it, nobody would have missed him, not for a while at least. He had a jar of moths and pill bugs and dead flies already in his backpack that he planned to use to show his mother later, when he got back, if she asked. Evidence. He liked what seemed to him to be the wiliness of this. Subterfuge. Camouflage. Decoy.

He'd find that shining thing—and at the same time he knew already, a part of him did, that whatever it was, it was going to be a disappointment. That it would not be what he'd been expecting. More likely much less than. Maybe nothing at all. He didn't care, though. It didn't matter. Glen wanted to do this anyway, no matter how it might turn out. He wanted to go there, and he would. Just for the doing. Just for the going.

He was following along the path between the trees, tracking the tangle of the trails. He'd come upon a small pond with tadpoles in it. Strings of frogs' eggs. Minnows swarming in the shallows, under the scum surface. And a clearing with a limestone fire pit. Beer bottles and cans. A downed tree furred with moss—its hollow trunk was big enough to climb into, which he had done, slipping down and wishing for somebody to come by so that he could prove to himself that he was as well hidden as he thought.

He heard the river. Its sound seemed to echo up to him through the trees, louder as he got that much closer to it. He crossed the swinging bridge, then climbed the slow rise of land and abruptly stopped.

Beyond a long flat yard was the tall and looming building of an old limestone barn and next to it a house, covered with ivy so that it was almost invisible, camouflaged in the trees. A car was parked in the driveway next to the house. A rusted truck was up on blocks, its two back tires gone. In the side yard, sheets had been strung out on a clothesline to dry.

Glen sneaked up closer, hiding behind the sheets. He scooted across the grass, scattered with dandelions, and ducked down into a window well. Dead bugs. Spiderwebs. He wasn't afraid, he told himself. He peered around—no one there. Faint sound of music. Slipped up onto the porch. On a mission now. Moving silently, the soft soles of his sneakers making no sound. He heard the voice of a woman singing somewhere inside the house. And some music, a radio playing softly.

He crouched at the window and peered in to see the same fat lady who had been doing all the yelling in the General yesterday—he recognized the flowered dress, the big arms, the folds of flesh at the back of her neck, her broad back, thick legs, puffy feet. She was at the sink, washing dishes. Her hair was in curlers—an odd sight, old-timey looking, like a magazine photo from the past. A man sat at the table near her, reading a newspaper. A little girl was crouched on the floor next to him, one hand cupped over the toe of his boot, as if she might be holding him in place. She was wearing the sundress that the woman had bought for her the day before. There was a bird in a cage on a stand. And a cat, looking impassively back at Glen.

The woman turned, and drying her hands on a towel, she walked heavily across the room toward the back door. Glen slipped down under the porch, squirmed in behind the broken trellis of its skirting, huddled in the dust there, with the woman above him, the floorboards creaking under her weight. He waited until she went back into the house again, and then he crept away.

How do you fuck a fat woman? he would ask Claire later. And when she didn't answer, he'd whisper, Roll her in flour, and laugh. It was a joke that he'd heard told at school. He didn't really get it, but when he told it to his sister, she would sneer at him in disgust, and as far as he was concerned, that was good enough.

Claire was counting on what she believed to be the fact that her brother couldn't have got very deep into the woods away from her and from the Riverhouse yet, just because he hadn't been gone all that long. Not ten minutes earlier she'd heard the back door smack itself shut after him, and she'd looked out to see him scuttle across the yard and step into the shadows of the trees and disappear there as if he had been swallowed in their midst. How ridiculous he looked, armored like a bug by his equipment, geared up for his hike. It would slow him down some, she guessed, all that stuff. Enough, anyway, that he ought still to be close enough for her to catch up without too much effort. She should have been able to hear the clatter of him even, she believed.

She stopped on the path and held her breath and listened, straining for some evidence of Glen not so far ahead but hearing only the cool shadowed silence of the woods instead, as it seemed to gather itself up and then fold back down over her. She peered into the trees for some glimpse of him, saw nothing but the dapple of sunshine and leaf shadow as it played around her. She sniffed at the smell of dirt and dank that seemed to be rising up to her from the ground and was in itself something like a remnant of the familiar boy-funk whiff of Glen himself.

When she came to the fire pit, she stopped again. Rain-stained blocks of limestone had been placed in a circle around a center of dampened ashes and the humpy blackened crumble of a half-burned log. The last remnants of an afternoon picnic or someone's midnight party maybe, left over from who knew when. Listening, craning past the huge hush of the woods, she thought maybe she could make out some far-off sound of Glen now, clanking and crashing his way through the brush, down along one of the paths toward the river. Like a knight on a quest, she thought, and knew that that was how Glen was seeing him-self. He was enthralled by the pretend of it, she understood that, and emboldened by the promising possibilities of his game of make-believe. She envied him some for this, she realized. Even as she was feeling herself to be superior to him, she was be-grudging him his heroism, his ability to become someone other than merely who he was, someone greater, or even just different, and what a relief it would be, she thought, if only she could find a way to escape her own more mundane self that way too. To be something other than Claire. To become nobody at all, even if that meant she had to turn herself into someone altogether else.

Glen had offered her a chance at this already. He'd invited her to play, had wanted her to go along with him, had practically begged her to join in on the game and the adventure. He'd talked about just about nothing else the night before, holding his flashlight up under his chin and making faces at her until she took it from him and snapped it off, so that what had been the twisted mask of his most distorted visage got turned back into only his harmless goofy smile instead. She'd been struck then by that same stab of regret that seemed to be growing out of her sense of the unstoppable progress in herself, the feeling she kept having that she'd maybe already gone off too far ahead of him, that she simply knew too much now and couldn't let go of herself enough to believe even for a while what he was telling her about what he might find.

But there she was then, the one who had been left behind and who was running to catch up to him, following what seemed to be the distant sound of him, going past the fire pit and back into the woods again, plunging as deeply down into them as she'd ever been before.

The rope bridge that had been strung up over the river was still swaying from the disturbance of Glen's recent passage across it. Below, the river water was deep and still. Claire stepped out onto the span, jarring its delicate balance with even her slight weight as her feet struck the worn boards and her hands grasped at the splintery ropes. Suspended above the water, she was shaken by a dizzying thrill of fear that pulsed through her, and as she bolted forward the bridge responded, swinging from side to side until she came to its other end and jumped off, skidding forward on her hands and knees. She picked herself up, heart pounding, and ran hard, away from herself and toward Glen, tearing down the ribbony path, her eyes stung by sweat, her shoes slipping on the wet leaves that littered the narrow trail. She stumbled again, but caught herself this time before she fell. She batted away a hanging branch, leaped over a fallen tree, felt the strength of her legs and the grace of her body, until she came to the end of the trail and burst out of the woods into the sunshine once more, at the edge of a wide grassy field.

Glen was not in sight. Claire stood gasping, breathless and hot.

She'd come the wrong way then, she thought. He should have been there somewhere, but he was not. She cupped her hands to her face and called out, screamed his name, sounded to herself like some wild screeching bird. And then she saw him appear, rising up from the deep grasses at the far side of the field as he clambered over the wire fence that edged its rim. Claire called to him again, but he didn't seem to hear her, didn't respond, didn't turn and didn't stop. She set off across the field toward him, snagged by burrs, tripped by gopher holes, startled by the grass-hoppers that clicked and leaped out at her, cursing Glen and herself too now, and her mother and everybody else besides, Deem and Ruth and even Grinnell, blaming them all for it, even her father, for everything, and sorry that she'd come here, this far, too far anymore to consider turning back. She was stopped again, by the fence this time, and climbing over it, she was caught in its barbed wire. It tore the back of her shirt and scratched at her bare leg.

When she finally caught up to Glen, he was at the edge of a grove of gnarled apple trees, hunched behind a mossy crumbling limestone wall and peering cautiously over its top. He turned and hissed at her to hush. Beyond him she could see the chain-link and razor wire that marked the Rampage Reformatory property edge.

"Glen?" she said, but he didn't answer, only waved at her behind his back and shook his head.

She crept up next to him. On the other side of the wall was crouched a battered Airstream camper, its dented sides gleaming and dazzling in the sun.

This was it, then—no diamonds, no spaceship, no wondrous gleaming glowing strange thing. Only an old aluminum husk, penned in by the fence on one side and the wall on the other, and an old woman, white-haired and age-withered, poised at the top of a ramp in its doorway, seated in a wheelchair, a cigarette burning in one hand, a glass of amber liquid cradled in the other. Her face was turned toward the wall and she was gazing blindly at it and through it and past it, at the children, at the trees, at the sky—leaning forward, squinting hard. She frowned and coughed and called out, "Hello?"—a brittle sharp sound that sent Glen tumbling backward from it, his equipment rattling with him. The woman stiffened. She lifted up one hand and cupped it to her ear, calling out again, "Hello?"

Ivy rolled down the ramp, wheels rattling, glass bouncing and spilled, its amber liquid seeping warmly into her lap. Whoever was out there seemed to be hiding in the trees, sucked back into those shadows, taken out of being like the smoky phantoms of her most baffling dreams.

"Are you there?" she called.

She sat with her head cocked, her face a frown of concentration and expectation at once. She listened, tried to hear past the watery mutter in her ears, and as she watched a shadow emerged, a sheer shape that took on solid form as soon as the boy stepped out into the sun. She thought she recognized him. Rafe's black-haired, black-eyed friend, wasn't it? What was his name? She couldn't remember. She'd have to ask Hannah later.

"Excuse me, ma'am," Glen said. He stood on the concrete looking at her, with his feet planted and his shoulders square. It was just an old lady. He was a soldier. A knight. He would not allow himself to be afraid. Behind him, Claire said his name, but he jerked his head hard to let her know she should shut up.

Ivy didn't notice anyway. She was smiling. "Come here, boy, come here," she said. Using both hands, with her elbows angled outward, she rolled herself over closer to him. Startled by her quick response, Glen took a step back. She reached out and snatched his wrist in her hand, held on tight so he wouldn't run away. She leaned forward, squinting past him toward the shadow that was Claire.

"You too," she said. "Come on over here where I can get a better look at who you are."

Glen turned and beckoned his sister forward. She stepped up then and stood near him. Ivy peered at the two of them, blinking, birdlike, at one and then at the other and then at the first again.

"Haven Cramer," she said finally, pursing her lips and nodding with some satisfaction as the name finally came back to her. She looked at Claire. "Madlen Malek." She squinted off toward the trees, seemed to try to see beyond them, to look more deeply in, then turned to the children again. "Where's Rafe?" she asked.

Glen looked at his sister. She shrugged.

"We're not who you think we are, I guess," she began, then stopped.

"I'm Glen and she's Claire," Glen said.

Ivy put her hand up and closed her eyes. Maybe she did have some small inkling of the fact that she'd made a fundamental mistake, but this was not a thing she cared to consider just at that moment. Here was the past, after all, it had come back to her the way that she'd been told by Hannah it never would and never could, but there it was posed before her in the flesh nevertheless, hair and skin and bone, and who was she to ask of it how or why? Better by far, she thought, not to waste time with questions that she didn't have to or even want to know the answers to.

"Never mind," she told Glen, waggling her old hand from

side to side and shaking her head as if to clear it of any doubt. "It doesn't matter." She smiled, gray-toothed. "Does it?"

"We don't mean to be bothering you," Claire said.

Ivy's smile widened, her face a craze of cracks. She tossed her head girlishly and laughed.

"No bother," she answered, and meant it.

She let go of Glen's hand and reared back and turned her chair and rolled it over toward the trees. He slipped his heavy pack off his shoulders, let it drop to the ground beside him. Ivy was leaning forward in the chair, gazing toward the shadows, peering blindly into them. She seemed to have drifted off, lost in thought.

Suddenly she sat up straight and cried out, "Listen!"

There was the creak of the crickets in the woods, the drone of an airplane in the distance, the rustle of leaves stirred by wind.

Glen looked at Claire, mouthed, "What?"

Claire shrugged again. She had no idea.

Ivy had closed her eyes and lifted her chin, tilted her face upward to hear better whatever it was. Something. She was listening to something, they could see it in her face.

At last Glen spoke up. "What is it?" he asked.

Ivy's eyes popped open. She smiled, cupped her hand behind her ear. "The river. Do you hear it? Listen!" She closed her eyes again. "Oh, it used to be so pretty here, didn't it?"

And at that moment she was seeing the twinkle lights strung up in the trees, white like stars glimmering in the canopy of the woods' thick dark overhanging leaves. Music was playing in the yard. Lanterns hung from the trees and candles glowed in crystal holders on the cloth-covered tables that had been set out on the grass. People came and went, the men in their crisp, broad-shouldered white jackets and the women bare-legged, bare-armed, bejeweled, their bodies snug in flower-colored dresses with wide watery flowing skirts. Jack had constructed a raised stage out on the grass for the band, and a floor next to it so that everyone, even the women in their sharp high heels, would be able to dance.

Her son Jack, standing on the porch in his tuxedo—how handsome he had been.

Ivy stopped. She picked up her empty glass, rolled it between her palms, dropped it back in her lap. She looked over her shoulder at the children, then beyond them, toward the shabby camper that was her home. "Not like now," she went on, turning to face them again. She raised herself up, sat straight. "It didn't used to be anything at all like this." The sweep of her hand was meant to encompass everything—the camper, the woods, the children, herself.

She tugged at the feathery wisps of her hair. Plucked at the fabric of her skirt in her lap. She dug down into her pocket and brought out her bottle of pills.

"You oughta stay away from the caves," she said. "How many times do you have to be told that?"

She shook some pills out into the cup of her palm. She opened her mouth and threw them back, swallowed them dry.

Glen was grinning at his sister. He rolled his eyes and waggled his tongue and turned his finger in a corkscrew at his temple. But Claire thought that she could see a sheen of tears gleaming in the old woman's eyes.

"I'm not all right," Ivy said, tucking the pill bottle back into her pocket again. "That's why they keep me here, you know. It's why they won't let me go."

"Who won't?" Claire asked.

But Ivy ignored the question. "I tell them, I only want to

look at the river again, that's all. I only want to see it. Before I get all the way blind. What's wrong with that?"

Glen shook his head. "Nothing, I guess." He was thinking of the storm.

"It wouldn't be hard, would it?" Ivy asked. "It's not that far. Just past the orchard. Through the barbed wire. Then just cut across the corner of the field and there it is, the water. Right?"

"Right."

"Maybe you would help me."

Glen shook his head. "Probably better not."

Ivy sighed. "You know, I don't know how to dance anymore," she said. "I wish I did. But I think by now I must have forgot."

Claire folded her arms and leaned back, regarding Ivy with one eyebrow raised. "Who are you, anyway?"

"My name is Ivy."

"You live here, Ivy?" Glen asked.

"Listen," the old woman said. "I told you already. I'm not all right."

"What's wrong with you?"

"Well." She pursed her lips. "I've been crazy."

Glen laughed. "That's what I thought!"

"You're okay," Claire said. "You look okay."

"But I'm not. I was nuts. Nutsy-cuckoo. Listen, you ever been nuts?"

Claire tried not to smile. "Maybe," she began. Then frowned, tossed her head. "No. I guess not." She squinted at the old woman. "What's it like?"

"I don't know," Ivy answered. "When you are, you can't know it at the time. So afterward it's hard to tell."

"How can you be so sure you ever really were, then?" Glen asked.

"Well, they put me in Cedarcrest for Christ's sake, didn't they? That oughta tell you something."

Jack had summoned the men to come and get her. He'd said he was fed up, he'd had enough, he wanted them, once and for all, to take her away. She didn't have any say in it. They were just doing what they'd been told. It wasn't their fault. She didn't blame them. They walked right into the camper and gathered her up out of her own bed, carried her outside into the yard. The light was bright. But she never did try to fight with them. Wouldn't have even if she could have, which she couldn't, because she'd been finding it so damned difficult to move. Lord, she'd been a mess. That embarrassed her when she thought about it now. Nightgown unbuttoned down the front, damp and rumpled and torn under the one sleeve, where she'd been picking at it. Hair a matted mess. Eyes bleary, hands limp. She hadn't eaten in days, Jack said, although she didn't know that for herself. Hadn't hardly even had the strength to get up to go pee.

She poked a finger at Claire. "What's the matter with you?"

Surprised, Claire stepped back.

Ivy rolled toward her. "You're a snotty little bitch, aren't you. Who told you to come here?" She glared at Claire. "Who asked you to butt in?"

"Nobody."

The old woman snorted in disgust. Claire said nothing. Glen was tugging at her arm.

"I ought to teach you a lesson," Ivy said. "Ought to take a stick. Whack!"

Claire smirked. "You wouldn't do that. You can't even walk."

Ivy turned to Glen. "Your father killed a man."

Glen slipped his hand into his pocket and fingered the green-handled knife that was there. "He did not."

"Yes, he did. Everybody knows it. In Linwood." Ivy wagged her head from side to side, and her hair wafted around her face like smoke. "And you!" she said, pointing at Claire. "Your damned mother!" She puckered her lips as if she'd tasted something sour. "That poor miserable hole. Grinnell. She was the one!"

Ivy raised her hands up in front of her face, palms pressed together as if in prayer, and peered past her fingertips at the children, the pinkish rims of her blue eyes widening. "Hit by a train," she went on, raising her gaze heavenward and slapping her hands together. The loud hard smack seemed to echo like a shot toward the thoughtful stillness of the trees. "Ha! It served her right!"

"Grinnell was not my mother," Claire said, her voice low. "She was my grandmother."

Ivy stared at her. "What difference does that make?"

"I'm not Madlen. I'm Claire."

"She did it. She did it on purpose. My son wouldn't have her. Told her to get. She deserved it."

"Did what on purpose?"

"Killed herself, you ninny! Walked in front of that train!"

"It was an accident," Claire said.

Ivy's hand snapped out and grabbed Claire's wrist, yanked down at it so that the girl stumbled to her knees beside the chair. "No, it wasn't, either," she said.

Glen had his knife out. He snapped open the blade and turned it so the metal caught the sunlight and gleamed.

"Glen!" Claire said. "Put that thing away."

"Let go of my sister, you old bitch," he said.

Ivy glared at him. "Get out of here." She pushed at Claire, who fell back. Ivy picked up the glass in her lap and held it up over her head. "Get! Go on! Get!" She flung the glass down and it shattered on the concrete just short of Glen as he picked up his pack and turned to run and Claire shrieked and rolled and skittered on hands and knees away.

The sun was hot on Rafe's back, so he stepped up onto the porch, into the shade where it was cool. He was watching the road, looking for the billow of dust that would be Madlen on her way over here in her father's truck. Jolie was near him, as always. She was playing with the marble that she'd been holding in her hand since yesterday. Because he'd told her that it was a cat's-eye, she believed that it had come out of a cat.

He took a deep breath, tried to calm down. Clenched both his fists, then unclenched them, then clenched them again. The girl was watching him, as always. He tried to smile but ended up only gritting his teeth, baring them. He shook his head, reached into his pocket, lit a cigarette, and felt better. He had to stay calm, he knew. He didn't want Jolie to sense that anything might be wrong. He needed for her to keep trusting him if he was going to keep from getting caught. He inhaled deeply and felt himself begin to relax, his jaw loosen, fists unclench, breath release. He'd come this far already, and now they were almost there.

Inside the house, Hannah was cutting out the pattern of a skirt. She was thinking that she could make a second use of the fabric of her own dresses to fashion some more clothes for Rafe's little girl, so she'd brought the old sewing machine out and set it up at the kitchen table. Her scissors followed the outline that she'd traced of the little sun frock she'd bought yesterday at the General. She looked up, looked out through the window to see Rafe outside there on the porch. There was some mystery for her, even in that clear sight of him there, as if she might have been only dreaming him up. She'd expected him never to come back here again and she'd thought when he left that she had reconciled herself to that fact, but here he was anyway, and it was hard for her to get used to it now.

Hannah hadn't been that much older than Rafe was now when Daggett died and they took Rafe away. He hadn't wanted to go, but it wasn't up to him. It wasn't even up to her. He couldn't go on living here, not with everyone talking the way they were about what had happened, as if Daggett's death had in some way been Rafe's fault. She would have gone away herself, she thought, if it hadn't been for Ivy. Not that the old woman couldn't have looked after herself, living down there by the river in her camper like a hermit, hardly ever coming out except to visit the doctor once in a while and the hospital that time when she fell and broke her hip. Not that Hannah could have thought of anyplace else for herself to go.

She supposed that the hardest part for Rafe must have been just the fact of having to walk through the doorway, back here into this house again. So many bad memories. It should have been a simple thing, surely would have been common enough for anybody else. In any other circumstance. The easiest thing in the world, people do it every day, don't they? They come home. Climb the steps, cross the porch, pull open the door, say hello again to whoever might still be left behind and waiting for their return. But the difference in it for Rafe was this: it wasn't really his home. And besides, he had never in his own mind meant to come back to Rampage. No, more than that: he'd meant never to come back.

He'd sworn as much to Hannah and to Daggett plenty of times. He'd flexed his muscles that way—proclaimed and promised that once he was old enough to be out on his own, then no matter what else happened, he'd be gone for good. Said exactly that to her that last time, with the social worker's car standing there in the driveway waiting, all set to take him, packed and loaded up. If Hannah didn't believe him completely, well, she didn't exactly blame him for the sentiment of it either. She would have done the same herself at one time, she thought. If only she'd been someone other than who she was. If she'd only known how.

But then what happens happened, and time passed and things changed, and so now here he was again, come back—it had come to this, a point where, he'd told her, he just had no other choice. That was the only simple part of it, if there was one. That there wasn't anyplace else he could think of that would be safe for him to be. If there were, well, he most likely would have turned up there instead, she supposed.

Over the years they talked on the phone sometimes, and he was pretty good about keeping in touch, letting her know what he was doing and where he lived. But she'd never met his wife, hadn't even been aware that he was married, much less that he had a kid. That had been a nice surprise. They sent each other cards on their birthdays and presents at Christmas. A letter now and then, just for the heck of it. Hannah had believed that it was just as well that Rafe went on about his business and kept his distance from here. It only brought bad memories back to him, she thought. A time in his life that was just as well forgotten, maybe. Until Haven died, it seemed that there wasn't any need for him to get tangled up in all that business with the Maleks again.

The only proof she needed to let her know she'd been right was in the fact that he seemed to be so nervous about it now, waiting to see Madlen again, and that he was doing his best to hide it. Out of pride probably, for one thing. And for another, she figured, the child. He wouldn't want the girl to know anything about how scared he was, wouldn't want her to start guessing that he might have a reason for being afraid, because then she might be afraid too, and inclined to go on beyond that and start to wonder why. He didn't want to spook her, he said. Get her missing her mother, maybe. Get her crying and feeling miserable. Well, Hannah sure didn't want that either.

Rafe needed for Jolie to keep on trusting him, he said, the way that she'd been doing all along, for his sake and also for her own. If she saw him falter, then she might falter too. And that would complicate everything, bring unwanted and unnecessary trouble to them all. He'd come right out and confessed up front that he wasn't supposed to have her. But if he'd broken the law by not going through the proper channels, by circumventing a process that was mean enough to keep making everybody miserable, and by bringing her here with him without her mother's knowledge and without the court's permission, that was because he was her father. And he had a solid need to have her with him. That was his God-given right, wasn't it?

Hannah believed that it was.

Besides, wasn't it all for the best? Everything else aside, he was only acting in the girl's best interests as he saw them. That was what he'd told Hannah, and he'd seemed to mean it, and she'd believed him. He'd rescued Jolie, he said. By removing her from what had been a very bad situation, he'd saved her. And that in itself was, had to be, for the good, the better, the best. Didn't it? How pleased she'd been when he had come to her for help.

Hannah had done the only thing that she could do, as far as she could see it, when he chose to come back here: she believed him. It was the least that she owed him, the simple benefit of doubt. He'd as good as been her own son for a while, for one thing. And for another, she couldn't think of any other reason for him to come back to live here in this place again. Unless it was Madlen.

Nevertheless, she watched him. She saw him seeming to bite down on his fear, and on his nervousness too. Recognized that he was working hard to hide what must have been the flutter in his stomach, what was the tremble in his hands. The girl was watching him too. He was on the porch, looking out toward the road, smoking a cigarette with his back to the house and to Hannah inside it. And the girl was sitting on the porch step below him, wearing those sunglasses, turning around now and then to look at him, keeping an eye on him as if she always needed to know just where to look, just how to find him, just exactly where he'd be.

Hannah slipped the fabric into the machine and clamped the foot down to hold it in place. And what, she wondered, must Rafe be thinking about her? As she flapped around him, around the house, around the yard like a wild bird. It must seem to him that she filled the house up with the presence of her own great self on purpose, to ward off the heartache of having to live here all alone. Well, she was larger now, that was true. And why not?

This was nothing new to Hannah. She was used to being looked at, ogled. She'd felt that same sort of scrutiny plenty of

times before, from strangers, from no one she knew or recognized, from no one she loved or who loved her, and they'd all
stared at her anyway, but why? Even when Daggett was alive.
They'd looked at her and wondered how a woman like that had
ever come to be that man's wife. The answer was easy: she was
his wife before he became the man they knew. After the Old
Barn was opened, Jack Daggett changed, but Hannah stayed the
same.

So she saw how Rafe had been studying her now too. She saw
how he paused, took a moment to take in the whole of what
she'd become. How he studied her, seemed to be appraising her,
trying to determine for himself, she supposed, whether she was
still a person that he could trust or not. And taking in the
changes in her at the same time, because he was remembering
how she'd been before, because he'd missed the slow and steady
alteration from that to this. He could only see it all at once, how
she'd been unfurled, how she'd been loosened maybe, how she'd
come undone and over the years had gone soft.

And how she'd aged, of course, at the same time. So he would
be seeing the same thing about her that she'd been seeing about
him, she knew, because time had passed through her just as
much as it had through him. He was older too, wasn't he? That
boy. Grown up hard and thin while she'd been expanding outward.

So Hannah watched Rafe watching her. She watched him
consider the fact of her, of her face, changed, and of her fat. As
well as of her hands, so capable, on the child.

"Who in the world cut this girl's hair?" she'd asked him the
first night.

His answer had been that he did it himself. Didn't want them
finding her right away, that was all, he reasoned, and Hannah

had believed him, because what else did she have? Jolie had been sitting on his lap, had seemed so comfortable there. Had made herself right at home here, had taken possession, made it hers. Without fear, it seemed. So what could there be that might be wrong, then? Hannah wondered. What Rafe had done had to be right and true, she reasoned, or wouldn't that little girl of his been somehow afraid?

Last night he talked to Madlen Cramer. He asked her to come by and see him here today. Hannah was glad for the company. It was good to have other people around again—Rafe and Jolie first, and now there would be Madlen too. She patted the curlers in her hair. Today felt like a holiday almost, she thought, smiling, running the cloth along under the needle's sharp silvery blur. There hadn't been a party here in too many years. Not since Rafe left, at least. Sure not since Daggett died.

And Jolie, if anyone were to ask her—but no one did—would for her part have said, quickly and with some assurance, that as a matter of fact she liked it that her hair was shorter now. Because for one thing, what a trouble it had been for everyone, herself included, with all those tangles, all that brushing and braiding of it every day. But more important, Jolie thought that she was able now to know an even bigger thing about herself besides her hair, and it was this: that she had become other and elsewhere, that because of what had happened she had been fundamentally and irrevocably changed. Whether or not she would ever be able actually to say how—what words could there be for her, at four years old?—well, that was something else. And another one's here and another one's here, and now this.

He'd held her while the wind blew outside the house; he'd

held her through the lightning and the thunder and the wind. It was a big storm. But he had never been afraid, and because of that, neither had she.

What Rafe had done when he took Jolie away, when he changed her from what she'd been to what she was now, was to give her a way to fall in love with herself as she'd never been able to before. She liked this thing that had happened to her. She liked this place. And she liked him too. That was a part of it, a big part—his blond hair, like straw, and his blue eyes, like stones. She liked it that her life had in that way been altered and started over. That she'd been able to become—she wasn't sure how, unless it was the hair and the sunglasses and the clothes—somebody other than whoever it was that she used to be. Before. That she was allowed to live there with him and Hannah. She loved them, she thought. It was as simple, or as complex, as that.

Yesterday morning she had waked up groggy and gazed at the window to see that it was raining softly, just as it had been that night when he took her, only warmer. The grayness of it was like the body of a cat curled up against the window screen, and that had been a comfort to her, in its way. It had seemed to dim everything around her down, just like when she had the sunglasses on. Edges softened. Corners round.

But then there'd been a sound, a footstep on the carpet, and a weight warm and bright beside her, and it had frightened her at first, sharpened and hardened things again, until she rolled over and saw that it was only Hannah come into the room, her white moon face smiling, one finger to her lips, telling Jolie, "Hush." Only Hannah, this big flowered and powdered woman, sitting on her bed, taking the girl's hand between her own softer two, holding it, smiling at her, speaking softly, and in that way calming her down. Asking, "Would you like to come along?"

Jolie had followed Hannah's big rubber boots down the stairs, past the front room where he was still in the chair, asleep. Why didn't he sleep in a bed? But Hannah had hushed her again. And taken her outside into the morning gray, into the warm soft rain. They'd walked up to the road, black and twiny as a licorice twist. This place, where the land rolled off in all directions, went away to nowhere, and the sky hung down around them like a wet rag, clouds gray and low.

Hannah had had a basket. Jolie had picked berries that she'd found there on the bushes, hers for the taking, like a treasure, a secret, waiting to be found out. Another one! And another! There had been more there than they needed, many more than she could pick. The basket was full, and that had seemed to be a miracle, such abundance. Enough and even more. Jolie had never seen anything like it.

Later there was breakfast—fresh berries and sugar and thick cream, as much as she wanted, no warnings here, no slaps. Then Rafe was awake again and he was sitting at the table too, with Hannah, while Jolie stayed close, on the floor, and played with the orange cat, pulling a bit of string for it to pounce at. Hannah said to him, She needs some clothes. So just like that Rafe gave her some money, no questions, no argument, no fight like there would have been between her foster parents, even if after a while the dad was usually more than likely to give in. Rafe just pulled that roll of bills out of his pocket and pinched off the rubber band wrapped around it.

Now Jolie was wearing the sundress that Hannah had bought for her. Its fabric was soft and cool against her skin. Her arms were bare. She was sitting on the porch step, watching Rafe as he studied the engine in Hannah's old broken-down truck. She held the marble that she'd found in the grass in the yard of the

Riverhouse. She opened and closed her fist around it. A cat's-eye, he'd told her it was. She took off the sunglasses and held the marble up to her own eye, tried to peer right through it, tried to see him in it, but she couldn't. She adjusted her glasses, smoothed the skirt of her dress over her knees, and went back to what she had been doing before, simply watching him. Because what would be worse would be if he was gone.

SEVEN

You Want to Be Careful About What You See

MADLEN WAS FINDING IT STRANGE, EVEN AS MANY TIMES in her life as she'd been here before, to be approaching the Old Barn in this way, from what seemed to be a wrong angle. She had hardly ever come upon it so, to the front from the road instead of to the back from the woods, the path, the river, the trees. The lighted sign was gone, and there was nothing anymore to indicate that this place had at one time been a popular party spot.

She maneuvered Deem's truck, struggling with it as it bounced in the hardened ruts of the drive and wishing that she had her rental car instead. Her skin was damp with sweat and her heart was pounding from the strain of trying to keep control, of herself and of the truck too, or maybe it was altogether something else. Maybe and more likely it was uneasiness over what she was doing there at all, over what a reckless step she had finally taken, coming here to see him. She would not be able to tell just exactly which.

Through the windshield she could see the dark structure of the barn looming, its high stone walls stained and streaked, the glass of its windows dimmed by layers of weather-borne grime, the broad lawn at its base overgrown with the season's crabgrass and dandelions, the overhanging trees that had at one time been starred with small white lights now tall and dense with shadows, the thickened branches and wide flat leaves leaning down closer than ever toward the rooftop peak of the smaller house nearby. And there on the wide veranda, where Jack Daggett himself had once stood to watch what went on at his establishment—the men and women gliding squares and eights and circles across the surface of the makeshift dance floor or sipping at iced drinks and playing at games of cards at the side tables or filling up plates of food at the smoking barbecue or sitting together on the cushioned wooden benches, laughing and talking, side by side—now standing in the place where Jack Daggett had stood, at the top of the steps, one hand on the post and the other raised up to his face to shade his eyes, was Rafe.

What could they have to say to each other, those two, Madlen and Rafe, brought back together again like this by the separate circumstances of their lives, after so much time and so much space had already come between them? Hannah watched them from the kitchen window—didn't mean to, couldn't help it. She leaned closer to the screen and listened, tried to hear what they were saying, but they'd lapsed into silence. They stood back and simply looked at each other, measuring up the distances, Hannah supposed, studying the change. He was looking at the old pickup, seemed to be marveling over the fact that Madlen's father was still driving it after all this time. She was looking around at the house and the yard, probably thinking something about how everything still looked just about the same, but that wasn't true and Hannah knew it. Nothing was the same.

Madlen turned to say hello to Jolie, but the little girl shied away. The two wide-slatted wooden chairs were still out there in the yard. Madlen sat down in one of them and Rafe went to pull a couple of bottles of beer from the cooler that he'd set out. He opened one and took it to Madlen, then opened the other for himself. He sat down. Jolie climbed up onto his lap and snuggled there with her head against his chest. She batted her fingers at the flap on the pocket of his shirt.

Hannah walked away from the window, tinkered with the loose handle on the cupboard above the sink, came back to the screen again, peered out. Madlen saw her and waved.

"Mrs. Daggett!" she called. "Hi!"

Hannah wasn't sure she wanted to be seen, not like this, without any makeup, with curlers still in her hair. But now there was no way for her to duck away and hide. She waved back, then came around to the door and stepped out onto the porch.

"Hello, Madlen," she said, patting her head. "It's sure nice to see you here."

Rafe was standing. "You want to sit with us?" he asked, and she could tell by the look on his face that he was hoping she'd say no. He lit a cigarette, squinted at her through the smoke.

"I guess I could sit for a while," she said.

"You want a beer?"

Hannah shook her head. "No, I don't." She took the chair that he'd got up from, filled it with herself, rested her arms on its arms, let the flesh of her legs and hips billow out over the surface of its seat. She fanned her face with her hand. She turned to Madlen. "I was awful sorry to hear about what happened to Haven," she said. She looked at Rafe. "All of us here were."

"Thank you," Madlen answered. She crossed her ankles under the chair and held her beer between her hands, demurely in her lap.

"I always liked him when he was a boy," Hannah went on.

Madlen smiled. "I know."

"Didn't see him again, though, after all that happened. Heard Doreen and him had moved away. Although we knew you two had gotten married when you did, of course. And we heard about it when you had your kids, too."

"I guess news still travels here."

Hannah nodded. "It does do that," she agreed. "Tell me, how's your dad?"

Madlen looked at her. "He's fine," she answered. "He's good. Fantastic, in fact. He's at the hospital today. His wife . . ."

"She's having a baby, I heard." Hannah was smiling. "Rafe said. Lucky for him."

Rafe dropped his cigarette in the grass and stepped on it. Jolie watched him, keeping an eye out from behind the darkened lenses of her glasses.

"Lucky for us all," Madlen replied.

Hannah stood up. "Well, I guess I'd best get back inside," she said. "Come on with me, Jolie. You can help me take these curlers out."

Jolie looked at Rafe. "Go on," he told her. "I'll be right here."

Hannah took the girl's hand and led her up to the house, onto the porch, and inside. The radio came on, and the sounds of music from it drifted out.

What Madlen had been noticing about Rafe was the tremble in his hands. His hair had darkened some, she thought, grown long and ragged, thinned. His jaw had hardened. His look was skittish; his eyes—blue flecked with amber—seemed to want to avoid hers.

Later Madlen would tell Sheriff Nicholls that she had started exchanging letters with Rafe sometime after her mother's accident, when he wrote to her to say that he'd heard about what happened and that he'd been saddened by the news. No, she'd answer, she never told her husband this, because she knew that it would upset him, and there was enough trouble in her marriage already without her bringing to it more.

They wrote back and forth to each other after that, infrequently, for a few years. He told her that he was married but about to be divorced, that he had a daughter, that he'd been drifting from job to job for a long time but had recently settled down and was working steadily for a shipping company up in Oregon. She'd tell Tom Nicholls that she had had no reason then to take what he said about himself for anything but the truth. No reason to suspect then that he might have been inventing that life for himself in order to convince her that he was like her and like Haven, that he wasn't different, that he wasn't bad, that he wasn't wrong.

Madlen picked at the paper label on her beer. The green silk dress that she wore was rumpled at the lap already. The emerald necklace that he'd given her glimmered at her throat. She realized that she should have put on something simpler, like sandals and slacks. She was overdressed for the situation, she knew.

When Rafe looked at her, she was held for a moment by the sharp dark blueness of his eyes. He offered her a cigarette, she declined, and he lit another one for himself.

Madlen sighed, closed her eyes, let the still blanket of the afternoon heat settle in around her. Rafe had sat back down again. She turned to him and smiled, wondering whether he had any idea what a relief this moment was to her. And whether he might be feeling any of the same sort of thing too. He was telling her that she looked good, saying that she looked just the same as she ever had to him, didn't seem to have much changed at all. She knew it wasn't true, but she was ready to accept the compliment anyway.

"You done with that?" he asked, nodding at the bottle in her hand.

She nodded.

"You want another one?"

She wasn't sure that it was right for her to be here; she knew her father wouldn't think so. But she didn't feel like making any move to go. She wasn't sure either what her children might be up to, but she didn't know that she cared. Deem could be trying to call her from the hospital, she realized. She probably ought to get home. And yet it felt so good to be relinquishing all of those responsibilities for a while that she couldn't bring herself to move. She wasn't ready to go back to the Riverhouse yet, and so she relaxed in her chair instead, leaned back, looked up through the trees at the sky, and felt as if she were being held here, cradled by the familiar serenity of this place and the pleasure of this moment, of having Rafe back in her life again, of the fullness and completion that his actual presence near her now seemed to be in some way summoning back.

She liked the sound of his voice. She liked the way he looked at her. She handed him the bottle and smiled and answered him drowsily, lazily: yes.

On an idle afternoon in early autumn Rafe had swiped a pint of gin from behind the bar inside the barn. He and Haven had met up with her at the fire pit behind the Riverhouse, and then they'd passed the bottle around from one to the other, swallowing it straight until it was all gone. Rafe had pulled a pair of black panties out of his pocket and waved them at his friends.

"Where'd you get those?" Haven asked.

Rafe shrugged. "Found them," he said.

Madlen took them from him and turned them over in her hands. Their silk was like a liquid on her fingers. She stretched the waistband between her thumbs and held the panties up to herself, swiveling her hips and pursing her lips.

"Ooh la la," she said.

Haven reached out and snatched them away from her and took off running. Rafe tore after him. They were all three crazy, drunk and howling, chasing along the narrow paths, dodging each other through the trees. It wasn't clear exactly how it happened, but Rafe hit Haven from behind, hard enough to knock the wind out of him. Haven sank to his knees, then rolled over sideways onto his back on the path, with one arm folded awkwardly underneath him. His eyes were closed, and he was still. Madlen and Rafe stood over him on either side, looking down at the limp body and placid face. Mouth hanging slack. Sunlight dappling his skin. Madlen knelt beside him. Nudged at his shoulder and pulled his arm out so he was lying flat. Put a palm on his chest, leaned her face in close to his to listen for the whisper of his breath.

She looked up at Rafe to see the fear that shadowed his eyes, turned them gray. Heard him murmur, "He's dead," as he backed away. Rafe believed that he'd killed his friend. But Madlen told him no, Haven had just passed out, that was all. Together they splashed water on his face to wake him up. They carried it up from the river in their shoes. But it didn't work, and Haven still didn't stir.

"He's just unconscious," Madlen insisted. "He's passed out."

But Rafe didn't believe her. "We have to bury him," he said. He'd started scratching at the ground, scooping up handfuls of leaves and dirt, sweeping them over toward Haven while Madlen didn't move, too bewildered by what Rafe was doing to do anything but stand helplessly and watch.

"Help me!" he cried, his face red, streaked with dirt and sweat.

Until finally Haven sat up, throwing off the debris, spitting and hollering, "I'm not dead." Then he'd screamed it even louder, his shrill voice cracking, sobbing: "Jesus Christ, Rafe! I'm not fucking dead!"

"Do you remember that time with the gin?" Madlen asked Rafe now, as he handed her another beer.

He smiled crookedly. "Yeah," he said. "That was dumb, wasn't it?"

She smiled back. "Yeah," she said. "It was."

"We were kids. It's okay to be dumb when you're a kid."

"I never did drink gin again."

"Nah, me neither."

She settled back in her chair and closed her eyes. "I forgot how much I like it here," she said. "I've missed it."

"Me too."

She turned to him. "What will you do now that you're back?" she asked.

He shrugged. "Go to work in Linwood, I guess." He said he'd had an offer from a storage and transfer company there, which she would later find out was an exaggeration. The truth was that he'd called them but they hadn't called him back. He told her that staying here with Hannah was only a temporary arrangement. Just until he could get himelf and his little girl situated. He was thinking that maybe he'd buy a house. Something big, with a yard, plenty of room to grow. He hated to throw good money away on rent.

"What about you?" he asked.

She frowned. She didn't know. Probably she'd stay put in Los Angeles.

"You like it that much there?" he asked.

"Not really."

"Then why go back?"

"Well, for the kids, I guess. They have their friends there. And their schools." She didn't want to unsettle them too much.

He sniffed. "It's a little late for that now, isn't it?" Hadn't they already been unsettled? And wouldn't it be better for them to be growing up here than in L.A.? Especially Claire, who was at that bad age. "You want to watch out for her, Madlen. She's a hot one. If you know what I mean."

Madlen blinked. Claire? Hot? "What did she say to you yesterday?" she asked.

He shrugged. "Nothing, really. Just said how much she misses her daddy."

She nodded.

"I guess you probably miss him too."

She nodded again, felt a sudden and surprising and unwanted sting of tears, which she quickly blinked back.

"Did he leave you any money?"

"Some. I have the house. His insurance paid the mortgage off."

"You could sell it then, use the cash to get yourself set up again here."

"I'd have to get a job."

"Doing what?"

She laughed. "I have no idea."

"Haven left you in a fix, didn't he?"

"Well, he didn't plan to die."

"No, I guess not. Still, it seems like it should have crossed his mind he might."

Jolie came out of the house and plodded down the porch steps into the yard. She had half a peanut butter and jelly sandwich in her hand, and one of Hannah's bristled curlers was pinned in her hair.

"You ought to stay here too, Madlen," Rafe was saying. Jolie scootched up next to him, crouched in the grass at his feet, and nibbled at the sandwich. "It's where we both belong. You know it, and I know it too."

"Maybe."

"Don't you think you would have come back here eventually anyway?" he asked. "After Haven moved out, I mean?"

She turned to him, startled. "What makes you think he was going to move out?"

"Well, he had that apartment, didn't he?"

244

"How do you know that?"

He shrugged. "I don't know. I guess you must have mentioned it."

"No, I didn't."

"Well, you must have."

"But I didn't. I'm sure I didn't." Had she told him? Had she told anyone?

Jolie was fiddling with the curler in her hair. Rafe was shaking his head. His eyes were steady now, fixed on Madlen's face.

"Did he have an apartment, Madlen?" he asked.

"Well, yes, but—"

"Then if you didn't tell me about it, how else did I know?"

He leaned toward her, blocked the sun. She felt the cool spread of his body shadowing hers as he brought his face so close that his breath brushed her eyes as she looked into his. For a moment she thought he might be going to kiss her, and she thought that this was how Haven must have felt too, that autumn afternoon as he lay on the ground in the leaves, drunk on gin, dizzy and breathless, his wind knocked away. With one finger Rafe touched her cheek, traced the line of her jaw.

"I'm here for you, Madlen," he said. "I would never do what he did. I would never leave you. I would never let you go."

The curler had become entangled in Jolie's hair, and she struggled with it, tugged and turned it, but the more she tried to roll it loose or yank it free, the more tightly ensnared it got, and she began to wail.

Rafe stood and scooped her up into his arms. Madlen held Jolie's head and gently worked the curler loose while Rafe rocked her from side to side and nuzzled her neck and whispered for her to hush, hush. Hannah had heard Jolie's cry and was standing at the screen door. She watched Rafe swing the child up and around onto his shoulders, then turn to Madlen, take her hand, and lead her across the grass, toward the barn.

Past the hanging barbed wire fence and across the gopher-pocked grassy meadow again, back over the rope bridge and then up along the web of paths through the woods between the river and the Riverhouse, two children, running. His shoes skittering over leaves, kicking up a spray of stones and sticks. The sticky prickle of burrs in her socks and on the sleeves of her shirt. His skin shiny with sweat, dusky with dirt. Hers freckled, pale, and pink.

Claire listened to the beat of her own hard breathing and of her feet hammering the ground. She felt the path roll off behind her, saw it unfold out before her as she rounded a curve, dropped down one slope, and then rose up another. Past the fire pit, which marked the halfway point between the river and the house, and then she'd crossed half of that again and half of that and half of that and half and half and half again—forever, it would seem.

Glen sloughed his gear off and dropped it down onto the grass at the bottom of the porch steps in a heap. That night, when their mother asked them what they'd done all afternoon while she was out, Claire would tell her that they'd gone exploring in the woods. They'd hiked all the way down to the river and beyond. Crossed the swinging bridge. Found a grove of apple trees and an old stone wall. Were stopped finally by the high chainlink fence at the edge of the reformatory grounds.

"Well, you stay away from there," Madlen would warn her

children, just as her parents had once warned her. "That's no place to play."

On a slab of concrete outside a battered metal camper, a woman in a wheelchair, going slack. Her head nodding forward to her chest, her body slumping groundward to the slab, the soft frictive hiss of cloth and skin as she falls, the dull crack and the slow sticky ooze of blood as her forehead strikes the baked cement.

Ivy wouldn't be found for four days, not until it occurred to Sheriff Nicholls that with Hannah gone, there was no one left to look after the old woman anymore and so he ought to send someone out to check and see that she was all right. But by that time she too would be dead.

On a white sheet on a steel table, beneath an icy circle of bright blue surgical lights, between the porcelain-pale thighs of a woman's spread legs, the crown of a baby's head, its dark hair slimed by a viscid bloody membrane.

A boy, the announcements in both the *Linwood Gazette* and the *Rampage Weekly* would read. Samuel Flynn Malek, five pounds, three ounces, nineteen inches, born at Saint Anne's Hospital to Ruth and Tim Malek of Rampage, Iowa, at 3:35 P.M. Baby thriving, mother doing fine.

In an ivy-covered stone house, a woman at a table sewing a hem into the fabric of a child's bright dress. The tight curls on her head bobbing with the movement of her body as she works. A dazzling yellow bird in a brass cage, shrieking. A radio on the counter; the deep baritone of an announcer's voice reporting the national news. The woman's thick fingers pulling the thread into a knot, her sharp white teeth biting the needle free.

Two days later, in the early morning hours after Rafe Ramsay was taken into custody, Rampage County Sheriff Tom Nicholls would send a deputy over to search the Daggett property, and Hannah Daggett would be found upstairs in her bed, and the mattress underneath her body would be soggy with her blood.

And in the cold and dark and huge and hollow space of the inside of an abandoned and dilapidated limestone barn, shadows moving. Rugged walls rising up into the even darker void of a hayloft overhead; hard shards of sunlight breaking through the narrow cracks in the roof's steep pitch and stabbing at the mote-swirled air.

The furnishings and equipment were all gone—Hannah had sold them off to a restaurant in Linwood soon after Daggett's death. The place was utterly vacant, a vast, empty shell. The stone floor, once scrubbed and polished every morning in antici-pation of the evening's entertainment, was caked now with dirt and droppings and debris.

The hard strong wave of longing and loss surged over Madlen like a physical cramp. It was an ache that rose up from the pit of her belly and seemed to squeeze her chest and her throat, her heart and her lungs, leaving her gasping, breathless, sobbing. Tears welled in her eyes as Rafe pulled her to him. He enfolded her, held her and rocked her and kissed her and hushed her, just as she had seen him hush his baby daughter moments before.

Birds' wings flapped in the rafters. Jolie, blind behind her sunglasses in the murky light, leaned against Rafe too, with one arm wrapped around his leg, holding on.

It was dark outside, long after dusk, when Deem finally left the hospital. He stood beside Madlen's rented car in the Saint Anne's parking lot and fumbled in his pockets, trying to find the key to start it. He looked up and counted the building's stories, searching for the window that he knew was on the sixth floor, three south of the corner, in the room where he'd left Ruth with the baby—three weeks premature, for which Evelyn Frye and the storm that she went out and drowned in would forever afterward be blamed.

He should go home and take a shower and change his clothes, he knew. Try to get back to normal again. Fix something to eat, talk to Madlen, let her know she had a brother—Rosemary had been wrong about that. Let her know the baby was okay—about that she had, thankfully, been right. And that Ruth was fine too, strong and solid, as Deem should have trusted all along that she would be.

But the truth was, he didn't want to talk to Madlen. He wished she weren't there, that when he got back home, she would somehow be gone. He didn't like it that he felt this way, but there it was. He wanted to be alone, he wanted to stop looking back, to leave the past behind him once and for all, move forward away from it, with Ruth and with his son, into the future, into their newly concocted life.

So he drove to Cedarcrest Retreat, thinking that he could take some refuge there now just as he'd done before, when it was the presence of Grinnell that he'd been dreading, when it was the chaos of his life with her that he'd been trying to avoid. He pulled in through the massive iron gates, past the high stone wall that enclosed the grounds, and on down the long black driveway that snaked across the front lawn. He parked in the employee lot behind the main house.

It was a massive Queen Anne, brick and concrete, with tall gabled windows and long thin chimneys and a pair of cement lions flanking the entryway stairs. Although the front light had been left on, the windows in the house were flat black—this late at night the patients would all be in their rooms, drugged, asleep.

He followed the path through the trees, past the duck pond, toward the white glow of the conservatory. And then, suddenly overcome by nausea, he stopped at the edge of the lawn and squatted, hands on his knees, to vomit onto the grass. He wiped at his mouth with the back of his hand. Around him, everything was quiet—serenity was supposed to be a part of the cure. He knelt at the edge of the pond to scoop water into his mouth and splash it over his face. He spit, coughed, spit again.

They'd told him that they were going to drain the pond. They'd fill it in with dirt, cover it over with grass. That would be simple, wouldn't it? But why? The water was not just picturesque, it was dangerous. Somebody might decide to take a swim in it. Somebody might drown. They didn't care that no one had done anything like that yet. There was always a first time, and so it was a hazard. There was insurance to worry about. Lawsuits. Liability. They'd said the same thing about the conservatory. It was old. It should be torn down.

What Deem needed, he knew, was a drink. A duck on the opposite bank, flat feet planted in the mud, watched him solemnly as he shook the water from his hands and wiped it from his face.

All along the path, the gardens had begun to bloom. Scott had planted marigolds along the edges. He'd even trimmed the roses. Next thing, Deem thought, they were going to want to pull those up, because somebody might try to kill herself with a thorn.

Near the white wooden trellis that arched gracefully over the roses was a plain wooden bench with Grinnell's name engraved on a brass plaque affixed to its back. It had been a gift from the doctors and nurses and patients in the retreat. "In loving memory," the plaque read. "Too briefly with us, too soon gone." Deem ran a finger over the letters, then turned and sat down, buried his face in his hands.

He'd found Grinnell hiding in the closet with Madlen one winter night when he'd come home, because she'd tried to light a fire and there'd been a bat in the chimney that swooped out at her the same way that she'd swooped out of the closet at him, screeching, hands waving around her like wings, her face pinched into a scrunch of anger and fear—where had he been, why was he never there when she needed him, how did he expect her to live in a house that was full of bats?—while Madlen stood behind her, holding a flashlight in one hand and a tennis racket in the other.

The bat had been clinging to the inside of the drapes in the living room. With Madlen's help, he killed it. He beat it with the racket, wrapped it in a paper sack, and dumped it in the garbage can outside.

"It's dead," he told Grinnell.

She'd changed her clothes. She was standing at the top of the stairs with a suitcase in one hand. "I can't live here," she said.

Madlen, still holding the tennis racket and the flashlight,

stepped toward her. "It's okay now, Mom. We got the bat. It's gone."

"I don't care about the bat."

He'd tried to apologize. He knew she'd been frightened, hiding in the closet, not knowing what to do. But she brushed past Madlen first, then him. Snarled when he tried to stop her. Went to the closet, got out her coat and hat. Wrapped a red scarf around her throat. Put on her gloves first, then her boots.

"Where are you going?" he'd asked her.

She didn't answer. Simply picked up her bag and walked through the house, to the kitchen, to the back door.

He followed, but Madlen hung back, listening and watching but still keeping a good distance, as if she knew that her mother was going to strike out at her if she got too close.

"Where are you going?" he asked again, and took hold of Grinnell's wrist to try to pull her toward him and then turn her around so that he could see her face. It was like touching an electrical wire, the shock, the force with which she shook him away.

"I'm leaving you," she said, then opened the door and stepped out into the snow.

He'd watched her tromp across the moonlit yard, suitcase banging her leg, and he hadn't tried to stop her. The red scarf had been a flash of color against the black back of her coat and the shadowy tangle of the trees, there for a moment, then gone, as she disappeared into the woods, following the path that would take her to Daggett's house at the Old Barn.

But now all that was over. He would stop thinking of it, of her. Everything would be, as Scott had said, copacetic. He was exhausted. He did need a drink.

Deem unlocked the door to the nearby shed and let himself

into the room that was his office there. He pulled the string on the overhead light to reveal a room full of tools and pots and sacks of dirt, with a bookcase and a desk pushed up against the far wall. Scott's tall rubber boots stood on the floor and one of his denim work shirts hung from a hook above them, so that for a brief moment Deem thought someone was standing there watching him, about to speak. Through the window at the back of the shed, the night was dark and still.

In the top drawer of his desk was his big ring of keys. In the bottom drawer, behind a pile of seed and fertilizer catalogues, was a pint bottle of scotch, half full, and a glass. Deem poured a shot, threw it back, then poured another one and threw that back too. He pulled off the happy-face T-shirt and wadded it up, tossed it toward a dark back corner of the room where he wouldn't have to look at it anymore. He lit a cigarette. He was feeling better now. He took Scott's work shirt down and put it on, cigarette clamped between his teeth, one eye squinted shut against the spiral of white smoke. The sleeves of the shirt were too long. He rolled them back. He took the bottle with him outside and up the short walk to the conservatory itself. Its glass panes glistened. Its door had been padlocked shut; Deem found the key on his ring and opened it.

The air inside the glass-walled, glass-domed room was moist and hot, lush with a carefully cultivated overgrowth of leaves and stems and branches, thick with the sharp clotted smell of fertilizer and flowers, wet brick and bark, and rich, freshly turned soil.

The seedlings that Scott had been working on were laid out in trays, ready to be set into the ground. Deem turned on the spigot to water them and the spray was a fine mist, pure white cloud. On the floor in a corner was the soot-black body of a dead bird. Deem poked at it with the toe of his boot. Not a sparrow but a starling. Must have got trapped. Must have flown into the window glass. Must have knocked itself out, died trying to get loose. He used a spade to scoop up the clump of feathers—loose, lolling head, shiny eyes, yellowish beak—and carried it over to the trash bin beside the door. He cranked open one of the upper windows, exposing a slice of night sky above his head, blacker even than the feathers of that bird. He hoped that Rosemary was right about that too. That whatever it was that was wrong here was eventually going to go away of its own accord.

On a stand at the center of the circular room was a sculpture that Rosemary had made and that Scott had mounted there. Another gift. It was an oblong block of layered porcelain, hardened strands and strata of fired white clay that had been laid out, fitted into place, and then bolted to a frame of backing boards. The colors of the glazes that she'd used on it were muted, blunt, deadened, and drab, shades of green and gray and brown. Mud colors—dirt, water, moss, and stone. Darker first, then lighter, then darker again, marking off clear distinctions within the depths and the gradations of the clay and its color strata—like the difference, she had explained, between the present and the past, between what was maybe then and what had been since then, and what was becoming now as well as what would be, or maybe could be, sometime soon. The muted colors reminded Deem of the stained limestone walls on the insides of the Rampage quarry wall. Or of the riverbank at the palisades at the end of summer, when the water was running low and the limestone caves were exposed.

Even this late at night, even with the windows cranked open, it was hot inside the conservatory. And quiet. He could hear the grinding of gears on the street outside; a truck crawled along the highway, growled down the hill. A fly had got itself trapped against a window, and it was beating itself, buzzing, against the glass. Deem listened to the sound of it, finding that he was able to take a kind of a comfort from the noise of its struggle. That was something, he believed, that he could understand.

He finished off the pint of scotch and tucked the bottle away in the bottom of the trash basket behind the door. He sighed. There was nothing left for him to do now but go home.

When he pulled into the Riverhouse driveway, he could tell from how she'd left it parked that Madlen had taken his truck out. Then he remembered that she had told him she'd been to town and that she'd seen Hannah Daggett there. He wondered if she'd seen Rafe yet. And if she hadn't, whether she would. He parked the rental car behind his truck. The lights were off inside the house, and he took that to be a good sign. A fan blew in an upstairs front window, billowing the white cotton curtains out into the air of the hot night. He listened, but there was no sound or movement that he could hear. They must be sleeping, then. He wouldn't wake them. Maybe he could be alone here for a while after all. Maybe he wouldn't have to talk to her right away.

He crossed the yard and stumbled up the steps to the door. He opened the screen, trying not to make too much noise, knowing that it squeaked. The weather door was locked—she'd bolted it from the inside. He cursed, kicked at it once, then raised his fist and began to bang on the wood, seemed to shake the whole big house with the fury of his pounding. He stopped and listened for a moment, then banged again. The noise and his own strength in making it had begun to please him.

A light came on inside and he stopped, listened again, waited for her to get the thing unlocked. She swung it open, and then there she was, standing there in her nightgown, letting him into his own house as if she had some kind of dominion here.

She looked too much like Grinnell for his taste—the mess of her hair, the shadowy bundle of her body inside the sheer fabric of her gown, the frown that crumpled her face, accusing him, it seemed, asking without saying so, Where have you been? Who have you seen? Why are you out so late? He pushed past her into the kitchen and then stopped, brought to a standstill by the unexpected starkness of the room. What the hell had she done to his house?

Her anger flared back at him. She hadn't done anything to it, she answered. She cleaned the kitchen for him, that was all. Was that a crime? Grinnell's face seemed to be a shadow behind the mask of Madlen's. He saw his first wife's anger in his daughter's eyes, and he shrank from it, turned his head away.

"No," he said. "It's not a crime."

She stood by the sink, waiting. "You have to admit it needed it, Dad. It was a mess."

He shrugged. Maybe. Maybe she was right. He sat down at the table. She fixed him a sandwich, poured him a glass of milk. He told her about Ruth and about the baby. That the labor had been long but not too long. Hard but not too hard. The kid was small but not too small. And they'd decided to name him Sam. She came over to him, bent and kissed the top of his head, brushed her fingertips across the weathered surface of his cheek.

"I'm glad."

And then she told him that she'd been over to the Old Barn and that she'd spent the afternoon there with Rafe. He swallowed his annoyance; he had expected this, hadn't he? So he shouldn't be surprised. It wasn't any of his business, he knew that, but he went ahead and said it anyway, because it was the truth—she shouldn't get herself messed up with Rafe Ramsay. He saw her stiffen, watched her mouth thin, her look sharpen, her shoulders square.

"Why not?" she asked him.

He was finding her defiance tiresome. She was an adult, after all. She didn't need his permission to do anything anymore. He sighed. "You know why not."

"You ought to at least give him a chance, Dad. You ought to find out that he's changed."

"Changed. From what, for Christ's sake? What was Rafe before?" Deem stood up, too quickly, bumped the table with his knee so the glass of milk tumbled over and rolled to the floor. He looked at it for a moment, then at her. "I don't want to talk about this anymore, Madlen," he said, turning, leaving the mess for her to clean up. "I'm tired of it. I'm tired."

He walked out through the dining room to the front hall, where he climbed the stairs slowly and clumsily, with both hands on the railings, as if he might be trying to pull himself up, drag himself out of some thick entrapping muck.

Madlen stayed in the kitchen, sponging up the milk, standing at the sink, rinsing off his glass and plate and putting them away in the dishwasher, and Deem understood that even after all this time, not much of significance here had been changed. Because just as Grinnell had always been talking to him and at the same time thinking about Jack Daggett, now there was his daughter with her own mind stuck on Rafe.

It was hot up on the sleeping porch, where Claire lay sleeping and wildly dreaming of that old crazy woman—of how she was getting her out of there, away from the camper and down through the woods to the river that she'd said she wanted so much to see. Claire had started with the wall, clawing and picking at it with her fingers, standing and pressing against it with her back, working to take it apart, stone by stone, to make an opening in it that might be wide enough for her to be able to push Ivy through. But the more she pulled away, the more there still was. She worked her hands into the stone; it crumbled under her fingertips like cheese.

She started again. Took hold of the ramp outside the camper door, dragged it over to the wall, and placed it there. Pushed Ivy's chair up to the top, where it teetered, tipped forward, fell away.

And so she started again. This time the chair was rolling over apples, snagging in the tangled grass, plowing through the high weeds. The back of Ivy's head, white-haired and pink-scalped, bobbed as Claire pushed her along, lurched over stones and rocks and bumps along the way. Claire bullied Ivy through mire and mud until the wheels were disentangled, jiggled loose and rolling freely, over firm dirt now and down a slope. It was as if the river were drawing them in, pulling them toward it, and Claire was being dragged along with the old woman. She stumbled and groaned, sweating, planted her feet, tried her best to hold back, but her grip weakened and her hands opened—she let go and Ivy sailed away, as if on her own momentum now, until she hit the wire fence, slammed into it, bounced and stopped, hanging, ensnared in a web of barbed wire, snagged.

Claire started again. This time Ivy's chair was already out there on the bluff, it was perched at the edge of a high palisade, and Claire was watching as it rolled forward, away from her. She felt it slip out of her hands, which were too small and too weak to hold on anymore, because Ivy had her own hands on the wheels and she was rolling her chair herself. Claire let go and Ivy moved on, away. She left the ground altogether, tumbled forward, was spilled from the chair. Claire dove off the edge after her. She would save her from the fall. She was calling out to Ivy, and the air all around was full of the sound of her voice; as if she thought that that might stop her, as if she believed that somehow its sheer sound was going to be enough to bring the woman back up to solid ground again, Claire was still crying out Ivy's name.

"I-i-i-i-vee-ee-ee!"

Clasped in an embrace, they landed in the river. They rolled and turned, were carried by the current across the languid depths of Sugar Bottom, were bouncing through the shallows, across the rocks, snagged in the grasp of an old downed tree for a moment, then dragged free and tumbled on, a snarl of arms and legs and hands and feet, two separate bodies broken and entwined and tangled into one.

She woke up, and she was crying. Ivy had told the truth— Grinnell had killed herself, Claire knew that now. She looked around and found that she was in her grandfather's bedroom, sitting on the bed, on the pink chenille spread fringed at the edges, soft in some places, woven stiff and hard in others. She must have walked here in her sleep. She remembered sitting on this bed before, watching as her grandmother tried on one dress and found it too fancy, tried on another and found it too plain. She remembered Grinnell standing in front of the mirror in her bare feet, regarding her reflection. She remembered riding off with Grinnell in her mother's car. She remembered a gray stuffed dog with a red collar.

Claire sat bent over herself, folded up with her head covered by her hands as the headlights from the rental car washed over the walls of the room. Deem was home. With her heart pounding, she scrambled off the bed and hurried out of the room, down the hall, and back to the sleeping porch, where she belonged. She stood at the screen and watched her grandfather walk across the yard toward the house. She heard him curse, heard him bang at the back door, heard her mother open it, heard their voices rising up to her—the baby had come, it was a boy, it was all right, Ruth was fine—and Claire felt relieved.

Glen was near her, on his own cot, asleep. Tonight he'd stayed inside. The Riverhouse was dark and quiet; it felt to Claire as empty as a cave. She looked at her brother and tried picturing her father, what he must have looked like when he was young, her age, when he was a boy scabbed and scarred, dirt-smudged and stinky like Glen. When she thought of Ivy now, Ivy's face was mixed up with that of the old woman they'd found drowned in the ditch after the storm.

Careful not to disturb him, Claire rummaged through Glen's clothes, looking for a cigarette. She found one hidden inside the toe of his shoe, and she took it out, smoothed it, lit it with the silver lighter. She supposed that now Deem was back, he was going to miss it and she was going to have to return it. She heard him come upstairs and go into his room and close the door. She stood near the screen again, blowing smoke out into the night.

It was as if she were looking into her own reflection at the red spark of a cigarette burning in Rafe's hand there at the edge of the woods. He was watching the house, it looked like. If he raised his eyes, he would be able to see her too. He dropped the cigarette on the ground and stepped on it. He pulled another from the pack in his shirt pocket, and as he lit it she saw him looking past the flame, seemed to see him looking through it, at the house and at her window and at her in it, watching him. He put his hand up to his mouth, and he whistled. Two long notes, one short.

The back door opened downstairs and Madlen stepped out onto the grass and crossed the lawn toward him. She was in her nightgown and she was barefoot and she skittered on her toes like a girl. As Claire watched, Rafe took Madlen's hand and turned and disappeared into the shadows of the trees, with Madlen following after, and then both of them were gone.

In Claire's mind now was swimming the vision of two boys' hands, clasped hard, upraised. Of the blood that pumped between them and ran down over their wrists. Of the flash of sunlight on an open knife blade dropped in the grass. And of her mother, white-haired and pale, poised at the edge of the palisade, brushed by the breeze of their passage as the boys raced by her, lunged forward, dropped down into the water, and then were gone.

She understood now why it was that Rafe had seemed familiar to her when he'd come by the Riverhouse to see her mother the day before. She knew him, all right, but not because of the brotherly connection that he'd had with her father when they both were boys. And she had seen him before, not in a photograph but in the flesh. Not here but there, at home, outside the house in California.

Why had she been awake that night? Because she was a roamer, her father used to say. A sleepwalker like her mother, nomad, wanderer, drifter in the dark. And this man, this other prowler like her, Rafe Ramsay, had been standing in the street under the same lamp that Dan Moorehead and his friends had broken with a rock on another night. Rafe had been smoking a cigarette then too, and he'd been watching the house, looking up at her window, seeing her in it watching him back. He hadn't seemed to care that he'd been seen. He'd smiled at her and waved and nonchalantly walked away. When she mentioned what she'd seen at breakfast the next morning, her father said it must have been another of her mysterious bad dreams. But she realized now that it was real.

Rafe was carrying a flashlight, and its beam flared into the trees ahead of him as he led the way and Madlen followed. The wildness of what they were doing felt welcome to her; it seemed to be taking her back again to what she could remember had been the lawlessness of the childhood she spent here, a time when you never knew why things had to be the way they were and didn't always even ask—when you didn't know and maybe didn't care what might be about to happen next to change everything that was familiar into something else.

They turned off onto a smaller path which took them around the fire pit and then on through the trees to a bluff above the river. The lights of the reformatory were burning on the flat land in the distance. Rafe switched off the flashlight and dropped it in the grass. When she looked at him now, she could see in the vague outline of his body and the shadowed features of his face the same boy that she'd always known. Around her throat was the emerald pendant that he'd given her, its stone a green spark against her skin. She wobbled, steadied herself, smiled, and said his name softly. "Rafe." His hands were tangled in the fabric of her nightgown. She pulled herself away, stumbled back toward the edge of the bluff, then turned and jumped off it, toward the river. She heard Rafe call out to her as she left the ground. She felt herself seem to hover there for a moment in thin air, with both hands raised up high above her head, before she fell, floating, drifting, with her nightgown blown out all around her, down.

Rafe followed. Moonlight shimmered on the surface of the water, then was shattered, frantic, as he moved toward her through it. Their bodies came together. His skin was warm against hers and the river flowed silky and cold around them. His hands were in her hair; his face was at her throat. She felt herself begin to soften, to loosen, to unfold toward him as he explored the landscape of her skin, hill and hollow, pucker and dimple, running his hands over her body's folds and mounds and curves, molding himself to her. Her knees softened, her legs rolled open, thighs fell apart, her head lolled back. She closed her eyes and let him hold her, let him lift and carry her toward the grassy bank, where he pulled her up out of the water and set her down. He was kneeling next to her. He was leaning toward her, bending his body over hers. His palms were flat against the grass, his arms were straight and hard, elbows locked, muscles taut, as he pressed his own flesh into hers, as his hips ground down on hers, as she tried for one last moment to writhe free and shift away from him, before she was caught, finally, and held. His pale skin seemed to her to be almost translucent in the dark. His hand was on her hip, cupping it. Her fists pushed against the small of his back as he moved, probing, trying to find her, trying to reach the center of her, Madlen, just for a moment, and then there was the one swift fleeting shudder when finally he found it, when finally he touched it, her, and then knowing that he had, he pressed himself farther into her, hard, as she raised her hips and arched her back and rocked against him, rocked with him, until he slowed and stopped and was still.

She leaned her head against his chest and listened to the

sounds of his body—heart beating, insides murmuring, breath breezing in and out. He ran his fingertip in circles across the milky skin on the inside of her upper arm. He thought he'd never felt anything so soft, he said. If she closed her eyes, the world would start to spin.

"I had a dream," she started to tell him, then stopped.

He wanted to hear it. He took her chin and lifted her face so she would look at him. "What was it?" he asked. He leaned closer to her, brushed his lips across her brow. "Tell me, please," he said.

She was trying to recall the details of it clearly. Groping for the words to describe how it had gone. A river, first. Then something floating. A boat of some kind. A house with a basement and an extra bedroom at the back. Green carpeting. A baby in a crib, sleeping, left alone, forgotten, for years and years and years. Remembering this part of it made her want to cry.

Rafe's finger had moved down to the pulse at Madlen's wrist. The moonlight ignited a flame of amber in his eyes. He touched her and turned her and made love to her again. He took her apart, tore at her seams, tried to undo her, to crack her open, touching her, licking her, probing her, reaching up into the deepest, most secret part of Madlen, until she arched back and cried out, knees bent and hips lifted, her weight on her heels and her hands clutching at the mattress of grass beneath her as her body rose upward again, to meet his.

Later Madlen would sneak back into the Riverhouse as if she were still a child, her hair wet and her nightgown sodden, clinging to her skin. She'd stand in the front foyer, shaking with cold and listening for some sound that might tell her whether anyone upstairs was still awake. But there would be nothing, only dark-ness and silence, and she would be reminded by the pounding pulse of her own wariness of those other nights long gone when she'd crept back upstairs to her room after an evening with her friends. Sleepwalking, Grinnell had said.

Madlen pulled the door shut after her and tiptoed up the stairs, past her father's bedroom, past the room where her chil-dren were asleep, down the hall to the bathroom. She was think-ing that she envied Claire and Glen in a way, for what she still kept letting herself believe to be their innocence, that dumb bliss of understanding nothing, only a dim memory now to her. She slipped off the wet nightgown and stood naked, ran her fingers through her hair, over her body, measured it up, tried to guess what Rafe might have felt, touching her, what he must have seen. She turned on the light then and gave her face a good hard study in the mirror. Her eyes, her lips, her skin. She inspected every line, poked at every pouch. What she was looking for in herself was not an indication of her age but a sign of her experi-ence, some expression there of who she was, of what had hap-pened to her, of where she'd gone and what she'd done.

She had tried this same thing after Haven died, looked to see whether she would find an imprint of her loss there on the surface of her face, some mark that would express in her what was otherwise past, a memory, over and done. But there had been nothing then and there was nothing now. She looked the same to herself and was relieved to see that she did seem to be unchanged.

Except change isn't always something sudden, and Madlen should have known this. It's more often a gradual shifting from this to that, a long and steady alteration that takes place over time, going so slowly from what was to what is that the difference between the two can hardly be recognized and is rarely even noticed until it's already been done. Madlen should have known that this is true. She'd seen it for herself—in her mother and in her father, in her husband and in her daughter and in her son. Why couldn't she see it in herself? Because, she would say later, there were things that she did not want to realize just then. There were things that she had chosen no longer to see.

Be careful what you look at, Doreen Cramer had warned, because the children made a game of spying on the adults. They took cover in the trees. They hid under the porch and listened to what was said. They sneaked up to open windows and peeked in. Mrs. Frye dancing. Grinnell trying on dresses. Doreen in a lounge chair on her belly, sunbathing in her scant back yard.

"Maybe it's better not to know too much," she'd told them, sitting up, shaking her hair, pulling a towel up to cover herself. "You want to be careful about what you see."

They were out in the woods and Madlen had crawled into the hollow tree that lay across the path not far from the fire pit to hide from the boys. She heard them scramble over her, listened to their war whoops dim and fade as they moved away, and then she waited for them to miss her, but they didn't. She knew that they'd ditched her, but she didn't want to think it. She was afraid of spiders. She thought that she felt ants and beetles crawling on her bare legs, up toward the high cuffs of her shorts. When she couldn't stand it anymore, she climbed out, stood in the middle of the path, blinking in the sunlight, then wandered down toward the river alone, wondering whether they'd second-guessed her and known she wouldn't last long, suspecting they might be waiting for her, hiding in the underbrush, and that any minute they'd come bounding out to pounce on her and make her shriek.

Her best guess was that they must have gone to the river to swim. She imagined the two of them laughing at her as they dove into the water, knowing all along that she was curled up over herself in the darkness of the insides of that old rotting tree trunk with the spiders and the beetles and the ants. Her only recourse would be to sneak up on them. Come from another direction and make them wonder whether maybe they'd been wrong. Cross at the bridge and climb down to the meadow near the corner of the reformatory fence, then show up on the other side, unexpectedly.

That meant passing Ivy's camper. Silver, it looked like a soup can with the paper torn off it. Ivy was at Cedarcrest then, so the camper was abandoned. Or should have been. But somebody was there, because the door was open and Madlen could hear music coming from inside. Maybe Ivy was back. She crept up closer and clambered onto the steps to look in through the open door. Or maybe the boys were inside, maybe they'd been coming here without telling her. It was a secret they'd been keeping. Something of their own that they hadn't planned to share with her. She peered through the screen expecting to see them there, sitting on the floor smoking cigarettes, maybe looking at the magazine that they'd swiped that morning from the General in town. She would surprise them. Now that she'd found out about it, they would have to let her in.

There didn't seem to be anyone in the front room. Only shadows. She opened the screen door and stepped inside. From the back of the camper came the sound of voices, someone talking, someone singing. The hallway was narrow and dark. The door to the bedroom was open. There was a table with a lamp on it. An old radio. A whisky bottle and a glass.

Later she wouldn't be able to remember exactly what she saw—the struggle that was going on between the two bodies on that bed. Limbs entangled, hands clasped. Her hair like tufts of straw against the green satin pillowcase. His shoulders, muscles knotted, moving. His hips slamming into hers. Her feet lifted, white, swimming in the air like fish. Daggett's straw hat on the seat of the chair and Grinnell's white leather sandals on the floor.

There was Madlen, poised in the doorway, her hands on the frame, scrabbling. And there was Grinnell, gasping, struggling free and jolting back, covering herself with the sheet pulled up to her chin. And there was Daggett, his long legs striding, and there was the stiffened stick of his penis, gleaming below his belly, as he bellowed, as he hobbled from the bed toward Madlen, cursing, scolding, and there was his hand on her arm, lifting her off her feet like a hard sweep of wind that turned her and hurled her, weightless, away.

EIGHT

Why Can't We Have This?

THE NEXT DAY MADLEN WAS AT THE TABLE ON THE screened porch, breaking up Ruth's unfinished mountainscape puzzle and putting it away. The afternoon's wet heat had bent and changed the pieces—they were swollen, sodden, and difficult to pull apart. The picture on their surface had started to peel off and curl back, so it was hard to tell anymore what fit together where.

Deem had taken Glen with him to Cedarcrest. Claire was upstairs napping—not feeling well, she said, and Madlen guessed that the heat must be getting to her too.

On the seat cushion next to Madlen was a copy of the Rampage weekly paper, folded open to the back page with its list of local obituaries, Mrs. Frye's among them. Sixty-two years old. A member of the First Presbyterian Church and the PEO. Survived by a sister and two nieces, all of them living elsewhere. On the front page was the news story about the storm, recounting what facts were known of Mrs. Frye's death by drowning, accompanied by a photograph of the house with its windows open, curtains billowing, and the tree that had cracked and fallen across the front porch. Madlen had been looking at that picture and thinking about that house, wondering what was going to happen to it now.

She put the lid back on the puzzle box and went upstairs. Claire was curled on her cot, eyes closed, asleep it seemed. Madlen reached out, touched her fingers to Claire's forehead. Her skin was cool. No fever, then. Claire opened her eyes, rolled over onto her back, folded an arm behind her head, and looked up at her mother. The silver handle of the mirror poked out from underneath the pillow.

Madlen pulled it out, looked at her own face in its glass, turned it around toward Claire. "Grinnell's," she said.

"I know," Claire answered, as if that were enough to explain to her mother why she had it here with her in her bed. She sat up. "She killed herself," Claire said.

Madlen frowned. "Who told you that?"

"I heard it. Did she?"

"It was an accident, Claire. She was walking on the tracks. She didn't hear the train." Madlen's look was hard. She wanted her daughter to believe what she was saying, but Claire knew better. She knew more.

They were running away, Grinnell had said that day as she pulled away from the Riverhouse in Madlen's car. Wasn't that an adventure, wouldn't it be fun? Claire, excited, had sat up on her knees and looked out the front window at the ribbon of road that seemed to be unraveling for them alone, a little girl and her grandmother, alongside the river, toward Rampage. She knew that Grinnell was not allowed to drive, that they'd only been playing a game of pretend travel, that they weren't supposed to go anywhere real. But there they were, running away, and it was fun. When they got to the train tracks, Grinnell stopped the car and turned the key, so the radio went off and the engine died and there was only emptiness and silence all around them, solid as a wall. Claire sat back and looked at her grandmother. Asked her, what were they going to do now? Why did she turn off the car? Why had they stopped? But Grinnell was listening to something else, and she didn't seem to hear Claire. She sat straight up in her seat, looking out ahead as if she were waiting for something to appear to her there, with her hands folded, fingers entwined, in her lap. When the crossing bells began to clatter and the red lights started to flash, Grinnell closed her eyes and smiled. Claire was looking down the tracks, and she saw the train, growing in size and sound as it neared.

She'd felt, she thought, the rumble of its approach—it shook the ground, shook the car, shook her. Still smiling, Grinnell had turned to Claire, calmly and slowly, and she'd reached out and touched her pale hair. Then she'd sat up and turned the key and started the car again, rolled it forward off the tracks as behind them the train's horn blared and its body thundered past.

Claire knew that her mother was lying about what Grinnell had done, not only to Claire but to herself. And she also knew that if Grinnell had decided to stay there on the tracks in the car with Claire on the seat beside her, there was nothing that Madlen could have done to stop it. Something like that was out of her reach, beyond the bounds of her control.

Claire's head hurt. She turned away and lay back down on the cot. She pulled the blanket up, felt chilled even though the room was damp and breathlessly hot.

"How are you feeling?" Madlen was asking.

Claire shrugged. "Okay, I guess," she lied.

Madlen would have liked to find a way to overcome what she saw as this continued sullenness of Claire's. She sat on the edge of the cot. "I thought I'd go over to the Frye house for a minute," she said, and smiled. "You want to come along?"

Claire frowned. "What for?"

"I don't know. To take a look at it, I guess. See what might be salvaged."

"I want to go home."

Madlen closed her eyes. "We're not going home, Claire, all right? Deem needs me here, for one thing." She looked at her daughter, touched the smoky wisps of her white hair. "Besides, don't you want to wait and see the baby?"

Claire shrugged again. "I guess."

"And I'd like to be here to help out when Ruth comes home."

"You don't even like Ruth." It was as if she had another self inside herself who did not know how to shut up. Madlen started to protest, but Claire stopped her by sitting up again. "It's okay, Mom," she said. "You don't have to make excuses. I know why you want to stay here. It's because of that man."

Claire hadn't meant to say this to her mother either. She didn't even know that she'd been thinking it until the words emerged, seeming to have been formed of themselves. It was as if she were outside herself, watching and listening, wondering as much as Madlen what might come drifting up into her mind and out of her mouth next.

Madlen's face was hot with color.

"Isn't that right?" Claire pressed on. She'd come this far, there didn't seem to be any reason to try to stop herself now.

"Claire . . ." Madlen didn't know how she was going to answer her daughter's accusation. She wasn't sure how much real knowledge might be behind it.

"Who is he, Mother?" Claire asked.

Madlen stood up, lifted to her feet by the directness of the question. She smiled, poked fingers at her hair. "Well, he's an old friend," she explained. "I thought you knew that. We grew up together here. Your father too." There seemed to her to be some innocence in this. She looked at her daughter, sitting up with the blanket pulled over her crossed legs, hands folded in her lap, chin tucked, one eyebrow raised, nostrils flared with contempt.

"I do know that," Claire was saying. "He told me that much himself already. But who is he really?"

Madlen stiffened. "He's just somebody I used to know, Claire," she said. "That's all. A friend, okay? Is it all right with you if I have friends?"

"He was in California," Claire said.

"What?"

"He was at our house. I saw him."

"When?"

"A long time ago."

And then she was telling Madlen about waking up at night and looking out the window of her bedroom and seeing Rafe outside under the streetlamp, as if it had happened to somebody else.

"But I wasn't dreaming," Claire insisted. "It was him."

Madlen frowned, waved her hands around. "I don't see how that could be," she said.

Claire didn't know what to say. It was as if she didn't know anything anymore—she couldn't tell the difference between what was true and what was not, and she didn't think she had the strength left to try to find out. She watched her mother work to put a smile of reassurance on her face.

"Look, Claire," Madlen said, "let's not talk about this right now, all right? Why don't we do something together instead? Why don't you come over to the Frye house with me?"

Her mother was trying one last time to make amends, but Claire couldn't bring herself to give in. "I don't want to," she said. Still the curled lip, raised brow. It was as if she had become her other self.

Madlen gave up. She turned toward the door. "All right, then," she said. "Suit yourself."

"Were you seeing him back there? Before Daddy died?"

Madlen stopped, shocked at what her daughter had been thinking, what she was implying. "No," she said. "What gave you that idea?"

"Daddy was leaving us, wasn't he?"

Madlen sighed. Resigned to Claire's questions. Accusations. Reproach. Maybe she did deserve it, after all. "He wasn't leaving you," she answered. "He was leaving me."

"Why?"

"It's complicated."

"Did you tell him to move out?"

Tears welled in Madlen's eyes. She swallowed. Shook her head. "No, Claire, I didn't. I didn't even know he was. I didn't find that out until after he was already dead. Okay? Are you happy now? Is this what you wanted?"

And before Claire could say no, that she was sorry, that she

wasn't trying to, had never meant to, didn't want to . . .
—before Claire could answer, Madlen had turned, was leaving
the room, was closing the door, was gone.

Driving over to the Frye house seemed to Madlen to be a rash
and dangerous thing for her to be doing. She pulled over onto
the road's grassy shoulder and parked there at an angle at the
bottom of the tidy gravel driveway, next to the mailbox, then
climbed the hill and clambered up onto the front porch, stepping
past the fallen tree, its leaves rustling in the breeze, and the
broken balustrade, its wood splintered and cracked like shattered
bone. She peeked in through the windows—all closed now—
with her hands cupped around her face. The storm-soaked curtains had been taken down, so she had a clear view into the
spoiled rooms, but there wasn't much to see. She dropped to the
ground again and went around to the back of the house, where a
yellow velvet chair had been left upturned in the yard, rain-
sopped and dejected, its skirts flipped and its legs poking up, the
torn black canvas square of its bottom side swollen and exposed.
She stood on the stoop and tried the back door, found it open,
and then without a second thought let herself in, supposing that
maybe it was meant to be this way, as if the house could be
offering itself up to her, an opportunity that she might decide to
take if that was what she wanted to do.

She walked through the sparsely furnished rooms, crossing the
bare wood floors and the watermarked oval rag rugs, startled by
the loud slap of her own sandals. She stopped to study her misshapen shadow, cast hugely on the flowery papered wall where
the sun was shining in aslant. She knelt and peered at the con-

centric circles of the carpet stains and the dried murk of mud marks on the kitchen's worn linoleum floor, as if they might, in their patterns, be able to tell her something about where she was and why.

Looking around, Madlen tried to imagine what it would be like to live here with the kids. Wondering, was there room? There were only two bedrooms upstairs. Maybe Claire and Glen could share? Impossible. She knew it even then. All the furniture that she had back in her California house wouldn't even begin to fit here, either, but maybe she could get rid of some of it. Put it in storage for the children, in case there was something they wanted or could use for themselves when they were grown up and had families of their own, later. Or just leave it all behind and set up a simplified, less cluttered life here.

She was admiring what seemed to her to be the bare restraint of Evelyn Frye's house, with its polished wood floors, straight-backed chairs, single bed, table, lamp in the bedroom upstairs. She thought that she might not mind such stripped simplicity, and at the same time understood that this must have been something of what Haven had been after too, when he had begun making his plans to leave her. Because it was so much the same as his apartment had looked to her—she'd been struck hard by the austerity of its barely furnished rooms.

Madlen stood in the front bedroom of Mrs. Frye's house and looked out the window at the lawn and the rolling fields beyond it and pictured a vegetable garden there, imagined herself working outside in it, barefoot, sleeves rolled up, arms muscled and brown. The fresh air would be good for the children too, she reasoned. Fresh air and hard work and good schools and straightforward, well-disciplined friends.

Because, after all, wasn't that how she had grown up herself? And Haven too? And Rafe? And so wouldn't that be best?

Blood brothers. They'd cut themselves with Rafe's knife, then pressed their hands together, clasped, before they turned to her. She'd lain down on her back in the grass, pulled her skirt up to her waist, lifted her hips to wriggle out of her underpants, bent her knees and opened her thighs, then let them press their palms against her, mingling their fresh blood with her own, viscous and bright.

Hannah was giving Jolie a bath. The tub was filled with bubbles, water, and fragrant foam. She rubbed Jolie's body all over with a big, misshapen sponge. Her soft hands moved through the warm water. Her hair, tied up, was damp. Jolie heard the front door slam shut downstairs and Rafe's car start up in the driveway outside. As he was backing out, she was struggling against the weight of Hannah's hands. Wet and slippery with soap, she slithered away, ran down the hall and down the stairs and across the house to the front door. There were sudsy Jolie footprints on the rug and on the floor. Her skin glistened with bathwater and her hair was wet, its tight curls pressed like paint against her scalp. Outside, at the end of the driveway, Rafe's car turned and then was gone. Inside, Jolie wailed.

"And then another one's here and another one's here and the next one's here and another one's here."

Holding on to her feet, Jolie rocked back and forth, bare bottom on the hardwood floor, head thrown back and throat taut, eyes shut tight and chin raised up. Hannah snatched her up naked and held her hard until after a while the girl quit, gave up and then was still. She was breathless in Hannah's arms, exhausted, buried in Hannah's flesh, as Hannah, on her knees, rocked her body back and forth and back and forth, murmuring, "Okay now, okay, it's okay, now it's okay, he'll be back, he's coming back to you, I promise, he will be back."

Rafe was on his way over to the Riverhouse, with his hair wet and combed back and his shirt crisp, boots polished and pants creased because Hannah had pressed them for him before he left. But when he saw Madlen's car parked at the bottom of the driveway at Mrs. Frye's, he pulled over there instead. Later Madlen would tell Sheriff Nicholls that she hadn't expected to meet Rafe there that afternoon, that he just showed up. That she saw him coming up the driveway. That even though it might look as if they'd planned it and as if she'd been waiting for him, still, she would insist, that wasn't how it was. Why would she have invited Claire to come with her if she knew that Rafe was going to be there? Unless she knew before she asked her that Claire's answer was going to be no. But there was no proof that she'd asked Claire, was there? Only Madlen's word.

She didn't go downstairs to greet him. She listened to him let himself into the house the same way she had, through the unlocked back door. She listened to the sound of his footsteps on the linoleum in the kitchen, the hardwood floor in the dining room, the braided rug in the living room. She heard him call her name, heard him climb the stairs toward her. And still she didn't turn but kept her place at the window, looking out over the cornfields, until he was behind her and had touched her, put his hands on her shoulders, until he was pressing his lips against the back of her neck. Only then did she turn. And saw as he seemed to wince that he was nervous. This endeared him to her. He ran his fingers through his hair, smiled crookedly, too much aware of himself, it seemed.

After it was all over, Madlen would admit to Sheriff Nicholls that yes, the sexual relations she had had with Rafe Ramsay had been consensual at first. But was that a crime?

He sat down on the bed and patted the place on the spread beside him. Madlen perched herself on the lip of the mattress, as if poised for flight, hands in her lap, fingers clenched.

"Relax," he said. He reached around and placed his hands on her shoulders. She closed her eyes, took a deep breath, felt her body begin to loosen at his touch.

He lay back and pulled her down next to him. "How about if you moved back here?" he asked.

Of course she'd already been thinking exactly this same thing. "With the kids?" she said, as if she hadn't gone so far as to consider this aspect of the possibility before.

He brushed a strand of her hair away from her face with his thumb. "It might be good for them," he said.

Again she felt herself second-guessed. "Except Claire. She'd never go for it."

Felt him tense. "Why not?"

"She says she hates it here."

He laughed. "She'll get over that."

She had to tell him then what Claire had said about seeing him in California. What did she expect? That he would deny it? That he would smile and try to explain it away, blame it on a girl's imagination gone wild? That he would be angry? That he would try to defend himself against it? That he would claim that

Claire was deluded, that he didn't know what she was talking about, that he had never been there, didn't even know exactly where *there* was?

He did none of these things. He sat up. He admitted that Claire was right. She had seen him. He had been there. He had been watching her, them, him.

She didn't like this. "Him?"

He leaned toward her; she shrank back.

"Haven," he said. Who else? He'd been watching Haven. Keeping an eye out, that was all. Following him for a few days, in fact. "I thought I was doing you a favor."

"How is spying on my husband doing me a favor?"

"Madlen. He was having an affair."

She was on her feet. How did he know that?

He sighed, resigned again. How could she be so stupid? When would she get it? When would she start to see?

"I followed him," he said. "I saw the other woman for myself. She was younger. Short dress. Too much makeup, a lot of curly hair. Someone that he worked with, probably."

Madlen was trying to remember, to think of who there was in Haven's office who looked like that.

"You're making this up," she said, even though she knew he wasn't. She already had the evidence of the apartment, after all.

"Madlen, don't act like you didn't know that it was happening. That's stupid. You don't have to pretend to me to be surprised," he said. His eyes were hard. He would have no sympathy for her in this part of it. He'd make her face the truth of what was what and then she would finally have to abandon Haven and her memories of him because of it.

In the statement that she gave the sheriff, Madlen said that she was worried for her daughter at that moment—because she'd doubted Claire and made Claire doubt herself. That she told Rafe she wanted to go home, and what she meant was back to the Riverhouse, where Claire was, upset and not feeling well.

But when he heard her say it, what he thought she meant was that she was going to leave him and go back to California. She claimed that this initial misunderstanding must have ignited his anger, because he said he couldn't believe that she would do that, how could she? After all that he'd gone through to get her there with him, to bring them that close together again, that far?

He stopped her before she could get away. Kissed her, still supposing she was going to respond and eventually give in, but when she continued to resist him, he caught her hair in the clench of his fist and dragged her back over to the bed, where he kicked her legs out from under her and pinned her down with one hand and tore at her dress with the other. Undid his belt, opened his pants, thrust himself into her, painfully, hard, and then stopped. Lay on top of her, was inside her, his mouth at her ear, his whisper telling her he was sorry, that he didn't mean to hurt her, that he loved her, and now it was all finally going to be all right for them, now it was all finally going to be good. She sobbed. Please.

"Why can't we have this?" he asked her. "Why?"

And then when he started to move, she was moving with him. She was holding on to him, crying out, and the muggy afternoon heat flowed over their bodies as if it were material, with density and weight. Madlen stretched herself out under the warmth and breadth of Rafe; she let herself be deafened by the rush of her own blood in her ears and rocked by the hard pounding of his heart in his body against hers.

Sheriff Nicholls wrote in his report that he saw the two cars parked outside the Frye house and stopped to investigate. That when he announced his presence from the yard, there was no response. He let himself in through the back door, the same way they had. They must have heard him coming. She was halfway down the stairs when he entered the living room of the house. He recognized her from before—she'd been there when they found the body of Mrs. Frye. He knew that she was Deem Malek's daughter and that her husband had been killed a year or so ago in a car wreck out in California. The strap on her dress was torn and hanging loose, and her hair was in some state of disarray. When he asked her if she was all right, she seemed surprised, and replied that she was just fine.

Did she know that she was trespassing here? She laughed at that, a little bit nervous about it maybe. Said she only came by to have a look at the place, see how salvageable it might be, that was all, no harm intended. And so he smiled back, answered, Well, it looks like no harm done.

She asked him if he knew what was going to happen to the house now. Did he think that Mrs. Frye's sister might decide to sell it?

He told her, because it was the truth, that he didn't know. Was she interested in buying?

She fiddled with that broken strap on her dress, smiled, and answered, Maybe, yes.

And then a man was there, his larger shadow looming at the top of the staircase behind her. When he came down into the light, the sheriff noted that his shirt was unbuttoned and its tails had come untucked but that otherwise he seemed to be composed. He was polite, deferential even. Introduced himself as Rafe Ramsay. Said he was staying over at Hannah Daggett's place with his daughter, but didn't bother to explain why. He had a look on his face that Tom Nicholls had seen before and so he figured he knew what the two of them had been doing up there, and he didn't exactly blame Rafe for it, because Madlen wasn't bad-looking, after all. They were both apologetic. And cooperative. Went on down to their separate cars and drove off, one in one direction and the other in the other.

It wasn't his fault what happened next, Tom Nicholls said. How was he supposed to know who Rafe was or what his connection to the Maleks had been? There was no way that the sheriff could have predicted or even guessed at what was coming. And there was also no way that he could have put a stop to it right then anyway, because as far as he could tell, it hadn't even started yet. He did everything there was for him to do, with the information that he had at the time. After they were gone, he called in on the radio to run the license plates and find out if there were any warrants out on Rafe Ramsay, but when the dispatcher came back to him, her answer was that the man was clean.

Madlen was scared, and her reflex was to run. Afraid, she realized, as much of herself as she was of Rafe. What was she doing? What had she done? The Riverhouse when she got back to it felt like a refuge of silence and shadow, its rooms as airless and fixed as her own held breath. Glen and Deem hadn't come back from Cedarcrest yet, and Claire was still upstairs in bed.

"Why can't we have this?" he'd asked. Meaning, why couldn't he have her?

Madlen was ready now to admit that Rafe might be a danger to her, just as Deem had warned her that he would be, and also that when she was with him she was a danger to herself. Because she didn't know the answer. Why not? Because she would have given herself to him, even if that meant that she had to abandon her family, her children. She only hoped it wasn't too late yet, that she might still be able to change her mind. That she and the children still could get away. She was afraid of Rafe and of herself and of the two of them together, and she was regretting what he'd done and what she'd done and what they'd done together, but she was still harboring some expectation that maybe it could all somehow still be all right. That maybe she would be able to leave Rampage behind her now, once and for all, pack up her bags and her children and go away, take them and herself back to California, which they never should have left, where she hoped they still belonged. That maybe Rafe would resign himself to staying here with his daughter and Hannah then, and that could be the end of it between them—a bad memory that over time would dim and fade until finally it was gone.

She stood in the front foyer of the Riverhouse with her back against the door and she crossed her arms and held herself, felt tears burning in her eyes, a sob hitching at her throat. One strap on her dress was torn and hanging. Her arms were bruised; her skin felt as if it had been scraped raw. She looked up to see her reflection in the foyer mirror and realized that this was what that sheriff had seen too—her hollow eyes, hanging mouth, snarled hair. A monster.

Well, she wasn't herself, she thought. Hadn't been since Haven's death. Surely she wasn't to be blamed for that, was she? The question rattled in the shuttered corners of her mind as she went upstairs to her room at the back of the house and emptied her drawers and her closet and began to pack her bag.

She didn't know how long Claire had been there watching her before she looked up from her work and saw the girl standing in the doorway with her hip cocked and her arms folded over her chest, scowling darkly. Her legs long and bare, in shorts, her arms and shoulders, in a tank top, pink with sunburn. Her white hair damp, standing up in spikes on her head. Eyes sparkling, face flushed and sheened with sweat.

"What's wrong?" Claire asked. "Mom, what are you doing?"

Madlen didn't want to alarm her. She held herself tight, her face hard, her body a clenched fist. Afraid to loosen, afraid to let her feelings give way.

"Nothing's wrong," she said. "Go pack your stuff."

Claire didn't move.

"You want to go home, don't you?" Madlen said.

"Mom?"

Madlen turned to her daughter, furious. Anger was going to have to be her last resort. "Just do it," she said, and watched, helpless, as Claire whirled away.

In the house at the Old Barn, Hannah was waiting for Rafe to come back home. She was sitting in the living room, holding Jolie's small bare body in the great soft amplitude of her lap. She was looking at Jolie's face and remembering Daggett's death. Remembering that everybody had blamed Rafe for it afterward, but she had never been able to believe that what had happened really was Rafe's fault. The official cause of death had been a stroke. She had an officially signed certificate to prove that. Natural causes is what it said. Daggett wasn't killed, he died. In a hospital, even. With doctors and nurses who had not been able to help him, who hadn't done one thing except to monitor him as he went. If they'd got to him sooner, maybe that would have made a difference. Or maybe not. Nobody could say anything about that for sure. He'd had a stroke. That's a common thing.

He smoked and he drank. People die from strokes every single day.

The child was swaddled in a towel as if she were a baby. Hannah rocked while Jolie watched her face, eyes solemn and wide. Silent because she was listening intently. She blinked at any sound. The bird fluttering in its cage. The house settling. Ice tumbling in the freezer in the kitchen. Wind shuffling along the treetops in the woods. And then when it was Rafe's car coming down the drive, Jolie kicked out and scrambled free and flew toward the door.

Hannah moved more slowly, hampered by her size. With some effort, she pulled herself up to her feet. She stopped and leaned against the chair back to catch her breath. Listened to the dull slow hammer of her heart. Heard the floor creak against her weight as she crossed it toward the front hall. She saw the door open and she saw the girl fly to him, saw her seem to float to him, with the billow of the white towel flowing out all around her, giving her wings.

It was a moment before he looked up from Jolie and realized that Hannah was there too. She'd stepped through the doorway, out of the shadows of the living room and into the front hall's brighter light.

Daggett had gone down to the river with the two boys, Rafe and Haven, to fish. It was a day like any other day. A day like this one, even. Summertime. Sunny. Muggy and hot. They took the old motorboat. Maybe they went too far downriver and so it took them a long time to get back. When Daggett toppled over, Rafe at first thought it was because of the sun. Or the cooler of beer that he'd been working on all afternoon. The boys ran the boat up onto the shore, then helped Daggett out. He wasn't unconscious, just weak, it looked like. Maybe only drunk. Loose, like. Wobbly. Together they walked him up the path to a cave in the bluff, where it was cool and he might revive.

Hannah looked at Jolie now, saw her holding on to Rafe. "She sure does cling to you," she said.

He had his hand on the girl's head, his fingertips circling her soft curls. "She's just a baby, Hannah," he answered. "And I'm all she's got."

"She threw a fit when you went out."

"Like I said. I'm all she's got."

She recognized the anger in him, saw it start to flare up in his eyes and burn there like a cold flame. Same as when he was a boy, thwarted, she thought. Those times when Daggett told him no.

Rafe said they didn't go for help right away because they weren't sure what was wrong, and besides, they didn't think Daggett ought to be left alone. Haven said he didn't go because Rafe told him not to. "Wait a minute," he'd told his friend. "Hold on."

And then had stood there looking down at the man slumped on the floor of the cave with his eyes wide open, rolling, fearful, like he knew. He wasn't dead yet, far from it, but there was definitely something wrong. He was breathing, but he wasn't talking. His face looked crooked somehow, and half his body seemed to be hanging limp. Rafe, seeing Daggett that powerless and that stupid, was laughing at him. Called him a damned old drunk. Said he'd shit his pants. Dapper Mr. Daggett, sitting in his own shit! Wouldn't the ladies at the Old Barn like to see that! Picked up a rock and lobbed it at him. Hit him in the forehead with it. Then again. This time on the cheek. Red welt. Daggett's mouth hanging open. Some kind of slobber sliming his lips and dripping down his chin. Rafe pulled off his belt and whacked it at the old man's head, his shoulders, arms and legs.

"I'll wallop you, mister! See if that don't make you learn!" Shoes scuffing in the damp dirt on the floor of the cave. Dancing. Like he was dancing.

How long was it before Haven finally took off, ran to the Riverhouse for help? Minutes? Hours?

Rafe had turned away from Hannah and was bent over Jolie. He picked her up gently and held her against his chest, carried her in his arms that way upstairs. When they came back down again, Jolie was in her white nightgown. He led her out into the kitchen. Made her a sandwich and some soup. Sat at the table drinking a beer, watched her eat.

Hannah watched him. "You remember all that about when Daggett died?" she asked.

He looked at her but said nothing.

"I know you do. The others all blamed you, but I never did. I blamed him."

"I didn't do anything wrong."

"I know that."

"I didn't kill him."

She nodded. Traced the flowered pattern on the tablecloth with her fingertip. "He never treated you the way you probably thought he should have. But he always believed that what he did for you was right."

"It wasn't right. I was just a kid."

"You always did have an answer."

He shrugged, drank his beer. "Everybody dies sometime, Hannah," he said. "Sooner or later, one way or another, the end is going to come."

When Haven got to the Riverhouse, he told them what Rafe was doing. Said that Daggett had been hurt and couldn't walk or talk. That Rafe had him holed up in a cave down under the palisade. Hannah had been out looking for them all already, worried because they weren't back yet and it was a Saturday and getting late and there was work to be done to set up for that night's dinner-dance. She was walking alongside the river, calling out to them, when she saw the boat pulled over onto the shore. There wasn't anybody around. She guessed the motor must have conked out again and this was as far as they'd got. She was about to turn around and go back home when out of the woods came Haven with the Maleks following after, and he led them all over to the cave where Daggett had been taken, but by that time Rafe was gone. It was Madlen who went looking for him, while Tim Malek picked Daggett up and carried him on his own shoulders back along the path up to the house. With Grinnell crying and carrying on as if it were her husband and not Hannah's that was hurt.

Now Hannah reached out, put her hand on Rafe's. When he was sent away from her, after Daggett's death, it was as if she'd lost everything, not only her husband but also the boy that she had hoped might be her son.

"I know you wouldn't lie to me, Rafe," she said. He looked at her, nodded, gave her a grateful smile, then turned to the child again. "And so I'm asking you this now, and I want you to tell me the truth. Is this little girl really yours?"

He didn't flinch. Only kept on watching Jolie, his eyes steady, bright, and blue, sharp as shattered glass.

"Because she doesn't look much like you," Hannah pressed on. She was telling herself that she was not afraid of Rafe. "Not in any way at all."

291

Jolie held the triangle of grilled cheese to her mouth with both hands and nibbled at it. Small gnawed fingers, sharp white teeth.

Rafe seemed to go soft. He relaxed his stiffened shoulders, dropped his chin. "What difference does it make, huh, Hannah?" he asked her. "I'm here, aren't I? And I'm taking care of her. Who else?" he went on. "Who else?"

Hannah didn't have any answer for that. She saw now that Jolie had stopped chewing and was watching her, waiting to see what she would say. She could tell that whatever the truth was, Rafe was sure that what he'd done was right. Wherever he'd got this child from, Jolie must be better off here with him than she ever was back where she'd been. Whatever else might have already happened, Rafe was finally about to put things right for himself, it looked like. He had it all worked out, it seemed. Maybe now all that had once been warped and twisted was finally about to be made clear and straight.

Glen told Sheriff Nicholls that when he and Deem returned to the Riverhouse, his mother was acting strange. She kept touching him, he said. Kept fussing over his hair and his clothes. She'd hurt herself somehow, too. There were red marks on her arms. She explained that she'd fallen, or something like that— she had some reason that she gave them, what it was now he wasn't sure. They'd brought her a bunch of fresh flowers from the Cedarcrest conservatory, where his grandfather worked. Deem told Madlen to get something to put them in. She went into the kitchen and found a vase and filled it with water, then came back out into the front room and told Glen that he should get packed, because they would be leaving in the morning. To get back to their lives, she said. So that Deem and Ruth could get back again to theirs.

Glen had been surprised to hear this, that they were going, but when he started asking questions, his sister told him he'd better just shut the fuck up. They both knew that something was wrong, but it was impossible at that time to tell exactly what.

It looked like Deem was sensing trouble too, and he wasn't afraid to make her tell him what was up. Why the sudden decision to leave? Why was she being so abrupt? What about the baby? Didn't she want to stay at least long enough to see him? He kept asking questions and dogging her with them and following her around the house from room to room. He wouldn't leave her alone, until finally he got her to admit that this man named Rafe had done something to her. He'd grabbed at her and pushed her, it sounded like. Or worse. It was hard for Glen to know exactly what his mother told Deem then, because she was screaming at him and Deem kept yelling back at her and slamming things around. In the kitchen he punched his fist into a wall and left a hole.

Claire and Glen stayed upstairs until things were quiet again. When they came down, Deem was sitting at the kitchen table with his hand in a bowl of ice. Madlen had made him a drink. She was standing at the counter fixing dinner, acting as if nothing had happened. She didn't say much. Just that they should all get to bed early because they'd be flying out of Linwood first thing in the morning. She'd changed their reservations. It was no big deal. Everything was going to be all right now, after all. It was over. They'd go home. Deem didn't need to worry. He didn't need to do anything or say anything. She didn't need his help. Didn't want it. She admitted he'd been right about Rafe, they all had. Rafe was insane maybe, dangerous certainly, but

that was all over with now. She was sorry that she hadn't listened
to him sooner, sorry it had started, sorry she'd allowed it to get
this far. She'd been stupid. She'd been wrong, but now it was
done, and all she wanted her father to do for her was to leave it
alone and let her go back home.

Who was Madlen kidding? Because for Rafe it was not done;
not by a long shot, it wasn't. He carried Jolie upstairs again after
she'd eaten and washed up. He helped her into bed, settled her
there, tucked the blanket in around her, and turned off the light.

Her name was Joliet Anne Ray. In the town that he'd taken
her from, nobody knew who he was, and there was no way to
trace her back to him. After a while the yellow ribbons that
they'd put up on the lampposts and the trees were going to start
to flap and unravel, fade and droop, until one day, early in the
morning, they'd be quietly removed. The flyers on the phone
poles would be bedraggled by the weather, sun and rain, get torn
and worn and weather-stained, covered over eventually by more
recent and more urgent-seeming announcements and bulletins
for yard sales or missing cats and dogs. After a while the people
of Monarch, Oregon, were going to drift right back to where
they'd been before he'd taken her, forgetful of what she looked
like, forgetful even of her name. They'd get back to going about
their same old ordinary daily businesses again, and even though
nobody would like to think they'd given up on her, that's what
they naturally would do. Because as long as no progress was
being made in finding her, then it would be hard for anyone
among them to muster much in the way of hope. She wasn't
even theirs, for one thing. No more theirs than his.

So who was there who might care enough to carry on the

cause for a missing little girl who didn't belong to anybody? No one had been close enough to either the family or their foster daughter to maintain the kind of obsession it was going to take to find out where she was. Maybe there'd be some momentary flurry of excitement when a body was found in the basement of an abandoned house, and the speculation for the first hours afterward would be that maybe it was her. Except then they'd find out that it was a boy. Some victim of something. An overdose. Or an accident. A murder, even. Something else. Someone else. Not her.

Rafe stood over Jolie, watching quietly with his hands folded and his head bowed until she closed her eyes and her breathing deepened and she seemed to be asleep. It was early, but she was tired.

Hannah hovered in the hallway, waiting. When Rafe came out of the room, she stopped him.

"You won't get away with it, you know," she said. "People will find out. They'll send you away again. Just like they did before. Except that this time it'll be for good."

"Are you planning to say something, Hannah?" he asked.

She trembled. "If I don't tell them, somebody else will."

He looked at her, his eyes cold and hard, his mouth tight, teeth grinding, muscles working in his jaw.

"I don't think I know what you're talking about," he said finally, turning from her, heading back downstairs. "Won't get away with what?"

She went to her room, lay down on her bed. Her heart was pounding hard. She felt dizzy, short of breath, afraid. Earlier that day she'd pulled the shades and drawn the curtains shut, so now the room was dark and hot. She had a fan set up on the dresser, but it didn't do much good. She was thinking about all the things that Rafe had said to her about the girl. Wondering why what he had told her in the first place couldn't still be true. More than anything, she wished that she could find some way to keep believing that it was. She'd always been like that with Rafe, hadn't she? Weak? Finding reasons and making up excuses. Daggett had warned her from the beginning, when Rafe had first come to live with them, that it wasn't going to be easy bringing up a foster child, especially one who was already as old as Rafe was then—nine. Daggett had been doing her a favor, letting her bring him home. But she wasn't supposed to get too attached to the boy, he told her, she was just supposed to take care of him— food, shelter, clothing, that was all. They were doing it for the money. Nobody ever said anything about love.

And so when Rafe made a mistake or if he did something wrong, it was Daggett who took care of it. If she protested—and she soon learned not to—he told her that it would be better for everybody if she could just be honest with the boy. Let him take the blame and the punishment he deserved. How else was he going to learn?

Daggett had made his office up in the hayloft of the old barn. He'd put a window in where the loft door had been, so he could see down into the yard when the guests were there. It was broken now, the glass long gone. The whole building had been left to fall to ruin over the years; just last month Sheriff Nicholls had warned Hannah that the place was getting to be a nuisance and she ought to sell it or get it fixed or at least have somebody fence it in and board the windows up, before some kids broke in and got hurt. She'd promised him that she'd get to that as soon as she could. She'd meant to mention it to Rafe, but she'd forgotten. Now maybe it was too late.

Daggett used to take Rafe up there to the office in the loft when he had some reason for it. Whack him with his belt; that was how it was done. For taking food off the party trays without asking first. For not finishing his chores. For swiping that bottle of gin from the bar and then coming home drunk and dirty and late.

That time, when Daggett went after him, Rafe tried to run, but Jack was bigger and faster and he caught him. Dragged him up the stairs into the loft with Hannah screaming at them both to quit. Rafe thrashing and struggling and spitting until Daggett threw him down and started to take off his belt. It was something about that gesture, the unbuckling, as if he were going to take off his pants, that made Rafe say it, Hannah guessed. Said that Madlen had seen Daggett in Ivy's camper with Grinnell Malek. Fucking her like a dog. Daggett let the belt go. He reached out and took hold of the back of Rafe's shirt with his fist. Rafe struggled some, but he was drunk and Daggett was stronger. In one smooth simple motion he lifted the boy up and out the open window, then just let go, dropped him down. Didn't even look to see how he'd landed, but turned around to Hannah with a question pleating his brow, a question that in combination with the jut of his chin she understood to be a challenge, asking, What? Do you want to be next? When she shrank away from him, he wrinkled his nose as if he smelled something bad and turned away. He kept on across the room and out and slammed the door hard after him. By the time she got down to Rafe in the yard, Ivy was there with him already and the doctor had been called.

She heard Rafe go outside now and then come back into the
house again. She listened to him climb the stairs. Saw his shadow
looming in the doorway. Saw him raise his arm, lift his hand to
point it at her. Something in it, hard and dark. Saw his finger
move, saw the flash and heard the sound, but that was all.

So maybe Rafe was insane, but Deem didn't believe it. Dangerous, maybe. Crazy, no. Leave it alone, Madlen had told him.
All right then, he would. Deem was sitting in the cushioned
wicker chair out on the back porch, listening to the crickets,
looking out at the first flicker of fireflies at the edge of the
woods, and brooding over the fact of Rafe Ramsay. Like chewing on a nail.

No, Deem thought, not insane. Not sick. Just selfish. Mean,
maybe. And smart. Pretty much the same as Jack Daggett had
been. Helping himself to whatever happened to come his way.
Taking what he wanted to, without stopping for a minute to
think about what kind of harm his taking or his wanting did to
everybody else. Never intending to give anything of his own self
in return. It had been hard for Deem to tell what part of it was
worse, what was the greater crime, the deeper sin: that Grinnell
had loved Daggett, that she'd given herself to him, or that Daggett had taken her and then not loved her back.

Oh, he'd known all about what they were doing. Pretty much
from the beginning of it; even though he didn't have any real
evidence, still he'd had a sense. Not that she ever came right out
and said so. Not that he ever came right out and asked. They
didn't talk about that because they didn't have to. It was like they
had an understanding, when she started sleeping with Daggett. If

that was what Grinnell needed, if that was what made her happy
. . . The truth was, Deem had been grateful for the peace.

Starting when? When she let Doreen Cramer cut off all her
hair? She'd come home from Rampage that afternoon like a
changed person, it seemed. Happier. Carefree. A girl again. It
wasn't the hair, of course, it was Doreen. When the parties
started up on weekends at the Old Barn? Grinnell and Doreen—
the two of them dancing with anybody who asked. That was
fine. Doreen's husband was locked up in the reformatory, so he
had no say. And Deem himself didn't mind. He had no plan to
get up there and do any dancing himself, and it was all right with
him if Grinnell wanted to have some fun. For those first few
times he went to the parties with her, but it wasn't long before
he got tired of it, and then he let her go alone. Told her to
behave herself. Only once or twice had to go out in the truck to
bring her home.

Meanwhile he had his flowers and his gardens. He had his
work. Grinnell seemed happy, and if she was happy, then it was
possible for there to be some tranquillity between them again.
They could have gone on that way for a long time, he thought.
It was a good arrangement. No harm done. Except for Daggett's
deciding it was time to move on. Taking up with somebody
else—a girl from Linwood, Deem had heard. Well, it was an old
story, wasn't it? Daggett was the kind of man who moved from
one woman to the next, without much holding on or looking
back. Grinnell had believed herself to be the exception to the
rule of that, but it turned out she was wrong. The only rule she
broke was that she couldn't let Daggett go. Kept coming after
him and coming after him. She'd made a big scene at the end,
although Deem was not supposed to know it.

Ivy Daggett had told him some of what had happened. The rest he'd had to guess. She said that Grinnell had showed up at the house with a suitcase in her hand on that winter night when the bat came flying out of the fireplace at her. She'd walked over through the snow from the Riverhouse expecting Daggett to take her in, but he'd said no. Shut the door on her. With Hannah standing there on the stairs watching, not knowing what to do, while Grinnell banged at the windows in the front of the house with her fists. Even broke a few.

Daggett called Deem and he went over in the truck to get her. Drove her back home to the Riverhouse again. She wouldn't talk to him about it. Didn't try to explain what had happened. Didn't have to, because he thought he knew. Then for the next fifteen years she just slowly fell apart, piece by piece by piece. She never did stop loving Jack Daggett, though, he didn't believe, not even after he was gone. That was why she'd killed herself, he guessed. And as hard as it was for him to admit it now, still the truth was that by the end it had been a relief to Deem when they called to let him know that his wife was dead.

In his statement to Tom Nicholls, Deem would say that he knew Madlen had got mixed up again with Rafe, in spite of the fact that he kept on trying to warn her against it. He suspected that she'd been mixed up with him for a long time before she even came back to Rampage that summer, maybe from even before Haven was killed. But even so, he explained, even though he was her father and still had some responsibilities toward her, he'd felt he had to draw the line at what his involvement in her personal affairs was going to be now. He didn't want to have anything to do with Rafe himself, for one thing. Not anymore. If Madlen had got herself into trouble now, then she was going to have to find a way to get herself back out. What Deem wanted just then was the whole fullness of his new life, not the shreds and remnants of his old one. He needed to be with Ruth. He needed to drive to Linwood to see her, to hold her, and to hold their newborn son. First he went upstairs to change his clothes. He'd had a drink, sure, maybe two, but he wasn't drunk. Sheriff Nicholls figured that by the time Deem had found his keys and gone outside and turned the pickup around to head out toward the road, Hannah was already dead, and Rafe was on his way.

Jolie had been sitting up, awake, in her bed in the room down the hall. She'd been listening. She'd been looking out the window. She'd been thinking back to her foster family, the mom and the dad, wondering, did she miss them in a way? Did she miss that house and her little room off the kitchen and the broken door and the mattress on the floor and the yellow star stickers that she'd pressed against the window glass herself? The barbecues on Sunday afternoons, the songs they sang together in the church, the rope swing in the tree in the back yard that she'd only just begun to learn how to pump at with her legs to get it going all by herself?

She decided that she didn't. Even though Jolie was more alone now than she'd been before. Even though nothing had changed for her, not really. Only the place of her loneliness, not its fact. She was still all by herself in a dark bedroom, supposed to be sleeping but awake and alert and watching at the window, waiting for something to happen.

She heard him go downstairs. She saw him go outside to his car, then come back inside again with the gun. She poked her finger into the hole in the screen. She heard the shot, and it was something like the first time, except that there was no solo singing sound here. And there was only that one single banging noise, no more. She was waiting for him to come and get her again. She was humming to herself, singing, "And another one's here and another one's here and the next one's here."

Then Rafe was in the doorway, as before. She thought he was beautiful, with the light from the hallway shining out behind him as it was. When he came for her, she reached for him. He lifted her up and carried her downstairs, outside, to his car. And then they were moving again, through the dark, just the two of them, just the same as they had been before.

Rafe came into the driveway of the Riverhouse at the same time that Deem was starting to turn his truck out onto the road. He pulled up alongside the pickup and rolled his window down.

"Hi there, Mr. Malek," he said. A smile on his face. His hand on the gun under his jacket on the seat next to him. Jolie belted in by the window on the other side.

Deem nodded. "Rafe."

"Heard your wife had a little boy yesterday."

"That's right."

"Well, congratulations!"

Deem nodded again. "Thank you."

"You on your way into Linwood to see them?"

"I was. I think maybe now I've changed my mind, though."

Rafe considered this. He reached into his shirt pocket, pulled out a pack of cigarettes, and offered one to Deem, who shook his head. He lit one for himself, blew smoke, coughed, and winced.

"I just came by to pay a visit to your daughter, sir," he said. "That's all."

Deem looked into the rearview mirror at the image of the Riverhouse reflected in its glass. "I don't guess that's such a good idea right now, Rafe," he said. "She's a little upset."

"I think you should go on into Linwood and see that wife and child of yours just like you planned, sir. It sure would be a shame if you had to disappoint them." He was smiling again, his teeth white. "If you don't mind my saying so, that is."

"I think they could hold off all right until tomorrow," Deem answered.

Rafe sighed. "Why don't you just pull on out onto the road now, Mr. Malek?" he asked. "Go see your wife and kid. Forget about all this here."

"You know I can't do that." Deem put in the clutch. Shifted into reverse, was turning to look behind him, was starting to back up.

But Rafe was out of the car and he was standing next to the window and the gun was in Deem's face. He flicked his cigarette away. "Get out."

Deem turned off the engine and climbed down from the truck. He held his hands out, palms up. "Best thing would be if you just went away now, Rafe," he said. "Before this goes too far. Quit while you're ahead, why don't you? It might not be too late."

Rafe shook his head. "I don't want to have to shoot you, old man."

"I know you don't."

Deem was looking past Rafe at the white shape of the little girl inside the car. He bent, leaned toward her. He waggled his fingers at her and smiled. He didn't see Rafe's hand come back. He didn't know that it already was too late, that it had been too late for a while. He didn't know that it already had gone too far for him to stop it, or even how far it had gone. He didn't know anything anymore, except that he was going down.

Glen was outside in the tent when Rafe's car pulled up. He turned his flashlight off and looked out through the flap to see a man get out of his car, put on his jacket, then disappear around the house as he headed up the front walk toward the porch. He'd left the lights on and the motor running, as if he weren't planning to stay there long. Glen had his knife in his pocket. He crawled out onto the grass and scooted across the yard toward the back door to slip inside the house.

Madlen was standing behind the screen in the oblong of light at the front door, and she was looking at Rafe as if she were surprised to find him there. She was seeing him as he was now and at the same time as he had been then—that afternoon when Daggett had had his stroke and she'd gone off into the woods to look for Rafe, had found him at the fire pit, huddled on a limestone block with his legs pulled up under him, his elbows on his knees, his face in his hands. Then he'd been a boy, powerless, scared, afraid of what he'd done and of what might be done to him. Not knowing whom to trust or where to run.

Then she'd had trouble making sense of what was wrong, what he was trying to tell her. That Daggett was in a cave, not dead but dying? Rafe didn't kill him; he'd tried to save him. It wasn't that she didn't believe Haven later, when he told them what he'd seen Rafe do to Daggett. It was only that she chose to disregard it. Because once Daggett was dead and Haven and his mother had gone back to Linwood and Rafe had been sent away, what difference did it make?

And now: that the little girl, Jolie, wasn't really his? That he'd taken her? But he'd only meant to rescue her, that was all, because she'd been in an impossible situation and she was better off here with him. That he hadn't taken her? That he'd saved her. And now he couldn't get caught. Not for his own sake but for hers, because they'd want to take her back?

"Come with us, Madlen."

She looked past him, through the screen, to see that Jolie was in the car, waiting, watching. She was fiddling with the window, pushing the button to roll it up and down. Her face there, not there, then there again.

Madlen turned back to Rafe. She shook her head. "No," she said. "I can't."

He put his hand out to her. "Come on. We don't have a lot of time."

She stayed behind the door. "I'm not going with you, Rafe."

He slammed his fist against the side of the house, spun away from her, then turned back. He hunched his shoulders and ducked his chin into the collar of his jacket, shut his eyes, took a deep breath, then opened them again.

"All right, Madlen," he said. "It wasn't supposed to happen this way, but it did. And there's nothing we can do about it now. Haven's dead, and that is not my fault. He brought it on himself. What he did to you. What he put you through. He deserved it."

"Go away, Rafe." Madlen reached to pull the inside door around and closed. Claire had come downstairs and was standing with her brother in the hallway, watching. Rafe nodded at them, smiled.

"You were right, Claire," he said. "I was in Los Angeles. You did see me there. I was at your house. And I was with your daddy when he died."

Madlen turned to the children. "Get upstairs."

But Glen's eyes were fixed on Rafe. The man that he'd seen inside the house with the fat lady and the girl. He stepped toward him. "What's that mean, you were with him?"

Rafe smiled at the boy. "You must be Glen," he said. "You look just like your dad did, do you know that?"

Glen was frowning. He tossed his hair back from his face. He fingered the knife in his pocket, rubbed at the smooth surface of its handle with his thumb. "Who are you?" he asked Rafe. "What do you want from my mom?"

Rafe's smile widened. "Well, I was your daddy's friend," he said. "And I just want to take care of her, now that he's gone."

Madlen had turned to Glen and taken hold of his shoulders. She pushed him back toward the stairs. "Go on," she said. And looked at Claire. "You too. Go." They didn't move. She put her hands up on her head, shouted at them. "Go!" But still they stayed.

Rafe was pacing back and forth outside on the porch. His footsteps seemed to shudder through the Riverhouse. He was talking as he moved, with his hands stuffed down into his pockets, explaining to Madlen and the children as well as to himself, it seemed—what had happened, what he'd done.

That Haven had been at the apartment and that Rafe had followed him there, had gone up and rung the bell and then told him how he knew all about what he was doing and how unhappy Madlen was too. Said that Haven ought to leave her; he should give her up and let her go. Make a clean break. It was only fair. It was the right thing to do, wasn't it? And Rafe would take care of her himself, if that was what he was worried about. He'd see to it that she was looked after, make sure that she was fine.

Rafe stopped. He looked at Madlen. "And I would have, too. I will." He shrugged and shook his head, as if in disappointment and dismay. "It didn't have to be this way, but you know how Haven was. He didn't want to hear what I was telling him. He wasn't going to listen to me. Told me to fuck off." Rafe slammed his fist against the house again. "I wasn't going to do that! All right?" He opened his hand and held it out, palm up, toward Claire, who hovered with her brother on the stairs. "We were blood brothers, remember?" The scar wormed over the mound below Rafe's thumb. "Me and Haven. And your mother too."

He followed the MG up the canyon, but when Haven saw that Rafe was behind him, he stopped and pulled over onto a turnout. Got out of the car. Told Rafe to leave him alone—to let his family be.

"He never was much of a fighter," Rafe said. "And he'd been drinking. He was slow and out of shape."

Claire's face was white. "You killed him," she said.

"I hit him a few times, that's all. Maybe kicked him once. Just to let him know I was serious."

Haven had pulled himself back up to his feet. His nose was bleeding, his face was cut, Rafe's boot had cracked a rib. Haven got into his car then, knowing he was beaten, and tried to get away.

"That was probably a mistake," Rafe said.

"You killed him," Claire said again.

Rafe shook his head. "No, I didn't. It was an accident. He was drunk, and he was hurt, and he was going too fast. He lost control of the car and it went off, just like the police report said."

Rafe had watched the MG miss the curve and slam through the guardrail. It had tumbled down the slope, and he had clambered after it, arms outflung for balance, feet skidding on the loosened rocks. He'd found the car settled in the brush with Haven unconscious behind the wheel, his head thrown back, mouth open, blood slicking his face and soaking into the crisp collar of his shirt. It was so quiet, Rafe said. It was as if he had gone deaf. He'd never heard so much silence as that before. Or ever since. He was going to pull Haven out, and if it hadn't been for all that silence, maybe he would have. He could have saved him if he'd wanted to, but he'd already decided that he was going to save Madlen instead.

He shrugged again, frowned, and seemed to reconsider. "If it hadn't been for the fire, I guess maybe Haven could have been all right. Even without any help of my own."

Claire was screaming, and Madlen was shouldering Glen back. She brought the inside door around and he heard the bolt turn as she locked it. He tore at the screen and kicked at the door. He stormed across the porch, howling Madlen's name. Saw Haven's head turn, saw his eyes open, saw him recognize his friend and realize his situation, heard the flurry of his struggle to get out of the car. Heard the twin bellows of Haven's anguish and his own, blended with the blast of whirled flames as the canyon burned and Rafe turned away and ran.

He picked up a flower pot and hurled it at the big window in the music room. He climbed in past the shattered glass, calling her name still as he raged from room to room to find her and stop her, hold her and make her understand.

"Madlen! Madlen!"

But she was gone. The back door stood open. She'd taken her children and escaped into the woods.

———

Jolie was watching from the car. She heard the girl's scream. She saw the boy lunge at the door just as the woman closed it. She saw Rafe smash the window and climb through it into the house. She heard him calling to the woman, saw the silhouette of his shadow moving past the lighted windows as he searched the house, saw him cross the yard out back and then disappear into the trees. She waited. Listened to the crickets and the cicadas, watched the fireflies sparking in the darkness and the moths circling in the light. When after a while he didn't come back, she was afraid that he was gone. So she got out of the car and she went after him.

Glen led the way along the path, with Claire and Madlen struggling after him, branches whipping at their faces, roots grabbing at their feet. They could hear Rafe storming on along behind them, crashing through the brush, calling Madlen's name. If they could just make it to the river, she thought. If they could cross the swinging bridge. If they got as far as Hannah's house, maybe she would help them, maybe she would call someone to come. Or they could run out to the road. Flag down a truck or passing car. Her foot slipped on a rock, her ankle twisted, cracked, and she fell, skidding forward into the clearing around the fire pit on her flattened hands.

She was screaming at the children to keep running. Told them not to stop for her—but how could they leave her, their mother, behind? They wavered in the shadows at the edge of the clearing as Rafe burst out of the trees. When she looked again, it seemed that they had done as she had told them and were gone. He was kneeling next to her. He was gently touching her. Brushing the hair away from her face. Taking her hand to help her up to her feet.

"I can carry you," he said. When she tried to pull away, he tightened his grip on her arm and yanked her up, held her close. "It's all right now. It's done." He kissed her throat, supported her body with one arm, moved his hand over her breasts and down across her belly, worked his fingers in between her thighs. She tried to wrench herself away from him, but pain tore through her leg and her ankle wouldn't hold her. As she fell, he caught her again and held her to him.

She cried out, and he shook her.

"Stop fucking with me, Madlen!"

She told Sheriff Nicholls that at that time the gun seemed to come out of nowhere. That he was holding on to her with one hand and in his other hand there was a gun, its barrel pressed against her cheek. He shook her again, shoved her away and then yanked her back, as if he wasn't sure anymore what exactly he wanted her to do.

Then Claire was screaming and Glen was charging from the shadows, springing out at Rafe from behind. He hurled himself up onto the man's back, locking his legs around his waist and his arm around his neck. The knife blade in Glen's hand rose and then fell against Rafe's side. Rafe howled and flung Madlen away from him, slammed her into Claire, and the two of them fell. He dropped the gun and brought his hands up behind him, clasped them around the back of Glen's head, tried to flip him over, but the boy held on, clinging to Rafe with his legs and his one arm while he worked and turned the buried blade in his other hand. Rafe arched backward, staggered, lost his footing, and tumbled down, landing on the dirt with Glen underneath. He rolled and began to raise himself up again on hands and knees, but before he could stand, Glen was on him once more. The boy still had hold of the knife, and as he embraced the man with his body he delved the blade into the soft flesh above Rafe's hip. Rafe surged upwards, bringing Glen with him. He backed away, still holding the boy, and took a step before his feet slipped out and he went crashing down again, hard against the ground. Both of them, the man and the boy, were still.

Madlen was on her knees. "Glen?"

He groaned and rolled away from Rafe. He lay on his back, panting. Rafe lumbered to his feet. His hand was on the knife that Glen had left buried in his side. Blood seeped between his fingers, soaked through the shining fabric of his white shirt, puddled in the pocket of his jacket.

Madlen had picked the gun up from the ground.

Groaning, Rafe pulled the knife out and tossed it down toward Glen. His face was glossy with sweat. He raised his hands and took a step toward Madlen. His lips were curled in a grimace of pain. He cocked his head at her. "What will you do now, Madlen?" he asked. "Shoot me?"

It was Claire who saw Jolie, a white shape that seemed to be floating down the path between the shadowed trees. Madlen raised the gun and pointed it at Rafe. Jolie, shrieking, was flying toward him. Just as Claire was leaping out to stop her. Just as the gun went off in Madlen's hand and her body absorbed the whole of its unforgiving force—the brightening, the bang, and the terrible knowledge that transformed Claire's face as she was struck. She caught Jolie in her arms and she held her, as if maybe she believed now that the girl she was saving was herself.

EPILOGUE

MOTHERS IN LINWOOD STILL TELL THEIR SONS THAT IF they don't watch out, shape up, behave themselves and stay out of trouble, they'll likely be sorry for it, maybe end up spending the best years of their lives in Rampage, locked behind bars at the reformatory there. Young kids caught shoplifting or spray-painting graffiti, smashing mailboxes or lobbing rocks at the windows of the abandoned factory buildings on the old west side of town, are driven out past the forbidding prison structure and made to gaze up at its high walls of blackened limestone, its barred windows, its tall guard towers, and the ribbon of razor-wired chainlink fence that describes the wide perimeter of the outer grounds, and they're asked to consider what it might be like to live there, locked up like an animal, caged in a cell inside for years and years, until they're old or dead.

But those mothers who think that they are only being honest with their wayward sons have not even begun to tell the truth. Because there are no boys in the Rampage Men's Reformatory, and the men who are there are not there to be reformed, they're there to be kept. More than fifteen hundred are incarcerated in double- and triple-bunk cells meant to hold only eight hundred and fifty men. And more than half of those are there for violent crimes, not against property but against persons—one hundred and twenty-seven of them, murderers and rapists, including Rafe Ramsay, for life. There is no death penalty in Iowa; there is only life.

What the girls in Linwood talk about is being taken away to Cedarcrest Retreat. They whisper to each other what they've heard about insulin shock treatments and electroconvulsive therapies, bed restraints, straitjackets, lithium and Thorazine, icewater baths, psychosurgery, lobotomies, an ice pick in the eye.

Everybody seems to know someone who has been at Cedarcrest sometime. Mothers or sisters or aunts who have had nervous breakdowns. They talk to themselves; they hear voices in their heads. Young women who drink too much or eat too little, who sleep too long or take too many pills. Who cry all the time, who can't take care of their babies, can't do their jobs, can't even get up out of bed in the morning and stay in their bathrobes and slippers and underwear all day. Some have tried to kill themselves, but no one likes to talk about that, to say precisely why or describe exactly how. Pills, mostly. Razor blades. Nutsy-cuckoo, as Ivy Daggett used to call it.

Deem Malek no longer works in the gardens at Cedarcrest Retreat, but his daughter has a room there, in a good wing, on a good floor, with a view of the gardens—the roses and the trellis and the bench with its brass dedication to the memory of Grinnell. The duck pond is gone; the conservatory has been torn down.

There is a dream that has been haunting Madlen ever since she came here—it's one that comes back to her again and again, and in it she's been taken. The fact that it won't leave her alone has made her wonder, does everybody have this dream, or is it only hers? When she asked another patient this, the woman thought about it for a moment and then answered no, she didn't think so. Anyway, not just exactly that. When she asked one of the doctors, he frowned and wanted to know why she would wonder such a thing. Sometimes, lately, she is afraid to go to sleep because she knows that she's going to have that dream.

At night her room in the old Queen Anne seems small, closed, and dark. She always leaves a lamp on when she goes to bed—it's something that her father gave to her for Christmas last year, a translucent porcelain square with an embossment of an angel on it, framed and clamped onto a plug and small bulb. He said when she unwrapped it that the angel's face reminded him of Claire. It's a simple thing, and the light that it casts is yellowy and shallow, but it's enough to let Madlen see what's where when she's up, awake, afraid, here in the utter darkness of the middle of the night.

Her dream will start with a shadow at the window. Then a stranger is looking in. He has his face pressed up against the glass, his nose is flattened by it, all his features look squashed. For a moment after that he's gone and she can't be sure that he was ever there at all, until his fist begins to hammer at the glass. The sound of this is loud. The whole building shudders under the solid force of each single blow. Madlen tries to turn away, but she can't. She tries to run away, but she can't. And then the window begins to crack and then the pane explodes. He's unlocking the latch and raising the sash, and then he's coming in.

In Madlen's dream, the man climbs into her room on the second floor of her house. Which house is it? Maybe it's the first one that she and Haven had, on Foxridge Road in Linwood. Maybe it's the house up in the canyon in L.A. Maybe it's Mrs. Frye's house. Or maybe it's the Riverhouse in Rampage, after all. That part of it is not altogether clear.

She can't say either just how it is that he gets up there. Maybe he has a ladder. And she also doesn't know why he isn't cut. Maybe he's wearing gloves.

He pulls her from her bed and he takes her into his arms and he carries her out the window and somehow down to the ground, off through the dark toward a place on the far side of the woods where he's left his car.

She runs with him along the path that twines between the trees. She can't quite see him clearly. He's not much more than a mere shape, large and dark, that moves ahead of her. Or sometimes he's a warmth, hard and close, and he carries her. Or it could be that he is behind her, that she's stumbling along ahead of him, or maybe he's dragging her with his hand wrapped tightly around her own.

That's all there is to that part of it, because then the dream will change to something else and she'll be driving the old black convertible MG. Haven is beside her. The top is down and the wind is blowing wildly in her hair. Glen is in the back seat, holding hands with Claire. Madlen is doing her best, trying to follow the road, which is something like the one that runs out past the Riverhouse on the way into Rampage, a road that swoops and circles and turns, then starts to become something else and ends up going to a place that Madlen doesn't think she's ever seen before and she doesn't know it and can't seem to recognize it, a place where she is certain she was never meant to be. There are airplanes swarming in the sky above her, but they've cut their engines so there is a silence that's like the silence before a storm, and she can tell that they're not going to be able to stay up much longer and then sure enough they start to dive at her, but even if she wanted to there would be nothing she could do to stop them from their spin and plummet down. And that's when she'll wake up.

Madlen pours a glass of water from a pitcher on the table by the bed. She wishes it were gin, without a lot of ice.

As always, she's just trying not to think too much; all she wants is to be left alone now, to be allowed to forget. The doctors here tell her it will harm her if they let that happen, but she doesn't believe them. What do they know? When they ask her something and she tells them that she can't remember, they reply that she isn't being honest. And until she starts being honest, they say, she is never going to get well. And until she gets well, she won't be able to go home.

What they don't seem to understand is that it isn't that Madlen can't remember. It's only that she won't. She doesn't want to. When they try to prod her on this, she willfully resists. She has no desire to go home, for Glen's sake even more than for her own. He's living with his grandfather and Ruth and their boy Sam now. Madlen has to believe that her own son is better off there with them than he would ever be with her.

She sits in her bed, her body propped up against the pile of pillows at her back, her skin yellowed by the jaundiced spill of light from the porcelain lamp. Her fingers fiddle with the emerald necklace at her throat. Her eyes are squeezed shut. Her hands are clenched in fists against her chest. It's always this way: the harder she struggles to forget what happened, the more sharply the images come back to her, images of things she didn't even see, things she only heard about, after it was all over—things she read in the newspapers, things that she was told of at Rafe's trial. Hannah's body as it lay bleeding into the bed. Ivy baking in the sunshine on the ground outside the camper, her blind eyes open to the sky and plagued by flies. Deem up on the dark road, struggling to his feet, stumbling down the driveway to the Riverhouse, too late. But this she did see: Jolie blood-soaked and screaming, pulling herself away from Claire and throwing her body at the man whom she believed to be her father like some frantic and wild red bird.

Be careful what you look at, Doreen Cramer had said. Maybe it would be better not to know too much.

Groaning, Madlen opens her eyes. When she looks at the visage of the angel in the lamp, she sees Claire again, sees herself. But another face is there too—Rafe's little girl, that beautiful child, small and dark-haired and dark-eyed and perfect, a splendid girlish apparition that will not stop glowing in the night.

It wasn't that he took her, not exactly. It was more that he tried to rescue her. It was more that she went. If anybody had asked Jolie—but no one did—she would, if she'd had the words for it, have argued this. It had seemed to her to be simple that way.

"And then another one's here and another one's here and the

next one's here and then another one's here and they all fall down."

He had come for her. He had climbed in through the window to her room. She had reached for him, he'd lifted her up, he'd pulled her close, and then he'd simply carried her away.

Acknowledgments

I would like to thank Betsy Lerner for her wise and patient guidance, Kim Witherspoon for her encouragement and support, and Liz Duvall for her meticulous reading. Thanks also go to my generous family and friends who so freely shared their knowledge and insights with me while I was working on this book: Al and Linda Taylor for that Wapsi River boat ride, Mary Susan Taylor for her deep understanding of Iowa, Robin and Meredith Taylor for those long country drives, Judy Miller for the images that her artwork has inspired, and my students in the 405 class at USC for their concerted suggestions and advice. Thank you to the women of The Lunch Group—Jo Giese, Linda Phillips Ashour, Judith Searle, Amanda Pope, Carolyn See, Doreen Nelson, Dale Pring MacSweeney, Jo Ann Matyas, Luchita Mullican, Janet Sternberg, Virginia Mullin, and Susan Suntree—who offered wine and empathy. Thank you to John Irving for his friendly mentoring over all these years. And, always, thanks to Tom, Parker, and Jesse, for their unflagging love.
—STC

Susan Taylor Chehak is the author of *The Story of Annie D.* (an Edgar Award nominee), *Harmony, Dancing on Glass,* and *Smithereens.* She was born and grew up in Iowa, and she received her M.F.A. from the Iowa Writers Workshop. Chehak teaches fiction writing at the University of California, Los Angeles. She recently opened an independent bookstore/coffeehouse in Keystone, Colorado, called inxpot. She divides her time between Colorado and Los Angeles.